HOW TO PLAY THE *NEW* REAL ESTATE SYNDICATION GAME

Richard R. Solem
Roger J. McClure

PRENTICE HALL
Englewood Cliffs, New Jersey 07632

Prentice-Hall International (UK) Limited, *London*
Prentice-Hall of Australia Pty. Limited, *Sydney*
Prentice-Hall Canada, Inc., *Toronto*
Prentice-Hall Hispanoamericana, S.A., *Mexico*
Prentice-Hall of India Private Limited, *New Delhi*
Prentice-Hall of Japan, Inc., *Tokyo*
Simon & Schuster Asia Pte. Ltd., *Singapore*
Editora Prentice-Hall do Brasil, Ltda., *Rio de Janeiro*

© 1988 *by*
PRENTICE-HALL, INC.
Englewood Cliffs, NJ

All rights reserved. No part of this
book may be reproduced in any form or
by any means, without permission in
writing from the publisher.

10 9 8 7 6 5 4 3 2 1

Printed in the United States of America

This publication is designed to provide accurate and authoritative information in regard to the subject matter covered. It is sold with the understanding that the publisher is not engaged in rendering legal, accounting, or other professional service. If legal advice or other expert assistance is required, the services of a competent professional person should be sought.

From the Declaration of Principles jointly adopted by a Committee of the American Bar Association and a Committee of Publishers and Associations.

Library of Congress Cataloging-in-Publication Data

Solem, Richard R. (Richard Ray), 1943-
   How to play the new real estate syndication game / Richard R. Solem, Roger J. McClure.
    p. cm.
   Includes index.
   ISBN 0-13-428178-0
   1. Real estate investment—Syndication—Law and legislation-
-United States. 2. Real estate investment—Taxation—Law and
legislation—United States. I. McClure, Roger J. II. Title.
KF1079.S65 1988
343.7305′46—dc19   88-19482
[347.303546]   CIP

ISBN 0-13-428178-0
ISBN 0-13-402223-8 PBK

PRENTICE HALL
BUSINESS & PROFESSIONAL DIVISION
A division of Simon & Schuster
Englewood Cliffs, New Jersey 07632

ACKNOWLEDGMENTS

Work on this book is very much an extension of my everyday work, developing my firm, Equity Fund Group, into a major force in the real estate syndication industry. I'd like to take this opportunity, therefore, to thank the EFG support group:

> Directors Neal Holtz and Bruce Mazzie, for their advice and encouragement over the years;
>
> Terry Smith, EFG's "cool under pressure" vice-president, for sharing the thrill and creative satisfaction that come from deal making; and
>
> Sanna, my wife, for her concern and loyalty during the hard times, when business was loneliest.

Together, we've made a lot of headway since the precursor to this book, *Getting Started In Real Estate Syndication,* was published in 1983. Thank you for your support.

Richard R. Solem

I'd like to thank Ray Solem for inviting me to participate in this revision and recasting of *Getting Started In Real Estate Syndication*, and Terry D. Gregory, Daisy Nappier, and Christine Moore for their assistance in review, preparation, and editing of the manuscript. I would also like to thank Simone Stephens for putting up with my absences as I wrote.

Roger J. McClure

THE *NEW* REAL ESTATE SYNDICATION GAME... AND HOW THIS BOOK HELPS YOU PLAY TO WIN

In the fall of 1986, gloom and doom prevailed in the offices of real estate syndication companies across the country. Massive tax reform and the subsequent crackdown on real estate tax write-offs was imminent, and scores of syndicators and their limited partners stood to lose their shirts. Yet, at the same time—and even two years prior to the Tax Recovery Act of 1986—savvy syndicators were already structuring real estate deals that took advantage of the new tax reforms.

What these smart real estate entrepreneurs realized is that real estate *was always* a sound economic investment even before it was a tax shelter and that it *will always* generate a competitive cash return. Some of these dealmakers were packaging lucrative investments in mobile home parks and industrial warehouses. Others began structuring deals for rehabilitating apartment complexes to provide a steady stream of income. Still others waited until the tax law took effect, rescued investor-abandoned properties and set them up on a new foundation of profitable operation.

As an active syndicator for the past ten years, I, too, have had my own share in the action. My experiences, along with the fortunes of resilient colleagues, have led me to believe that there is no greater, more exciting time to get into real estate syndication than right now. This book, *How to Play the New Real Estate Syndication Game*, will give you proven insights and strategies for getting in, playing by the new rules, and coming out a winner. For instance, you'll discover:

- How to structure your syndication deal so that your partners will receive their share of net income each quarter or year with a portion or most of it free from current taxation.
- How to use an "all equity" approach for putting together syndications that can produce a 12% or higher cash ROI.
- How you can take advantage of tax credits earned from low-income housing and rehabilitation expenditures for qualified

or historic structures to bypass the passive income pass-through restrictions. . .plus at least a dozen other tactics for coming out ahead.

But first, let's be realistic. Winning the real estate syndication game is not, and never has been, easy. Because the stakes are higher and because the money of a number of people is involved, the risk and the burden of responsibility is much greater. You'll need guts, energy, and knowledge to stay in the game. In this book I will show you where guts and energy are required, so that you can judge whether you're up to the task. Most important, however, I'll share with you the insider's *knowledge*—accumulated during my own struggle to build a successful real estate syndication business from the ground up.

In addition, the path from investment opportunity to public or private offering is filled with blind alleys and obstacles in the form of complex state and federal tax, securities, and partnership laws, as well as all the legal restraints and practices which typically encumber investment real estate. *How to Play the New Real Estate Syndication Game* leads you through this legal and economic maze *without taking any shortcuts*. In fact, I've even added something that I have never seen offered in a book of this type: an opportunity for you to hear a dissenting opinion: *You get advice from a practicing real estate and tax attorney for every strategy and technique discussed.*

One of the most confusing aspects of the syndication business is that there are few certainties and, thus, there is often the need for making judgments. This environment of uncertainty sets up a continual conflict between the syndicator and his or her legal counsel. In *How to Play the New Real Estate Syndication Game* this syndicator/attorney conflict is brought to the forefront by the inclusion of commentary by my own favorite real estate and tax attorney—so that you may see the conflicts firsthand. The attorney, Roger McClure, and I argue all day long on these very issues, so it was only natural that I invite him to point up the precautions you must take, the liabilities you assume, and the pitfalls and legal traps for the unwary and uninformed.

You'll find both my guidelines and Roger's comments organized into four sections which, taken together, will provide you with a solid foundation upon which to build a syndication business or work with those who are building one:

Part One, "The Syndicator as Dealmaker," gives you a quick rundown of the critical social and economic roles the syndicator plays in our current economy, and some of the benefits of working with investor funds. Discussed are the power of leveraging time, operating in larger transactions, and allocating investment benefits among different parties for a greater overall return.

Part Two, "Understanding the Legal and Regulatory Framework of Limited Partnerships—Making It Work for You," provides you with a critical look at the sometimes confusing maze of laws, regulations, guidelines, regulators, and trade associations that populate the world of investment syndication today. In this section, you'll gain some of the following insights:

- *Important advantages of the limited partnership vehicle* as a means of ownership including limited liability, favorable tax treatment, control by the general partners, and easy title transfer.
- Four reasons *why you should seriously consider the use of the trust* format for smaller investment offerings.
- The *elements that distinguish limited partnerships from corporations and from general partnerships* (as well as the role of key laws and regulations governing partnerships).
- *The importance of securities laws and regulations* such as the *Securities Act of 1933* (the basis for all regulation of offering disclosure whether private, intrastate, or public) and the *Securities Act of 1934* (the basis for regulation of offering sales: e.g., broker-dealer definition and registration).
- How federal and state regulatory bodies are organized and what they can do *for* you as well as *to* you.

Part Three, "Techniques for Successful Syndication," is where the real insider secrets are shared. In this section you will learn how to put together successful real estate syndication offerings in the post-1986 tax reform economy. You'll discover:

- What you should watch out for when making private offerings (and how to know whether you should use the public offering instead).
- Why nonspecified "blind pool" offerings are the fastest-growing segment of the real estate syndication industry (and how the professional dealmakers sell those hard-to-sell intangibles).
- How to use my "33/33/34" formula for ensuring a mutually satisfying and profitable division of profits with a co-general partner (plus how the 1986 TRA impacts on allocation to selected partners).

- How to structure the limited partnership for maximum financial return, optimal allocation of benefits among investors, and easy sale of the "interests" to investors.
- How to convert most investment ideas into a powerful preliminary analysis document within 24 hours at a cost of under $250.00.
- A host of new ways for structuring syndication deals to take advantage of the 1986 TRA (including a formula for getting maximum use of investment losses and gains).
- How to use SEC's Guide 5 to translate your ideas into a set of first-class offering agreements *and* cut your legal fees in half (and you'll discover where to get and how to use model documents employed by your competitors in the business).
- What kind of specialists you need to make the deal work, where to find them, and how to get the most out of them at the least cost.
- Tips on typing and printing your offering materials that can save you thousands on each offering made.
- Strategies for selling your own offerings privately or publicly, and advice on dealing with broker-dealers where they are used.
- How to manage the partnership investment process while keeping your limited partners adequately informed.

Part Four, "Sample Documents You Can Tailor for Your Own Use," provides you with a real "live" transaction to review and refer to when you assemble your own offerings. This section is comprised of an illustrative General Partner Understanding, a Preliminary Analysis Document, and a complete Offering Memorandum with appendices. Use of model documents is the single most valuable technique you can learn in the investment packaging business, and the sample documents offered herein give you a first start on your own collection.

Appendices to this book continue in the same spirit of providing you, the reader, with the basis to operate successfully in the business. Provided is a mini-reference library on real estate syndication, including the key legislative and administrative guidelines, forms, and directories for the practitioner. If you want to "hold your own" with your attorney, familiarize yourself with these appendices. You will communicate more effectively while achieving greater understanding; and your bills will drop in the process.

Get Ready, Get Set, Go—and Good Luck!

As you can see from the foregoing, Roger and I have tried to give you as much guidance as possible—the type of guidance I wish I'd had ten years ago when I first started out. Of course, no matter how much help we give you, the winds of politics, tax legislation, or sheer chance will affect the outcome of your syndication endeavors. Yet, whether you are an investor, broker, attorney, or accountant, if you want to profit from real estate syndication, this book will get you started in the right direction.

Richard Solem

CONTENTS

The *New* Real Estate Syndication Game . . . and How This Book Helps You Play to Win iv

PART I THE SYNDICATOR AS DEALMAKER 1
    Introduction to Part I • 2

Chapter 1 How You Can Fulfill the Need for Syndicators 5

Chapter 2 Three Reasons for Getting Into Real Estate Syndication . 7
Higher Returns on Time Invested • 7
Potential for Bigger Deals • 10
Allocation of Investment Benefits to Maximize Returns • 10

PART II UNDERSTANDING THE LEGAL AND REGULATORY FRAMEWORK OF LIMITED PARTNERSHIPS . . . MAKING IT WORK FOR YOU 13
    Introduction to Part II • 14

Chapter 3 Four Important Advantages of the Limited Partnership Vehicle 17
Limited Liability • 17
Favorable Tax Treatment and the Four Qualifying Tests • 18
Control by the General Partner • 21
Easy Title Transfer • 21

Chapter 4 Laws and Regulations Governing Partnerships 27
Uniform Partnership Act • 27
Uniform Limited Partnership Act • 28

Chapter 5 Laws and Regulations Governing Preparation of Investment Offerings 32
The Securities Act of 1933 • 33
The Securities and Exchange Act of 1934 • 43
Tax Shelter Registration with the IRS • 48
State Securities Laws • 49
Organizational Framework for Securities Regulation • 51

PART III TECHNIQUES FOR SUCCESSFUL SYNDICATION 55

x

Contents   xi

Chapter 6   Winning Investor Confidence 56
Private Versus Public Offerings • 57
Specified Versus Nonspecified Offerings • 62
Establishing Investment Objectives • 69
Defining Your Market • 70

Chapter 7   How to Set Up the General Partner Relationship 74
Reasons for Choosing a Co-General Partner • 74
Rules of Thumb for Structuring the General Partner Understanding • 76
Use of a Corporation as Co-General Partner • 81

Chapter 8   Structuring the Limited Partnership 84
Determining How You Will Make Money • 85
Deciding How Returns Will Be Shared • 87
How to Determine If You Can Sell the Limited Partnership Interests • 93
Preparing a Preliminary Analysis Document • 95
Structuring Under the Tax Recovery Act of 1986 • 99

Chapter 9   Packaging Your Investment Proposal 103
Organizing the Offering Documents • 103
NASAA Guidelines—Regulators Share Their Own Rules of Thumb • 111

Chapter 10   Engaging and Controlling Specialists 114
Understanding the Need for Control • 114
Identifying Competent Advisors • 121
Preparing for Meetings with Specialists • 125

Chapter 11   Useful Tips on Typing and Printing 132
Importance of Appearances • 132
How to Minimize Costs • 134

Chapter 12   Selling the Securities 136
When to Make Private Offerings • 136
Profitable Tips on Public Offerings • 137
Success-Tested Ways to Obtain Marketing Assistance • 142

**Chapter 13   Do's and Don'ts of Successful Investing and
               Reporting** 149
Guidelines for Investment Decisions • 149
Walking that "Fine Line" Between Too Much and Too Little Information • 151

Chapter 14   Helpful Tips on Partnership Record Keeping 154
Setting Up the Accounting File • 154
Establishing and Using a Specimen Documents File • 155
Organizing a Subject File • 157

PART IV SAMPLE DOCUMENTS YOU CAN TAILOR FOR YOUR OWN USE 159

Chapter 15 Pre-Offering Documents 160
Overview • 160
  SAMPLE DOCUMENTS:
  General Partner Understanding • 162
  Preliminary Analysis Document • 165

Chapter 16 The Offering Package 175
Overview • 175
  SAMPLE DOCUMENTS:
  Offering Memorandum • 181
  Attorney Opinion for Offering Memorandum • 235
  Agreement of Limited Partnership • 253
  Certificate of Limited Partnership • 287
  Subscription Agreement and Materials • 293
  Partnership Management Agreement • 315
  Selling Agreement • 317

APPENDICES 327

Appendix A Rules 146, 240 and 242 • 328
Appendix B Regulation D and Form D • 356
Appendix C Rule 147 • 383
Appendix D Regulation A • 389
Appendix E Form S-11 • 426
Appendix F Guide 5 • 435
Appendix G Form U-4 • 461
Appendix H State Security Administrators • 468
Appendix I Work of the SEC • 477
Appendix J NASAA Guidelines • 507
Appendix K NASD Offices • 552
Appendix L Glossary • 553
Appendix M Survey of NASAA Real Estate Guidelines • 557

INDEX 562

PART I

THE SYNDICATOR AS DEALMAKER

This book is written for realtors, attorneys, accountants, financial planners, builders, developers, investors, and the like, who have experience in real estate investment for their own accounts, but who yearn to participate in larger transactions—to grow faster. The purpose of this book is to help you reexamine where you are going professionally and suggest a new option that may be appealing.

If you will give me a few hours of your time, together we will explore a part of the real estate industry you may have thought out-of-reach—the exciting world of investment syndication. Whatever your investment background, you can probably increase your income and your net worth by learning to leverage into larger transactions through application of other people's money.

There is a great need for people with good real estate knowledge to make real estate investments available to moderate income people. Where is the typical professional couple, earning $50,000 per year, with $5,000 to invest, going to place that money? For a great many Americans their first choice is real estate. They're not asleep! They know that with the effects of leverage, inflation, and capital gains treatment, real estate has savings certificates beat "hands down." The figures below, illustrating that difference for a 28% bracket taxpayer, are known intuitively by most of us.

	Savings Certificates (8%)	Real Estate (Equity)
Cash Invested	$5,000	$ 5,000
Assets Controlled	$5,000	20,000[1]
Inflation Effect (5%)	-0-	1,600
Tax Savings Due to Depreciation	-0-	133[2]
Cash Flow	-0-	140[3]
ROI Year 1 (Before Taxes)	400	1,740
ROI Year 1 (After Taxes)	$ 288[4]	1,252[5]
Percent Return (After Taxes)	6.0%	25%

---

[1] Assumes a loan equal to 75% of purchase price is placed against the property acquired.

[2] Assumes 75% of property is depreciable via 31½ years S/L, i.e. $15,000 x 0.03175 = $476.25 x 0.28 tax bracket = $133.35

[3] Assumes rent slightly exceeds depreciation.

[4] Interest income is taxed at ordinary income rates and cannot be offset by depreciation. Assumes 28% tax bracket.

[5] Assumes $1,740 ($1,600 gain plus $133.35 of recaptured depreciation plus $6.65 taxable income) taxed at ordinary income rate = $1,252.50 after tax.

Despite these impressive figures, nine times out of ten the investor with $5,000 places his money in savings certificates, or listed stocks in companies he knows nothing about. Why?

You know why! With $5,000 it is very difficult to make a straightforward real estate investment, particularly if ability to "carry itself" (no negative cash flow) is a requirement. People are forced to make uneconomical investments because the market has failed to provide them with good ones. That's where the syndicator comes in.

Needed are people with interest in and knowledge of real estate to provide investment syndication services at a local level. Syndicators are needed to identify investment opportunities, reveal them to reluctant savers, package them in a legally sufficient, economically sound way, and manage them to the benefit of all involved.

My objective in writing this book is to get you thinking about the syndication option and to tell enough about it that you can decide whether it interests you.

Until about fifteen years ago real estate investment through syndication was largely a "rich man's game." With rare exceptions, funds were raised privately with shares priced in the tens of thousands of dollars, thus precluding participation by people of moderate income. Then, in the late 1960s, a dozen or so farsighted individuals resolved to bring the industry to middle-class Americans. They formed public, limited partnerships and offered interests priced at $5,000 and less. The response has been awesome. Last year more than a dozen major public syndicators raised in excess of $50,000,000—each—from middle income investors. The demand is still growing.

Happily, you don't have to be a national syndicator to get into the business. Many investors would rather deal in local real estate with a nearby firm. They want to deal with someone they know and property they can drive by, but they need you to make it possible. If you *know how to make* prudent real estate investments, *enjoy working with people*, and *can develop a few specialized skills*, you can provide the alternative. If you've done well in real estate you may already have the first two qualifications. This book will start you on the road toward the third—development of specialized skills. Realtors who are also syndicators enjoy some particular advantages over their competitors. These are:

1. Captive acquisition commissions, because they are acquiring with their own funds.
2. Captive property management commissions, because they are managing their own property.

3. Captive sales commissions, because they are selling their own property.
4. Best of all, participation in profits from the real estate investments made.

Sound scary? Seem too sophisticated for you? Heard horror stories about dealing with the securities regulators? Relax! Investment syndication is like everything else. If you contemplate the entire task at once it looks insurmountable, but if you just apply yourself, and take one step at a time, it is not difficult. And it can certainly make life interesting!

Chapter 1

How You Can Fulfill the Need for Syndicators

A journey of a thousand miles must begin with a single step.
—Lao Tzu

In 1976 I switched gears. Acquisition and rehabilitation of single-family homes was no longer fulfilling. I was making money, and the road to modest wealth and security seemed assured. I had developed a skill and was practicing it successfully. But I was bored.

The transactions, I reflected, were just too small and routine. With my personal assets and borrowing ability alone, it would be years before I could make large-scale investments.

I also felt lonely and in need of the inspiration of compatriots. As an individual investor/rehabilitator in one-house-at-a-time deals I could ill-afford the advice and participation of partners, attorneys, accountants, architects, builders, etc. It was just me against the world. Exhilarating and satisfying at first, but now knowing that I had learned it and that the road I was on might never lead anywhere, I wanted more challenge, and some colleagues to share it with.

What I really wanted to do was build resort hotels in great vacation spots, rehabilitate magnificent old structures so that they might be enjoyed for years to come, or construct office buildings right in my own community. These things were being done every day. But by whom, and how? Were the people involved in such projects smarter than I, or somehow different? I had to know, so I set out to learn. In the process I discovered the exciting world of real estate syndication.

America, I learned, was built by syndicators. Most of the great commercial companies in our land, as well as the great real estate projects, were assembled by syndicators who, in many cases, brought little or none of their own wealth to the transaction. Rather, they contributed the essential role of entrepreneur and packager. Without them, large transactions would rarely be made.

Who, among us, could build an Empire State Building from personal assets? Financing even a small, roadside Holiday Inn is beyond the capabilities of most individuals. Yet they are built daily, and they are built mostly by people who are far from wealthy. Engineers, doctors, attorneys, government workers—all these people are building America, and they are doing so through real estate syndications.

How do they do it? The key is always the deal maker, entrepreneur, syndicator. By whatever name he is described, he is the spark that converts ideas into reality. He is the person who can make it happen, who can pull all the essential ingredients together into a whole which is greater than the sum of the parts.

Chapter 2

Three Reasons for Getting Into Real Estate Syndication

Let each man pass his days in that wherein his skill is greatest.
—Sextus Aurelius Propertius

HIGHER RETURNS ON TIME INVESTED

Most of us have a special function we perform in society. This function is assigned a value. An attorney's time may be worth $100 per hour. With 10 billable hours per week (the other 30, 40, or 50 hours spent trying to generate billable hours), he may earn $50,000 per year. An accountant may earn $50 per hour, a plumber perhaps $25 per hour. The thing to remember is that our time is most productive and valuable when we work within our specialties. When we leave our area of special expertise we become less efficient.

What if a medical doctor earning, say, $150,000 per year (approximately $50 per hour, assuming 60 billable hours per week), wishes to invest in real estate so that he can reduce his income taxes and enjoy wealth accumulation through appreciation. Should he go out and purchase a rental house and manage it? Is that the best use of his time? How much of his $50 per hour time will he invest in property selection, arranging financing, seeking tenants, maintenance, and so forth? If he spent his time on his medical practice instead, wouldn't he be further ahead financially?

Property selection, financing, and leasing are done by realtors who, on the average, earn substantially less than doctors. Maintenance is done by tradesmen who also earn less. The effect of the doctor's direct intervention into the real estate profession, therefore, is that he has resolved to work for a lesser wage in exchange for the benefits afforded to real estate investment. He has drawn the fallacious conclusion that in order to benefit from real estate investment one must practice real estate. That fallacy has the effect of reducing the doctor's overall return on the investment. This concept is illustrated by the table below:

	Rate Per Hour	Hours Per Year	Cost Per Year	Gross Gain Per Year	Net Gain Per Year
Prof. Services	$18[1]	104	$1,880	$10,000[2]	$8,120
Realtor	20	40	800		
Manager	15	52	300		
Tradesman	25	12	780		
Doctor Services	50	104	5,200	10,000	4,800
TOTAL SAVINGS DUE TO USE OF PROFESSIONAL SERVICES.............					$3,320

[1] Weighted average hourly rate, rounded to nearest dollar.

[2] Assumed gain due to a combination of appreciation, tax benefits, and cash flow.

In the direct investment scenario the doctor, in order to enjoy the $10,000 in appreciation and tax savings, invests two hours per week in a combination of realtor/manager/tradesman activities at an average savings of $18/hour. The effect therefore is a loss of $100 in physician's time to save $36 in realtor/manager/tradesman time—a net loss of $64 per week or, assuming 52 work weeks per year, $3,328 per year. The true yield from the real estate investment is clearly much higher when related services are performed by the appropriate professionals.

What does all this have to do with real estate syndication? To answer that, let's look at another scenario. Same doctor, same desire to invest in real estate so that he can reduce his income taxes and enjoy wealth accumulation through appreciation. In this scenario, however, he elects to invest indirectly, through the services of a real estate investment syndicator, and passively, by leaving all the related services to real estate professionals. The roles are all being played by performers who have trained for them. The person who makes it all possible, the real estate syndicator, is at the center of things, making it all come together.

Now the doctor who, left alone, might have limited his investment options to single-family homes in his own neighborhood (because of the limitations of his own acquisition, financing, leasing, and maintenance skills) can consider hotels (which might have far greater tax benefits), shopping center development (which might offer better appreciation prospects), or anything else that interests him. The service people involved in this scenario are likewise better off because in dealing with the syndicator they have the comfort of knowing that he is a professional and thus able to skillfully evaluate the risks and tradeoffs along the way. Everyone, from the doctors to the maintenance person, is doing precisely what he is trained to do, and is being paid for it at market rates. The syndicator, for his role as director, typically participates in profits, if any are earned.

That is how America was built, and is being built today. Syndicators with courage and vision are blending all the diverse elements into a whole greater than the sum of its parts, with everyone benefiting in the process.

What does all this mean to you, the reader? What I'm trying to communicate is a way of looking at opportunities around you. If you realize, one day, that there is a dearth of hotel rooms in your community, don't mutter "somebody should build a hotel here" and then put it out of your mind. Instead, ask yourself: "What are the financial benefits from a successful hotel? Do I know people who could benefit from such an investment? Do I know anyone who could locate a good site, build it, operate it? How could I structure such a package so that my personal risk (time and money) is minimized? Given those considerations, is investment of my time (as a syndicator) in developing a hotel syndication as remunerative as it would be in doing another kind of project?"

In other words, don't arbitrarily cut yourself off from opportunities which you see around you because they seem too large. Don't spend your life slaving for brokerage commissions if you really desire, and have the ability, to purchase and manage investments. If you can think, write, and calculate, you can structure and package a limited partnership offering. If you can deal with risk, you can contract for and finance property. If you can inspire the confidence of others in yourself, you can raise investor money. If you have common sense, you can manage partnership assets.

POTENTIAL FOR BIGGER DEALS

You can band together with your friends to buy a better investment than you could afford individually. For example, a person may have $50,000 to invest and could buy an apartment building with ten apartment units. But with a ten-unit building, you often can't afford professional management, a resident manager, or a maintenance staff. Also, you will pay more per unit for a ten-unit building than for a 200-unit building. By pooling $50,000 investments from five or ten friends, you might be able to buy a 200-unit building at a lower per unit cost and be able to afford professional management, a resident manager, and some maintenance personnel. Buying a large building may be crucial to obtaining enough cash income necessary to reap the benefits of the new tax provisions.

Syndication offers the passive investor the opportunity to hire a professional real estate entrepreneur to take over the headaches of real estate management and development. Because the entrepreneur's profits are not guaranteed and are dependent on how well the deal goes, the entrepreneur is motivated by his own self-interest to provide a higher return for the investor. Typically, an investor may be able to get only a 5–10% after-tax return on his or her money by investing it on his own. By going into a syndication, the investor "hires" a real estate pro who knows how to get returns of 15% and higher. The syndicator benefits by using the investor's money to acquire larger, more challenging and profitable properties.

ALLOCATION OF INVESTMENT BENEFITS TO MAXIMIZE RETURNS

Each piece of investment real estate can provide four distinct and different benefits: (1) appreciation, (2) income, (3) tax shelter, and (4) amortization. "Appreciation" is the increase in the value of the real estate caused by inflation, rehabilitation of the property, shifts in the local or world economy, or actions by the owners to increase rental income. "Income" derives from the excess of rental income over expenses, and for the well-designed project, can be munificent. I know of one real estate entrepreneur who bought enough apartment buildings so that his surviving widow now receives $2,000,000 a year in income from the apartments. Real estate may provide "tax shelter" in the form of deductible expenses and depreciation; often, the income from this and other real estate investments and from certain limited sources may be sheltered from taxation. "Amortization" is the pay down of the loans and mortgages on the property over a 15- to 30-year period. If you sign a million-dollar 30-year mortgage on a piece of real estate, in thirty years—even with no inflation, appreciation, or tax benefits—you will be a millionaire.

Through syndication, you can split up the four benefits of investment real estate among your partners. Often you want a larger share of appreciation than you are able or willing to pay for with cash. The passive investor gets the major portion of the tax shelter, professional management of assets, and appreciation. The income from the real estate can be used to pay lenders and provide a base of steady income with which to pay your overhead and your limited partners. Amortization might be split off from the investment and sold to a pension fund or family trust.

ATTORNEY COMMENT

Specialization

I endorse Ray's concept that by specializing in your own area of expertise, you are less likely to make mistakes and more likely to be efficient. Also, you must understand that in many instances you *must* use specialists. For example, many states require that you have a real estate license to sell property or to lease property owned by others; in a syndication, the partnership owns the property and you don't. Some securities regulations require that you have an attorney's opinion as to tax aspects of the partnership and a CPA's certification of accounting statements. In certain states, where you use a particular type of private offering exemption, you must have a securities license even to sell one of your partnership interests.

Bigger Deals Mean Greater Risks

By syndicating, you can participate in bigger real estate deals and thereby gain larger profits and wider experience. However, you are also subject to much greater business, legal, and emotional liabilities. First, when you use the typical limited partnership form, you are then subject to all applicable securities laws. This means that if you do not provide the required disclosure or you do not take necessary precautions, you will be required to refund all the money that you and your investors provided if the deal goes sour. Second, you are subject to scrutiny for civil and criminal securities law penalties. You must conform to applicable partnership laws and principles in setting up and operating your venture. Most of these requirements are not present when you invest on your own account or with a few friends.

By syndicating, you also expose your hard-earned assets. Syndicators must already have had some experience in operating, owning, and selling real estate before they go into this business. They should have built up some assets. You could lose a large portion or all of these hard-earned assets if your syndication blows up. Will you be able to sleep if you owe $2,000,000?

With an investment in a single-family house, you can always sell if you get into financial trouble. You may even take a loss, but generally it may not be for more than a few thousand dollars. With a syndication, if you sign a contract to buy a 100-unit apartment building with a $100,000 nonrefundable deposit, but are unable to raise the remaining $200,000 required for the down payment, you will lose the entire $100,000. I know of a recent example where a syndicator forfeited a $120,000 deposit because he couldn't complete the deal.

Even if you get the money together to buy that $5,000,000 office building, you could still run into negative cash flow and virtually forfeit your estate if your major tenant moves out and you can't make a $6,000 monthly mortgage payment. If you lose the building to foreclosure, your limited partners could sue you for their money back if you did not disclose in your offering materials that you and the partnership did not have the cash reserves to take care of major vacancies.

Be Careful With Special Allocations

You have to be very careful in syndications as to how you allocate tax benefits, how you structure the fees, and how you split profits. Contrary to popular belief, you cannot simply allocate all the tax benefits to your limited partners and all the economic profits to yourself and expect to survive a tax audit. None of these problems are insurmountable. All of them have standard, understandable, and practical solutions as we show you in Chapter 3, "Four Important Advantages of the Limited Partnership Vehicle."

PART II

UNDERSTANDING THE LEGAL AND REGULATORY FRAMEWORK OF LIMITED PARTNERSHIPS—Making It Work for You

Law is order and good law is good order.
—Aristotle

The key word in the title of this book, "syndication," is a general term which, according to *Webster's New World Dictionary*, means "an association of individuals or corporations formed to carry out some financial project." There is no implicit reference to limited partnerships or to real estate. One can syndicate investments as diverse as newspaper columns, films, restaurants, oil wells, or race horses. You name an investment, and I'll show you someone who makes a living syndicating such investments.

The form of syndication with which we are dealing in this book is very specific, however. We are dealing with limited partnerships. Indeed, we are even more specific. We are dealing only with real estate limited partnerships. The operational distinction, from a legal and regulatory viewpoint, is limited partnership, not real estate. The laws and organizations that govern the industry are directed to the form of ownership, not to the object of the investments. Therefore, the syndicator who masters the limited partnership vehicle has a powerful skill—a skill that can enable him to organize and operate virtually any kind of investment. As long as the syndicator knows enough about his target transaction to inspire investor confidence, place the funds wisely, and manage competently, he can do what he pleases.

The inventory of laws, regulations, and organizations governing real estate limited partnerships is very complex because real estate limited partnerships encompass several distinct bodies of the law.

There is no need for you to get hopelessly lost in the complex body of partnership, securities, and tax laws that surround syndication. In its essence, these laws basically require you to be honest and up front in your dealings and to follow the golden rule with your partners. In the beginning, you have to do it; as you get more experience, it becomes like second nature. In return, they trust you with their money in expectation of the benefits you promise them. You are in charge, but bear all the ultimate responsibilities.

Partnership law is based upon the simple notion that each general partner has the power to bind the business in his dealings with the public. Each general partner is generally liable for all partnership debts. Each general partner has a veto on all partnership decisions unless otherwise agreed. These restrictions and multiple liabilities are well suited only to small and easily controlled businesses. The grand tradition of general partnership law still defines the relationships between two general partners in a limited partnership. The general partnership has largely been abandoned (with some notable exceptions) by most modern businesses for the corporate form.

The limited partnership meets the challenge of the corporate form by eliminating the power of limited partners to bind the partnership with outside parties and by preventing limited partners from having anything to say about day-to-day business matters. A major distinction between a partnership interest and an interest in real estate is that a partnership interest is not real property and does not have to be transferred with all the formalities of the transfer of real property. It is treated as personal and not real property for state law purposes. But, like a chameleon, it changes its apparent coloring and becomes like owning real property for federal tax law purposes.

ATTORNEY COMMENT
Layers of Regulations Often Create Confusion

Real estate limited partnership encompasses state statutory laws on limited partnerships, state and federal securities laws (mainly statutes), state and federal tax codes, and state judge-made law on real property, misrepresentation, and fraud. It initially appears complex because it encompasses not only different legal specialties (partnerships, securities, tax, real property) but also different governmental authorities (federal and state) and different lawmaking bodies.

The limited partnership is a relatively new form of business and did not exist in the common law, but instead has been invented by state legislatures. With these limited partnership statutes, state legislatures authorize the formation of a limited partnership, define the rights and liabilities of general and limited partners, and require that a minimal amount of information be provided the state and the public about the structure and participants in the limited partnership.

State statutes and state judges have expounded on the common law in developing general partnership law, which governs the relationships between general partners in a limited partnership. In general, there is no federal partnership law governing limited partnerships.

Limited partnership interests are considered to be securities and the promotion of limited partnerships is governed by both *federal and state* securities statutes and also by rules and regulations issued by administrative bodies which regulate the sale of securities. These statutes and regulations affect when, how, and to whom you can sell your limited partnership shares. Fortunately, the security regulators have provided ways in which you can relatively easily and economically conform to these strictures. In addition, state common law can impose liability on you if you engage in misrepresentation and fraud.

Federal tax law has a major impact on real estate limited partnerships because often a syndicator uses this legal form to provide investors with a magic combination of substantial tax benefits, equity growth, no management responsibilities or control, and limited liability. This near miracle is not available in other business forms such as a corporation and the general partnership. Even with recent tax legislation, there are ways in which limited partnerships can be used to shelter passive income.

In the following sections, the authors will explain the basics of this interplay of state and federal laws and regulations both from the syndicator's and the lawyer's perspective.

Chapter 3

Four Important Advantages of the Limited Partnership Vehicle

There are some very important advantages that have been enjoyed by the limited partnership investment form in recent years. Several of these are explored below.

LIMITED LIABILITY

For the classic, passive investor, nothing is more appealing than the idea of being able to take a chance on an investment scheme with the hope of substantial profits while secure in the knowledge that in case of failure one needn't fear lawsuits, loss of home or business, or any other repercussion beyond the amount of the initial investment.

What this means, in practical terms, is that the moderate and high income dentist, engineer, or government worker can occasionally take a chance in an area where he has no special expertise without threatening the fruits of an entire life's work. Filling teeth can become boring if you've been doing it for twenty years. It might be fun to invest in a sailboat marina or a new apartment building, provided, however, that someone else does all the work and downside loss is limited to an affordable amount.

This is what the ownership vehicle known as the limited partnership will do for you. Gone is the fear of losing everything one has worked for. In the case of real estate, gone also is the fear of liability on mortgages, often in amounts two to four times the cash investment. The only thing necessary is to limit cash input to an amount one can afford to lose, and to seek an investment manager (general partner) in whom one has confidence and trust.

FAVORABLE TAX TREATMENT AND THE FOUR QUALIFYING TESTS

A consideration of tremendous importance in virtually all investments one can choose in America today is the relative tax treatment. This is so because America's tax laws provide for substantial discrimination against certain types of investments and in favor of others. Although there are advantages to a corporate form of ownership from the viewpoint of a corporation's principles (the limited liability provisions), for the passive shareholder it is hard to justify.

The biggest problem passive investors have with the corporate ownership form is the double taxation of profits, first as they are earned by the corporation and taxed at corporate rates, and second as they are passed through to investors in the form of dividends and taxed at personal income rates. In a small, closely held corporation this double taxation characteristic can be ameliorated by paying out earnings as salaries or spending them on perquisites such as company autos, club memberships, and the like. In a large corporation where there is no direct involvement of investors with the corporation's activities, however, the double taxation is unavoidable.

Thus, the second main reason for the popularity of limited partnerships—favorable tax treatment. Partnerships, general or limited, are not subject to payment of federal income taxes. Rather, they are treated as conduits of cash flow gains and losses. Only the investors/partners pay taxes on profits. Likewise, it is the investors/partners who enjoy the benefits of any tax losses, not the partnership itself.

These profit and loss "pass-throughs" are particularly popular in the real estate business where a wide range of appealing tax losses is also available. Under the limited partnership format, the individual limited partner can use these losses to shelter income from other passive investments or, lacking such passive income, can accumulate these losses and use them to reduce taxes on the eventual gains from sales of partnership property.

A word of caution with regard to the tax treatment issue is in order. Tax treatment as a partnership, rather than as a corporation, cannot be automatically assumed just because you call your entity a limited partnership and file your documentation as such in your state. The Internal Revenue Service (IRS) has its own ideas about what constitutes a corporation (for tax purposes), and the reader will be well advised to consider the IRS viewpoint on this matter in structuring his ownership entity. Recognition by your state as a legally constituted partnership is not safe haven from treatment as a corporation by the IRS.

Treasury regulations set forth six characteristics that are found in corporations:

- associates
- an objective to carry on business and divide the gains
- continuity of life
- centralization of management
- limited liability
- free transferability of interests

The first two of these characteristics apply to all partnerships as well as to corporations. The last four, however, may or may not exist in a partnership. The position of the IRS, therefore, has been to look closely at a business entity that claims tax treatment as a partnership to see whether it has more than two of those last four corporate characteristics. In structuring a limited partnership entity, therefore, one should take care to consider these four tests of limited partnership status.

Continuity of Life

This is an easy corporate characteristic to avoid. Simply state clearly in your partnership agreement that "the limited partnership is automatically dissolved upon the resignation, expulsion, bankruptcy, retirement, insanity, or death of a general partner unless the remaining general partners agree to continue" or, in case there are no additional general partners, "unless the limited partners agree to continue." The other technique which helps to avoid failure of the continuity of life test is to choose a date at which time the partnership will absolutely terminate (a requirement anyway). In doing this, consider that partnership creditors will be reluctant to make thirty-year loans to a partnership with a five-year term. On the other hand, partnership investors will be reluctant to tie up their funds for periods as long as 30 years. A practical compromise here is to have a legal termination date set for a period in excess of the anticipated mortgage terms and an operational termination target of, say, five years from inception.

Centralization of Management

This test is a hard one to avoid in the case of limited partnerships. In a corporation, management is left to directors and officers, with remaining shareholders having no say in day-to-day operations. In a limited partnership, management is left to the general partners. Were the limited partners to violate this convention and become active in day-to-day decision making, they would risk loss of their limited liability status—in effect, becoming general partners in their own right. To attempt to structure a limited partnership which avoids meeting the centralization of management test would risk losing the limited liability feature.

Limited Liability

This corporate characteristic can be avoided if some person or entity in the limited partnership entity has personal liability for the partnership's obligations and if that person or entity has substantial assets. In the case of an individual general partner, the test of substantial assets is not well defined. Clearly, an "indigent" would not be classified as having substantial assets, but there is no clear-cut minimum net worth test.

Where the sole general partner is a corporation, the IRS has been more precise so as to avoid a situation in which a general partner could cloak himself in a "dummy corporation" and thus avoid personal liability. The IRS's rule of thumb with regard to sole corporate general partners is that they must have a net worth of the lesser of $250,000 or 15 percent of capital raised for partnerships, or less than $2,500,000 or 10 percent of capital raised for partnerships of $2,500,000 or more.

Free Transferability of Interests

This is another corporate test that your limited partnership can easily be designed to fail. IRS regulations provide that free transferability of an entity's interests exists if an interest holder can transfer his interest at his own volition without permission from other interest holders or managers of the entity.

The best way to structure your limited partnership to avoid meeting this corporate test is to build in restrictions on transferability. The strongest would be a provision that limited partnership interests may not be sold or assigned without the express written consent of the general partners, and that such consent may be withheld at the sole discretion of the general partners.

There are "master limited partnerships" which are structured so as to allow their shares to be sold on national stock exchanges. This recent investment vehicle will probably not be used by the beginning syndicator.

Clearly, the key to receiving favorable tax treatment as a limited partnership is to ensure that you are viewed as a limited partnership not only under state law but also by the IRS. It is not uncommon that there is conflict between the two. Compliance with state limited partnership laws does not protect you from treatment as a corporation by the IRS. Be aware of IRS rulings and case law in this area and structure your partnership accordingly. Loss of the advantages of partnership tax treatment can go a long way toward contravening the effects of lots of hard work on your part. Be careful!

CONTROL BY THE GENERAL PARTNER

In a limited partnership, the general partner is the Board of Directors and the Chief Executive rolled up into one. The general partner makes all major decisions, generally without consultation with the limited partners, and in states that do not require "partnership democracy" can stipulate that limited partners cannot remove the general partner. The general partner has this tremendous power even though he has only a very small initial investment in the partnership and the limited partners put up all the money.

In contrast, in the normal small business corporation, the investors own most of the voting stock, can vote out the Board of Directors at a shareholders' meeting and can change the management. Although corporations can be set up so that ownership and control are split as in a limited partnership, this is often impractical for business, legal, and tax reasons.

EASY TITLE TRANSFER

If you buy a piece of real estate in your own name and later decide to bring in additional partners, you may have to pay substantial local transfer and recording charges to record their interest in the deal, go through another real estate settlement, and run the risk of violating the due-on-scale clause in any mortgages or deeds of trust in the loans on the property. By taking the property as a limited partnership, you can bring in limited partners later without paying any recording or transfer taxes or going through another settlement. Also, most lenders will tell you that they will not call the loan when you take title as a limited partnership, and you later take in limited partners, even though the limited partners will in substance own most of the property. In a properly designed limited partnership, you usually have to get the signatures of only the general partners to deed the property rather than having to locate each general and limited partner and get them all to agree to sign the deed. By using the limited partnership format, you save thousands of dollars in legal fees and costs and weeks of potential aggravation and frustration.

ATTORNEY COMMENT

Even while acknowledging the many charms of the limited partnership as a legal vehicle for real estate investments, there are a number of administration and tax considerations that should be noted.

Added Paperwork increases Overhead

There are present disadvantages to the limited partnership format which make it the wrong choice for certain transactions. An attorney will probably charge you anywhere from $500 to $3,000 to set up a limited partnership. You must document the limited partnership arrangements and file them with state or county officials prior to taking title at settlement. The costs and trouble of this may not be warranted for just one single-family home or other small investment. Also, limited partnerships are subject to complex federal tax regulations that require you to prepare an annual partnership return based upon some of the most challenging and difficult portions of the tax code. You are limited in how you allocate depreciation in limited partnerships.

The passive investor has very little control or authority in the limited partnership. If the real estate project is going broke because of mismanagement, a limited partner cannot step in to straighten out the mess without losing his status as a limited partner. If he does step in, he then becomes a general partner and acquires liability for all the debts of the failing project. The problem is solved only in partnerships in which the limited partners have the power to vote out the general partner, an unusual provision in a private syndication.

For small investments with only two or three investors, serious consideration should be given to the use of the trust format. The trust format can provide pass-through of tax benefits, some limited liability, centralized or shared management, and no title problems (caution— check with your title advisors first). The trust can be set up so that it is or is not a taxable entity. In limited cases where the proper procedure is followed, no annual tax return need be prepared and filed for the trust. Large sophisticated syndicators sometimes use the Real Estate Investment Trust over a limited partnership for tax and other reasons; however, the REIT is impractical for beginning syndicators because of the IRS requirement that such a trust have more than 100 investors.

Fiduciary Controls

You cannot treat syndicated property as your private reserve and draw out funds when you need them as you might do with your own property. The partnership agreement will restrict when and how much money you can take out of partnership accounts and determine your share of profits at the end. Under nationally recommended guidelines in effect in some states for public offerings, you are discouraged from taking more than 25% of the final profits from the deal and that only after your limited partners receive all their money back plus at least a 6% cumulative return. You may be restricted in the amount you can charge as real estate brokerage fees (usual maximum of 6%) and the amount of money you can take out as initial set-up fees. State partnership law will require that you maintain partnership accounts separately from your own personal accounts, and that these partnership accounts must be open and available for inspection by a limited partner at all reasonable times upon reasonable notice.

Important Features of the Tax Recovery Act of 1986

The Tax Recovery Act of 1986 (TRA) will change the way the real estate industry uses limited partnerships in syndications in several important ways.

Limits on Loss Pass-Throughs

The most important change—limits on loss pass-throughs—prescribes that, with a few exceptions, passive losses from real estate investments may only be used to offset passive investment income. In the past, a limited partner might receive a $20,000 tax loss from his limited partnership interest and then deduct this from his ordinary earned income from his job or business. Under the TRA, a limited partner will not be able to take his losses from a partnership, called "passive losses," and deduct them from his job or business income. Instead he will have to carry these losses forward until they can be offset against income from passive investments. This income may be from a partnership he is in that starts to produce taxable income, from another partnership that produces income, or from the gains from sales of partnership property. In most cases, this means the limited partner still gets to take these losses against real money coming in the door, except that his deduction comes later rather than earlier.

There are two major exceptions to this rule. First, for investments made prior to the enactment of the TRA, there is a phase-in rule for limitation on passive investment losses. In 1987, the limited partner can deduct 65% of the losses from his job or business incomes. In

1988, the deductible percentage is 40%; in 1989, 20%; in 1990, 10%; and in 1991, 0%. Second, where an individual actively participates in the management of his real estate (excludes all limited partners), he would be able to deduct up to $25,000 in income and credits from real estate investment losses as long as his adjusted gross income is less than $100,000. This $25,000 deduction ceiling phases out for incomes between $100,000 and $150,000 and is calculated before taking such passive losses into account. These are the ceilings for married individuals; the ceiling for single people starts at $50,000.

This new loss limitation has been anticipated by the syndication industry. For a year or more prior to the TRA enactment, many syndicators switched to doing partnerships which produced substantial income rather than tax shelter. A limited partner who is locked into a deep shelter partnership can buy into one of these income partnerships and thereby fully use all the deductions available from the pre-TRA deep tax shelter. Indeed, through this tactic, an investor can reap the benefits of a remaining high tax shelter partnership and lower ordinary income rates.

In fact, the TRA may encourage the use of limited partnerships for owning of income-producing assets. If you get an 8% return from a certificate of deposit, you have no way to shelter that 8% interest income under the TRA as a passive investor. However, if you get an 8% return from a rental property held by a limited partnership, you could shelter all of that 8% return by using tax losses earned on investments in other real estate limited partnerships.

Reduction of Personal Tax Rates

A second major feature of the TRA has been the reduction in the top tax rates from 50% to 38.7% in 1987 to a hypothetical 28% in 1988. The theory is that tax shelters will be less valuable because they will provide fewer benefits due to rate reductions. A $1,000 deduction is worth $500 in a 50% bracket, $385 in the $38.5% bracket and $280 in the 28% bracket. However, these numbers are deceptive because people who heavily invested in tax shelters often had reduced their tax rate to an effective rate of 30% or lower prior to the TRA. With the multiple restrictions of the TRA, tax shelter investors will find that their effective tax rates are actually higher. Also, the rate of 28% is actually up to 33% due to the phasing out of various deductions in the higher income brackets. Finally, with continuing budget deficits projected, effective tax rates will, in my personal opinion, be increased in the next few years to raise more revenue.

Lengthening of Depreciation Schedules

A third major change brought about by the TRA is the lengthening of depreciation schedules. Property bought during the period 1981 through 1985 could have a depreciation schedule of 15, 18, or 19 years, with the Accelerated Cost Recovery System of 175% available for residential and commercial properties and the ACRS of 200% for low income rental properties. This depreciation system will remain on buildings purchased in these years. For purchases after 1987 (and not subject to any transition rule), there will be only straight-line depreciation of 27.5 years for residential and 31.5 years for commercial projects. This reduction in depreciation will affect all real estate and, combined with other TRA changes, will basically end the use of high write-offs to subsidize cash flow losses on properties. Now, many real estate projects will be structured so that the income from the project comes close to matching or exceeding all deductions, including depreciation. Depreciation will then shelter the income from real estate. As shown in the example, this will still give investors in a real estate limited partnership a higher pretax and after-tax return than that from a certificate of deposit even where the real estate has a lower cash flow and appreciation rate than the interest rate on the CD.

Also, limited partners will not be able to deduct more interest passed through to them than the total of their net investment income plus certain other expenditures. This also will limit the amount of tax losses available. Again, this can be solved by investment in a limited partnership that produces enough income to enable the investor to take full advantage of his tax shelter deductions.

Changes in "At-Risk" Rules

The TRA will no longer allow syndicators to borrow a lot of money from the seller of the property on a nonrecourse basis so as to add that debt to the basis of the limited partners. This means that a limited partner could not include any part of seller-provided mortgages on partnership property in his or her tax basis unless he or she was personally liable on the mortgage. In affected real estate syndications, this would result in a substantial postponement in tax benefits. To regain such tax benefits, the limited partner would have to give up some of his or her "limited liability" by accepting personal liability to pay on some or all of the loans on the property. Many limited partners will refuse to sign a $1,000,000 loan so that they can get a $50,000 tax benefit.

This "at-risk" limitation will not apply to financing provided by third parties such as banks, savings and loans, mortgage companies, and other lenders. These at-risk limitations can even be avoided when a partner has a lending business and the partner's lending company makes a loan to the partnership at commercially reasonable rates and terms similar to those made by unrelated persons. Thus, for many projects, limited partners in real estate syndications retain the advantages of nonrecourse financing.

Elimination of Capital Gains

The TRA eliminated capital gains for real estate and all other investments. This means that the maximum tax on real estate gains will go from 20% to 28% or higher. This may result in higher taxes being paid by all real estate investors. However, if a limited partner has losses that he cannot take in a particular year, he will be able to carry forward such losses and use those losses to reduce his tax on the sale of the property. In a partnership that produces cash flow always equal to cash expenses, a limited partner who always carried forward his share of the depreciation would pay no taxes on that unused depreciation. Under the law prior to TRA, he would have had to pay taxes on depreciation at capital gains and ordinary income rates at the time of sale.

Creative Techniques for Damage Minimization

A true disadvantage of the limited partnership format is that it will be difficult to use a tax-free exchange of partnership interests. Under the Tax Reform Act of 1984, limited partners could no longer exchange partnership interests. However, a person who has a percentage interest in a piece of real estate will be able to defer his taxes on a real estate sale by an exchange, thereby substantially lessening any effect of the elimination of capital gains rates for direct real estate investments. If planned properly, there may be opportunities to dissolve a limited partnership and take advantage of the exchange format.

All the changes do not mean that real estate syndication is dead. The basic reasons for syndication remain, and substantial tax benefits also remain. These changes do mean that syndicators will be more creative in their use of limited partnerships as discussed above. In some instances, one might elect to break an investment property into individual units such as a condominium and have each investor own one or several of the actual property units for apartments, offices, hotel or motel rooms. Before using the limited partnership format, you must consult with competent tax counsel as to the best approach.

Chapter 4

Laws and Regulations Governing Partnerships

Who will pay for the shoe of a partnership horse?
—American Indian Proverb

The general partnership form goes back centuries and is a product of centuries of judge-made law in England. When this country was formed, all the states adopted the English common law on partnerships except for Louisiana, which was more influenced by the French Napoleonic Code. With the growth of interstate commerce and businesses, businessmen and their lawyers decided they couldn't tolerate fifty different sets of partnership laws and lobbied for the enactment of virtually identical statutes on partnerships in the form of the Uniform Partnership Act and the Uniform Limited Partnership Act.

UNIFORM PARTNERSHIP ACT

In 1914 the laws and conventions regarding treatment of partnerships were pulled together in the Uniform Partnership Act (UPA). Since then the UPA, or some variation of it, has been adopted in most of the states.

According to the terms of the UPA, a general partnership is any association of persons formed for the purpose of carrying on a business. It may be composed of natural persons, other partnerships or associations, or corporations. No formal written agreement is required. If there is no understanding to the contrary, the sharing of profits and losses is assumed to be on an equal basis between the partners, regardless of relative ownership/investment. Each and every partner in a general partnership is considered to be fully liable for all the partnership's debts. Should a creditor choose to proceed against only one of the general partners for a partnership obligation, it may do so.

Management responsibility may be delegated to just one or to several of the partners. Without an agreement, however, decisions are to be made by a majority vote.

UNIFORM LIMITED PARTNERSHIP ACT

The Uniform Limited Partnership Act (ULPA) of 1916 provides the basis for state regulation of limited partnerships. All states except Louisiana have adopted the provisions of this act in one form or another. Amendments have been made to the ULPA and many states have enacted the revised version, called the Revised Uniform Limited Partnership Act (RULPA). Check with your state to determine whether it has ULPA or RULPA.

Following is a brief rundown of certain essential provisions of the RULPA.

Documentation Needed to Form a Limited Partnership

Unlike the general partnership vehicle, a limited partnership is not assumed to exist unless it is formally and legally established. Required is the preparation, signing, and filing with the governing state authority of a certificate of limited partnership. Such certificate may be the entire agreement between general and limited partners concerning partnership arrangements, or it may confine itself to certain essential elements required by the state's limited partnership law. Without a formally filed certificate, the partnership may be looked upon as a general partnership with each partner having unlimited liability with respect to partnership actions and obligations. For precise information concerning the essential elements of a certificate of limited partnership in your state, write to your secretary of state. Alternatively, you can go to your public library and see your state code, looking under "limited partnerships."

Control by the General Partners

An essential element in any general partner/limited partner relationship is that control over operation of the partnership must be vested in the general partners. This is the tradeoff the passive investor makes in order to attain limited liability.

Unfortunately, there is considerable ambiguity concerning the question of what constitutes control. Limited partners clearly have the right to review partnership records, receive reports, seek dissolution of the partnership, and receive predetermined profits and/or losses from operations. Beyond this, the law is imprecise. Sometimes, limited partners are given the right to vote on certain major partnership decisions, such as refinancing or sale of partnership assets. The RULPA sets forth which actions a limited partner can take and still avoid being classified as a general partner. If not listed in the RULPA, a limited partner's action could threaten his or her claim to limited liability. Case law experience in every state can be different, and the results, in terms of current and potential future rulings, may vary accordingly.

In an effort to minimize areas of ambiguity, the original ULPA was revised to indicate certain rights that may be safely given to or exercised by limited partners without threat of losing their limited liability status. These include, in addition to the items mentioned in the preceding paragraph, a change in partnership business and removal of the general partner. Limited partners can act as a consultants, employees, or sureties of the partnership and vote on amendments to the partnership agreement and other items, such as removal of a general partner, sale of partnership assets, incurrence of indebtedness, and admission of a new general partner. The revised ULPA does not mean to limit limited partners' rights by such provisions, but rather to define a basic set of minimum rights that partners may enjoy without fear of losing their limited liability.

Control in a limited partnership lies with the general partners. They alone are responsible for day-to-day partnership management, in the course of which they act as fiduciaries to the partnership. In the event of default by the partnership, the general partners alone must stand behind partnership obligations. The only real limits to general partner control are that (1) they may not commit criminal acts, and (2) any and all restrictions imposed by the limited partnership agreement must be adhered to.

ATTORNEY COMMENT

General Partnerships Can Be Dangerous

The rather dangerous business form of the general partnership may be easily entered into. If two persons agree to carry on a business for their mutual benefit and one of them provides the capital, the other works in the business, and they both agree to share any profits that might be derived from the business, then they will be deemed under the law to have formed a general partnership and will become jointly and severally liable to all creditors of the firm. This can be true even though they never put anything in writing, they never intended to form a general partnership, and they never told anyone that they were partners. Fortunately, in most states, the standard real estate ownership forms of joint tenancy, tenancy in common, or tenancy by the entireties do not establish a general partnership.

The general partnership has multiple disadvantages. You are liable for your partner's actions while on partnership business. Your potential liabilities are awesome. The general partnership can be an unstable form. The expulsion, death, or bankruptcy of any one partner, unless otherwise agreed, causes the dissolution of the partnership. It does not have the advantages of a corporation as to limited liability for corporate debts, centralized decision making, and the ability of the business to carry on after the death or bankruptcy of its owners. In short, the consequences of not using the right documentation for a limited partnership means that you will be classified as a general partnership, a potentially disastrous situation.

How to Form a Limited Partnership

To avoid being classified as a general partnership, you must file the correct form of a limited partnership certificate. Under the RULPA, the certificate must contain the following: the name and purpose of the limited partnership; the name and address of the resident agent and signature of each partner and the location of the principal business address; the amount of cash or other property to be contributed by each limited partner; the events which cause an additional contribution to be made; the authority of a limited partner to assign his interest; the ability and terms for a limited partner to withdraw from the partnership and get his money back; the rights of partners to receive distributions, profits, and a return of contributions; the events which would cause the partnership to be dissolved and any right of a remaining general partner to remain if one of the general partners withdraws. Other provisions may be included. In many private syndications, the certificate contains only general statements on each of these items with the true meat of the partnership arrangements being reserved for the nonpublic partnership agreement. In contrast, publicly registered partnerships tend to put the certificate and agreement together in one document.

In the model documents, discussed in Part IV, you can see how each of the requirements for a certificate is typically met. When doing a certificate, I prefer to list the information in the same order and with the same numbers as the state statute so that the clerk reviewing the certificate will clearly and quickly understand how it complies with state law. As for the agreement, the model documents contain many suggested provisions. If you are subject to NASAA guidelines, there are many provisions which you *must* include in your partnership agreements.

GP/LP Decision-Making Arrangements Are Critical to Success

As a beginning syndicator doing a private offering (defined later), you will want to structure your limited partnership so that you retain control of the partnership business. Most likely, you will want to be able to make all major decisions, including a sale or refinancing of the property, without consulting or receiving the consent of the limited partners. You will also want to prevent the limited partners from voting you out as a general partner. In general, these partnership provisions are common in private offerings and consistent with applicable laws. Your attorney must check applicable state securities regulations on this. Nationally recommended guidelines require you to grant certain rights to your limited partners in public offerings. If your limited partners organize and are represented by counsel before they join your syndication, they could insist on the rights permitted under the RULPA and NASAA guidelines, but not typically found in private offerings.

Chapter 5

Laws and Regulations Governing Preparation of Investment Offerings

Limited partnership interests are considered securities. As such, their issuance, sale and transfer come under the purview of federal and state securities laws. In most circumstances general partnership interests are not considered securities and are thus not subject to securities laws. Why the distinction?

In any investment there is an expectation of, or hope for, profit. This is true of either a general or a limited partnership investment. In a limited partnership investment, however, there is the additional characteristic of obligatory reliance upon others for the entrepreneurial or managerial effort. You, the general partner, are being relied upon by your limited partners, and because of this you are in the securities business.

What is the practical effect of being in the securities business? What special regulatory provisions does it entail? In the remainder of this chapter we shall briefly review the Securities Act of 1933 (regulating securities issues), the Securities and Exchange Act of 1934 (regulating securities issuers and sellers) and the role of corresponding state securities laws.

――――――――― **ATTORNEY COMMENT** ―――――――――

The Origins of Our Securities Laws

The securities laws come out of the U.S. Constitution, federal legislation and regulation, state legislation and regulation, the common law, history, and ultimately Judeo-Christian ethics. Attempts to prevent stock fraud schemes go back as early as the 1720 Bubble

Act of the British Parliament. The securities legislation of 1933 and 1934 were depression-era reforms designed to prevent stock manipulations such as those that led to the great stock market crash and subsequent depression of 1929. These and other reforms earned liberal President Franklin Delano Roosevelt, the title of "the savior of capitalism." It could be said that the securities laws arise out of basic tenets of traditional American culture: under these securities commandments, you shall not bear false witness to your investor and you shall not steal your investor's money.

Under the U.S. Constitution, the federal government is a limited government which has only those powers granted to it by the states in the Constitution. This lofty abstract principle of constitutional law has direct practical meaning to the syndicator. You have to conform to federal securities regulation only if your operations go beyond one state. But, conformance with federal laws and regulations does not necessarily mean that you have conformed to state laws and regulations. In our federal system, you must always comply with applicable federal *and* state statutes, rules, and regulations.

THE SECURITIES ACT OF 1933

The Securities Act of 1933 (1933 Act) requires that any securities must be registered with the U.S. Securities and Exchange Commission (SEC) prior to sale unless there is some legal exemption from such registration. The basic premise of the law is that in the case of investments wherein individuals are relying upon the services of others for success, the government should intervene on behalf of the general public to ensure that all critical aspects of such investments are fully disclosed.

The intent of this regulation is not to preclude certain types of activities, but rather to ensure that investment sponsors are honest and open about critical aspects of the partnership, the investment itself, and the background and experience of the sponsors/managers. Exemptions from registration are provided in cases where it is felt that there is no practical need for registration or the benefits of such registration are considered to be remote.

From a regulatory viewpoint, there are four broad classes of limited partnerships: private offerings, intrastate offerings, small public offerings, and large public offerings. Each of these broad classes is reviewed briefly below, followed by a discussion of disclosure documents and the SEC's Guide 5 (formerly Guide 60).

ATTORNEY COMMENT

The Key Word Is Disclosure

The key word for the Securities Act of 1933 is *disclosure*. Generally, the American system of protecting securities investors from stock frauds and snake oil salesmen requires disclosure of all important aspects of the particular business deal. Stock frauds have a history and tradition older than this country. And today, nearly every month the *Wall Street Journal* reports how some swindler raised millions of dollars by promising high returns from a proposed investment scheme. In reality the promoters intended to buy themselves a luxury home on a Caribbean island, a Rolls Royce, and a Lear jet for a fast getaway when they ran out of bribe money to give local officials in an attempt to resist extradition to the United States. To decrease the number of such charlatans and to encourage people to release their hard-earned dollars from savings accounts, the federal and state governments have primarily adopted the approach of requiring promoters to provide adequate information to potential investors and of imposing strong punishment for failure to disclose business plans, experiences, and conflicts of interest.

Private Offerings

Sections 3(b) and 4(2) of the Securities Act of 1933

Sections 3(b) and 4(2) of the 1933 Act provide that securities issues offered to small groups of sophisticated and financially able investors may be allowed exemption from registration with federal regulators provided that there is no general solicitation. Determination as to whether this exemption applies turns on questions such as number of offers made to potential investors, number of actual investors, ease of access to investment managers/sponsors, availability of information regarding the investment, ability of investors to assess investment viability, ability of investors to bear the economic risk, manner of solicitation, and restrictions on transfer of securities after the initial sale.

Were the language of the 1933 Act better defined, we might still be operating with this as our sole guideline for the private offering exemption from registration. The intent of the 3(b) and 4(2) exemptions was to define an area within which a syndicator could operate without the need for public oversight. If the syndication could confine himself to raising funds among a few well-to-do, financially sophisticated friends with whom he had regular contact, by one-on-one solicitation, he could clearly operate safely under these exemptions.

Rules 146, 240, and 242

Unfortunately, borderline cases abounded, lawsuits proliferated, and the need for further elucidation of the path to achieving the private offering exemption became clear. In 1974 the SEC obliged by issuing Rule 146, clarifying the intent of Section 4(2) of the 1933 Act, and Rules 240 and 242, defining exempt small issues as authorized by Section 3(b). These rules were a big help to syndicators wishing to pursue the private offering exemption and probably contributed substantially to the growth of capital formation during the 1970s. Nevertheless, practitioners' complaints of overregulation, particularly for small-size offerings, and of problems with specific provisions of Rules 146, 240, and 242 led to further clarification by the SEC in 1982 via Regulation D.

Regulation D

According to SEC Release No. 33-6389, the intent of Regulation D is "to simplify and clarify existing exemptions, to expand their availability, and to achieve uniformity between federal and state exemptions." What it does, in essence, is rescind Rules 146, 240, and 242 and related forms, and replace them with a revised and restated regulation covering the same ground, hopefully in clearer language and with less cumbersome restrictions. Regulation D covers, in effect, all the ground rules for the private offering exemption from registration with the SEC. To the extent that the SEC is able to accomplish its goal "to achieve uniformity between federal and state exemptions" it may also be accepted by many of the individual state securities administrators as their ground rules. Until that happens, there will continue to be some differences in private offering exemption requirements at the federal and state levels. Following is a brief outline of the priorities of the SEC's Regulation D. For a look at the regulation itself, see Appendix B.

Rule 501—Definitions and Terms Used in Regulation D

Rule 501 provides an alphabetical listing of all definitions necessary to an understanding of the regulation. Generally, these definitions follow the same lines as those used in Rules 146, 240, and 242. An important departure is expansion of the "accredited investor" concept, which bears review if you expect to raise funds from certain institutions or wealthy persons.

Rule 502—General Conditions to Be Met

Rule 502 sets forth conditions relating to all Regulation D offerings. These include: (1) guidelines for determining whether a series of ostensibly separate securities offerings may be judged to be parts of a larger offering (integrated), (2) specific disclosure requirements, (3) limitations on manner of conducting initial sale, and (4) subsequent resale of securities in the offering.

Rule 503—Filings of Notice of Sales

Rule 503 provides a uniform notice of sales form for use in offerings under both Regulation D and Section 4(2) of the 1933 Act. Issuers furnish information to the SEC by checking appropriate boxes on the form, and indicating which exemption they claim.

Rule 504—Exemption for Offers and Sales Not Exceeding $500,000

Rule 504 replaces the old Rule 240. Relying upon Section (b) of the 1933 Act, it provides exemption from registration for certain offers and sales of securities not exceeding $500,000 to an unlimited number of investors (under Rule 240 the limit was $100,000 in securities to 100 investors). There are no specific disclosure requirements, although it should be emphasized that absence of disclosure requirements does not exempt issuers from federal and state anti-fraud and civil liability laws.

Rule 505—Exemption for Offers and Sales Not Exceeding $5,000,000

Rule 505 replaces the old Rule 242. Relying upon Section 3(b) of the 1933 Act, it provides exemption from registration for offers and sales to no more than 35 purchasers that are not "accredited" where the aggregate offering price over 12 months does not exceed $5,000,000. Under Rule 242 the offering limit was $2,000,000 aggregated over a six-month period.

As a beginning syndicator promoting a partnership not already registered with the SEC, you will have to provide the same information required in Part I of the SEC Form S-18 registration statement and certain financial statements for you, the partnership, and the property when using Rule 505. Partnerships already registered under the 1934 Act must provide the documents required under Rule 502 of Regulation D. For existing partnerships, you must provide an audited financial statement and for a new partnership, an unaudited statement. Corporate general partners must provide an audited balance sheet unless it is not material. You have to provide either an audited balance sheet or a net worth statement on yourself in the offering. Depending on whether you can meet the conditions in Item 21(g) of Form S-18, you need to provide audited income statements for one to two years for the property. In compliance with Guide 5, you must disclose your track record in prior syndication.

Rule 506—Exemption for Offers and Sales Without Regard to Dollar Amount

Rule 506 replaces the old Rule 146. Relying upon Section 4(2) of the 1933 Act, it provides exemption from registration for certain offerings regardless of the offering amount. Among the specific requirements to qualify for a 506 exemption are (1) the number of offers and sales cannot exceed 35, excluding "accredited" investors, (2) only purchasers need the "sophistication" requirements (under Rule 146 all "offerees" had to be deemed "sophisticated" before they were spoken to, whether or not they eventually invested), and (3) the "economic risk" test has been eliminated altogether (under Rule 146 offerees and purchasers were required to meet certain wealth or income tests).

If your partnership cannot use Form S-18 under a Rule 506 offering, you must furnish the same kind of information required in Part I of Form S-11, the financial information in S-11, audited balance sheets on all general partners, and one to two years of audited financial information on the property. The audited statement requirement may be dropped only if the audited requirement is not material. You must discuss your track record in a Guide 5 format.

--- **ATTORNEY COMMENT** ---

If you put together a public offering, you must submit it for review to the Securities and Exchange Commission for completeness of its disclosure, but not necessarily for accuracy. After you have gone through this very expensive, arduous and time-consuming process, you are then permitted to use public advertising of your units or stocks and to sell them to strangers. Of course, these *public* offerings may be sold through the public stock exchanges or through licensed broker-dealers.

Some Things to Watch Out for When Making Private Offerings

Typically, as a beginner, you will not be selling your limited partnership interests through a public offering. This is in large part due to Regulation D which allows you to raise up to and over $5,000,000 without going through the expense and travails of a public offering.

When you use a private placement, the SEC and state authorities generally do not look over your documents to see whether you have provided all the necessary disclosures. As a result, these authorities are not going to let you sell your deal to the average Joe who isn't sophisticated enough to be able to spot a con artist. With a private placement, you cannot use public advertisements; you may only sell to your friends or business acquaintances, and your purchasers must be sophisticated and wealthy enough to withstand a loss of all their money. You can sell to unsophisticated but wealthy individuals only if they use sophisticated advisors to review your deal.

By limiting the types of people to whom you can sell your private offering, the regulators hope that your investors will have the sophistication to be able to protect themselves against you. If you slip up and sell your partnership to someone who is not wealthy and sophisticated or if you cannot prove you knew the person before your partnership offering, then you lose the protection of Regulation D. When you lose the Regulation D exemption, then you have just sold an unregistered security and everyone involved in the promotion becomes personally subject to a fine up to $10,000 and up to five years in jail for each violation. In addition, in a developing area of the law, you could be potentially liable to pay back three times what your investors put into the project plus their attorneys fees for using you under the Racketeer Influenced and Corrupt Organizations Act.

Complying with the Securities Act of 1933 is a two-step process for a private placement. First, you must comply with the exemption requirements of the federal government and the states in which you will sell your partnership. This generally means complying with Regulation D and its state versions, except where the state has "merit" review. If your state has merit review for your particular offering, they will actually pass judgment on the investment merit of your deals before letting you sell it to other people. Second, you must provide sufficient written disclosures to satisfy your liability for false or fraudulent statements or for failing to disclose significant details. Even if you meet all the exemption requirements, this does not mean that you are protected from lawsuits on the basis that you omitted to state a material fact required to understand the risks of the undertaking.

Do not believe that you can use Rule 504 for a series of similar offerings to avoid using Rule 505 for larger offerings. Under the securities laws, there is a concept of "integration." This means that if you offer the exact same type of partnerships, one right after another, the securities regulator will aggregate and integrate all your very similar offerings into one offering and then make you comply with the rules applicable to a combined group of partnerships. For example, let's say you complied with Rule 504 in February and raised

$400,000 and in April did another Rule 504 offering raising $300,000, using the same business plan and partnership format. If these two are "integrated" together, you will have a combined offering of $700,000 and will be required to comply with Rule 505 for both offerings.

Again, the rules in this area are complex, but the solutions are relatively simple and easy. If you always follow the highest standards of disclosure and file all applicable notices, you will find yourself protected and in compliance with your moral and legal responsibilities.

Intrastate Offering Exemption From Registration

Section 3(a)(11)

Section 3(a)(11) of the 1933 Act provides exemption from registration for "any security which is . . . offered and sold only to persons resident within a single State or Territory, where the issuer . . . is a person resident and doing business within . . . such State or Territory." This sounds pretty straightforward, doesn't it? Well, in practice it proved not to be. Determination of whether the "intrastate" exemption could be applied turned on various terms which the 1933 Act failed to define. The meaning of "resident" and "doing business within" were the sore points. Who was to say where the offeree and issuer resided when they maintained homes and/or did business in more than one jurisdiction? How much business did the issuer have to do in a "foreign" jurisdiction to risk losing his intrastate exemption?

Because of such issues, and the difficulty and expense of resolving them via the courts, in 1974 the SEC promulgated Rule 147 to further define the intent of the 1933 Act with regard to intrastate offerings.

Rule 147

Rule 147 stipulates that any securities offering or sale made in compliance with the rule will be deemed to satisfy the conditions of the 3(a)(11) intrastate offering exemption. It then proceeds to clarify the ambiguities of the 1933 Act in several areas.

Resident

For an issuer, "residence" was defined in Rule 147 as the state of organization and registration, i.e. in the case of limited partnerships, the state whose partnership laws apply. For offerees and purchasers, "residence" was defined as the state where their principal residence is located or, in the case of a business entity, where its principal office is located. Temporary residency does not suffice, and the burden of proof of state of residency is upon the issuer.

Doing Business Within

For an issuer to be deemed to be "doing business within" a state it must have its principal offices within the state, and 80% of its gross revenues earned, assets held, and proceeds of sales invested, must be within that state.

Because Rule 147 and the underlying Section 3(a)(11) of the 1933 Act do not preclude public offering and sales, such public offering is permitted provided that it does not contravene resident state requirements. It is therefore possible to do an intrastate public offering which qualifies for an exemption from registration with the SEC based upon the 3(a)(11) and Rule 147 exemption provisions. See Appendix C for a statement of SEC's rule 147.

Small Public Offerings

Section 3(b) of the 1933 Act provides for a modified registration procedure for certain small public offerings. Regulation A from the Code of Federal Regulations (Appendix D) elaborates on that. Worth noting is that per the terms of Regulation A, up to $1,500,000 in securities can be sold in a twelve-month period under this exemption. Although the documentation requirements are much the same as for a fully registered public offering, registration is handled through the appropriate regional office of the SEC and a "fast track" review is pursued whereby, if reviewer comments are not received within ten days, compliance by the regulators can be assumed.

With the widespread use of Regulation D for raising amounts up to and over $5,000,000, Regulation A has fallen into relative disuse.

Large Public Offerings

For securities offerings where it is desired to raise large amounts of money in more than one state from more than 35 nonaccredited investors, the only permitted approach is to comply with all the requirements of a full SEC registration. As a rule, such SEC registration is a very expensive process involving substantial legal, accounting, typing, and printing costs in complying with both federal requirements and requirements in the individual states where the offer is to be marketed. For a review of the requirements for a full public offering registration see Form S-11 from the Code of Federal Regulations (Appendix E).

Guide 5 Disclosure Standards

The documentation required by federal and state regulators for explanation of the syndication offering to prospective investors (offerees) is variously described as the "disclosure document" or the "offerings package." In offerings seeking a private placement exemption from registration this package is called the "offerings memorandum." Where an intrastate exemption is sought the package is called an "offerings circular" and in interstate public offerings (both under Regulation A and Form S-11) it is called a "prospectus."

Unfortunately for practitioners, there is no uniform standard of documentation for private offerings (by far the greatest bulk of all offerings), and the standards for intrastate public offerings (the next most common offering type) vary with each state. Only Regulations A and Form S-11 offerings have uniform disclosure standards.

The existence of uniform disclosure standards turns out to be one of the greatest appeals of operating public limited partnerships. In a business where the laws are so very complex, and where judicial interpretations can introduce new perspectives overnight, it is very reassuring to have concise and understandable standards. In the realm of public real estate limited partnerships, that standard is known as Guide 5.

Whatever you may think about Guide 5, it is clearly a well-crafted and thorough document. You don't have to be an attorney to understand it, because it is written in simple English, without use of esoteric, legal phraseology. What's more, it is so thorough that if you follow its dictates, and are truthful, the likelihood of inadvertently overselling your proposal to an investor is very small. Indeed, if it can be faulted, it is because it goes to extremes to encourage negative disclosure (i.e., emphasis on risks, potential conflicts of interest, sponsor fees, and so forth).

Guide 5 disclosure standards are not required for the bulk of limited partnership offerings. As a result, often they are not followed. Because there are no comparable standards for private offerings, the result is a veritable "hodgepodge" of offering documents, many seriously lacking in legal sufficiency.

Worse, the absence of official disclosure standards for private offerings has led many syndicators to believe that they do not come under the purview of the securities regulators at all. This is a terrible mistake!

When one of your investors is upset with you and claims that you didn't properly disclose a potential risk, your reply that there was no such disclosure requirement will not protect you.

The same standards apply to all syndicators, private or public. The only difference is that private offerings are not normally reviewed by regulators in advance so a syndicator can, in effect, get by with anything he pleases until someone (generally an irate investor) summons the attention of the proper authorities.

My advice to all prospective syndicators is to take advantage of the existence of the excellently crafted Guide 5 standard and employ it in your own offerings, whether they are offered under the private offering exemption (Regulation D), the intrastate offering exemption (Rule 147), Regulation A, or Form S-11. Never mind that it is a rigorous standard, and that it forces you to put heavy emphasis on risks. The prospective investors you lose because of risk disclosure are often the ones who will give you the most trouble when things go wrong. Truly sophisticated investors will appreciate your thoroughness in complying with Guide 5 disclosure and will be attracted to your offering because of it.

Beyond that, what magnificent assurance it gives you, knowing that you've lived by the highest standard of the land. You don't have to wonder if your attorney followed a good model offering document and, provided you follow it faithfully, you don't need to worry whether you should have disclosed this or that. Best of all, in case of investor disputes, you can point to the fact that you followed the official SEC public offering standard. For a complete statement of SEC's Guide 5, see Appendix F. Use it as your own guide next time you package a limited partnership offering.

──────────────── **ATTORNEY COMMENT** ────────────────

Getting a Straight Answer From the Regulators

Regulation D sets forth only in very general terms what information you must disclose in a private offering to be able to qualify for the protection of the Regulation D exemption. For offerings under $500,000 (Rule 504), the lack of specific information requirements is very frustrating. As a beginning syndicator, you will probably fall under Rule 504. I have called both the SEC and state regulators to ask them what I can advise my clients as to what they must disclose in a Rule 504 offering. The SEC staffs have pointed out to me that to qualify for the Regulation D exemption under Rule 504, no specific disclosure is required. I am on my own as to what I think the client needs to put in the document to avoid lawsuits for misrepresentation.

My conversations with state authorities have compounded my frustration: Me to state regulator: "What information does a syndicator have to put in the disclosure documents to avoid civil liability for misrepresentation in a Rule 504 offering?" State Staffer: "Well, we have no written rules or guidelines for 504 offerings, but they must state every material fact." Me: "Well, this guy is only raising $100,000 and doesn't want a 100-page document costing him $10,000. What can I leave out of a Guide 5 type disclosure?" State Staffer: "We couldn't possibly answer such a question over the telephone." Me: "Okay, I'll write you and send you all of the documents and you can give me an advisory opinion." State Staffer: "We don't grant advisory opinions on what must be included in a nonpublic offering under Rule 504." (!) After this phone conversation, they made me feel like the syndicator who was left out in the cold.

Why You Should Follow Guide 5

In my practice, I am forced to advise beginning and small syndicators that I cannot tell them what they can safely omit from their private offering memorandum that is required in Guide 5 for public offerings. This is because their "fraud" liability under the securities laws extends to include not only untrue statements but also omission of material facts. Leaving items *out* can be as dangerous as putting false items *in* the documents. The risks in being subjected to a lawsuit based on these vague and shifting standards are high if you omit anything suggested by Guide 5. As a practical matter, you really have no protection from misrepresentation lawsuits unless you follow Guide 5. And, as a practical matter, with the development of new and cheaper computerized word processing systems, once you make the investment of putting together a Guide 5 type offering, you can use much of it again in your later offerings, thereby effectively amortizing the high initial costs over several deals. If you don't follow Guide 5, *you* will become the syndicator left out in the cold.

Finally, you should understand that a few states will require you to follow Guide 5 in private placements, and others have a state policy of recommending use of Guide 5 without directly requiring its use in private deals. This is an area where the law is evolving from state to state.

THE SECURITIES AND EXCHANGE ACT OF 1934

The Securities and Exchange Act of 1934 (1934 Act) requires that persons engaged in the business of selling securities are subject to regulation by the SEC, and that persons who fit the SEC's definition of "brokers" or "dealers" may be required to register as such with appropriate authorities. In the following paragraphs, we shall review the highlights of the 1934 Act vis-à-vis issuers of real estate limited partnership interests.

Broker-Dealer Defined

The 1934 Act defines the term "broker" as meaning any person "engaged in the business of effecting transactions in securities for the account of others" and it defines the term "dealer" as meaning any person "engaged in the business of buying and selling securities for his own account." For the purposes of regulation, it does not matter whether the securities are traded publicly or privately. What is important is that one is in the business.

In the case of most private securities offerings, the interests are often sold by the issuer himself. In such cases, is an issuer a broker and/or dealer under the terms of the 1934 Act?

It depends. If he is charging commissions for such sales it certainly looks like he "is in the business of effecting transactions for the account of others" (i.e., a sponsor or employee earning commission from a limited partnership) and thus falls under the broker definition. If he is continually making such offerings and selling the securities himself, it begins to look as though he is in the business of selling securities and therefore is a broker-dealer.

Registration Requirements

If it is determined that registration of the securities issuer with regulatory authority as a broker-dealer is appropriate, there are several registration options available: registration at the state level only, provided that all his securities business is done within the state, or registration at the federal and state levels if securities business is to be done in more than one state. Though state registration may be in lieu of federal registration where a broker-dealer confines activities to one state, federal registration is never in lieu of state registration. A federally registered broker-dealer must also register in every state in which he or she operates.

Until recently, federal broker-dealer registration could be handled either directly by the basic regulatory agency, the Securities and Exchange Commission (SEC), or by the industry's self-regulatory body, the National Association of Securities Dealers (NASD). The SEC registration option, called "SEC Only" (SECO), was phased out in 1983 however. The NASD, with its highly competent staff in the Washington, D.C. headquarters as well as in regional offices, has done such a fine job over the years that SEC activity in this area of regulation was judged redundant.

Through its nationwide network of offices, the NASD offers as efficient a portfolio of member services as any trade association in the nation, and it simultaneously serves as a tough but fair industry regulator.

First-time applicants for a broker-dealer license find the NASD assistance in dealing with forms, testing, bonding, and miscellaneous other requirements invaluable. Registration with individual state governments is much facilitated as well, thanks to the NASD uniform testing and application procedures.

To get a better idea of the specifics of broker-dealer registration, see Appendix G for a statement of the SEC's Form U-4. For background on the broker-dealer business in general, see two recent books by John D. Ellsworth titled *How to Register as a Broker-Dealer* and *How to Operate the DPP Broker-Dealer*. These are down-to-earth "how-to" books that will save you lots of time and money should you be considering the business. Both are available through the Real Estate Securities and Syndication Institute in Chicago (312-670-6760).

Exemptions From Registration

There are a great many issuers of real estate limited partnership interests today who are not registered or NASD broker-dealers. How do they avoid registration? There are two basic paths one can follow.

Intrastate Exemption

This is the approach discussed briefly above. If you are clearly operating, or intend to operate, as a broker-dealer per the terms of the 1934 Act, the only way to avoid registration with the NASD is to confine your activities solely to your state of residency. You must do all your business—buying, selling and soliciting—within the state, with residents of the state. In determining residency, the SEC will look to the standards developed under Section 3 (a) (11) of the 1933 Act and Rule 147 thereunder.

One can operate as an intrastate broker-dealer, but you've got to be very careful in selecting transactions and clients alike, and compliance with federal regulations continues to be a requirement.

Issuer's Exemption

If you do not meet the definition of a broker-dealer, but you wish to sell the securities in your own offerings from time to time, you may qualify for an issuer's exemption. For issuers making private offerings the question of an issuer's exemption doesn't arise because the regulatory authorities are not required to approve the issue. Indeed, in many states the securities administrators are not even informed of private offerings, and interests in them are sold without their knowledge. It is only in the event of difficulties, typically when a limited partner is looking for a way to get back at a general partner, that the question of whether a sponsor needed a license is likely to arise.

For issuers making public offerings, however, the question of need for a license must be faced at the very outset because, in reviewing the issue for compliance with legal requirements, the regulators also review the issuer. The issuer test is the definition of broker-dealer. To fail the test, i.e., be classified as a casual issuer rather than as a broker-dealer, an issuer must be able to demonstrate that he is not "dealing for the account of others" and is not "in the business of buying and selling." If you sell only your own securities and do it only occasionally (no more than once every two years) you can generally avoid the requirement of registration with state and federal authorities.

─────────── **ATTORNEY COMMENT** ───────────

Who Can Legally Sell Those Partnership Interests

People new to the syndication industry find it very hard to understand the strict requirements imposed on sellers of securities. If you hire or use anyone other than a co-general partner to sell your limited partnership interests on a commission basis, they must have a broker-dealer license. There are restrictions on your ability as a co-general partner to sell partnership interests without a license. If you employ the common practice of using an accountant or attorney to sell your partnership interests to their clients, the attorney and accountant cannot receive a commission from you unless they have the required broker-dealer license. A violation of the Securities Exchange Act of 1934 can subject you and your unlicensed seller to a fine of up to $10,000 and a jail term up to five years. You could lose your exemption from registration under Regulation D by using unlicensed salesmen. The unlicensed seller and you will be subject to civil lawsuits including damages and a requirement to refund any money put into the deal by the limited partners.

You do not have an unlimited right to sell your own limited partnership interests. The rule of thumb under the federal securities laws and in many states is that if you are selling two or less limited partnership interests in eighteen months or less and your offering complies with Regulation D guidelines, then you are not considered to be a broker-dealer and do not need to get a broker-dealer license.

Should you sell three different limited partnership offerings in a year, you could be considered to be in the business of selling securities and have to be appropriately licensed. However, in some states, depending upon the registration exemption you claim, you may have to sell all partnership interests through licensed brokers dealers.

Does this mean you cannot talk to all of those attorneys and accountants who have clients who may want to get into your deal? No, but it does mean that they can't be the "sellers" of the deal. They can be "purchaser's representatives" who receive a fee for reviewing your memorandum and advising the prospective limited partner as to the economic, tax, or legal soundness of your offering. You can pay their fees for reviewing the material and advising the prospective limited partner only if they conform to their obligation to represent the purchaser, reveal that their fees are being paid by you, and disclose any past relationship they have had with you in the last two years.

The NASD Limited Securities License

To facilitate sales of limited partnerships in real estate, oil and gas, and other "tax shelter" type investments, the SEC has adopted a limited licensing provision. This limited license (the NASD Direct Participation Program [DPP]) lets you offer securities solely in the tax shelter area but not stocks and bonds generally. The examination for the DPP license emphasizes the tax shelter area. Your state may or may not impose additional examination and licensing requirements beyond those for the federal DPP examination and license. If you are regularly syndicating properties, you should get a DPP license and could form a separate corporation which will operate as a registered broker-dealer separate and apart from your syndication activities. Properly disclosed, your new broker-dealer corporation can collect brokerage commissions and serve as another source of cash income from your syndication business.

Be Sure to Check Investor Residency

As for intrastate exemptions, my experience has lead me to generally recommend filing a Form D with the U.S. Securities and Exchange Commission even where you expect to sell all your partnership shares in one state. If you sell to twenty different partners, and one partner just happens to live in another state, you have blown your intrastate exemption and may be subject to penalties and recisions by your investors for failure to file the Form D with federal authorities. You can advertise in interstate periodicals, but you must sell only to residents in the state to retain your intrastate status. The problem is where do people really reside? If you sell to a military officer on temporary assignment, does he or she really reside in your state? I have seen syndicators fooled by investors as to their residence even when the syndicator made the investor swear in the offering questionnaire that he lived in the state. It later turned out that the investor in fact did not live in the state and then it was too late to timely file the Form D.

TAX SHELTER REGISTRATION WITH THE IRS

In Section 6111 of the Internal Revenue Code, effective for partnership interests offered after September 1, 1984, each syndication must be registered with the IRS on its first day of sale if it is a certain type of "tax shelter." You can be subject to substantial fines if you fail to register, either (1) if you are the promoter of the syndication, or (2) if you have an equity interest and work as a professional with the partnership and the promoter fails to register the tax shelter.

Section 6111 and the promulgated regulations under it set forth criteria for defining the type of tax shelter covered. First, the shelter has to have a two-to-one ratio. This two-to-one ratio is calculated taking all tax benefits promised and totaling them for each year of the first five years of the partnership. You do *not* deduct any income from the property from these total tax benefits. After determining total possible annual deductions and multiplying all tax credits by 300%, you calculate the total invested by each partner each year. If the syndication organizer helped the limited partner find financing for the contributions of the limited partner, then only the amount directly put into the partnership which was not borrowed can be counted each year as a contribution to the partnership. Then, you must divide the total tax benefits for *each* partner by that partner's calculated contributions for each year. If *any* partner for *any* one year has a 2-to-1 write-off as defined above, then the entire partnership has a 2-to-1 write-off.

To be required to register, the project must also meet a second test having to do with the type or size of the syndicate. Virtually all limited partnerships and any other type of organization deemed a "security" must register. Also, any organization that must file a Form D or any other exemption form with any state or federal securities authority also meets this second test. Finally, even if you have a general partnership which is totally exempt from any securities requirements, if the aggregate amount of the partnership units offered for sale is expected to exceed $250,000 and five or more investors are expected to invest, then the second test is also met. If you use a limited partnership form and you have an average type of real estate syndication, then you will probably have to register as a "tax shelter" by filing

Form 8264 with the IRS. The penalty for failure to register will be 1% of the total amount invested in the shelter with no limitation.

ATTORNEY COMMENT

The IRS "tax shelter" requirements are so broadly defined that they will require registration of virtually all syndicated real estate limited partnerships. Fortunately, the registration requirement is relatively easy and inexpensive. For more information, please consult "Why Most Real Estate Deals Must Register As a Tax Shelter," by Roger J. McClure, in the November 1985 issue of *The Practical Real Estate Lawyer* (a publication of the American Bar Association) ALI-ABA, 4025 Chestnut Street, Philadelphia, PA 19104.

STATE SECURITIES LAWS

Offers and sales of securities must be made in compliance with the laws of the state in which they occur. Compliance with federal regulations (the 1933 Act and the 1934 Act) does not guarantee compliance at the state level, and the states do not defer to federal securities administrators. If you're going to offer limited partnership interests in a state, you'd better learn the regulatory framework of that state before you do anything.

It is true that most states' securities laws (called "blue sky" laws) are closely patterned after the federal statutes, and if you learn and comply with the federal laws, you will be off to a good start. There are important differences, however, and if you don't know the differences in a state where you are operating, you can get into lots of trouble.

A very important point, for example, is that whereas the SEC is empowered by law only to define and require full disclosure of the material facts regarding a securities offering, some states' securities administrators have the legal authority to review the merits of a securities issue to decide whether it is a good or bad deal, fair or unfair. If you are operating in a state where the securities administrator has such authority, you'd better plan to get to know him and his staff well, because you can't do anything without his possible intervention.

Another important point regarding the role of state securities administrators is that they may relate differently to the SEC. Most states are "registration by coordination" states, meaning that where one is making SEC registered offerings, the state will accept the SEC review as meeting their standards and will not impose additional requirements. A number of other states, however, are "qualification" states. What that means to the issuer is that registration and compliance with federal regulators notwithstanding, the state securities administrator will review the issue separately and may require adjustments as a condition to making the offering in his state. Where the "qualification" state empowers its securities administrator to review securities offerings on their merits as investments, anything can happen.

This discussion of state securities laws is very brief, not because it isn't important but rather because, with fifty separate and equal jurisdictions, it is extremely complicated. If you want to "know the score" in a given state, the only real way to learn it is to read that state's code. To facilitate your "tracking down" state laws, or asking specific questions, see Appendix H, a list of the addresses and telephone numbers for the various state administrators.

―――――――――― **ATTORNEY COMMENT** ――――――――――

What to Do When State and Federal Securities Laws Differ

Compliance with federal securities laws does not necessarily mean you have complied with state securities laws. (Please read this sentence again and again until you understand it.) We have a federal system of government and the states have nearly limitless powers to impose their own type of securities regulation. You must comply with the state securities laws and regulations in each state in which each of your limited partners resides. If you are so unlucky as to have twenty limited partners residing in twenty different states, you have to comply with the laws of each of those twenty states. As a beginning syndicator, your activities may be too small to be worthy of the allocation of resources by federal enforcement agencies. However, I know of a case where state securities regulators have done "undercover" work by calling investment ads in to newspapers and posing as investors to determine whether someone is selling real estate securities without securities registration or complying with exemption requirements. You may find that some state requirements are so burdensome that you will refuse to sell your partnership units in some states. The simple solution here is to learn the requirements of your state and neighboring states. You will probably be doing a Regulation D offering and many states have adopted regulatory schemes similar to Regulation D. Some states require you to file a Regulation D type notice with them. If you are in a "merit" state which insists on reviewing the merits of your particular proposal, then you are going to have to allocate substantial funds to the effort of getting your syndication approved. In addition, compliance with federal securities sales licensing requirements does not mean that you have complied with state securities licensing requirements.

The state securities regulators are developing a uniform limited offering exemption similar to Regulation D at the federal level. This will make compliance with state securities regulations standardized from state to state and facilitate interstate offerings.

ORGANIZATIONAL FRAMEWORK FOR SECURITIES REGULATION

Along with the complex system of federal and state laws, rules, and practices discussed under "regulatory framework" above, there is also a system of federal, state, and industry organizations that one must deal with and/or be influenced by when in the securities business. In this section I shall touch on four such organizations very briefly and refer you to sources of further information should you desire to dig deeper.

Securities and Exchange Commission

At the very heart of the whole business is the SEC. Established by law in 1934, it is the central regulatory body for securities transactions in the United States. Relying upon the federal government's constitutional right to regulate interstate commerce, it is the ultimate authority on all securities transactions that transcend state boundaries. Given the mobility of the American people, and the highly integrated system of interstate transportation and communication which we enjoy, the great majority of securities transactions today fall under the aegis of interstate commerce.

The SEC itself is composed of five commissioners, appointed for five-year terms by the president, with the advice and consent of the Senate. Terms are staggered so that no more than one appointment need be filled each year.

The Commission maintains a staff of attorneys, accountants, other professional, clerical, and secretarial personnel in nine regional offices geographically dispersed throughout the U.S. The headquarters office is in Washington, D.C. For an excellent rundown on the SEC, see the pamphlet "Work of the SEC" in Appendix I.

North American Securities Administrators' Association

The North American Securities Administrators' Association (NASAA) was formed early in the twentieth century as a voluntary organization, comprising most of the state securities administrators. It was organized in recognition of the ever-increasing need for dialogue between federal and state administrators/regulators concerning matters of interstate commerce.

In subsequent years, a number of the NASAA state administrators formed an additional, more active group interested in the problems of securities regulation. This group, which came to be called the Mid-West commissioners, eventually developed voluntary standards for review of new securities offerings within their respective jurisdictions. These standards came to be known as the Mid-West Guidelines.

In 1980, when the need for strong representation of the states in development of nationwide regulatory standards had become widely accepted, the Mid-West Commissioners merged completely with the NASAA, bringing a revised version of their by-then-famous Guidelines with them. Reviewed extensively by a NASAA committee, and updated and modified where judged appropriate, the bulk of the Mid-West Guidelines was reissued in 1982 as the NASAA Guidelines, thus providing a uniform standard for state guidelines nationwide.

The important thing to keep in mind with regard to the North American Securities Administrators Association is that it is a sort of state level counterpoint to the SEC. It enables states to negotiate more effectively with the SEC in development of rules and regulations. It also greatly helps the industry through its efforts to standardize state securities laws so as to make the national system more efficient and less costly for practitioners to deal with. See Appendix J for a complete statement of the 1986 version of the NASAA Guidelines.

National Association of Securities Dealers

The National Association of Securities Dealers (NASD) is a nationwide industry association, established in 1935 for the purpose of promoting the securities broker-dealer business. NASD endeavors to do this by establishing high standards of practice, and assisting its members to live up to such standards. NASD's membership comprises all of the major securities broker-dealers in the U.S. and a great majority of the other companies operating intrastate. For addresses of NASD's national and regional offices, see Appendix K.

Real Estate Securities and Syndication Institute

Because it is an association of broker-dealers, NASD does not necessarily represent the viewpoint of issuers themselves. The great majority of small issuers are not broker-dealers at all. Rather, they are realtors, attorneys, accountants, etc. Because they are occasional issuers, normally of private offerings, until very recently they found themselves operating very much alone, without the benefit of association membership. Establishment of the Real Estate Securities and Syndication Institute (RESSI) in 1972 has rapidly been changing that.

Organized as an "institute" within the powerful National Association of Relators, RESSI could easily have developed itself as an exclusively realtors' organization. It did not. Rather, RESSI opened its doors via "affiliate" membership to all professionals interested or engaged in the business of issuing real estate securities. In the process, it has established itself as an effective and respected spokesman for the real estate securities industry.

The distinctions between NASD and RESSI are important, so, I shall reiterate them here. NASD is an industry-wide representative of securities broker-dealers. RESSI deals only with real estate securities, and it is composed primarily of the issuers themselves (syndicators). RESSI members who wish to become broker-dealers may join NASD for representation in that area, and NASD members who wish to become real estate securities issuers (syndicators) may join RESSI. NASD is a government-sanctioned, industry self-regulating body with delegations of authority from the SEC. RESSI is purely a trade association affiliate with no official governing authority.

RESSI has its national headquarters at 430 North Michigan Avenue, Chicago, IL. It also has membership chapters throughout the USA. Addresses for persons in the state chapters may be obtained by calling RESSI's national office in Chicago.

ATTORNEY COMMENT

Keep One Eye on the NASAA Guidelines

The NASAA Guidelines (Appendix J) have been adopted as state guidelines for *public* offerings. You will notice that they go beyond Guide 5 and require more than mere disclosure. The NASAA Guidelines require that certain provisions be placed in your partnership agreement, such as the right of the limited partners to vote you out of office as the general partner. These guidelines also restrict you in how much and when you can charge for brokerage fees, how much you can charge for property management and partnership management, the share of any profits you can take as general partner, and the extent to which you can use staged payments and extra assessments.

These restrictions apply to public and not to private syndications. However, you should have a good reason for deviating from the suggested guidelines even in a private placement. A common example of where many private placements do not follow NASAA guidelines is their stance on *partnership democracy*. Typically the limited partners do not have the power to vote the general partner out of office. However, it is common in private placements as in NASAA Guidelines to require that all the contributions of the limited partners be paid back first, plus some percentage return, before any profits at the end of the deal are paid to the general partners. You must check in your state the extent to which guidelines similar to those of the NASAA will be imposed on your transaction. In Appendix M, we have included a survey showing a state-by-state implementation of NASAA guidelines (as of 1987) and showing, also, which state has a merit or disclosure approach or securities regulation.

PART III

TECHNIQUES FOR SUCCESSFUL SYNDICATION

Chapter 6

Winning Investor Confidence

The beginning is the most important part of the work.
—Plato, The Republic

So you think you may try your wings as a real estate syndicator. Now what? Where should you begin? What kind of deal do you want to make? What are the choices?

The first consideration relates to you as an individual dealmaker: Always trade on your strengths! If you're a real estate broker who specializes in purchasing and selling single-family homes, and you feel that you are truly competitive in that area, consider single-family home investments as the objective of your first syndication offering. If you are a commercial broker, with twenty years' experience selling and leasing office buildings, focus on finding a good office building investment for your first offering.

Winning investor confidence in your first effort is no easy matter. There are many alternative choices for investments, and if your clients feel the least bit uneasy about your ability to earn them high returns on their hard-earned money they will take it elsewhere. Packaging a transaction in which you are an established expert is absolutely essential. Don't delude yourself that your first offering will "sell itself." If that happens, it is probably because you have failed to make adequate disclosure of the overall partnership setup. This typically occurs when the syndication is sold to old friends, via telephone presentations which focus on the property itself, while passing over the partnership arrangement.

If you operate correctly, and disclose to prospective investors all the implications of purchasing the property via a limited partnership vehicle, it may be difficult to raise money for your first syndication. With proper disclosure your friends will be made abundantly aware that an investment in XYZ Partnership is really an investment in you, the Sponsor/General Partner. They will know that if you are flawed in some way (insufficient experience, too many other activities, a poor manager) the prospects for success, even with a very good investment property, are not good. What you're really selling is yourself, and the attractive investment property goes along in the bargain.

So let's assume that you want to trade on your strengths—that you are serious about becoming an investment syndicator and you want to develop an approach that will give you long-term staying power. What are your options for approaching the business within that framework?

ATTORNEY COMMENT

The Importance of a "Track Record"

There are many legal reasons why you should always trade on your strengths. In the disclosure document, you must disclose your background and experience in real estate and business and list the status and types of your previous syndication offerings. Regulation D requires that you list your track record in Guide 5 format for private offerings raising more than $500,000. NASAA guidelines for public offerings prohibit you from providing services to the partnership unless you independently provide such services as an ordinary part of your ongoing business. For NASAA regulated nonspecified offerings, you must have at least five years of executive experience in the real estate industry and at least two years of experience in the type of property you are syndicating. In my opinion, a failure to disclose that you do not have any previous experience in the particular type of investment vehicle could be construed as a material omission subjecting you to potential fraud liability.

PRIVATE VERSUS PUBLIC OFFERINGS

One of the choices rarely faced in a systematic way by beginning syndicators is that of making public offerings versus making private offerings. Normally, in the syndication business, one starts off with a small transaction offered privately to a few friends. One thing leads to another, and in the process most of those who have taken the first step withdraw from the business altogether because of a bad experience—typically, poor relations with the limited partner investors. Of those who stay in the business, the great majority limp along from deal to deal without any real direction or growth. Only a very few progress to different, larger, and ultimately, publicly offered transactions.

Why, I am often asked, do you bother with the hassle of registering your syndications with the state and federal securities administrators? Isn't it terribly expensive? Don't they require all sorts of horrendous disclosures, making it difficult to raise money?

It is always hard for me to know where to begin when barraged with such questions, because they are based on a profound misunderstanding of the business and are reflective of an unjustifiably defensive attitude.

Legal Rationale for Avoiding Registration

Let's look at the last question first—disclosure requirements. As we discussed in Part II of this book, disclosure requirements for securities offerings are based primarily upon: the 1933 Securities Act; successor regulations and guides at the federal level; additional, largely corresponding laws, regulations, and guides at the federal level; and additional, largely corresponding laws, regulations, and guides from fifty sovereign states. These laws, regulations, and guides do not apply solely to public offerings, however. They apply to all securities offerings, public or private.

The fact that one is not required to subject a private offering memorandum to review by the regulators prior to offering commencement does not mean that one is not subject to the regulations. The standards for disclosure are there anyway. The important difference between making private offerings, versus making public offerings, is that in registering a public offering one is benefiting from a gratis review by the very regulators one will have to deal with anyway, should he or she get into trouble.

A notable benefit of this prior review approach is that it effectively gives official sanction for the documents so that one cannot be faulted later for, say, being unduly optimistic in projections, failing to disclose risks that should have been perceived, etc. In effect, by registering an offering, the syndicator is buying insurance against a major area of legal vulnerability—inadequate disclosure. He need only live by the promises he makes and operate in a legal fashion, and he is safe from investor reprisal.

Economic Rationale for Avoiding Registration

What if I'm not worried about lawsuits from disenchanted investors? What if my investors are all friends, and the deals we wish to make are so simple that long and burdensome disclosure is unwanted by everyone involved? Isn't it really wasteful of investor money to prepare a "razzle-dazzle" offering document?

Here, again, popular misconceptions have led to improper conclusions. If your transaction involves a relationship between limited and general partners it is not simple, no matter what the real estate aspects. There are a great many general partner responsibilities, and restrictions on both the general and limited partners' behavior, which need to be clearly stated. Granted, most of them are based on common sense, Judeo-Christian ethics, and our common-law traditions, so you will probably abide by them unconsciously, but others are less obvious. The irony is that it is often the least sophisticated person, the one most likely to err, who is most convinced that he needs no guidance in these matters.

What about the cost of preparing first-class disclosure documents, and of public registration itself? Isn't it unfair to one's investors to accrue and pass on such high costs?

The notion here is that if a document is professionally prepared, it must cost more, and if one wants to cut costs, one needs simply to lower standards. In medicine, that would be akin to trying to cut the cost of dealing with a health problem, say the need for heart surgery, by looking for the cheapest surgeon.

It never ceases to amaze me that so many people try to cut legal bills by going to an attorney just out of law school who may work for $50 per hour, or a neighborhood general practitioner who charges only $75 per hour, when there is a nearby specialist who charges $100 per hour. Forgotten by these misguided "bargain hunters" is that the specialist will do superior work in a fraction of the time. He doesn't have to "go to school on you." He already knows the rules and has his models. In the securities business, as in medicine, plumbing, and lots of other businesses, the specialist will do a better job for you at less cost, not more.

The Importance of Full Disclosure

Another self-defeating way of cutting legal bills is to keep the disclosure very brief, often by starting from "scratch" and discussing only the few items you feel are germane to your specific offering. You know what you want to do and if you can lay it out in three pages that is better, right?

Wrong! Starting from "scratch" is like reinventing the wheel. There are reasons for all that mystifying language you see in the expensive public disclosure documents, and in SEC's Guide 5. If you read them, and you don't appreciate the rationale for every section, you need to "go back to school." Read some more. Buy an hour's lecture from a first-rate securities attorney, or take a syndication course from RESSI. When you've acquired a bit more knowledge, you'll understand the need for disclosure, and you'll be glad you took the time. You'll avoid lots of grief and aggravation if you learn to do things right from the outset.

Is it really more costly to prepare a first-class disclosure document suitable for registration with the state and/or federal securities administrators? Of course not. You need only: (1) use a good guide, and (2) get the advice of experts (especially an attorney) who have done it before. You, or your attorney, can "mark-up" a model document taken from an available public offering with less investment of time than if you create one from scratch. Alternatively, or in addition, you can use the SEC's approved formula for public offerings (Guide 5) and essentially fill in the blanks.

Using Guide 5 Disclosure in Private Offerings

Think of the benefits you will derive from preparing your offering documents in this way. Guide 5 and your model public offering documents will draw your attention to issues that may otherwise never have crossed your mind. What an education to see the myriad, sometimes mystifying, securities regulations applied to something that you yourself are doing. When you see them in this context, they will take on meaning.

So, having dealt with the classic objections to full, public offering quality disclosure, and concluding that irrespective of one's intent with regard to marketing the offering (publicly or privately), full disclosure *is* desirable, on what other bases should one evaluate the decision to operate publicly or privately?

To my mind, the most important considerations are where you want to go in the business, and how you plan to get there. First of all, how big do you want to be? Your first offering may be very small, perhaps you and several friends purchasing a house, but is that where you want it to end? If so, if that is the extent of your syndication ambitions, then plans to move someday into a public offering mode are probably not indicated.

What if you are thinking of a single-house syndication with several friends as a start, which you hope can lead to much larger offerings later on? Then you have to think carefully about prospects for raising all your funds privately. Do you have the right friends? Do you have a relative or partner who is so "well connected" with well-to-do passive investors that your fund-raising ability is essentially limitless among people already known to you? If so, then you may be able to plan on operating privately indefinitely. You'll have to be mindful about the manner of offering (e.g. no public meetings) and take care not to develop a string of offerings so similar that the securities administrators could argue that they are all really one (called integration), thus violating the maximum number of investors rule (thirty-five in most states), but you can feasibly do many offerings over the years without registering any of them.

What if you don't have rich friends, or your ambitions are so great that even a few rich friends can't be relied upon to meet all your capital requirements? What if you know people with money, and they would trust you with it, but you don't want to get into that kind of relationship with them. You prefer to keep a certain distance from your investors. If these are considerations that are important to you, then you should think about preparing to do public offerings. Even if your first offering is very small, effectively presold, and you are committed to doing it privately, you can at least start thinking about a public mode. Future plans with regard to a public or private offering mode will affect your operation in many ways, ranging from disclosure documents, to bookkeeping, to reports. If you anticipate "going public" one day, practice on your friends in the small, private offerings. Develop systems that can be expanded for dealing with large numbers of investors and learn to use them. In the process you'll learn whether such a business approach really suits you.

Above all, don't let your friends, attorney, or the regulators themselves intimidate you with the query: "Why do you want to go to all the trouble of doing a public offering when you're raising so little money?" The decision of public versus private is much more complicated than the size of your current offering and it is yours to make, not theirs. You alone have the liability and the responsibility, and you alone have the "big picture" with regard to where you want to go.

ATTORNEY COMMENT

*Some Practical Problems
With Making Small Public Offerings*

There are several legal considerations as to why the beginning syndicator will probably use a private versus a public offering. There are many restrictions applicable to public syndications that generally are not applicable to private syndications. Under the NASAA guidelines for public syndications, you must raise at least $1,000,000 for nonspecified offerings, you must give your limited partners the right to vote you out of office, you are restricted in the property management fees you can charge, you are limited in how much you can charge in up-front fees and how much you can take as part of the ultimate profit. Additionally, you must have at least two years' experience in the type of property to be acquired, and you must have a net worth of $50,000 or 5% of the gross amount of all offerings sold within the prior 12 months; if capital contributions are paid on an installment basis, the front-end fees paid to the sponsor must be paid only as the installments come in; you must invest a minimum amount of the money raised in the property; and you must first pay back all contributions plus at least a 6% return before you can receive any profits from the sale of the property.

In a private offering, not subject to NASAA guidelines, you have flexibility on each of these issues, absent contrary state regulation.

How to solve the dilemma that a private placement is better for you but the best legal guidelines for placement documentation come from the public placement guidelines? Do a private placement, following the disclosure guidelines of Guide 5 and the NASAA guidelines, but structure your deal in a way that makes sense to you without the straightjacket imposed by public offering requirements.

SPECIFIED VERSUS NONSPECIFIED OFFERINGS

Another choice that one should evaluate when considering a career in the investment syndication business is that of specified versus nonspecified offerings. Probably 90% of all syndicators are not even aware that there is such a choice—that one can raise money for investment in certain objectives (nonspecified offering) versus a specific property, (specified offering). Well, there is such a choice, and there are some very important tradeoffs between the two approaches.

In dealing with the specified versus nonspecified offering tradeoff, the first thing one must come to terms with is a recognition that there is a big difference between investing in real estate and syndicating real estate investments. Most of us who have worked in the real estate business are used to focusing on investment properties per se—houses, office buildings, shopping centers—very tangible items which can be evaluated for profitability through a variety of quantitative analyses.

At the point that an investment property is acquired by a limited partnership, however, it takes on a far less tangible nature. Ownership is in a security, rather than real property, and is subject to a host of restrictions and considerations that influence its value and convertibility into cash or other consideration. By investing in a limited partnership to purchase the investment property, versus investing directly (either outright or through a general partnership), we have made a big step toward the world of intangible investments.

Now let's go one step further. Let's invest in a limited partnership which has as its goal the acquisition, operation, and sale for profit of an as-yet-undetermined investment property or properties. Sound crazy? Is it intangible enough for you? Would anybody ever invest in such a partnership?

What we have just described is a nonspecified, limited partnership offering and, indeed, people do invest in such partnerships in very large numbers. As a matter of fact, there are more than a dozen syndicators in the United States who are raising $50 million or more per offering, sponsoring one such limited partnership every year. Nonspecified property offerings are a very big business today, perhaps the fastest growing segment of the real estate syndication industry. There are some very good reasons why you should consider nonspecified offerings as your own approach to the syndication business.

Advantages of Specified Offerings

The advantages of doing specified offerings are fairly straightforward. Essentially they relate to the relative ease of raising funds. If a potential investor can drive by a property, or perhaps even walk through it and "kick the bricks," he can be encouraged to focus on the property per se rather than on the less tangible true investment—a security in a limited partnership. Even in America, with its highly developed securities market and the amazing level of trust that we have in intangible investments, it is much harder to get someone to part with his hard-earned cash for a piece of paper (a limited partnership interest) than for a building. So, it is easier to raise money for a specified offering.

Drawbacks to Specified Offerings

There are some real drawbacks to the specified offering approach, however. What if, for example, you tie up that investment property with a deposit and then find yourself unable to raise enough investor funds to go to settlement? What if you raise the targeted amount of investor funds but your financing falls through? What then? Not only might you lose your deposit, but you also lose the money you spent organizing the limited partnership and, even more serious, you lose some credibility as a dealmaker with your stable of potential investors. If your investor friends went to the trouble to sell stocks or savings certificates (possibly paying taxes and/or an early withdrawal penalty) to invest in your limited partnership and the partnership never "gets off the ground" they aren't going to be happy with you.

Another drawback to the specified offering relates to the viewpoint of the seller of that investment property. How easy is it going to be to deal with him if, in your approach, you request that he accept a low deposit and long review period. You need the low deposit consideration because at this point it is your own money you're working with. You need a long review period because in addition to assessing the property, you have to form a limited partnership, prepare disclosure documents, and raise funds. Each task, in itself, is an expensive, time-consuming, costly endeavor. You might not succeed. You might go through all the steps of forming a partnership and preparing disclosure documents and fail to raise sufficient funds.

You can't assume that the seller is stupid. If you approach him with no money and no partnership, he's going to be wary. Do you think it will influence the price and terms he will agree to? You bet it will! If he has a really marketable property and your track record for raising money is short, or blemished, he may not agree to deal with you at all. Alternatively, he may insist on a higher price, a nonrefundable deposit, or an "acceleration" clause in case a more "qualified" buyer appears on the scene.

If you are of only modest means, without the capability to personally guarantee meeting minimum offering proceeds from personal funds, these drawbacks of specified offerings can be very restrictive indeed. They may not keep you out of the business altogether, but they will definitely limit your growth to larger offerings. They will also probably cause you to miss out on really well-priced properties because your contracts will, of necessity, have too many contingencies, and you may have to settle for inferior terms.

To summarize, specified offerings have the advantage of making it easier to raise funds because the investment is relatively more tangible. On the other hand, they entail high up-front costs during the period between contract and closing (the riskiest phase, during which risk is borne by the syndicator alone), and they often result in the partnership's paying top dollar for its acquisitions.

Advantages and Disadvantages of Nonspecified (Blind Pool) Offerings

What about the alternative—doing nonspecified offerings? What are the advantages and disadvantages of this approach?

The advantages and disadvantages of nonspecified offerings are almost a mirror image of the advantages and disadvantages of specified offerings. First, where specified offerings are relatively easier to sell because there is tangible, real property to evaluate, nonspecified offerings are hard to sell because you are dealing with intangibles. Offered to your investors is a concept (e.g., investment in a half dozen rental houses), certain parameters (e.g., District of Columbia Metropolitan Area, stable neighborhoods slated for subway impact), investment objectives (e.g., return on investment from appreciation, tax losses, cash flow, and loan amortization) and a strategy (buy low, maximize financial leverage, lease for five years while taking tax losses, and sell for a profit). This degree of intangibility is particularly difficult for those of us who are closely identified with the real estate industry. We are often incapable of disassociating the realty from the security, and it creates all sorts of problems for us as a result.

How to Sell Those Hard-to-Sell Intangibles

Yet nonspecified funds are marketed every day by the public syndicators and associated securities dealers who sell the major public, nonspecified funds alluded to earlier. How do they do it?

Sell the General Partners

The technique used is to concentrate first on the intangible (concept, parameters, objectives, and strategy) and then create some sort of tangible to take the place of specified realty, which is lacking. This is done in several ways. First, they sell the general partners and their organization. Then they provide some illustrative realty (e.g., pictures and description of either a past investment or one representative of those planned for the current offering). These are both tangible items that a prospective investor can embrace and from which he can derive security.

Sale of the general partners and their organization is handled differently for a major nationwide public offering than for a small public or private offering. A national syndicator sponsor might stress name recognition, association with an even better known underwriter, track record, and impressive biographical sketches of a large staff. In a small, area-specific offering the sponsor is more likely to sell his reputation in the community for honesty and competence, his track record in whatever business he has been in, and his determination to do well for his investors.

The thing to stress, in both cases, is that although no specific property is promised to the investor, the concept, parameters, objectives, and strategy are known, and the general partners are being "retained" by the investors to carry them out. The created tangible is thus the general partners themselves. Investors are encouraged to look at their records and to invest in them.

Sell the Concept

The other tangible that is created to take the place of specified realty is the illustrative property. Some companies will slip this into the offering materials in the form of a brochure showing investments made by previous partnerships. Others will place contracts on the first two or three of, say, ten projected investments and present profiles of these as illustrative investments. Investors are still buying into a nonspecified fund, and if the offering documents are done appropriately they will be reminded of this repeatedly, but their attention will continually return to the illustrative investment.

How to Minimize Your Risk

With regard to the issue of up-front risk, and the difficulty of obtaining good terms from sellers, the nonspecified offering has great advantages over its counterpart, the specified offering.

Low Minimum Offering Size

Up-front risk can be minimized in nonspecified offerings by setting the minimum offering size at a level that is easily within the means of the syndicator to meet. In a partnership proposing to invest in houses, you might establish your minimum at, say, $50,000 (perhaps enough funds to buy two or three houses) and your maximum at $250,000 (enough for ten or fifteen houses). If you're proposing to acquire shopping centers, you will be looking at larger numbers, of course, but the basic premise is the same. Set a low enough minimum so that you can: (1) purchase at least one of your target investments, and (2) be assured of raising the minimum so that your up-front organization costs can be passed along from the sponsor to the partnership.

Become a Cash Buyer

The other form of up-front risk that is virtually eliminated by the nonspecific property approach is the risk of losing one's deposit on a realty acquisition for a nonspecified fund until you have the necessary funds to consummate the transaction. In effect, you transfer from being a person with a dream but no money, to a qualified, institutional buyer with cash in hand and the ability to move very quickly.

The other advantage of the nonspecified offering is an outgrowth of this. When you are a cash buyer, able to move very quickly, you abruptly move into the category of "qualified buyer." Now you are able to dictate terms, take advantage of foreclosure sales, and all the other things that go with buying smart.

So where should you come out on the specified versus nonspecified offering tradeoff? Is there any easy answer—a right way and a wrong way? Not really. Not one that applies to everyone. What I hope you do conclude, however, is that the nonspecified offering route is a viable option—just because your attorney, accountant, and business associates may never have heard of it or are confused by it, does not make it impracticable. In my own syndication business, the nonspecified offering has been my "strong suit." It has enabled me to work at my own pace (rather than against the time constraints of contract settlement deadlines), to carefully select my investors (to assure compatibility with me and with partnership objectives), and to make judicious investments on favorable terms.

If you can learn to do nonspecified funds, you'll be richer and wiser for the experience. It will not prevent you from doing specified offerings concurrently, or in the future, but it will provide a "product line" that will enable you to always be in the marketplace, both as a syndicator/securities offeror and as a real estate buyer. It will also give you a perspective on the securities business you may never acquire if you limit yourself to specific realty offerings. It is worth learning to do.

ATTORNEY COMMENT

Securities Regulators Are Distrustful of Nonspecified Offerings

Before doing a nonspecified offering, check with your state regulatory authorities as to any restrictions on nonspecified offerings. Securities regulators fear that nonspecified offerings can be a fraud just waiting to happen. For example, for public offerings subject to NASAA guidelines, you must raise a minimum of $1,000,000, you must have at least two years of experience in the particular type of real estate to be syndicated, you are restricted in the extent to which you can invest in raw land and notes and mortgages, and you can't extend your money-raising period beyond one year. Guide 5 requires that you disclose that it is a nonspecified offering. I think that regardless of the size of your nonspecified offering, you must disclose that fact and what you intend to use the money for. And, once raised under those promises, you *must* use the money to invest in the type of properties you described in your offering memorandum. Regulation D's basic requirements do not change depending upon whether if is nonspecified or specified.

Cash Buyers Sleep Better

Usually, you are working at a tremendous disadvantage in a specified offering if you need the offering to fund the purchase of the property. Typically, your seller will require you to place a nonrefundable deposit with him to tie up the property. Usually, this money comes from your own resources. If the syndication fails and you can't find enough investors, you forfeit your money, and you will probably lose any lawsuit to recover it. I know of one local large syndicator who recently forfeited $120,000 on a specified offering because they were unable to go to closing. I know of a beginning syndicator, who on the morning of the day of closing, realizing that he didn't have enough funds raised, dashed out his front door to spend the whole day raising money, only to find his car had died on him at the worst possible moment. He dashed to a local car dealer, bought a new car, chased around all day for money and arrived at the closing breathlessly clutching the last necessary dollars in his hands. After that horrifying close call, he went into semiretirement from syndication.

Nonspecified Offerings Are a Tough Sale for Beginners

As attractive as the nonspecified offering is from the perspective of relieving pressures to "settle" on an acquisition at a certain time, I would usually recommend against someone doing a nonspecified offering if his or her first syndication involves apartment buildings or commercial properties. A nonspecified offering memorandum can be more difficult to write for someone inexperienced in compiling abstract documents because he can't talk about a specific property. NASAA guidelines effectively prohibit beginners from doing a public nonspecified partnership. You have no track record to point to or to make your investors feel comfortable with in giving you their money. State regulation may severely hinder you. In general, as a first-timer, you don't have the experience necessary to handle the problems with the nonspecified form for the large properties. You are probably stuck with the risk that failure to raise the necessary funds will result in loss of your deposit. On the other hand, if you are starting out with a syndication of single-family homes, and are an experienced single-family home investor, the nonspecified offering may be the only practical and sensible alternative.

ESTABLISHING INVESTMENT OBJECTIVES

A third choice worth evaluating systemically is that of investment objectives. This is a choice one faces whether operating publicly or privately, via specified or nonspecified offerings. What kind of investments do you want to specialize in with your limited partnership offerings? Do you want to invest in single-family houses for appreciation, apartment buildings, or shopping centers for cash flow, deteriorated historic and commercial properties for value added from rehabilitation and tax writeoffs? How do you decide in what to specialize?

This choice should also be evaluated and made very systematically, and the final decision should be a function largely of two factors: (1) your field of expertise, and (2) a projection of your potential investors' demands/needs. Don't start off by targeting on a property you feel is well priced and then endeavor to adapt your expertise and your investors' needs to the challenges and rewards presented by that property. If you do, you will end up doing a half-baked job on a potentially good investment (good for another syndicator and another group of investors) and, worse, you'll establish a pattern of being out of control. You must never be out of control in business, especially when you're responsible for other people's money.

The focal point of all your decisions should be investment objectives, not the investment property itself. Your responsibility, as an investment syndicator, is to optimize the use of your investors' money. You should, therefore, build your entire decision framework around your investors and their needs.

What if you have never syndicated an investment, so you don't have investors to cater to? In that case, you focus on your perception of needs among the type of investors you feel you are most likely to reach. Do you live in a community where there are lots of high-income, mid-career professionals? Then consider investments with major tax savings benefits. Do you know a lot of retired people with low current incomes but substantial savings? Then consider investments that generate high cash flow.

There is a big, wide world of potentially lucrative investments out there. The most successful syndicator, over time, will be the one who recognizes that the investors must take precedence. Serve them well, and there will always be business for you.

ATTORNEY COMMENT

If You Don't Understand the Investment, Don't Syndicate It

I cannot tell you that you are legally required to syndicate properties only within your real estate expertise. But, given the disclosure requirements, your personal liability for large partnership debts as a general partner, the likelihood that the project will have trouble if you are a neophyte to that property type, and the probability that you will return all your investors' money if the project fails, it is foolhardy for you to syndicate properties with which you have little experience. In a syndication, the limited partners "hire" you to manage their money, due to your superior expertise.

As an attorney, I see a lot of the "dark side" of real estate. I can assure you that there are crooks and people just waiting to take the money of someone who is inexperienced in their specialized type of property or marketplace. I have seen syndicators who were highly successful in their own marketplace but who failed in a neighboring market and state only ten miles away. This usually infallible syndicator made a disastrous investment in an unfamiliar market.

DEFINING YOUR MARKET

Before you buy your property or put your syndication together, you should define your market. This is not the real estate market, but an entirely different market—the market for your limited partnership units. You must decide which type of person will be interested in the type of property in your syndication, and how they will want you to structure your syndication. And, most important, you have to decide *who* will sell the partnership units *before* you buy the property.

Putting Your Investor's Needs Ahead of Your Investment Opportunities

I have seen excellent syndications completely fail to sell to investors even though the economics of the deal were far superior to other available deals being sold. I have seen other deals sell out in a couple days even though the partnership structure virtually prohibited any substantial return being gained by the limited partners.

From these experiences, I have concluded that it is not the deal which is the most important factor, but the people involved in the deal, especially the person who is selling the partnership. Partnership units are sold based upon respect for the seller's abilities and judgment. A client of an accountant may buy any syndication recommended by the accountant to the client. Some investors will buy limited partnership interests if they are sold to them by their stock broker or financial planner.

Discovering What Securities Dealers Are Looking For

In a small deal, say where you are raising less than $500,000, you or your partner will probably be the person who will sell the partnership units. This is true because to hire someone else to sell it, you may have to pay an 8 to 10% commission to raise the funds and the deal may not have enough profit in it to allocate that much to commissions. Also, if you do use someone else to sell your units, they must have the required securities licenses. Someone with such a license will have to protect themselves by doing "due diligence," which means they have to investigate you and your deal. Due diligence takes so long and costs so much that there have to be minimum commissions in the deal and in future business with you to make it worthwhile for the broker-dealer to become involved.

If you are raising $300,000 to $1,000,000, you may be able to use the services of a financial planner or insurance agent who has the proper securities credentials. For larger offerings, you may be able to graduate to a local or regional brokerage house. The large national syndication companies often use a large national brokerage house to sell their partnership units.

Fad Investments and Investment Size

Another major factor to consider in marketing your units is the property type. For awhile, many investors only wanted to buy new shiny office buildings in high-growth cities in the sunbelt. Other investors only trust investments in single-family homes within a fifty-mile radius of their home. Others only like shopping centers in suburban areas. In a private placement, you can sell only to the clients of your broker-dealer and to your friends and acquaintances. You have to match your prospective partnership purchasers with your property type.

A further important factor is how much money you expect from each investor. If you are going to sell the partnership to your friends who usually have only about $5,000 to invest, then you should not structure the partnership so that the minimum contribution is $50,000. If you do not want to deal with a lot of small, unsophisticated investors, then you may want to have a minimum contribution of $50,000 or more.

Also, if you can have only thirty-five investors who are not accredited, then if you want to raise $1,000,000, you should not offer minimums less than the amount necessary to raise the $1,000,000 from only thirty-five investors. If you need to raise these larger sums, then your investors must be able to financially withstand the loss of their entire investment and meet appropriate suitability standards.

Once you have determined your strengths as far as the type of property you will syndicate, meet with the person who will sell your units. If you are going to sell them, make a list of all your friends and business acquaintances. Go down the list and write beside each name how much money that person is likely to invest with you. Your total should at least be 50% more than you need. Talk to a sample to see how good you have estimated your chances. If using a broker-dealer, get a similar estimate from him or her. You need to constantly think about and consult with your unit sales agent through the whole syndication process, beginning with the acquisition of the property and the structuring of the syndication. If you do this, you will find it much easier to raise money and to insure that you get only qualified investors into your partnership.

ATTORNEY COMMENT
---

*Who Should Sell Your Partnership Interests,
and to Whom Should They Be Sold?*

Your reaction to this section may be that you know of many instances where tax shelters are sold by salesmen who don't have licenses or by advertisements in the paper to people who should not have invested in these schemes. It is just plain illegal for an unlicensed person who is not an active general partner to sell a public or private offering subject to the securities laws; these people are operating outside of the law. Just because burglary is common, doesn't mean that it is appropriate behavior that will escape punishment. In a private placement, regardless of whether you are selling the units or you have a licensed salesperson, it is unethical and possibly illegal to sell to someone an interest in a real estate investment that is not suited to them.

"Suitability" is a concept of securities law which encourages you to match up the property benefits with the financial needs of your investors. NASAA guidelines impose suitability standards on syndication promoters. You must set forth in your offering materials the investment objectives of your program, a description of the type of person who could benefit from your syndication and the suitability standards to be applied in your marketing. Such factors as high leverage, tax write-offs available, amount of cash flow, all affect suitability. If your partnership provides deductible tax losses of 50% or more of the contributions of an investor, then these units should only be sold to persons in a high tax bracket who can use these write-offs. For public offerings, the federal and state regulators will review your statement of suitability standards.

An elderly retired person who mainly needs income should generally not be sold a high-risk, low-income partnership with substantial tax benefits. A high-income middle-aged person who pays substantial taxes may benefit little from a partnership producing only income and no tax benefits, unless sold to his or her self-directed pension plan. A "good deal" is only a good deal for those persons who need the benefits it is producing. If you put together a private partnership which you will market yourself, you should sell it only to your friends and business acquaintances if it is suitable to them.

Chapter 7

How to Set Up the General Partner Relationship

Every man shall bear his own burden.
—St. Paul, Galatians

So you've taken a hard look at your own abilities and the needs of your target investors, and you've selected an investment property. The next question that frequently arises is: "Can I do this deal alone, or do I even want to do it alone?"

In my own experience, there has been another general partner in each syndication. The individuals or entities have varied from transaction to transaction, but always there has been somebody to help make the deal, and later to share the heavy burden of responsibility for operating it. In this section, we will discuss some of the reasons why one might elect to share the general partner responsibilities, and benefits (typically a percentage of any profits earned) with a co-general partner, and we will look at some ideas on how to structure that relationship.

REASONS FOR CHOOSING A CO-GENERAL PARTNER

Perhaps the most common reason for choosing a particular individual as a co-general partner is because the person contributes control of a desirable property that fits the syndicator's expertise and the needs of his target investors. You may recall from our discussion of specified versus nonspecified offerings that control of the investment property is one of the major up-front risks borne by syndication sponsors. Do you have a colleague who meets all or many of the requirements you may have for a co-general partner, who can resolve this risk himself? If so, such a contribution may well be worth a share in the general partnership interest. Control may be attained through fee ownership (in effect, joint venturing with the owner of a property to acquire it for the partnership), contract ownership (your partner has tied up a property with a purchase contract), even, in some cases, through an exclusive listing. In the latter case, consider requiring the partner to bear all the economic burden of misspent organizational expenses in the event that another party buys the property before the syndication can do so. Without such an agreement he really hasn't removed from your shoulders the risk of losing control.

Another basis for selection of an individual as a co-general partner is his or her ability to contribute some skills which you perceive as critical if the sponsors are to represent themselves as experts. In effect, whatever qualities your co-general partner brings to bear are blended with your own as part of the general partnership whole. If you see an opportunity to develop a nursing home, and you know such a project will meet the investment objectives of your target investors, but you don't have expertise in this area, consider giving a portion of the general partner interest to someone who can contribute that expertise. The same approach might apply to a whole range of investments, particularly where some change in the use or form (through rehabilitation or development) of a property is envisioned.

A third, very common basis for selection of a co-general partner is his or her ability to contribute to raising investor funds. Perhaps you have a transaction in mind which can be unusually remunerative for a certain target investor group but you don't know how to reach these investors yourself, or the deal is simply too large for you alone. Maybe you know someone who is a major center of influence among your target investors who, with the incentive of a share in the general partnership interest, would raise substantial investor funds for the partnership.

A good source for a "fund-raising" co-general partner is from among your colleagues who are engaged in financial planning, insurance, law, or accounting. Perhaps the best general source of such assistance, although it is also the least attainable because of competition from other syndicators, is the local securities broker-dealer community. These people raise money for a living, so they know with a fair degree of certainty what products they can sell, and in what quantity. They also participate in ownership relatively infrequently, so if you can make them feel secure with you as a co-general partner, and with the transaction as an investment for their clientele, they may be a useful ally not only on one, but perhaps on many future transactions.

The above list of reasons why one might choose to share a general partnership interest is merely illustrative. With some thought, another dozen valid reasons could be developed. The next consideration is how to structure a relationship with a co-general partner, if such a relationship is deemed worthwhile. The decision on how general partners are to relate, and be rewarded, over the life of a limited partnership is too important to leave to chance. A methodology for making that decision is very much needed. Poor planning at this stage of the syndication has probably "taken the bloom off," if not destroyed, more partnerships than any other mistake. Following is a discussion of two rules which, if obeyed, can greatly enhance your prospects for long-range mutual satisfaction with your co-general partner arrangement.

ATTORNEY COMMENT

General Partner Assets Are Important

One of the factors which the IRS looks at to determine whether an entity should be treated as a partnership for tax purposes is whether the general partners have sufficient personal assets in relation to the risks posed by the project. If you are a beginner with no assets, you might consider bringing in a "money man" to help qualify the partnership for partnership tax treatment and to obtain the necessary financing. Also, for marketing and management purposes, it is wise for the general partners to have sufficient assets in relation to the size or risk of the syndication. The greater the size or risk, the greater the need for a strong general partner financial statement.

RULES OF THUMB FOR STRUCTURING THE GENERAL PARTNER UNDERSTANDING

Each Party Should Be Paid for What He or She Contributes (And No More)

Scratch a seasoned syndicator and the probability is about 90% that he broke this rule in his early years and lived to regret it. What is the most common approach to taking on a partner in an enterprise? A 50/50 split in work, risk, and rewards, right?

Where in the world did that notion come from? Does it make sense? Are two people likely to be equally able to perform work and take risks, thus justifying the 50/50 split?

Using the Formula Approach

Don't fall into the automatic, unthinking 50/50 split mode. It bears no relationship to the realities of what is needed to construct a successful co-general partner arrangement. It is neither pragmatic nor equitable to arbitrarily divide things 50/50 because there are two of you, or 25/25/25/25 because there are four of you. Division of the general partner interest should be on the basis of what is contributed by each party to the transaction. In order to systematically determine the value of the various contributions, one must list them and evaluate them.

In my own syndication practice I have a rough, rule-of-thumb approach for deciding on sharing of the general partnership interest. It is a crude rule which, in practice, requires much refinement. I'll lay it out in its simplest form first, and we'll discuss refinements later. First, for perspective, we'll look at the general partnership interest in relationship to the overall partnership. Then we'll look at how that general partner interest might be split between several general partners.

GENERAL PARTNER/LIMITED PARTNER DIVISION

Return of Capital: 100% given back to investors based upon their contributions. If general partners have made cash contributions they too shall have equal claim on this return of capital.

Allocation of Profits and Losses: 75% given to limited partners in return for their capital contributions and 25% given to general partners in return for their direction of the partnership.

SUBDIVISION OF GENERAL PARTNERSHIP INTEREST

	PERCENT
For contributing control of the investment property	33
For raising investor capital	33
For structuring, packaging, and directing the offering	34
	100

As you can see from the above, the value of the entire general partnership interest is really not known at the outset of a syndication offering because it is subordinated to return of the investors' capital. This is preferred to simply taking ownership at the outset because (1) it doesn't take anything away from the investors, (2) it doesn't allow payment to the general partners for their direction of the partnership unless that direction is successful and results in profits, and (3) by subordinating the return to a percentage of profits there is no tax liability for the general partners until such profits are earned. If a share of the investment were taken at the outset, the general partners would have a taxable event even though no funds had yet been received. What we must concern ourselves with here, however, is how to allocate shares in that interest among the various persons who perform the overall general partner role.

Gathering the Critical Elements for Success

My 33/33/34 formula is a convenient way to commence a dialogue. Oftentimes colleagues in the real estate business tell me about a property they have listed at a very good price, or one with great potential which can be bought cheaply. If it fits within my area of expertise and interest, and if I think I know the investor clientele to whom it can be marketed, I respond: "I'm interested. Instead of finding a buyer for it and settling for a real estate commission, why don't we buy it for a limited partnership? If you can tie it up (control it) for three to six months I'll take you as a partner and we'll buy it ourselves." If that stimulates interest, I next lay out my methodology for sharing the general partner interest. In the process of discussing that, we do a pretty good job of analyzing the various elements that go into forming a successful limited partnership.

When I hear from other colleagues who feel they can raise substantial amounts of money for good investments, I speak to them in the same way.

The truth, you see, is that there are many individuals who possess some of the critical skills to sponsor a limited partnership and can pull all these elements together into a coherent, administratively viable package. The skills to perform that brokerage function are generally in the third element: structuring, packaging, and directing the offering. If you have those skills, you should be able to identify a transaction appropriate to investor needs and sponsor abilities, and to assemble the optimal partnership structure around it.

The refinements on the 33/33/34 split are fairly apparent. Common, for example, is a situation in which more than one of the general partners participates in raising money. All who so participate might then be expected to share in the 33% interest attributed to fund raising, perhaps on the basis of a pro rata share of funds raised.

Another item I frequently "break out" is the cost of partnership structuring and packaging. On the surface, this would seem to be the natural responsibility of the person performing those services for a 34% general partner interest.

On reflection, however, one realizes that a great deal of the structuring and packaging time occurs at the earliest stages of pulling a limited partnership together, at the most vulnerable time in the entire transaction. What happens if the structurer/packager spends 100 hours of his or her time and $5,000 in cash at this phase and then learns that the person he counted upon to control the investment, or the person he counted upon to raise the funds, has failed? Who has lost 100 hours' time and $5,000? The structurer/packager alone.

More conducive to success, and ensuring seriousness on the part of all parties to the transaction, is to require that some minimum portion of the up-front structuring/packaging be handled by the other partner or partners. The structurer/packager is certain to take the enterprise seriously because he must invest so much of his time up front. The property contributor and/or money raiser will likewise approach the transaction seriously if he is in a position to lose money in the event of failure.

The idea is that if you have an equitable and pragmatic methodology for sharing the responsibilities and benefits of general partnership ownership, you can better understand the skills that must be brought to bear and can take steps to assure that all the principals in the transaction are paid only for what they contribute.

ATTORNEY COMMENT

*No Legal Requirements
for General Partner Structuring*

There are no legal requirements or guidelines as to how a general partnership interest must be split up. There is no requirement in partnership law that someone who puts up 50% of the money gets 50% of the profits. Thus, the allocation formula (whether 33/33/34 or 50/50) is simply a matter of agreement; there is tremendous flexibility in designing an allocation formula. But, once it is set, then profits and tax losses are usually required to be allocated according to the selected formula.

Put Your Agreement in Writing

A big problem in the limited partnership business is that the focus of attention is so much on documenting all aspects of the transaction that relate to the limited partners and, to the securities requirements, that documentation of the understanding between the sponsors/general partners is overlooked. It sounds strange, but there is no place in the officially sanctioned disclosure documents where clarification of the general partners' relationship between themselves is made. All treatment of general partners in the disclosure documents relates to their dealings with the limited partners.

The best way to handle this is to create your own formal documentation requirement for the general partner understanding. I say formal because it should be written, signed, and witnessed or notarized. The relationship between general partners is too important to leave on a verbal basis alone. With many partnerships lasting five years or more, the time horizons are too long for a reliance upon memory.

An ideal "boilerplate" general partner understanding is a very simple straightforward document that spells out in a few paragraphs who is committed to do what and for what consideration. An illustration of a very perfunctory general partner understanding is offered in Part IV, "Sample Documents You Can Tailor for Your Own Use."

ATTORNEY COMMENT
A Partnership Is Like a Marriage

You can save yourself a lot of grief and litigation by putting your general partnership agreement in writing. Entering a partnership with someone can be almost like getting married, and the number of partnership breakups may exceed the divorce rate. Certainly, the emotional turmoil between ex-partners can equal the acrimony of former spouses. Ask anyone who has been in a partnership that failed what it was like. Remember that your co-general partner can create liabilities for you that expose your entire personal estate. You are often personally liable for the deeds and misdeeds of your co-general partner while he or she is on partnership business.

By putting it in writing, you will have automatically paved the way for a smoother drive down the partnership highway and will have put your prospective partner to a crucial first road test. If your partner is someone who "never puts anything in writing," then be sure you are dealing with someone who is honest. A wise banker once recommended to me that you should exchange confidential credit reports with anyone with whom you are planning to go into partnership. If they have bad credit and don't pay their bills, you will find out then, not later when you are turned down for crucial loans needed to close a deal and before you are tarnished with the bad reputation of a potential partner.

Keep Your Agreement Simple

Sometimes it is very hard for a lawyer to agree with the Keep It Simple Stupid (KISS) principle. It is extremely important to get the basic outlines of agreement between the general partners in writing. This should be regarded only as a *preliminary outline*, and it should be followed by a separate, more detailed agreement between the parties. In particular, this more detailed contract should spell out: how to resolve differences of opinion; what happens if a general partner fails to perform his or her duties; the events requiring or permitting withdrawal; allocation of profits and liabilities for losses in the event of withdrawal; and a listing of the duties of each general partner. I know of two former general partners who communicate with each other only when they are bickering over who is responsible to personally repay the losses of their failed limited partnership.

USE OF A CORPORATION AS CO-GENERAL PARTNER

A favorite structuring technique of mine, when I commence a limited partnership investment transaction on my own, is to negotiate and contract the general partner agreement between myself individually and a new corporation which I wholly own. Sound crazy? Not at all! This approach can greatly simplify the complicated and often awkward early stages of structuring a transaction. How does it work?

Say, for example, that I have taken control of a strip shopping center by executing a contract with 90 days' absolute right of review and 180 days to settle. The transaction worries me in several respects: (1) I really don't know if I can raise sufficient cash to take title, (2) I'm concerned about my ability to place a high loan to value first trust given the illiquidity of my personal financial statement, and (3) the strip center needs a major rehabilitation and I have little knowledge of the area. These major worries strongly suggest the need for a co-general partner, but at the moment I have no one in mind and I'm eager to get on with the transaction.

Do I have to sit on my hands until "Mr. Right" comes along, possibly losing valuable time in packaging of my offerings memorandum, partnership agreement, subscription materials, etc.?

Absolutely not! Create a corporate general partner with 100% of the stock assigned to you, write a general partner agreement spelling out the terms of the relationship, file your certificate of limited partnership immediately making you, your spouse, or the corporation the original limited partner, and begin the offerings package even as you seek the assistance needed.

The worst that can happen from this "get right down to business" approach is that you subsequently withdraw from the contract and you've wasted a few hours and several hundred dollars forming a corporation, writing a partnership agreement, and filing a certificate of limited partnership. On the positive side, you've established high momentum for your transaction, creating the "mystique" and image of inevitability that goes with that, and you've lost no flexibility whatever.

How is that possible? How can you still be flexible to seek the missing strengths needed when you already defined the general partner interest and relationship? You do it by assigning shares in the corporation. Here's how it works.

Assume that you divided the general partner interest 33% for yourself as individual general partner for controlling the investment and 67% to the corporate general partner. Two weeks later the deal begins to "jell." Maybe you've found a bank that will lend 90% of the money but they want 33% of any profits realized. Assign them half of the shares in the corporate general partner. What if you meet a person with very "deep pockets" who will guarantee a 100% bank loan? Assign him some shares. What if you meet a securities broker-dealer who will raise all the money for a 10% commission, but also wants a 20% participation in profits, or an investor with all the cash needed who wants to be invisible to creditors, tenants, and others?

Get the idea? By going forward with your disclosure documents, loan applications, etc., with the individual and corporate general partners you have gained momentum and time and given up absolutely nothing.

---——— **ATTORNEY COMMENT** ———---

Warning On "Shell" Corporations

Be warned that you should not use such a "shell" corporation (a corporation without assets) as a sole general partnership. If you do, then your partnership will have one more corporate characteristic (limited liability of the principals) and become more likely to be taxed as a corporation, not a partnership. However, you can use an assetless corporation as a co-general partner as long as you, as the second and individual general partner, have adequate assets.

Once you complete your incorporation of your co-general partner and go ahead with the partnership, you should take all steps necessary to make certain that the corporation will be treated as a corporation for tax and liability purposes. This includes conducting a first meeting where you make capital contributions and loans to the corporation, adopt bylaws, elect directors, appoint officers and issue stock. You also need the required business licenses and tax identification numbers. Failure to take these steps may cause the IRS to challenge your corporate status during subsequent tax audit or permit a creditor to "pierce" your corporate veil.

Chapter 8

Structuring the Limited Partnership

For the purposes of this discussion, let us separate the two main phases of an offering—structuring and packaging. Structuring involves the basic economic decisions that a limited partnership sponsor must deal with at the early stages of resolving whether or not to engage in an investment syndication. Packaging entails the subsequent administrative, legal, and economic decisions that he must make after he has decided to go forward and is preparing to deal with his target investors.

The structuring phase, it seems, is very self-centered and pragmatic. It is the point at which the potential syndication sponsor weighs all his options for time, risk and capital investment and decides whether the proposed syndication measures up to competing opportunities. It is extremely important to be "hard-headed" at this stage. If you're not, you may find yourself drifting from deal to deal with neither a pattern nor an overall goal. Such drifting will impede long-term growth.

If you haven't sponsored your first syndication yet, this may not seem so serious. When you've done one or two, however, you will see what happens. Everyone that you know, and lots of other people as well, will become aware that you are a person who can "make it happen"—who can convert an idle dream into a reality. Many of them will bring you their dreams. If you maintain discipline and control, measuring the various proposals against your own goals and structuring the best ones to meet your own needs, you can benefit from this attention even while aiding your colleagues. If you are led off course by them, all of you will lose.

Structuring the Limited Partnership

What are the basic questions that one deals with at the structuring stage? Essentially, they are the following:

- How will the investment generate returns?
- How might such returns be split?
- To whom can the limited partnership interests be sold?

In assessing the answers to these three questions you, as the potential syndication sponsor, can decide the following.

- Is the investment viable?
- Is it worth your while from an economic standpoint?
- Do you know where and how to raise investor funds?

Implicit in all these questions is the overall consideration: Does this proposal fit into your overall business development plans? Let's not lose sight of that because of the charms of an individual transaction.

ATTORNEY COMMENT
Structuring As a Circular Process

Structuring involves the creative combining of your projected profits from the real estate, your calculation of likely tax benefits, your contractual relationship with your co-general partner and your list of potential suitable investors. It is the first step of the syndication process and all else flows from it. You have to combine legal and business aspects of the deal. For example, for public offerings affected by NASAA guidelines, you will have to create a structure that pays back your investor's contributions plus a 6% return, which limits your percentage of eventual profits, and which conforms to other NASAA requirements. It starts with goals, proceeds to an analysis of how a partnership can be structured to meet those goals, and ends with analysis of the market for such a partnership. If the market does not exist, you may have to start over and change your goals to meet the market. It is a circular process which you continue to transverse until everything fits together. At each stage, legal considerations and business requirements are built into the model.

DETERMINING HOW YOU WILL MAKE MONEY

In addressing this question, you must give the investment's economics a hard look. Does the transaction primarily promise cash flow, tax benefits, or long-term appreciation? Few investments will give you all three types of returns, but many will give you two out of three. Can it be structured to give greater emphasis to one or another of these types of returns? High leverage, for instance, tends to minimize cash flow while maximizing tax benefits and appreciation potential. An all-cash transaction, or all-cash above an existing loan, can frequently result in a lower acquisition price. This may be important when quick resale, or major rehabilitation or development is foreseen. Can you arrange an installment purchase, thus minimizing cash requirements in the first year? If this is possible, the syndicator may be able to raise substantially more money by taking investor money in installments as well, thus increasing their leverage and tax benefits.

In assessing the structuring tradeoffs, the syndicator must be ever mindful of both what type of structure will best serve his own long-term growth objectives and what is good for his target investors. Most important, however, is overall investment viability and predictability. A novice investment syndicator can ill-afford a losing transaction or, for that matter, even a transaction that is profitable but less profitable than predicted. Investors will probably not praise you for performing above expectations, but very likely will complain if you perform below expectations. You are, after all, representing yourself as the expert and are asking investors to trust in you. If you violate that trust in any way, expect a strong, negative reaction. It isn't just the investors' money you will have lost.

My personal approach to structuring is very conservative. I offer it here simply as an illustration of where one syndicator comes out on the structuring issue, not as a model.

I never sponsor a transaction that I can't live with in a "worst case" scenario, and I constantly remind investors that a "worst case" scenario can and may happen. This screens out from my consideration a great many terrific investment opportunities where, say, the location is unstable (if it improves you look like a genius; if it worsens you're out of business) or the eventual users or purchaser is not clearly identifiable (eliminating most novel ideas). I don't do this because it suits my personal investment philosophy. It doesn't. Rather I do it because I see a successful career in syndication of real estate investment as assured if one can avoid making mistakes.

Given this premise, the wise syndicator will choose and structure his investments giving equal emphasis to profit optimization and loss avoidance. This diminishes the likelihood of permanent setback in the case of one losing syndication, even while appealing to the conservative nature of many passive investors. They may not place a major portion of their personal assets into your syndication because they believe it is the deal that will "turn their lives around," but they will give you some of their funds—perhaps that portion that is invested in a certificate of deposit or a poorly performing stock.

ATTORNEY COMMENT

Different Structures Yield Different Results

The same piece of real estate can be structured in totally different deals depending upon the goals of your structurings. A 100% financed purchase of a 100-unit apartment building with built-in negative cash flow will be a tax-oriented partnership. However, the same apartment building could be bought by a partnership which buys it for all cash, thereby producing very little tax shelter, but a lot of cash flow. Thus, your goals and the needs of your investors will greatly affect the price, terms, and acquisition methods of the properties you purchase for your partnership.

DECIDING HOW RETURNS WILL BE SHARED

In reviewing the limited partner/general partner split of investment proceeds, the syndicator has to trade off a number of considerations. First, and foremost, can the transaction be structured so that both general and limited partners emerge as winners? In a sense, the two sides can be viewed as competitors for some finite amount of investment returns. If the general partner can't find a way to meet his minimum needs, he won't bother to sponsor the offering. If the target limited partners can't be shown how they will meet their minimum rate of return requirements, they can't be counted upon to invest.

Perhaps the best technique for structuring to assure maximum compatibility between general and limited partners is to bring together people with different objectives. In this way the various benefits (e.g., tax losses, cash flow, appreciation) can be parceled out to the parties that most desire them. To illustrate, in the case of an investment in historic property for rehabilitation, there may be very major tax benefits due to (1) credits for money spent on rehabilitation, (2) donation of an historic easement on the facade, and (3) depreciation. At the same time, with major rehabilitation there may be prospects for high appreciation due to value added. The trick in this transaction is to structure it so that your many limited partners with high need for tax benefits and less need for appreciation are teamed with general partners who don't need the tax benefits (they are already "sheltered up") but desire a larger portion of the appreciation, or vice versa. Thus, neither side is hurting the other. To a limited partner in the 28% tax bracket, every dollar of tax loss is worth 28 cents. If the general partner is paying no taxes anyway, he can give away his share of those losses without sacrifice.

A seasoned syndicator can deal from either side on the tax benefits issue, giving them away in one transaction (while selling the offering to high tax rate taxpayers) and keeping them in another case (while selling the offering to people already "sheltered-up" or in need of cash flow).

Structuring can truly be an art form. You must decide on your structuring objectives before you buy the property because your purchase terms will facilitate your proposed structure. Suppose, for example that you want to offer sheltered cash flow to your investors. To do this, you have to make sure that the investment will quickly start producing more cash flow than actual expenses, but not more cash flow than tax deductions available from the property. This makes your real estate investment similar to a tax-free bond with a good potential for upside appreciation, but with the caveat of the eventual taxation of taxable gains. On a $1,000,000 apartment building that has a break-even cash flow, you could have about $30,000 of depreciation in the first year. If you have another $20,000 in first-year deductible expenses not paid from cash flow, you could distribute $50,000 in cash, "tax deferred," to your limited partners.

I could provide additional illustrations of structuring to assure overall compatibility, but I don't think it is necessary. Examples of your own will come to mind. A word of caution, however. When you "experiment" with formulas for allocating tax benefits, you are not entirely free in your choice. The Internal Revenue Service does provide restrictions. To be safe, while you are in the structuring stage review your plan with a first-class tax accountant or tax attorney before going forward. Meantime, until you are ready to buy professional time to look at your own specific transaction, I'll share with you two general rules which will get you through 80% of the potential pitfalls of working out tax allocation formulas: (1) there must be an economic reason for the allocation, and (2) taxpayers cannot take tax losses in excess of their basis in the investment. Both of these rules are somewhat esoteric so I'll explain them further.

"Economic Reason" Under IRS Rules

What the IRS is saying here is that tax benefits have to be shared by those who pay for them. You can't, for instance, arbitrarily give one limited partner in an apartment building investment all of the tax losses and another limited partner all of the cash flow—not unless there is an economic reason for it.

How could you restructure such an investment to accomplish the same effect? Look for an economic reason. One way might be to break the limited partnership into two segments, with investors in one segment buying the land beneath the building (nondepreciable) and earning a strong rental income from it and investors in the other segment buying the building itself. The contrast of returns could be further magnified in this model if the land buyers were to pay all cash for their portion while subordinating their title to a high-leverage loan on the building. Another approach to this same model would be to divide your limited partnership interests between purchaser interests and lender interest, with the former having access to cash flow and tax losses and the latter receiving the promise of a fixed income return.

In either of the above models the benefits of appreciation in the value of the assets upon sale can be shared between the two segments. In the case of the landowner/building owner breakdown, it would be prudent to award the appreciation on a pro rata (land value/building value) basis. In establishing that ratio, keep in mind that any departure from the tax assessor's evaluation must be defensible. This is important not only when dividing profits from appreciation, but also when allocating values at the time of purchase.

In the case of the purchaser/lender breakdown you are much freer to decide how to divide appreciation profits. Through an "equity participation" loan, for instance, the lenders might earn 25 or 50 or 75% of the appreciation, depending entirely upon what was agreed to in the loan documents.

How to Establish and Increase "Investment Basis"

The IRS prohibits taxpayers from taking tax losses from an investment in excess of their tax basis in the investment. Therefore, if nineteen limited partners and one general partner invest $5,000 each, for a total of $100,000, and the investment is an all-cash transaction, everyone's basis is $5,000. If, however, the limited partnership borrows another $400,000, so that a $500,000 property can be purchased, another $400,000 in basis is available. Who gets that? It depends on how the transaction is structured.

Basis	Equity[1]	LPs	GPs
All Cash	$100,000	$ 95,000	$ 5,000
$400,000 Loan/Recourse to GP	100,000	95,000	405,000
$200,000 First Trust/Recourse to All + $200,000 Second Trust/Recourse to GP	100,000	285,000	215,000
$400,000 Loan/Nonrecourse	100,000	475,000	25,000
All Cash With $100,000 Pro Rata Call	100,000	190,000	10,000

[1] LPs invested $95,000 and GP invested $5,000 for total of $100,000

If the general partner alone signs for the note, he gets it all. In effect, his $5,000 investment qualifies him for $405,000 in tax losses. It doesn't necessarily follow that he may take 81% ($405,000/500,000) of the losses as they are accrued however. The partnership may be structured to give the limited partners all or, say, 95% of the losses except that at the point that losses taken equal their combined basis of $95,000, they cannot take more. There are two factors at play here: (1) your relative share of losses per the terms of the partnership agreement, and (2) the amount of such losses that can be passed through per the terms of your basis allocation. The first figure is a function of the partnership agreement, constrained by certain tax principles such as the economic reason test. The latter figure is a function of IRS rules with regard to basis allocation.

Taking another approach to the same transaction, if the limited partners join the general partner in signing the note, then their basis is increased by the amount of their liability. It is possible for the limited partner to sign for only a portion of a note (say, the bottom 50%) via special agreement, or in the case of multiple trusts perhaps only the first trust (safest position), thereby taking on additional risk and the basis that goes with it.

Limited partners may also increase their basis by agreeing, in the Partnership Agreement, that they will provide additional equity if called upon to do so. If this call is for an additional $5,000 each, then the investors' bases would be increased by $5,000 each.

Structuring the Limited Partnership

Finally, there is a technique for increasing the limited partners' bases with no increase in liability at all. This can be done via what is known as a "nonrecourse" loan. A "nonrecourse" loan agreement states, in effect, that the lender shall have no recourse to signer's personal assets, but rather shall limit his recourse to the assets of the partnership. The IRS's view is that tax basis accompanies a loan, but if no one has signed for the loan as an individual, no one can be selected as having more liability than the others. Therefore, the liability is solely with the partnership and the basis thus earned belongs to the owners of the partnership pro rata.

Having understood this, it is easy to see that the idea of nonrecourse borrowing for limited partnership investments is very appealing. Unfortunately, it is also difficult to arrange in smaller transactions. Lenders for large buildings and developments (insurance companies, pension funds, etc.) have a tradition of looking solely to the assets against which their loans are placed, so nonrecourse loans from them are common. In recent years they have begun to insist upon participation in appreciation, however, and this can go a long way toward mitigating the benefits of a nonrecourse loan.

Your typical lender on small projects, unfortunately, often doesn't even know what a nonrecourse loan is. Community savings and loans and commercial banks are so accustomed to looking to the personal assets of the borrower that they may give a borrower guarantee more consideration than their assessment of the investment itself. Don't plan on arranging nonrecourse financing from your community savings and loan unless you have discussed it very carefully with everyone from the chairman of the loan committee to the president and his legal counsel, because they do not, as a rule, understand such an approach and they fear it. You can't use the seller for nonrecourse financing because seller nonrecourse financing can not be used to increase the basis of limited partners.

As a final structuring tip regarding investment basis, consider a scenario in which you have arranged for very heavy tax benefits, you cannot arrange nonrecourse financing, and the limited partners don't want to sign loans "going in." An alternative way of handling this situation is to start business with the general partner receiving most of the basis, pass your tax deductions and credits through per your agreed formula (say, 95% to the limited partners), and when you reach the point that the limited partners have taken benefits equal to their basis, go back to them with a choice. They can continue to be free of liability on partnership borrowings, thus giving up that portion of the overall basis, or they can join the general partners on all or a portion of the loan(s). This situation would not normally be reached in the early stages of a partnership anyway, so the limited partners should be in a good position to evaluate the additional risk against potential for future tax savings.

ATTORNEY COMMENT

Impact of the 1986 Tax Recovery Act

The allocation of tax benefits to selected partners is a very complex and developing area of the tax law. At this writing, controversial regulations on allocations of tax benefits have been promulgated by the IRS. The basic concept of these proposals is that your allocation of tax benefits must have "economic effect"; the IRS has adopted a "capital account" analysis as a guideline for determining the requisite economic effect.

This means that all tax losses, income, deductions, and distributions must relate to the capital account. The capital account is maintained for each partner and starts out equal to the partner's contribution plus the partner's share of liabilities. It is adjusted by distributions, gains, losses, and additional contributions and debts. The IRS recommends that at the end of the partnership, if some of the partners have a negative balance in their capital accounts, the partnership agreement should require the partners with a negative balance to make up the balance for the benefit of partners with a positive balance. You may be able to painlessly comply with these proposals in a partnership where there will never be a negative capital account. However, in planning deep shelter partnerships, you should be very careful in making allocations of tax benefits.

You often may be able to justify making an allocation of eventual gains from the sale different from ownership interests; but rarely will you be able to justify allocations of operating income different from the allocation of tax benefits. For example, let us say that the limited partners own 95% and the general partners 5% of the partnership. If you have good reasons for it, it is likely that you will be able to justify giving the limited partners 95% of the current tax deductions at the same time you plan to pay the limited partners only 75% of the eventual gains from the sale of the partnership property. You as general partner receive 5% of the operating cash flow, but 25% of the profits from the eventual property sale. This will pass IRS scrutiny if the allocation is done pursuant to each partner's capital accounts and substantially affects the actual profits realized by partners. Unless you are willing to engage in some expensive and risky tax planning, you will probably not be able to get away with taking 25% of operating cash flow when you have only 5% of the tax benefits as general partner and your limited share of 95% of tax benefits. In such instances where you take 25% of operating cash flow, the IRS may reduce the tax benefits of the limited partners to 75%, and issue deficiency notices for unpaid taxes together with penalties and high interest charges to your frightened and angry (at you) limited partners.

For syndications of single-family homes, there is one way you might be able to get nonrecourse financing. If the house has an assumable loan insured by the Veteran's Administration or the Federal Housing Administration, when you buy the property you can take the property "subject to" rather than "assume" the old loan. The lenders will not like you for it, but there is little they can do about it.

HOW TO DETERMINE IF YOU CAN SELL THE LIMITED PARTNERSHIP INTERESTS

In assessing how and to whom a proposed investment should be offered, the syndicator should take a long view. It is very tempting, in any transaction, to look only to the transaction under review. From that perspective, the syndicator's only concern would be "Do I know where to raise enough money to pull this deal together?" Many small syndicators start out with a few financial sources with whom they have "good will"—family members or close friends—and they turn to these people for every transaction that comes along. That is dangerously shortsighted.

It's great to have "anchor" investors, but never bring them into a deal that doesn't precisely meet their needs. If your uncle needs cash flow and you can't structure your investment to give him good cash flow, leave him out of it. Your "anchor" investors should be cherished and cared for above all others because they are the ones who are most likely to reinvest profits in future syndications. This seems obvious, yet many beginning syndicators take these people for granted and, to make one deal work, do them a disservice. The result, often, is loss of "good will" built up over a lifetime.

The other side of assessing how and to whom you should sell a given offering involves consideration of your long-range ambitions for target investor clientele. If you have a really good product that involves unusual tax benefits, give some thought to using that product to advertise yourself. See if you can reach people who are potential "centers of influence" with that product. If you do well for them, they may be able to help you reach additional investors at a future date. Sometimes a small investment from an accountant with a large tax clientele, or from a leader in a professional association, can reap greater long-term dividends for you than can a large investment from a "loner."

Another target investor type who can be helpful over the long run is the local media, sports, or political celebrity. Many passive investors have a strong social instinct. They invest in real estate through limited partnerships because they don't have confidence in their own investment skills. They look to see what others are doing to decide what is good for them. A celebrity investor, especially someone judged to be knowledgeable or "well connected," can have a strong drawing effect upon such people. When you get a great product, don't fail to at least make an effort to reach some of these "drawing card" investors.

From a substantive point of view, the structuring phase of limited partnership formation is clearly the most dynamic, creative, and important. At no other point in the five to ten years of a typical limited partnership transaction will you make more important decisions. At this point the "die is cast" for the entire life of the deal. Take it seriously, talk about it with colleagues, buy an hour's advice from your accountant, attorney, financial planner—whoever you deal with that has a strong background in such things. You can make or break the investment at the all-important structuring phase, so it is no time to be careless or "penny-wise" with expert time.

How much money to raise? Don't raise so much money that the potential return from cash flow and appreciation is spread over so many dollars that no one gets a good return. Also, don't raise so little money that there is not enough to pay for managing and maintaining the property, managing the partnership itself, and maintaining an adequate reserve account. Solely as a guideline, many syndicators will raise cash equal to between 20 and 40% of the price of the property purchased.

There are many competing computer software products on the marketplace that will greatly aid you in structuring your partnership. You can buy one of these programs, or hire a computer specialist, for reasonable sums to help with your structuring. These computerized reports will be helpful in selling your plans to lenders and investors alike.

ATTORNEY COMMENT

Be Sure That Your Investors Are Qualified

Your investors must be *qualified* to invest in your property. You should get each limited partner to fill out an investor qualification questionnaire, and you should read it. The typical elderly widow should not put all her life savings into a risky real estate venture. However, an elderly widow who just happens to be a millionaire retired real estate mogul could be qualified to risk $100,000 on your real estate deal. If your investor's standard of living would be substantially changed if all the money invested were lost, then you should refuse to take the money. Your partnership also must meet federal- and state-imposed suitability requirements in terms of investor income, net worth, and sophistication.

PREPARING A PRELIMINARY ANALYSIS DOCUMENT

Just as it is useful to commit yourself to paper when working on an understanding with a co-general partner, likewise it is important to write down your notions, however preliminary, with regard to the relationship between general and limited partners. A good way to do that is to prepare what I call a Preliminary Analysis Document.

The preliminary analysis step in the packaging phase can be thought of as an educational process focused on the needs of the syndicator. There are a lot of questions he needs to find answers to before committing his time and money to any investment offering. Should he go directly into preparation of offering documents, he could easily invest several months' time and $5,000 to $20,000 on attorneys, accountants, typing, printing, etc., before receiving answers to those questions. Preliminary analysis work can be done for a fraction of the cost, and most of it can subsequently be utilized in the preparation of the formal offering documents.

What are the questions the syndicator wants to seek answers to at the preliminary analysis stage? What does the preliminary analysis look like?

In my practice, the preliminary analysis is like a trial balloon. I don't know for sure how I feel about an investment property until I have described it on paper, so I analyze the property. I don't know for sure how I, and my intended co-general partner, feel about structuring issues until the proposed arrangements are thoroughly discussed and written down, so I do that in the preliminary analysis. Finally, I don't know for sure how my target investors will receive the proposal, or even who they should be, so I summarize the overall transaction, with visual aids (maps, photos, and the like), and "run it by" prospective investors for reactions.

Perhaps this "staged" process of committing to a syndication activity is unnecessary for some, but it has served me very well. It is a wonderful way of converting that abstract idea that you, your partner, and your target investors have "waxed eloquent" about into an immediate reality with which they must deal. It is very sobering. It "separates the wheat from the chaff" and lets you know whether you really can, or want to, make the deal work. And it costs you very little money.

A good preliminary analysis may only be ten or twenty pages long, much of it fairly pro forma (e.g., your summary partnership arrangements, economic analysis, maps and photos), and it needn't be subjected to expensive legal and accounting scrutiny because you aren't using the document to raise funds. That is not to say that you shouldn't buy expert time to help you understand structuring issues or whatever else you need help on, but you need do it only to help clarify your own understanding. That kind of help costs much less than written opinions or review of written materials.

Following are some guidelines on preparation of the preliminary analysis.

Preparing the Preliminary Analysis Quickly and Cheaply

If you're going to do investment syndications on a regular basis, you should develop a system for converting the most appealing investment proposals you encounter into writing, quickly and at minimal cost. Most of the ideas that come to you, perhaps nineteen out of twenty, you can screen in minutes, just from talking them over. Either they are intrinsically flawed, the timing is wrong, or for some other reason they don't fit your plans. One out of twenty ideas, though, will really excite you. You will think it is something you would like to do and are capable of doing. In the real estate business sometimes that exciting idea revolves around the use of a "hot" property—something priced very low, an imminent foreclosure, a unique opportunity. Whatever the reason, you often have to be able to move fast to be able to take advantage of it. If you can't decide quickly, you can't participate.

For my own business, I have developed a pro forma preliminary analysis format that I can address very efficiently. It provides a place to deal with all the important considerations, and enables me to get things on paper quickly. As a result, I can convert most investment ideas into an analysis document within 24 hours at a cost (mostly word processor time) of under $250. The last thing accomplished is usually development of the film of photographs taken. I print perhaps twenty of these preliminary analyses for review by potential co-general partners—attorney or accountant friends who may desire some involvement or have some contribution to make—and potential investors. Remember, a nicely printed analysis pays dividends. People are far more likely to take you seriously if your package looks finished. They are also less likely to give you false assurances under such circumstances.

Discuss Alternative Structures and Strategies

The preliminary analysis is no place to make final decisions. Rather, it is a document to help you to discover the universe of potential decisions. During your initial discussions you probably rejected a number of alternatives out of hand, but it is likely that there are still several that hold promise. Review each of the promising ones in your preliminary analysis document. This is important because in your discussions with colleagues you'll receive more and better feedback if your options are still open. Maybe you'll find, for instance, that the approach you feel best about is rejected by everyone you speak to, or that someone especially important to you (a major target investor or a potential co-general partner capable of raising lots of money) likes an alternative you would have ranked below.

This is not to say that you should be completely "mushy" about your plans. It is important, from a psychological viewpoint, that your preliminary analysis convey the idea that this is a transaction that is going forward, and that the only questions are details.

At the same time, your reader should be made to feel privileged at the opportunity to discuss the details with you before they are finalized and, if there is mutual interest, join with you in the investment at some future date.

Don't Use the Preliminary Analysis to Raise Funds

For the preliminary analysis to be a really useful tool for the syndicator, it must be something he can prepare very quickly. It should also be flexible in format, and free from a lot of miscellaneous constraints. If it is all these things, then it cannot meet the disclosure requirements of securities regulators. If you don't meet such disclosure requirements, you can't use the preliminary analysis to raise money from consumers.

In practice, from time to time you will see your competitors circulate preliminary analysis documents calling for an investment commitment, an expression of interest, or something roughly equivalent. Tread very carefully when you get into this area. Remember, to the extent that your preliminary analysis is used for marketing to consumers, as opposed to decision making by the sponsors, it comes under the purview of securities regulators. Try to take your initial investor soundings without requesting written responses.

If you don't feel comfortable with this, if you are absolutely convinced that you cannot be assured of serious replies unless they are in writing, then develop an informal "expression of interest" letter for your preliminary analysis package. In doing so, however, remember the rules. You cannot sell securities to consumers unless you provide adequate disclosure, so try not to do anything to allow a conclusion that the sale occurred at the preliminary analysis stage. You might try to cover yourself on this by explaining to your target investors that no binding commitment is requested or, indeed, even permitted, based upon reading the preliminary analysis—that no sale or commitment can be made until the appropriate offering documents have been read and understood.

See Part IV for an illustrative preliminary analysis document. Please don't view it as something to be emulated. You may find far better models elsewhere. I include it here only because I have found in my own experience that illustrations (model documents) are terrific teaching tools. If you've understood the theoretical and legal framework, and have a model document as a point of departure, you can very quickly learn to function on your own. It is much like learning to ride a bike from books alone, versus learning from a combination of book learning and first-hand experience. There is no one way to write a preliminary analysis. However, if you understand the basic usefulness of the document, and the parameters of what you can do with it, and then take a look at one prepared by someone else, you can quickly decide your feelings on the subject and can develop your own version.

ATTORNEY COMMENT

You Can't Accept Funds Until You Deliver a Prospectus

For Regulation D sales under Parts 505 and 506, you must deliver all the disclosure documents prior to sale and during the course of the offering. This means that you cannot take the investor's money until they have had an opportunity to review the prospects. Even if your investors want to quickly get in your deal, and they shove their money at you after seeing your preliminary analysis, you should politely decline, telling them that you would love to have them in the deal, but that federal regulation prohibits you from taking their money until all the legal necessities have been followed.

STRUCTURING UNDER THE TAX RECOVERY ACT OF 1986

A new element you have to take into account is the Tax Recovery Act (TRA) of 1986. The TRA has many complicated provisions which restrict using syndication to provide big tax deductions for limited partners. The simple answer to these complicated provisions is that you will want to design your partnership so it has a small taxable cash flow right from the beginning.

Passive Losses Can Be Used Only to Offset Passive Income

Under the 1986 provisions, your limited partners will be able to deduct their tax losses from your syndication (up to the amount of income available) only from your syndication and from their other passive income investments. Most simply, your limits will be able to immediately deduct only the amount of interest paid and other deductions, such as depreciation, equal to the income allocated to them. One exception is where it is a partnership that bought the property prior to the enactment of the TRA and that can take advantage of the phase-in of the passive loss limitations. Also, where your partners have other passive income, such as income from an all-cash real estate limited partnership, they can use the other passive income against the deductions generated by your partnership. Any deductions they cannot immediately deduct can be carried forward until the partnership produces some taxable income. To avoid these problems for your partners, you need to provide income to your investors at least equal to all deductions.

Here's an example. Let's say you buy a strip shopping center for $1,000,000. You raise $300,000 from your syndication, with $200,000 for the down payment, $30,000 for closing costs and financing fees, and $70,000 for some cosmetic repairs. You get an $800,000 loan on it with monthly payments of about $8,000 per month. Your tenants pay all their own utilities. Your operating costs are $3,000 per month (taxes, insurance, maintenance, management fees, common utilities), with monthly depreciation of about 2,100. You will want to collect rent equal to or in excess of your loan payments ($8,000), plus operating expenses ($3,000), plus depreciation ($2,100) for a total of $13,100. You can make sure that the numbers work right by buying the property for a reasonable price or by raising the rents, or by improving the property so that you can attract higher rents.

By doing this, your partners will receive their share of the net income each quarter or year with a portion or most of it without any current taxation. Because income equals or slightly exceeds total deductions, there are no carry-forwards, all interest can be deducted, and you have sheltered most of the income they receive from the partnership. Except for the problem of capital gains, this eliminates most of the tax problems imposed on limited partnerships by the TRA.

Getting Maximum Use of Investment Losses and Gains

This is a formula to follow when putting together a partnership:
1. Calculate your annual loan expenses.
2. Estimate your annual operating expenses from the property.
3. Compute the depreciation available from the property.
4. Add items 1, 2 and 3.
5. Estimate total rental and other income from the property.
6. If rents under 5 are higher than the total under 4, take out a larger loan, increase your rehabilitation efforts or increase depreciation or syndication expenses which can be written off over time. If total rents are less than the total in item 4, raise more money so as to lower loan costs. Lower operating expenses by better management or by requiring tenants to pick up more expenses such as paying their allocated share of real estate taxes, insurance, and common area maintenance expenses, or by repairing or replacing high-maintenance items. You could also lower your depreciation by using a higher value for land and lower deductible expenses by not taking any fees up front. By taking all or some of these steps, you can bring rent and total deductible expenses into equilibrium.

Another approach will be to do a syndication that relies heavily on equity rather than borrowed capital. For that $1,000,000 strip center, you may decide to put $500,000 or even $1,000,000 down depending upon the rate of return. In the past, due to the tax laws, it made sense to borrow money at 12% to purchase a property which only produced an 8% return from rents on the total money invested. Now with the TRA of 1986, if the building produces 8% return on the money invested, whether by debt or by equity, it may often make no sense to borrow money at 12% to buy it. Instead, it may make more sense to raise enough equity capital to buy it without debt as long as the investors are willing to accept 8% on their money; you can point out to them that their cash return is partly sheltered and will be higher then 8% when taking appreciation into account. Large national syndications have successfully used the "all equity" approach on properties that may produce a 12% or higher cash return on equity invested.

If you are planning to buy a property, fix it up, and resell it in a three-year period, it may make sense to have a lot of tax losses in that partnership. Your losses would then exceed your income and your partners would not be able to take all the losses available in the first year and would have to postpone them to later years. But, if you sell the property in the third year, your investors would be able to take these unused losses and use them against their profits on sale. Because sale profits are taxed at ordinary income rates, these losses would be valuable in the year of sale. You don't want to have a lot of deferred losses in a long-term partnership because you would have to wait too long to use them. A variation on this would be to incur a lot of losses in the rehabilitation and tenant turnover period which would be used to shelter income when the property starts to produce a lot of cash flow.

Another opportunity under the TRA is tax credits from low income housing and rehabilitation expenditures for qualified or historic structures. There is a 4% credit for new construction and rehabilitation of low income housing financed with federal subsidies and on a 9% credit when not financed with other federal subsidies. These 4% and 9% credits are for each year for 10 years. There is also a 4% credit for 10 years for the acquisition of low income housing. A new 10% credit is available for rehabilitation of commercial buildings placed in service prior to 1936 and a 20% credit for historic structures. These credits are not subject to the passive income restrictions and can be used by your limited partners to offset their active earned income up to certain maximum amounts. You can use these credits very effectively because a credit is a dollar-for-dollar offset against tax liability. Thus, these credits are very powerful even at the lower tax rates.

ATTORNEY COMMENT

Structuring With the Tax Act in Mind

The TRA of 1986 will not destroy the syndication business or even prevent further growth of it. The TRA of 1986 will require syndicators to structure their partnerships differently. The above approaches show that you have many planning opportunities; however, this presentation greatly simplifies for the purpose of clarity many new complex additions to the Internal Revenue Code. This means that it will be necessary to put your attorney and accountant team together in the beginning of the syndication so that they can advise you of the best methods for property acquisition. If you acquire the property with too much debt, you may have some passive losses that some of your limited partners cannot immediately use and which must be carried forward. Also, if your partnership does have passive losses, you should consider whether these passive losses are suitable for your potential limited partners.

Chapter 9

Packaging Your Investment Proposal

To know just what has to be done, then to do it, comprises the whole philosophy of practical life.
                                            -Sir William Osler

ORGANIZING THE OFFERING DOCUMENTS

We move now to the part of the business that is most intimidating to novice investment syndicators, yet is really not at all difficult. The problem with this phase (packaging of your ideas into a form suitable for reading and analysis by target investors, their attorneys and accountants, regulators, and the judge (if you get into trouble), is that most people think it is esoteric.

Granted, limited partnership packaging is esoteric up to a point. There are a number of rather technical aspects that are not quickly understood by the layman. They are understandable with thought, however. Indeed, when the legal basis for them is revealed, they make perfect sense. The securities laws of our nation, and the fifty states, are just as much an outgrowth of our Judeo-Christian and common law traditions as are all our other laws and customs.

The important thing to remember in preparing your offering materials for target investors is that at the packaging stage you are dealing with consumers. The U.S. legal system has a strong tradition of consumer protection—protection from you. Get used to that. Let it sink in. You, the syndicator, are the person everyone is worried about. You are regarded as the sophisticated one—the one who might take advantage.

How do you handle that? Do you make excuses for yourself? Do you protest that you are really just a "regular guy" like everyone else, and you're just trying to do your investors a favor?

No! That whole approach is counterproductive. Even if you're new in the business and you don't feel different from the investors from whom you expect to raise funds, don't think that way. Force yourself, if necessary, to make the mental adjustment from "regular guy" to professional operator in a highly regulated industry.

Understand and accept the need for the regulation, especially the heavy disclosure requirements. Master them, and become their proponent. If you do, you'll soon find yourself not feeling burdened but, in fact, helped by them. You'll find, for instance, that most of your competitors don't understand and accept all the rules; they take potentially dangerous "short cuts." You will find yourself winning investor confidence by your mastery of, and willingness to play by, the rules.

As I stated earlier, the primary purpose behind all securities regulation is consumer protection. The regulators have attempted to accomplish this by requiring heavy disclosure. All aspects of the investment offering must be discussed. This must be done in a coldly analytical way that does not generate a false sense of security. If there is a bias in the regulations toward influencing conclusions from analysis of offering material, it is toward influencing negative conclusions. Throughout the offering documents, the syndicator is encouraged to emphasize downside risk from economic setback, poor judgment, fraud, acts of God, whatever. Don't let that bother you. Understand the philosophy behind it, master it, and later in this section, I'll teach you how to "close" your investors on such disclosure—in effect, to make it work for you.

There are two logical stages in the packaging phase of a limited partnership offering: The first, very important to the syndicator but problematical because of its potential for misuse, is the preliminary analysis phase. The second, much more clearly laid out and conventionally handled, is the offering documents phase.

Where the preliminary analysis was characterized as an education process focused on the needs of the syndicator, the offering documents can be characterized as an education process focused on the needs of the consumer. There are a great many considerations that the consumer needs to evaluate in making an intelligent limited partnership investment decision, many of which will come to his mind from the outset, and others that he will later wish he had asked. Over the past fifty years (since the 1933 Act) federal and state securities regulators have developed a standard for offering document disclosure (items that should be discussed to reveal and explain an investment) to assure that consumers (target investors) are given a realistic look at the transaction before committing themselves.

In the remainder of this section, we will take all these scary laws, regulations, and guidelines and show you how to deal with them. You will learn to evaluate your own investment proposal in their light, and translate your ideas into a set of first-class offering documents that you need not fear sharing with anyone—attorneys, accountants, regulators, or the judge.

ATTORNEY COMMENT

The Prospectus As "Memorandum to Plaintiff's Counsel"

Securities lawyers are fond of calling the offering document a "memorandum to plaintiff's counsel." If you are sued under the securities law for fraud or misrepresentation by one of your investors, then your proof that you provided adequate disclosure is your offering document. Your investor's lawyer will be plaintiff's (the suer's) counsel; offering documents are like a long memorandum to plaintiff's counsel showing how you made all the necessary disclosures. The fantasy of your lawyer (defense counsel) is that as soon as he hands the offering documents to plaintiff's counsel, plaintiff's counsel will quickly look through them, see that everything is covered, and then beat a hasty retreat from the courtroom battlefield.

Using Guide 5 As a Recipe for Success

The first step in building self-confidence in anything is knowledge of the subject. The securities regulators have attempted to convey knowledge of standards for practice partly by writing their codes, and partly by establishing standard forms. Perhaps the most useful standard form in the entire spectrum is the guideline for public offering documents—Guide 5. Although it is offered as a recommended format (deviations are allowed where the regulator can be persuaded they are justified) only for registered public offerings, it is, in my experience, an excellent format for any offering. Yet there are a great many syndicators doing private offerings today whose offerings don't even approach Guide 5 disclosure standards. Many private offering syndicators are raising investor money with documents that are so lacking in disclosure that a legal judgment against them is a certainty if they ever find themselves in court. Their offerings are time bombs, waiting to explode.

Why do so many novice syndicators ignore the officially sanctioned guidelines and proceed on instinct when the price of miscalculation is so high?

I think that the main reason is that they haven't seen the guidelines in the first place. I myself worked as an investment syndicator for two years, doing one private and one intrastate public offering, before I became aware of it. I had purchased and read a dozen books on the subject and never encountered it. I had spent many hours with attorneys and was not told about it. I didn't know there was an officially sanctioned guideline for real estate limited partnership offerings so I operated on instinct.

Another reason so few novice syndicators use Guide 5 is because they are discouraged from doing so. They are discouraged by their own instincts that they should "keep things simple" because, after all, "it's just me and a few close friends doing this and we don't need all that technical stuff." Others are discouraged by their attorneys. They are told, "Stick with me, Mr. Syndicator, and I'll take care of you. Tell me what kind of transaction you want, and I'll package it for you, and if anyone has questions about the details you call me, or have them call me directly, and I'll have the answers."

Do you have any idea how much it will cost you to let your attorney "package it for you" and, in the process, establish himself as the only one who understands the offering document, so you must call him whenever a question comes up? No wonder he doesn't give you a copy of Guide 5 and encourage you to prepare the first draft yourself.

If you're forceful, and insist on drafting your own documents, your attorney may alternatively suggest that you check with him periodically with questions about specifics, and allow him to judge whether it is good enough. Not that he's offering any guarantees, mind you. In the final analysis your attorney's opinion is of no value to you at all if the regulators and the judge disagree with it.

Have I belabored the point sufficiently? Is there anyone who still wants to ignore Guide 5 and operate on instinct? Is there anyone who still thinks the best course is to turn over all the packaging details to the attorney and let him "turn-key" the offering documents? I hope not.

ATTORNEY COMMENT

The Pros and Cons of Writing Your Own Documents

I have seen novice syndicators attempt to write their own disclosure document from scratch and nothing happens because they get writer's cramp or are so confused that they don't know where to start. Most people go through life without ever taking on a large writing project such as a disclosure document. If you haven't previously written a large report for a government agency or corporation, you may never get your project off the ground until you hire an attorney to do your first memorandum. Once you have gone through your first offering with an experienced attorney, you then may be ready to do the initial drafting on your second.

I work with a lot of people who draft their own initial documents and who hire me to review them for legal sufficiency. Some of them are so bad, it's cheaper for me to start from scratch. Others have carefully prepared documents from good models and saved themselves lots of money by having me just review their drafts.

A major drawback of having non-attorneys prepare the documents is that the non-attorney may have left something out. You could be held liable for misrepresentation under the securities laws if you omit necessary information even if it was done unintentionally or in ignorance that it should have been included. By following Guide 5, you at least have a checklist of what ought to be included. No attorney can assure you that you have complied with all the disclosure requirements unless you as syndicator and the attorney work together in putting together the disclosure documents.

The formula provided in Guide 5, if followed, will provide you with an offering document that meets the highest standard of disclosure in the industry. It will give you a valid sense of security because it has been developed by the regulators themselves. It will also save you lots of money in expert time because, with it as a guide, you'll be able to prepare your own offering documents and confine expert time to review and advise on details.

Time Is Money So Don't Waste It

If you are an experienced syndicator, with many large projects, you probably earn more per hour than the attorney preparing the documents. If the attorney charges you $30,000 for 200 hours of work, and you can make $100,000 by spending 40 hours of your time on a real estate deal, it obviously is more economical to let the attorney do it. Doing your own documentation is probably most economical for the syndicator who has done at least one syndication but who does not syndicate on a full-time basis and who does not yet have a large cash flow from his projects.

To me, the important issue here is not cost, but time. Typically, you need the documents in a week so you can start raising money; but the attorney says it will take a month. Let me let you in on a secret not always understood by non-lawyers. As a group, attorneys are among the greatest procrastinators. But, if a judge tells them to produce a forty-page brief in three days, they can do it. Any law firm worth its salt should be able to turn out a disclosure memorandum in a week! They just have to assemble a team and work night and day. They do it all the time when a judge tells them to do it. Go to your attorneys and tell them that this is what you want, agree to pay extra for the cost to them of ignoring their other clients' work, and give them a big retainer up front so that they will have the cash flow to pay for the overtime of their staff. If they can't give your syndication top priority, then consider taking your business elsewhere. But do not expect to get such extraordinary service unless you agree to pay for it up front.

Sources for Good Model Documents

Another tremendous aid to packaging your offering documents is the use of models. Well-chosen models can be very helpful and poorly chosen models can cause problems. How do you ensure that you've chosen a good model, that is, one which is legally sufficient? Within that spectrum of legally sufficient models, how do you find the one that can be most useful to you in packaging your specific investment?

With regard to legal sufficiency you have two excellent tests. If it is a SEC-registered public offering you're "home free." It has already been tested by the regulators themselves. They reviewed it by comparing it point by point for conformance with Guide 5 and found that it qualified. If it is a private offering, then you will have to do precisely what the regulators did. Compare it with Guide 5. You won't be as expert at this test as the regulators are, but you can do well enough. Guide 5 is very concisely and clearly written.

With regard to appropriateness of the model to your specific investment the process is less straightforward. You're going to have to rely on your own judgment here. If your investment plan is to purchase and manage an apartment building, then look for models of apartment building offerings. That will get you close. Among the spectrum of apartment building offerings, however, some will be structured for optimization of cash flow, others for tax benefits, and others for appreciation. You'll also have projects so much larger or so much smaller than yours that they don't apply well. That is where the judgment comes in. You'll have to sort all that out and decide what parts of the model to emulate and what parts to modify.

——————— ATTORNEY COMMENT ———————

Overreliance on Models Can Be Hazardous

Everyone starts with models, but you should never end up relying completely on a model. You are under an obligation to disclose all the risks of your particular venture. If you are renovating a decaying shopping center dependent on a nearby freeway to provide customers for your tenants and you know about serious proposals to reroute the freeway away from your shopping center, you should mention these rerouting proposals. Your model documents may never have had that problem and therefore you didn't think about putting it in your document. Your model may not have had recourse financing, but you do, so you have to talk about the tax impacts of recourse financing. Also, your model may simply not have provided adequate disclosure or it may contain statements about tax impacts that are no longer correct. In the last five years, there have been four massive revisions of the tax laws and there may be more equally significant revisions in the next several years. A model is like a car; as a tool, it can get you where you want, but if you don't use it carefully, you can injure yourself and all these around you.

Where does one find model syndication documents? Following are numerous sources, listed in the approximate order of preference.

Your Attorney

Probably the first source that comes to mind is your attorney. He's a good source if he's willing to go along with you. He works from models himself. If he's a specialist in securities he'll have good models. If he's not a specialist, there is no telling what he'll come up with.

Here's a revealing test you can give your attorney. Ask him for a model offering document. As a minimum, you'll find out the answers to two important questions: (1) Is he willing to be open with you, and (2) Does he know anything about the business? His refusal to question #1, incidentally, will not be "I'm not willing to be open with you." Rather, it will be something like: "We don't use models" or "All offering documents are protected by client confidentiality." Whatever the nature of his refusal, you will have learned something.

If he is cooperative, then what? Check out the model against Guide 5. See if it "stacks up." Ask your attorney questions to see what he knows. If he's comfortable with securities he will know answers to your questions, and probably the "case law" behind the answers.

If your attorney passes these tests—of sharing a model or helping you to put your hands on one elsewhere, and then being able to explain it to you—count your blessings. You'll know not only that your attorney respects you and is willing to deal with you in a collegial fashion, but also that he knows what he's doing. You will be off to a great start in mastering the investment syndication business.

―――――――――――― **ATTORNEY COMMENT** ――――――――――――

An attorney does have a serious problem with providing you with an example of a private placement that he recently did for a client. Private placements are not public documents, and often contain confidential financial statements about a particular deal. How would you like your attorney showing your competitors all the details of your latest deal? If your attorney does share such a document with you, he is assuming that you can be discreet with it and treat it as confidential. If he doesn't know you and this is your first meeting, I believe it is entirely appropriate for him to refuse to show you any prior private placement on the basis of client confidentiality. Attorneys believe that successful business people don't consult lawyers with loose tongues.

Your Local Securities Broker-Dealer

The quickest and easiest way I know for picking up first-rate model offering documents is to call your friendly broker at Merrill Lynch, E. F. Hutton, or the like. Most securities broker-dealers these days are selling limited partnership offerings. The most commonly available are nonspecified offerings from major U.S. public syndicators. These are beautifully packaged, well-crafted documents that represent tens of thousands of dollars in legal and accounting fees and many years of experience. You can also find at your broker-dealer, less frequently, specified public offerings of all sorts, as well as private offerings. You'll want to subject the private offerings to your Guide 5 review, of course, but if you obtain the documents from a large broker-dealer firm the odds are pretty good that they have already been subjected to close scrutiny for legal sufficiency.

―――――――――――― **ATTORNEY COMMENT** ――――――――――――

My experience is that if you pose as a potential investor in a real estate limited partnership at meetings with your local securities dealers, you will soon be deluged with sample offering material. It's so easy to get inundated with this stuff, it's like turning on a faucet.

Your Trade Association

If you're in the real estate business and a member of the National Association of Realtors (NAR) you have a tremendous asset at your disposal. Pick up your telephone, call NAR headquarters in Chicago, and ask for the library. On tap there is a large collection of syndication-related materials including a number of books that contain model documents. The librarian can locate what you need and mail it to you, postage paid, for 30 days' use. The NAR librarian helped me tremendously when I was getting started in the syndication business, and she would like to help you. You may reach the NAR library at 430 North Michigan Avenue, Chicago, IL 60611, telephone 312-329-8200.

Your State Securities Administrator

Call the office of your own state securities administrator and ask if his files on registered offerings are available for public review. Chances are they can be perused on the premises, and in many states they will have copying facilities for you. Some of the documents found on file in this way will be intrastate public offerings which may not conform with Guide 5 requirements, and others will be full registrations which do conform. Addresses and telephone numbers of the state securities administrators can be seen in Appendix H.

Regional Office of the SEC

If you're within reach of one of the eight regional offices of the SEC, stop by there. They will have copies of all SEC registered offerings from their jurisdiction and will allow public perusal as well as copying service. Addresses of the regional offices of the SEC can be seen in Appendix I.

National Headquarters of the SEC

If you're fortunate enough to be within reach of SEC's headquarters in Washington, D.C., stop by their public information office. At this location there is a wealth of model documents, all available for public scrutiny. There are also staff people available who will copy whatever you wish to remove at a nominal cost per page. As a Washington, D.C. based syndicator, I rarely do an offering without stopping by to see the most recent model on file. I've saved many thousands of dollars in legal and accounting fees by starting my information search there, locating at a good "point of departure" document, and "marking it up" to reflect my own specific objective. The Public Reference Section of the National Headquarters of the SEC is at 450 5th Street, N.W., Washington, D.C. 20549, telephone 202-272-7460.

NASAA GUIDELINES—REGULATORS SHARE THEIR OWN RULES OF THUMB

The final aid to preparing a first-class set of offering materials for a limited partnership is a little-known document called the North

American Securities Administrators Association "Statement of Policy Regarding Real Estate Programs" or, more commonly, the NASAA Guidelines. The NASAA Guidelines are not laws that you must obey, such as a federal or state securities codes. Nor do the Guidelines provide you with a "cookbook" such as Guide 5 does. They are nothing more than what the title suggests—guidelines on how to structure and package real estate limited partnerships.

The NASAA Guidelines can be tremendously useful when you are packaging your limited partnership offering because they give insights into the thinking of the state securities regulators—their views of what is fair and appropriate. Developed in committee by the securities commissioners from many different states and continually reviewed and updated to reflect changing attitudes and business realities, the NASAA Guidelines provide the best bellwether available for present and developing attitudes with regard to acceptable behavior and structuring of deals by syndication sponsors.

I like to kick off efforts in packaging a new limited partnership offering by laying before me (1) a copy of Guide 5, (2) a model of a similar offering with very recent tax and legal opinion, and (3) the NASAA Guidelines. I then lay a copy of my own latest offering at the center, and work through every document page by page, comparing the treatment of each document toward the various components of an offering, e.g. suitability standards, source and use of proceeds presentation, etc. With all this backup material before me, the task of creating first-class offering materials is really quite simple.

The complete limited partnership offerings package consists of a half-dozen discrete components, each meeting a special purpose, and each very simple in its own right. In Part IV, we have provided a summary of each component, explored its part in the overall presentation, and then produced a real-life example of such a package used in an offering. Compare the sample documents with the copy of Guide 5 in Appendix F and the NASAA Guidelines in Appendix J.

ATTORNEY COMMENT
Regulation of Securities Offerings

NASAA guidelines require you to meet the requirements of Guide 5 in your disclosure memorandum. They also specify how and to what extent you can use forecasts of projected profits, the content and assumptions of those forecasts, and what provisions you should have in your partnership agreement. These guidelines encourage you to clearly document the suitability of your deal for the investors who

Packaging Your Investment Proposal **113**

put up their money. Even if not subject to NASAA guidelines and Guide 5 for public offerings, an offering under Regulation D, parts 505 or 506, must make certain disclosures as previously discussed.

NASAA guidelines require all real property acquisitions to be supported by an appraisal by a qualified independent appraiser. They also require a balance sheet for any corporate general partner examined and reported by an independent CPA in accordance with generally accepted accounting principles. These guidelines essentially mandate that you must have a legal opinion that your partnership will be taxed as a partnership for federal tax purposes, that the partnership units are duly authorized or created and issued interests in your partnership and that your limited partners will have limited liability. A state administrator may request an additional opinion of counsel as to further tax aspects of the offering.

Regulation of Attorneys and Accountants

Regulators of attorneys and accountants have been tightening the requirements for opinions of attorneys and accountants in offering documents. The American Bar Association has issued ethical opinion 346 which requires a lawyer to make an adequate factual investigation, to state whether the tax benefits will or will not be realized, to take steps to insure that all material tax factors have been considered and to conform to other ethical requirements imposed by the opinion. A lawyer who violates any of these ethical guidelines could be disbarred or suspended from practice by state authorities who follow this opinion. The IRS has promulgated circular 230 which governs what attorneys must state in tax shelter opinions. Accountants are governed by generally accepted accounting principles and state boards of accountancy. Accountants are under restrictions regarding projections of future benefits to be gained from your partnership. Appraisers can suffer penalties from the IRS for overly inflated appraisals used for tax purposes. The impact of all of these requirements is that your attorney, accountant, and appraiser are restricted in what they can say, are required to make certain statements, and are encouraged to realize that they must have their own professional agenda different from yours as a syndicator, if they wish to retain their professional licenses.

Chapter 10

Engaging and Controlling Specialists

Exercise yourself in what lies in your power.
—Epictetus

It seems that requesting, receiving, and paying for advice regarding syndication of investments ought to be very straightforward—not something worth belaboring in a book. We all know how to ask questions, don't we? So what is there to worry about?

Plenty! To be a successful syndicator you have to be an "in-charge" person. You have to know where you are going, how and when you'll get there, and at what cost. If you don't, investors will be unwilling to trust you with their money (more than once), and you'll be unsuccessful at making and managing investments. Yet a great many syndicators fail the "in-charge" test and most often it is at the stage of engaging specialists that they do so. How and why does this happen? How can it be avoided?

UNDERSTANDING THE NEED FOR CONTROL

There is a broad spectrum of specialists who may become involved to some degree in organization of your investment syndication. Prominent among them are attorneys, accountants, securities broker-dealers, and real estate brokers. These are all people who work at the periphery of your transaction—who play very critical but highly specialized roles. Each specialist is contributing his work toward a larger, overall effort. None of these contributions is an end in itself. If it doesn't fit into the large picture it is useless. The coordinator and director of all such contributions is the investment syndicator. He must pull it all together into something of value. Therefore, he must have the final say.

Logical, you're probably thinking. Well, if it is so logical then why do so many first-time syndicators fail on this point? Why do they go into what they often hope is the first of a long line of successful syndications and fail miserably because they let one of their specialists take control away from them. Let's examine that.

Handling Fear of Controlling the Undertaking

Probably the single greatest reason why syndicators lose control is fear that they will do something wrong if they take control. Fear may be instilled in them in many ways, by many people. Ironically, the worst perpetrators of such fear are the very specialists that the syndicator employs to help him.

It can be done in many ways. The real estate broker may persuade the syndicator that if he attempts to make acquisition decisions without his okay, failure is sure to follow. The securities broker-dealer may persuade the syndicator that prospects for raising funds on his own, or via someone other than the broker-dealer, will doom him to failure. The accountant may argue that terrible financial miscalculations, or tax consequences, will follow if the syndicator doesn't structure his investment or his projections of financial return in a certain way. Fear may cause the syndicator to give up control to any of these experts.

The worst offender on the issue of fear, however, is the attorney. He is an expert at taking control by instilling fear, and he seems to have the entire American legal system in his corner.

Why does your attorney want control? Since he is your attorney, why not give it to him?

The big struggle with your attorney will typically occur at the packaging stage. The differences you and your attorney have in responsibilities (he for helping you to protect yourself against possible investor lawsuits while satisfying disclosure and registration requirements, and you for everything from raising money to making and managing investments) provide his motive for seeking to take control. The complexity of the U.S. securities laws provide him his lever.

Your attorney, you see, doesn't have the same objectives that you have. If he wants to be a big success as an attorney he's got to avoid at all costs a situation wherein a disgruntled investor successfully sues the sponsor/general partners for money, rescision of his investment, or anything else. Were such a suit brought successfully it might reflect poorly upon the attorney. It might even require gratis attorney's time in litigation of the suit (if it can be shown that the suit is a result of improper legal work). In such an event, the entire transaction will be judged a disaster by the law firm even if the investors and the partnership make a nice return on their investment.

See the contrast? The attorney's interests are different from the investors' interests. The syndicator's and investors' interests are the same. The attorney, typically, is paid on an hourly basis irrespective of whether the offering raises the minimum proceeds necessary for activation of the partnership and irrespective of whether the investments are profitable. The syndicator, on the other hand, is typically going to lose money (his personal assets) if he can't raise the minimum offering proceeds and, likewise, will lose incentive for sponsoring offerings if he doesn't earn investors a profit which he can share.

Because you, the syndicator, have interests most clearly matching those of the investors, you must insist on taking and keeping control no matter how terrifying. If you can't handle the fear, then get out of the business. If your attorney tells you that a $5,000 tax opinion (by him, of course) would virtually eliminate any possibility of future problems with the IRS and failure to insert an opinion could result in disaster for one and all, you—the syndicator—must weigh the tradeoffs. Does the offering present problems vis-à-vis taxes, and if so, are they large enough to justify a $5,000 opinion? Ultimately, it is the investors who will pay for this. If you overload your offering with such costs you may make it impossible to sell, or you may dilute profits unnecessarily. Neither of these eventualities is going to cost your attorney any money but either one can put you out of business permanently.

Your attorney may counsel you to play it safe with securities regulators and not hold investor meetings, or to avoid projections, or to set very high investor qualification standards, etc. These and a thousand other things might be construed as protecting you even as they render your partnership impossible to sell.

Remember, in the investment syndication business there are right and wrong ways of doing things, but there are also many grey areas where your specialists, particularly your attorney, will play on your fears. There are many judgments to be made at all stages of the life of a syndication and the best person to make those judgments is the sponsor/general partner. It is he who is most closely identified with the investors. He should listen to his specialist advisors, of course, but he must not let them frighten him into backing away from making the final decisions.

ATTORNEY COMMENT

Why Attorneys Say All Those Terrible Things

I know that attorneys often use fear as a technique to gain people's attention. Otherwise, the attorney's advice gets ignored and the syndicator ends up taking unnecessary risks or just plain ignoring the law. An attorney would rather dispassionately state how the law applies to your particular situation without having to resort to fear to motivate you to comply with applicable legal principles. But, in many an attorney's experience, they find they have to use fear to properly motivate you. If you want to avoid being scared out of your wits, learn how to show your attorney you know how to sensibly deal with important risks and to ignore unimportant risks.

In my experience, some people can intellectually and emotionally handle taking risks and others can not. In the syndication business as in the real estate business generally, you can be sued for no good reason. You can even lose a lawsuit where the facts and the law are on your side, if your conduct offends your local community's sense of right and wrong. You need to take reasonable steps to minimize the likelihood of a successful lawsuit against you, but if you took every possible legal step to protect yourself, you'd never do any business. It is the duty and responsibility of your attorney to warn you of every possible and potential legal liability, even if such liability is remote and unlikely. It is your job, with your attorney's help, to sort out the likely risks, do something about them, and take a chance on the unlikely risks.

Dealing With Personal Lack of Knowledge

The next biggest reason why syndicators lose control of their own syndications is lack of knowledge. To a large extent, it is this lack of knowledge that leads to the fear we discussed above. If the syndicator felt confident that he knew the tradeoffs between the various possible approaches he wouldn't fear making the judgments himself.

There is another aspect to the lack of knowledge that has nothing to do with fear, however. The syndicator may simply recognize that he doesn't know enough about some aspect of his investment syndication and coolly opt, on that basis, to rely on an expert entirely. Rather than educate himself to the point that he can critically review the expert's advice and make the final decisions himself, he may deliberately evade his responsibility to his investors for reasons of short-term convenience.

Sound unlikely to those of you who are still deliberating doing your first syndication? Well, it's not unlikely at all. It is common.

First-time syndicators, you see, are just like regular folks. Some of them are attorneys and know lots about the law and very little about accounting. Their time is dear, and quantitative analysis may never have come easily, so they deliberately decide to rely on an accountant for all financial aspects including structuring. Others are real estate brokers who know nothing about the law. They are also busy, and they have a friend who practices law, so they rely on him for the securities work.

The problem is much less severe among experienced syndicators. This is because: (1) many of the first-time syndicators who took the knowledge shortcut had an unsatisfactory experience and left the business, and (2) most of those who survived the first offering despite the knowledge shortcut realized the error of their ways and began to educate themselves.

What is it that experienced syndicators learn that persuades them of the importance of broad knowledge? Once again, we are back to the "in-charge" question.

Without a fairly good understanding of the various aspects of the investment syndication business the syndicator cannot be in control. He cannot protect his investors. If the attorney persuades the syndicator to let him "turn-key" the offering documents, for example, where does that leave the syndicator? Throughout the entire life of the business it will be necessary to turn to the attorney to answer investor questions. During the operating phase this will be merely expensive—lots of attorney time billed to explain things the general partners ought to know themselves. During the offering phase, when you are raising money, failure to be able to answer simple questions about your documents will cost you credibility and may, as a result, prevent you from raising the necessary funds.

Likewise, overreliance upon your accountant (to make and answer questions about your projections or tax treatment), securities dealer (to raise money), or real estate broker (to handle acquisitions and sales) can be fatal. You, the syndicator, are responsible for all aspects of the investment and you must be knowledgeable of all aspects. If you are not willing to acquire that knowledge, then you shouldn't be in the business.

ATTORNEY COMMENT

Greater Knowledge Spells Lower Fees

It is much easier for an attorney to advise a knowledgeable and sophisticated syndicator than an uninformed one. When dealing with the knowledgeable syndicator, the attorney has some confidence that he or she will understand the attorney's advice and be able to sort out important from insignificant problems. The attorney believes he or she can be candid and can risk a close working relationship with that person. The attorney can use legal jargon and quickly go over the fine points with some confidence that this educated syndicator understands what the attorney is saying. However, when an attorney works with a novice syndicator who refuses to take the time to educate himself, the attorney has to take a more conservative, doctrinaire and less candid approach because the attorney has no confidence that this person has good judgment or is able to intelligently handle ambiguous situations.

Attorneys, as a profession, tend to look for the worst possible thing that could happen. Their day is filled with the instances in which the unexpected disaster occurred. This naturally clashes with the entrepreneur/syndicator whose very nature is to see the positive aspects of the investment. This results in a predictable and natural clash over just how extensively the offering memorandum should discuss the many things that could go wrong with the project.

The syndicator wants to avoid putting all that bad news in the offering memorandum and wants to use the offering memorandum as a sales tool. The attorney sees the offering memorandum not as a sales tool, but as a legal document designed to protect the syndicator (and his attorney) in the event of litigation if the deal goes sour. A balance is achieved by the general partner showing his enthusiasm through his direct (oral) discussions with the investor about the proposed investment together with the simultaneous providing of the offering memorandum. The syndicator's presentation should be the forum for the sales pitch, and not the offering memorandum. In my opinion, the syndicator is making a bad mistake if he tries to "take control" of the syndication by turning the offering memorandum into a sales tool.

Overcoming Laziness and Taking Charge

Another reason why investment syndicators fail to take charge is laziness. They know that control is essential and they can usually see that knowledge would give them the ability and confidence to take control, but they are simply unwilling to invest the time and effort. These are the people who do their first investment syndication on a whim. Some have succeeded in another business without great effort or attention to detail. For a number of reasons, such people are likely to have very short careers as investment syndicators.

Syndicating on a whim is a terrible mistake. If that whim only affected the syndicator it would not be so bad. Unfortunately, by definition, investment syndications involve the use of other people's money. Seldom can a syndicator count on his investors being tolerant of a whimsical approach. Investors are usually deadly serious about seeing a good return on their investment, and expect the same seriousness of the sponsor/general partner.

Likewise, it is a big mistake to think that you can be engaged in the investment syndication business without making a substantial personal effort involving constant attention to detail. Visualize a business in which there are twenty or thirty bosses who give very little guidance but have definite expectations for performance, and one employee who must either personally perform, or administer the performance (via contract assistance), of all the work. If expectations are met, then everyone is happy. If they are not, then everyone looks to the single employee for blame. He may simply be "blacklisted" from future employment, or his bosses may seek to impose, often without merit, civil or criminal sanctions against him, requiring him to spend his own time and money in the courts defending himself.

That is what the syndication business is like. The bosses are your investors and they are unforgiving in the extreme. There are few second chances, and if there is evidence that failure to meet objectives was due to laziness on the part of the syndicator, heaven help him!

If one wishes to operate as an investment syndicator it is essential to recognize that only the syndicator/sponsor is positioned to have overall responsibility, and as such only he can be allowed to maintain control. Often the specialists he works with in organizing and operating his syndication will want to take control, especially of that portion of the activity they are involved in. This must not be permitted for any reason. You've got to take heart (overcome fear), educate yourself (overcome lack of knowledge), and work diligently to take and maintain control. Never forget that the specialists with whom you are dealing may be your competitors for control and in all your dealings with them you must handle yourself accordingly.

With that stern admonition as background, let's discuss some techniques for locating competent specialists and getting the most out of your dealings with them at the lowest cost.

IDENTIFYING COMPETENT ADVISORS

Knowing which specialist to employ for help is also a major problem faced by most new syndicators. Who are the experts you should turn to? How do you know if you're getting good or bad advice? Let's discuss some of the pitfalls in a few paragraphs, then turn to techniques to help you find the best help you can afford.

It is in the field of securities law that the problems of dealing with specialists are most severe. A lot of people have such a vague notion of the law that they don't distinguish among the skills of attorneys. If they do distinguish, it may be only between civil and criminal law or, in civil law, only between business and personal injury law.

Too often the would-be investment syndicator (say he's a real estate broker), on deciding to form a limited partnership, turns to an old friend who is practicing personal injury law, or an associate who specializes in real estate settlements, to provide the necessary legal advice and services. The friend or associate, maybe because he needs the work or because he wants to learn about syndication himself, agrees to do the job. The result is "the blind leading the blind" but with a twist. In this instance one of the blind now claims to be able to see and, furthermore, is charging an hourly fee for the time he spends groping his way through the maze of the highly specialized state and federal securities code.

The accounting profession is far less specialized than the legal profession, but even there it is helpful to deal with an expert who has background in the type of investment you are packaging. A CPA who has a general practice is unlikely to be really knowledgeable about structuring a real estate limited partnership for maximum tax benefits. Yet lots of those CPA general practitioners would love to learn at the syndicator's expense.

The problem is then compounded by what the attorneys and accountants refer to as "professional ethics." They don't like to advertise, and they are reluctant to tattle on one another. The result is that you have a hard time finding out who the competent people are.

Does it really make any difference who the first-time syndicator turns to for legal, accounting, and real estate brokerage services? You bet it does! No matter how small your offering and how friendly your investors, you are still governed by state and federal securities laws, and you are still expected to make some money for your investors. If you fail to meet either expectation you can be fairly certain that your career in the investment syndication business will be ended. It is worth your while finding legitimate experts and working with them.

How do you find such experts? Following are some tips.

Attorneys

These guys are difficult to deal with, largely because of their general reticence to advertise. I can give you some tips, however. First, never use a nonspecialist for securities work if you have an option. If you live in a small community and don't have any way to access a specialist, then educate yourself via study of the federal and state codes and textbooks on syndication so that you and the attorney can do the work together—you with the specialized knowledge on syndication and your attorney with a general background in the law.

Here is a tip for checking out the attorney who claims to be an expert. Read up on some point of securities law, and ask him his opinion on it. If he really practices securities law he'll have an immediate and long-winded answer. Also, per advice given in our discussion of packaging, ask him about model offering documents. If he fares poorly with either of these queries tell him flatly that you intend to retain a specialist in securities and would be grateful for a reference.

――――――――― **ATTORNEY COMMENT** ―――――――――

A Specialist Will Save You Money in the Long Run

The practice of law has become very specialized. You should *never* retain a general practitioner to do your securities work. An ethical attorney will not accept your work if he or she is not qualified.

Most state bar associations have corporation and real estate subdivisions and the members of such divisions or sections will know people who specialize in securities work. The active specialists will not advertise to the general public, but will often let you know about them by writing articles or giving speeches and seminars for attorneys and other specialists. Join your local RESSI chapter and you will be likely to find a specialist there.

You shouldn't automatically dismiss an attorney who doesn't answer all your questions immediately. First off, attorneys are trained not to "give it away" and are in the business of selling answers. They may only sell you the answers when you are prepared to pay for them. Secondly, syndication involves complex issues in federal tax law, federal and state securities law, and state partnership and real estate law. No one attorney can now be current in all these areas, and syndication attorneys tend to be very knowledgeable in certain of these areas and less well informed in others. The size of the law firm and its prestige in the community is no guide as to whether you will get competent, timely, and reasonable legal services for your particular syndication. Look for the individual attorney and not the firm.

Accountants

Accountants who are knowledgeable about securities are easier to find. This is because in the accounting profession most large firms have a business services department with specialists in syndication. The safe bet with accountants, therefore, is to approach the several largest firms in your area and ask them for their specialist. When you reach him, ask him "point-blank" what his syndication experience is, and for what clients. You might also ask him a fine point of partnership accounting from a recent newsletter or textbook you've seen.

ATTORNEY COMMENT

Try to find an accountant who has prepared balance sheets for prior syndications. Ask your attorney or securities broker for some references.

Securities Broker-Dealers

Dealing with securities broker-dealers presents a wide range of pitfalls—more, perhaps, than any of the other key experts with whom a syndicator typically does business. The reason for this is that the broker-dealer people are so very diverse, both in professional background and approach to the business.

People who call themselves securities broker-dealers may be employees or principals of stock brokerage houses, financial planners, insurance agents, even realtors (with the advent of the NASD limited license). What they all have in common is that they work for commissions (so they are salespeople) and they spent at least two days in a licensing course. What many of them have in common is a greatly exaggerated idea of their knowledge of real estate investments and a tendency to make extraordinary demands for their participation.

My experience is that people who are accustomed to working with investment capital tend to associate control with money rather than control with knowledge. Coming from this perspective, the classic broker-dealer will often demand far more remuneration and influence than is warranted in an investment transaction he brings an investor to. This is very dangerous because the money only gets a person into a deal. It takes knowledge to make it work.

Do not allow your broker-dealer colleagues to (1) negotiate excessive front-end remuneration and/or profit participations, or (2) have control over partnership decision making. Be assured that if the investment goes awry, *you*—the sponsor—will be held accountable, and if you signed for partnership credits it is *your estate* that will be sold to make up any shortfalls. To the extent that your investors are overcharged for partnership organization and management, or given a poor management performance because you, their fiduciary, were not free to manage well, the greater is the likelihood of disaster.

So how do you determine if your broker-dealer expert can do the job for you? Ask him qualifying questions such as: (1) Who, precisely, will raise the money required—himself? employees? cooperating institutions? (2) From whom will it be raised? (3) How much has been raised in prior, similar, transactions by this same team? (4) Who can formally commit the broker-dealer to the task? and (5) What is the nature of the commitment—all or nothing? best efforts? To the extent that your broker-dealer colleague is (1) relying upon others to raise the funds, (2) hoping to raise them from sources previously untapped or little used by him, (3) committing to a larger amount than previously raised, (4) dependent upon some third party to perform due diligence and make the final decision and (5) unwilling to make some form of guarantee to raise the funds—you should take great care in relying upon him. A realistic guarantee you should negotiate for is some share of your front-end expense in organizing the partnership, all of which will be lost to you should your broker-dealer fail to raise the necessary funds.

ATTORNEY COMMENT

You should find out how long it typically takes for your broker-dealer to do due diligence review and whether it is done locally or by someone else you will never meet. Obviously, you should employ a broker-dealer only if he or she has all the necessary licenses for each state in which you plan to sell your partnership. You should have a written agreement with your broker-dealer.

Real Estate Brokers

Distinguishing between real estate brokers on the basis of experience in the type of acquisitions you have in mind is not so difficult these days. First, and most important, realtors advertise. One can thus look at their yellow pages advertisements, their listings, or any other method to see what type of practice they have.

Beyond that, however, the National Association of Realtors has a number of specialty realty institutes which publish names and addresses of their degree candidates and graduates. Holders of and candidates for the Certified Commercial Investment Member (CCIM) designation are perhaps the best examples. Likewise you can expect to find considerable expertise among candidates and designees from the Investment Counselor, Farm and Land and Real Estate Securities and Syndication Institutes. To get guidance on the above institutes call the national Association of Realtors in Chicago (312-440-8000). Ask for the appropriate institute by name, and ask that institute's representative for their membership directory, or for several name references in your area.

ATTORNEY COMMENT

The realtors who are knowledgeable about local and commercial property love to show off their knowledge. Find out about some recent local sale of significance. Chat informally about it with your prospect. If he or she doesn't know about it, your potential choice may not be current on the marketplace. Individual realtors often change companies for one reason or another. Find a realtor who works hard for you and be loyal to that broker. Carefully review any agreement that you sign with a realtor. While I believe that it is both morally required and a good business strategy to make sure that your realtor is often rewarded for his or her hard work with ample commissions, you should not agree to pay a commission if the realtor had nothing to do with obtaining the property or the sale.

PREPARING FOR MEETINGS WITH SPECIALISTS

So you've figured out who the local experts are and you've made appointments. Now what?

Never walk into a meeting with an expert advisor without thinking in advance about what you want to accomplish. Remember, all these people are potential adversaries in the battle to control your syndication. Many would be delighted to maneuver you into a position of total dependence upon them for the services they have to sell. Remember also that in most cases (particularly with the attorney and the accountant) they are working on an hourly basis at very substantial fees. You are not serving yourself or your investors well if you incur unnecessarily high expert/consultant bills.

What does all this means in terms of dealing with the experts? First, prepare yourself for the encounter. Think about what you want to accomplish and write it down. You may have three or four major points you want to clarify in your first meeting. Perhaps there are several questions which will lead you into each. When I go to see a new expert I always follow a certain pattern.

Determine Expertise

This is a great way to start because it puts you "in the saddle." He will probably be on his turf, behind his desk, with you at his feet, but you are evaluating him. This is very important to do, and do well. Even if you've "checked him out" with someone else ask him a bit about his background and experience. Don't let him pontificate unduly at this point. He may want to show off. Try to get short responses to specific questions.

Establish the Working Relationship You Desire

The vast majority of people buying services from experts allow themselves to be put into a position of subservience. It probably comes from a combination of dealing in the expert's subject matter (where he can overwhelm you) and on his turf (where the entire office arrangement is designed to intimidate). Don't let that happen. Don't ask the expert how he does things, tell him how you do things and ask him if he can accommodate you on that basis. You, after all, are the customer, paying for the service, and he is the vendor, selling the service. It might be okay, sometimes, for a shopper to go into a clothing store and say to the salesman, "Please give me whatever you think is good for me" but it is never prudent for the syndicator to do that with his attorney, accountant, securities broker, or realtor. It isn't prudent because the syndicator is responsible for more than himself—he's responsible to the investors. They expect him, not his experts, to make the decisions.

Examples of things to cover in discussing the working relationship might include (for attorneys) models, whether the syndicator or the attorney does drafting, who relates to the regulators, involvement in investor meetings; (for accountants) use of projections, handling of reports and investment analyses; (for securities broker-dealers) copies of prior offerings sold and a sales performance report, and a copy of their model sales agreement; (for real estate brokers) acquisitions policies, property management, etc.

Discuss Fees

Virtually everyone stumbles at this point, and it makes no sense. You wouldn't buy a suit without asking the price. You probably wouldn't agree to have your home painted, or a new roof installed, without knowing the price. Why do so many people fail to discuss fees with expert consultants, before becoming obligated to them for time spent?

Who Gets Flat Fees

Flat fees for either hours spent or "piece work" (also called "value billing") are most common among attorneys and accountants. You need to deal with these people being ever aware that they expect to be paid whether your transaction comes to fruition or not, which really means that you are engaging them with *your personal resources*. They expect to be paid on the basis of what *they do*, not on what your transaction does. Knowing this, you be sure that what they do is no more and no less than what the transaction needs. Do not let them sell you work that is really a monument to their own egos, and do not allow them to waste your money on work you don't need.

Many of these people just sell hours. With such people, at your very first meeting, indeed even before the meeting, you should discuss rates. When you first call the attorney who is selected by you, tell him you want to "buy one hour's time" to discuss a possible retainership on an investment syndication offering. Don't try to get the first meeting free. It takes away your control, putting you into a supplicatory position. Over the long-run that will cost you more than you have saved.

Going in you've already taken the initiative on rates. If you're paying $1 or $2 per minute for the initial meeting, you'll get yourself organized for it, and you will make the most of it.

When the time comes at your meeting to discuss fees (after you've determined his expertise and discussed your relationship), tell him what you expect. By doing so you will establish the reference point from which your discussion will depart. If he is sitting across from you thinking $20,000 in billable time and you tell him you expect a bill not to exceed $5,000, suddenly he must adjust and prepare to try to move you up from $5,000 rather than you moving him down from $20,000.

There is no fixed price for expert fees on a syndication offering. The hourly rate may be fixed, but the number of hours logged can vary dramatically depending upon how the work is divided between syndicator and expert and, especially with attorneys, the extent that you want to buy increased insurance with legal opinions for which you hope the firm will take responsibility in event of future problems.

By establishing your target price at the outset you will save everyone lots of time. Based upon your conversation up to that point, the expert will know whether you are a person for whom he can provide the necessary services for $5,000 in fees. If it is legal work it may require allowing the syndicator to do the initial drafting and typing, or perhaps all the dealings with the regulatory officials (these can be time consuming). If it is accounting work it may require letting the syndicator set up the financial projections, with the accountant only reviewing them. Whatever, your expert will know how long it takes to do things and when you tell him your price expectation he'll be able to calculate quickly what that means in terms of how you will work together.

Who Gets Commissions

The securities broker-dealers and realtors tend to be accustomed to working on a straight commission basis. This has the advantage of assuring the syndicator that he will have no expense unless the transaction is consummated, thus enabling him to pay the fees from its proceeds, and the disadvantage of translating to often very high rates for expert time spent. Happily, these rates can generally be known upfront and negotiated to an acceptable level.

Summarize for Clarity

Finally, before you conclude your first meeting with prospective experts review what you discussed and summarize it in your own language. If you can't do that, then you probably didn't understand it, and it is too soon to leave. Another advantage of summarizing everything in your own language is that it reasserts your control of the situation at the point of departure. Securities attorneys, especially, are likely to try to close things out by saying: "This is very complicated stuff, Mr. Syndicator, but if you rely on me I'll get you through it."

That is not the way to finish! It is the expert's job to make you understand everything because you are the person responsible for knowing it. If he hasn't made you feel you understand it, then he hasn't done his job.

The best way to know if you understand something is to try to verbalize it in your own language—relate it to something in your own experience. Finish your meeting by summarizing what you learned and asking for validation. Then go home and think it over for a few days, or talk to competitors, before making a decision. That puts the control (and responsibility) where it belongs—squarely on your shoulders.

ATTORNEY COMMENT

How to Get the Most for Your Legal Bill

I sincerely believe that many attorneys try hard to do a good job in delivering reasonably priced services that will genuinely help and promote their client's business. I'm aware that most of the public does not think that this is true. What the public doesn't know, is that many experienced attorneys don't trust the public either. In fact, the lawyers in the big firms often refuse to take individual clients. If you want to get good, efficient, and prompt services from your attorney, you have to know how to separate yourself from the crowd so that you get around the adverse reaction many attorneys have to the public. If you are able to prove that you will be a competent and reliable client, then the attorney will be motivated to go the extra mile for you, will want to keep you in control of your syndication, and will even refer investors and good deals to you.

The more you prepare for your meetings and work with the attorney, the more you can get done and the less it will cost you. If you show that you are well organized, careful, reasonable, and capable of understanding risks, then your attorney should be willing to be less fearful of releasing his grip on your syndication. If the attorney can't trust your judgment and discretion, he will have to maintain control over the syndication efforts if he is going to avoid having both you and him being sued.

You must understand that an attorney or other expert might be personally liable for some of the statements in the offering memorandum. The bar associations and courts which regulate attorneys are tightening up on what an attorney may or may not do in a legal opinion for a syndication. More and more professionals are being sued, disbarred, and charged with crimes. In the current atmosphere, an attorney must constantly temper all his or her actions and advice based upon whether or not he or she could be liable for what he or she said or did. If you want control over the syndication documents through mutual respect from the attorney, you have to show that you can be trusted as a co-professional.

Syndication is like no other legal work in its capacity to bring legal liability to the attorney. Indeed, lawyers often have to pay extra premiums for legal liability insurance if they do work for syndicators. Each year, the attorney may have to give a special written explanation to his liability insurance carrier as to what steps he takes to avoid malpractice claims for securities work.

The insurance carrier may or may not provide professional liability insurance for only some of the securities work of the lawyer. The securities attorney is always aware of his or her potential liabilities. He or she would be a fool to let you totally control the syndication documentation if you are inexperienced or have bad judgment.

A second important tip in getting the most out of your attorney is to pay your legal bills on time, without complaining. There are legions of people out there who are ready to cheat and rip off attorneys by not paying their bills. Each practicing attorney quickly learns to constantly protect himself from being exploited. Unless you have worked in a professional office before becoming a syndicator, you will have very little idea of the large and constantly growing costs of maintaining even a modest law office. The way to avoid being sent into a state of shock over a legal bill is to set the fees up front, get a written retainer agreement, and clearly specify the work that you want done. If you constantly complain about "excessive" attorneys' bills, you are training your attorney to think of you as an unpleasant person. Many attorneys love legal work and hate to discuss fees and hate to think of themselves as businessmen. They find the whole subject of fee disputes extremely distasteful. Attorneys hate to deal with people who constantly complain about fees.

An attorney may be able to review a syndication for only $5,000 if you prepare all the basic documentation and you have demonstrated that you are a competent, sophisticated, and honest professional. An attorney will charge this much lower rate only if you have gained his or her confidence through dealings prior to the syndication and he does not have to write a tax opinion. If you are not organized, gloss over important details, and show that you are not capable of organizing the production of a 100-plus page disclosure memorandum, or if this is the first time you have worked with this attorney, the attorney may charge you $30,000 and up because he can't trust you to carefully do the work. Part of the fee charged by the attorney when he writes the memorandum and a tax opinion is for "legal insurance" rather than just the time and expenses incurred to produce the documents. Expect to pay high fees if you expect to buy insurance from an attorney by requiring him to produce a tax opinion. Depending upon the applicable regulations, you may have to have a tax opinion, thereby greatly increasing your legal costs.

Chapter 11

Useful Tips on Typing and Printing

I'm sure that a lot of the "hard chargers" among my readers are going to skip this topic. "Typing and printing! How interesting or useful can that section be? I'll leave those details to my secretary."

If that is your attitude you are sorely mistaken. Granted the subject of typing and printing might not be as exciting as others that the syndicator must deal with, but it is no less important. No chain is any stronger than its weakest link. The syndication process is like that chain, beginning with the initial concept of the investment and continuing through finding a partner, structuring, packaging, selling the security, acquiring the investments, managing the partnership, liquidating the property, and liquidating the partnership. The typing and printing element is a critical component in forging the "packaging and selling" links and must not be treated in a cavalier fashion.

Why are typing and printing important? There are several reasons.

IMPORTANCE OF APPEARANCES

When a would-be investor considers placing his hard-earned cash with someone he doesn't know well, if at all, he wants a lot of assurances that the person he is relying on to manage the investment (the general partner) knows what he is doing. If the would-be investor is an expert on the type of investments your syndication was formed to make, he has no problem. All he has to do is study the investment itself. If he's an expert, though, chances are he won't be joining someone else's syndication as a passive investor. He will be making his own deals.

No, it is more likely that the subject of the investment will be something he knows very little about. Or perhaps the syndication is a nonspecified fund, with the general partners having sole discretion as to use of funds. Then there is no investment to study. It is in this environment (nonexpert investor and/or nonspecified property funds) that the printing and typing become especially important.

Everyone wants to evaluate the investment in some way, and the way that occurs to almost everyone is to look at the package itself. Does it contain typographical errors? Was it typed double space and copied on a dirty machine? You'd be surprised how many private syndication offerings fit this description.

What kind of impression does that leave? Careless, right? Do you want to entrust your hard-earned cash to a careless person—a person who doesn't pay attention to details? Not me! Remember, if the investor doesn't know the general partner, and can't evaluate the technical and economic merits of the proposal for lack of expertise, then he's going to evaluate those things he knows how to evaluate and project his conclusions regarding them to all other aspects of the deal. That's human nature.

I recall several years ago two colleagues of mine came to me very excited, saying that they had an opportunity to join a limited partnership with some very bright and successful developers who sounded extremely knowledgeable. Interested, I asked to look at the offering documents. They were replete with typographical errors, double spaced, had jagged margins, were copied on a dirty copying machine and stapled in the corner. This worried me, but I feared that my friends would disregard an opinion based upon such observations. Then I noted that the syndicator's sloppiness had spilled over into a critical substantive area—the assumptions upon which investment viability was based. He assumed that rent control in his property's jurisdiction would end that year, thus allowing rental adjustments to market rates.

I spoke to my friends. I explained how my feelings with regard to packaging details made me very nervous regarding the syndicator, and the rent control assumption confirmed my fears. They went forward anyway. Rent control was not terminated. The partnership begin to "take water" and "sink." Indeed, my feelings based upon the typing and printing had been right.

If you're going to optimize marketing effort, don't give short shrift to typing and printing. Don't leave it to your secretary. Maybe your disinterest in such things is not an indication of sloppiness in your case, but if people think it is you're going to be hurt. You may find yourself unable to raise sufficient funds. When you think about it, sloppiness in the typing and printing task is a poor reason to fail. So don't. Do it right.

ATTORNEY COMMENT

When your investors give you their hard-earned $10,000 or $50,000, all they get is the offering memorandum and a letter from you welcoming them into the partnership. Make sure your offering memorandum shows due respect for their money by being a quality production. I've seen many instances where beginning syndicators made up for their relative inexperience by providing a high-quality offering memorandum.

HOW TO MINIMIZE COSTS

Another surprise for many new syndicators is that typing and printing of the offering documents, when done well, can be very costly. As a matter of fact, once you get to know what you are doing, have your own model documents, and know your way around the legal and accounting issues, you may spend more money on typing and printing than on anything else.

Given that it is a costly item, you should give some thought about how to minimize it. There are a number of very easy and helpful things to do.

Use of Word Processors

Instead of wrestling with doing your documents over and over on standard desk typewriters, use a word processor. This will help you in two ways. First, it will greatly cut your costs of editing as you move from first to second, third, and fourth drafts. If you're going to do a good job on your offering package, you'd better figure on lots of changes as you, your partners, your attorney, your accountant and, in the case of public offerings, the regulators, pass it back and forth. If you accept the reality going in, and plan for it by putting your document on a word processor, you'll save lots of time and money.

A second way that the word processor will save you time and money is in replacing the typesetter. Although virtually all printers these days use electronic typesetting machines (essentially word processors), they will charge for the work though it were done by hand. One full page of typesetting can easily cost $100. The same page, done on a word processor, might cost $5. What is the difference in appearance? Well, until recently there was plenty. Only the typesetters could line up the margins on both right and left sides, change from standard type to italics or bold, center, etc. Now many word processor systems have the same capability. As a matter of fact, if a paper is carefully planned and the word processor operator is good, it is possible to prepare an offering package on a word processor that is equal in appearance to a typeset document, and at a fraction of the cost.

A third way you can benefit from the word processor is less direct. You've got to wait until your next offering to realize it. Save the magnetic disk on which your final document is recorded so that next time around you'll have your model already typed. All you'll have to do is mark up your last offering, making appropriate changes (modest in certain sections and major in others) and give the disk and the markup to your word processor operator for a quick, very reduced cost first draft. Neat, huh? And the time and money saved are all yours because normally, at the packaging stage, the syndicator is still in the partnership formation stage where he carries the cost on his shoulders alone.

Supervision of the Process

A second item of concern relating to packaging is the question of who should oversee the typing and printing process. It is very common for larger law offices to be equipped with word processors. If they are, expect your attorney to offer to relieve you of the burden of supervising the typing and editing process. He may even tell you it is free—included in his fee. Don't let yourself be tempted!

Giving up control of the typing and printing process will prevent you from being the ultimate authority on what has gone into your offering package. You can't afford to give that up. It will create dependence for a long time to come.

Likewise, the offer to do it free is dubious. Possibly the word processor operator's time isn't billed, or is billed only at cost. That may be true. What is always billed, however, is the attorney's time. If you turn over to him supervision of the typing operation you will be paying him $100 per hour to do something you, or your assistant, could do with equal alacrity in your spare moments.

──────────── **ATTORNEY COMMENT** ────────────

Attorney's offices often have some of the best word processing teams available. If you have a joint working relationship with your attorney, you may be able to work with his word processing people and lessen supervision time for the attorney. Also, it is often more efficient to have it done in the same office where your attorney is located rather than having to run all over town between the word processor and the attorney. I think you can have the attorney's office do the typing and not lose control.

Chapter 12

Selling the Securities

So you have made it to the selling stage. You located what appears to be a good investment. You found an appropriate individual with whom to share general partner responsibilities. You structured it to optimize returns for your target investors. You packaged it in accordance with the best models and guidance available. Your offering materials are as neat, clean, and professional looking as any on the street. Now comes the moment of truth. It is time to raise investor money.

Fund raising can be an enormous challenge. For the occasional syndicator, or the one who structures only small transactions that he can purchase himself if need be, it isn't such an important hurdle. If you want to be active, however, always working on a new transaction, and if you want to make large investments, beyond your personal capacity, you will have to give serious thought to the question of systems for fund raising. In this section we're going to talk about raising investor money privately (for offerings in which you seek exemption from securities registration), as well as publicly (for registered offerings), and we're going to discuss some of the selling arrangements that can simplify your task.

WHEN TO MAKE PRIVATE OFFERINGS

The reason most syndicators seek exemption for their limited partnership offerings from registration with state and federal regulators is desire to avoid the burden of paperwork and red tape and the expense they entail. For the most part they view the difficulties of registration as greater than they are, and thus choose not to register their offerings. Others seek private offering exemptions for their syndications because they genuinely have no need or desire to offer them to the public. They may have an extended family from which to draw funds, a large circle of well-to-do friends, or possibly just a penchant for privacy.

It has been my observation that some of the most successful private offering syndicators have great "noses" for making good investments but poorly developed skills for economic analysis and writing. This would seem to indicate that they may have chosen to keep everything on an informal basis to avoid exposing such weaknesses. The alternative, to learn the requisite skills or to be able to deal in a more structured environment, might have seemed too great a challenge, or not worth their while.

This is not to put down the syndicator/investor who makes his decisions based upon instinct rather than analysis, and raises money based on familiarity with the investors rather than good packaging. If you have either of those gifts (a good investor instinct, or rich family or friends) for heaven's sake trade on them! However, if you don't have those gifts, or you have them but wish to go further than they alone will take you, you'll also have to develop economic analysis and writing skills.

PROFITABLE TIPS ON PUBLIC OFFERINGS

If you don't have rich family members or friends to draw upon for investment capital, you may want to reach out to a wider audience. The best way to do that is by registering your offerings with appropriate state and federal regulators and offering them to the general public. Registration doesn't mean you can do anything you please vis-à-vis marketing the offering, but it does give you far greater flexibility. It opens the door to newspaper advertisements (albeit carefully controlled ads), public meetings, unlimited numbers of investors, etc. The price you pay for this greater freedom is that you must submit your offering material to the regulators for review to ensure that they comply with the law.

Keep in mind, please, that even syndications offered privately, with exemption from registration requirements, are obliged to comply with the law. The only differences are (1) some minor variations in disclosure requirements, and (2) the regulator is unlikely to look at your private offering package until you are in trouble. At that point, however, if you are not in compliance you receive much more than advice on disclosure. You may also be subjected to civil or criminal liability for your shortcomings.

Some years ago I spoke with a syndicator colleague from another state. He had been sponsoring real estate limited partnerships for about ten years and had gradually withdrawn from making private offerings. He now registered all his new transactions, no matter how small. I knew that he was raising a lot of his money from a small circle of friends so I asked him why he bothered with public registration. He replied that: (1) he was using high standards of disclosure anyway, and (2) by registering his offerings he was insuring himself against investor lawsuits in the event of future difficulties (inadequate disclosure can't be claimed if the offering materials have been judged worthy by the regulators).

ATTORNEY COMMENT
A Word of Caution on Public Offerings

I agree that the safest way to go is public registration. However, I think there are several factors which mitigate in favor of private syndications for the syndicator in the early stages of his or her career: (1) avoidance of the application of NASAA guidelines if adopted as law in your state; (2) the cost and delay in public registration; (3) the annoyance in dealing with state regulators; and (4) the ability to exclude "crackpots" from private syndications. This is discussed more fully in previous comments.

Let's assume that you have paid the price of somewhat higher organization costs, have registered your offering and received permission to market it to the public. Now what? Do you have an approach, a marketing strategy, that will enable you to persuade complete strangers, or perhaps people you know only slightly through your work, church, club, or whatever, to invest with you? Believe me, it is not an easy task, particularly if your firm is small and your track record is short. Following are some approaches to consider.

How to Handle Advertising

Public advertising of limited partnership offerings is very tightly regulated by state and federal securities administrators. Regulation is so severe, in fact, that the classic advertisement which meets regulator approval is known as a "tombstone ad," that is, you can't say any more on it than the few vital statistics that are characteristic of tombstone inscriptions. Flowery or enthusiastic language is not allowed, and gimmicks such as free toasters with each share purchased are frowned upon. Essentially, you are allowed to state the partnership name, date, and amount of the offering, minimum investment, and similar details. That's all.

The key to successful use of direct mail advertising is to come up with the mailing lists that can bring you high response ratios. How do you find these? The easiest and most obvious way is to purchase subscriber lists from publications that seem to be appropriately targeted. If there is such a publication your mailer might be inserted in the publication itself, or sent separately. On another level, you can turn to mailing list wholesalers. There are many of these around the country, some with very detailed catalogues of their mailing list offerings. They can sell you almost any list you can think of, normally broken down into zip code areas.

ATTORNEY COMMENT

Pitfalls in Advertising

You should always pass all proposed advertisements, both the copy and the distribution method, to your legal counsel for review. Otherwise, you will not know if your advertisements conform to securities strictures.

You may say, "Why be so cautious? I see those ads in the paper stating 'Attention Investors,' three-to-one write-off and no money down. Call now.'" As for these ads, either (1) they are not selling securities, just real estate, or (2) they are in reality selling a security and are grossly violating the law.

I would be wary of an investor who responds to newspaper advertisements, tombstone ads or mailings. They may not understand (or want to understand) the risks of real estate and they have no personal connection to you. They may want out or want to sue you if the project goes through a rough period. Are they truly qualified to invest? Will a qualified wealthy person respond to a mailing? A beginning syndicator would be better advised to build up his or her investors through personal contact with people in organizations likely to contain prospects for investors. I know one syndicator who slowly builds up his investor base by taking them to lunch one by one and talking to them about real estate investing.

Organizing and Conducting Investor Meetings

Making presentations to large groups is another tool that is off-limits to private offering syndicators but very acceptable when one is marketing public offerings. These might be made via short talks on the regular programs of your local Rotary club, an investment society, etc., or you might conduct special seminars. A very common technique in many cities is to offer a luncheon or evening seminar on the subject of the limited partnership offering (i.e., tax shelter, equity growth) to catch people's attention. With a group thus assembled, the syndicator can discuss the advertised subject first, then lead into his investment offering.

The problems of selling to large groups are many, however, and you could spend a lot of time, energy, and money failing before "hitting your stride" and beginning to get results.

First, you have to figure out how to get the groups together. This may be done via your response to ad calls and direct mail feedback. Rather than trying to answer questions via the telephone, or mailing materials to callers sight-unseen, or meeting each caller one-on-one, try scheduling meetings on a regular basis. You can then respond to calls by saying: "We're going to be meeting to discuss that on Thursday night. Would you like to attend, hear the general partners describe the investment firsthand, and pick up copies of the offering materials?"

Because the materials which comprise the average public offering package are expensive, and because many callers on advertisements are competitors (fellow syndicators) or service vendors (lawyers, accountants, and brokers) rather then potential investors, a practice of mailing materials to each caller will prove very expensive. It is far better, I think, to attempt to channel the caller into a group meeting. If they don't want to come to such a meeting you can usually figure that they are either not serious about looking for an investment, or in one of the noninvestor categories.

For the potentially serious investor the group meeting has much appeal because it provides less pressure (more anonymity) than a one-on-one session, while allowing the investor to "size up" the sponsors firsthand. Remember, though, that you are just as responsible for what you say in investor meetings as you are for what you write in your official offering materials. You should not paint an unreasonably optimistic picture of things or make projections you don't feel you can meet. The consumer protection laws that govern the securities offering package govern other aspects of the offering as well. Expect to be held accountable, and play by the rules.

If you're one of those promoters who gets so carried away with enthusiasm for your product (many of us do) that you can't help making overly optimistic claims and projections, for heaven's sake make sure there are not tape recorders in the room. The syndication business is perilous enough without having to deal with investors who tape your conversations.

ATTORNEY COMMENT

Things to Be Wary of at Investor Meetings

NASAA guidelines for public offerings require that you clearly state in the notice for a meeting to sell your partnership units the purpose of your meeting, the minimum purchase price of your units and the names of the partnership sponsor, underwriter or selling agents. You cannot offer any cash or any other item of value to induce them to attend such a meeting (providing coffee and cookies, without prior announcement is probably okay); you can't give away free or bargain trips to visit the property. You must submit all written handouts, slides, placards, and scripts in advance for review not more than three business days prior to the meetings.

A common practice of promoters of private offerings is to give seminars on real estate investments in general with no specific mention of a particular offering. Later, after the meeting, the syndicator contacts the participants on an individual basis to discuss a specific offering. This approach, properly executed, may be acceptable in many states.

Using Public Relations to Get the Media Working for You

Another tool for marketing public offerings that is used very effectively by major public syndicators is publicity. The objective is to get into the target investor's newspapers and magazines as news, rather than in costly advertisement form. A news story about your offering is far more effective than a tombstone advertisement. It also has the advantage of not being regulated. If the writer thinks what your partnership is doing is exciting, or filling a great consumer need, or potentially lucrative, he can say so.

How do you get into the media as news? The first step is to hire a media consultant. You needn't spend a lot of money on this, but if you get the right person the investment can pay large dividends.

Few of us know enough about the very esoteric world of reporting the news to do a competent job of handling our own publicity. The professional media consultant knows (1) what publications will reach your target investor, (2) who are the people running them, (3) what kind of material they will use, and (4) how to bring you, or your story, to their attention. Do what the major public syndicators do, and what some small public syndicators like myself have done: engage a media consultant. Your results may be slow in developing—they may even be indirect—but over time you'll find the results of a professionally directed public relations campaign more lucrative than any of your other approaches, and complementary to all of them.

SUCCESS-TESTED WAYS TO OBTAIN MARKETING ASSISTANCE

Whether your company's approach is to sponsor private offerings or public offerings, you should give serious consideration to complementing your own sales effort with the help of others in related fields.

Who are these other people who might be helpful in marketing your limited partnership offerings, and how do they work? For the purposes of this discussion we will focus on two basic types of arrangements, finders and sellers, and we'll look at some of the professional groups who typically work under such arrangements.

Finders

Finders, under securities laws, are people who identify (find) potential investors for a securities offering but do not sell the security itself. Rather, they pass the name to the appropriate selling agent in return for a fee or other consideration. It is very important to keep the distinction between finders and sellers clear because the business of securities selling is highly regulated whereas finding is not. Selling of securities for a fee requires a license—finding does not.

If you are going to engage someone as a finder, be sure that you review the distinction between finding and selling with him. A clear understanding of the difference will help to keep both of you out of trouble.

What if your finder makes such a persuasive pitch for the offering he is "finding" for that the investor decides to invest before he has even seen the offering documents or met with the offeror or his legitimate sales representative? Has the finder acted solely as a finder? It can certainly be argued to the contrary. What might such an innocent misunderstanding mean?

To begin with, keep in mind that quarrels over such points rarely arise except in cases of dispute. Normally such disputes arise only when there are economic problems with the investment. When things are going well investors rarely complain about fine points. When things are going poorly, however, investors and their attorneys sometimes go to great lengths to identify potential points of vulnerability. Sloppy implementation of your finder arrangements, as in the above case, could prove to be a fatal mistake should the courts insist on "rescision" of the investors' original contributions at a time when that can be least afforded. It could also expose the finder, and his syndicator sponsor, to civil penalties for unlicensed securities selling, and sponsorship of such unlicensed selling.

Got the distinction between finding and selling? It's grey, isn't it? There is one little trick, rather nonsubstantive on the surface, that can help to buoy the syndicator's and finder's arguments that finding is all that was going on. That is to distinguish between fee amounts for finding and selling. There is a well-defined market rate fee for selling limited partnership securities. It is an amount equal to around 10% of the purchase price of the security. For finding, the rate is not so well defined. Indeed, in many state securities codes finder arrangements are not even mentioned. It seems reasonable to assume, however, that a finding fee should be less than a selling fee. In my own business when I have paid finders I paid them half the going rate for sellers—5%. The rate didn't attract a lot of finders, but then I'm not sure that 10% would have either. At least I felt secure.

Another technique that can help you protect yourself in dealing with finders is to formalize the arrangement with a written agreement that clearly spells out their role, reminds them of the difference between finding and selling, and gives them an opportunity to affirm, by their signature, that they understand the restrictions on their behavior and will live by them.

Now that we've reviewed some of the pitfalls concerning use of finders and decided to work with them, let's see who they are and how we locate them.

Finders come from all fields of endeavor. Generally speaking, the things they have in common are that (1) they feel they know people with money to invest, (2) they think that such people are interested in their referrals of investments to look at, and (3) they are willing to refer your investment in return for a consideration. More often then not the would-be finder is wrong about the second assumption. You can't learn that, without giving him a try, however, so brace yourself for frequent disappointment with finders and maybe, over time, you'll develop a few procedures.

Who are the most effective finders? Generally, they come from fields of endeavor which have given them credibility regarding the second assumption (they think that people are interested in their referrals of investments). These people are often attorneys, accountants, insurance agents, or financial planners.

Attorneys can be effective as finders because many people regard them as knowledgeable about business. They are also effective as finders because in dealing with many clients in business relationships they often learn the client's investment interests and capabilities. They get a pretty good feel for who can afford to do what, and for their level of financial sophistication.

On the negative side of the ledger, some attorneys simply refuse to "find" for a fee. They consider it a potential conflict of interest. If your attorney won't take a fee, then you'd better have some other way of making him feel appreciated (maybe you can send lots of legal business his way) or he'll lack incentive to "find" for you. Attorneys have to make a living, too.

CPAs are much like attorneys vis-à-vis people's perceptions of them and their resultant effectiveness as finders. They also have the professional ethics problem regarding taking a fee. If it is a nonspecified offering you're doing you'll have a terrible time attracting accountants as finders. Accountants love numbers and pride themselves on being able to evaluate the quantitative aspects of an investment. In a nonspecified offering there are none to evaluate so they tend to feel that the whole thing is unreal. Don't plan on attracting accountants as finders for your nonspecified offerings.

Insurance agents can be among your very best finders because (1) they often know a lot about their clients' assets, (2) a good agent is trusted by his clients, and (3) insurance agents are skilled salespeople with a strong fee orientation. For many agents, "finding" for syndicators is part of a natural progression from selling insurance to selling securities, or even to sponsoring their own investment offerings.

Financial planners are probably your very best finders. All the characteristics which render attorneys, accountants, and insurance agents effective in this endeavor apply to them as well. However, they also present a problem. Many of them are licensed securities dealers as well as financial planners, and are accustomed to taking full sales commissions which are likely to be more remunerative for them than finder's fees.

--- **ATTORNEY COMMENT** ---

How To Avoid Trouble With Finders

Do not plan to be able to get around requirements for a broker-dealer by using "finders." If someone has a substantial participation in the transaction or continuously acts as a finder for you, then they may be classified as acting as an unregistered broker-dealer. In some instances, a finder can be held to underwriter liability. NASD takes the position that no NASD licensed salesman can pay finder's fees to a non-NASD licensed salesman. If the finder gives investment advice he may be required to register under the Investment Advisors Act.

For you to avoid problems with finders, you should have your finder certify in writing that he has given no advice on the merits of your offering, that he has made no representations about your deal, that he has not negotiated the sale, that he has complied with all applicable federal and state securities laws, that he has not been paid as a finder for more than two offerings in the past two years, and that he agrees to hold the partnership and you harmless for his activities. This is an area where it is not clear what the finder can do to avoid liability. Actions beyond a mere introduction of the prospect to you could cause him to lose his status as finder. Work closely with securities counsel if you intend to use finders.

Sales Agents

The other way to get some help in selling your offering is to engage sales agents. This is expensive, but it is probably worthwhile if you're going to be selling syndication offerings on a regular basis. There are several different approaches to this, and the distinction between them is very critical.

The first approach applies where the sponsor is selling his own offering either privately, with an issuer's exemption from registration assumed, or publicly, with an official issuer's exemption letter from the affected state securities administrators. No one can sell a security for a commission consideration unless he is licensed by regulatory authorities to do so. When a nonlicensed syndication sponsor sells his own private offering with an issuer's exemption assumed, or his public offering under a formal issuer's exemption letter, it is understood that he is not charging a sales commission. His consideration for selling the interest is taken in other ways, e.g., participation in investment returns. So long as others in his firm are not paid sales commissions, they too can help with the sales effort. They can't take orders (fill out the subscription agreements), but they can do almost anything else. The thing to remember is that they can't be remunerated on the basis of sales performance. Their payment must be even, like salary, and preferably related to other normal and usual tasks done under the sponsor's other business activities.

The second approach applies when the sponsor engages a licensed securities broker-dealer to market his product. Then he becomes involved in a very formal procedure. Commissions for selling are negotiated with certain parameters (8 to 10% of proceeds raised being the norm), sometimes exclusive agency is insisted upon (meaning that no matter who identifies investor funds the securities broker-dealer takes a commission of the sale), sometimes participation by the broker-dealer in profit from the syndication is insisted upon, and always the securities broker-dealer will engage in some form of "due diligence." Due diligence is a term that means the broker-dealer has looked the syndication over carefully and satisfied himself that it was legally and professionally organized, that it represents itself honestly, and that it offers a reasonable investment for those to whom it is directed.

Since "due diligence" is done by and for the securities broker-dealer, it seems logical that it is paid for entirely by the securities broker-dealer. Logical, maybe, but wrong! The due diligence process can be easy or hard, fast or slow, depending upon how the securities broker-dealer operates. If you are a low-overhead syndicator used to doing things quickly and efficiently and you get involved with a securities broker-dealer who operates at the other extreme, heaven help you! Your time, and the time of your attorney and accountant, will be required throughout the process and all of these will cost you money.

Having said all that about selling through licensed securities broker-dealers, however, it is still often a good deal for the syndicator to make if he can. Raising investor money is a very specialized business. It is not something that your average syndication sponsor, with background in law, accounting or real estate, is necessarily good at. He may be able to do so up to a point, but before long most syndicators run out of family and friends they can tap and have to go to the general public. Then they are in a tough "ball game"—one which the securities broker-dealer alone is trained to play.

My advice is to get involved with a securities broker-dealer as soon as you can, at whatever price. When he's sold your product successfully a time or two he'll have more confidence in you, and you can cut a better deal (perhaps diminish his profit percentage). The expense involved in meeting his due diligence requirement will also drop dramatically following the first transaction. If he doesn't become easier to deal with at that point you can talk to other broker-dealers. They will be more inclined to work with you if you have a track record with one of their competitors than if you are an unknown.

Another thing to remember about licensed securities broker-dealers: if they have been in business a few years they generally know what they can do—how much money they can raise for a given venture, and from whom. That is valuable knowledge to have. One of the most worrisome points of the syndicator's business is making all that "up-front" investment in organizing the partnership without knowing for sure that he can raise the funds necessary to consummate the transaction. A good securities broker-dealer can do much to relieve you of that worry. That's worth a lot.

ATTORNEY COMMENT

Some Precautions to Take in Use of Sales Agents

Regulation D prohibits both you and your sales agent from any form of public advertising for your private offering. When you alone, as syndicator, sell your offering, you may sell it only to people who are your friends or business acquaintances. However, by hiring a licensed sales agent, your sales agent can contact his clients, friends, and business associates to present to them your private offering.

If you employ licensed sales agents, you must be sure that they don't make untrue or distorted representations you will be stuck with later. You should have them sign an agreement that they will state only what is correct about your offering, that they will not violate any securities laws in their offering and that they will hold you harmless if you are sued due to an unauthorized representation by them. You should require them to keep a listing of each person they contact, whether they gave them a copy of the offering materials and the result of the contact. If the person ends up investing in the partnership, your sales agent should have records showing that the investor received a copy of the offering materials, had an opportunity to ask questions, filled out the suitability questionnaire and is in fact qualified to invest in your partnership. NASAA guidelines require you and your sales agent to make every reasonable effort to insure that the people offered or sold your partnership are suitable investors and that your project is appropriate for the customer's investment objectives and financial situation. You should have a contract with your sales agent which spells out the responsibilities and restrictions on them.

You should have documentation showing that your investors have the capacity to understand your partnership offering through employment experience, education, access to experts, or experience with similar prior investments. Your sales agents and you have to be able to prove that the investor understands the fundamental risks and hazards of the investment, the lack of liquidity, the control to be exercised only by you, and the tax consequences of the investment. You need to be able to show that each investor can benefit from your offering. NASAA guidelines impose a minimum annual gross income of $30,000 and a net worth of $30,000, or in the alternative a net worth of $75,000 for your investors. The suitability standards are higher for high-risk or high write-off offerings. Your state may have different suitability requirements. Your limited partners should all sign a form showing that all this is true. This is normally done by using an offeree questionnaire, an example of which is found in Part IV, Exhibit C. If your investor has an advisor, have the advisor fill out an offeree advisor questionnaire, particularly where the investor must rely on the sophistication of the advisor to understand the risks of your proposal.

Chapter 13

Do's and Don'ts of Successful Investing and Reporting

Nothing astonishes men as much as common sense and plain dealing.
—Ralph Waldo Emerson

For the reader who automatically associates formation and operation of a real estate investment syndication with acquisition and management of a specific piece of realty, this section may seem somewhat esoteric. After all, what is there to know? You make the investment for which you formed the syndication, and you send your investors their cash flow, tax loss, and profit allocations as they are available. Right? Well . . . yes. It can get far more complicated than that, however, particularly when you get involved over long periods of time, or in nonspecified investment funds.

In the following several pages, we'll discuss these two important subjects in general terms. I don't believe that specific guidance on how to handle the investment and reporting functions can be given, but the spirit of good investment and reporting policies can be discussed. Perhaps the critical nature of the investment and reporting functions, which are so often given short shrift in syndication firms (especially reporting policies), can be thus highlighted.

GUIDELINES FOR INVESTMENT DECISIONS

Rule 1 on limited partnership investment policies is always do what you said you were going to do in your offering documents. If you organized your partnership with a certain property and financial structure in mind, follow through on that basis. Often in nonspecified offerings, and occasionally in specified offerings, something changes and another investment approach may seem more desirable. You really don't have a right to make those changes—not unless you discussed such eventualities in your offering documents.

Sure, it can be argued that technically as general partner, you can do anything you please, as long as you don't violate laws. So you make unforeseen investments, win the argument in court, but anger your investors. What happens then? You've lost anyway.

My approach, in the long-term (four to seven years) nonspecified property offerings I have made is to establish investment objectives that relate not to the realty itself, but rather to investor goals. For example, rather than say that the partnership's objective is to purchase and rehabilitate an old commercial building, I say that the objective is to make investments that will provide the limited partners with (1) long-term appreciation taxed, (2) substantial tax shelter of property income from credits and depreciation, (3) modest cash flow distributions, and (4) slight equity buildup due to principal amortization. Such goals might be met in any number of specific investments, so the general partners can then exercise their discretion in choosing among opportunities without fear of violating investor trust.

Suppose you had taken the other approach, focusing your partnership investment strategy on the realty rather than the investor, and in the course of rehabilitation study you learned that you could "flip your contract" on the commercial building for a quick, short-term gain. Alternatively, suppose you did the rehabilitation, took the appropriate tax credits, operated the building for five years, then sold. You could be faithful to your problems about purchasing and rehabilitating the building in either scenario, but each has very different effects on the investor. The former scenario, with a quick short-term gain taxable at ordinary income rates, would result in no shelter of other income and in heavy tax consequences in the year the investment was made. The latter scenario, with tax credits, 31.5 year depreciation, very minor cash flow, and probably a substantial gain in five years, would result in tax benefits and good long-term equity buildup. Each scenario is suitable to very different investors. The person investing in anticipation of scenario #1 would be unhappy with scenario #2, and vice versa.

Always remember that the investment itself is of no consequence. It is merely a means to an end.

The syndicator's primary responsibility is to his investors and their needs and expectations. They put their confidence in the syndicator, and he must earn and keep that confidence. The way to do that is by setting investment objectives with the target investor in mind (income, shelter, or equity growth), make sure that all investors match the target investor profile, then see to it that every specific investment made is structured to provide the desired effects.

When I talk to investors on acquisitions policy, I refer them to our partnership's investment goals, pointing out their order of importance and relative weights, and I tell them it is my convenant with them. I, in my capacity as general partner, promise to make my best effort to accomplish such investment goals on their behalf. If they don't share such goals, or if they feel they can accomplish them better on their own, then they shouldn't invest in the partnership.

ATTORNEY COMMENT
NASAA Guidance on Reporting Policies

NASAA guidelines seek to impose a fiduciary duty on the syndicator of a public offering as to the use of funds of the program. The sponsor is required to commit a substantial portion of the investor's capital contributions to the property and is limited in the amount that can go into front-end fees. A minimum of 67% of capital contributions must go into the property and lesser percentages depending upon the financing on the property. You are restricted to joint ventures with partnerships which have the same objectives as your proposal.

In a nonspecified offering, NASAA guidelines require a statement as to what types and sizes of properties you intend to invest in. If you propose to invest in shopping centers, you must so state and must invest a high percentage of funds in shopping centers. A partnership formed to invest in warehouses probably couldn't invest in apartment units. State requirements can limit you in your ability to invest in unimproved land, nonincome-producing properties, or junior trust deeds. For investments in private offerings under Regulation D, you could be liable for misrepresentation or even fraud if you invest in different types of property than you set forth in the offering materials.

WALKING THAT "FINE LINE" BETWEEN TOO MUCH AND TOO LITTLE INFORMATION

The spirit of a good reporting policy, I think, is to practice full disclosure. This doesn't mean that you bore your investors with all sorts of inconsequential details concerning matters that won't affect their "bottom line." If they were interested in the details they would have invested directly. As general partner, you are being paid to handle small details.

What the limited partners do want to know is everything that will affect their personal stake in the partnership. If you're experiencing problems in obtaining appropriate financing, and it is "dragging on," tell them about it and what you are doing to resolve the situation. That way, if you end up accepting a loan at a very high rate, they won't be surprised. If you're having serious tenant problems at a building that threatens catastrophe, tell your investors about it before catastrophe strikes.

Sure they will worry. Some may even call you to express concern. Even so, informing them is preferable to protecting them from bad news until the worst happens. You don't want to be seen as "holding out on them." Over the long run if you share your really substantive travails as you work through them, in a concise, matter-of-fact, non-alarming way, your investors will welcome your honesty, empathize with you, and appreciate what you are doing to earn your share of the partnership profits.

What about reporting at regular intervals just to be reporting? That has some appeal, and in certain public offerings there are legal requirements for periodic reporting.

The one periodic report you should plan on in any syndication is an annual report concerning tax consequences of the investment. That is unavoidable. It is both legally required and substantively useful to the investor. He can't file a complete personal tax return without it.

The next most popular interval for periodic reporting is quarterly. There is a basis for this in the regulatory requirements for a full-registration SEC offering. Full-registration offerings are generally very large in size so there is nearly always something substantive going on. The quarterly report requirement thus actually tends to limit the frequency of reports in such offerings rather than increase it. Reporting is time consuming and expensive, so a legal rationale for limiting it to four times per year is welcome.

In very small offerings, however, particularly those of long duration wherein one really just purchases and manages a property or two, quarterly reporting can be rather pointless. There may be nothing more to report than a minor furnace repair, or a late rent check. Don't invest time and money in passing that type of information along to your partners.

What I do in my own small offerings is tell investors in the offering documents, and verbally in oral presentations, that the general partners will report only when they have something of consequence to say, but no less than annually, at tax time. I then go on to explain what I think will be the activity cycle of the partnership based upon my best guess, that is, lots of activity and reporting during the investment and rehabilitation phase, little activity and reporting during the property management phase, and moderate activity and reporting at the liquidation phase. That is a truthful, no-nonsense disclosure of a policy you needn't strain to live by—it will come naturally.

ATTORNEY COMMENT
NASAA Guidance on Reporting Policies

NASAA guidelines require you to agree to provide any report or statement to state regulatory authority on demand which you are required to distribute to limited partners. For all NASAA-affected partnerships, you have to provide all the information necessary for the preparation of a limited partner's tax return within 75 days of the end of the fiscal year. Within 120 days, you have to provide an annual report containing a balance sheet, income statement, cash flow statement, a statement of activities, a table comparing previous forecasts to actual results, and an explanation of the sources of funds distributed to limited partners. In the annual report, you have to provide a breakdown of the reimbursement of costs by the partnership to you. Your CPA has to verify these allocations. Each limited partner also has access to partnership records. Within sixty days after the end of each quarter in which you acquired property, you have to send a detailed report to the investors describing each property acquired, the proposed method of financing and a statement that you have acquired title insurance and the necessary bonds. Registered programs require quarterly reports to investors. Regulation D does not have such detailed reporting requirements for private offerings.

I completely agree with Ray that you should keep investors informed about your setbacks. I know one beginning syndicator who couldn't meet his mortgage payments due to tenant problems. He failed to keep his investors informed until he finally lost the building to foreclosure. Then, he was faced with having to deliver a much worse message. If he had informed them and perhaps brought them in on what was happening, he might have been able to either rally the partnership to save the building or to lessen the eventual wrath of his investors.

Chapter 14

Helpful Tips on Partnership Record Keeping

There are at least three good reasons why you should be conscientious about keeping records for your investment syndications: (1) it will help you manage better, (2) it will reassure any other general partners and your limited partner investors, that you're "on top of things," and (3) it will protect all of you, in the case of challenge by tax authorities, irate investors, or whomever. The systems that I use to accomplish this are the following.

SETTING UP THE ACCOUNTING FILE

This is a very simple ledger system on which I keep a running record of the status of my financial accounts. It shows where the money is stored, from whom it is received, and to whom it is disbursed. Dispersals are further broken down into various categories of expenditures so that, at year's end, the task of the tax accountant is much simplified. Expert fees are much reduced that way. An illustration of this ledger system is shown below.

Date	To/ From	Chk. No.	Trans.	Rec'd Sav.	Rec'd Chk.	Dis- bursed	Prop. Acq.	Prop. Mgmt.	Prop. Improv.	Mort. PITI	Partnership Mgmt.	Misc.

ESTABLISHING AND USING A SPECIMEN DOCUMENTS FILE

This file is unorthodox, but extremely useful. Essentially, it is a collection of copies of all the key documents in the life of the syndication, pulled together into a loose-leaf binder. Here's how it works.

At the beginning of each new syndication, purchase one four-inch wide, heavy-duty, loose-leaf binder for each general partner. Prepare a table of contents to include all the major categories of documents which are expected to be developed, and a divider for each category. Then, as you move through the phases of syndication formation, marketing, investing, managing, and liquidation, you will have an outline of where you are headed and a very efficiently organized repository for all the documentation required along the way.

These "specimen files" are terrific aids in several ways.

For General Partner Communication

If you're the managing general partner in one limited partnership you can probably keep pretty good track of where you're going, and where you've been, just from memory. In such event, very quick access to records is not too critical. If you're managing three or four partnerships, however, it gets more complicated. The investments, the problems, even the investors, are harder to keep track of. Some of the details tend to blur.

If it is tough for you as the managing general partner, imagine how difficult it must be for the other general partner. He may also receive investor inquiries, or have occasion to go over in his mind the status of partnership mortgages, or its general portfolio. If he has to travel to the office of the managing general partner to learn these things he's going to feel "put upon." After all, if he has liability for partnership activities shouldn't he be informed?

A notebook containing copies of all the major partnership documents is a terrific general partner communication tool. Without taking up more than a few inches on the general partner's bookshelf it puts at his fingertips a complete history of what is going on. No more does he have to respond to investor inquiries with the embarrassed reply: "I don't remember that, but I can check with the managing general partner and get back to you." The format of the "Specimen Documents" file is as follows:

- General Partner Agreement
- Offering Documents
- Certificate of Limited Partnership and Amendments
- Limited Partner Subscription Agreement
- Registration Materials (a section for each security administrator)
- Property Acquisition (settlement papers and feasibility studies)
- Property Management (contracts)
- Partnership Reports (from GPs and accountants)

As a Memory Device

Another nice use of this file is as a very quick and efficient reference document. My own experience has been that 90% of the inquiries the general partners receive regarding partnership affairs can be answered from the loose-leaf specimen documents file. These inquiries result not only from need for knowledge about the partnership itself, but also from a need for models for future partnerships. Say you're thinking of drafting a general partner agreement and you want to see what you've done in past partnerships. Pull your specimen documents files off the shelf and line them up. If you're ready to do a report and you want to see what you projected in your last report, the quickest way to check up on yourself is to go to this file. No need to mess up your file jackets. Most of the items you'll need to refer to are organized in the loose-leaf binder.

As an Investor Selling Tool

An unexpected benefit of the specimen documents files we keep is their usefulness as an investor fund-raising tool. We are regularly contacted by potential investors, finders, and broker-dealers to inquire about specific investments. They want to ask a few more questions, and they want to look us over—see if we look like we know what we are doing. When they pose a memory question such as "Have you ever sponsored a partnership before?" or "Do you report to the investors?" I simply pull one of the specimen document binders off the shelf and direct them to the appropriate section. It works great. The visitor feels calm because you've shown him more than he bargained for, and it's all well organized. The general partner also feels good because it keeps him in control, directing the conversation along constructive lines.

ORGANIZING A SUBJECT FILE

Finally, originals are kept of all documents, filed by subject. These files parallel the categories in the specimen files, but will also include correspondence and ancillary documents related to each major item. When I commence work on an acquisition, for example, a file is established and all materials related to the acquisition are filed there. When the acquisition is completed, I make two copies of the settlement documents, punch three holes in them, and send one set to the other general partner for his specimen documents files, file one in mine, and place the original in the jacket file.

To those who hate files, or have elephantine memories, this three-file approach may seem extreme. It is not. It takes very little extra time once you learn to do it. Once you have such a system developed it will pay dividends in good will with your general and limited partners as well as in efficiency.

─────────── **ATTORNEY COMMENT** ───────────

NASAA and RULPA Guidelines on Partnership Records

The Revised Uniform Limited Partnership Act (RULPA) requires you to maintain: (1) a full list of the names and last-known home or business addresses of all the limited partners, listed in alphabetical order, (2) a copy of the certificate of limited partnership and executed powers of attorney, (3) copies of federal, state, and local income taxes of the partnership for the last three years, (4) copies of the limited partnership agreement and the last three years' financial statements, and (5) the partnership books. NASAA guidelines and the RULPA require you to grant the limited partners reasonable access to all your partnership records. The IRS requires you to keep a listing of each person who invests in your tax shelter. By following Ray's advice, you can avoid being embarrassed by having someone go through a disorganized set of records.

PART IV

SAMPLE DOCUMENTS YOU CAN TAILOR FOR YOUR OWN USE

Chapter 15

Pre-Offering Documents

OVERVIEW

The documentation required to move from the *idea* of an investment to the point where one is ready to engage attorneys, accountants, and others to prepare the formal offering documents is what I call the pre-offering phase. It consists of the following two concise, "written-down" understandings:

1. General Partner Understanding
2. Preliminary Analysis Document

Neither of these documents is required by any law or regulation. Both have only one purpose—to help you clarify the understandings (1) between you and any co-promoters, and (2) between the promoters and any limited partner investors. These documents can, therefore, be as formal or informal as you like. The only requirement for usefulness is that they be thoughtful and communicative.

The documents that follow in this chapter are not offered as models to be emulated. Rather, they are simply illustrations of how one syndicator has approached a specific transaction. They represent a real investment. They have not been "touched-up" for publication. It is my hope that by perusing them, and by reading the sometimes critical Attorney Comment for each, you will get a feel for the role of each document in the process and how each relates to the whole.

―――――― **ATTORNEY COMMENT** ――――――

The sample documents that follow provide an example of what we have been discussing in previous chapters. These documents are basically sound and highly usable for their purpose. Although they can be used as "model" documents, they are subject to all of the caveats previously set forth concerning model documents. My comments on each are intended only to highlight particularly significant points and to add additional cautionary notations so as not to interrupt the flow of the presentation. There is an Attorney Comment for each major section.

1. General Partner Understanding

The General Partner Understanding is one of the very first steps in the syndication process. Once you have decided to create a limited partnership investment opportunity, you need to get down to the practical aspects of bringing the necessary funds and talent to bear on the task. Often this translates into finding a co-general partner.

In Part III, "Techniques for Successful Syndication," we explored some of the reasons for selecting a co-general partner and some of the ways you might elect to divide the responsibilities and ownership. The sample General Partner Understanding presented in this chapter depicts a scenario in which the syndicator does not yet know where, or from whom, he will find the necessary talent to help him make the syndication work. Therefore, he has created a corporate general partner which he wholly owns to share the general partner interest. As pointed out in Chapter 7, this then enables him to get on with forming the limited partnership and preparing offering materials even as he continues to "shop" the remainder of the general partner interest.

The General Partner Understanding does not have to be filed with any official authorities, and it is not subject to securities regulations. As such, the General Partner Understanding can be a very brief, nononsense document that just covers the high points of a relationship. How the wholly owned corporate general partner is titled is of no consequence. In the example offered below the corporate general partner happens to have a title suggesting that it is the second in a sequence of such corporate general partners. The corporation could just as well have been named for the investment itself, e.g., Chillum Terrace Associates, Inc., or the like.

ATTORNEY COMMENT
GENERAL PARTNER UNDERSTANDING

As mentioned in Chapter 8, I think it is vital to get a basic General Partner Understanding in writing. However, once you find your general partner, you should put together a more detailed agreement and include this detailed agreement as an appendix to the offering memorandum. In your General Partner Understanding and your Limited Partnership Agreement, you should consider providing active management roles for both general partners so that both can use the $25,000 exemption from the passive loss limitations as allowed under the 1986 TRA for active management of real estate.

SAMPLE DOCUMENT:
GENERAL PARTNER UNDERSTANDING

GENERAL PARTNER UNDERSTANDING

GENERAL PARTNER UNDERSTANDING

This is to record the understandings between Equity Fund Profit Sharing Associates, Inc. #2 and Richard Ray Solem with respect to their relationship as co-general partners in the formation and operation of a real estate limited partnership to be known as Equity Fund/Chillum Terrace Limited Partnership.

1. The general partner interest will represent 50 percent of the profits and 2 percent of the tax losses from the enterprise.

2. Ownership of the general partner interest will be split per the following terms:

   50 percent to Solem individually, and

   50 percent to Equity Fund Profit Sharing Associates, Inc. #2 corporately.

3. Solem shall serve as managing general partner for the enterprise and shall take a fee for such services as subsequently determined in the Limited Partnership Agreement.

4. All decisions with regard to the limited partnership to be formed and any changes in the General Partner Understanding are to be by consensus between the parties.

5. Should either general partner wish to dispose of his interest in the partnership he must first offer such interest to the other. In the event that the terms of such sale cannot be agreed to between the parties a third party arbitrator chosen by both parties shall determine them.

Date: _____   _____

                                                     Richard Ray Solem
                                                   Individual General Partner

Date: _____   _____

                                                   Richard Ray Solem, President
                                                 Equity Fund Profit Sharing
                                                 Associates, Inc. #2
                                                 Corporate General Partner

2. Preliminary Analysis Document

The purpose of the Preliminary Analysis Document is (1) to help the syndicator look objectively at the proposed enterprise by committing it to writing, and (2) to begin the process of creating some reality for the proposal. Everyone you know has investment ideas, but very few of your colleagues are able to get beyond talk. Talk is cheap and easy, and it is also very common. Unless the syndicator is already an established investment sponsor he will not be able to really understand a transaction until he begins to write it down and analyze it. Unless he has a very strong track record for performance, his friends and associates will not give him an honest and critical answer to his investment inquiry based upon words alone. It is too easy to say, "Sure, I'm always interested in a good investment." You don't want to spend a lot of time packaging a limited partnership offering based upon assurances lightly given—and they may indeed be lightly given if you yourself present the opportunity in a light and nonserious vein.

With this in mind, the sample Preliminary Analysis Document in this chapter is offered as illustrative of a relatively efficient way to traverse this vital step. The elements of the preliminary analysis are very simple and include:

1. *The Partnership Business.* This section describes what you plan to buy, what you plan to do with it, and how you will make money.
2. *Summary of the Offering.* This section describes the security, i.e., what the limited partners are being offered. It lays out the terms of the limited partner/general partner relationship.
3. *General Partner Bio Data.* This section informs potential investors about the individuals upon whom they will depend to make the enterprise a success. For new syndicators, this is an important opportunity to let folks know your qualifications without seeming to boast.
4. *Confidential Offeree Questionnaire.* If you are serious about using the Preliminary Analysis Document to test the waters for potential investors, this section is important. It requires your friends who may mislead you by saying, "Sure, I'm always looking for a good investment," to disclose some personal information. That has two uses for you: It tells you if they can afford to be serious investors, and it forces them to think. If your colleagues are just talking when they say they are interested, their interest will fade quickly when you put the form in front

of them. You need to know if they are just talking, and the Preliminary Analysis Document is a low-cost way for you to get this information.

5. *Letter of Intent.* This is the ultimate test of investor seriousness and also, therefore, of your ability to raise the necessary funds for the investment under consideration. It requires the investors to actually sign a letter saying how much they are prepared to invest. Take care with this letter of intent that you aren't actually selling the offering; it should be crystal-clear that the investment decision is to be made only when all appropriate disclosure documents have been presented. The Preliminary Analysis Document is not a disclosure document and thus is not a sufficient basis for an investment decision. Don't take money at this letter-of-intent stage, and don't ask for promises that must be kept.

ATTORNEY COMMENT
PRELIMINARY ANALYSIS DOCUMENT

There are no legal guidelines as to what has to be in a Preliminary Analysis Document, since it is basically a means to test the waters and cannot serve as a basis to raise money. The comments below refer to particular items in the following Preliminary Analysis Document.

Confidential Offeree Questionnaire

At all times, you must treat your investor's financial information with the highest confidentiality. Your investors expect you to be discreet and to conform to state and federal privacy laws.

Letter of Intent

Letters of intent have a murky status under the law. They are like an agreement to attempt to agree and in many instances, unenforceable. In the context of the securities laws, you do not want any implication that this letter of intent would be enforceable in court if your investor later backed out on his or her promise to invest with you. The sentence in the third paragraph should be amended to delete the intention to acquire a certain number of units and that a sum is to be advanced to the partnership. It should be replaced with a statement that "I am strongly interested in participating in this partnership. I have complete discretion to withdraw from this letter of intent at any time for any reason upon review of the offering memorandum or any independent research." The fourth paragraph should be deleted. (*See "Letter of Intent," page 174.*)

> SAMPLE DOCUMENT:
> PRELIMINARY ANALYSIS DOCUMENT

PRELIMINARY ANALYSIS DOCUMENT

PRELIMINARY ANALYSIS DOCUMENT
EQUITY FUND/CHILLUM TERRACE LIMITED PARTNERSHIP

This summary does not constitute an offer to sell or the solicitation of an offer to buy any securities. Any offering of interests, when and if made, will be made only by means of appropriate descriptive materials, and only to persons who have satisfactorily completed the attached Confidential Offeree Questionnaire or provided other satisfactory information and who meet applicable legal requirements.

Page 1   SAMPLE DOCUMENT: PRELIMINARY ANALYSIS DOCUMENT

I. THE PARTNERSHIP BUSINESS

The Partnership business is defined as the purchase of the strip shopping center and adjacent property known as 5904-5926 Riggs Road and 905 Sheridan Street, Hyattsville, Maryland, and the increase of its potential for long-term appreciation in value. The appreciation in value is to be accomplished through physical rehabilitation of the premises to give it a new look and possibly convert to a condominium ownership form, followed by either the re-leasing or selling of the units therein. The business will be conducted in the following steps:

1. Purchase

The Partnership will take down the property on June 7, 1985 using a $225,000 loan from the General Partners to make the down payment of $200,000 and pay approximately $25,000 in settlement and related costs.

2. Syndication of Equity for Development Costs

Additional Partnership Interests totalling $750,000 in value will be made available privately, through this offering, to finance rehabilitation and development of the property without need for additional borrowing by the Partnership. General Partner loans for acquisition costs and contingency expenses will be repaid from such offering proceeds.

3. Development Study

The Operating Partner will study the development potential of the property to determine its highest and best use. Recasting the property as a more "up-scale" retail center, or alternately as a professional office park, is most likely. In either event, conversion to a condominium ownership form is expected due to its positive effect on resale value to users and investors alike.

4. Implementation of Development Plan

Once the highest and best use has been determined, the rehabilitation and condominium conversion will be carried out. Even as such work is underway, the new space will be offered for sale or lease at its higher value. It is anticipated that all physical work will be completed within twelve months and leasing/sale activities within eighteen months of settlement.

5. Refinancing and Benefits

With rehabilitation completed, the Partnership will place new financing on the property. Given an appraised value of the property at settlement of $743,000, and completion of an estimated $500,000 in improvements, a new loan in the amount of $750,000 should be obtainable. This amount will be used to pay off the seller-held first trust of $400,000, the remaining General Partner note of $200,000, and leave some $150,000 for reserves or distribution to the Limited Partners.

Limited Partners are expected to benefit from this investment in four ways:

   a. Tax Benefits

Substantial tax benefits are projected from taking a 15% tax credit on rehabilitation costs (property is over 30 years old) in addition to tax losses from (1) amortization of Partnership costs, and (2) depreciation of the improvements.

   b. Refinance Proceeds

If the rehabilitated property can be refinanced at the projected $750,000 level, the rents support such a mortgage, then a distribution of all or a part of such funds beyond what is required to pay off any Partnership debt may be distributed to investors as a tax-free return of capital.

   c. Cash Flows

Provided rents exceed amounts required for debt service and contingencies, any excess will be distributed to Limited Partners on a periodic basis.

   d. Gains Upon Sale

If the rehabilitation, possible condominium conversion and leasing efforts have the expected effect of increasing the property's value, then profits will be realized upon sale. Current tax laws make it impossible to predict whether such gains will result in ordinary income or capital gains treatment to investors, but in all events, the General Partners will seek to maximize overall returns on an after-tax basis.

II. SUMMARY OF THE OFFERING

General Partners	Richard R. Solem, 7512 Whittier Boulevard, Bethesda, Maryland 20817, and Equity Fund Profit Sharing Associates, Inc. #2, 7512 Whittier Boulevard, Bethesda, Maryland, 20817.
State and Date of Organization	The Partnership is a limited partnership organized on June 1, 1985 pursuant to the Maryland Revised Uniform Limited Partnership Act.

> **SAMPLE DOCUMENT:**
> **PRELIMINARY ANALYSIS DOCUMENT**

Partnership Business	The Partnership intends to purchase and develop that existing retail/professional office complex known as Chillum Terrace Shopping Center at 5904-5926 Riggs Road, Hyattsville, Maryland. It is anticipated that a physical rehabilitation of the premises will occur within twelve months of acquisition, which rehabilitation will qualify for 15% investment tax credits, and that the property may also be converted to a condominium form of ownership. Upon completion of rehabilitation/conversion work, the property will be leased at higher rents or sold at appreciated prices, resulting in either increased cash flow from operations or substantial profits from sale.
Partnership Objectives	The Partnership objectives are to provide (1) cash flows generated from anticipated increases in rental income or proceeds from sale of condominium units, and (2) tax benefits to Limited Partners from tax credits on rehabilitation expenditures, amortization of organization expenses, and depreciation of property improvements.
Partnership Management	Partnership management will be handled by the General Partners. Where appropriate, and in the sole discretion of the General Partners, Affiliates of the General Partners may also provide services to the Partnership.
Compensation to General Partners and Affiliates	The General Partners and their Affiliates will receive substantial compensation from the Partnership for services performed pursuant to Partnership objectives.
Returns to Limited Partners	Cash flows and tax losses from Partnership operations and proceeds from sales and refinancing shall be distributed and allocated at least annually, and at the termination of the Partnership, according to the following formula:

(1) Cash flows in excess of those required for Partnership debts and reserves for future project requirements, if realized, will be distributed first to the Limited Partners until they have received an amount equal to 8% per annum return (based upon their prior year net investment), if earned, and the balance, if any, distributed 50% to the Limited Partners and 50% to the General Partners as a supplementary fee for successful management.

(2) Tax losses and credits from Partnership operations and sales shall be allocated 98% to the Limited Partners and 2% to the General Partners.

(3) Proceeds from refinancing and sales shall be distributed first to the Limited Partners until they have received an amount equal to their cash investment, and the balance, if any, distributed 50% to the Limited Partners and 50% to the General Partners.

Depreciation Method	To the extent the Partnership acquires depreciable assets, it intends to use the straight-line method of depreciation.
Maximum Leverage	It is anticipated that rehabilitation costs will be paid largely from Partnership equity, and that when such improvements are completed the property will be refinanced in an amount sufficient to pay off the seller held first trust as well as the General Partners second trust loan. In no event is leverage within the Partnership expected to exceed 80% of the appraised value of all partnership assets.
Termination	The Partnership will terminate on December 31, 2020 or earlier upon the sale of all Partnership assets. It is expected that such termination will take place between the third and tenth years of Partnership operation.

III. GENERAL PARTNER BIO DATA

Richard Ray Solem

Richard R. Solem, 41, is President of Equity Fund Group, a central service corporation for six distinct companies formed to support his activities in real estate syndication. Equity Fund Realty, Inc., of which he is Broker of Record, is licensed to practice real estate in Maryland, the District of Columbia, and Virginia. Equity Fund Management, Inc. is a property management firm, Equity Fund Investors, Inc. specializes in partnership management, Equity Fund Construction, Inc. is a general construction firm, Equity Fund Mortgage, Inc. is a newly organized commercial loan origination/brokerage firm, and Equity Fund Securities, Inc. is an inactive securities broker-dealer firm.

A graduate of the University of Texas (BA & MA) and the Foreign Service Economics and Commercial Studies Institute, Mr. Solem was employed in 1968 as a Project Design Officer with the Agency for International Development (AID), serving in Latin America, Africa and Washington, DC.

Mr. Solem entered real estate in the D. C. Metropolitan Area in 1971 as an investor/renovator of single family residences. In 1977 he became a licensed Realtor Associate employed with Century 21 Kadow, Inc., and in 1980, upon receipt of his Maryland real estate broker's license, he established the Equity Fund Group.

A member of the National Association of Realtors, Mr. Solem is a holder of the SRS designation from the Real Estate Securities and Syndication Institute as well as a Director of its Chapter for Maryland, District of Columbia and Delaware. Mr. Solem also serves as a Director of the Lafayette Federal Credit Union in Washington, D.C., lectures in real estate syndication at Montgomery College, Montgomery County, Maryland, and is author of a text book on real estate syndication titled <u>Getting Started in Real Estate Syndication</u>, Acropolis Books, Ltd., 1983.

Mr. Solem has been actively engaged in real estate syndication since 1978, acting as a sponsor and general partner in CTS Investment Group (1978), Maryland Residential Investors (1979), Equity Fund Residential Investors (1980), Equity Fund Properties (1981), Equity Fund/Fox Ridge (1983), Equity Fund/Viers Mill (1984), and Equity Fund/Annapolis Road (1985).

Equity Fund Profit Sharing Associates, Inc. #2

Equity Fund Profit Sharing Associates, Inc., #2 is a newly organized Maryland Corporation formed for the sole objective of serving as Corporate General Partner in the Partnership. Wholly owned by Richard R.

Solem, who also serves as its president, the purpose of the corporation is to provide a vehicle whereby Solem can assign partial ownership in the general partner interest to employees and advisors to Equity Fund Group, Inc. In the event that such interests (corporate shares) are assigned, they shall be nonvoting so that control of the Corporate General Partner stays with Solem, its current sole shareholder and president.

IV. CONFIDENTIAL OFFEREE QUESTIONNAIRE

The purpose of this questionnaire is to obtain certain information about your present financial position in order to help determine whether you are qualified to receive offers of and to participate in the purchase of limited partnership interests in the Partnership. This Questionnaire may also help us to determine whether such an investment is suitable for you.

Any private placement of securities, when and if made, will be made pursuant to the exemption from registration provided for in Section 4(2) of the Securities Act of 1933, or under Regulation D under Section 4(2).

One of the requirements of Regulation D is that the persons involved in the offering and sale of the securities must have reasonable grounds to believe that each person subscribing to the offering either:

(1) has such knowledge and experience in financial and business matters that he is capable of evaluating the merits and risks of the prospective investment, or

(2) is able to bear the economic risk of the investment.

This Questionnaire will assist in compliance with the legal requirements of Section 4(2) and Regulation D for the protection of all concerned.

Your answers to this Questionnaire will be kept strictly confidential. The Sponsors of the Offering may present this Questionnaire to legal counsel and to other persons who may be legally responsible for the Offering, who also will be required to maintain confidentiality. If necessary, this Questionnaire may be presented to appropriate parties in order to establish the availability of an exemption under applicable securities laws.

> SAMPLE DOCUMENT:
> PRELIMINARY ANALYSIS DOCUMENT

CONFIDENTIAL OFFEREE QUESTIONNAIRE

Name: _____

Home Address: _____

_____

Occupation: _____

Employer's Name: _____

Business Address: _____

_____

Telephones: Home _____ Business _____

Estimated Income 1984
(all sources): _____

Estimated Income 1985
(all sources): _____

> SAMPLE DOCUMENT:
> PRELIMINARY ANALYSIS DOCUMENT

V. LETTER OF INTENT

Mr. Richard Ray Solem
Equity Fund/Chillum Terrace Limited Partnership
7512 Whittier Boulevard
Bethesda, Maryland 20817

Dear Mr. Solem:

With this letter I declare my intention to join in the real estate Limited Partnership known as Equity Fund/Chillum Terrace Limited Partnership, whose objective is to purchase, rehabilitate, operate and sell for profit that strip shopping center known as Chillum Terrace, located on Riggs Road in Hyattsville, Maryland.

I understand that Equity Fund/Chillum Terrace Limited Partnership is a Maryland Limited Partnership, that I will be investing as a Limited Partner, that the Managing General Partner will be Richard Ray Solem, and that the details of this offering will be set forth in an Offering Memorandum with a separate Subscription Agreement to accompany such Memorandum.

Provided that the details of the Offering Memorandum are to my satisfaction and my personal investment situation has not changed materially, I intend to acquire _____ Limited Partnership Interests in such offering at a cost of $ _____ .

This Letter of Intent is for the purpose of enabling you to assess Limited Partner interest in the structure of the transaction only. It will become null and void if (1) I decide not to become a Limited Partner or (2) the proposed transaction is materially changed from the form described herein.

Date: _____   Signature: _____

Chapter 16

The Offering Package

OVERVIEW

The complete limited partnership offering package consists of a half dozen discrete components, each meeting a special purpose. This overview presents a brief look at each component, exploring its part in the overall presentation given to investors.

The components of a limited partnership offering package are the:

1. Offering Memorandum
2. Partnership Agreement, which can also include a separate Certificate of Limited Partnership
3. Subscription Agreement and Materials
4. Project Documents
5. Partnership Management Agreement
6. Selling Agreement, also called the Soliciting Dealer Agreement

Items 2 through 6 are frequently included as exhibits with the Offering Memorandum, and so I have included them as Exhibits A through F following the Offering Memorandum in the Sample Document section of this chapter. Also, note that Attorney Comments to each of the offering components have been interspersed throughout the various documents, highlighting sensitivities and differences of opinion concerning approaches taken.

1. Offering Memorandum

The purpose of the offering memorandum (a.k.a. private placement memorandum, offering circular, and prospectus) is to describe the limited partnership investment to potential subscribers. It is, therefore, a selling document. Because limited partnership interests are considered securities, the document through which they are offered to the market is subject to securities regulations. It is the jurisdiction of these securities regulators that has led to most of the myriad laws, regulations, and guidelines one associates with limited partnerships.

The common thread that winds through all regulations treating offering memorandums is an emphasis on *disclosure*. Limited partnership sponsors are assumed to be sophisticated people who need to be closely watched, and limited partnership investors are assumed to be "innocents" in need of protection. As a result, a "full disclosure" offering memorandum is likely to look more like a "red flag" than an invitation to join up.

ATTORNEY COMMENT

From the attorney's perspective, the offering memorandum is not a selling document but a legal document. It is the "memorandum to plaintiff's counsel." From a business perspective, it is a lousy selling tool because it is designed to be so negative. It is better to accompany your offering memorandum with a short summary with lots of pictures of the real estate and a summary of benefits of the investment for the limited partner. This "executive" type summary must always be accompanied by the offering memorandum if distributed to prospective purchasers. Under limited circumstances, you can deliver just this executive summary to licensed selling agents.

An illustrative Offering Memorandum, as well as the attorney opinion, begins on page 181 in the Sample Document section of this chapter. (*See* SAMPLE DOCUMENT: OFFERING MEMORANDUM; *also*, SAMPLE DOCUMENT: ATTORNEY OPINION FOR OFFERING MEMORANDUM.)

2. Partnership Agreement

The purpose of the partnership agreement is to record the understandings between general and limited partners. It may be recorded in one document alone, or in two, one being a summary agreement that covers only the essential items required by the respective state's limited partnership act (Certificate of Limited Partnership) and the other going into detail on the whole range of relationships in the particular transaction (Partnership Agreement).

The important thing to keep in mind concerning the partnership agreement is that it is not a securities document, regulated by securities laws, but rather a partnership contract, regulated by the parent state's limited partnership act. Whereas securities regulations emanate from both federal and state securities administrators, partnership regulations are all at the state level. Though the Uniform Limited Partnership Act is a model for all the fifty states, its legal application is on a state-by-state basis and it is only through a legal action under the state law that enforcement can be brought.

My practice, with regard to the partnership agreement, is to have two separate agreements. The certificate of limited partnership is a several page form that covers basic points required by law to be a legal certificate of limited partnership which must be filed with the state of registration. It becomes the partnership agreement of record and is public information for all to see. I then prepare a far more detailed understanding that treats all aspects of the general partner/limited partner relationship, called the partnership agreement, and share this only with my investors. Some syndicators elect to prepare only one document and so prepare only the more detailed version. That is fine, but it must be filed with the applicable state or local officials. You may not want to put such a detailed filing in the public records.

ATTORNEY COMMENT

You can save work and money by using basically the same agreement from partnership to partnership. The large national syndicators often use a combined certificate and agreement which specifically discusses only that particular partnership.

An illustrative Partnership Agreement, as well as a Certificate of Limited Partnership, begins on page 253 in the Sample Document section of this chapter. (*See* SAMPLE DOCUMENT: PARTNERSHIP AGREEMENT.)

3. Subscription Agreement and Materials

The purpose of the subscription agreement is to document the investment transaction and to ensure that limited partner investors are properly screened. Securities regulators have some fairly strict conventions concerning who can or should buy what investment.

Depending on the form of offering (private, intrastate, or public) and type of investment (tax shelter, income or capital gains objectives), the securities regulators have different rules and guides. In a private offering, for example, the subscription agreement might provide a means to count the number of offerees so to record compliance with the 35 investor limitation. In an intrastate offering, the subscription agreement will provide for screening as to legal residency. In all three forms of offering there should be screening to match investor and investment objectives; e.g., widows with income or mid-career professionals with tax shelter. This is done through a statement of suitability standards.

If the offering provides a means for investors to make their equity contribution in stages, or to borrow a portion of their investment, documents to record these arrangements will be in the subscription materials. Likewise, if the partnership sponsor wishes to allow for use of offeree representatives to qualify potential investors, he can provide questionnaires toward this end in the subscriptions package.

ATTORNEY COMMENT

I have seen too many beginning syndicators try to skip using subscription agreements. They seem to think that their investors don't want to do all the work of filling in the questionnaire; and further, the beginning syndicator is embarrassed at having to review private financial data of friends and acquaintances. This is a mistake, because without the subscription agreement, you have no easy proof: (1) that the investor received and read your costly and belabored offering materials, (2) that your limited partner was suited for the investment, and (3) that your investors met the minimum qualifications which would have permitted them to invest in your venture.

An illustrative Subscription Agreement and other subscription materials begin on page 293 in the Sample Document section of this chapter. (*See* SAMPLE DOCUMENT: SUBSCRIPTION MATERIALS.)

4. Project Documents

The purpose of this section is to provide materials by which the investment itself can be evaluated. Standard features typically include a description of the investment and, if a specified offering, financial projections and an appraisal. The idea is to provide enough objective data concerning the investment to enable a rational evaluation thereof.

ATTORNEY COMMENT

Under a NASAA regulated offering, you may have to have an appraisal and to disclose it in the offering materials. An appraisal is also valuable to prove value for IRS purposes if it was not an arm's length purchase. You may have to provide certain financial projections.

In the Sample Documents section of this chapter, I have included a sample cover sheet for the project documents that would be part of the Offering Memorandum. (*See* SAMPLE DOCUMENTS: PROJECT DOCUMENTS.) Documents that were part of this particular offering were the Purchase Contract, the Property Appraisal Report, the Preliminary Builder Estimate, and Financial Illustrations. However, because these are not of general interest but are, rather, very particular to each offering, I have not included the documents themselves.

5. Partnership Management Agreement

This is straightforward as well. How an offering sponsor intends to provide for partnership management is a material consideration in a prospective limited partner's investment decision, so the terms and conditions of that arrangement are an important aspect of disclosure. What better way to disclose partnership management arrangements than to include that agreement in the offering package.

An illustrative Partnership Management Agreement begins on page 315 in the Sample Document section of this chapter. (*See* SAMPLE DOCUMENT: PARTNERSHIP MGMT. AGREEMENT.)

6. Selling Agreement

In cases where a limited partnership offering is being offered to investors through a selling agent, it is wise to disclose the terms of such agreement. Here again, what better way to disclose than to share the actual agreement with prospective investors.

An illustrative Selling Agreement, also called a Soliciting Dealer Agreement, begins on page 317 in the Sample Document section of this chapter. (*See* SAMPLE DOCUMENT: SELLING AGREEMENT.)

ATTORNEY COMMENT

If you have a General Partnership Understanding, either the terms of it or the actual document should be disclosed. If you are hiring a management company to manage the property, you should include the agreement with the management company. If you have a tax opinion from an attorney or audited CPA statements, you should attach those. It is also common to include the purchase contract and realtor-produced site maps. If you are financing the contributions of your investors, you should include copies of your investor note forms.

> SAMPLE DOCUMENT:
> OFFERING MEMORANDUM

OFFERING MEMORANDUM

EQUITY FUND/CHILLUM TERRACE LIMITED PARTNERSHIP

750 Limited Partnership Interests

$1,000 Per Interest . . . Minimum Purchase 25 Interests ($25,000)

Equity Fund/Chillum Terrace Limited Partnership (the "Partnership") is a Maryland limited partnership formed June 1, 1985. Its address is 7512 Whittier Boulevard, Bethesda, Maryland, 20817. The Partnership has been formed to purchase the property known as Chillum Terrace Shopping Center, Hyattsville, Maryland, to rehabilitate such property to give it a new look, possibly converting it to a condominium form of ownership, and to rent or sell spaces therein at a price allowing for profits. The investment objectives of the Partnership will be to provide cash flow from the operation of the center, to provide tax benefits to Limited Partners, including rehabilitation credits, to the extent permitted by law, and to provide the potential for capital appreciation to be realized at the time of sale.

> THESE SECURITIES INVOLVE A HIGH DEGREE OF RISK. IF INCREASED RENTAL INCOME DOES NOT RESULT FROM PLANNED DEVELOPMENT AND MARKETING EFFORTS, ALL FUNDS INVESTED TOWARD SUCH ENDS COULD BE LOST. FOR A FURTHER DISCUSSION OF THESE AND OTHER RISKS SEE "RISKS," PAGES 17 To 23.

> THESE SECURITIES ARE OFFERED PURSUANT TO CERTAIN EXEMPTIONS UNDER FEDERAL AND STATE SECURITIES LAWS, AND THEREFORE HAVE NOT BEEN REGISTERED. THESE SECURITIES HAVE NOT BEEN REVIEWED BY ANY STATE OR FEDERAL SECURITIES AGENCY. INVESTORS ARE URGED TO OBTAIN ADVICE FROM INDEPENDENT COUNSEL AS TO THE POSSIBLE LEGAL, FINANCIAL AND TAX CONSEQUENCES ASSOCIATED WITH AN INVESTMENT IN THIS PARTNERSHIP.

	Price to Public(1)	Securities Commissions(2)	Proceeds to Partnership
Per Limited Partnership Interest	$ 1,000	$ 100	$ 900
Minimum Offering	500,000	50,000	450,000
Maximum Offering	$ 750,000	$ 75,000	$ 675,000

(1) Until the required minimum in subscriptions is received, funds paid by subscribers will be held in a Partnership account at Suburban Bank in Bethesda Maryland. If the required minimum is not obtained by September 30, 1985, funds will be refunded with interest. See "Subscription For And Sale Of Interests," page 50.

(2) The Limited Partnership Interests are offered for sale through a "best efforts" selling agreement with registered NASD Broker-Dealers who elect to participate in this offering under the terms of the "Soliciting Dealer Agreement" (Exhibit F).

The date of this Offering Memorandum is July 1, 1985.

SUITABILITY

An investment in the Partnership involves certain risks. There is not expected to be any public market for Limited Partnership Interests, and the sale or transfer of Interests may result in adverse tax consequences. Further, any tax benefits of investment in Interests will be better realized by individuals in the higher Federal income tax brackets. Accordingly, Interests will only be sold to individuals who represent in writing that they have adequate means of providing for current needs and personal contingencies and have no need for liquidity of this investment. Furthermore, each individual must warrant that he has: (1) a net worth (excluding home, home furnishings, and automobiles) of at least $50,000 and estimate that (without regard to investment in the Partnership) he will have gross income during 1985 of at least $50,000, and does not expect any significant decrease in taxable income during the next four succeeding years, or; (2) a net worth, (excluding home, home furnishing, and automobiles) of at least $200,000 irrespective of current income. An investment in the Partnership by a qualified pension or profit-sharing plan involves certain additional risk factors which should be considered by the fiduciary prior to making the investment. (See "Risks—

Investments by Qualified Pension and Profit-Sharing Trust," page 19, and "Tax Aspects of the Offering—Unrelated Business Income," page 43.

HOW TO SUBSCRIBE

An investor who meets the qualifications set forth above may subscribe for Interests by completing and signing the materials contained in Exhibit C of the Offering Memorandum and delivering them to the General Partners through their selling agent, United Securities and Investment Corporation, together with a check and promissory note for the full purchase price of the Interests being subscribed for. The check and promissory note should be made payable to Equity Fund/Chillum Terrace Limited Partnership.

DESCRIPTION OF REAL ESTATE INVESTMENT

The Partnership intends to invest the proceeds of this offering (after deductions for securities commissions, and other offering expenses) in the purchase and development of that property known as Chillum Terrace Shopping Center, 5904- 5926 Riggs Road, Hyattsville, Maryland. The investment's viability depends upon the relationship of the Partnership's purchase price to current market conditions, the successful development of planned improvements for the subject property, and the market conditions at time of eventual resale. For a more detailed description of the proposed investment see "The Partnership Business," page 27. Also see Exhibit D, "Project Documents," outlined below:

D-1 Purchase Contract
D-2 Property Appraisal Report
D-3 Preliminary Builder Estimate
D-4 Financial Illustrations

A. SUMMARY OF THE OFFERING

General Partners	Richard R. Solem, 7512 Whittier Boulevard, Bethesda, Maryland 20817, and Equity Fund Profit Sharing Associates, Inc. #2, 7512 Whittier Boulevard, Bethesda, Maryland, 20817.
State and Date of Organization	The Partnership is a limited partnership organized on June 1, 1985 pursuant to the Maryland Revised Uniform Limited Partnership Act.
Partnership Business	The Partnership intends to purchase and develop that existing retail/professional office complex known as Chillum Terrace Shopping Center at 5904-5926 Riggs Road, Hyattsville,

Maryland. It is anticipated that a physical rehabilitation of the premises will occur within twelve months of acquisition, which rehabilitation will qualify for 15% investment tax credits, and that the property may also be converted to a condominium form of ownership. Upon completion of rehabilitation/conversion work, the property will be leased at higher rents or sold at appreciated prices, resulting in either increased cash flow from operations or substantial profits from sale. See "Risks," page 17 and "The Partnership Business," page 27.

Partnership Objectives

The Partnership objectives are to provide (1) cash flows generated from anticipated increases in rental income or proceeds from sale of condominium units, and (2) tax benefits to Limited Partners from tax credits on rehabilitation expenditures, amortization of organization expenses, and depreciation of property improvements.

Partnership Management

Partnership management will be handled by the General Partners. Where appropriate, and in the sole discretion of the General Partners, Affiliates of the General Partners may also provide services to the Partnership.

Compensation to General Partners and Affiliates

The General Partners and their Affiliates will receive substantial compensation from the Partnership for services performed pursuant to Partnership objectives. See "Compensation to General Partners and Affiliates," page 8.

Returns to Limited Partners

Cash flows and tax losses from Partnership operations and proceeds from sales and refinancing shall be distributed and allocated at least annually, and at the termination of the Partnership, according to the following formula:

(1) Cash flows in excess of those required for Partnership debts and reserves for future project requirements, if realized, will be distributed first to the Limited Partners

until they have received an amount equal to 8% per annum return (based upon their prior year net investment), if earned, and the balance, if any, distributed 50% to the Limited Partners and 50% to the General Partners as a supplementary fee for successful management.

(2) Tax losses and credits from Partnership operations and sales shall be allocated 98% to the Limited Partners and 2% to the General Partners.

(3) Proceeds from refinancings and sales shall be distributed first to the Limited Partners until they have received an amount equal to their cash investment, and the balance, if any, distributed 50% to the Limited Partners and 50% to the General Partners.

Depreciation Method	To the extent the Partnership acquires depreciable assets, it intends to use the straight-line method of depreciation. See "Tax Aspects of the Offering—Tax Deductibility and Accounting Methods," page 34.
Maximum Leverage	It is anticipated that rehabilitation costs will be paid largely from Partnership equity, and that when such improvements are completed the property will be refinanced in an amount sufficient to pay off the seller held first trust as well as the General Partners second trust loan. In no event is leverage within the Partnership expected to exceed 80% of the appraised value of all partnership assets.
Termination	The Partnership will terminate on December 31, 2020 or earlier upon the sale of all Partnership assets. It is expected that such termination will take place between the third and tenth years of Partnership operation.
Promissory Notes	Partnership Interests will be purchased partly with cash and partly with a promissory note

earning interest at approximately 14% per annum. Upon subscription each Limited Partner will execute such note for Interests acquired, committing to four principal plus interest installments per year for four years at $62.60 per $1,000 Interest. Breakdown of these installment arrangements is given below, looking at initial investment and per annum costs per $1,000 Interest and per $25,000 minimum subscription:

PER $1,000 INTEREST

	Payment	Principal	Interest	Balance
Initial Investment	$ 250.00	$ 250.00	$ -0-	$ 750.00
End Of Year 1	245.94	150.34	95.60	599.66
End Of Year 2	245.94	172.80	73.14	426.86
End Of Year 3	245.94	198.60	47.34	228.26
End Of Year 4	245.94	228.26	17.68	-0-
Totals	$ 1,233.76	$ 1,000.00	$ 233.76	

PER $25,000 MINIMUM SUBSCRIPTION

	Payment	Principal	Interest	Balance
Initial Investment	$ 6,250.00	$ 6,250.00	$ -0-	$18,750.00
End Of Year 1	6,148.46	3,758.57	2,389.99	14,991.43
End Of Year 2	6,148.46	4,319.89	1,828.57	10,671.54
End Of Year 3	6,148.46	4,965.03	1,183.43	5,706.51
End Of Year 4	6,148.46	5,706.51	441.95	-0-
Totals	$30,843.84	$25,000.00	$ 5,843.94	

In the event that any Limited Partner fails to pay such notes in timely fashion all of the Partnership Interests acquired by such Partner are subject to seizure by the Partnership and subsequent resale to satisfy the requirements related thereto. Limited Partners are free to purchase Interests for cash or, in the event that they pay for a portion of their Interests with a promissory note, to pay off such notes at any time prior to maturity without prepayment penalty. See Exhibit A, "Agreement of Limited Partnership," Article 8.

B. USE OF PROCEEDS

	Minimum Offering		Maximum Offering	
Gross Offering Proceeds	$500,000	100.00%	$750,000	100.00%
Less Offering Expenses:				
Selling Commissions (1)	50,000	10.00%	75,000	10.00%
Organization Expenses (2)	42,500	8.50%	63,750	8.50%
Investor Note Financing Fee (3)	7,500	1.50%	11,250	1.50%
Total Offering Expenses	$100,000	20.00%	$150,000	20.00%
Amount Available For Investment:				
Acquisition Fees/Commissions (4)	$ -0-	-0-	$ -0-	-0-
Acquisition Expenses (5)	25,000	5.00%	25,000	3.33%
Down Payment (6)	-0-	-0-	-0-	-0-
Development Studies (7)	25,000	5.00%	25,000	3.33%
Rehabilitation Cost (8)	300,000	60.00%	500,000	66.67%
Reserve For Contingencies	50,000	10.00%	50,000	6.67%
Total Available For Investment	$400,000	80.00%	$600,000	80.00%
Plus Offering Expenses	$100,000	20.00%	$150,000	80.00%
Total Application Of Proceeds	$500,000	100.00%	$750,000	100.00%

(1) Selling Commissions are paid to participating broker-dealers under a "best efforts" selling agreement. See Exhibit F, "Soliciting Dealer Agreement."

(2) "Organization Expenses" includes all legal, accounting, typing and printing costs associated with preparation of the offering as well as the professional fees associated with preparation of Exhibit D, "Project Documents." Any funds remaining after payment of these "hard costs" will be paid to the General Partners for their time and effort in directing such work.

(3) "Investor Note Financing" is paid to the lender providing promissory note financing to Limited Partner subscribers. The charge for such financing is 2% of loan disbursal.

(4) Subject property was offered for sale by American Investment Properties. Inc. (AIP) a Maryland real estate brokerage with offices in Bethesda, Maryland. AIP will receive a real estate

commission equal to six percent (6%) of the purchase price, which commission will be split 80% to AIP and 20% to Equity Fund Realty, Inc., a Maryland real estate brokerage wholly owned by the Individual General Partner. Therefore, there is no charge to the Partnership for "Acquisition Fees/Real Estate Commissions" because all such costs will be borne by the seller.

(5) "Acquisition Expenses" is an estimate of actual costs of taking title to subject property (state and county transfer and recording fees, legal, title insurance and miscellaneous costs) and operating it until syndication.

(6) "Down Payment" represents all the cash required to purchase property with $400,000 in seller financing. Because this was paid by a General Partner loan made prior to this offering, there is no deduction from Partnership equity.

(7) "Development Studies" will be conducted prior to commencement of design and construction activities. Plans are to develop the shopping center around existing tenants with a view to minimal disruption and rent loss.

(8) In the minimum offering scenario, $200,000 of the rehabilitation costs are borrowed.

C. COMPENSATION OF GENERAL PARTNERS AND AFFILIATES

The compensation to be received by the General Partners has not been determined by arm's-length negotiations with the Partnership.

Set forth below is a description of all compensation that may be received by the General Partners and their Affiliates from the Partnership or in connection with the investment of the proceeds of this offering. References in this Offering Memorandum to the receipt of real estate commissions or other compensation by the General Partners also include the receipt of such compensation by its Affiliates.

FORM OF COMPENSATION - RECIPIENT ENTITY	METHOD AND AMOUNT OF COMPENSATION
	Organization Stage
Organization Expenses - The General Partners	A charge to the Partnership of 8.50% of the gross offering proceeds, will be paid to the General Partners as reim-

	bursement for the hard and soft costs of the offering.
Selling Commissions - Equity Fund Securities, Inc.	A charge to the Partnership of 10% of the gross offering proceeds, will be paid to NASD broker-dealers under soliciting dealer arrangements. If Equity Fund Securities is successful in completing its licensure prior to completion of this offering, it may participate in such commissions.

Operation Stage

Partnership Management Equity Fund Investors, Inc.	An annual charge equal to 1% of the gross offering proceeds. From this fee Richard R. Solem acting through Equity Fund Investors, Inc., a company wholly owned by him, will serve as Partnership Manager, overseeing all study, rehabilitation, marketing, property management and eventual resale efforts, and reporting on these to the Limited Partners.
Development Studies - Equity Fund Construction, Inc.	Final arrangements for conducting market and condominium conversion studies have not been made at the date of this offering. The General Partners may elect to utilize services from Equity Fund Construction, Inc., a company wholly owned by the Individual General Partner, for all or a portion of this work. In such event services will be provided by them at rates and on terms no less favorable to the Partnership than those customary for similar services in the area.
Loan Origination - Equity Fund Mortgage, Inc.	Construction and permanent loans for property improvements have not been made as of this date. The General Partners may elect to arrange such financing through Equity Fund Mortgage,

	Inc., a company partly owned by the Individual General Partner. In such event, services will be provided by Equity Fund Mortgage, Inc. at rates and on terms no less favorable to the Partnership than those customary for similar services in the area.
Leasing and Management - Equity Fund Management, Inc.	Final arrangements for leasing and management have not been made at the date of this offering. The General Partners may elect to utilize staff from Equity Fund Management, Inc. (EFM), a company wholly owned by the Individual General Partner, for this task. In such event, services will be provided by them at rates and on terms no less favorable to the Partnership than those customary for similar services in the area.
Percentage Share of Tax Losses - The General Partners	Tax losses and credits shall be awarded 98% to the Limited Partners and 2% to the General Partners.
Percentage Share of Cash Flows - The General Partners	After the Limited Partners have received a priority annual return on investment equivalent to 8% (based upon prior year net investment), the General Partners shall receive 50% of any remaining balance for that year as a supplementary fee for successful management.

Upon Refinancing or Sale

Percentage Share of Proceeds - The General Partners	After the Limited Partners have received an amount equal to their investment in the Partnership, 50% of any remaining balance shall be distributed to the General Partners as their share of sales or refinancing proceeds.

Page 11 — SAMPLE DOCUMENT: OFFERING MEMORANDUM

Real Estate Commissions Upon Sale - Equity Fund Realty, Inc.

It is anticipated that the property will be listed for sale through Equity Fund Realty, (EFR), a company wholly owned by the individual General Partner. In such event the commission charged to the Partnership is expected to be 6% in the event of a sale through a cooperating real estate broker (3% to EFR and 3% to the cooperating broker) or 4% in the event of a direct sale by EFR.

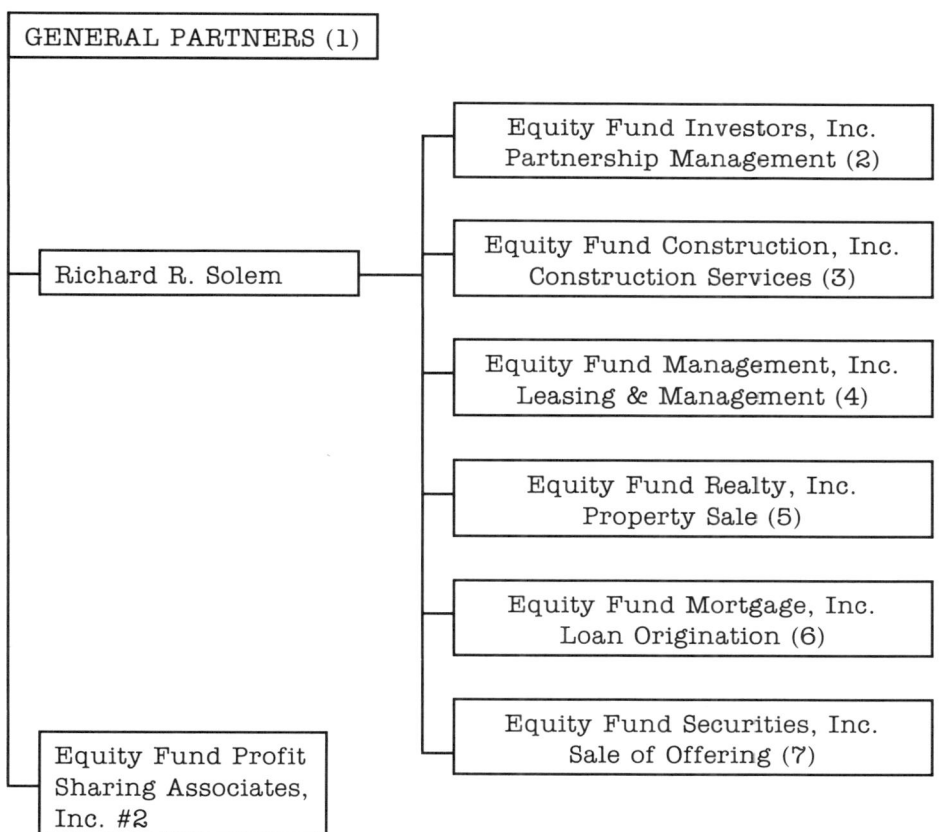

(1) The General Partners of Equity Fund/Chillum Terrace Limited Partnership are Richard R. Solem and Equity Fund Profit Sharing Associates, Inc. #2. Solem is the owner of Equity Fund Investors, Inc., Equity Fund Construction, Inc., Equity Fund Management, Inc., and Equity Fund Realty, Inc. and half owner of Equity Fund Mortgage, Inc., all of which may be called upon to provide services to the Partnership.

Equity Fund Profit Sharing Associates, Inc., #2 is a Maryland corporation newly formed for the purpose of serving as Corporate General Partner in the Partnership. The President and sole initial stockholder of Equity Fund Profit Sharing Associates, Inc., #2 is Richard R. Solem.

(2) Equity Fund Investors, Inc. is a Maryland corporation organized in 1980 and wholly owned by Richard R. Solem. The normal business of Equity Fund Investors, Inc. is management of limited partnerships sponsored by Solem. In this Partnership, Equity Fund Investors, Inc. will provide partnership management services.

(3) Equity Fund Construction, Inc. is a Maryland Corporation organized in 1982 and wholly owned by Richard R. Solem. Equity Fund Construction, Inc. completed a 10 unit historic rehabilitation in Annapolis, Maryland in 1983, is providing contruction management services on a Rockville, Maryland shopping center rehabilitation project now underway, and is making preparations for an early 1985 project to contruct 208 detached homes in Leesburg, Virginia.

(4) Equity Fund Management, Inc. is a Maryland Corporation organized in 1980 and wholly owned by Richard R. Solem. The business of Equity Fund Management, Inc. is to provide leasing and management services for properties owned or controlled by the Equity Fund companies and clients thereof.

(5) Equity Fund Realty, Inc. is a Maryland Corporation organized in 1980 and wholly owned by Richard R. Solem. Equity Fund Realty, Inc. is primarily involved in the acquisition and sale of investment properties in Maryland, however it is licensed to operate in the District of Columbia and Virginia as well.

(6) Equity Fund Mortgage, Inc. is a Maryland Corporation organized in 1984 and partly owned by Richard R. Solem. Equity Fund Mortgage, Inc. is expected to provide financial packaging and loan origination services to the Partnership.

(7) Equity Fund Securities, Inc. is a Maryland Corporation organized in 1980 and wholly owned by Richard R. Solem. Equity Fund Securities is in the process of attaining licensure as an NASD

broker-dealer in Maryland, the District of Columbia and Virginia. If such licensure can be accomplished prior to completion of the offering it may participate in marketing of the offering.

D. ALLOCATION OF CASH FLOWS AND TAX LOSSES

Cash flows from Partnership operations and or proceeds from refinancings and sales in excess of those required for continued project operations shall be distributed at least quarterly, and at the termination of the Partnership, according to the following formula:

(1) Cash flows in excess of those required for Partnership debts and reserves for future project requirements, if realized, will be distributed first to the Limited Partners until they have received an amount equal to 8% per annum return on investment (based upon prior year net investment), if earned, and the balance, if any, distributed 50% to the Limited Partners and 50% to the General Partners as a supplementary fee for successful management.

(2) Tax losses and credits from Partnership operations and sales shall be allocated 98% to the Limited Partners and 2% to the General Partners.

(3) Proceeds from refinancings and sales shall be distributed first to the Limited Partners until they have received an amount equal to their cash investment and the balance, if any, distributed 50% to the Limited Partners and 50% to the General Partners.

E. CONFLICTS OF INTEREST

The Partnership is subject to various conflicts of interest arising out of its relationships with the General Partners and their Affiliates. Because the Partnership was organized and will be operated by the General Partners, these conflicts will not be resolved through arm's-length negotiations but through the exercise of the General Partners' judgment consistent with their fiduciary responsibilities to the Limited Partners and the Partnership's investment objectives and policies. See "Fiduciary Responsibility of the General Partners," page 16 and "The Partnership Business," page 27.

1. <u>Other Activities of the Managing General Partner and Affiliates</u>

The Individual and Managing General Partner, Richard R. Solem, has formed CTS Investment Group, Maryland Residential Investors, Equity Fund Residential Investors, Equity Fund Properties, Equity Fund/Fox Ridge, Equity Fund/Viers Mill, and Equity Fund/Annapolis Road, all of which are limited partnerships investing in real estate. To the extent that any of these earlier partnerships makes acquisitions at the same time that Equity Fund/Chillum Terrace Limited Partnership is operating, there may be competition between the various entities for management resources. In addition, the Individual General Partner and his Affiliates are forming and expect to form and to manage or advise additional public and private real estate investment entities. The Partnership may involve itself with past, present or future buyers, sellers or other affiliates of the General Partner. The Individual General Partner has engaged in and will continue to engage in other business activities and therefore will not manage the Partnership as his sole and exclusive function.

2. Acquisition and Development of Chillum Terrace Shopping Center

Equity Fund/Chillum Terrace Limited Partnership is the assignee of a contract to purchase the parcel of land identified as 5904-5926 Riggs Road, Hyattsville, Maryland which is known as Chillum Terrace Shopping Center. The purchase price was determined by the seller although the MAI appraised value of the property was higher. As a part of attaining the objectives of the Partnership, a development study will be undertaken to determine the best use of the Center. Although any agreements which the Partnership may enter into for either this study or in brokerage agreements will be on terms no less favorable than those customary for similar services in the area, considerable fees could be earned by Equity Fund Investors, Inc.

3. Leasing and Management

The Managing General Partner, Richard R. Solem, owns Equity Fund Management, Inc., a Maryland property leasing and management company. Although any agreements the Partnership might enter into for leasing and management services will be on terms and conditions no less favorable to the Partnership than those customary for similar services in the area, considerable fees could be earned by Equity Fund Management, Inc. should it be awarded the leasing and/or management contract.

4. Construction

The Managing General Partner, Richard R. Solem, owns Equity Fund Construction, Inc., a Maryland general contracting firm that may be called upon to provide Construction Management services. Although any agreements which the Partnership may enter into for construction services will be on terms no less favorable to the Partnership than those customary for similar services in the area, considerable fees could be earned by Equity Fund Construction, Inc.

5. Real Estate Brokerage

The Managing General Partner, Richard R. Solem, owns Equity Fund Realty, Inc., a Maryland real estate brokerage. Although any agreements the Partnership might enter into for real estate brokerage services will be on terms and conditions no less favorable to the Partnership than those customary for similar services in the area, considerable fees could be earned by Equity Fund Realty, Inc. should it be selected to provide such services. In no event, however, will Equity Fund Realty, or affiliates thereof, receive real estate commissions on resale in excess of 3% of the gross sales price in case of a cooperative sale, or 4% of the gross proceeds in case of a direct sale.

6. Mortgage Brokerage

The Managing General Partner, Richard R. Solem, and Neal E. Holtz, executive Vice President of H. "Manny" Holtz Construction, Inc. are the co-owners of Equity Fund Mortgage, Inc., a Maryland mortgage brokerage. Solem serves as president of Equity Fund Mortgage, and Holtz serves as its director. Although any agreements the Partnership might enter into for mortgage brokerage services will be on terms and conditions no less favorable to the Partnership than those customary for similar services in the area, considerable fees could be earned by Equity Fund Mortgage, Inc. should it be selected to provide such services. In no event, however, will Equity Fund Mortgage, Inc. receive mortgage brokerage commissions in excess of 1% of the gross amount of loans placed by it.

7. Determinations by the General Partners

The General Partners have certain specified interests in the Net Cash Receipts, Sale or Refinancing Proceeds, and Profits and Losses of the Partnership per the terms of the Partnership Agreement. Various determinations for the Partnership regarding the timing and amount of Net Cash Receipts, Sale or Refinancing Proceeds, and Profits and Losses may represent a conflict of interest in as much as they affect the General Partners interests.

8. Devotion of Time by the General Partners

The Partnership will not have independent management and it will rely on the General Partners and affiliates for the management of the Partnership. The General Partners and affiliates will devote only so much of their time to the business of the Partnership as in their judgement is reasonably necessary. The General Partners and affiliates will have conflicts of interests in allocating management time, services and functions between various existing partnerships sponsored by them and any future partnerships which they may choose to sponsor, as well as other business ventures in which they are or will be involved. The General Partners believe that the General Partners and affiliates have sufficient staff personnel to be fully capable of discharging its responsibilities to the Partnership and to any other business entities for which they may be responsible, and they will employ additional persons for such purpose if required. The General Partners and affiliates may engage for their own account, or for the account of others, in other business ventures, whether in real estate or otherwise, and neither the Partnership nor any Limited Partner shall be entitled to any interest therein solely by reason of any relationship arising from the Partnership.

F. FIDUCIARY RESPONSIBILITY OF THE GENERAL PARTNERS

The General Partners are accountable to the Partnership as fiduciaries and, consequently, must exercise good faith and integrity in handling Partnership affairs. A provision has been made in the Partnership Agreement that the General Partners will not be liable to the Partnership or any Limited Partner for any action taken or failure to act, on behalf of the Partnership within the scope of the authority conferred on them by this Agreement or by law unless such act or omission was performed or omitted fraudulently or in bad faith or constituted gross negligence.

In addition, the Partnership Agreement provides for indemnification by the Partnership of the General Partners for liability resulting from errors in judgment or certain acts or omissions, disclosed or undisclosed. Therefore, the Limited Partners may have a more limited right of action against the General Partners than they would have had absent these provisions.

In the opinion of the Securities and Exchange Commission, indemnification for liabilities arising under the Securities Act of 1933 is contrary to public policy and therefore unenforceable. See "Summary of the Partnership Agreement — Limitation on the Liability of the General Partners," page 46.

This is a rapidly developing and changing area of the law, and Limited Partners who have questions concerning the rights and duties of the General Partners should consult their own counsel.

Further, and subject to the foregoing, the Partnership Agreement also provides that, to the extent permitted by law, the Partnership shall indemnify the General Partners against liability and related expenses (including attorney's fees) incurred in dealing with third parties, provided

Page 17

that the conduct of the General Partners is consistent with the standards described in the preceding paragraphs. A successful claim for such indemnification would deplete Partnership assets by the amount paid. The Partnership shall not pay for any insurance covering liability of the General Partners and their Affiliates or any other persons for actions or omissions for which indemnification is not permitted by the Partnership Agreement, provided, however, that this shall not preclude the naming of the General Partners or their Affiliates, employees or agents, as additional insured parties on policies obtained for the benefit of the Partnership.

G. RISKS

Investment in the Interests offered herein is speculative, entailing a high degree of risk. This offering endeavors to set forth those risk factors which seem paramount, but it should be noted that no amount of planning can anticipate all of the possible unfavorable eventualities which may affect the outcome of this investment. In addition to the factors set forth in "Conflicts of Interest" and elsewhere in this Offering Memorandum, prospective investors should consider the following:

1. <u>No Market for Interests</u>

There is no public market for the Interests. Although the Interests may be transferable, subject to certain limitations, it is not anticipated that any public market will develop. See "Summary of Partnership Agreement — Transferability of Interests," page 47. Consequently, holders of Interests may not be able to liquidate their investment in the event of emergency or for any other reason, and Interests may not be readily accepted as collateral for loans. In addition, the transfer of interests may result in taxable income for the transferor. See "Tax Aspects of the Offering — Disposition of Partnership Interests," page 40.

2. <u>Economic Risks of Investing in Real Estate</u>

The business of investing in real estate development is highly competitive and is subject to numerous inherent risks, including changes in general or local economic conditions, neighborhood values, interest rates, availability of mortgage funds, real estate tax rates, the uncertainty of cash flow to meet fixed obligations, changes in the relative popularity (and thus the relative price) of the Partnership's product when compared to other similar opportunities, adverse local market conditions due to changes in general or local economic conditions or neighborhood values, changes in motor vehicle traffic patterns, the financial condition of tenants and sellers of properties, changes in operating expenses, acts of God and other factors which are beyond the control of the General Partners.

3. Competition

The Partnership will meet with competition in the market place from numerous other real estate investment partnerships, as well as from individuals, corporations, banks, insurance companies, foreign investors and other entities engaged in real estate development and management in Hyattsville and the nearby market area. Such competition could create an oversupply of comparable space, and result in the inability to rent the retail space developed by the Partnership or to eventually sell the proposed project.

4. No Request for a Tax Ruling

The Partnership has not requested and does not intend to request a tax ruling from the Internal Business Service ("Service") that the Partnership or any joint venture in which it invests will be taxed as a partnership. In the absence of such a ruling, there can be no assurance that the Partnership will not be taxed as a corporation. Investors should recognize that they might be forced to incur substantial legal and accounting costs in resisting a challenge by the Service.

If the Partnership were classified as an association taxable as a corporation, the Partnership would be subject to federal income tax on any taxable income at regular corporate tax rates. The Limited Partners would not be entitled to take into account their distributive share of the Partnership's deductions or credits, and would be subject to tax on their share of the Partnership's income to the extent distributed either as dividends out of current or accumulated earnings and profits, or as a return of capital in excess of the tax basis of their Limited Partnership Interests. Classification of the Partnership as an association, taxable as a corporation, would result in a substantial reduction in yield and cash flow to Limited Partners. For a further discussion of this risk, see "Tax Aspects of the Offering," page 29.

5. Federal Income Tax Risks

The Tax Return Act of 1984 was recently signed into law. Prospective investors would be ill-advised to rely unduly on the prospect that tax benefits provided in the past will continue to be afforded to them in the future. Tax benefits of investment in the Partnership could be lost and/or substantial tax liabilities incurred by reason of recent changes in the tax law and proposed Regulations. There are no assurances that anticipated tax benefits will not be challenged by the Service and possibly disallowed. Moreover, there is no assurance that changes in the interpretation of applicable income tax laws will not be made by administrative action which will adversely affect the law consequences of an investment in the Partnership. In addition, there can be no assurance that the current

Federal income tax treatment accorded an investment in the Partnership will not be modified or eliminated by other legislative action at any time. Any such changes could be retroactive with respect to transactions prior to the effective date thereof. Each potential Limited Partner should seek and must rely on the advice of his own tax advisors with respect to the possible impact of the 1984 Act on his proposed investment.

6. <u>Powers Granted Limited Partners — Effect on Limited Liability</u>

Authority as to the management and conduct of the business and affairs of the Partnership is vested exclusively with the General Partners. Prior to purchasing interests in the Partnership, purchasers should satisfy themselves that the General Partners and their affiliates possess the requisite experience and abilities to adequately manage and otherwise conduct the business and affairs of the Partnership. No limited partner will be personally liable for the debts or obligations of the Partnership beyond the amount contributed by such Limited Partner to the capital of the Partnership, unless he takes part in the management and/or control of the business of the Partnership. In such case he could be deemed to be a General Partner of the Partnership and, therefore, generally liable for the debts and obligations of the Partnership. In compliance with the securities laws of the state of Maryland, the Partnership Agreement provides that a majority in interest of the Limited Partners are empowered to amend certain provisions of the Partnership Agreement without the consent of the General Partners, to dissolve the Partnership without the consent of the General Partners, to consent to the disposal of substantially all of the assets of the Partnership and to remove one or all of the General Partners. Removal of any General Partner must be by unanimous written approval. The Partnership has been organized under the Maryland Revised Uniform Limited Partnership Act, which specifically authorizes such powers without subjecting Limited Partners to liability as General Partners.

7. <u>Investments by Qualified Pension and Profit-Sharing Trusts</u>

In considering an investment in the Partnership by a trust of a pension or profit-sharing plan qualified under Section 401(a) of the Internal Revenue Code and exempt from tax under Section 501(a), a fiduciary should consider (1) whether the investment satisfies the diversification requirements of Section 404(a)(3) of the Employee Retirement Income Security Act of 1974 ("ERISA") and (2) whether the investment is prudent, since Interests are not freely transferable and there may not be a market created in which he can sell or otherwise dispose of the Interests. An investment in the Partnership may also produce unrelated business income which may cause the trust to pay a tax on that income if it exceeds $1,000 in any year of the trust. See "Tax Aspects of the Offering — Unrelated Business Income." ERISA requires that the assets of a plan be valued at their fair market value as of the close of the plan year, and it may not be possible to adequately value the Interests from year to year since there will not be a market for those Interests and the appreciation of any property may not be shown in the value of the Interests until the Partnership sells or otherwise disposes of the property.

8. Environmental and Regulatory Problems

The cost of rehabilitation and operation of properties in which the Partnership may invest may be adversely affected by legislative, regulatory, administrative and enforcement action at the local, county, state and national levels in the areas, among others, of housing and environmental controls including air and water quality standards, noise pollution and indirect environmental impacts such as increased motor vehicle activity.

9. Energy and Supply Shortages

The Partnership expects to undertake construction of various improvements on the subject property. Timely construction may be adversely affected by local or national strikes and shortages in materials, insulation, building supplies, energy and fuel for equipment, which shortages may result from national or local shortages and other factors. Such construction delays and the disruption related thereto, could have an adverse impact on any existing tenants and cause unexpected vacancies, lawsuits, or other action potentially costly to the Partnership business.

10. Reliance on Management

All decisions with respect to the management of the Partnership will be made exclusively by the General Partners. Limited Partners have no right or power to take part in the management of the Partnership. Accordingly, no person should purchase Interests unless he is willing to entrust all aspects of Partnership management to the General Partners. See "Management," page 25.

11. Uninsured Losses

While the Partnership will carry insurance on its properties, including fire, liability, and extended coverage, certain risks exist which are uninsurable or not insurable on terms which are economical. The General Partners will use discretion in determining coverage limits and deductibility provisions on insurance, with a view to obtaining appropriate insurance on Partnership property at an appropriate cost and on suitable terms. This may result in insurance coverage which will not cover, in the event of a substantial loss, the full current market value or current replacement cost of a property. Additionally, due to inflation, and changes in building codes and ordinances, it may not be feasible to replace the property with the insurance proceeds. Under such circumstances, the receipt of the insurance proceeds by the Partnership may not suffice to place the Partnership in the same economic position it was in immediately before the property was destroyed.

12. Non-Liability of General Partners

Under the Partnership Agreement, the General Partners are not liable to the Partnership or the Limited Partners for the performance of any act or for their failure to act, so long as such act or failure to act was performed in good faith and in a manner determined by them to be within the scope of their authority and in the best interest of the Partnership, and so long as they were not guilty of negligence, misconduct, or breach of their fiduciary obligations. In addition, under certain circumstances, the General Partners and their officers, directors, trustees, agents and employees will be entitled to indemnification from the Partnership. See "Summary of Partnership Agreement, Limitation on the Liability of the General Partners," page 46.

13. Construction

The Partnership intends to rehabilitate the Property, Chillum Terrace Shopping Center, 5904-5926 Riggs Road, Hyattsville, Maryland, engaging in substantial construction activities in developing the property. Any such construction activity may subject the Partnership to various risks, including the inability to obtain building and use permits or necessary zoning changes, construction delays, inability to complete construction at projected costs and to fund any excess construction costs, strikes, adverse weather conditions, unavailability of building materials, inability to refinance construction financing on favorable terms or to meet preconditions for permanent financing and other conditions beyond the control of the Partnership. Therefore, uncertainties may exist with respect to the timing of commencement or completion of construction of the mini storage facility, when lease revenues from any such facility might commence, and when construction financing will be released.

14. Market

The General Partners will be making judgments about how, and to whom, the Partnership property should be marketed during and after completion of development. If they are incorrect in their judgments certain development expenditures could prove inappropriate. Likewise, efforts to increase rents could create vacancies by existing tenants, or render it impossible to attract new tenants, thus adversely affecting the economic viability of the overall project. In any of these events, the value of the Partnership's assets would be adversely affected.

15. Investment through Promissory Notes

Limited Partners who purchase a portion of their Partnership Interests with Promissory Notes (Notes) issued on behalf of the Partnership incur special risks in that their entire position in the Partnership will depend upon their ability to promptly meet all obligations thereunder. Limited Partners will be purchasing their Interests partly with cash and partly with promissory notes. Amortization of the Notes for 25% of the Partnership investment is shown below on an annual basis, though payments will actually be made quarterly:

$375,000 LOAN - MINIMUM OFFERING

	Payment	Principal	Interest	Balance
Initial Investment	$125,000.00	$125,000.00	-0-	$375,000.00
End Of Year 1	122,969.14	75,171.46	$ 47,797.68	299,828.54
End Of Year 2	122,969.14	86,397.73	36,571.41	213,430.81
End Of Year 3	122,969.14	99,300.53	23,668.61	114,130.28
End Of Year 4	122,969.14	114,130.28	8,838.86	-0-
Totals	$680,901.76	$550,000.00	$130,901.76	

$562,500 LOAN - MAXIMUM OFFERING

	Payment	Principal	Interest	Balance
Initial Investment	$187,500.00	$187,500.00	$ -0-	$562,500.00
End Of Year 1	184,453.72	112,757.20	71,696.52	449,742.80
End Of Year 2	184,453.72	129,596.58	54,857.14	320,146.22
End Of Year 3	184,453.72	148,950.80	35,502.92	171,195.42
End Of Year 4	184,453.72	171,195.42	13,258.30	-0-
Totals	$925,314.88	$750,000.00	$175,314.88	

In the event that a Limited Partner shall fail to make timely payment of principal and interest due on such Note, the Limited Partner will be deemed to be in default. In the event of a default, the holder of a Note may, at his option, accelerate all payments due under the Note. The defaulting Limited Partner will be subjected to personal liability for payments due on the Note, as well as any costs of collection plus legal fees.

Further, the defaulting Limited Partner's Interests will be subject to purchase and resale by the General Partners and the Partnership. Should such resale result in an amount less than the Limited Partner's obligation to the Partnership, the General Partners may elect to demand repayment from other assets for the delinquent Limited Partner. Whatever the proceeds of resale, first priority shall be the satisfaction of any obligations to the Partnership. (See "Agreement of Limited Partnership," Exhibit A.)

H. PRIOR PERFORMANCE OF THE GENERAL PARTNERS

Individual General Partner

The Individual General Partner, Richard R. Solem, has been involved in seven prior real estate limited partnerships, in all cases as the Managing General Partner.

1. CTS Investment Group

A privately offered Limited Partnership, CTS Investment Group (CTS) was marketed between May 1, 1978 and April 30, 1979. Proceeds of $85,000 were raised through the sale of 17 Interests to 14 limited and 2 general partners at $5,000 per interest. The objectives of CTS are to:

(1) preserve and protect the Partnership's original invested capital through real estate investment,

(2) provide capital gains through potential appreciation of the Partnership's properties.

(3) provide annual allocations and distributions from operations in the form of income and/or losses, and

(4) provide build-up of equity through amortization of mortgage loans on the Partnership's properties.

CTS limited itself to new and existing residential property. Investments made to date have been 3 detached, single family homes. Two have subsequently been sold at a profit and the third is currently leased and operating at a nearly break- even cash flow. The sponsors of this offering were Richard R. Solem as Individual General Partner and CTS Associates, Inc. (owned in equal shares by Richard R. Solem, Norman Cohen and Graham Thompson) as Corporate General Partner.

2. Maryland Residential Investors

A public limited partnership offered to Maryland residents only, Maryland Residential Investors (MRI) was marketed between March 15, 1979 and September 15, 1979. Proceeds of $67,500 were raised through sale of 27 Interests to 16 limited partners at $2,500 per interest. The objectives of MRI are the same as for CTS above.

MRI limited itself to new and existing residential property. Investments made to date have been 1 detached, single family home and 2 condominium apartments. The detached home was sold during 1982, with the Partnership taking back financing, and the 2 apartments are leased at a break-even cash flow. The sponsors of this offering were Richard R. Solem as Individual General Partner and Group Investors, Inc. (owned in equal parts by Richard R. Solem, Brian Kadow and Kevin Kadow) as Corporate General Partner.

3. <u>Equity Fund Residential Investors</u>

A privately offered limited partnership, Equity Fund Residential Investors (EFRI) was marketed between August 15, 1980 and November 15, 1980. Proceeds of $85,000 were raised through sale of 34 Interests to 12 Limited Partners at $2,500 per Interest. The objectives of EFRI are the same as those for CTS above.

EFRI limited itself to new and existing residential property. Investments made, to date have been 3 condominium townhouses. Making the acquisitions under land contract arrangements, the Partnership was able to minimize transaction costs while assuming 8% and 9% mortgages. All properties are currently leased, and the cash flow is negative. The sponsors of this offering were Richard R. Solem as Individual General Partner and Rick Wolfe and Associates, Inc. as Corporate General Partner.

4. <u>Equity Fund Properties</u>

A publicly offered limited partnership (under Regulation A of the Securities Act), Equity Fund Properties (EFP) was marketed between October 1, 1981 and June 30, 1982. Proceeds of $250,000 were raised through sale of 250 Interests to 26 Limited Partners at $1,000 per Interest, 5 Interests minimum. The objectives of EFP are the same as for CTS above.

EFP made one acquisition, an historic building in Annapolis, Maryland, and carried out a major rehabilitation and conversion of that property to 10 apartment units. The sponsors of this offering were Richard R. Solem and Norman Cohen as Individual General Partners.

5. <u>Equity Fund/Fox Ridge</u>

A privately offered limited partnership, Equity Fund/Fox Ridge (EF/FR) was marketed between September 2, 1983 and December 31, 1983. Proceeds of $370,000 were raised through the sale of 74 Interests to 25 Limited Partners at $5,000 per Interest.

The objective of EF/FR is to earn profits from the sale of homes constructed by the Partnership at Fox Ridge Subdivision in Leesburg,

Virginia. It is anticipated that most, if not all, Partnership income from the EF/FR project will be taxable at ordinary income rates, and that little, if any, tax losses will be earned.

EF/FR is currently in the midst of site plan revision and development of home designs. There has been no construction as of the date of this offering, nor has there been any Partnership income.

6. Equity Fund/Viers Mill

A privately offered limited partnership, Equity Fund/Viers Mill (EF/VM) was marketed between February 13, 1984 and April 15, 1984. Proceeds of $1,200,000 were raised through sale of 1,200 Interests to 3 Limited Partners at $1,000 per Interest, each taking 400 Interests. The objective of EF/VM is to earn profits through rehabilitation, operation and resale of a 60,000 square foot shopping center in Rockville, Maryland. As of the date of this offering, rehabilitation of the center is underway, and several new leases have been signed or are in negotiation at substantial rent increases.

7. Equity Fund/Annapolis Road

A privately offered limited partnership, EF/AR was marketed between February 8, 1985 and March 15, 1985. Proceeds of $300,000 were raised through sale of 300 Interests to 7 Limited Partners at $1,000 per Interest. Limited Partners were offered Promissory Notes to finance 60% of their purchase.

The objective of EF/AR is to earn profits from the rehabilitation, operation and resale of an office building in Lanham, Maryland. As of the date of this offering, deferred maintenance items are being contracted for and several new leases have been signed.

I. MANAGEMENT

The General Partners will have responsibility for all aspects of the Partnership's operations. Limited Partners will be kept apprised of Partnership activities and financial status through semi-annual reports as well as at the time that tax losses are allocated and proceeds from cash flow, refinancing or sale are made.

Partnership management (reporting, accounting and general direction) will be the responsibility of Richard R. Solem, the Individual General Partner, working in consultation with the Corporate General Partner. For his services as Managing General Partner, Solem will be paid an annual fee equal to 1% of the proceeds of this offering, payable in equal quarterly installments. Solem will provide this service through Equity Fund Investors, Inc., a partnership management firm wholly owned by him.

Development studies, and subsequent implementation of the development plan will be closely supervised by Solem, with specific tasks contracted out to various experts. Tentative plans are to rely upon third party architects, engineers and market analysts to perform design, construction, and market feasibility services during the study phase. It is also planned to contract with a third party contractor for construction of any improvements, although such work may be done at competitive rates by Equity Fund Construction Inc., an affiliate firm, if the General Partners shall deem such to be in the best interests of the Partnership.

In the event that a third party general contractor is selected, Equity Fund Construction, Inc. may provide construction management services. It is expected that this arrangement will result in lower general contracting costs and/or higher likelihood of successful completion of the overall task, and any fees paid for such construction services will be on terms no less favorable to the Partnership than those customary for similar services in the area.

Prior to termination of the Partnership, the investment property will be offered for sale. Plans are to market the property through Equity Fund Realty, Inc., a Maryland real estate brokerage wholly owned by Solem. In the event of a cooperative sale (involving a third party real estate broker) a standard 6% real estate commission will be charged to the Partnership and split between the cooperating brokers. In the event of a direct sale by Equity Fund Realty, Inc., the commission charged to the Partnership shall be reduced to 4% of the sale price.

Biographic data and relevant business experience concerning the General Partners follows:

1. Richard R. Solem, Individual General Partner

Richard R. Solem, 41, is President of Equity Fund Group, a central service corporation for six different companies formed to support his activities in real estate syndication. Equity Fund Realty, Inc., of which he is Broker of Record, is licensed to practice real estate in Maryland, the District of Columbia, and Virginia. Equity Fund Management, Inc. is a property management firm, Equity Fund Investors, Inc. specializes in partnership management, Equity Fund Construction, Inc. is a general construction firm, Equity Fund Mortgage, Inc. is a newly organized commercial loan origination/brokerage firm, and Equity Fund Securities, Inc. is an inactive securities broker-dealer firm.

A graduate of the University of Texas (BA & MA) and the Foreign Service Economics and Commercial Studies Institute, Mr. Solem was employed in 1968 as a Project Design Officer with the Agency for International Development (AID), serving in Latin America, Africa and Washington, DC.

> SAMPLE DOCUMENT: OFFERING MEMORANDUM

Mr. Solem entered real estate in the D. C. Metropolitan Area in 1971 as an investor/renovator of single family residences. In 1977 he became a licensed Realtor Associate employed with Century 21 Kacow, Inc., and in 1980, upon receipt of his Maryland real estate broker's license, he established the Equity Fund Group.

A member of the National Association of Realtors, Mr. Solem is a holder of the SRS designation from the Real Estate Securities and Syndication Institute as well as a Director of its Chapter for Maryland, District of Columbia and Delaware. Mr. Solem also serves as a Director of the Lafayette Federal Credit Union in Washington, D.C., lectures in real estate syndication at Montgomery College, Montgomery County, Maryland, and is author of a text book on real estate syndication titled <u>Getting Started in Real Estate Syndication</u>, Acropolis Books, Ltd., 1983.

Mr. Solem has been actively engaged in real estate syndication since 1978, acting as a sponsor and general partner in CTS Investment Group (1978), Maryland Residential Investors (1979), Equity Fund Residential Investors (1980), Equity Fund Properties (1981), Equity Fund/Fox Ridge (1983), Equity Fund/Viers Mill (1984), and Equity Fund/Annapolis Road (1985).

2. <u>Equity Fund Profit Sharing Associates, Inc., #2, Corporate General Partner</u>

Equity Fund Profit Sharing Associates, Inc., #2 is a newly organized Maryland Corporation formed for the sole objective of serving as Corporate General Partner in the Partnership. Wholly owned by Richard R. Solem, who also serves as its president, the purpose of the corporation is to provide a vehicle whereby Solem can assign partial ownership in the general partner interest to employees and advisors to Equity Fund Group, Inc. In the event that such interests (corporate shares) are assigned, they shall be non-voting so that control of the Corporate General Partner stays with Solem, its current sole shareholder and president.

J. THE PARTNERSHIP BUSINESS

The Partnership business is defined as the purchase of the strip shopping center and adjacent property known as 5904- 5926 Riggs Road and 905 Sheridan Street, Hyattsville, Maryland and the increase of its potential for long-term appreciation in value. The appreciation in value is to be accomplished through physical rehabilitation of the premises to give them a new look and possibly conversion to a condominium ownership form followed by either the re-leasing or selling of the units therein. The business will be conducted in the following steps.

1. Purchase

The Partnership will take down the property on June 7, 1985 using a $225,000 loan from the General Partners to make the down payment of $200,000 and pay approximately $25,000 in settlement and related costs.

2. Syndication of Equity for Development Costs

Additional Partnership Interests totaling $750,000 in value will be made available privately, through this offering, to finance rehabilitation and development of the property without need for additional borrowing by the Partnership. General Partner loans for acquisition costs and the contingency expenses will be repaid from such offering proceeds.

3. Development Study

The Operating Partner will study the development potential of the property to determine its highest and best use. Recasting as a more "up-scale" retail center, or alternatively as a professional office park, is most likely. In either event, conversion to a condominium ownership form is expected due to its positive effect on resale value to users and investors alike.

4. Implementation of Development Plan

Once the highest and best use has been determined, the rehabilitation and condo conversion will be carried out. Even as such work is underway, the new space will be offered for sale or lease at its higher value. It is anticipated that all physical work will be completed within twelve months and leasing/sale activities within eighteen months of settlement.

5. Refinancing and Benefits

With rehabilitation completed, the Partnership will place new financing on the property. Given an appraised value of the property at settlement of $743,000, and completion of an estimated $500,000 in improvements, a new loan in the amount of $750,000 should be obtainable. This amount will be used to pay off the seller-held first trust of $400,000, the remaining General Partner note of $200,000, and leave some $150,000 for reserves or distribution to the Limited Partners.

Limited Partners are expected to benefit from this investment in four ways:

    a. Tax Benefits

Substantial tax benefits are projected from taking a 15% tax credit on rehabilitation costs (property is over 30 years old) in addition to tax losses from (1) amortization of Partnership costs and (2) depreciation of the improvements.

b. Refinance Proceeds

If the rehabilitated property can be refinanced at the projected $750,000 level, and rents support such a mortgage, then a distribution of all or a part of such funds beyond what is required to pay off any Partnership debt may be distributed to investors as a tax-free return of capital.

c. Cash Flows

Provided rents exceed amounts required for debt service and contingencies, any excess will be distributed to Limited Partners on a periodic basis.

d. Gains Upon Sale

If the rehabilitation, possible condominium conversion and leasing efforts have the expected effect of increasing the property's value, then profits will be realized upon sale. Current tax laws make it impossible to predict whether such gains will result in ordinary income or capital gains treatment to investors, but in all events the General Partners will seek to maximize overall returns on an after tax basis.

For a picture of the anticipated property development scenario in numerical terms, see "Financial Illustrations," Exhibit D-4.

ALTHOUGH THE PARTNERSHIP STRUCTURE IS FELT TO BE CONSERVATIVE, THERE CAN BE NO GUARANTEES THAT PARTNERSHIP DEVELOPMENT OBJECTIVES WILL BE ATTAINED. STUDY FINDINGS MAY SUGGEST ALTERNATIVE APPROACHES, OR FINANCIAL AND ECONOMIC CONDITIONS MAY PREVENT EXECUTION IN TIMELY FASHION. THE PROPOSED DEVELOPMENT PLANS, AND THE FINANCIAL ILLUSTRATIONS PRESENTED IN EXHIBIT D-4, ARE FOR ILLUSTRATIVE PURPOSES ONLY, AND SHOULD NOT BE RELIED UPON EXCLUSIVELY IN MAKING ANY INVESTMENT DECISIONS.

K. TAX ASPECTS OF THE OFFERING

This section relates to Federal income tax and other tax matters. The analysis contained herein is not intended as a substitute for careful tax planning, particularly since certain aspects of the income tax consequences of an investment in the Partnership will not be the same for all taxpayers. Accordingly, prospective investors are urged to consult their tax advisers with specific reference to their own tax situation.

1. No IRS Ruling Requested as to Classification as a Partnership

No advance ruling has been sought from the Internal Revenue Service as to the tax classification of the Partnership. Based upon existing laws and regulations, as well as Revenue Ruling 79-106, in which the IRS announced that it would follow the decision of the United States Tax Court in Phillip G. Larson 66 T.C. 159 (1976),acq.1979-1 C.B.1 in classifying organizations, it is assumed that the Partnership will be classified as a partnership for tax purposes. However, in the past Regulations have been proposed and withdrawn that would have resulted in classification of the Partnership as an association taxable as a corporation for Federal tax purposes. The IRS may change its position at any time, perhaps with retroactive effect.

Further, the Tax Reform Act of 1984, H.R. 4170, (the "Act") was signed into law by the President on July 18, 1984. The Act, as drafted by Congress, affects a significant number of Internal Revenue Code provisions. Consequently, there can be no assurance that partnership status will not be challenged in the future, whether as a result of IRS regulations issued in response to the Act, as a result of changes in applicable law, or as a result of the manner in which the Partnership is operated. Any such changes in applicable law may or may not be retroactive with respect to transactions consummated prior to the date such changes are announced.

Should the Partnership be deemed an association taxable as a corporation, then it will be subject to Federal income tax rates and rules applicable to corporations generally, and the Limited Partners will be treated as if they were corporate shareholders. In such event, investors could be subject to the substantial adverse effects of corporate taxation. Corporations are required to pay taxes on their taxable income and capital gains, distributions to investors are taxable at ordinary income tax rates to the extent of earnings, and corporate losses are not permitted to be included in the individual tax returns of investors. INVESTORS ARE URGED TO CONSULT WITH INDEPENDENT TAX COUNSEL FOR ADVICE AS TO THE FEDERAL AND STATE TAX CONSEQUENCES ARISING FROM THE PURCHASE OF INTERESTS IN THIS PARTNERSHIP.

2. Taxation of Limited Partners

The Partnership, as an entity, will not be subject to any Federal income tax and each Limited Partner will be taxed on his allocable share of the Limited Partnership's taxable income, whether or not distributed to him. Thus, a Limited Partner's tax liability may exceed the cash distributed to him in a particular year. Each Limited Partner will be entitled to deduct on his own income tax return his allocable share of the Partnership's net losses, if any, to the extent of the tax basis of his Partnership interest at the end of the Partnership year in which such losses occur.

If the Partnership should be treated as an association taxable as a corporation for Federal income tax purposes in any taxable year, income and losses of the Partnership would be reflected only on its tax return rather than being passed through to the holders of Interests, and all or a portion of the distributions made to holders of Interests could be taxable as dividend income (to the extent of current or accumulated earnings and profits) or treated as a return of capital (to the extent of the holder's basis for his Interests) or capital gains income, none of which would be deductible by the Partnership.

The IRS is paying increased attention to the proper application of the tax laws to partnerships, including partnerships investing in real estate. It should therefore be noted that if adjustments are made to Partnership income or loss as the result of an audit of the Partnership's income tax return, the returns of the Limited Partners will probably be reviewed by the IRS. Such review may lead to IRS audits of the Limited Partners' returns, which might result in adjustment both in related and unrelated items.

3. Basis of Limited Partnership Interests

Generally, the tax basis of any Limited Partnership Interest is equal to its cost, reduced by the Limited Partner's share of Partnership distributions and losses and increased by his share of Partnership income. In addition, the tax basis of a Limited Partner's Interest would be increased by his proportionate share of liabilities to which Partnership assets are subject, but for which no Partner has any personal liability (such as real estate acquired subject to a mortgage which is not assumed by the Partnership or any of the Partners). A decrease of a Limited Partner's share of the aforementioned type of liability (as, for example, when a mortgage is paid off in whole or in part, the liability is discharged through foreclosure, the Partnership sells the property subject to a mortgage or a Limited Partner sells or otherwise transfers his Interest) is treated for tax purposes as though it were a cash distribution.

If the cash distributions to a Limited Partner by the Partnership in any year (including his share of any reduction in liabilities, as described above) exceed his share of the Partnership's taxable income for that year, the excess will constitute a return of capital to the Limited Partner. A return of capital will not be reportable as taxable income by a recipient for Federal income tax purposes, but it will reduce the tax basis of his interest in the Partnership. If the tax basis of a Limited Partner's interest, including his share of Partnership liabilities, should be reduced to zero, his share of any cash distributions for any year (including his share in any reduction in liabilities as described above) in excess of his share of Partnership taxable income will be taxable to him as though it were a gain on the sale or exchange of his Partnership interest, some of which may be taxable as ordinary income.

The tax basis of a Limited Partnership Interest is important because a Limited Partner may not deduct his share of Partnership losses to the extent that they exceed his tax basis. However, where the mortgage liabilities with respect to Partnership properties are of the type on which neither the Partnership nor any Partner is personally liable, such liabilities will be considered in determining a Limited Partner's tax basis, as discussed above. The tax basis is also important because it is used in measuring gain or loss upon cash distributions and partial or complete dispositions of Limited Partnership Interests.

4. Section 754 Election

Because of the complexities of the tax accounting required, the Partnership does not presently intend to file an election under Section 754 of the Internal Revenue Code to adjust the basis of Partnership property in the case of a transfer of an interest. As a consequence, the transferee of an interest may be subject to tax upon a portion of the proceeds of sales of Partnership property which represents as to him a return of capital, if the purchase price for his interest exceeded his share of the adjusted basis for all Partnership properties.

5. Allocations of Profits and Losses

Under the Tax Reform Act of 1984 (the "Act"), for partnerships using the cash basis method of accounting items of income, gain, loss, deduction, credit or special items will be allocable to a partner only if they are paid to or by the Partnership during that portion of the year in which he is a member of the Partnership. In determining whether any of these items have been paid prior to a Partner's entry, the Partnership must allocate such items ratably on a daily basis. However, a review of the legislative history of the Act reveals that regulations to be issued should provide for the use of a monthly convention whereby partners entering during the first 15 days of the month will be treated as entering on the first day of the month, and partners entering after the 15th day of the month will be treated as entering on the first day of the next month. In addition, the IRS may provide for other conventions or deny the use of any conventions if significant tax avoidance could result. To the extent permissible under law, all investors who become Partners during a particular 30 day period will be treated equally in accordance with the proposed monthly convention.

In accordance with the Act, with respect to Partnership expenses incurred subsequent to March 31, 1984, deductions for such expenses will be allocated to the month (or day) of the year in which they were incurred, and thus to those investors who are Limited Partners at that time, regardless of the period of the taxable year in which such expenses are actually paid.

The Partnership, in the course of any development of the subject Property, may participate in various joint ventures. The profits and losses of any such joint venture are based upon the terms of each joint venture agreement. The Partnership's share of the profits and losses of any joint venture will be allocated to the partners of the Partnership as if the items of income and expense had been realized or incurred by the Partnership.

The allocation of income, gain, loss, deductions, credits and special items among the Partners as set forth in the Partnership Agreement and any joint venture agreement will be recognized if the allocation may have a substantial economic effect. If the allocation has no substantial economic effect or the Partnership Agreement or joint venture agreement does not provide for a method of allocation, then income and losses or items of income, gain, loss, deduction or credit will be allocated among the partners on the basis of the partner's interest in the Partnership or joint venture (determined by taking into account all facts and circumstances), the result of which allocation could be an increase or decrease in each partners' share of Partnership items. In computing income, gain, loss deductions, credits and special items, approximately 98% of all items of Partnership income, gain, loss, deductions, credits and special items will be allocated among the Limited Partners in proportion to their respective investments, and approximately 2% will be allocated to the General Partners. Because this allocation applies in all instances, it is assumed that such allocation has "substantial economic effect" within the meaning of Section 704(b) of the Code and any regulations promulgated with respect thereto.

It is further assumed that the IRS will agree that any Partnership Management fees paid to Equity Fund Investors, Inc., any Property Management Fees paid to Equity Fund Management, Inc., and any Construction Management Fees paid to Equity Fund Construction, Inc., will be treated as payments for services rather than as Partnership distributions. Under the Act, new rules apply to the treatment of payments to partners for services performed, as addressed in Internal Revenue Code Section 707(a). If a partner engages in a transaction with a partnership other than in his capacity as a member of such partnership, the transaction shall be considered as occurring between the partnership and one who is not a partner. It is assumed that any provision of services to the Partnership by companies wholly owned by the General Partners will be characterized as described above. A Senate Committee Report lists factors to be used in determining whether or not a partner is receiving an allocation and distribution in his capacity as a partner. They are as follows: (1) whether the payment is subject to an appropriate risk as to amount; (2) whether the partner status is transitory; (3) whether the distribution and allocation are close in time to the partner's performance of services; (4) whether under all the facts and circumstances, it appears that the recipient became a partner primarily to obtain tax benefits for himself or the partnership that would not have been available to him in a third party capacity; and (5) in the case of service performed, whether the value of the recipient's interest in general and continuing partnership profits is small in relation to the allocation in question. However, the Act authorizes the IRS to prescribe regulations as may be necessary to make any judgments as to characterization of services rendered by a partner. Therefore, no assurances can be made that the IRS will not recharacterize any such Partnership Management, Property Management or Construction Management fees, if any at all, as Partnership distributions, with the principal result being that a portion of the Partnership's claimed deductions, previously allocated to the Limited Partners would be disallowed to them, and instead allocated to the General Partners.

In the event that new regulations are proposed, promulgated, or new Federal legislation enacted which would have an adverse impact on the Partnership's method of allocating (or on any other term in the Partnership Agreement), the General Partners may amend the Partnership Agreement to cause it to comply with such regulations or legislation.

6. Tax Deductibility and Accounting Methods

The Partnership's fiscal year will be the calendar year, and it expects to file its tax returns on a cash basis.

a. Depreciation Method

Depreciation will be calculated under the Accelerated Cost Recovery System (ACRS) for any new and used, real and personal property acquired by the Partnership. Under ACRS, depreciation deductions are designed to permit the recovery of the cost of the asset over a specified period of time, which period is generally shorter than the actual useful life of the property. Non-residential real property, other than land, can be depreciated using either the straight-line method or an accelerated method. Pursuant to the Act, properties acquired after March 15, 1984 must be depreciated using an 18-year recovery period. Depreciation taken pursuant to an accelerated method for non-residential real property is subject to full recapture upon sale or disposition of the Property (see "Recapture of Depreciation," item 6.b below).

Any personal property acquired by the Partnership in the course of development of the Property may be assigned a 5-year useful life, and the Partnership may use the equivalent of a 150% declining balance method of depreciation. The Partnership may depreciate personal property under the accelerated method.

Since the Partnership may have both taxable and tax-exempt entities as limited partners, the 1984 Act imposes a new restriction upon ACRS depreciation benefits. Internal Revenue Code Section 168(j)(9), as added by the Act, requires that a Partnership having both taxable and tax-exempt entities as partners to depreciate the tax-exempt entities proportionate share of the partnership's property over a 40-year recovery period, using the straight-line method of depreciation. The tax-exempt limited partner's proportionate share of the partnership's real property will be determined by the tax-exempt entity's share of partnership items of income or gain, whichever item results in the largest proportionate share, measured at any time during the life of the partnership. It is not anticipated that Tax-Exempt Limited Partners will be afforded special allocations of income or gain at any time during the life of the Partnership. Therefore, it is expected that the Partnership will be able to depreciate its real property using an 18-year recovery period. Similarly, IRC Section 168(j)(9) will assign a different recovery period for personal property acquired by the Partnership.

While the Internal Revenue Service will not be allowed to dictate the method of depreciation to be selected, they may, at some future time, determine the allocation of costs between personal property, real property, and land, which could result in a reduction of allowable depreciation.

The Partnership will use methods of depreciation that the General Partners consider appropriate in development of the subject Property.

    b. <u>Recapture of Depreciation</u>

When non-residential real estate has been depreciated by the Partnership through the use of an accelerated method and is then disposed of through sale, foreclosure or otherwise, all of such depreciation is subject to full recapture and hence taxable as ordinary income. When non-residential real estate has been depreciated through use of the straight-line method, any gains on disposition by sale or otherwise is taxable at capital gain rates.

Further, the Act requires that all ordinary income recaptured upon the sale or other disposition of real or personal property after June 6, 1984 be recognized in the year of such transaction, even though the balance of any such gain may be included in future income under the installment method as payments are received. Prior to the Act, income from depreciation recapture on an installment sale of property generally has been recognized only as the seller received principal payments. After the Act, depreciation recapture will be recognized and fully taxed in the year of the sale, even if no payments are received in that year. This new provision applies to sales of both real and personal property. Consequently, in the event of an installment sale of Partnership property, Limited Partners might be required to recognize some ordinary income in the year of such sale without receiving sufficient cash to pay the resulting tax due in that year. The General Partners will give consideration to this possibility in selecting methods of depreciation and planning the timing of any disposition of property in an attempt to insure that Limited Partners will have sufficient cash to pay resulting Federal taxes as they come due.

    c. <u>Commitment Fees and Preparing Costs</u>

The Partnership may pay standby commitment fees to the seller of the subject Property, his affiliates, or other lenders, in connection with the acquisition of the Property. Once the commitment is exercised, these fees will be amortized over the term of the loan, if the loan is funded through the commitment.

Further, certain other business expenses incurred in 1985 and prior to the time in which Partnership operations generate income, but ordinary and necessary to Partnership operations, will be deducted in 1985, the year in which they were incurred. The IRS may later attempt to require the disallowance and capitalization of the expenses because they were paid by the Partnership in the pre-opening period. If the IRS is upheld, then the deduction of the substantial portion of such payments made in 1985 would be deferred to later years.

It is expected that the IRS, in response to the Act, will develop regulations that more clearly define when an active trade or business is deemed to begin for purposes of determining whether a particular expense is a pre-opening cost. Expenses which are determined to be pre-opening costs, may be either capitalized by the Partnership or amortized over a 60-month period.

    d. <u>Recharacterization of Property Acquisition</u>

Since the purchase by the Partnership of the property in question will not be the result of arm's length negotiations between unrelated parties, the IRS could attempt to deny interest and other deductions to be taken by the Partnership based upon payments to the seller by attempting to recharacterize the property acquisition; the payments to be made by the Partnership on the purchase price. Because such recharacterization depends on various facts and circumstances which may be viewed subjectively, there can be no assurance that the IRS may not attempt to recharacterize certain payments and deductions in whole or in part. If the IRS were successful, the disallowance of deductions for such payments would result in a proportionate increase in the taxable income or decrease in the tax loss of the Limited Partners from the Partnership, with no associated increase in cash flow with which to pay resulting increase in tax liabilities.

e. Construction Period Interest and Taxes

The Partnership anticipates that substantial construction activities will be a part of any development program for the Property, and that certain costs, in the form of hard and soft construction costs, interim and standby loan fees, leasing commissions, and appraisal fees, among others, will be incurred during the construction period. Certain restrictions exist regarding the deductibility of interest and taxes paid with respect to construction of real property or improvements thereto. Interest and taxes which relate to the construction period must be capitalized and amortized over a 10-year period. Other costs may not be fully deductible in the year of payment, but must be capitalized and added to the basis of the property or amortized over a period of years.

For purposes of determining whether or not expenses are incurred during the construction period, the construction period will commence on the date that construction commences and end on the date that the particular property or improvement thereto is ready to be placed in service. Payment of interest and taxes prior to commencement of the construction period will be fully deducted by the Partnership in the year paid, or in the future years to which they relate.

f. Deductibility of Interest and Financing Fee

With respect to the acquisition of some properties, the Partnership may pay mortgage financing fees and interest, which payments would be applicable to years subsequent to the year of payment. Such payments would be deductible by the Partnership in the future years to which they relate, as compared to the year in which paid. Deductibility of such payments is also subject to the limitations on the deductibility of construction period payments as discussed above.

g. Accrual of Original Issue Discount

Although it will use the cash basis method of accounting, the Partnership might be subject to the Original Issue Document (OID) rules, which were substantially expanded under the 1984 Act, with respect to any installment sale of Partnership property. Recognition by the Partnership of OID as an item of income in any year will have the effect of either reducing losses, if any, allocable to Limited Partners from the Partnership or increasing the amount of income which Limited Partners must report from the Partnership without the receipt of cash distributions with which to pay any tax resulting from the reporting of such income.

h. Deduction of Management Fees

The Partnership will be deducting fees for various management services which it will pay to the General Partners or an affiliate thereof. The IRS may examine closely any deductions for management fees payable to the General Partners, joint venture partners, their affiliates, or any other party, and may challenge such deductions based upon the payment being excessive, based upon a recharacterization of the payment, or based upon the payment being to a partner in its capacity as a partner rather than in some other capacity. If the IRS were successful, the disallowance of the deductibility of such fees would result in a proportionate increase in the taxable income of the Limited Partners from the Partnership, with no associated increase in cash flow with which to pay any resulting increase in tax liabilities.

i. Syndication and Organization Expenses

The General Partners will be reimbursed for offering expenses up to certain limits. The portion of offering expenses which represent Syndication Expenses are required to be capitalized and, thus, cannot be deducted by either the Partnership or the Limited Partners. The portion of the offering expenses which represent organization expenses may be amortized ratably over a period of not less than 60 months as may be selected by the Partnership persuant to IRC Section 709.

There is considerable uncertainty as to the proper allocation of expenses among non-deductible syndication expense, amortizable organization expense, amortizable "start-up" expenditures, deductions with respect to the property to be acquired, and when the 60 month period for amortization commences. While the General Partners intend to assert positions that are well supported, there can be no assurance that the IRS will not successfully challenge such allocation, amortization or deduction.

7. Disposition of Property by the Partnership

Any profit or loss which may be realized by the Partnership on the sale of any of the Partnership's real properties (except to the extent that it represents depreciation recapture, taxable as ordinary income as described in paragraph 6 (g) (above) will be treated as capital gain or loss under the Internal Revenue Code unless it is determined that the Partnership is a "dealer" in real estate for Federal income tax purposes. To the extent that assets sold constitute "Section 1231 assets" (i.e., real property and depreciable assets used in a trade or business and held for more than six months), gains or losses would be combined with any other Section 1231 gains or losses incurred in that year and the net Section 1231 gains or losses would be allocated to the Limited Partners and combined with any other Section 1231 gains or losses incurred by the Limited Partners in that year. For 1984, a Limited Partner's net Section 1231 gains or losses would be taxed as capital gains or constitute ordinary losses, as the case may be. Beginning in 1985, the Act requires that a Limited Partner treat his net Section 1231 gain as ordinary income to the extent of any "non-recaptured net Section 1231 losses." Non-recaptured net Section 1231 losses are defined as the aggregate net Section 1231 losses reported by a taxpayer in the five most recent prior years beginning after 1981, less the portion of such losses already taken into account, in converting Section 1231 gain into ordinary income. In the event the Partnership is deemed a "dealer" and its investment in a particular property is not considered to be a capital asset or Section 1231 asset, any gain or loss on the sale or other disposition of such property would be treated as ordinary income or loss. The Partnership will attempt to operate in such a manner as not to be deemed a "dealer" in real estate for Federal income tax purposes, but there can be no assurance that it will be successful in this respect.

In the event the Partnership acquires unimproved land and decides to develop any such properties, it may be deemed a "dealer" with respect to such properties. If the Partnership engages in a substantial amount of sales which could generate ordinary income, such activity could be a factor in causing the Partnership to be deemed a "dealer" in real estate for Federal income tax purposes with respect to other real estate properties or interests held by the Partnership.

It should be noted that the Limited Partners may realize taxable income upon sale of Partnership assets without receiving a sufficient cash distribution to enable them to pay the tax liability resulting from their allocable share of the Partnership's income from the sale. Additionally, a foreclosure is treated as a sale for tax purposes. It is therefore possible for the Partnership to realize taxable income upon a foreclosure without receipt of any cash.

8. Dissolution or Liquidation of the Partnership

In the event of a dissolution of the Partnership prior to the expiration of its term, the Partnership might be required to liquidate all of its properties during a limited period of time. This might cause the Partnership to sustain substantial losses (determined in terms of its original cost). Nevertheless, the Limited Partners might be required to recognize taxable income on such sales as a result of the reduction in the tax basis of Partnership properties by depreciation deductions previously taken as well as prior cash distributions.

9. Disposition of Partnership Interests

Gain or loss realized on the sale of a Limited Partnership Interest by a Limited Partner who is not a "dealer" in securities and who has held such Interests for more than six months will be long-term capital gain or loss. However, the proceeds of a sale, as well as cash deemed distributable, will be taxed at ordinary income rates to the extent attributable to the Limited Partner's share of substantially appreciated inventory items and unrealized receivables. The Federal income tax payable upon sale of an Interest could exceed the actual cash proceeds of sale because, upon sale or other disposition of an Interest, a Limited Partner is deemed to receive a cash distribution to the extent of the reduction of his proportionate share of liabilities to which Partnership assets are subject (see "Basis of Limited Partnership Interests," paragraph 3 above).

The gift of an Interest by a Limited Partner may result in Federal income tax (as well as Federal Gift tax) liability to the donor. The gift is likely to be classified by the IRS as wholly or partially a sale where the Limited Partner's basis for the Interest is less than his proportionate share of Partnership nonrecourse liabilities, and to the extent that it constitutes a sale, the Federal income tax consequences are as set forth in the preceding paragraph.

Under the Internal Revenue Code the Partnership would be considered as terminated if, within a 12-month period, there is a sale or exchange of 50% or more of the total interest in Partnership capital and profits. If that occurs, there would be a loss of accelerated depreciation and other tax benefits.

Therefore, there is a restriction upon the transferability of Limited Partnership Interests in order to prevent a termination of the Partnership. See "Summary of the Partnership Agreement-Transferability of Interests," page 47.

10. Interest Limitation Provisions

A limitation is placed upon the deductibility of interest on funds borrowed to acquire or carry investment assets (investment interest). In general, investment interest is deductible by non-corporate taxpayers only to the extent that it does not exceed the sum of the following items: (1) $10,000 (but only $5,000 for a married taxpayer filing a separate return and zero for a trust); and (2) net investment income, i.e., the excess of non-trade or business income from interest, dividends, rents, royalties and net short-term capital gain from investment property, excluding any long-term gains, over expenses including straight-line depreciation incurred in earning such income. Investment interest which is disallowed as a deduction may be carried over to subsequent years within certain limits. Interest incurred in real estate ventures may be regarded as Investment interest, subject to disallowance, rather than business interest, which remains fully deductible. Thus, under certain circumstances the full amount of mortgage interest passed through from the Partnership to the Limited Partners might not be allowable as a deduction to some or all of the Limited Partners where property is rented by the Partnership under a net lease. Payments of interest by the Partnership out of pocket from the proceeds of the offering should not constitute investment interest although the Partnership may incur investment interest as a result of interest payments from other cash sources.

11. Section 183

Section 183 of the Code limits deductions attributable to "activities not engaged in for profit". The term "activities not engaged in for profit" means any activity other than one that (1) constitutes a trade or business, or (2) is engaged in for the production or collection of income for the management, conservation, or maintenance of property held for the production of income. The determination of whether an activity is engaged in for profit is based on all facts and circumstances, and no one factor is conclusive.

If the gross income derived from an activity for two or more of five consecutive taxable years exceeds the deductions attributable to such activity, the activity is presumed to be engaged in for profit for the second profit year and all subsequent years within the five-year period, unless the Commissioner of Internal Revenue establishes to the contrary. Under certain conditions, a taxpayer may elect to defer the determination of whether the foregoing presumption applies in each of the five taxable years involved. However, the regulations under Section 183 indicate that an organization can satisfy the requirement of a profit motive even if the five-year test is not met. The Partnership anticipates that it will be able to satisfy the profit motive requirement. However, since the test of whether an activity is deemed to be "engaged in for profit" is based on facts and circumstances that exist from time to time, no assurance can be given that Section 183 may not be applied in the future to disallow deductions of the Partners from partnership operations. The IRS is paying increased attention to the application of Section 183 to partnerships, and has recently ruled that Section 183 applies to the activities of a partnership (rather than its partners), and that the provisions of Section 183 are applied at the partnership level.

Page 42

12. Alternative Minimum Tax

The Tax Equity and Fiscal Responsibility Act of 1982 ("TEFRA") replaced the "add on" minimum tax and the previous alternative minimum tax with a new alternative minimum tax for tax years beginning after December 31, 1982. The alternative minimum tax is intended to reduce the ability of taxpayers to totally avoid income taxes through the combination of the special treatment of long-term capital gains and the availability of tax shelter deductions and credits. The alternative minimum tax is imposed at a flat 20 percent rate on a taxpayer's alternative minimum tax base in excess of $40,000 for joint returns, $30,000 for individual returns, and $20,000 for estates, trusts and married individuals filing separate returns. Beginning in 1985, the Act requires tax payers liable for the alternative minimum tax to make estimated tax payments.

The alternative minimum tax base is computed by increasing a taxpayer's adjusted gross income by the total of all tax preference items. Tax preference items include: (i) the excess of accelerated depreciation over straight-line on real property; (ii) accelerated depreciation on personal property subject to a lease; (iii) the excess of a 60-month amortization of certain pollution control facilities over depreciation otherwise allowable; (iv) the excess of percentage depletion over the adjusted basis of the property, (v) intangible drilling costs in excess of the amount that they would have been deductible with respect to such costs and the taxpayer's net income from production; (vi) the long- term capital gains deduction; (vii) interest and dividends excluded under the $100 dividend exclusion and the 15% net interest exclusion (after 1984); (viii) the excess of expensing over 10-year amortization of mining exploration and development costs, research and development costs and magazine circulation expenditures; and (ix) the excess of the fair market value of stock received on the exercise of an incentive stock option over the exercise price. (Section 57(a) of the Code.)

Solely for the purpose of the alternative minimum tax, net investment income takes into account all income derived from interests as limited partners in limited partnerships and from interests in S Corporations where the taxpayer does not actively participate in management. Furthermore, interest expenses incurred to acquire or carry out an interest as a limited partner in a limited partnership, or an interest in an S Corporation where the taxpayer does not actively participate in management are not taken into account in arriving at adjusted gross income, but rather are considered itemized deductions for these purposes, and therefore are subject, for purposes of the alternative minimum tax, to the net investment income limitation. (Section 55(e)(8) of the Code.) The effect of the alternative minimum tax may be to reduce the benefit to any Limited Partner of long-term capital gains attributable to the Properties.

13. Reports

Within 75 days following the close of each fiscal year, or as soon thereafter as all necessary documentation can be arranged, the Partnership will provide the Limited Partners with information as to their share of income and losses of the Partnership, as well as certain other information, which will be sufficient to prepare their individual Federal income tax returns.

14. State and Local Taxes

In addition to the Federal income tax consequences described above, a Limited Partner's distributive share of the taxable income or loss of the Partnership may be required to be included in determining his reportable income for state and local tax purposes in the jurisdiction in which he is a resident. In addition, certain jurisdictions in which the Partnership may own and operate real estate investments may require the Partnership to file tax returns and, in some jurisdictions, the Partnership may be required to pay a tax. These jurisdictions may also impose a tax on nonresident partners determined with reference to their pro-rata share of Partnership income derived from such jurisdiction. On the other hand, tax losses derived through the Partnership from properties in such jurisdictions may be available to offset income from other sources within the same jurisdiction. To the extent that a nonresident Limited Partner pays a tax to a jurisdiction by virtue of Partnership operations within that jurisdiction, he may be entitled to a deduction or credit against tax owed to his jurisdiction of residence with respect to the same income. A Limited Partner may also be subject to estate or inheritance taxes in jurisdictions in which the Partnership does business.

15. Unrelated Business Income

A qualified tax-exempt person or profit-sharing plan is subject to tax on its unrelated business income. Unrelated business income is the gross income derived by an exempt organization from any unrelated trade or business regularly carried on by it or by a partnership of which it is a member. Specific deductions which are directly connected with the carrying on of such trade or business, computed with modifications, are allowed. Since the Partnership carries on a trade or business, any exempt organization including the trust of a qualified plan, which invests in the Partnership would be considered to be regularly carrying on the business of the Partnership and any income produced by the Partnership may be unrelated business income. The trustee of each qualified plan is allowed in the aggregate $1,000 annual exemption from tax on its unrelated business income. Therefore, if the trust has unrelated business income from other investments, only a portion of the $1,000 exemption will be available to offset taxable income, if any, from the Partnership.

Also, when a property is debt financed, the deduction for depreciation is limited to the amount computed by use of the straight line method, even if accelerated depreciation is used by the business. See "Tax Aspects Of The Offering-Depreciation," page 34, concerning the Partnership's possible use of accelerated depreciation methods.

When the Partnership disposes of a property, a Limited Partner which is an exempt organization will be required to pay a tax on the gains that were attributable to the borrowed funds.

16. Partnership Decisions in the Event of an Audit

Before the Tax Equity and Fiscal Responsibility Act of 1982 ("TEFRA"), the IRS was required to grant each partner of a partnership administrative and judicial review of such partner's tax return independently of any review of another partner in the same partnership. This procedure raised considerable administrative burdens for the IRS in enforcing the tax laws. TEFRA changed the procedures dramatically in this respect.

Under the new rules, a General Partner of the Partnership is to be designated as the "Tax Matters Partner". Treasury Regulations to be produced will require the Tax Matters Partner to advise the other partners of all administrative and judicial proceedings concerning the proposed adjustment at the partnership level of partnership items of income, deduction or credit. All partners may participate in any proceeding, although the time and place is set by the Tax Matters Partner and the Tax Matters Partner will have authority to bind all partners with respect to any settlement or other resolution of a tax dispute with the IRS at the administrative level.

17. IRS Registration

The 1984 Act requires the General Partners to register the Partnership as a "tax shelter" with the IRS and thereby obtain an identification number. The identification number will be furnished to Limited Partners after their purchase of Interests in the Partnership. Temporary regulations for tax shelter registration have been promulgated by the IRS, requiring the following statement to be made to all Limited Partners:

> You have acquired an interest in the Equity Fund/Chillum Terrace Limited Partnership. The General Partners have applied to the Internal Revenue Service for a tax shelter registration number. The number will be furnished to you as soon as it is available to the General Partners. You must report the registra-

tion number as well as the name and taxpayer identification number of Equity Fund/Chillum Terrace Limited Partnership on Form 8271. FORM 8271 MUST BE ATTACHED TO THE RETURN ON WHICH YOU CLAIM THE DEDUCTION, LOSS, CREDIT OR OTHER TAX BENEFIT OR REPORT ANY INCOME. ISSUANCE OF A REGISTRATION NUMBER DOES NOT INDICATE THAT THIS INVESTMENT OR THE CLAIMED TAX BENEFIT HAVE BEEN REVIEWED, EXAMINED OR APPROVED BY THE INTERNAL REVENUE SERVICE.

L. GLOSSARY OF TERMS

"Adjusted Original Capital" means Original Capital as reduced from time to time by the amount of distributions on Interests from Net Cash Proceeds.

"Net Cash Proceeds" means the cash proceeds realized by the Partnership upon the sale or refinancing of Partnership properties after: (1) payment of all expenses of such refinancing or sale, including brokerage commissions, if applicable, and (2) the payment of indebtedness relating to the property sold or refinanced.

"Net Cash Receipts" shall mean all cash revenues of the Partnership (other than capital contributions or proceeds of any sale or refinancing of Partnership properties) less the sum of the following to the extent made from such cash revenues received by the Partnership: (1) all principal and interest payments on mortgage or other indebtedness of the Partnership and all other sums paid to lenders and (2) all cash expenditures incurred incident to normal operations of the Partnership business.

"Original Capital" means $1,000 per Interest outstanding, less the amount of any capital contributions which have not been invested in properties and have been returned to holders of Interests.

Other items capitalized in this Offering Memorandum or the Partnership Agreement are defined in the Partnership Agreement.

M. SUMMARY OF THE PARTNERSHIP AGREEMENT

The Partnership Agreement to be executed by the General Partners and each Limited Partner is included as Exhibit A to this Offering Memorandum and it is recommended that each prospective investor read it in full. The following briefly summarizes certain provisions of the Partnership Agreement. All statements made below and elsewhere in the Offering Memorandum relating to the Partnership Agreement are hereby qualified in their entirety by reference to the Agreement.

Page 46

1. Responsibilities of the General Partners

The General Partners are responsible for the exclusive management and control of all aspects of the business of the Partnership. In the course of their management, the General Partners may, in their absolute discretion, acquire, mortgage, encumber, hold title to, pledge, sell, release or otherwise dispose of real and personal property and interests therein when and upon such terms as they determine to be in the best interests of the Partnership, borrow money and give security therefore and employ such persons, including, under certain circumstances, affiliates of the General Partner, as they deem necessary for the efficient operation of the Partnership.

2. Liability of Partners to Third Parties

The General Partners will be liable for all general obligations of the Partnership to the extent not paid by the Partnership. The Partnership Agreement provides that no Limited Partner shall be personally liable for the debts of the Partnership beyond the amount committed by him to the capital of the Partnership. However, a Limited Partner will be liable to the Partnership and to its creditors to the extent of any distribution made to him if, after such distribution, the remaining assets of the Partnership are not sufficient to pay the Partnership's then outstanding liabilities. See "Risks, Powers Granted Limited Partners—Effect on Limited Liability," page 19.

3. Limitations on the Liability of the General Partners

The General Partners will not be liable to the Partnership or the Limited Partners for any act or omission performed or omitted by them in good faith pursuant to the authority granted to them by the Agreement, but only for negligence, gross negligence, fraud or bad faith. The Partnership shall indemnify the General Partners, their agents and employees and each partner and officer for any loss or damage incurred on behalf of the Partnership or in furtherance of the Partnership's interests without relieving the General Partners and such related persons of liability for intentional wrong-doing, gross negligence, fraud or bad faith. Insofar as indemnification for liabilities under the Securities Act of 1933 may be permitted to the General Partners, the Partnership has been advised that in the opinion of the Securities and Exchange Commission such indemnification is against public policy as expressed in the Act and is therefore unenforceable. Notwithstanding the foregoing, neither the General Partners nor any agent or employee thereof shall be indemnified from any loss or damage incurred by them in connection with any judgement entered in or settlement of any lawsuit involving allegations that federal or state securities laws were violated in connection with the offer or sale

Page 47

of Partnership Interests unless: (1) where the lawsuit is not settled, the General Partners or any partner or officer thereof is successful in defending such action; and (2) such indemnification is specifically approved by a court of laws which shall have been advised as to the current position of the Securities and Exchange Commission regarding indemnification for violations of securities laws.

4. Transferability of Interests

Interests may be transferred by the purchasers thereof, subject to the limitations set forth below. To transfer Interests, a form which will be available from the General Partners must be signed by both the transferor and transferee and approved by the General Partners. Each transfer will be effective as of the last day of the month during which the form is received and approved by the General Partners. For information regarding allocation of Partnership income, gain, loss, deduction, or credit to the Interests transferred see "Tax Aspects of the Offering—Retroactive or Special Allocations of Profits or Losses," page 32.

If necessary to avoid premature termination of the Partnership for tax purposes, the effectiveness of any transfer will be deferred if it would result in 50% or more of the Interests having been transferred within a 12-month period. The transferor will be notified in such event and any deferred transfers will be effected (in such reasonable order as the General Partners may determine, if necessary) as of the first day of the next succeeding calendar quarter as of which such transfers can be effected without premature termination of the Partnership for tax purposes. In the event transfers should be suspended for the foregoing reason, the General Partners will give written notice of such suspension as soon as practicable to all Limited Partners.

It is not anticipated that a market for Interests will develop. Upon request, the General Partners will endeavor to assist a Limited Partner desiring to transfer his Interests and it may utilize the services of broker-dealers in this regard. The price to be paid for the Interests, as well as the commission to be received by the broker-dealer, will be subject to negotiation by the Limited Partner.

5. Dissolution and Liquidation

The Partnership will be dissolved on December 31, 2020, or earlier upon the prior occurrence of either of the following events: (1) the disposition of all interests in real estate of the Partnership, including notes received in connection with sales of real estate; or (2) bankruptcy or termination of a General Partner, subject to the rights of the remaining General Partner to continue the Partnership as set forth in the agreement.

Upon dissolution of the Partnership, all assets will be liquidated and the proceeds of liquidation will be applied first to the payment of obligations of the Partnership, to third parties and the expenses of liquidation, and to the setting up of any reserves for contingencies which the General Partners consider necessary. Any remaining proceeds of the liquidation and any other funds or properties of the Partnership will then be distributed as described under "Plan of Distribution," page 50, and "Compensation to General Partners and Affiliates," page 8.

N. REPORTS TO LIMITED PARTNERS

Financial information contained in all reports to the holders of Interests will be prepared on a cash basis of accounting and will include, where applicable, a reconciliation to information furnished to the holders of Interests for income tax purposes.

Semesterly, beginning on December 31, 1985, or as soon thereafter as all necessary information can be arranged, the General Partners shall send to each person holding Interests a regular report detailing the status of development, leasing and management activities and the Partnership's financial status. Included in this report shall be any distributions of cash flow which the General Partners shall elect to make to Limited Partners.

Within ninety days of completion of the rehabilitation effort, or as soon thereafter as all necessary information can be arranged, the General Partners shall send to each person holding Interests a special report detailing a breakdown of costs and an update on the results of the Partnership's leasing effort.

Within 75 days after the end of each fiscal year, or as soon thereafter as all necessary documentation can be arranged, the General Partners shall send to each person who was a holder of Interests at any time during the fiscal year then ended such tax information as shall be necessary for the preparation by such holder of his Federal income tax return, and state income and other tax returns with regard to jurisdictions in which the Partnership is formed or qualified.

O. TRANSFER OF LIMITED PARTNERSHIP INTERESTS

Limited Partners may sell, assign or otherwise transfer their Interests under the following conditions:

(1) An instrument of assignment executed by both the assignor and the assignee of the Interests, satisfactory in form to the General Partners, shall be delivered to the General Partners.

(2) Each assignment shall be effective as of the date that the General Partners indicate they accept and approve of the in-

strument of assignment by affixing their signatures thereon.

(3) No assignment shall be effective if such assignment would, in the opinion of the General Partners, result in the termination of the Partnership for purposes of the then applicable provisions of the Internal Revenue Code of 1954.

(4) No assignment shall be effective if the assignment would, to the knowledge of the General Partners, violate the provisions of any applicable federal or state securities law.

(5) No assignment to a minor or incompetent shall be effective in any respect.

(6) No assignment shall be effective unless approved by the General Partners. Approval or disapproval is in the sole discretion of the General Partners.

There is no assurance that Limited Partnership Interests can be sold for their original price, if at all. Any and all expenses incurred by the Partnership in facilitating the sale or transfer of such Interests shall be borne by the selling Limited Partner.

P. CAPITALIZATION

The capitalization of the Partnership as of the date of this Offering Memorandum and as adjusted to give effect to the sale of and full payment for the minimum and maximum number of Interests offered hereby is as follows:

Title of Class Sold	As of the Date Hereof	Total Interests
Limited Partnership Interests ($1,000 per Interest)	$100 (1)	$ 750,000
General Partnership Interests ($100 per interest)	200 (2)	200

(1) Purchased by Richard R. Solem as the Original Limited Partner in connection with the filing of the Certificate of Limited Partnership. When the Partnership closes its subscription period the Original Limited Partner will have his capital returned to him and cease to be a Limited Partner. Each Limited Partner and the Original Limited Partner hereby consent to this act and waive and release the Original Limited Partner from any right, claim or action that any of them may have against him for the return of such capital contribution. All subsequent Limited Partners shall contribute to the Partnership

in multiples of $25,000, with a minimum contribution of $25,000 (25 interests) per investor.

(2) Only two General Partnership interests are authorized and both have been sold.

Q. PLAN OF DISTRIBUTION

Subject to the terms and conditions set forth in this Offering Memorandum, the "Partnership Agreement" (Exhibit A) and the "Soliciting Dealer Agreement" (Exhibit F), the $750,000 in Interests offered herein shall be marketed for the Partnership on a "best efforts, all or none" basis by cooperating NASD licensed broker-dealers for a total commission of 10% of the proceeds thus raised. Provided that Equity Fund Securities, Inc. is successfully licensed as an NASD broker-dealer while this offering is in progress, it is anticipated that securities sales shall be handled through that entity, whether directly or through cooperation arrangements with other NASD firms.

The offering period will commence on the date of this Offering Memorandum (July 1, 1985) and will terminate when all Interests have been sold or on October 30, 1985, whichever first occurs. Should the required minimum of $550,000 in Interests not be sold by October 30, 1985, the offering will be terminated and all funds collected and returned to Limited Partner investors with interest.

R. SUBSCRIPTION FOR AND SALE OF INTERESTS

Every person desiring to purchase Interests will be required to subscribe therefor by completing and signing the Execution Copy of the Subscription Agreement contained in the Offering Memorandum (on pages C-3 and C-4) and delivering it to their soliciting NASD broker-dealer together with a check and promissory note for the full purchase price of the Interests being subscribed for. The check should be made payable to Equity Fund/Chillum Terrace Limited Partnership. Complete instructions for subscribers are contained in the Subscription Agreement attached as Exhibit C to this Offering Circular.

The purchase of the Interests is suitable only for persons of adequate means who have no need for liquidity in their investments. Every subscriber for the purchase of Interests will be required to make the representations set forth under "Suitability", on page 2 of this Offering Memorandum, and in the Subscription Agreement.

The proceeds of the offering will be retained in a Partnership escrow account at Suburban Bank in Bethesda, Maryland for the benefit of investors and used only for the purposes set forth under "Use of Proceeds" and "The Partnership Business." When the required minimum of 550

Interests have been subscribed for, such funds (including any interest earned thereon) may be paid over to the Partnership for utilization as described under "Use of Proceeds," page 7.

The General Partners have the unconditional right to accept or reject any subscription. If the General Partners reject any subscription, they will return to the subscriber the funds paid by him, without interest. Purchasers of Interests will become Limited Partners in the Partnership upon release of their subscription funds from escrow.

> SAMPLE DOCUMENT:
> OFFERING MEMORANDUM

J. T. BRAY AND COMPANY
ACCOUNTANTS AND FINANCIAL PLANNERS
8030 WOODMONT AVENUE
BETHESDA, MARYLAND 20814
(301) 657-9322

Equity Fund/ Chillum Terrace Limited Partnership
7512 Whittier Blvd.
Bethesda, MD 20817

Gentlemen:

We have prepared for the Maryland partnership, Equity Fund/Chillum Terrace Limited Partnership, a PROFORMA Balance Sheet which is attached herewith.

The Partnership's only transaction to date is to open an operating checking account to deposit funds received from investors and to enter into a contract to purchase the property known as Chillum Terrace Shopping Center, 5904-5926 Riggs Road, Hyattsville, Maryland, for $600,000, for which they have made a deposit of $60,000, which is being held by the Seller.

There is no Statement of Operations presented as the partnership has not had any operating transaction.

The Balance Sheet of Equity Fund/Chillum Terrace Limited Partnership presents fairly the statement of financial condition as of that date in accordance with generally accepted accounting principles.

Respectfully submitted,

> SAMPLE DOCUMENT:
> OFFERING MEMORANDUM

EQUITY FUND/CHILLUM TERRACE LIMITED PARTNERSHIP

BALANCE SHEET

ASSETS

CURRENT ASSETS:

Cash in Suburban Bank operating account number	$	300
TOTAL CURRENT ASSETS:	$	300

INVESTMENT:

Purchase of Chillum Terrace Shopping Center		*618,470
TOTAL ASSETS	$	618,770

LIABILITIES AND PARTNERS' EQUITY

CURRENT LIABILITIES:

Due at settlement of purchase of Chillum Terrace Shopping Center	$	618,470

PARTNERS' EQUITY:

General partners	$	200
Limited partner		100
TOTAL PARTNERS' EQUITY	$	300
TOTAL LIABILITIES AND PARTNERS' EQUITY	$	618,770

SEE LETTER OF TRANSMITTAL

*Includes $18,470 in settlement costs.

> SAMPLE DOCUMENT:
> ATTORNEY OPINION FOR OFFERING MEMORANDUM

ATTORNEY OPINION

FOR OFFERING MEMORANDUM

> SAMPLE DOCUMENT:
> ATTORNEY OPINION FOR OFFERING MEMORANDUM

Roger J. McClure & Associates, P.C.

Admitted to Practice
Maryland, Virginia
District of Columbia

Counselors and Attorneys at Law
1317 King Street
Alexandria, Virginia 22314

Telephone (703) 684-3995

July 29, 1985

Mr. Richard R. Solem
Equity Fund/Chillum Terrace Limited Partnership
7512 Whittier Boulevard
Bethesda, Maryland 20817

RE: Equity Fund/Chillum Terrace Limited Partnership

Dear Sirs:

We have acted as special counsel to you in regard to the proposed operations of Equity Fund/Chillum Terrace ("Chillum Terrace"), a limited partnership formed under the laws of the State of Maryland. Chillum Terrace intends to acquire a fee simple interest in a shopping center known as the Chillum Terrace Shopping Center at 5904-5926, Riggs Road, Hyattsville, Maryland. You have asked for my opinion as to a portion of the federal tax consequences of Chillum Terrace, specifically whether or not Chillum Terrace will be classified as a partnership for federal income tax purposes.

In formulating this opinion, this office has reviewed the Private Placement Memorandum, an executed and filed copy of the Certificate of Limited Partnership of Equity Fund/Chillum Terrace Limited Partnership and the Agreement of Limited Partnership of Equity Fund/Chillum Terrace Limited Partnership; the executed copy of the agreement of sale of the office building to the Equity Fund Group, and or assigns, the net worth of General Partner Richard R. Solem, the Articles of Incorporation of General Partner Equity Fund Profit Sharing Associates, Inc. #2, and such other instruments and documents this office deems necessary and relevant to the rendering of this opinion.

In providing this opinion, we are relying upon, without independent verification the following representations, among others, you have made to this office:

    (1)   Except as provided in (2) below, the Chillum Terrace Agreement of Limited Partnership will not be modified in any way

which would affect the statements in this opinion and that the Partnership Certificate, as filed, has constituted the partnership as a valid limited partnership under the laws of the State of Maryland.

(2) The Chillum Terrace Partnership Agreement will be amended to admit additional limited partners; and

(3) Chillum Terrace will constitute a valid limited partnership, under the laws of the State of Maryland, will be operated in accordance with the laws of the State of Maryland, and will be operated pursuant to the Partnership Agreement, as amended in (2) above; and

(4) Mr. Richard R. Solem has substantial assets as a general partner, other than his investment in Chillum Terrace, that he has the means to satisfy a significant portion of the projected business obligations of Chillum Terrace, that substantial sums will be placed in the operating account of Equity Fund Profit Sharing Associates, Inc. #2, and that Richard R. Solem will actively direct, individually and as Chief Executive Officer of Equity Fund Profit Sharing Associates, Inc. #2, the Chillum Terrace partnership; and

(5) It will be policy of Chillum Terrace to invest most of the assets of the partnership in the shopping center and that the general partner believes that the center has a possibility in appreciation in value.

The opinion expressed in this letter is also based upon the information and representations contained in the Memorandum. It is our understanding that said Memorandum presents an accurate and complete description of the proposed plans of the Partnership and the facts and circumstances of its business operations. Any change in the Partnership Agreement, the major assets of the Partnership and the designated general partners of the Partnership may be so substantial as to materially affect the applicability of the conclusions stated in this letter.

Classification of Chillum Terrace as a Partnership

The tax consequences to Chillum Terrace and its general and limited partners depend upon whether or not Chillum Terrace is classified as a partnership or an association taxable as a corporation for federal income tax purposes. Section 7701 (a) (2) of the Internal Revenue Code of 1954 as amended (the "code") states:

> The term 'partnership' includes a syndicate, group, pool, joint venture, or other unincorporated organization through or by means of which any business, financial operation, or

venture is carried and which is not, within the meaning of this title, a trust or estate or corporation; and the term 'partner' includes a member in a syndicate, group, pool, joint venture, or organization.

The income tax regulations of the U.S. Department of Treasury ("regulations") in Section 301.7701- 3(b) provide that a partnership, even though it qualified as a limited partnership under state law, may be classified either as a partnership or as an association for the purposes of the Code. If the partnership more resembles a corporation than a partnership under the principles set forth in the regulations, then the IRS will take the position that it should be taxed as a corporation. If taxed as a partnership, all profits and losses are passed on to the partners. If taxed as a Sub-chapter C Corporation, all profits and losses will be captured by the corporate entity and not directly passed onto the partners.

The regulations in Section 301.7701-2 (a) (3) provide that an unincorporated organization shall not be classified as an association taxable as a corporation unless such organization has more corporate characteristics than non-corporate characteristics. In making such a determination, the regulations provide that characteristics common to both types of organizations shall be disregarded. The regulations provide further that an organization having associates and an objective to carry on a business and to divide gains therefrom are examples of characteristics generally common to both corporations and partnerships, and therefore are not to be considered. Accordingly, the determination as to whether an organization formed as a partnership will be treated as a partnership for federal income tax purposes depends on whether, or to what extent, there exists the four corporate characteristics of (1) continuity of life, (2) centralization of management, (3) limited liability, and (4) free transferability of interests. Each of these factors may bear equal weight. Chillum Terrace will be classified as a partnership for federal income tax purposes if it lacks at least two (2) of the four (4) corporate characteristics described above, and if it has no other corporate characteristics which are significant in determining its classification.

1. Continuity of Life

Section 301.7701-2 of the regulations provides that an organization has "continuity of life" if the bankruptcy, insanity, retirement, resignation, death or expulsion of any member of the limited partnership will not cause dissolution of the partnership. If the death, retirement or insanity of a general or limited partner causes a dissolution of the partnership, then the entity does not have continuity of life. This is true unless all remaining members agree to continue the partnership or unless the remaining general partners agree to continue the partnership. An agreement whereby the partners may continue the business in the event of a withdrawal or death of any member does not mean that the partnership has continuity of life if under local law the death or withdrawal of any member would cause a dissolution.

In Philip G. Larson, 66 T.C. 159, 175 (1976), appeal withdrawn 9th Cir. 1978, acq. 79-1 C.B. 1, the Tax Court noted that a limited partnership would probably always fail to qualify as having continuity of life. This was so in that case because, under California law, the bankruptcy of the sole general partner would cause a dissolution of the partnership.

On the other hand, the regulations state that if the partnership agreement provides that the organization is to continue a stated period or until the completion of a stated transaction, the organization has continuity of life if the effect is that no member can dissolve the organization. But if under local law, such as the Uniform Limited Partnership Act, a member has the power to dissolve the partnership, then the organization lacks continuity of life.

Section 17.1 of the Chillum Terrace Limited Partnership Agreement provides that the dissolution, withdrawal or bankruptcy of a General Partner shall dissolve the Partnership. There are two General Partners which are Raymond Solem, an individual, and Equity Fund Profit Sharing Associates, Inc. #2, a corporation. However, the remaining general partner has the option to continue the partnership. But, if the remaining general partner becomes bankrupt, the Partnership shall dissolve unless all limited partners unanimously vote to elect a substitute General Partner. Under Section 14.3 of the partnership agreement, the death or legal incapacity of a limited partner shall not cause the dissolution of the partnership.

It is the opinion of this office that it is more likely than not that a reviewing court will find that the Chillum Terrace Limited Partnership lacks the corporate characteristics of continuity of life. The partnership agreement provides for the dissolution of the partnership if any of the general partners dissolves, withdraws or becomes bankrupt. But, if a general partner remains, and it is within the first ten years of the partnership or as long as the partnership still retains the original property, then the remaining general partner will continue the partnership. If there is only one remaining general partner, the partnership would dissolve. Under the condition of two remaining general partners, then it might be said that the partnership has continuity of life. However, under Section 10-802 of the Maryland Code, any partner has the power to petition a court to dissolve the partnership. Under Section 10-402, unless otherwise provided in the Certificate, the bankruptcy of a general partner is a withdrawal and therefore a dissolution of the partnership under Section 10-801. In addition, under Section 10-603, a limited partner is permitted to withdraw from the partnership if a contrary intention is not, as it is not, expressed in the Certificate of Chillum Terrace. However, a withdrawal of a limited partner does not cause the partnership to dissolve. Additionally, Chillum Terrace was formed under the Maryland version of the Uniform Limited Partnership Act. For these reasons, Chillum Terrace lacks continuity of life.

2. Centralization of Management

Section 301.7701-2 (c) (1) of the regulation provides that if any person, or group or persons has continuing exclusive authority to make the management decisions necessary for the conduct of the business, then the organization has one corporate characteristic of centralization of management. Section 301.7701-2 (c) (4) states that centralization of management in a limited partnership does exist where substantially all of the interests of the partnership are owned by limited partners. Another factor is the power of some or all of the limited partners to remove the general partner.

Under Article 15 of the partnership agreement, the general partner have the exclusive authority to manage the operations and affairs of the Partnership, and to make all decisions regarding partnership business. Under the partnership agreement, the limited partners have no authority to remove the general partner. The Maryland Limited Partnership Act does not give the limited partners the power to remove any general partner.

The regulations do not define what "substantially all" of the interests of the partnership means. In Larson and Zuckman v. United States, 524 F. 2d 729, 737-39 (Ct. Cl. 1975), the Courts interpreted the regulations to mean that a partnership will not have centralization of management if the general partners have a "meaningful proprietary interest," even where there may be centralization of management.

It is the opinion of this office that a court would more likely than not find that the Chillum Terrace Limited Partnership has the corporate characteristics of centralization of management. This is because "substantially all" of the interests in Chillum Terrace are owned by the limited partners within the meaning of Larson and Zuckman and the management of the partnership is centralized in the general partners.

3. Limited Liability

Section 301.7701-2 (d) (1) of the regulations states that an entity has the corporate characteristics of limited liability if under local law no member of the organization is liable for the debts of the partnership. In the case of a partnership under the Maryland Limited Partnership provisions, personal liability exists with respect to each general partner with certain exceptions. Personal liability does not exist where a general partner has no assets such as a dummy corporation with no assets. If a corporation is a general partner, it should have substantial assets other than its interest in the partnership for personal liability to exist for the corporation. If the partnership is engaged in financial transactions which involve large sums of money, and if the general partner has substantial assets, personal liability exists although the assets of the general partners would be insufficient to satisfy any substantial portion of the obligations of the organization. The term "substantial assets" is not defined in the regulations. If the limited partnership agreement provides that a general partner is not personally liable for the debts of the partnership, the IRS presumes that personal liability does not exist unless local law nullifies that portion of the partnership agreement. Also, if the general partner merely serves as a "dummy" for the limited partners, personal liability may not exist.

Chillum Terrace has two general partners, Raymond Solem and Equity Fund Profit Sharing Associates, Inc., #2, (EFFSA #2, Inc.). Mr. Solem has significant assets in the form of a personal residence, bank accounts and interests in a variety of real estate investments. Most of the assets of EFPSA #2, Inc. are that corporation's interest in the partnership. Section 15.8 of the partnership agreement provides that the partnership will indemnify and hold harmless the general partners from any loss, expense, damage or injury for actions which were in the best interest of the partnership. General partners are not indemnified for actions which involve bad faith, fraud, intentional wrong doings, and state or federal securities law violations. There is no provision in the partnership agreement which states that the general partner shall not be liable for debts of the partnership. Section 10-403(b) of the Maryland Limited Partnership Act prohibits a general partner from limiting a general partner's liability to persons other than his partners or the partnership. A general partner in a Maryland Limited Partnership has the same liabilities as a general partner in a general partnership i.e., personal liabilities for recourse partnership debts. Since under the Chillum Terrace agreement, the general partners make the decisions for the partnership, operate partnership property, and can not be removed by the limited partners, the general partners do not serve as dummies for the limited partners.

Based upon the representations by Richard Solem as to his assets and that he will not be acting as a dummy for the limited partners, and based further on the representations that Richard Solem will be actively involved in the business of the partnership, it is our opinion that it is more likely than not that a Court would find that Chillum Terrace lacks the corporate characteristics of limited liability.

4. Free Transferability of Interests

Section 301.7701-2 (e) (1) provides that an organization has the corporate characteristics of free transferability of interests if members owning substantially all of the interests in the organization have the power, without consent of other members, to substitute for themselves, a non-member of the group. A member must be able to provide the substitute for all of the rights and benefits of his partnership interest. A right to only assign profits, without consent of the other members, does not result in free transferability. Under Section 301.7701-2 (e) (2), if a member can transfer his interest to a person who is not a member of the entity only after having offered such interest to other partners at its fair market value, the IRS may assert that a modified form of free transferability exists.

The Tax Court in Larson dealt with partnership agreements which permitted the assignment of a limited partner's income interest with the consent of the general partner, which consent could not unreasonably be withheld. The Tax Court concluded that an assignee of a limited partner's interest could acquire all the rights of a substituted limited partner without discretionary consent, and accordingly found that the corporate characteristic of free transferability of interest existed. The Court of Claims in Zuckman held that free transferability of interest did not exist where the consent to a transfer was required by all the limited partners.

The Chillum Terrace partnership agreement permits an assignment by a limited partner of his limited partnership interests if and only if certain conditions set forth in Section 16.1 of the agreement are satisfied. The assignment must be on a form satisfactory to the general partner and is only effective upon approval by the general partner. Most of the partnership interests are owned by the limited partners. The general partners may approve or disapprove the assignment in their sole discretion. No assignment may take place if such an assignment would result in the termination of the partnership under the Internal Revenue Code in the opinion of the general partner. No assignment would be effective if it would violate the provisions of any applicable state or federal securities laws or would be to a minor or incompetent. Other limited partners do not have to consent to the assignment of the limited partnership interest. The new substitute limited partner has the full rights and liabilities of the original limited partner. Most of the partnership interests are owned by the limited partners. The transfer of a general partnership interest is subject to the dissolution provisions in Article 17 of the partnership agreement as discussed in part (B) above.

The limited partners are not entities or individuals controlled by the general partners according to the representations of the general partners.

It is the opinion of this office that it is more likely than not that a court would find that the partnership does not possess the corporate characteristic of free transferability of interests. This is based upon the fact that a limited partner does not have an unlimited right to transfer his interest without the consent of the General Partners, which consent can be withheld or given at the sole discretion of the General Partners. Another factor is that a new substitute general partner may not enter the partnership without the consent of a majority of the limited partners.

Other Factors

Section 301.7701-2 (a) (1) of the regulations provides that in addition to the major characteristics set forth above, other factors may be significant in classifying an organization as a corporation or a partnership. If the particular circumstances of a particular organization are such that the organization more nearly resembles a corporation than a partnership, it will be treated as a corporation. The Court of Claims in Outlaw v. United States 494 F. 2d 1376 (Ct. Cl. 1974), cert. denied, 419 U.S. 884 (1974) indicated that the financing of an organization through an offering memorandum in a manner similar to the marketing of corporate securities was an additional corporate characteristic. The Tax Court in Larson, however, indicated that such a method of marketing was not critically significant in a case where the organization lacked two of the four major characteristics. The regulations indicate that if a limited partnership has only two of the major corporate characteristics and no other corporate characteristics which are significant, then such a limited partnership may not be classified as an association taxable as a corporation.

Conclusion

For the reasons described above, under present law, as of this date, it is our opinion that the Equity Fund/Chillum Terrace Limited Partnership will be classified and treated as a partnership for federal income tax purposes. The foregoing opinion is based upon the existing regulations which the courts have specifically held to be valid, but which may be subject to challenge in later cases and subject to lawful amendment by the Internal Revenue Service.

On January 5, 1977, the Internal Revenue Service published notice that it proposed to amend the regulations relating to the classification of limited partnerships for federal income tax purposes. The proposal, however, was withdrawn almost immediately to permit further consideration. On January 14, 1977, the Department of Treasury announced that the proposed amendments would not be re-proposed, and that the existing regulations remain in force and effect. There can be no assurance, however, that the withdrawn regulations will not be re-proposed, and if re-proposed, that they will not be applied retroactively.

The Internal Revenue Service has also issued Revenue Procedure 74-17, 74-1 C.B. 438, which states that the Internal Revenue Service will not consider a request for issuance of an advance ruling that a limited partnership will be taxable as a partnership for federal income tax purposes if, among other matters, the aggregate deductions to be claimed by all partners as their distributive shares of partnership losses for the first two (2) years of operation of the limited partnership will exceed the amount of equity capital invested in the limited partnership.

According to the Internal Revenue Service, the Revenue Procedures are to be applied only in determining whether advance rulings will be issued and are not intended as substantive laws for the determination of partnership status, nor are the requirements to be applied as criteria for the audit of a taxpayer's return. Chillum Terrace does not expect to apply for a ruling as to its status as a partnership for income tax purposes. Should the Internal Revenue Service succeed in advancing the criteria of the Revenue Procedure as propositions of substantive law, Chillum Terrace may not be able to meet all the tests advanced in the Revenue Procedure.

Except as may be set forth above, this office has made no independent verification of the facts and representations referred to above. Any misrepresentations by a general partner, any amendment to the documents (except as referred to above) or other material adverse change in the affairs of Chillum Terrace after the date of this letter may have the effect of changing all or a part of this opinion. Based upon the information and documents that have been made available to us, it is our conclusion that it is more likely than not Chillum Terrace will be classified as a partnership under federal income tax law.

The foregoing opinion is based on and limited to tax issues discussed and based on the present provisions of the Code and Regulations, court decisions, and upon the information and representations made by the general partners. Consequently, future events, including adoption of proposals in the Congress, its committees, the Department of Treasury, and the Internal Revenue Service, or the invalidity of the

Page 10   SAMPLE DOCUMENT: ATTORNEY OPINION FOR OFFERING MEMORANDUM

information and representations of the general partners, may result in different federal income tax treatment of Chillum Terrace and the limited partners than described above.

Whether any economic or income tax benefits will ultimately be derived by a limited partner as a result of his interest in Chillum Terrace will, of course, depend upon the actual operation of Chillum Terrace. We have not commented upon any state income tax issues relating to this offering.

Very truly yours,

Roger J. McClure

ATTORNEY COMMENT
ON OFFERING MEMORANDUM

(*Author's Note*: Each of the following comments is keyed to a particular section of the Offering Memorandum, as indicated by the heading. Please refer back to the Offering Memorandum and to the particular section indicated for a full understanding of the comments.)

Introductory Statements

For partnerships which must be registered as a tax shelter, I recommend that the following be added to the ALL-capitalized portion of the first page or two:

THIS OFFERING MUST BE REGISTERED WITH THE INTERNAL REVENUE SERVICE AS A TAX SHELTER. INVESTORS IN THIS OFFERING MUST FILE A FORM 8271 STATING THAT THEY INVESTED IN A TAX SHELTER WITH THEIR TAX RETURNS. THIS MAY INCREASE THE LIKELIHOOD OF AN AUDIT OF AN INVESTOR'S TAX RETURN. THE FACT THAT THIS PARTNERSHIP IS REGISTERED WITH THE IRS CANNOT BE USED TO IMPLY IN ANY MANNER THAT THE IRS HAS REVIEWED THE CONTENTS OF THIS OFFERING OR IN ANY WAY APPROVED IN ANY MATTER THE CLAIMS OF TAX BENEFITS OR ANY OTHER MATTER DISCUSSED IN THIS OFFERING.

Suitability

NASAA Guidelines are lower; these guidelines only require a minimum gross income of $30,000 and net worth of $30,000 or in the alternative, net worth of $75,000. Regardless of whether these guidelines are applicable to your transaction, you should rarely go below these very minimal amounts because individuals below these income levels *generally* do not have funds left over from living expenses which they could afford to lose in a business venture. Your state may impose higher suitability standards. You are not prohibited from using higher minimum standards; many "blue chip" offerings may require a $100,000 minimum annual income. Guide 5 requires a discussion of the importance of the investor's federal income tax bracket and your methods to insure use and enforcement of suitability.

How to Subscribe

The promissory note may be made payable to a financial institution if the institution is financing the investor notes. If you use investor notes, it is likely that you will have to register with the IRS as a tax shelter.

Summary of the Offering

This is a "specified offering" because it is designed to raise money solely for a specified property. The investor's money can only be used for this project and no other investment.

Here, the general partners have only a 2% interest in the partnership, but will receive 50% of the profits after the limited partners receive a return of their contributions plus an 8% per annual return. If the 50% residuary profits turn out to be large in relationship to total profits made by the partnership, this allocation may be considered as aggressive tax planning. An aggressive tax position which allocates economic benefits different from tax could be the subject of an IRS audit. It is difficult to decide this issue for this partnership due to the impossibility of knowing exactly how much the 50% residuary share will be in comparison to the 8% priority returns. You should consult tax counsel before using a 50% residuary allocation formula. This 50% residuary share is above what NASAA considers as presumptively reasonable in a syndication.

Note that this refers to 80% of "appraised" value. Another interpretation could be that the property was acquired using virtually 100% financing provided by a seller first trust and a second trust from the general partners.

Compensation of General Partners and Affiliates

There are several points to be made here. First, you must reveal each instance in which you or one of your organizations are making money in the deal. Do not attempt to "hide" a $50,000 fee taken by you or one of your corporations from your investors. Attempting to hide such fees is unethical and possibly illegal and will greatly harm or even end your syndication career. Ethical potential partners will not do business with you. Guide 5 requires you to reveal if you previously had an interest in the partnership property. Secondly, some investors will refuse to invest with you if they feel you will be taking too many up-front fees. You have to sell them on the tax and business reasons for your fees. NASAA guidelines restrict the amount of fees you can take and will only permit you to take fees for businesses in which you regularly provide such services at prevailing rates pursuant to locally required licenses and regulations. Thirdly, you *should* take fees for each function you perform. As your business expands, so will your costs, office rent and staff salaries. If you do not include such expenses in your syndication, you may go broke; a bankrupt sponsor is a disaster for his investors. Finally, as long as you reveal all of the fees, how they create conflicts of interest, and stay within applicable regulations, there is generally no prohibition in your receipt of such fees for providing a multitude of services.

Conflicts of Interest

You should frankly spell out each conflict of interest you have for all of the roles you will play in the partnership. In addition, NASAA guidelines may require you to obtain an opinion from an outside unaffiliated expert that any loan by a mortgage loan syndication program to an affiliate of yours is fair and at least as favorable to the program as a loan to an unaffiliated borrower in similar circumstances. NASAA regulations otherwise prohibit loans by a program to you or an affiliate. They also forbid rebates, kickbacks and reciprocal arrangements and commingling of funds. See the NASAA guidelines at Appendix L Part V for further restrictions. Guide 5 contains suggested language which spells out fiduciary responsibilities.

Risks

NASAA guidelines prevent any indemnification provision in a partnership agreement for any loss or liability suffered by you, the sponsor, unless (1) you have determined in good faith that the conduct causing the loss or liability was in the best interest of the partnership, (2) the loss or liability was not due to your negligence or misconduct, *and*, (3) the indemnification only comes from partnership finds and not from the limited partners. These NASAA standards are stricter than those described in the offering memorandum.

These are the normal risks associated with virtually all limited partnerships. Each of these risks should be listed in your offering memorandum. Guide 5 contains a list of disclosure requirements for risk factors and you should discuss each applicable risk factor listed.

There may be risks which particularly apply to your offering. You should list each of these specific risks.

Prior Performance of the General Partners

Guide 5 requires you to provide a narrative summary of your "track record" in prior syndications. In its Appendix II, it sets forth a format for you to reveal use of proceeds of prior programs, compensation to sponsors, operations and sales of properties of prior programs. Guide 5 discourages you from touting your real estate successes in general.

Management

Guide 5 requires a discussion of management personnel, including any substantial reliance on an outside management company, but does not require production of a management plan. If your partnership agreement provides for a change in management, you must describe how such a change would be accomplished. NASAA guidelines put a maximum cap on property management fees: 5%

The Offering Package

for residential and 1–6 % for commercial and industrial properties. NASAA provisions severely restrict or prohibit fees for program management.

The Partnership Business

Guide 5 requires a statement of investment objectives and policies and a description of the real estate investment. Both Guide 5 and NASAA guidelines discourage any projection of a rate of return for an investment in non-specified properties. If during the sale period for a non-specified offering there is a reasonable probability of acquiring a property, you may have to provide additional disclosures on the particular property. In the specimen document, Ray Solem has provided some projections of partnership profits but with very strong caveats.

Tax Aspects of the Offering

Guide 5 requires an extensive discussion of the tax aspects of the offering. In many memorandums, this is the largest section. It is typically written by partnership legal counsel. This sample document discusses each category listed in Guide 5. Although you might try to use a model's discussion of tax aspects, you dare not rely on the accuracy of such a previous exposition. Congress has gotten into the habit of regularly making massive changes to the tax laws in recent years. Even without these seemingly endless Congressional "reform" efforts, the IRS and the courts are continuously changing the details of the tax laws. Also, the tax aspects of your offering may be different from those of your sample.

It is commonly the practice not to apply for an opinion as to partnership status from the IRS and it is unlikely that you will apply for such a ruling after consultation with counsel. IRS requirements for a ruling often don't make it sensible for you to apply and adverse IRS rulings have not always been consistent or justified by current and applicable legal standards.

If you use recourse loans on any of your properties in your partnership, you should illustrate how a limited partner can not include this loan in his or her basis if he or she is not liable on that loan. You should also mention that you can not include non-recourse loans from the seller under new at-risk rules.

This is a very brief discussion of the special allocations issue. In this particular partnership, where 50% of the profits will go to the general partners after a payment of an 8% return to the limited partners, it might have been appropriate to more fully discuss whether this allocation met the substantial economic effect test. For example, the discussion could have pointed out that the partnership agreement requires the maintenance of capital accounts and restoration of negative capital account balances. These partnership provisions are recommended by IRS regulations setting forth how to use capital accounts to insure that partnership special allocations have "substantial economic effects."

The direct deductibility of fees taken by general partners and the relationship of such fees to special allocation formulas are current battlegrounds between the IRS and syndicators. Syndicators are constantly creating new fees which may trigger IRS scrutiny.

In using the limited partnership format, you are required to use the calendar year unless you receive IRS approval to do otherwise. Unless you have clear business reasons to justify a fiscal rather than calendar year, the IRS will deny your request in most instances. The 1986 TRA further limits partnerships to the average tax year of their partners.

Congress passed legislation which changed 18 year ACRS to 19 year ACRS for all real estate bought on or after May 8, 1985, with certain exceptions. This discussion would be more informative if it stated that the partnership will not use ACRS but will use straight line depreciation for the real estate portion of the shopping center. For *commercial* property, if you used ACRS, *all* depreciation was recaptured at ordinary income rates. If you used straight line depreciation for commercial property, all depreciation was recaptured at capital gains rates. As a result, your net profits are usually higher using straight line depreciation for commercial buildings such as shopping centers. Ironically, if you used ACRS with a commercial building you might come out ahead due to the abolition of the special capital gains rate. For properties bought after 1986, unless subject to transition rules, the depreciation available for residential properties will be 27.5 years straight line and 31.5 years straight line for commercial properties.

The TRA of 1986 has uniform capitalization rules for certain costs incurred in connection with non-inventory property and self-use property.

The TRA of 1986 limits the deductibility of interest by limited partners.

I believe that a discussion of the alternative minimum tax should be in virtually every offering memorandum. It can impose on one of your investors an unexpectedly large tax bill in the year of sale of the partnership properties. The TRA of 1986 expands the coverage of the Alternate Minimum Tax and increases the rate to 21%.

Glossary of Terms

Guide 5 requires you to provide a glossary of technical or ill-defined terms. It recommends using the NASAA definitions in the glossary.

Summary of the Partnership Agreement

Guide 5 requires you to include a brief summary of your limited partnership agreement.

Reports to Limited Partners

Guide 5 requires a disclosure of all of the reports you will provide your investors, including a statement as to whether your financial reports will be audited by a CPA. NASAA guidelines require certain reports, as previously discussed.

Transfer of Limited Partnership Interests

Paragraph 16 of Guide 5 requires a disclosure of restrictions on transferability of limited partnership interests. These restrictions arise from applicable securities and tax laws; for example, you want to restrict ease of transferability so as to retain this non-corporate aspect of a partnership to protect your partnership tax status.

Capitalization

Paragraph 17 of Guide 5 requires a discussion of any right by the General Partner to redeem or repurchase interests in the limited partnership. Because no such rights exist in this Chillum Terrace offering, there is no need for a redemption or repurchase discussion.

Plan of Distribution

A plan of distribution is required by Guide 5. If a purchase by a general partner of limited partnership units can be counted towards the minimum number of required units, you must disclose whether you later plan to resell such units after you have met your minimum sales goal.

Subscription for and Sale of Interests

This section is not specifically required by Guide 5, but it helps investors by telling them what is expected of them and it assures them that their money will be held in escrow until the deal is firm. There is no summary in this offering memorandum of the promotional and sales material, as required by paragraph 19 of Guide 5, because Solem did not prepare and use such material in this offering. Also, a paragraph 20 "undertaking" of Guide 5 is not included because these "undertakings" refer to promises made by the syndicator to securities regulators in a public offering. Such undertakings are generally not required for most Regulation D offerings at the federal level. Check with your local state securities regulator to decide if you must provide any such assurances to state officials.

PARTNERSHIP AGREEMENT

EXHIBIT A

AGREEMENT OF LIMITED PARTNERSHIP

AGREEMENT OF LIMITED PARTNERSHIP
OF
EQUITY FUND/CHILLUM TERRACE LIMITED PARTNERSHIP

AGREEMENT OF LIMITED PARTNERSHIP, made and entered into by and between Richard R. Solem and Equity Fund Profit Sharing Associates, Inc., #2, the General Partners, and those other parties who from time to time execute this Agreement or counterparts hereof as limited partners (the "Limited Partners").

ARTICLE 1
FORMATION OF LIMITED PARTNERSHIP

The parties hereby enter into a limited partnership under the provisions of the Revised Uniform Limited Partnership Act of the State of Maryland, and the rights and liabilities of the Partners shall be as provided in that Act except as herein otherwise expressly provided.

ARTICLE 2
NAME

The business of the Partnership shall be conducted under the name of Equity Fund/Chillum Terrace or such other name as the General Partners shall hereafter designate in writing to the Limited Partners.

ARTICLE 3
DEFINITIONS

"Affiliate" of the General Partners shall mean: (1) any corporation, partnership, trust or other entity controlled by/or under common control with the General Partners; and (2) any officer, director, trustee, general partner, employee or holder of 10% or more of the outstanding voting securities of any corporation, partnership, trust or other entity controlled by or under common control with the General Partners.

"Agreement" means this Agreement of Limited Partnership, as amended, modified or supplemented from time to time.

"General Partners" means Richard R. Solem and Equity Fund Profit Sharing Associates, Inc., #2 but, in the event that such party or parties are at any time no longer acting as General Partners, the term shall mean the party or parties then acting in such capacity.

"Limited Partners" means the other parties who execute this Agreement or counterparts hereof as Limited Partners and any party admitted as substituted Limited Partner pursuant to Article 16.

"Participating Percentage" means, as to each holder of an Interest or Interests at any particular time, the percentage arrived at by dividing the total number of Interests held by such party by the total number of Interests outstanding hereunder and multiplying the quotient thereof by one hundred (100).

"Partners" means the General Partners and all Limited Partners, where no distinction is required by the context in which the term is used herein.

"Partnership Interest" or "Interest" means the interest in the capital of the Partnership representing a capital contribution of $1,000.

ARTICLE 4
PURPOSE

The purpose of the Partnership is to purchase and develop the Chillum Terrace Shopping Center, known as 5904-5926 Riggs Road, Hyattsville, Maryland with the objective of earning profits from rental income and subsequent sale.

ARTICLE 5
NAMES AND ADDRESSES OF PARTNERS

The names and addresses of the General Partners and the names and addresses of the Limited Partners are as set forth in Schedule A attached hereto and incorporated herein by reference.

ARTICLE 6
TERM

The term of the Partnership shall be from June 1, 1985 to December 31, 2020, unless sooner terminated as hereinafter provided.

ARTICLE 7
PRINCIPAL PLACE OF BUSINESS

The principal place of business of the Partnership shall be at 7512 Whittier Boulevard, Bethesda, Maryland 20817. The General Partners may from time to time change the principal place of business and, in such event, the General Partners shall notify the Limited Partners in writing within 30 days of the effective date of such change. The General Partners may in their discretion establish additional places of business of the Partnership.

ARTICLE 8
CAPITAL AND CONTRIBUTIONS

SECTION 8.1 GENERAL PARTNERS. The capital of the Partnership and the General Partner contributions shall be the amount stated to be such from time to time in Schedule A attached hereto and incorporated herein by reference.

SECTION 8.2 GENERAL PARTNER'S RIGHT TO ACQUIRE INTERESTS. The General Partners have the right, but are not obliged, to acquire Interests and become Limited Partners with all the rights and obligations thereof, and on the same terms and conditions as other Limited Partners. All references in this Agreement to Limited Partners shall, if applicable, include General Partners in their capacity as Limited Partners.

SECTION 8.3 ORIGINAL LIMITED PARTNER. The Original Limited Partner shall contribute $100 to the Capital of the Partnership as reflected in Schedule A attached hereto.

SECTION 8.4 LIMITED PARTNERS. The General Partners have the right to admit one or more, but no more than 35 persons as Limited Partners at any time without the consent of other Limited Partners. Each Limited Partner admitted to the Partnership shall contribute a minimum of $1,000 per Interest multiplied by the total number of Interest to be purchased. Each Limited Partner is required to purchase at least 25 Interests, representing a total Capital contribution of $25,000, unless the General Partners permit lesser subscriptions. The General Partners may sell fractional Interests to any Limited Partner.

SECTION 8.5 Persons who become Limited Partners shall pay in cash the amount set forth in Schedule B, Section 1 attached hereto, to the Partnership, or the amount set forth in Schedule B, Section 2, in cash together with the delivery of a negotiable, interest-bearing promissory note, or an acceptable letter of credit, or an investor bond, or other cash equivalent satisfactory to the General Partners and evidencing the Limited Partner's promise to pay the remainder of his minimum capital contribution.

SECTION 8.6 Limited Partners who make a Schedule B, Section 2 cash payment coupled with a promissory note shall make the note payable to the order of the Partnership, with the principal terms set forth in form and substance satisfactory to the General Partners. The execution and delivery of the note to the Partnership shall occur simultaneously with the execution and delivery of the Subscription Agreement. The General Partners may, at their sole discretion, at anytime and without notice to the maker, negotiate or otherwise transfer the Note to any person, with or without recourse or warranties.

SECTION 8.7   Pending the receipt of subscriptions for the entire 550 Interests, all subscription proceeds shall be kept by the General Partners separate and apart from all other funds, and shall be deposited and held in trust in one or more interest-bearing or non-interest-bearing bank accounts or temporarily invested in bank certificates of deposits, bankers acceptances, short-term government obligations, time and demand deposits and similar investments, commercial paper and securities of mutual funds which invest exclusively in "money market" instruments with maturities generally not exceeding one year, all at the discretion of the General Partners. At such time as subscriptions for 550 Interests have been received and accepted by the General Partners, the proceeds from such subscriptions may be utilized by the General Partners to pay expenses incurred in connection with the offering and for such other proper Partnership purposes as the General Partners may determine necessary and proper. Purchases of Interests shall become Limited Partners in the Partnership upon release of their subscription funds from escrow. If, for any reason whatsoever, the Partnership has not received subscriptions to purchase 550 Interests by September 30, 1985, the General Partners shall terminate the offering, and all monies therefor deposited by subscribers shall be promptly refunded in full to the subscribers with interest.

SECTION 8.8   In the event that a Limited Partner fails to pay in full to the Holder of his promissory note the accrued interest and/or principal amount owed when due, the General Partners may then give such Limited Partner notice of default and demand immediate payment.

SECTION 8.9   In the event such defaulting Limited Partner fails to make a full payment of the amount due within ten days after notice and demand by the General Partners, the principal amount owed by such Limited Partner plus interest, shall become immediately due and payable without further demand. If the defaulting Limited Partner does not immediately pay the total amount due the Partnership on the Note or Notes in question, then the General Partners, may exercise, on behalf of the Partnership, any and all remedies at law or in equity that may be available to the General Partners, the Partnership, or the Holder of such Note or Notes. Possible remedies might include but shall not be limited to the following:

    (a)   The General Partners may offer to any or all non-defaulting Limited Partners the option to purchase the defaulting Limited Partner's Interests or the option to personally assume his obligations to the Partnership then due,

    (b)   The General Partners may offer to other persons or to themselves the opportunity to purchase the defaulting Limited

Partner's Interests on the term set forth in Article 8 of this Agreement.

(c) The General Partners may sue for and recover from a defaulting Limited Partner the full amount due and payable on any Note or Notes in default, together with all costs and expenses of collection, including attorney's fees.

None of these possible remedies are exclusive and the use of any one or all of them shall not preclude the exercise of any other remedy.

Each Limited Partner hereby agrees that if his Interests are sold at the time of his default, to any person, Limited Partner(s), or General Partner(s), then he will immediately execute in good faith all necessary or appropriate instruments associated with such a transfer. Otherwise, the General Partners may do so pursuant to the irrevocable power of attorney given to them pursuant to the terms of this agreement.

SECTION 8.10   Except as otherwise provided in this Agreement, the General Partners shall have sole and complete discretion in determining the terms and conditions of the offering and sale of Interests, and the General Partners are authorized and directed to do all things which they deem to be necessary, convenient, appropriate or advisable in connection therewith.

ARTICLE 9

DISTRIBUTIONS AND COMPENSATION

SECTION 9.1   The following definitions shall be applicable to the terms set forth below as used in this Article 9 and elsewhere in this Agreement:

"Adjusted Original Capital" shall mean Original Capital, as reduced from time to time by the amount of Distributions on Interests from Net Cash Proceeds.

"Net Cash Proceeds" shall mean the cash proceeds realized by the Partnership upon the sale or refinancing of Partnership properties after (1) payment of all expenses of such refinancing or sale, including real estate commissions, if applicable and (2) the payment of indebtedness relating to the property sold or refinanced.

"Original Capital" shall mean $1,000 per Interest outstanding less the amount of any capital contributions which have not been invested in properties and have been returned to holders of Interests.

SECTION 9.2   The General Partners may set aside as a reserve for contingencies or expend for any Partnership purpose any portion of Net Cash Receipts and/or Net Cash Proceeds which the General Partners in their sole discretion deem reasonably necessary or appropriate for the operation of the Partnership.

SECTION 9.3   As Net Cash Receipts become available for distribution, subject to section 9.2 herein, holders of Interests shall receive distributions in proportion to their Participating Percentages as of the record date for such distributions according to the terms of Article 10 of this Agreement.

SECTION 9.4   Partnership distributions, if any, will be made at least annually to the persons recognized on the books of the Partnership as the holders of Interests.

SECTION 9.5   Except with respect to matters as to which the General Partners are granted discretion hereunder, the opinion of the independent public accountants retained by the Partnership from time to time shall be final and binding with respect to all disputes as to computations and determinations required to be made under this Article 9 (including computations and determinations in connection with any distribution pursuant to Article 18) or under Section 15.4 hereof.

ARTICLE 10
ALLOCATIONS OF PROFITS AND LOSSES

SECTION 10.1   Cash flows and tax losses from Partnership operations and proceeds from sales and refinancing shall be distributed and allocated at least annually, and at the termination of the Partnership, according to the following formula:

(a) Cash flows in excess of those required for Partnership debts and reserves for future project requirements, if realized, will be distributed first to the Limited Partners until they have received an amount equal to eight percent (8%) per annum return (based upon prior net investment), if earned, and the balance, if any, distributed fifty percent (50%) to the General Partners as a supplementary fee for successful management.

(b) Tax losses and credits from Partnership operations and sales shall be allocated ninety-eight percent (98%) to the Limited Partners and two percent (2%) to the General Partners.

(c) Proceeds from refinancings and sales shall be distributed first to the Limited Partners until they have received an amount equal to their cash investment and the balance, if any, distributed fifty percent (50%) to the Limited Partners and fifty percent (50%) to the General Partners.

SECTION 10.2   The liability of each Limited Partner shall be limited to the amount of capital contributions which each Limited Partner is required to make in accordance with the provisions of Article 8 of this Agreement or the amount by which any Limited Partner is required to restore his Capital Account Deficit as provided in Section 10.5. None of the Limited Partners shall have any further personal liability to contribute money to or in respect of the liabilities or obligations of the Partnership, nor shall the Limited Partners be personally liable for any obligations of the Partnership. If any distribution or distributions shall have been made to the Limited Partners at any time when there shall be any unpaid debts, taxes, liabilities or obligations of the Partnership, and if the Partnership shall not have sufficient assets to pay or meet such debts, taxes, liabilities or obligations, then each Limited Partner, and successor to such Limited Partner's Interest, shall be obligated to repay all or part of any such distributions theretofore made to such Limited Partner or successor. Any repayment of distributions or make-up of a Capital Account Deficit provided for pursuant to this Section 10.2 shall be made to the Partnership within 30 days after the General Partners shall have delivered to such Limited Partner written notice requesting such repayment, together with a statement of the aggregate amount and the amount chargeable to such Limited Partner to be repaid and an explanation of the necessity for such repayment.

SECTION 10.3   A capital account shall be maintained for each Partner and shall be increased by the amount of his contribution(s) to the capital of the Partnership, by his distributive share of Net Profits, and by his distributive share of income of the Partnership exempt from tax; and shall be decreased by his distributive share of Net Losses, by the amount of any distributions to him pursuant to Article 10 of this Agreement, and by his share of expenditures of the Partnership not deductible in computing taxable income (allocated according to his interest in the Partnership). Loans to the Partnership by any Partner shall not be considered contributions to the capital of the Partnership. Furthermore, in the event of a termination of the Partnership for tax purposes under Section 708 of the Code, the Capital Accounts of the Partners as calculated above shall govern the constructive liquidation, and the Capital Account of each Partner shall thereafter be determined as set forth above. A Partner shall be liable to the Partnership in damages for the withdrawal of any part of his capital account, except as provided in this Agreement.

SECTION 10.4   All profits and losses shared by the Partners shall be credited or charged, as the case may be, to their Capital Accounts as provided in Section 10.2 herein.

SECTION 10.5 In connection with the distribution of proceeds from the sale or other disposition of all or substantially all of the Partnership properties, other than from operations, in the event that following such distribution any Partner or Partners continue to have a Capital Account Deficit, as calculated under Section 10.2 herein, and any other Partner or Partners have at that time a positive Capital Account, such Partner with a Capital Account Deficit is hereby required to restore the amount of such deficit to the Partnership. This amount shall be distributed to those Partners with positive Capital Accounts or paid to creditors. Such Capital Account Deficit make-up shall be effected in accordance with Section 10.2 herein. This requirement shall not apply if, following such distribution of proceeds, all Partners have Capital Account Deficits or their Capital Accounts are zero.

SECTION 10.6 Notwithstanding the provisions of Section 10.1, in the event of the sale or other disposition of all or substantially all of the Partnership Property and/or the Partnership Investment, income or losses arising therefrom shall be allocated as follows:

(a) Income shall be allocated among the Partners in the following order or priority:
  (i) first, an amount of income equal to the aggregate negative balances in the Capital Accounts of the Partners shall be allocated to the Partners having such negative balances, pro rata, in proportion to such negative balances, until the balance in the Capital Account of each such Partner equals zero, and
  (ii) second, to the Partners in the proportion that they share sale or refinancing proceeds pursuant to Section 10.1.

(b) Losses shall be allocated among the Partners as follows and in the following order of priority:
  (i) first, an amount of losses equal to the aggregate positive balances in the Capital Accounts of the Partners shall be allocated to the Partners having such positive balances, pro rata, in proportion to such positive balances, until the balance in the Capital Account of each such Partner equals zero; and
  (ii) second, any remaining losses shall be allocated among all Partners, pro rata, in proportion to their respective percentages of Partnership Interest.

(c) Notwithstanding the provisions of these subsections 10.6(a) and (b), any depreciation recapture recognized pursuant to I.R.C. Sections 1245 and 1250 or investment tax credit recapture recognized pursuant to I.R.C. Section 47 shall be deemed to have been allocated to the Partners in the same proportions that the depreciation deductions and investment tax credits giving rise to such recapture were allocated among such Partners or their respective predecessors-in-interest.

SECTION 10.7 Richard R. Solem is hereby designated the Tax Matters Partner. Without the consent of the Limited Partners owning a least fifty percent (50%) of the total Percentage of the Limited Partnership Interests, the Tax Matters Partner shall have no right to extend the statute of limitations for assessing or computing any tax liability against the partnership of the amount of any Partnership tax item.

In the event the Tax Matters Partner elects to file a petition for readjustment of any Partnership tax item (in accordance with I.R.C. Section 6226(a)), such petition shall, unless the Limited Partners owning at least fifty percent (50%) of the total percentage of the Limited Partnership Interests agree otherwise, be filed in a court chosen by the Tax Matters Partner upon advice of counsel.

Any reasonable costs incurred by the Tax Matters Partner for retaining accountants and/or attorneys on behalf of the Partnership in connection with any Internal Revenue Service audit of the Partnership shall be expenses of the Partnership. Any accountants and/or lawyers retained by the Partnership in connection with any Internal Revenue Service audit of the Partnership shall be selected by the Tax Matters Partner in his sole discretion.

SECTION 10.8 It is the intent of the parties of this Partnership agreement that all allocations discussed in Article 10 will occur within the bounds of Internal Revenue Code Section 704(G). The General Partners reserve the right to correct any allocations at any time so that all allocations conform to the requirements of Section 704, regardless of any contrary language or terms contained elsewhere in the Partnership Agreement.

ARTICLE 11
BOOKS OF ACCOUNT, RECORDS AND REPORTS

SECTION 11.1 Proper and complete records and books of account shall be kept by the General Partners in which shall be entered fully and accurately all transactions and other matters relative to the Partnership's business as are usually entered into records and books of account maintained by persons engaged in businesses of a like character. The Partnership books and records shall be prepared in accordance with accepted accounting practice, consistently applied, and shall be kept on the cash basis method of accounting, except in circumstances where the General Partners determine that the accrual basis of accounting will be in the best interest of the Partnership. The books and records shall at all times be maintained at the principal office of the Partnership and shall be open to the inspection and examination of the Partners or their duly authorized representatives during reasonable business hours. The Partnership shall furnish a list of names and addresses of and Interests held by all Partners to any Limited Partner who requests such a list in writing for any proper purpose, such cost to be borne by the requesting Limited Partner.

SECTION 11.2 Semesterly, beginning on October 30, 1985, or as soon thereafter as all necessary information can be arranged, the General Partners shall send to each person holding Interests a regular report detailing the status of development, leasing and management activities and Partnership financial status. In this same report shall be included any distribution of cash flow which the General Partners shall elect to make to Limited Partners.

SECTION 11.3 Within ninety days of settlement on the Partnership investment, or as soon thereafter as all necessary information can be arranged, the General Partners shall send to each person holding Interests a special report detailing the results of marketing and rehabilitation studies, progress on leasing and progress on rehabilitation.

SECTION 11.4 Within ninety days of completion of the rehabilitation effort, or as soon thereafter as all necessary information can be arranged, the General Partners shall send to each person holding Interests a special report detailing a breakdown of costs and an update on the results of the Partnership's property leasing effort.

SECTION 11.5 Within 75 days after the end of each fiscal year, or as soon thereafter as all necessary documentation can be arranged, the General Partners shall send to each person who was a holder of Interests at any time during the fiscal year then ended such tax information as shall be necessary for the preparation by such holder of his federal income tax return, state income and other tax returns with regard to jurisdictions in which the Partnership is formed or qualified.

ARTICLE 12
FISCAL YEAR

SECTION 12.1 The fiscal year of the Partnership shall be the calendar year; provided, however, that the General Partners may change the fiscal year at any time after the first fiscal year upon 30 days' written notice to the holders of Interests.

ARTICLE 13
PARTNERSHIP FUNDS

SECTION 13.1   The funds of the Partnership shall be deposited in such bank account or accounts, or invested in such interest-bearing or non-interest-bearing investments, as shall be designated by the General Partners. All withdrawals from any such bank accounts shall be made by the duly authorized agent or agents of the General Partners. Partnership funds shall not be commingled with those of any other person.

ARTICLE 14
STATUS OF LIMITED PARTNERS

SECTION 14.1   The Limited Partners shall not participate in the management or control of the Partnership's business nor shall they transact any business for the Partnership, nor shall they have the power to act for or bind the Partnership, said powers being vested solely and exclusively in the General Partners. The Limited Partners shall have no interest in the properties or assets of the General Partners, or any equity therein, or in any proceeds of any sales thereof by virtue of acquiring or owning Interests of the Partnership.

SECTION 14.2   No Limited Partner shall have any personal liability whatever, whether to the Partnership, to any of the Partners or to the creditors of the Partnership, for the debts of the Partnership.

SECTION 14.3   The death or legal incapacity of a Limited Partner shall not cause a dissolution of the Partnership, but the rights of such Limited Partner to share in the profits and losses of the Partnership, to receive distributions of Partnership funds and to assign a Partnership Interest pursuant to Article 16 hereof shall, on the happening of such an event, devolve on his personal representative, or in the event of the death of one whose Limited Partnership Interest is held in joint tenancy, shall pass to the surviving joint tenant, subject to the terms and conditions of this Agreement, and the Partnership shall continue as a limited partnership. The estate of the deceased Limited Partner or such surviving joint tenant, as the case may be, shall be liable for all of the obligations of the deceased Limited Partner. However, in no event shall such personal representative or surviving joint tenant become a substituted Limited Partner, except in accordance with Article 16 hereof.

SECTION 14.4   Pursuant to the terms of the Maryland Revised Uniform Limited Partnership Act, a majority of interest of the Limited Partners may be empowered to amend certain provisions of the Partnership Agreement without the consent of the General Partners, to dissolve the Partnership without the consent of the General Partners, to consent to the disposal of substantially all of the assets of the partnership and to remove one or all of the General Partners. Removal of any General Partner must be by unanimous written approval.

ARTICLE 15
POWERS, RIGHTS AND DUTIES OF THE GENERAL PARTNERS

SECTION 15.1   The General Partners shall have exclusive authority to manage the operations and affairs of the Partnership and to make all decisions regarding the business of the Partnership. Pursuant to the foregoing, it is understood and agreed that the General Partners shall have all of the rights and powers of general partners as provided in the Maryland Revised Uniform Limited Partnership Act and as otherwise provided by law, and any action taken by the General Partners shall constitute the act of and serve to bind the Partnership. In dealing with the General Partners acting on behalf of the Partnership, no person shall be required to inquire into the authority of the General Partners to bind the Partnership. Persons dealing with the Partnership are entitled to rely conclusively on the power and authority of the General Partners as set forth in this Agreement.

SECTION 15.2   The General Partners are hereby granted the right, power and authority to do on behalf of the Partnership all things which, in their sole judgment, are necessary, proper or desirable to carry out the aforementioned duties and responsibilities, including but not limited to the right, power and authority: to incur all reasonable expenditures; to employ and dismiss from employment any and all employees, agents, independent contractors, real estate managers, brokers, attorneys and accountants; to let or lease all or any portion of any property for any purpose and without limit as to the term thereof, whether or not such term (including renewal terms) shall extend beyond the date of the termination of the Partnership and whether or not the portion so leased is to be occupied by the lessee or, in turn, subleased in whole or in part to others; to create, by grant or otherwise, easements and servitudes; to borrow money and as security therefor to mortgage all or any part of any property; to construct, alter, improve, repair, raze, replace or rebuild any property; to obtain replacements of any mortgage or mortgages related in any way to the property owned by the Partnership, and to prepay in whole or in part, refinance, recost, modify, consolidate or extend any mortgages affecting any such property; to do any and all of the foregoing at such price, rental or amount, for cash, securities or other property and upon such terms as the General Partners deem proper; to place record title to any property in its name or in the name of a nominee or a trustee for the purpose of mortgage financing or any other convenience or benefit of the Partnership and to execute, acknowledge and deliver any and all instruments to effectuate any and all of the foregoing.

SECTION 15.3   The General Partners shall have the right, power and authority to lease, sell, exchange, refinance, resyndicate or grant an option for the sale of all or any portion of the real and personal property of the Partnership, at such rental, price or amount, for cash, securities or other property and upon such other terms as the General Partners in their sole discretion deem proper. The General Partners shall have the right to transfer Partnership capital to a separate partnership, comprised of the same Partners with the same Interests, which Partnership could acquire and lease other properties.

SECTION 15.4   The General Partners shall devote such time to the Partnership business as they, in their sole discretion, shall deem to be necessary to manage and supervise the Partnership business and affairs in an efficient manner; but nothing in this Agreement shall preclude the employment, at the expense of the Partnership, of any agent or third party to manage or provide other services in respect to the Partnership properties subject to the control of the General Partners.

SECTION 15.5   The General Partners and their Affiliates shall not be required to manage the Partnership as their sole and exclusive function and they may have other business interests and may engage in other activities in addition to those relating to the Partnership, including the rendering of advice or services of any kind to other investors and the making or management of other investments.

Neither the Partnership nor any Partner shall have the right to participate in, or be entitled to any interest in other ventures or activities of the General Partners and their Affiliates solely by virtue of this Agreement or the partnership relationship created thereby. The pursuit of such other ventures by the General Partners, even if competitive with the business of the Partnership, shall not be deemed wrongful or improper. Furthermore, neither the Partnership nor any of the Partners shall have any rights to income or profit derived from such independent activities of the General Partners and their Affiliates.

SECTION 15.6   The validity of any transaction, agreement or payment involving the Partnership and any Affiliate of the General Partners otherwise permitted by the terms of this Agreement shall not be affected by reason of the relationship between the General Partners and such Affiliate.

SECTION 15.7   The General Partners shall not be liable, responsible or accountable in damages or otherwise to the Partnership or any Limited Partner for any action taken or failure to act on behalf of the Partnership within the scope of the authority conferred on the General Partners by this Agreement or by law unless such act or omission was performed or omitted fraudulently or in bad faith or constituted negligence or gross negligence.

SECTION 15.8   The Partnership shall indemnify and hold harmless the General Partners, and the agents and employees of each, (herein the "Indemnified Parties") from and against any liability, loss, expense, damage or injury suffered or sustained by them by reason of any acts, omissions or alleged acts or omissions arising out of their activities on behalf of the Partnership or in furtherance of the interests of the Partnership, including but not limited to any judgements, awards, settlements, reasonable attorney's fees and other costs or expenses incurred in connection with the defense of any actual or threatened action, proceeding or claim and including any payments made by the General Partners pursuant to any indemnification agreement, if the acts, omissions or alleged acts or omissions upon which such actual or threatened action, proceeding or claims are based were for a purpose reasonably believed to be in the best interests of the Partnership and were not performed or omitted fraudulently or in bad faith or as a result of intentional wrong doing or gross negligence by such indemnified party and were not in violation of the General Partner's fiduciary obligation to the Partnership.

The Partnership shall not pay for any insurance covering liability of the General Partners, their agents and employees for actions or omissions for which indemnification is not permitted hereunder; provided, however, that nothing herein shall preclude the Partnership from purchasing such types of insurance, including extended coverage liability, casualty, health and workmen's compensation, as would be customary for any person engaged in a similar business, or from naming the General Partners and any of their Affiliates, agents and employees as additional parties insured thereunder.

If, at any time, the Partnership has insufficient funds to furnish indemnification as herein provided, it shall provide such indemnification if and as it generates sufficient funds and prior to any distribution to the Limited Partners of cash flow operations and cash from sales or refinancing.

SECTION 15.9   Notwithstanding the foregoing Paragraph 15.8 of this Agreement, the General Partners shall not be indemnified for any loss or damage incurred by them in connection with any judgement entered in or settlement of any lawsuit involving allegations that federal or state securities laws were violated by the General Partners in connection with the offer or sale of Partnership Interests unless: (1) where the lawsuit is not settled, the General Partners seeking indemnification are successful in defending such lawsuit; and (2) such indemnification is specifically approved by a court of law which shall have been advised as to the current position of the Securities and Exchange Commission regarding indemnification for violations of securities laws.

SECTION 15.10   The General Partners may, in their sole discretion, make or revoke the election referred to in Section 754 of the Internal Revenue code of 1954 or any similar provision enacted in lieu thereof. Each of the Partners will upon request supply the information necessary to properly give effect to such election.

SECTION 15.11   The General Partners will not voluntarily withdraw from the Partnership unless a general partner acceptable to a majority of the holders of Interests is substituted.

SECTION 15.12   In the event of the withdrawal of one of the General Partners, his interest as General Partner in the Partnership up through the date of such withdrawal shall be appraised by two independent appraisers, one selected by the remaining General Partner and one by the withdrawing General Partner. In the event that such two appraisers are unable to agree on the value of the General Partner interest, they shall jointly appoint a third independent appraiser whose determination shall be final and binding. This interest shall first be offered to the remaining General Partner on terms to be agreed upon between the parties. If the remaining General Partner is unable, or unwilling, to purchase such interest, the Partnership shall pay the General Partner for the value of his interest, as so determined by delivery of a promissory note bearing interest at the rate of ten percent (10%) per annum, with interest payable annually and principal payable, if at all, from any cash distribution which the removed General Partner otherwise would have been entitled to receive pursuant to Article 9 of this Agreement. Any amounts received pursuant to this Section 15.17 shall constitute complete and full discharge for all amounts owing to the General Partner on account of his interest in the Partnership.

SECTION 15.13   The Managing General Partner shall be reimbursed for his services as day to day Partnership Manager, payable quarterly, at an annual rate of five thousand five hundred dollars ($5,500), which amount is equivalent to one percent (1%) of the Partnership's total offering proceeds.

In addition, the General Partners shall be entitled to charge the Partnership, and to be reimbursed by it, for any and all costs, overhead, and expenses incurred by them in connection with the Partnership. Those reimbursable items include, but are not limited to, expenses incurred for the Partnership's organization, the sale of Interests therein, the conduct of its business, the performance of their duties as General Partners, and an allocable portion of overhead and expenses incurred by them in connection with Partnership activities.

SECTION 15.14   The General Partners, or any entity affiliated with any General Partner, shall have the right to contract with and perform services for the Partnership. The General Partners hereby agree that if they or any Affiliates do provide services, such services will be provided on terms and at rates no less favorable to the Partnership than those customary for similar services by independent third parties. In addition, as disclosed in the Offering Memorandum, the General Partners and their Affiliates may be paid fees, commissions, or other forms of compensation in connection with any sale, exchange, or refinancing of the subject development or any part thereof.

ARTICLE 16

TRANSFER OF INTERESTS BY LIMITED PARTNERS

SECTION 16.1   A Limited Partnership may assign the whole or any part of his Interests in the Partnership (but only in whole Interests), and such assignment shall confer upon the assignee the right to become a substituted Limited Partner, in the following manner and subject to the following conditions:

(a) An instrument of assignment executed by both the assignor and the assignee of the Interest satisfactory in form to the General Partners shall be delivered to the General Partners.

(b) Each assignment shall be effective as of the date that the General Partners indicate this receipt and approval of the instrument of assignment by affixing their signatures thereon.

(c) No assignment shall be effective if such assignment would, in the opinion of the General Partners, result in the termination of the Partnership for purposes of the then applicable provisions of the Internal Revenue Code of 1954.

(d) No assignment shall be effective if the assignment would, to the knowledge of the General Partners, violate the provisions of any applicable federal or state securities law.

(e) No assignment to a minor or incompetent shall be effective in any respect.

(f) No assignment will be effective unless approved by the General Partners, who, in their sole discretion, have the right to approve or disapprove such assignment for any reason deemed appropriate by them.

SECTION 16.2   Upon effectiveness of an assignment of Interests under Section 16.1, the General Partners shall execute, file and record with the appropriate governmental agencies such documents (including amendments to this Agreement) as are required to accomplish the substitution of the assignee as a substituted Limited Partner. In no event shall the consent of any Limited Partner (other than the assignor) be required to effect such substitution. The Partnership shall treat such person entitled to become a substituted Limited Partner pursuant to the provisions of Section 16.1 as the substituted Limited Partner with respect to the Interests assigned from the date such assignment is effective under Section 16.1, notwithstanding the time consumed in preparing and filing the necessary documents with governmental agencies necessary to effectuate the substitution.

SECTION 16.3   Any person admitted to the Partnership as a substituted Limited Partner shall be subject to and bound by all the provisions of this Agreement as if originally a party to the Agreement.

SECTION 16.4   If any Limited Partner uses a promissory note to purchase part or all of his limited partnership interests, that Limited Partner will be personally liable for payment of interest and principal due under such notes in timely fashion, subject to the terms and conditions of Article 8.

ARTICLE 17

DISSOLUTION OF THE PARTNERSHIP

SECTION 17.1   The dissolution, bankruptcy or withdrawal from the Partnership of a General Partner shall dissolve the Partnership unless within 90 days thereafter the remaining General Partner shall elect to continue the Partnership business. In the event of such election, the Partnership shall not be dissolved, but shall continue with the remaining General Partner as sole General Partner. In the event no such election is made, the Partnership shall be dissolved and terminated in accordance with Article 18 hereof. In the event of the bankruptcy, dissolution or withdrawal of either of the General Partners during the first 10 years of the Partnership or during such time as the Partnership retains its original properties, whichever is shorter, the remaining General Partner will elect to continue the Partnership for such period. In the event of the bankruptcy, dissolution or withdrawal of a General Partner at any time during the life of the Partnership, the remaining General Partner shall promptly give the Limited Partners notice of the occurrence of an event constituting such bankruptcy, dissolution or withdrawal. The sole remaining General Partner shall give the Limited Partners 60 days' prior written notice of his intent to voluntarily withdraw as a General Partner of the Partnership.

SECTION 17.2   The happening of any one of the following events shall work an immediate dissolution of the Partnership:

(a) the bankruptcy of the last remaining General Partner unless, if permitted by law, a substitute General Partner is elected by unanimous vote of the Limited Partners;

(b) the disposition of all interests in real estate of the Partnership, including notes received from sales of real estate; or

(c) the expiration of the term of the Partnership as provided in Article 6 of this Agreement.

SECTION 17.3   For purposes of this Agreement, the "bankruptcy" of a General Partner shall be deemed to have occurred 60 days after the happening of any of the following: (1) the filing of an application by such General Partner for, or a consent to, the appointment of a trustee of his assets, (2) the filing by such General Partner of a voluntary petition in bankruptcy or the filing of a pleading in any court of record admitting in writing his inability to pay his debts as they come due, (3) the making by such General Partner of a general assignment for the benefit of creditors, (4) the filing by such General Partner of an answer admitting the material allegations of, or his consenting to, or defaulting in answering a bankruptcy petition filed against him in any bankruptcy proceedings, or (5) the entry of an order, judgement or decree by any court of competent jurisdiction adjudicating such General Partner bankrupt or appointing a trustee of his assets, and such order, judgement or decree continuing unstayed and in effect for such period of 60 days.

ARTICLE 18

ADDITIONAL PROVISIONS CONCERNING DISSOLUTION OF THE PARTNERSHIP

SECTION 18.1   In the event of the dissolution of the Partnership for any reason, the General Partners (or in the event that the General Partners have become bankrupt or terminated, a liquidator or liquidating committee selected by a majority in interest of the Limited Partners) shall commence to wind up the affairs of the Partnership and to liquidate its investments. The holders of the Interests shall continue to share profits and losses during the period of liquidation in the same proportion as before the dissolution. The General Partners (or such liquidator or liquidating committee) shall have full right and unlimited discretion to determine the time, manner and terms of any sale or sales of Partnership property pursuant to such liquidation having due regard to the activity and condition of the relevant market and general financial and economic conditions.

SECTION 18.2 Following the payment of all debts the liabilities of the Partnership and all expenses of liquidation, and subject to the right of the General Partners (or such liquidator or liquidating committee) to set up such cash reserves as they may deem reasonably necessary for any contingent or unforeseen liabilities or obligations of the Partnership, the proceeds of the liquidation and any other funds of the Partnership shall be distributed in accordance with Article 10 hereof.

SECTION 18.3 Within a reasonable time following the completion of the liquidation of the Partnership's properties, the General Partners shall supply to each of the Partners a statement audited by the Partnership's independent accountants which shall set forth the assets and the liabilities of the Partnership as of the date of complete liquidation, each Interest holder's pro rata portion of distributions pursuant to Article 10, and the amount paid to the General Partners pursuant to Article 10.

SECTION 18.4 Each holder of an Interest shall look solely to the assets of the Partnership for all distributions with respect to the Partnership and his capital contribution thereto and share of profits or losses thereof, and shall have no recourse therefor (upon dissolution or otherwise) against the General Partners or any Limited Partner.

SECTION 18.5 Upon the completion of the liquidation of the Partnership and the distribution of all Partnership funds, the Partnership shall terminate and the General Partners shall have the authority to execute and record a Certificate of Cancellation of the Partnership as well as any and all other documents required to effectuate the dissolution and termination of the Partnership.

ARTICLE 19
NOTICES

SECTION 19.1 All notices and demands required or permitted under this Agreement shall be in writing and may (except in the event of a mail strike) be sent by first class mail, postage prepaid, to the Partners at their addresses as shown from time to time on the records of the Partnership. Any Partner may specify a different address by notifying the General Partners in writing of such different address.

ARTICLE 20

AMENDMENT OF LIMITED PARTNERSHIP AGREEMENT

SECTION 20.1   This Agreement may be amended from time to time by the General Partners without the consent of any of the Limited Partners (1) to add to the representations, duties or obligations of the General Partners or surrender any right or power granted to the General Partners herein, for the benefit of the Limited Partners; (2) to cure any ambiguity, to correct or supplement any provision herein, or to make any other provisions with respect to matters or questions arising under this Agreement which will not be inconsistent with the provisions of this Agreement; and (3) to delete or add any provision of the Agreement required to be so decided or added by the Staff of the Securities and Exchange Commission or other Federal agency or by a State "Blue Sky" commissioner or similar such official, which addition or deletion is deemed by such Commission, agency or official to be for the benefit or protection of the Limited Partners; provided, however, that no amendment shall be adopted pursuant to this Section 20.1 unless the adoption thereof (1) is for the benefit of or not adverse to the interests of the Limited Partners; (2) is consistent with Article 15 hereof; (3) does not alter the interest of the General Partners or holders of Interests in profits or losses or in cash distributions of the Partnership; and (4) does not, in the opinion of counsel for the Partnership, by its terms alter the limited liability of the Limited Partners or the status of the Partnership as a partnership for Federal income tax purposes.

SECTION 20.2   Notwithstanding any other provisions of this Agreement, the General Partners shall have the right to modify Article 10 hereof or any other provision of this Agreement without the consent of the Limited Partners, if in the opinion of counsel and the General Partners, such modification is necessary to: (1) cause the allocations contained in Article 10 to have substantial economic effect in accordance with the most recently proposed or final regulations relating to Section 704 of the Internal Revenue Code, or (2) cause the provisions of this Agreement to comply with any applicable Federal legislation enacted subsequent to the date of this Agreement.

SECTION 20.3   In the event this Agreement shall be amended pursuant to this Article 20, the General Partners shall amend the Certificate of Limited Partnership to reflect such change if it deems such amendment of the Certificate to be necessary or appropriate.

ARTICLE 21
POWER OF ATTORNEY

SECTION 21   The Limited Partners, by their execution hereof, jointly and severally hereby irrevocably constitute and appoint the General Partners, with full power of substitution, their true and lawful attorney-in-fact, in their name, place and stead to make, execute, sign, acknowledge, record and file, on behalf of them and on behalf of the Partnership, the following:

- (a) a Certificate of Limited Partnership and any other certificates or instruments which may be required to be filed by the Partnership or the Partners under the laws of the State of Maryland and other jurisdictions whose laws may be applicable;
- (b) a Certificate of Cancellation of the Partnership and such other instruments or documents as may be deemed necessary or desirable by the General Partners upon the termination of the Partnership business;
- (c) any and all amendments of the instruments described in subsection (a) and (b) above, provided such amendments are either required by law to be filed, or are consistent with this Agreement or have been authorized by the particular Limited Partners; and
- (d) any and all such other instruments as may be deemed necessary or desirable by the General Partners to carry out fully the provisions of this Agreement in accordance with its terms.

The foregoing grant of authority:

- (a) is a Special Power of Attorney coupled with an Interest, is irrevocable and shall survive the death or incapacity of the Limited Partner granting power;
- (b) may be exercised by the General Partners on behalf of each Limited Partner by a facsimile signature or by listing all of the Limited Partners executing any instrument with a single signature as attorney-in-fact for all of them; and
- (c) shall survive the delivery of an assignment by a Limited Partner of the whole or any portion of his interest.

ARTICLE 22
MISCELLANEOUS

SECTION 22.1   The Partners agree that the Partnership properties are not and will not be suitable for partition. Accordingly, each of the Partners hereby irrevocably waives any and all rights that he may have to maintain any action for partition of any of the Partnership property.

SECTION 22.2   This Agreement constitutes the entire agreement among the parties. It supersedes any prior agreement or understandings among them, and it may not be modified or amended in any manner other than as set forth herein.

SECTION 22.3   This Agreement and the rights of the parties hereunder shall be governed by and interpreted in accordance with the laws of the State of Maryland.

SECTION 22.4   Except as herein otherwise specifically provided, this Agreement shall be binding upon and inure to the benefit of the parties and their legal representatives, heirs, administrators, executors, successors and assigns.

SECTION 22.5   Wherever from the context it appears appropriate, each term stated in either the singular or the plural shall include the singular and the plural, and pronouns stated in either the masculine, the feminine or the neuter gender shall include masculine, feminine and neuter.

SECTION 22.6   Captions contained in this Agreement are inserted only as a matter of convenience and in no way define, limit or extend the scope of intent of this Agreement or any provision hereof.

SECTION 22.7   If any provision of this Agreement, or the application of such provision to any person or circumstance, shall be held invalid, the remainder of this Agreement, or the application of such provision to persons or circumstances other than those to which it is held invalid, shall not be affected thereby.

SECTION 22.8   This Agreement may be executed in several counterparts, each of which shall be deemed an original but all of which shall constitute one and the same instrument. In addition, this Agreement may contain more than one counterpart of the signature page and this Agreement may be executed by the affixing of the signature of each of the Partners to one of such counterpart signature pages; all of such counterpart signature pages shall be read as though one, and they shall have the same force and effect as though all of the signers had signed a single signature page.

IN WITNESS WHEREOF, the undersigned have executed this Agreement as of this ____ th day of _____ , 1985.

          INDIVIDUAL GENERAL PARTNER:

          _____

          Richard R. Solem

On this _____ day of _____ , 1985, before me, a Notary Public in _____ , duly commissioned and sworn, personally appeared _____ , known to me to be the individual named in and subscribing to the foregoing AGREEMENT OF LIMITED PARTNERSHIP, and he, being by me duly sworn, did depose and say that he subscribed to such document.

IN WITNESS WHEREOF, I have hereunto set by hand and affixed by official seal the day and year in the certificate first above written.

          _____

(SEAL)   Notary Public

          My Commission Expires: _____

          CORPORATE GENERAL PARTNER:

          _____

          Richard R. Solem
          President
          Equity Fund Profit Sharing
          Associates, Inc. #2

On this _____ day of _____ , 1985, before me, a Notary Public in _____ , duly commissioned and sworn, personally appeared _____ , known to me to be a duly authorized representative of Equity Fund Profit Sharing Associates, Inc., #2, the corporation named in and subscribing to the foregoing AGREEMENT OF LIMITED PARTNERSHIP, and he, being by me duly sworn, did depose and say that he subscribed to such document.

IN WITNESS WHEREOF, I have hereunto set by hand and affixed by official seal the day and year in the certificate first above written.

          _____

(SEAL)   Notary Public

          My Commission Expires: _____

> SAMPLE DOCUMENT:
> PARTNERSHIP AGREEMENT

ORIGINAL LIMITED PARTNER:

_____

Richard R. Solem

On this _____ day of _____ , 1985, before me, a Notary Public in _____ , duly commissioned and sworn, personally appeared _____ , known to me to be the individual named in and subscribing to the foregoing AGREEMENT OF LIMITED PARTNERSHIP, and he, being by me duly sworn, did depose and say that he subscribed to such document.

IN WITNESS WHEREOF, I have hereunto set by hand and affixed by official seal the day and year in the certificate first above written.

_____

Notary Public

(SEAL)

My Commission Expires: _____

> SAMPLE DOCUMENT:
> PARTNERSHIP AGREEMENT

(EXECUTION COPY)

SIGNATURE PAGE

EQUITY FUND/CHILLUM TERRACE LIMITED PARTNERSHIP

_____   _____
DATE   ADDITIONAL LIMITED PARTNER

_____   _____
DATE   WITNESS

SAMPLE DOCUMENT: PARTNERSHIP AGREEMENT

(SPECIMEN COPY)

SIGNATURE PAGE

EQUITY FUND/CHILLUM TERRACE LIMITED PARTNERSHIP

_____   _____
DATE   ADDITIONAL LIMITED PARTNER

_____   _____
DATE   WITNESS

> SAMPLE DOCUMENT:
> PARTNERSHIP AGREEMENT

SCHEDULE A

CAPITAL
CONTRIBUTION

INDIVIDUAL GENERAL PARTNER

    Richard R. Solem.................................$100
    7512 Whittier Boulevard
    Bethesda, Maryland 20817

CORPORATE GENERAL PARTNER

    Equity Fund Profit Sharing Associates, Inc. #2......$100
    7512 Whittier Blvd.
    Bethesda, Maryland 20817

ORIGINAL LIMITED PARTNER:

    Richard R. Solem.................................$100
    7512 Whittier Boulevard
    Bethesda, Maryland 20817

> SAMPLE DOCUMENT:
> PARTNERSHIP AGREEMENT

SCHEDULE B

SECTION 1: All Cash

Limited Partner Minimum Total Capital Contribution of $25,000.

SECTION 2: Promissory Note(s)

Limited Partner Minimum Total Capital Contribution of $25,000:

	Payment	Principal	Interest	Balance
Initial Investment	$6,250.00	$6,250.00	$ -0-	$18,750.00
End Of Year 1	6,148.46	3,758.57	2,389.99	14,991.43
End Of Year 2	6,148.46	4,319.89	1,828.57	10,671.54
End Of Year 3	6,148.46	4,965.03	1,183.43	5,706.51
End Of Year 4	6,148.25	5,706.51	441.95	-0-
Totals	$30,843.84	$25,000.00	$5,843.94	

Principal and interest payments are due quarterly on the 15th day of the month preceding quarter's end, beginning on December 15, 1985. An interest rate of 14 percent is selected for projection purposes only. Investors are advised that these numbers will vary according to a final rate quote from the cooperating lender.

ATTORNEY COMMENT
ON AGREEMENT OF LIMITED PARTNERSHIP

(*Author's Note*: Each of the following comments is keyed to a particular section of the Agreement of Limited Partnership, as indicated by the heading. Please refer back to the limited partnership agreement and to the particular section indicated for a full understanding of the comments.)

Formation of Limited Partnership

The syndicator forms a limited partnership by making himself and his corporation general partners and making himself the sole limited partner. After the partnership units are sold, the new limited partners are brought into the partnership by an amendment to the partnership agreement. You also may wish to have a table of contents preceding the text of the partnership agreement to make it easier to research the agreement.

Definitions

You may wish also to have a "Managing General Partner" in the event there are two individuals involved as general partner and one person will be making the daily operating decisions. Consult with tax counsel as to the possible use of the active management exception to the passive loss rules under the 1986 TRA before using a managing general partner. Other terms that could be defined include capital account, capital contribution, cash flow, affiliate, cash from financings, cash from operations, cash from assets and net income.

Purpose

This partnership is solely for the purpose of acquiring, operating and selling one property. You would have a more general description in a non-specified offering. Also, it is better to put in a longer list of powers and purposes to make it clear that the partnership can engage in all necessary businesses and may take all steps necessary to make the partnership property profitable.

Term

A partnership should have a definite ending date so as to not have the corporate characteristic of unlimited life. Also, a real estate limited partnership rarely functions beyond 15 years with 5 years a common life span for a particular deal. Make sure that you will have plenty of time here, usually in the range of 20-25 years, but not much longer. If need be, you can extend it later by agreement.

Principal Place of Business

State law will probably require you to have an address for the service of process in the state where the property is located. You can typically use your home address. Your choice of office addresses might be influenced by county or state business or gross receipts taxes.

Capital and Contributions

The limitation to a total of 35 investors may be wise if required to comply with a state securities exemption. Under federal Regulation D, you can have 35 investors plus any number of "accredited" investors. You decide through your structuring analysis what you consider is a reasonable minimum investment.

You should have a provision setting forth a remedy in the event of a failure of a partner to make a contribution. I have seen partnerships which fell apart, with one of the partners left with substantial liabilities to meet, where there was no such default provision. NASAA Guidelines discourage heavy penalties for investor defaults and circumscribe the toughness of the terms you can use in investor notes. There can be no confession of judgment provisions.

Distributions and Compensation

As a good practice, you should always plan to have a reserve of funds. Real estate investments are always presenting surprises which call for emergency use of funds.

Allocations of Profits and Losses

In general, I take a more conservative tax approach and never allocate operating income differently from the percentages used to allocate tax losses.

Although a limited partner has limited liability, a limited partner can be required to refund to partnership creditors any repayments to him of his capital contributions. The reasons for the requirement to make up capital account deficits is to conform to IRS regulations on how special allocations are to have substantial economic effects through adjustments to capital accounts.

Books of Account, Records and Reports

If subject to NASAA reporting requirements, you will make a NASAA delineated annual report to limited partners.

Status of Limited Partners

As long as you are not governed by NASAA Guidelines or similar state requirements, you can prevent the limited partners from removing you as general partner by not giving them the power to do so in the partnership agreement. Under the Revised Uniform Limited Partnership Act, limited partners can exercise certain powers by vote without subjecting themselves to general partnership liability.

Powers, Rights and Duties of the General Partners

The general partner should also have the power to borrow funds from the general partner or any limited partner when needed for partnership operations. These funds could be in the form of interest bearing partnership notes and take a priority in distribution before any profits are returned to the limited partners. Without such a provision, it may be necessary to obtain the written consent of all limited partners before the partnership can borrow needed emergency funds from a partner.

This standard of indemnification is similar to NASAA Guidelines. The major difference is that NASAA guidelines do not permit indemnification for regular negligence or for misconduct of the sponsor. This partnership agreement could be interpreted to allow indemnification for negligence and misconduct, which are less grave acts than intentional wrong doing or gross negligence.

It may be wise to include a mechanism to elect a new general partner in the event of the death, disappearance, dissolution, or bankruptcy of a general partner. Otherwise, such events could trigger the winding up of the partnership business at a time when the real estate market was weak or when the property is in the middle of rehabilitation. When using such provisions, you should not make them automatic so as to give the partnership continuity of life, a corporate characteristic. This is done in Section 17 of the agreement.

Transfer of Interests by Limited Partners

Restrictions on transferrability, although often necessary for tax and securities reasons, are generally disfavored by NASAA. NASAA only permits them to the extent necessary to preserve the tax status of the partnership and any restriction must be supported by an opinion of counsel. NASAA prohibits restrictions on assignments.

Additional Provisions Concerning Dissolution of the Partnership

Under the ULPA, a limited partner has a right to receive a return of his contribution from partnership assets after payment of partnership debts. To protect yourself as a general partner, you should make it clear that you have no personal liability to return capital contributions.

Amendment of Limited Partnership Agreement

This amendment paragraph does not state that amendments may be made by simple majority of all partnership units, thereby leaving the implication that you must have unanimous consent to any amendment of the partnership agreement. To avoid this inefficient and cumbersome interpretation, the partnership agreement should say that it can be amended by a vote of a majority in interest of the partners. "A majority in interest" refers to the number of units, not partners, in the partnership. For example if 5 partners have 21 out of 40 total units, these 5, voting together, would have a majority in interest even though there are 20 partners in the partnership. As general partner, you will want an exception to the majority in interest rule by requiring unanimous consent to a removal of a general partner and unanimous consent to a change in general partner's share of profits, losses or income, powers or authority.

Power of Attorney

This power of attorney is necessary to amend the partnership agreement to add the investors as limited partners. Otherwise, you may have to get all limited partners to sign the amendment admitting them as general partners, a very cumbersome practice. It is best to have the limited partners each execute a recordable and notarized separate power of attorney in a form acceptable to the clerk who reviews partnership amendments.

> SAMPLE DOCUMENT:
> PARTNERSHIP AGREEMENT

EXHIBIT B

CERTIFICATE OF LIMITED PARTNERSHIP

CERTIFICATE OF LIMITED PARTNERSHIP
OF
EQUITY FUND/CHILLUM TERRACE LIMITED PARTNERSHIP

This is to certify that the undersigned, have formed a limited partnership, pursuant to the Revised Uniform Limited Partnership Act of the State of Maryland this 30th day of May 1985, per the following terms.

1. The name of the Limited Partnership is EQUITY FUND/CHILLUM TERRACE LIMITED PARTNERSHIP.

2. The business of the Partnership is to invest in, acquire, hold, maintain, operate, improve, develop, sell, exchange, resyndicate, lease, refinance, grant an operation and otherwise use real property and interests therein for profit, and to engage in any and all activities related or incidental thereto.

3. The location of the principal place of business is 7512 Whittier Boulevard, Bethesda, Maryland 20817. The resident agent is Richard Ray Solem whose home address in 7512 Whittier Boulevard, Bethesda, Maryland 20817.

4. The name and place of residence of each of the General and Limited Partners is set forth on Schedule A attached hereto.

5. Each of the General and Limited Partners is contributing in cash the amount set forth opposite his name on Schedule A attached hereto.

6. The General Partners may not assess the Limited Partners for additional capital contributions to the Partnership.

7. Each Limited Partner shall have the right to assign or otherwise dispose of his interest in the Limited Partnership as set forth in the Partnership Agreement and such assignee as may become a substituted limited partner with the consent of the General Partners, subject to the provisions of the Partnership.

8. A Limited Partner has no right to demand the return of his capital contribution, except that, to the extent such funds are available after all debts and liabilities of the Partnership have been paid, the contributions of each Limited Partner are to be returned upon, and not before, dissolution and winding up of the Partnership.

9. The Limited Partners have no right to demand and receive property other than cash in return for their capital contribution.

10. No Limited Partner has priority over any other Limited Partner as to contributions or as to compensation by way of income.

Page 2

SAMPLE DOCUMENT: PARTNERSHIP AGREEMENT

11. The term of the Partnership shall be from May 30, 1985 until December 31, 2020, unless earlier dissolved upon the occurrence of either of the following events:

    a. the disposition of all of the interests in real estate of the Partnership, including notes received from sales of estate; or

    b. the bankruptcy of the General Partners (unless a substitute General Partner is elected).

12. In the event of withdrawal of a General Partner for any reason, the remaining General Partner will have full rights to continue the Partnership according to the terms of the Partnership Agreement and applicable laws of the State of Maryland.

13. The Limited Partners, by their execution hereof, jointly and severally hereby irrevocably constitute and appoint the General Partners, with full power of substitution, their true and lawful attorney-in-fact, in their name, place and stead to make, execute, sign, acknowledge, record and file, on behalf of them and on behalf of the Partnership, the following:

    a. Certificate of Limited Partnership and any other certificates or instruments which may be required to be filed by the Partnership or the Partners under the laws of the State of Maryland and other jurisdiction whose laws may be applicable;

    b. a Certificate of Cancellation of the Partnership and such other instruments or documents as may be deemed necessary or desirable by the General Partners upon the termination of the Partnership business;

    c. any and all amendments of the instruments described in subsection (a) and (b) above, provided such amendments are either required by law to be filed, or are consistent with this Agreement or have been authorized by the particular Limited Partners; and

    d. any and all such other instruments as may be deemed necessary or desirable by the General Partners to carry out fully the provisions of this Agreement in accordance with its terms.

The foregoing grant of authority:

    a. is a Special Power of Attorney coupled with an interest which is irrevocable and shall survive the death or incapacity of the Limited Partner granting the power;

> b. may be exercised by the General Partners on behalf of each Limited Partner by a facsimile signature or by listing all of the Limited Partners executing any instrument with a single signature as attorney-in-fact for all of them; and
>
> c. shall survive the delivery of an assignment by a Limited Partner of the whole or any portion of his interest.

14. The undersigned agree that this Certificate may be executed and sworn in multiple counterparts, each of said counterparts constituting an original and all together one certificate.

INDIVIDUAL GENERAL PARTNER:

_____
Richard R. Solem

On this day of _____ day of _____ 1985, before me, a Notary Public in _____ , duly commissioned and sworn, personally appeared Richard R. Solem, known to me to be the individual named in and subscribing to the foregoing CERTIFICATE OF LIMITED PARTNERSHIP, and he, being by me duly sworn, did depose and say that he subscribed to such document.

IN WITNESS WHEREOF, I have hereunto set by hand and affixed by official seal the day and year in the certificate first above written.

_____
NOTARY PUBLIC

(SEAL)

My Commission Expires: _____

> SAMPLE DOCUMENT:
> PARTNERSHIP AGREEMENT

CORPORATE GENERAL PARTNER:

_____

Richard R. Solem, President
Equity Fund Profit Sharing
Associates, Inc. #2

On this _____ day of _____ 1985, before me, a Notary Public in _____ , duly authorized and sworn, personally appeared Richard R. Solem, known to me to be a duly authorized representative of Equity Fund Profit Sharing Associates, Inc. #2, the Corporation named in and subscribing to the foregoing CERTIFICATE OF LIMITED PARTNERSHIP, and he, being duly sworn, did depose and say that he subscribed to such document.

IN WITNESS WHEREOF, I have hereunto set by hand and affixed by official seal the day and year in the certificate first above written.

(SEAL)

_____
NOTARY PUBLIC

My Commission Expires: _____

ORIGINAL LIMITED PARTNER:

_____
Richard R. Solem

On this _____ day of _____ 1985, before me, a Notary Public in _____ , duly commissioned and sworn, personally appeared Richard R. Solem, known to me to be the individual named in and subscribing to the foregoing CERTIFICATE OF LIMITED PARTNERSHIP, and he, being by me duly sworn, did depose and say that he subscribed to such document.

IN WITNESS WHEREOF, I have hereunto set by hand and affixed by official seal the day and year in the certificate first above written.

(SEAL)

_____
NOTARY PUBLIC

My Commission Expires: _____

> SAMPLE DOCUMENT:
> PARTNERSHIP AGREEMENT

SCHEDULE A

CAPITAL
CONTRIBUTION

INDIVIDUAL GENERAL PARTNER

    Richard R. Solem.................................$100
    7512 Whittier Boulevard
    Bethesda, Maryland 20817

CORPORATE GENERAL PARTNER

    Equity Fund Profit Sharing Associates, Inc. #2......$100
    7512 Whittier Blvd.
    Bethesda, Maryland 20817

ORIGINAL LIMITED PARTNER:

    Richard R. Solem.................................$100
    7512 Whittier Boulevard
    Bethesda, Maryland 20817

SAMPLE DOCUMENT:
SUBSCRIPTION MATERIALS

SUBSCRIPTION AGREEMENT AND MATERIALS

EXHIBIT C

SUBSCRIPTION MATERIALS

EXHIBIT NO.	EXHIBIT TITLE
C-1	Subscription Agreement
C-2	Purchaser Questionnaire
C-3	Purchaser Representative Questionnaire
C-4	Limited Partnership Notes

Page 1

SAMPLE DOCUMENT:
SUBSCRIPTION MATERIALS

EXHIBIT C-1

EQUITY FUND/CHILLUM TERRACE LIMITED PARTNERSHIP
SUBSCRIPTION AGREEMENT

TO: Equity Fund/Chillum Terrace Limited Partnership

1.   Application for Interests

By executing or having executed on my behalf this Subscription Agreement and submitting payment, I hereby make application to become a Limited Partner in the Equity Fund/Chillum Terrace Limited Partnership (the "Partnership"). I agree to purchase _____ Interests (minimum of 25 Interests per Limited Partner) at $1,000 per Interest, for a total payment of $ _____ . By executing this Subscription Agreement, I further:

    a.   acknowledge receipt of a copy of the Offering Memorandum, of which this Subscription Agreement is a part, and understand that the Interests being acquired will be governed by the terms of the Agreement of Limited Partnership set forth as Exhibit A therein, and the Certificate of Limited Partnership set forth as Exhibit B, and that the transferability of the Interests is subject to restrictions as set forth in the Partnership Agreement as well as by the Maryland Securities Act;

    b.   accept and agree to be bound by the Agreement of Limited Partnership as set forth in Exhibit A to the Offering Memorandum, and as it may be amended from time to time by the General Partners and in accordance with applicable State and Federal laws;

    c.   represent that I am of majority age;

    d.   represent that I have adequate means of providing for my current needs and personal contingencies; have no need for liquidity of this investment; and through employment experience, educational level attained, access to advice from qualified advisors, prior experience with similar investments or a combination thereof, (i) understand the risks and possible financial hazards, lack of liquidity, and tax consequences of an investment in the Partnership, and (ii) realize that the Partnership will be directed and managed by the General Partners;

Page 2

    e.   represent that I am able to satisfy the suitability standards as set forth in the Offering Memorandum;

    f.   agree to fully indemnify and hold the Partnership, the General Partners, their affiliates and employees, harmless from any and all claims, actions, and causes of action whatsoever; and

    g.   represent that I am acquiring Interests herein for long-term investment purposes, and that the General Partners have the right, in their sole discretion, to refuse to consent to the assignment of Interests.

2. Payment of Capital Contribution:

I enclose herewith (1) my check in the amount required to be paid at subscription as set forth above, and (2) my executed promissory notes (the "Notes") payable to the Partnership and in the aggregate balance stated.

I agree and understand that I am responsible to: make payments for principal and interest due on the Notes, as billed by the Partnership on a quarterly basis. If principal and interest payments are outstanding for 30 days or more from the date of the Partnership billing, then I will be subject to certain liabilities at the sole option of the General Partners as set forth in the Agreement of Limited Partnership, including among other remedies, acceleration of my Notes, and sale of my entire Partnership Interests to the other Limited Partners. My obligations to pay amounts pursuant to this paragraph shall survive any transfers of my Interests.

I acknowledge that third parties may rely on this Subscription Agreement and the information set forth herein. I further agree not to modify or alter any of the Notes in any way. I hereby waive the right to interpose any defense, set-off or counterclaim of any nature or description in any litigation in which the Partnership or any holder of the Notes shall be an adverse party arising from or pertaining to the Notes or the payment of any portion of the principal thereof or interest thereon.

In addition, I understand that I may tender, at the time of subscription, the entire capital contribution (without reduction) for the number of Interests being purchased, instead of executing promissory notes.

3. Additional Investor Information

The undersigned represents and warrants that the following information and responses are true and correct.

Page 3

a. Name(s) in which Interests are to be registered and manner of ownership: _____

_____

_____

b. Social Security Number(s): _____

_____

_____

c. Place of residence: _____

_____

_____

4. Investor Suitability

   a. I (we) have either (1) a net worth (excluding home furnishings and automobiles) of at least $50,000 and estimate that (without regard to investment in the Partnership) I (we) will have gross income during the current year of at least $50,000, and do not expect a significant decrease in taxable income during the next four succeeding years; or, (2) a net worth (excluding home furnishings and automobiles) of at least $200,000 irrespective of current income.

   b. I (we) represent that in acquiring an Interest in Equity Fund/Chillum Terrace Limited Partnership I am (we are) acquiring such interest for long-term investment purposes.

> SAMPLE DOCUMENT:
> SUBSCRIPTION MATERIALS

NOW THEREFORE, I (we) agree to all of the foregoing and agree to become a Limited Partner in Equity Fund/Chillum Terrace Limited Partnership and to contribute money as set forth above. (Each party whose name will appear on the Partnership records must sign here.)

Signature: _____

Print Name: _____

Signature: _____

Print Name: _____

Signed this _____ day of _____, 198____ ,

at _____

Accepted and agreed to as of this _____ day of _____ , 198___ .

_____ _____
Richard R. Solem   Richard R. Solem, President
Individual General Partner   Equity Fund Profit Sharing
                                      Associates, Inc. #2 Corporate
                                      General Partner

INVESTOR QUALIFICATION FORMS

EQUITY FUND/CHILLUM TERRACE LIMITED PARTNERSHIP

    It is important for the General Partner and any Selling Agent to determine potential investors' qualifications and suitability for the offering being made. Each Purchaser must be able to evaluate the merits and risks of the investment and be able to bear the economic risk. Prior to acceptance of investor funds, the General Partner and the Selling Agent, if any, must determine to their own satisfaction that the Purchaser, or his representative, is capable of evaluating the merits and risks of the prospective investment and that the Purchaser is able to bear the economic risk.

> SAMPLE DOCUMENT:
> SUBSCRIPTION MATERIALS

EXHIBIT C-2

PURCHASER QUESTIONNAIRE

1. Name:
2. Address:

   Principal Residence

   _____
   _____
   _____

   Business

   _____
   _____
   _____

3. Phone Number: Residence (_____) _____

   Business (_____) _____

4. Social Security Number or I.D. Number:

   _____

5. Occupation: _____

   Employer and Position: _____

   _____

6. Previous Investment Activity

   Oil and Gas investments: _____

   Approximate amount: _____

   Real estate investments: _____

> **SAMPLE DOCUMENT: SUBSCRIPTION MATERIALS**

    Approximate amount: _____

    Other investments, please identify:

    _____

    _____

7. Educational Background

    College Degree: _____

    University: _____

    Graduate Degree: _____

    University: _____

    Specialization or Training: _____

8. If a corporation, trust, partnership association or other entity:

    Owners of, or parties in, interest of such entity:

    _____

    _____

    Such entity was incorporated or organized on:

    _____

    and is existing under the laws of the State of _____ .

9. Tax Status:

    Taxable Income for 1984: $ _____

    Projected Taxable Income for 1985: $ _____

    Filing Status for 1984: _____

    Filing Status for 1985: _____

10. Present net worth (exclusive of home, furnishings, and automobiles:

    _____

11. Do you anticipate that your current level of income will change in the foreseeable future and, if so, when, why, and to what level will it change?

    _____

    _____

> SAMPLE DOCUMENT:
> SUBSCRIPTION MATERIALS

12. Do you feel you have sufficient knowledge of real estate investments to evaluate the risks associated with Equity Fund/Chillum Terrace Limited Partnership? _____ If so, why?

   _____

13. A. Do you have a Purchaser Representative to aid you in evaluating your investment? Yes _____ No _____

    B. If so, what is his name and address?

    _____

    _____

14. Have you been furnished a copy of the Offering Memorandum?

    Yes _____ No _____

15. Have you read it? Yes _____ No _____

    If you have a Purchaser Representative, has he read it?

    Yes _____ No _____

16. Have you or your Purchaser Representative (if you have one) been afforded an opportunity to ask questions of a qualified representative of the Partnership regarding this investment, the Partnership, the Partnership's properties, the Partnership's methods of doing business?

    Yes _____ No _____

    If so, have you received satisfactory answers to your questions?

    Yes _____ No _____

17. Are you purchasing these securities for your own account?

    Yes _____ No _____

_____   _____
DATE   PURCHASER

_____   _____
DATE   WITNESS

> SAMPLE DOCUMENT:
> SUBSCRIPTION MATERIALS

EXHIBIT C-3

PURCHASER REPRESENTATIVE QUESTIONNAIRE

Name and Address of Issuer: Equity Fund/Chillum Terrace Limited Partnership
7512 Whittier Boulevard
Bethesda, Maryland 20817

Name and Address of Purchaser: _____
_____
_____

    The undersigned Purchaser Representative hereby acknowledges, represents, and warrants to the General Partner that he has been retained by the above named Purchaser to act as such person's Purchaser Representative and that he qualifies as such under Regulation D under the Securities Act of 1933, as amended (the "Act"). By reason of the knowledge and experience of the undersigned in business and financial matters in general, and investments in the same type of security as the Securities of the Limited Partnership in particular (a summary of all of such experience, education, and business background being attached hereto and incorporated by reference herein), the undersigned is capable of evaluating and has, in fact, evaluated an investment in the Securities on behalf of the above-named prospective purchaser.

    The undersigned further acknowledges that he has received a copy of the Offering Memorandum of the Limited Partnership, and all exhibits thereto setting forth information relating to the General Partner, the Limited Partnership and the terms and conditions of an investment in the securities, as well as any other information he deems necessary or appropriate to evaluate the merits and risks of an investment in the securities. The undersigned further acknowledges that he has had the opportunity to ask questions of, and to receive answers from, representatives of the General Partners concerning the terms and conditions of the offering and the information contained in the Offering Memorandum.

    The undersigned further acknowledges, represents, and warrants that he has disclosed in writing to the above named Purchaser details regarding all material relationships, if any, between him and his affiliates and the General Partner and his affiliates. A copy of such written

SAMPLE DOCUMENT: SUBSCRIPTION MATERIALS

disclosure, if any, is attached hereto and incorporated by reference herein.

To the best of the knowledge of the undersigned, all of the statements made by the above named Purchaser in the foregoing Purchaser Representative Questionnaire are true, complete, and accurate. The undersigned represents and warrants to the General Partner that the information contained in this Purchaser Representative Questionnaire is true, complete, and correct.

Purchaser Representative must, in addition to the above representations, complete the following questionnaire fully, attaching additional sheets if necessary.

1. Name: _____

   Age: _____

   Business Address: _____

   _____

   Business Phone: (_____) _____

2. Present occupation or position, indicating period of such practice or employment and field of professional specialization, if any:

   _____

   _____

3. Describe briefly all positions held during the past 10 years related to business and financial matters:

   _____

   _____

   _____

   _____

4. List any business or professional education, indicating degrees received, if any:

   _____

   _____

   _____

> **SAMPLE DOCUMENT:**
> **SUBSCRIPTION MATERIALS**

5. List any professional licenses or registrations (including bar admissions, accounting certifications, real estate broker-dealer registrations) held by you:

   _____

   _____

6. Have you had prior experience in advising clients with respect to an investment of this type? _____ Yes _____ No

   Explain: _____

   _____

   _____

   _____

7. Describe generally any professional, business, financial or investment experience which would help you to evaluate the merits and risks of this proposed investment:

   _____

   _____

   _____

   _____

8. State how long you have known the Purchaser and in what capacity:

   _____

   _____

9. For purposes of this questionnaire, the term "affiliate" of a person means a person that directly or indirectly through one or more intermediaries, controls, or is controlled by, or is under common control with such person. Except as set forth below, neither I nor any of my affiliates have any material relationship with the General Partner or any of his affiliates, no such material relationship has existed at any time during the previous two years, and no such material relationship is mutually understood to be contemplated:

   _____

   _____

   _____

If a material relationship is disclosed above, indicate the amount of compensation received or to be received as a result of such relationship:

_____

_____

10. Please state whether you are an affiliate, director, officer or other employee of the General Partner or any of his affiliates:

_____

_____

_____

11. In advising the Purchaser in connection with the Purchaser's prospective investment in the Limited Partnership, I will be relying in part on the Purchaser's own expertise in certain areas.

_____ Yes _____ No

Explain: _____

_____

12. In advising the Purchaser in connection with the Purchaser's prospective investment in the Limited Partnership, I will be relying in part on the expertise of an additional representative or representatives.

_____ Yes _____ No

If "Yes," explain and give the name and telephone number of such additional representative or representatives:

_____

_____

_____

> **SAMPLE DOCUMENT:
> SUBSCRIPTION MATERIALS**

In furnishing the above information I acknowledge that the General Partner and others will be relying thereon in determining, among other things, whether there are reasonable grounds to believe that I qualify as a Purchaser Representative under Regulation D, for the purposes of the proposed investment to which this questionnaire relates.

Date: _____ , 19_____

_____
Signature

_____
(Please print name)

> SAMPLE DOCUMENT:
> SUBSCRIPTION MATERIALS

EXHIBIT C-4

LIMITED PARTNERSHIP NOTES

Equity Fund/Chillum Terrace Limited Partnership has made arrangements for loans to qualified persons who wish to purchase their interests on an installment basis. To participate in this program, you must complete the following:

1. Fill out PROMISSORY NOTE AND SECURITY AGREEMENT.
2. Fill out FINANCIAL STATEMENT.
3. Provide TAX FORMS for the last two years.

Page 1   SAMPLE DOCUMENT: SUBSCRIPTION MATERIALS

EXHIBIT C-4-1

PROMISSORY NOTE AND SECURITY AGREEMENT

Date:_____

$1,000.00 Per Interest x _____ (insert number of Interests subscribed for) = $ _____ (cash disbursed).

For value received, the undersigned maker or makers hereof (collectively, the "Maker") jointly and severally promise to pay to the order of Equity Fund/Chillum Terrace Limited Partnership ("Lender") at the principal office of the Lender located at 7910 Woodmont Avenue, Bethesda, Maryland 20814 or at such place as the holder hereof shall direct in writing, the principal sum of $1,000.00 times the number of Interests set forth above (the "Principal Sum") in level principal plus interest installments as follows:

      Payment Date   : Quarterly from 12/15/85 till 09/15/89
      Payment Amount: $61.49 Per Interest x _____ Interests =
      $ _____ .

The loan is four years' term, fully amortizing, 14% interest compounded monthly, with payments made quarterly beginning December 15, 1985 and continuing until maturity (whether by acceleration or otherwise).

All payments pursuant to this Promissory Note and Security Agreement ("Note Agreement") shall be made in lawful money of the United States of America.

Maker has subscribed for one or more limited partnership Interests in Equity Fund/Chillum Terrace Limited Partnership, (the "Partnership"). The Maker authorizes Lender to disburse $1,000.00 per Interest of proceeds under this Note Agreement to the Partnership upon written instruction from the General Partner of the Partnership in connection with closing of the sale of such Interests to the Maker as part of the undersigned's obligation to the Partnership to make capital contributions to the Partnership.

Each of the following events shall constitute an Event of Default hereunder:

    (1)   The Maker fails to make any payment in full when due under this Note Agreement:

    (2)   The Maker makes any materially false representation, statement, certificate, warranty, or other assertion in this Note

Agreement or in the Qualification Questionnaire which has been delivered to Lender and the Partnership together with the delivery of the Note Agreement to the Lender;

(3) The filing of a petition in bankruptcy by or against the maker or the commencement of any proceedings in bankruptcy, or any legislative acts relating to the relief of debtors, with respect to the Maker;

(4) The appointment of a receiver for any property of the Maker; and

(5) Any default by the Maker under the Promissory Note (the "Promissory Note") to the Partnership evidencing the Maker's obligation to make additional capital contributions to the Partnership.

Upon the occurrence of any Event of Default hereunder, all amounts owing under this Note Agreement shall become immediately due and payable without notice, presentation, or demand of any kind, all of which are hereby waived.

Upon the occurrence of an Event of Default, the Lender may demand payment from the Maker for the unpaid principal balance under this Note Agreement, plus accrued interest. Upon the occurrence of an Event of Default, the unpaid principal balance of this Note Agreement shall bear interest at the prime interest rate charged by Sovran Bank, N.A., from time to time plus two percent (2%) per annum or at the highest interest rate permitted by applicable law, whichever is lower. Such interest shall accrue from the date on which an Event of Default shall have occurred until the unpaid principal balance on this Note Agreement has been paid in full.

The Maker shall pay to Lender, on demand, all costs and expenses incurred to collect any indebtedness evidenced hereby, including, without limitation, court costs and reasonable attorneys' fees.

(1) The Maker represents and warrants that except by the terms of this Note Agreement, no part of his Interests in the Partnership ("Pledged Interests") is subject to any prior lien, pledge, or encumbrance.

(2) As security for the prompt payment of this Note Agreement to Lender, the Maker hereby grants to Lender a security interest in the Pledged Interests, and the Maker hereby authorizes Lender to execute and file a UCC Financing Statement with the Maker's signature (or, if permitted by applicable law, without Maker's signature) or any other document or instrument necessary to evidence and perfect

Lender's security interest granted under this agreement. Maker agrees that a carbon, photographic, photostatic, or other reproduction of this Note Agreement or of a financing statement is sufficient as a financing statement. The Maker acknowledges that Lender shall be under no duty with respect to the Pledged Interests, except as may otherwise be required by law.

(3) Upon or after the occurrence of an Event of Default hereunder, in addition to its other remedies, Lender is hereby authorized and empowered to sell, assign, or deliver all or any part of the Pledged Interests at private sale, either for cash or on credit, without assumption of any credit risk, without demand or adjustment (unless otherwise required by law) and without any requirement of notice to the Maker. In the event of such sale, the enforcing party shall deduct all costs and expenses of every kind including interest on the Note Agreement and thereafter, it shall apply the residue of the proceeds of sale to the payment or reduction, either in whole or in part, of the Note Agreement and then to the Partnership for any sums due it from the Maker, returning the surplus, if any, to the Maker or his successors in interests. The Lender shall not incur any liability as a result of any private sale of the Pledged Interests. The Maker hereby waives any claims which may arise by reason of the fact that the price at which the Pledged Interests are sold at private sale is less the price which would have been obtained at a public sale or sales or is less than the amount of this Note Agreement, even if the enforcing party accepts the first offer received and does not offer the Pledged Interests to more than one offeree. Notwithstanding the above, the enforcing party shall not sell, assign, or deliver such Pledged Interests in violation of any federal or state law or regulation.

(4) Upon an Event of Default of the Maker, if Lender either pays any amount or incurs any expenses on behalf of the Maker, such amounts paid or incurred shall be repaid to Lender immediately upon demand, together with interest thereon at the prime interest rate charged by Sovran Bank, N.A., from time to time, plus two percent (2%) per annum, or, if less, the maximum rate of interest permissible by applicable law from the date the same is disbursed until the same is repaid to Lender.

(5) The Maker, for himself and his successors in interest, hereby covenants and agrees that this instrument shall be deemed to impose a claim against his assets and estate with the same force and effect as any other debt.

(6) All notices and other communications hereunder shall be in writing and delivered, telegraphed, or mailed (certified mail, return receipt requested, postage prepaid) to:

(a) if to the Maker;

_____

_____

_____

(b) if to the Lender:

_____

_____

_____

(7) No delay by Lender in exercising any right or remedy hereunder or afforded by law shall operate as a waiver thereof.

(8) If any provision of this Note Agreement is held void or unenforceable under the laws of any place governing its construction or enforcement, this Note Agreement shall not be void or vitiated thereby, but shall be construed to be in force with the same effect as though such provisions were omitted.

(9) The Maker hereby agrees that this Note Agreement shall be deemed to have been executed in the State of Maryland, and the rights and liabilities of the parties hereto shall be determined in accordance with the laws of the State of Maryland. Any action or proceeding of any kind against the maker arising out of or by reason of this Note Agreement may be brought in any state or federal court of competent jurisdiction in any County or City in the State of Maryland in addition to any other court in which such action might properly be brought.

(10) If the Maker shall in any manner acquire any additional Limited Partnership Interests in the Partnership, such

Limited Partnership Interest shall forthwith be included within the meaning of "Pledged Interests" for all purposes.

(11) Without the consent of Lender, the maker will not sell, assign, transfer, or otherwise dispose of, grant any option with repect to, mortgage, pledge (except pursuant hereto) or otherwise encumber any of the Pledged Interests.

(12) Provided that the maker has made all payments under this Note Agreement when due, Lender shall release the maker from this Note Agreement and shall execute and deliver all documents and instruments required for such release.

(13) This Note and any installment payment of principal due hereunder may not be prepaid without the consent of the Lender.

(14) The provisions of this Note Agreement shall insure to the benefit of and be binding upon any successor to the Maker, or any assignee hereof, and shall extend to any holder hereof.

(15) The Maker acknowledges that all of Lender's right, title and interest in and under this Note Agreement, including but not limited to its right to all moneys due or to become due under this Note Agreement, may be assigned to another party by the holder hereof. The obligation to pay said assignee hereunder shall be absolute and unconditional and the rights of said assignee hereunder shall not be subject to any defense, setoff, counterclaim or recoupment which Maker may exert against the Lender or by reason of any indebtedness or liability at any time owing by the Lender to the Maker. This Note Agreement shall in all respects be governed by, construed and enforced in accordance with the laws of the State of Maryland.

(16) Without the consent of the holder hereof, the Maker shall not sell, assign, transfer or otherwise dispose of, grant any option with respect to, mortgage, pledge (except pursuant hereto) or otherwise encumber any of the Pledged Interests.

Print or type name of Maker

Print or type name of Additional Maker

Signature of Maker

Signature of Additional Maker

By: _____
(signature of authorized
officer, trustee, general
partner or other authorized
representative if Maker is
a corporation, trust,
partnership or other entity)

By: _____
(signature of authorized
officer, trustee, general
partner or other authorized
representative if Maker is
a corporation, trust,
partnership or other entity)

_____
(Please print name of person
signing and title, if
applicable.)

_____
(Please print name of person
signing and title, if
applicable.)

Lender: _____

By: _____

Title:_____

> SAMPLE DOCUMENT:
> PROJECT DOCUMENTS

PROJECT DOCUMENTS

EXHIBIT D

PROJECT DOCUMENTS

EXHIBIT NO.	EXHIBIT TITLE
D-1	Purchase Contract
D-2	Property Appraisal Report
D-3	Preliminary Builder Estimate
D-4	Financial Illustrations

Author's Note: The above documents were included as part of the offering for the Equity Fund/Chillum Terrace Limited Partnership. However, because these are not of general interest but are particular to each offering, I have not included the documents themselves in this section.

PARTNERSHIP MANAGEMENT AGREEMENT

EXHIBIT E

PARTNERSHIP MANAGEMENT AGREEMENT

> SAMPLE DOCUMENT:
> PARTNERSHIP MGMT. AGREEMENT

PARTNERSHIP MANAGEMENT AGREEMENT

Equity Fund/Chillum Terrace Limited Partnership hereby agrees to contract with Richard R. Solem, Individual General Partner, to serve as Managing General Partner. Solem's duties as Managing General Partner shall be to arrange for and supervise (1) the feasibility studies, (2) development, (3) leasing, (4) operation, and (5) eventual resale of all Partnership assets at 5904-5926 Riggs Road, Hyattsville, Maryland, and when such tasks are completed to take necessary actions to close the Partnership. In carrying out such duties, Solem will report faithfully to the Limited Partners as per the terms of the Partnership Agreement, and will look to the Corporate General Partner for advice and consent on all matters of a non routine nature.

For his services as Managing General Partner Solem will be paid on an annual fee of $5,500, payable $1,375.00 per quarter beginning December 30, 1985. Checks will be made payable to Equity Fund Investors, Inc., a partnership management company wholly owned by Solem.

Date: _____

                                        Richard R. Solem
                                        Individual General Partner
                                        Equity Fund/Chillum Terrace

Date: _____

                                        Richard R. Solem, President
                                        Equity Fund Profit Sharing
                                            Associates, Inc. #2
                                        Corporate General Partner
                                        Equity Fund/Chillum Terrace

Date: _____

                                        Richard R. Solem
                                        President
                                        Equity Fund Investors, Inc.

SELLING AGREEMENT

EXHIBIT F

SOLICITING DEALER AGREEMENT

> SAMPLE DOCUMENT: SELLING AGREEMENT

SOLICITING DEALER AGREEMENT

EQUITY FUND/CHILLUM TERRACE LIMITED PARTNERSHIP
($750,000 In Limited Partnership Interests)

Dear Sirs:

Equity Fund/Chillum Terrace Limited Partnership (the "Partnership"), and its general partners, Richard R. Solem and Equity Fund Profit Sharing Associates, Inc. (the "General Partners"), propose to offer and sell, through you and other securities dealers (collectively the "Soliciting Dealers"), to selected persons acceptable to the General Partners, upon the terms and subject to the conditions set forth in the enclosed offering memorandum, 750 Limited Partnership Interests in the Partnership (the "Interests") aggregating $750,000.

The Partnership and General Partner hereby confirm their agreements with you as follows:

1. Sale of the Interests

    a. Each person desiring to purchase Interests will be required to complete and execute a combined subscription agreement and limited partnership agreement signature page ("Subscription Agreement") and to return the same to you, together with a check in the full amount of the purchase price of such Interests and any other documents that may be required under the Registration Standards established by the General Partner. You shall ascertain that each Subscription Agreement has been appropriately completed and executed and shall promptly return to subscribers any incorrectly completed subscriptions.

    b. Until subscriptions for the minimum offering of 500 Interests have been received and accepted subscriptions shall be deposited and held in a special escrow account with Suburban Bank, Bethesda, Maryland as Escrow Agent. Until telegram or written notification from the General Partner of the receipt and acceptance of subscriptions for 500 Interests, subscribers' checks shall be made payable to "Suburban Bank — Escrow Agent for Equity Fund/Chillum Terrace, Account No. . . ." You shall transmit the original of the Subscription Agreement to Equity

Fund/Chillum Terrace, 7512 Whittier Boulevard, Bethesda, Maryland 20817, Attention: Subscription Processing; and the yellow copy of the Subscription Agreement, together with the check, to Suburban Bank, ... Wisconsin Avenue, Bethesda, Maryland 20814, not later than the close of business on the next business day following receipt by you. The pink copy of the Subscription Agreement shall be retained for the Registered Representative's files; and the gold copy for the Investor's files. Notwithstanding the foregoing, if your final internal supervisory review is conducted at a different location (the "Final Review Office") your branch offices receiving subscriptions may transmit checks and subscriptions to your Final Review Office not later than the close of business on the next business day following receipt by such branch office, provided that your Final Review Office then transmits such check and appropriate copies of the Subscription Agreement, if properly completed and executed, to the Escrow Agent not later than the close of business on the next business day following receipt thereof by the Final Review Office, and simultaneously transmits the appropriate copies of the Subscription Agreement to Equity Fund/Chillum Terrace Limited Partnership.

 c. Following telegram or notification from the General Partner of the receipt and acceptance of subscriptions for 550 Interests, subscribers' checks shall be made payable to "EQUITY FUND/CHILLUM TERRACE LIMITED PARTNERSHIP." You will transmit all Subscription Agreements and checks properly completed and executed to Equity Fund/Chillum Terrace Limited Partnership as specified above by the close of business on the next business day following receipt by you.

 d. The General Partner, upon receipt of a Subscription Agreement, will determine promptly whether it wishes to accept the proposed purchaser as a limited partner in the Partnership. Should the General Partner determine to reject the tender of the Subscription Agreement, it will promptly notify in writing the prospective purchaser and you and return or direct the Escrow Agent to return, as applicable, the tendered Subscription Agreement and check to the prospective purchaser.

 e. In the event that subscriptions and payments for the minimum subscription of 500 Interests shall not have been received and accepted by the General Partner within three months of the date of this offering this Agreement will terminate and neither the Partnership nor the General Partner shall have any further obligation or liability hereunder to you or any other Soliciting Dealer. In the event of such termination, all subscription payments deposited with Suburban Bank as Escrow Agent shall be returned to the subscribers and no selling commissions will be payable.

2. Compensation

a. For your services in soliciting and obtaining purchasers of the Interests the Partnership agrees to pay you a selling commission of $100 for each Interest sold by the Partnership through your efforts, payable as follows: (1) promptly following the date that the minimum number of subscriptions are paid and accepted, the Partnership will pay the commissions payable with respect to the Interests purchased on or before such date; and (2) commissions will be paid with respect to Interests purchased thereafter, substantially concurrent with the acceptance of the purchaser as a limited partner by the General Partner.

b. You and other Soliciting Dealers may be reimbursed by the Partnership, on terms to be agreed upon, for expenses in connection with due diligence activities; provided, however, that the total amount of such reimbursements shall be made in the sole discretion of the General Partner and in any event shall not exceed 0.5% of the gross proceeds of the offering.

c. You will not be entitled to a selling commission in any case in which it is determined that your solicitation or obtaining of purchasers was made in violation of the securities laws of any state or other jurisdiction.

3. Agreements of the Soliciting Dealer

a. You covenant and agree to comply with the requirements of the Act, the Securities Exchange Act of 1934, the rules and regulations of the Commission, and the Rules of Fair Practice of the National Association of Securities Dealers, Inc. ("NASD"). You confirm that you are a member in good standing of the NASD. You agree that you will not reallow commissions to any other broker/dealer.

b. You will not give any information or make any representation in connection with the offering of the Interests other than those contained in delivery to a prospective purchaser ("Supplemental Literature"). You agree not to deliver the Supplemental Literature to any person unless the Supplemental Literature is accompanied or preceded by the Offering Memorandum. You agree not to publish, circulate or otherwise use any other advertisement or solicitation material. You are not authorized to act as agent of the Partnership or the General Partner in any connection. You agree that, if and when the General Partner supplies you with copies of any supplement to the Offering Memorandum, you will affix such copies of such supplement to copies of the Offering Memorandum already in your possession, and that thereafter you will only distribute Offering Memorandum containing such supplement and that you will accept subscriptions only from investors who have received a copy of the Offering Memorandum containing such supplement. You further agree to comply with all instructions from the General Partner concerning the destruction of out-dated Offering Memorandum and the use of supplemented or amended Offering Memorandum.

c. You agree (1) to solicit purchases of the Interests only in the states and other jurisdictions in which the Blue Sky Memorandum furnished to you indicates that such solicitation can be made and in which you are qualified to so act, (2) to solicit purchases of the Interests only from those persons to whom offers and sales will be made by the Partnership as described in the Offering Memorandum under "Who Should Invest" and in the Subscription Agreement, (3) to inform each purchaser of the applicable suitability standards and the risks of a purchase of Interests and the illiquidity and marketability thereof, and (4) to maintain in your files appropriate records and documents disclosing the basis upon which the determination of suitability was reached for each such purchaser. You shall not execute the purchase of Interests in any discretionary account without specific prior written approval by the purchaser.

d. In arranging transfers of Interests, you shall comply, with respect to the purchase by the transferee, with clauses (2) and (3) of Paragraph (c) hereof and the other suitability requirements of Section 3 of Appendix F, Article III Section 34 of the NASD's Rules of Fair Practice, (Appendix F) to the same extent as if the transferee were an original purchaser of Interests.

e. To the extent that information is provided to you marked "For Broker/Dealer Use Only — Distribution to the Public Prohibited," you covenant and agree not to provide such information to prospective investors.

f. Prior to participating in the offering you shall obtain and review all material information relevant to the offering, but may rely upon results of inquiry conducted by other NASD members, to the extent permitted by Section 4 of Appendix F.

4. Indemnification

a. The Partnership and the General Partner, jointly and severally, agree to indemnify and hold harmless you and each person, if any, who controls you (within the meaning of the Act) against any losses, claims, damages or liabilities, joint or several, to which you or such controlling person may become subject, under the Act or otherwise, insofar as such losses, claims, damages or liabilities (or actions in respect thereof) arise out of or are based upon (1) any untrue statement or alleged untrue statement of a material fact contained (a), in the offering memorandum or any post-effective amendment thereof or (b) in any Supplemental Literature (as defined above) furnished to you for use in selling the Interests, or (c) in any blue sky application or other document executed by the Partnership specifically for that purpose or based upon written information furnished by the Partnership filed in any state or other jurisdiction in order to qualify any or all of the interests under the securities laws thereof (any such application, document or information being hereinafter called a "Blue Sky Application"), or (2) the omission of alleged omission to state in the offering memorandum or any post-effective amendment therefore (or supplement to the Offering Memorandum) or in any Supplemental Literature or in any Blue Sky Application, a material fact required to be stated therein or necessary to make the statements therein not misleading, and will reimburse you or such controlling person for any legal or other expenses reasonably incurred by you in connection with investigating or defending any such loss, claim, damage, liability or action. The foregoing indemnity agreement is subject to the condition that, insofar as it relates to any untrue statement, alleged untrue statement, omission or alleged omission made in the Offering Memorandum but eliminated or remedied in any amendment or supplement thereto, such indemnity agreement shall not inure to your benefit (or to the benefit of any person who controls you) if a copy of the Offering Memorandum (or of the Offering Memorandum as so amended or supplemented) was not sent or given to such person at or prior to the time the subscription of such person was accepted by the General Partner. This indemnity agreement will be in addition to any liability which the Partnership and/or the General Partner may otherwise have. Notwithstanding the foregoing provisions of this paragraph 4,a, the Partnership shall not indemnify any Soliciting Dealer which is an "Affiliate" of the General Partner, as that term is defined in the Limited Partnership Agreement of the Partnership, or any controlling person thereof, for any losses or damages incurred by them in connection with any judgement entered in or settlement of any lawsuit involving allegations that federal or state securities laws were violated by such affiliated Soliciting Dealer or controlling person thereof in connection with the offer or sale of Partnership Interests unless: (1) where the lawsuit is not settled, the affiliated Soliciting Dealer or controlling person thereof seeking indemnification is successful in defending such lawsuit; or (2) such indemnification is specifically approved by a court of law which shall have been advised as to the current position of the Commission, regarding indemnifications for violations of securities laws.

    b. You and each other Soliciting Dealer severally agree to indemnify and hold harmless the Partnership and the General Partner against any losses, claims, damages or liabilities to which the Partnership or the General Partner may become subject, under the Act or otherwise, insofar as such losses, claims, damages or liabilities (or actions in respect thereof) arise out of or are based upon any offers and/or sales of the Interests effected by you other than in accordance with the Offering Memorandum and any supplements thereto, and this Agreement, and will reimburse any legal or other expenses reasonably incurred by the Partnership or the General Partner in connection with investigating or defending any such loss, claim, damages, liability or action. This indemnity agreement will be in addition to any liability which you or such other Soliciting Dealer may otherwise have.

c. You and each other Soliciting Dealer agree to indemnify each of the other Soliciting Dealers to the extent and in the manner each other Soliciting Dealer agrees to indemnify the Partnership and the General Partner in subparagraph (b) of this Paragraph 4.

d. Promptly after receipt by an indemnified party under this Paragraph 4 of notice of the commencement of any action, such indemnified party will, if a claim in respect thereof is to be made against any indemnifying party under this Paragraph 4, notify in writing the indemnifying party of the commencement thereof; and the omission so to notify the indemnifying party will relieve it from any liability under this Paragraph 4 as to the particular item for which indemnification is then being sought, but not from any other liability which it may have to any indemnified party. In case any such action is brought against any indemnified party, and it notifies an indemnifying party of the commencement thereof, the indemnifying party will be entitled to participate therein, and, to the extent that it may wish, jointly with any other indemnifying party, similarly notified, to assume the defense thereof, the indemnifying party to such indemnified party of its election so to assume the defense thereof, the indemnifying party will not be liable to such indemnified party under this Paragraph 4 for any legal or other expenses subsequently incurred by such indemnified party in connection with the defense thereof other than reasonable costs of investigation. Any such indemnifying party shall not be liable to any such indemnified party on account of any settlement of any claim or action effected without the consent of such indemnifying party.

5. Effective Date and Termination

a. This agreement shall become effective on the later to occur of (1) such time as the General Partner shall first release the Interests for sale to the public or (2) your execution and delivery of a counterpart of this Agreement. For the purpose of this Paragraph 5 the Interests shall be deemed to have been released for sale to the public upon notification by the General Partner to the Soliciting Dealers.

b. This Agreement will terminate at the close of business on the date that the General Partner shall notify you that the offering of Interests by the Partnership has terminated.

Any notice referred to above may be given at the addresses specified in Paragraph 7 hereof in writing or by telegraph or telephone, and if by telegraph or telephone, shall be immediately confirmed in writing.

6. Survival of Indemnities, Warranties and Representations

The respective representations, warranties and agreements of the Partnership, the General Partner, you and other Soliciting Dealers contained in this Agreement shall remain operative and in full force and effect, regardless of any termination or cancellation of this Agreement, and shall survive the delivery of and payment for the Interests, and any successor of yours or the General Partner or any such controlling person or any legal representative of any such controlling person, as the case may be, shall be entitled to the benefit of the respective indemnity agreement.

7. Notices

Except as otherwise provided in this Agreement, whenever notice is required by the provisions of this Agreement or otherwise to be given to the Partnership, such notice shall be in writing addressed to Equity Fund/Chillum Terrace Limited Partnership, 7512 Whittier Boulevard, Bethesda, Maryland 20817; and whenever notice is required by the provisions of this Agreement or otherwise to be given to you, such notice shall be in writing addressed to you at such address as you shall have included in the counterpart of this Agreement which you shall have signed and delivered to the General Partner, or at such other address as you shall have furnished in writing to the General Partner for the purpose of such notice.

8. Persons Entitled to Benefit of Agreement

This Agreement is made solely for the benefit of you, the Partnership and the General Partner or controlling persons referred to in Paragraph 4 hereof, and their respective successors and assigns, and no other person shall acquire or have any right by virtue of this Agreement, and the term, "successors and assigns", as used in this Agreement, shall not include any purchaser, as such purchaser, of any of the Interests.

> SAMPLE DOCUMENT:
> SELLING AGREEMENT

9. Not a Separate Entity

Nothing herein contained shall constitute the Soliciting Dealers or any of them, an association, partnership, unincorporated business, or other separate entity.

- - - - - - - - - - - - -

Please confirm your agreement to become one of the Soliciting Dealers under the terms and conditions herein set forth by signing and returning both of the copies of this Agreement at once to Equity Fund/Chillum Terrace Limited Partnership, 7512 Whittier Boulevard, Bethesda, Maryland 20817.

Sincerely,

EQUITY FUND/CHILLUM TERRACE LIMITED PARTNERSHIP
By Richard R. Solem, Managing General Partner

By: _____
          Managing General Partner

Accepted: _____
              Firm (Please type or print)

By: _____
          Signature of Authorized Officer

        Please type or print name of Authorized Officer.

Date of Acceptance: _____

> SAMPLE DOCUMENT:
> SELLING AGREEMENT

SOLICITING DEALER INFORMATION SHEET
(sign and return)

Equity Fund/Chillum Terrace Limited Partnership
7512 Whittier Boulevard
Bethesda, Maryland 20817

Dear Sirs:

    We hereby confirm our acceptance of the terms and conditions of the accompanying Soliciting Dealer Agreement. We hereby acknowledge receipt of the Offering Memorandum, and confirm that in executing this confirmation we have relied upon such Offering Memorandum and the accompanying Sales Literature and upon no other representations whatsoever, written or oral. We confirm that we are registered and are in good standing as a broker or dealer under the laws of all states into which we will direct offers or make sales of Limited Partnership Interests of Equity Fund/Chillum Terrace Limited Partnership. We further confirm that we are a member in good standing of the National Association of Securities Dealers, Inc. and we will comply with the Rules of Fair Practice of that Association.

Firm (Please type or print)
By: _____
Signature of Authorized Officer

(Please type or print name of Authorized Officer)

Date of Confirmation: _____

Employer Identification Number _____

Kindly have checks representing commissions forwarded as follows. (Please type or print.)

Name of Firm: _____

Address: _____
Street

City   State   Zip Code

Telephone Number

Attention: _____

APPENDICES

APPENDIX A: Rules 146, 240 and 242

APPENDIX B: Regulation D and Form D

APPENDIX C: Rule 147

APPENDIX D: Regulation A

APPENDIX E: Form S-11

APPENDIX F: Guide 5

APPENDIX G: Form U-4

APPENDIX H: State Security Administrators

APPENDIX I: Work of the SEC

APPENDIX J: NASAA Guidelines

APPENDIX K: NASD Offices

APPENDIX L: Glossary

APPENDIX M: Survey of NASAA Real Estate Guidelines

APPENDIX A

Rules 146, 240 and 242

§230.146. Transactions By An Issuer Deemed Not To Involve Any Public Offering, As Amended [17 C.F.R. §230.146]

Preliminary Notes

1. The Commission recognizes that no one rule can adequately cover all legitimate private offers and sales of securities. Transactions by an issuer which do not satisfy all of the conditions of this rule shall not raise any presumption that the exemption provided by section 4(2) of the Act is not available for such transactions. Issuers wanting to rely on that exemption may do so by complying with administrative and judicial interpretations in effect at the time of the transactions. Attempted compliance with this rule does not act as an election; the issuer can also claim the availability of section 4(2) outside the rule.

2. Nothing in this rule obviates the need for compliance with any applicable state law relating to the offer and sale of securities.

3. Section 5 of the Act requires that all securities offered by the use of mails or other channels of interstate commerce be registered with the Commission. Congress, however, provided certain exemptions in the Act from such registration provisions where there was no practical need for registration or where the public benefits of registration were too remote. Among these exemptions is that provided by section 4(2) of the Act for transactions by an issuer not involving any public offering. The courts and the Commission have interpreted the section 4(2) exemption to be available for offerings to persons who have access to the same kind of information that registration would provide and who are able to fend for themselves. The indefiniteness of such terms as "public offering," "access" and "fend for themselves" has led to uncertainties with respect to the availability of the section 4(2) exemption. Rule 146 is designed to provide, to the extent feasible, objective standards upon which responsible businessmen may rely in raising capital under claim of the section 4(2) exemption and also to deter reliance on that exemption for offerings of securities to persons who need the protections afforded by the registration process.

In order to obtain the protection of the rule, all its conditions must be satisfied and the issuer claiming the availability of the rule has the burden of establishing, in an appropriate form, that it has satisfied them. The burden of proof applies with respect to each offeree as well as each purchaser. See "Lively v. Hirschfeld," 440 F.2d 631 (10th Cir. 1971). Broadly speaking, the conditions of the rule relate to limitations on the manner of the offering, the nature of the offerees, access to or furnishing of information, the number of purchasers, and limitations on disposition.

The term "offering" is not defined in the rule. The determination as to whether offers, offers to sell, offers for sale, or sales of securities are part of an offering (i.e., are deemed to be "integrated") depends on the particular facts and circumstances. See Securities Act Release No. 4552 (November 6, 1962) (27 FR 11316). All offers, offers to sell, offers for sale, or sales which are part of an offering must meet all of the conditions of Rule 146 for the rule to be available. Release 33-4552 indicates that in determining whether offers and sales should be regarded as a part of a larger offering and thus should be integrated, the following factors should be considered.

(a) Whether the offerings are part of a single plan of financing;

(b) Whether the offerings involve issuance of the same class of security;

(c) Whether the offerings are made at or about the same time;

(d) Whether the same type of consideration is to be received; and

(e) Whether the offerings are made for the same general purpose.

4. Rule 146 relates to transactions exempted from section 5 by Section 4(2) of the Act. It does not provide an exemption from the anti-fraud provisions of the securities laws or the civil liability provisions of section 12(2) of the Act or other provisions of the securities laws, including the Investment Company Act of 1940.

5. Clients of an investment adviser, customers of a broker or dealer, trusts administered by a bank trust department or persons with similar relationships shall be considered to be the "offerees" or "purchasers" for purposes of the rule regardless of the amount of discretion given to the investment adviser, broker or dealer, bank trust department or other person to act on behalf of the client, customer or trust.

6. The rule is available only to the issuer of the securities and is not available to affiliates or other persons for sales of the issuer's securities.

7. Finally, in view of the objectives of the rule and the purposes and policies underlying the Act, the rule is not available to any issuer with respect to any transactions which, although in technical compliance with the rule, are part of a plan or scheme to evade the registration provisions of the Act. In such cases registration pursuant to the Act is required.

(a) <u>Definitions</u>. The following definitions shall apply for purposes of this rule.

(1) <u>Offeree representative</u>. The term "offeree representative" shall mean any person or persons, each of whom the issuer and any person acting on its behalf, after making reasonable inquiry, have reasonable grounds to believe and believe satisfies all of the following conditions:

(i) Is not an affiliate, director, officer or other employee of the issuer, or beneficial owner of 10 percent or more of any class of the equity securities or 10 percent or more of the equity interest in the issuer, except where the offeree is:

(a) Related to such person by blood, marriage or adoption, no more remotely than as first cousin;

(b) Any trust or estate in which such person or any persons related to him as specified in paragraph (a)(1)(i)(a) or (c) of this section collectively have 100 percent of the beneficial interest (excluding contingent interests) or of which any such person serves as trustee, executor, or in any similar capacity; or

(c) Any corporation or other organization in which such person or any persons related to him as specified in paragraph (a)(1)(i)(a) or (b) of this section collectively are the beneficial owners of 100 percent of the equity securities (excluding directors' qualifying shares) or equity interest;

(ii) Has such knowledge and experience in financial and business matters that he, either alone, or together with other offeree representatives or the offeree, is capable of evaluating the merits and risks of the prospective investment;

(iii) Is acknowledged by the offeree, in writing, during the course of the transaction, to be his offeree representative in connection with evaluating the merits and risks of the prospective investment; and

(iv) Discloses to the offeree, in writing, prior to the acknowledgement specified in paragraph (a)(1)(iii) of this section, any material relationship between such person or its affiliates and the issuer or its affiliates, which then exists or is mutually understood to be contemplated or which has existed at any time during the previous two years, and any compensation received or to be received as a result of such relationship.

Note 1: Persons acting ad offeree representatives should consider the applicability of the registration and anti-fraud provisions relating to brokers and dealers under the Securities Exchange Act of 1934 and relating to investment advisers under the Investment Advisers Act of 1940.

Note 2: The acknowledgement required by paragraph (a)(1)-(iii) of this section and the disclosure required by paragraph (a)(i)(iv) of this section must be made with specific reference to each prospective investment. Advance blanket acknowledgement, such as for "all securities transactions" or "all private placements," is not sufficient.

Note 3: Disclosure of any material relationships between the offeree representative or its affiliates and the issuer or its affiliates does not relieve the offeree representative of its obligation to act in the interest of the offeree.

(2) <u>Issuer</u>. The definition of the term "issuer" in section 2(4) of the Act shall apply, provided that notwithstanding that definition, in the case of a proceeding under the Bankruptcy Act, the trustee, receiver, or debtor in possession shall be deemed to be the issuer in an offering for purposes of a plan of reorganization or arrangement, if the securities offered are to be issued pursuant to the plan, whether or not other like securities are offered under the plan in exchange for securities of, or claims against, the debtor.

(3) <u>Affiliate</u>. The term "affiliate" of a person means a person that directly or indirectly through one or more intermediaries, controls, or is controlled by, or is under common control with such person.

(4) <u>Material</u>. The term "material" when used to modify 'relationship" means any relationship that a reasonable investor might consider important in the making of the decision whether to acknowledge a person as his offeree representative.

(b) <u>Conditions to be met</u>. Transactions by an issuer involving the offer, offer to sell, offer for sale or sale of securities of the issuer that are part of an offering that is made in accordance with all the conditions of this rule shall be deemed to be transactions not involving any public offering within the meaning of section 4(2) of the Act.

(1) For purposes of this rule only, an offering shall be deemed not to include offers, offers to sell, offers for sale or sales of securities to the issuer pursuant to the exemptions provided by section 3 or section 4(2) of the Act or pursuant to a registration statement filed under the Act, that take place prior to the six month period immediately preceding or after the six month period immediately following any offers, offers for sale or sales pursuant to this rule, Provided, That there are during neither of said six month periods any offers, offers for sale or sales of securities by or for the issuer of the same or similar class as those offered, offered for sale or sold pursuant to the rule.

(2) Transactions by an issuer which do not satisfy all of the conditions of this rule shall not raise any presumption that the exemption provided by section 4(2) of the Act is not available for such transactions.

Note: In the event that securities of the same or similar class as those offered pursuant to the rule are offered, offered for sale or sold less than six months prior to or subsequent to any offer, offer for sale or sale pursuant to the rule, see Preliminary Note 3 hereof as to which offers, offers to sell, offers for sale or sales may be deemed to be part of the offering.

(c) <u>Limitation of Manner of Offering</u>. Neither the issuer nor any person acting on its behalf shall offer, offer to sell, offer for sale, or sell the securities by means of any form of general solicitation or general advertising, including but not limited to, the following:

(1) Any advertisement, article, notice or other communication published in any newspaper, magazine or similar medium or broadcast over television or radio;

(2) Any seminar or meeting, except that if paragraph (d)(1) of this section is satisfied as to each person invited to or attending such seminar or meeting, and, as to persons qualifying only under paragraph (d)(1)(ii) of this section,

Appendix A: Rules 146, 240 and 242

such persons are accompanied by their offeree representative(s), then such seminar or meeting shall be deemed not to be a form of general solicitation or general advertising; and

(3) Any letter, circular, notice or other written communication, except that if paragraph (d)(1) of this section is satisfied as to each person to whom the communication is directed, such communication shall be deemed not to be a form of general solicitation or general advertising .

(d) <u>Nature of offerees</u>. The issuer and any person acting on its behalf who offer, offer to sell, offer for sale or sell the securities shall have reasonable grounds to believe and shall believe:

(1) Immediately prior to making any offer, either:

(i) That the offeree has such knowledge and experience in financial and business matters that he is capable of evaluating the merits and risks of the prospective investment, or

(ii) That the offeree is a person who is able to bear the economic risk of the investment; and

(2) Immediately prior to making any sale, after making reasonable inquiry, either:

(i) That the offeree has such knowledge and experience in financial and business matters that he is capable of evaluating the merits and risks of the prospective investment, or

(ii) That the offeree and his offeree representative(s) together have such knowledge and experience in financial and business matters that they are capable of evaluating the merits and risks of the prospective investment and that the offeree is able to bear the economic risk of the investment.

(e) <u>Access to or furnishing of information</u>.

Note: Access can only exist by reason of the offeree's position with respect to the issuer. Position means an employment or family relationship or economic bargaining power that enables the offeree to obtain information from the issuer in order to evaluate the merits and risks of the prospective investment.

(1) Either:

(i) Each offeree shall have access during the course of the transaction and prior to the sale to the same kind of information that is specified in Schedule A of the Act, to the extent that the issuer possesses such information or can acquire it without unreasonable effort or expense; or

(ii) Each offeree or his offeree representative(s), or both, shall have been furnished during the course of the transaction and prior to sale, by the issuer or any person acting on its behalf, the same kind of information that is specified in Schedule A of the Act, to the extent that the issuer possesses such information or can acquire it without unreasonable effort or expense. This condition shall be deemed to be satisfied as to an offeree if the offeree or his offeree representative is furnished with information, either in the form of documents actually filed with the Commission or otherwise, as follows:

(a) In the case of an issuer that is subject to the reporting requirements of section 13 or 15(d) of the Securities Exchange Act of 1934:

(1) The information contained in the annual report required to be filed under the Exchange Act or a registration statement on Form S-1 under the Act or on Form 10 under the Exchange Act, whichever filing is the most recent required to be filed, and the information contained in any definitive proxy statement required to be filed pursuant to Section 14 of the Exchange Act and in any reports or documents required to be filed by the issuer pursuant to section 13(a) or 15(d) of the Exchange Act, since the filing of such annual report or registration statement, and

(2) A brief description of the securities being offered, the use of the proceeds from the offering, and any msterial changes in the issuer's affairs which are not disclosed in the documents furnished;

(b) In the case of all other issuers, the information that would be required to be included in a registration statement filed under the Act on the form which the issuer would be entitled to use, <u>Provided</u>, <u>however</u>, That:

(1) The issuer may omit details or employ condensation of information if, under the circumstances, the omitted information is not material or the condensation of information does not render the statements made misleading.

Appendix A: Rules 146, 240 and 242

Note: The issuer would have the burden of proof to show that, under the circumstances, the omitted information is not material and that any condensation does not render the statements made misleading.

(2) If the issuer does not have the audited financial statements required by such form and cannot obtain them without unreasonable effort or expense, such financial statements may be furnished on an unaudited basis, provided that if such unaudited financial statements are not available, and cannot be obtained without unreasonable effort or expense, the financial statements required by Regulation A under the Act may be furnished.

(3) If the financial schedules required by Part II of the registration statement have not been prepared, they need not be furnished.

(c) Notwithstanding paragraph (e)(1)(ii)(a) and (b) of this section exhibits required to be filed with the Commission as part of a registration statement or report need not be furnished to each offeree or offeree representative if the contents of the exhibits are identified and such exhibits are available pursuant to paragraph (e)(2) of this section;

(d) If the aggregate sales price of all securities offered in reliance upon this rule does not exceed $1,500,000, the information requirements of paragraph (e)(1)(ii) may be satisfied by furnishing the disclosure required by schedule I of regulation A under section 3(b) of the Act; and

(2) The issuer shall make available during the course of the transaction and prior to sale, to each offeree or his offeree representative(s) or both, the opportunity to ask questions of, and receive answers from, the issuer or any person acting on its behalf concerning the terms and conditions of the offering and to obtain any additional information, to the extent the issuer possesses such information or can acquire it without unreasonable effort or expense, necessary to verify the accuracy of the information obtained pursuant to paragraph (e)(1) of this section; and

(3) The issuer or any person acting on its behalf shall disclose to each offeree, in writing, prior to sale:

(i) Any material relationship between his offeree representative(s) or its affiliates and the issuer or its affiliates, which then exists or mutually is understood to be contemplated or which has existed at any time during the previous two years, and any compensation received or to be received as a result of such relationship;

(ii) That a purchaser of the securities must bear the economic risk of the investment for an indefinite period of time because the securities have not been registered under the Act and, therefore, cannot be sold unless they are subsequently registered under the Act or an exemption from such registration is available; and

(iii) The limitations on disposition of the securities set forth in paragraph (h)(2)(3) and (4) of this section.

Note: Information need not be provided and opportunity to obtain additional information need not be continued to be provided to any offeree or offeree representative who, during the course of the transaction, indicates that he is not interested in purchasing the securities offered, or to whom the issuer or any person acting on its behalf has determined not to sell the securities.

(f) <u>Business Combinations</u>. (1) The term "business combination" shall mean any transaction of the type specified in Paragraph (a) of Rule 145 under the Act and any transaction involving the acquisition by one issuer, in exchsnge solely for all or a part of its own or its parent's voting stock, of stock of another issuer if, immediately after the acquisition, the acquiring issuer has control or the other issuer (whether or not its had control before the acquisition).

(2) All the conditions of this rule except paragraph (d) and paragraph (h)(4) of this section shall apply to business combinations.

Note: Notwithstanding the absence of a written agreement pursuant to paragraph (h)(4), any securities acquired in an offering pursuant to paragraph (f) are restricted and may not be resold without registration under the Act or an exemption therefrom.

(3) For purposes of paragraph (f) only, the issuer and any person acting on its behalf, after making reasonable inquiry shall have reasonable grounds to believe, and shall believe, at the time that any plan for a business combination is submitted to security holders for their approval, or in the case of an exchange, immediately prior to the sale, that each offeree either alone or with his offeree representative(s) has such knowledge and experience in financial and business matters

that he is or they are capable of evaluating the merits and risks of the prospective investment.

(4) In addition to information required by paragraphs (e) and (f)(2) of this section, the issuer shall provide, in writing, to each offeree at the time the plan is submitted to security holders, or in the case of an exchange, during the course of the transaction and prior to the sale, information about any terms or arrangements of the proposed transaction relating to any security holder that are not identical to those relating to all other security holders.

(g) <u>Number of purchasers</u>. (1) The issuer shall have reasonable grounds to believe, and after making reasonable inquiry, shall believe, that there are no more than thirty-five purchasers of the securities of the issuer from the issuer in any offering pursuant to the Rule.

Note: See paragraph (b)(1) of this section, the note thereto and the Preliminary Notes as to what may or may not constitute an offering pursuant to the rule.

(2) For purposes of computing the number of purchasers for paragraph (g)(1) of this section only:

(i) The following purchasers shall be excluded:

(a) Any relative or spouse of a purchaser and any relative of such spouse, who has the same home as such purchaser; and

(b) Any trust or estate in which a purchsser or any of the persons related to him as specified in paragraph (g)(2)(1)-(a) or (c) of this section collectively have 100 percent of the beneficial interest (excluding contingent interests);

(c) Any corporation or other organization of which a purchaser or any of the persons related to him as specified in paragraph (g)(2)(i)(a) or (b) of this section collectively are the beneficial owners of all the equity securities (excluding directors' qualifying shares) or equity interest; and

(d) Any person who purchases or agrees in writing to purchase for cash in a single payment or installments, securities of the issuer in the aggregate amount of $150,000 or more.

Note: The issuer has to satisfy all the provisions of the rule with respect to all purchasers whether or not they are included in computing the number of purchasers under paragraph (g)(2)(i).

(ii) There shall be counted as one purchaser any corporation, partnership, association, joint stock company, trust or unincorporated organization, except that if such entity was organized for the specific purpose of acquiring the securities offered, each beneficial owner of equity interests or equity securities in such entity shall count as a separate purchaser.

Note: See Preliminary Note 5 as to other persons who are considered to be purchasers.

(h) <u>Limitations on disposition</u>. The issuer and any person acting on its behalf shall exercise reasonable care to assure that the purchasers of the securities in the offering are not underwriters within the meaning of section 2(11) of the Act. Such reasonable care shall include, but not necessarily be limited to, the following:

(1) Making reasonable inquiry to determine if the purchaser is acquiring the securities for his own account or on behalf of other persons;

(2) Placing a legend on the certificate or other document evidencing the securities stating that the securities have not been registered under the Act and setting forth or referring to the restrictions on transferability and sale of the securities;

(3) Issuing stop transfer instructions to the issuer's transfer agent, if any, with respect to the securities, or, if the issuer transfers its own securities, making a notation in the appropriate records of the issuer; and

(4) Obtaining from the purchaser a signed written agreement that the securities will not be sold without registration under the Act or exemption therefrom.

Note: Paragraph (h)(4) of this section does not apply to business combinations as described in paragraph (f) of this section. Notwithstanding the absence of a written agreement, the securities are restricted and may not be resolved without registration under the Act or an exemption therefrom. The issuer for its own protection should consider, however, obtaining such written agreement even in business combinations.

(i) <u>Report of offering</u>. At the time of the first sale of securities in any offering effect in reliance on this rule the issuer shall file three copies of a report on Form 146 with the Commission at the Commission's Regional Office for the region in which the issuer's physical business operations are conducted or proposed to be conducted in the United States. The copies of such report with respect to an issuer having or proposing to have its principal business operations outside the United States shall be filed with the Regional Office for the region in which the offering is primarily conducted or proposed to be conducted. No report need be filed for any offering or offerings in reliance on Rule 146 the proceeds of which total, cumulatively, less than $50,000 during any twelve-month period. If any material change occurs in the facts set forth on the report on Form 146 filed with the Commission, the person who filed the statement shall promptly file with the Commission, at the Regional Office of the Commission in which the original report on Form 146 was filed, three copies of an amendment Form 146 disclosing such change.

(Secs. 4, 19, 203, 209, 48 Stat. 77, 85, 906, 908; sec. 6, 68 Stat. 684; sec. 12, 78 Stat. 580; sec. 308(a)(2), 90 Stat. 57; 15 U.S.C. 77d(2), 77s(a), 77sss(a).)

[39 FR 15266, May 2, 1974, as amended at 40 FR 21710, May 19, 1975; 43 FR 10550, Mar. 14, 1978; 43 FR 41194, Sept. 15, 1978.]

§230.240 Exemption Of Certain Limited Offers And Sales By Closely Held Issuers.

Preliminary Notes

1. Rule 240 relates to transactions exempted only from section 5 of the Act by section 3(b) of the Act. It does not provide an exemption from the anti-fraud provisions of the federal securities laws or from the civil liability provisions of Section 12(2) of the Act or other provisions of the federal securities laws.

2. Nothing in this rule obviates the need for compliance with any applicable state law relating to the offer and sale of securities.

3. Purported reliance on this rule does not act as an election; the issuer can also claim the availability of any other applicable exemption.

4. The rule is available only to the issuer of the securities and is not available to affiliates or other persons for resales of the issuer's securities. The rule provides an exemption only for the transactions in which the securities are offered or sold by the issuer, not for the securities themselves. The securities acquired in a transaction effected in reliance on the rule are unregistered securities and are deemed to have the same status as if they were acquired in a transaction pursuant to section 4(2) of the Act.

5. In view of the objectives of the rule and the purpose and policies underlying the Act, the rule is not available to any issuer with respect to any transactions which, although in technical compliance with the rule, are part of a plan or scheme to evade the registration provisions of the Act. In such cases registration pursuant to the Act is required.

6. While a transaction may be exempt pursuant to Rule 240, the same transaction may be part of a larger issue of securities and may affect the availability of a different exemption for other transactions which are a part of such larger issue. See Securities Act Release No. 4552 (November 6, 1962) (27 FR 11316) concerning the integration of transactions.

(a) <u>Definitions</u>. For purposes of the rule only, the following definitions shall apply.

(1) <u>Securities of the issuer</u>. The term "securities of the issuer" shall include all securities issued by the issuer and by any affiliate of the issuer. Securities issued by partnerships with the same or affiliated general partners and fractional undivided interests in oil or gas rights created by the same or affiliated persons shall be deemed to be included as "securities of the issuer."

(2) <u>Affiliate</u>. The term "affiliate" of or "affiliated" with a person means a person that directly or indirectly through one or more intermediaries, controls, or is controlled by, or is under common control with such person.

(3) <u>Executive officer</u>. The term "executive officer" means the president, secretary, treasurer, any vice president in charge of a principal business function (such as sales, administration or finance) and any other person who performs similar policy-making functions for the issuer.

(4) <u>Promoter</u>. The term "promoter" includes: (i) Any person who, acting alone or in conjunction with one or more persons, directly or indirectly takes the initiative in founding and organizing the business or enterprise of an issuer; or (ii) any person who, in connection with the founding or organizing of the business or enterprise of the issuer, directly or indirectly receives in consideration of services or property 10 percent or more of the proceeds from the sale of any class of securities. However, a person who receives such securities or proceeds either solely as underwriting commissions or solely in consideration of property shall not be deemed a promoter within the meaning of this paragraph if such person does not otherwise take part in founding and organixing the enterprise.

Note: Commissions may not be paid or given for soliciting buyers or in connection with sales of securities pursuant to the rule. See paragraph (d).

(b) <u>Conditions to be met</u>. Transactions by an issuer involving the offer and sale of its securities in accordance with all terms and conditions of this rule shall be exempt only from the provisions of section 5 of the Act pursuant to section 3(b) of the Act; provided, however, that the issuer is not an investment company registered or required to be registered under the Investment Company Act of 1940.

Notes: 1. Each individual transaction effected in reliance on the rule must meet all the terms and conditions of the rule; the availability of the rule will not be affected by other transactions effected in reliance upon the rule but which do not meet all its terms and conditions.

    2. This rule is available only for offers and sales by issuers of their securities. See Preliminary Note 4.

    (c) <u>Limitation on manner of offering</u>. The securities shall not be offered, offered for sale or sold in reliance on this rule by any means of general advertising or general solicitation.

    (d) <u>Prohibition of remuneration paid for solicitation or for sales</u>. No commission or similar remuneration shall be paid or given directly or indirectly for soliciting any prospective buyer or in connection with sales of the securities in reliance on this rule.

    (e) <u>Limitation on aggregate sales price</u>. The aggregate sales price of all sales of securities of the issuer as defined in subparagraph (a)(1) in reliance on this rule or otherwise without registration under the Act within the twelve months preceding the point in time immediately after the last such sale shall not exceed $100,000.

    Notes: 1. The calculation of the aggregate sales price may be illustrated as follows: If an issuer sold $50,000 of its securities on June 1, 1975 in reliance on the rule, and an additional $25,000 on September 1, 1975, the issuer would be permitted to sell only $25,000 more until June 1, 1976 since until that date the issuer must count both prior sales toward the $100,000 limit. However, if the issuer made its third sale on June 1, 1976, the issuer could sell $75,000 of its securities since the June 1, 1975 sale would not be within the preceding twelve months.

    2. If a transaction relying on the rule fails to meet the limitation on the aggregate sales price, it does not affect the availability of the rule for the other transactions considered in applying such limitation. For example, if the issuer in the prior note made its third sale on May 31, 1976 in the amount of $30,000, the rule would not be available for that sale; but the exemption for the prior two sales would be unaffected.

    3. The calculation of the aggregate sales price would include all consideration received for the issuance of securities of the issuer, including cash, services, property, notes, or other consideration.

For purposes of computing the dollar amount of securities sold, the following shall be excluded:

(a) All securities of the issuer registered or exempt from registration under the Act, if such securities were sold prior to the effective date of this rule.

(b) The following securities if sold in reliance on an exemption from registration other than this rule:

(i) Nonconvertible notes or similar evidences of indebtedness (1) representing a purchase money mortgage or (2) issued to a bank, savings institution, trust company, insurance company, investment company registered under the Investment Company Act of 1940, Small Business Investment Company or Minority Enterprise Small Business Investment Company licensed by the U.S. Small Business Administration, or pension or profit sharing trust; or

Note: The exclusion set forth in this subparagraph does not apply to arrangements where nonconvertible notes are issued with warrants or other rights enabling the purchaser to acquire an equity interest in the issuer.

(ii) Securities sold to any promoter, director, executive officer, or full-time employee.

Note: It should be noted that this subparagraph (ii) only provides an exclusion for the computation of the aggregate dollar amount of securities sold; persons named in this subparagraph are not excluded from the computation of the number of beneficial owners in paragraph (f).

(f) <u>Limitation on Number of Beneficial Owners</u>. Both immediately before and immediately after any transaction in reliance on this rule, the issuer shall, after reasonable inquiry, have reasonable grounds to believe, and shall believe, that the securities of the issuer as defined in subparagraph (a)(1) are beneficially owned by 100 or fewer persons. For purposes of this provision:

(1) the following shall be deemed the same and not a separate beneficial owner:

(i) Any relative or spouse of a beneficial owner and any relative of such spouse, who has the same home as such beneficial owner;

(ii) Any trust or estate in which a beneficial owner or any of the persons related to him as specified in subparagraphs (f)(1)(i) or (iii) collectively have 100 percent of the beneficial interest (excluding contingent interests); and

(iii) Any corporation or other organization of which a beneficial owner or any of the persons related to him as specified in subparagraphs (f)(1)(i) or (ii) collectively are the beneficial owners of all of the equity securities (excluding directors' qualifying shares) or equity interests;

(2) There shall be counted as one beneficial owner any corporation or other organization, except that if such entity was organized for the specific purpose of acquiring the securities offered, each beneficial owner of equity interest or equity securities in such entity shall count as a separate beneficial owner; and

(3) There shall be excluded from the computation any owner of only a purchase money mortgage and any bank, savings institution, trust company, insurance company, investment company registered under the Investment Company Act of 1940, Small Business Investment Company or Minority Enterprise Small Business Investment Company licensed by the U.S. Small Business Administration, or pension or profit sharing trust which purchases or holds only nonconvertible notes or similar evidences of indebtedness of the issuer.

Notes: 1. The exclusion set forth in this subparagraph does not apply to arrangements where nonconvertible notes are issued with warrants or other rights enabling the purchaser to acquire an equity interest in the issuer.

2. It should be noted that subparagraph (e)(2)(ii) only provides an exclusion for the computation of the aggregate dollar amount of securities sold; persons named in that subparagraph are not excluded from the computation of the number of beneficial owners.

(g) <u>Limitation on resale</u>. In determining the availability of an exemption from registration for resale of securities acquired in a transaction effected in reliance on this rule, such securities shall be deemed to have the same status as if they had been acquired in a transaction pursuant to section 4(2) of the Act and they cannot be resold without registration under the Act or exemption therefrom. The issuer shall exercise reasonable care to assure that the purchasers of the securities are not underwriters within the meaning of section

2(11) of the Act, which reasonable care shall include, but not necessarily be limited to:

(1) Making reasonable inquiry to determine if the purchaser is acquiring the securities for his own account or on behalf of other persons;

(2) Informing the purchaser of the restrictions on resale; and

(3) Placing a legend on the certificate or other document evidencing the securities stating that the securities have not been registered under the Act and setting forth or referring to the restrictions on transferability and sale of the securities.

(h) *Filing of notice of sales.* (1) During each calendar year, within ten days after the close of the first month in which a sale in reliance on this rule is made, the issuer shall file with the Regional Office of the Commission for the region in which the issuer's principal business operations are conducted three copies of a notice on Form 240 which shall be signed by a duly authorized officer of the issuer or by a person acting in a similar capacity for a noncorporate issuer.

(2) Notwithstanding the foregoing, the exemption provided by this rule will be available for the first $100,000 of the securities of the issuer as defined in paragraph (a)(1) sold by the issuer if the sale of such securities complied with all the conditions of this rule other than the notice requirement. However, the exemption provided by this rule will not be available for any subsequent sale of securities by such issuer unless such issuer files:

(i) Prior to such subsequent sale in reliance on this rule, a notice on Form 240 covering the prior sale of all securities for which reliance on this rule is claimed; and

(ii) A notice on Form 240 covering such subsequent sale.

[40 FR 6487, Feb. 12, 1972]

§230.242 Exemption Of Limited Offers And Sales By Qualified Issuers.

Preliminary Notes

1. Rule 242 relates to transactions exempted from section 5 of the Securities Act of 1933 (the "Act") [15 U.S.C. 77a et seq., as amended] under section 3(b) of the Act. It does not provide an exemption from the anti-fraud provisions of the federal securities laws or from the civil liability provisions of section 12(2) of the Act or other provisions of the federal securities laws.

2. Nothing in this rule obviates the need for compliance with any applicable state law relating to the offer and sale of securities.

3. Reliance on this rule does not act as an election; the issuer can also claim the availability of any other applicable exemption.

4. This rule is available only to the issuer of the securities and is not available to affiliates or other persons for resales of the issuer's securities. The rule provides an exemption only for the transactions in which the securities are offered or sold by the issuer, not for the securities themselves. The securities acquired in a transaction effected in reliance on the rule are unregistered securities and are deemed to have the same status as if they were acquired in a transaction pursuant to section 4(2) of the Act.

5. In view of the objectives of the rule and the purposes and policies underlying the Act, the rule is not available to any issuer with respect to any transactions which, although in technical compliance with the rule, are part of a plan or scheme to evade the registration provisions of the Act. In such cases registration pursuant to the Act is required.

6. Section 5 of the Act requires that all securities offered by the use of mails or other channels of interstate commerce be registered with the Commission. Congress, however, provided certain exemptions from the registration provisions in section 3(a) of the Act and in section 3(b) allowed the Commission to exempt other securities if it finds that registration is not necessary in the public interest and for the protection of investors by reason of the small amount involved or the limited character of the public offering. Rule 242 is

Appendix A: *Rules 146, 240 and 242*

promulgated under section 3(b) and is designed to help certain corporate issuers raise limited amounts of capital from the public by providing objective requirements which are less burdensome than those found in other exemptions from registration under different sections of the Act.

In order to obtain the protection of the rule, all sales which are part of the same issue must meet all of the conditions of the rule. The issuer claiming the availability of the rule has the burden of establishing, in an appropriate forum, that it has satisfied all of the conditions. Broadly speaking, the conditions of the rule relate to limitations on the manner and amount of the issue, the furnishing of information, the number of purchasers, and the filing of notices of sales.

The term "issue" is not defined in section 3(b) or in the rule. Generallly, the determination as to whether separate sales of securities are part of the same issue (i.e., are deemed to be "integrated") depends on the particular facts and circumstances. The following factors should be considered in determining whether separate sales are part of the same issue for purposes of section 3(b) and Rule 242:

(a) Whether the sales are part of a single plan of financing;

(b) Whether the sales involve issuance of the same class of security;

(c) Whether the sales have been made at or about the same time;

(d) Whether the same type of consideration is received; and

(e) Whether the sales sre made for the same general purpose.

These same factors are applicable to a determination of whether offers and sales should be integrated for purposes of the exemption under section 4(2) of the Act. See Securities Act Release No. 4552 (NOvember 6, 1962) (27 FR 11316).

(a) <u>Definitions</u>. For purposes of this rule only:

(1) <u>Accredited person</u>. The term "accredited person" shall mean any person who the issuer and any person acting on its behalf have reasonable grounds to believe and believe, after making reasonable inquiry, comes within any of the following

categories at the time of the sale of the securities of the issuer pursuant to this rule:

(i) Any bank as defined in section 3(a)(2) of the Act whether acting in its individual or fiduciary capacity; insurance company as defined in section 2(13) of the Act; employee benefit plan within the meaning of Title I of the Employee Retirement Income Security Act of 1974 if the investment decision is made by a plan fiduciary, as defined in section 3(21) of such Act, which is either a bank, insurance company or registered investment adviser; investment company registered under the Investment Company Act of 1940; Small Business Investment Company licensed by the U.S. Small Business Administration under section 301(c) or (d) of the Small Business Investment Act of 1958.

(ii) Any person who purchases $100,000 or more of securities of the issuer per issue sold pursuant to this rule for any combination of: (A) Cash, or (B) an obligation to pay which provides for full recourse against the purchaser of the securities and for discharge of the obligation within 60 days of the first issuance of the securities, or (C) the cancellation of any indebtedness owed by the issuer to the purchaser; and

(iii) Any director or executive officer of the issuer of the securities being offered pursuant to this rule.

(2) <u>Affiliate</u>. The term "affiliate" of a person shall mean a person that directly or indirectly, through one or more intermediaries, controls or is controlled by, or is under common control with such person.

(3) <u>Executive officer</u>. The term "executive officer" shall mean the president, secretary, treasurer, any vice president in charge of a principal business function (such as sales, administration, or finance) and any other person who performs similar policy-making functions for the issuer.

(4) <u>Predecessor</u>. A "predecessor" of an issuer shall mean: (i) A person the major portion of whose asserts have been acquired directly or indirectly by the issuer or (ii) a person from which the issuer acquired directly or indirectly the major portion of its assets.

(5) <u>Qualified issuer</u>. The term "qualified issuer" shall mean any corporation which is incorporated under the laws of the United States or Canada or any State or Province thereof, and has or proposes to have its principal business operations

Appendix A: Rules 146, 240 and 242

in the United States, if a domestic corporation, or in Canada or the United States if a Canadian corporation, and which:

(i) Is not an investment company;

(ii) Does not engage or intend to engage in oil and gas related operations which exceed the criteria for exemption specified in §210.4-10(k) of Regulation S-X.

(iii) Does not engage or intend to engage in significant mining operations;

Note: For purposes of this rule, the criteria for exemption specified in §210.3-18(k) of Regulation S-X for oil and gas operations shall be considered by analogy as an appropriate test for determining the significance of mining operations.

(iv) Is not a majority-owned subsidiary of an issuer which does not meet the qualifications for use of this rule as specified in paragraph (a)(5)(i), (ii), or (iii) of this rule.

(v) Is not an issuer described in §230.252(c), (d), (e), or (f) under the Act; Provided, however, That for purposes of this section only:

(A) The term "filing of the notification required by §230.255" as used in §230.252(c), (d), (e) or (f) under the act shall mean the first sale of securities in any issue in reliance on this section; and

(B) The term "underwriter" as used in §230.252(d) or (e) under the act shall mean a person which has been or will be paid or given directly or indirectly any commission or similar remuneration for solicitation of purchasers in connection with sales of securities in any issue offered in reliance on this section;

Provided, further, That paragraph (a)(5)(v) of this section shall not apply to any issuer if the Commission determines, upon a showing of good cause, that it is not necessary under the circumstances that the exemption under this section be denied. Any such determination by the Commission shall be without prejudice to any other action by the Commission in any other proceeding or matter with respect to the issuer or any other person.

(6) <u>Securities of the issuer</u>. The term "securities of the issuer" shall mean:

(i) All securities issued by a qualified issuer;

(ii) All securities issued by any predecessor of a qualified issuer; and

(iii) All securities issued by any affiliate of a qualified issuer which was organized or became such an affiliate within the preceding twelve months.

(b) <u>Conditions to be met</u>. All sales which are part of the same issue of securities offered or sold by a qualified issuer in compliance with all the conditions in paragraphs (c) through (h) of this rule shall be exempt from registration under section 5 of the Act pursuant to section 3(b) of the Act. For purposes of identifying which securities constitute a single issue, sales of securities occurring more than six months prior to the commencement of an issue of securities pursuant to this rule and sales of securities and offers in connection therewith occurring at any time after six months from the completion date of the issue pursuant to this rule, shall not be considered part of the same issue so long as there are during neither of said six-month periods any offers or sales of securities by or for the issuer of the same or similar class as those offered or sold pursuant to this rule, other than offers or sales of securities pursuant to any section 3(b) exemption from registration or any employee plan as defined in paragraph (d)(1) of Rule 16n-3 under the Securities Exchange Act of 1934 which meets the conditions in paragraphs (a) through (c) of that rule.

Note: In the event that the issuer offers or sells securities as to which the safe harbor described in paragraph (b) of this rule is unavailable, see Preliminary Note 6 hereof as to which offers or sales may be deemed to be part of the same issue.

(c) <u>Limitation on aggregate offering price of each issue</u>. The aggregate offering price of an issue of securities of the issuer by a qualified issuer shall not exceed $2,000,000, less the aggregate gross proceeds from all securities sold pursuant to an exemption from registration provided by Regulation A pursuant to any employee plan as defined in paragraph (d)(1) of Rule 16b-3 under the Securities Exchange Act of 1934 which meets the conditions of paragraphs (a) through (c) of that rule) six months prior to the commencement and during the offering of the issue of securities pursuant to this rule.

Note 1: The calculation of the aggregate offering price may be illustrated as follows: If an issuer sold $500,000 of its securities on June 1, 1980 in reliance on this rule, $50,000 on September 1, 1980 pursuant to Rule 240, and an additional $200,000 on October 1, 1980 pursuant to Regulation A, the issuer would be permitted to sell only $1,250,000 more until December 1, 1980, since until that date the issuer must count all three prior sales toward the present section 3(b) $2,000,000 limit. However, if the issuer made its fourth sale under this rule on December 1, 1980, the issuer could sell $1,750,000 of its securities, since the June 1, 1980 sale would not be within the preceding six months.

Note 2: The calculation of the aggregate offering price includes all consideration received by the issuer for the issuance of securities of the issuer, including cash, services, property, notes, cancellation of debt, or other consideration. Where securities which have no determinable market value are offered in exchange for outstanding securities, claims, property, or services, the aggregate offering price thereof shall be computed at the public offering price of securities of the same class for cash, or if no cash offering is to be made, then upon the basis of the value of the securities, claims, property, or services to be received in exchange, as established by bona fide sales made within a reasonable time, or in the absence of such sales, upon the basis of the fair value of the securities, claims, property, or services to be received in exchange as determined by some accepted standard.

(d) <u>Limitation on manner of offering</u>. Neither the issuer nor any person acting on its behalf shall offer or sell securities pursuant to this rule by means of any form of general solicitation or general advertising, including, but not limited to, any advertisement, article, notice or other communication published in any newspaper, magazine or similar medium or broadcast over the television or radio.

(e) <u>Limitation on number of purchasers</u>. (1) The issuer shall have reasonable grounds to believe, and after making reasonable inquiry, shall believe, that there are no more than 35 purchasers of each issue of the securities of the issuer from the issuer pursuant to this rule.

Note: See paragraph (b) of this rule and Preliminary Note 6 as to what may or may not constitute an issue pursuant to this rule.

(2) For purposes of computing the number of purchasers for paragraph (e) only, the following purchasers shall be excluded:

(i) Any relative, spouse, or relative of the spouse of a purchaser who has the same home as the purchaser;

(ii) Any trust or estate in which a purchaser or any of the persons related to him as specified in paragraph (e)(2)(i) or (iii) of this section collectively have 100 percent of the beneficial interest (excluding contingent interests);

(iii) Any corporation or other organization of which a purchaser or any of the persons related to him as specified in paragraph (e)(2)(i) or (ii) of this section collectively are the beneficial owners of all the equity securities (excluding directors' qualifying shares) or equity interests; and

(iv) Any accredited person as defined in paragraph (a)(1).

Note: The issuer must satisfy all the other provisions of the rule with respect to all purchasers whether or not they are included in computing the number of purchasers under this paragraph.

(3) There shall be counted as one purchaser any corporation or other organization, except that if such entity was organized for the specific purpose of acquiring the securities offered, each beneficial owner of equity interests or equity securities in such entity shall count as a separate purchaser for all provisions of this rule.

(f) _Furnishing of information_. (1) If the issuer sells an issue of securities pursuant to this rule only to accredited persons, the rule does not specify what information must be furnished to such persons. In any offering of an issue of securities involving only non-accredited persons, or both accredited and non-accredited persons, the issuer shall furnish the following information to all purchasers in writing during the course of such offering and prior to sale:

(i) The same kind of information as that specified in Part I of Form S-18, to the extent material to an understanding of the issuer, its business, and the securities being offered; _Provided_, _however_, That only the financial statements for the issuer's most recent fiscal year must be certified by an independent public accountant or a certified public accountant.

(ii) Such further material information, if any, as may be necessary to make the required information, in the light of the circumstances under which it is furnished, not misleading.

(iii) An issuer that is subject to the reporting requirements of section 13 or 15(d) of the Securities Exchange Act of 1934 may satisfy the informational requirements of paragraph (f)(1)(i) by furnishing purchasers with the information contained in its most recent annual report, definitive proxy statement, and any other reports or documents required to be filed by the issuer pursuant to section 13(a) or 15(d) of the Securities Exchange Act since the filing of such annual report, except that the information required by items 1, 2, 3, and 14 of Part I of Form S-18, if applicable, shall also be provided.

(2) The issuer also shall make available to each offeree, during the course of the transaction and prior to sale, the opportunity to ask questions of, and receive answers from, the issuer or any person acting on its behalf concerning the terms and conditions of the offering and to obtain any additional information, to the extent that the issuer possesses such information or can acquire it without unreasonable effort or expense, necessary to verify the accuracy of the information obtained pursuant to paragraph (f)(1).

(3) At a reasonable time prior to the purchase of securities by any non-accredited person in a transaction pursuant to this rule, the issuer also shall furnish such purchaser a brief description in writing of any written information obtained from the issuer in connection with the offering by any accredited person prior to the date of purchase by the non-accredited person. The issuer shall furnish any portion or all of such information to such non-accredited person upon his written request if made prior to the date of his purchase.

(g) <u>Limitation on resale</u>. In determining the availability of an exemption from registration for resale of securities acquired in a transaction pursuant to this rule, such securities shall be deemed to have the same status as if they had been acquired in a transaction pursuant to section 4(2) of the Act and cannot be resold without registration under the Act or exemption therefrom. The issuer shall exercise reasonable care to assure that the purchasers of the securities are not underwriters within the meaning of section 2(11) of the Act, which reasonable care shall include, but not necessarily be limited to:

(1) Making reasonable inquiry to determine if the purchaser is acquiring the securities for his own account or on behalf of other persons;

(2) Informing the purchaser of the restrictions on resale; and

(3) Placing a legend on the certificate or other document evidencing the securities stating that the securities have not been registered under the Act and setting forth or referring to the restrictions on transferability and sale of the securities.

(h) <u>Filing of notice of sales</u>. (1) The issuer shall file with the Commission five copies of a notice on Form 242 [17 CFR 239.242]:

(i) No later than 10 days after the completion date of the offering of such issue: <u>Provided</u>, <u>however</u>, That only one notice need be filed for purposes of paragraphs (h)(1)(i) and (ii) under this rule if the offering of the issue is completed within the 10-day period described in paragraph (h)(1)(i) and the notice is filed no later than at the conclusion of that period but subsequent to the completion of the offering of the issue; and

(iii) Every six months after the first sale of securities in the issue is made in reliance on this rule, unless the final notice required by paragraph (h)(1)(ii) of this rule has been filed.

(2) Every notice on Form 242 shall be signed by a duly authorized officer of the issuer and shall contain an undertaking by the issuer to furnish to the Commission, upon the written request of its staff, the information furnished by the issuer to any non-accredited person pursuant to paragraph (f)(1) of this rule.

(3) If more than one notice is required to be filed pursuant to paragraph (h)(1) of this rule as to any issue of securities offered in reliance thereon, notices other than the original notice need only report the information required by Part C and any material change in the facts from those set forth in Parts A through B of the original notice.

(4) A notice on Form 242 shall be deemed to be filed with the Commission for purposes of paragraph (h)(1) of this rule:

(i) As of the date on which it is received at the Commission's principal office in Washington, D.C., or

(ii) As of the date on which the notice is mailed by means of United States registered or certified mail to the Commission's Office of Small Business Policy, Division of Corporation Finance, at the Commission's principal office in Washington,

D.C., if the notice is delivered to such office after the date on which it is required to be filed.

(Secs. 3(b), 4(1), 19(a), 48 Stat. 75, 77, 85; sec. 209, 48 Stat. 908; 59 Stat. 167; sec. 6, 68 Stat. 684; sec. 12, 78 Stat. 580; 84 Stat. 1480; sec. 308(a)(1), (2), (3), 90 Stat. 56, 57; sec. 18, 92 Stat. 275; sec. 2, 92 Stat. 962; 15 U.S.C. 77c(b), 77d(1), 77s(a))

[45 FR 6367, Jan. 28, 1980, as amended at 45 FR 71776, Oct. 30, 1980; 46 FR 13508, Feb. 23, 1981; 46 FR 18532, Mar. 25, 1981; 46 FR 18950, Mar. 27, 1981]

APPENDIX B

Regulation D and Form D

Regulation D - Rules Governing the Limited Offer
and Sale of Securities Under the Securities Act of 1933

Preliminary Notes

1. The following rules relate to transactions exempted from the registration requirements of section 5 of the Securities Act of 1933 (the "Act") [15 U.S.C. 77a et seq., as amended]. Such transactions are not exempt from the antifraud, civil liability, or other provisions of the federal securities laws. Issuers are reminded of their obligation to provide such further material information, if any, as may be necessary to make the information required under this regulation, in light of the circumstances under which it is furnished, not misleading.

2. Nothing in these rules obviates the need to comply with any applicable state law relating to the offer and sale of securities. Regulation D is intended to be a basic element in a uniform system of federal-state limited offering exemptions consistent with the provisions of sections 18 and 19(c) of the Act. In those states that have adopted Regulation D, or any version of Regulation D, special attention should be directed to the applicable state laws and regulations, including those relating to registration of persons who receive remuneration in connection with the offer and sale of securities, to disqualification of issuers and other persons associated with offerings based on state administrative orders or judgments, and to requirements for filings of notices of sales.

3. Attempted compliance with any rule in Regulation D does not act as an exclusive election; the issuer can also claim the availability of any other applicable exemption. For instance, an issuer's failure to satisfy all the terms and conditions of Rule 506 shall not raise any presumption that the exemption provided by section 4(2) of the Act is not available.

4. These rules are available only to the issuer of the securities and not to any affiliate of that issuer or to any other person for resales of the issuer's securities. The rules provide an exemption only for the transactions in which the securities are offered or sold by the issuer, not for the securities themselves.

Appendix B: Regulation D and Form D

5. These rules may be used for business combinations that involve sales by virtue of Rule 145(a) (17 CFR 230.145(a)) or otherwise.

6. In view of the objectives of these rules and the policies underlying the Act, Regulation D is not available to any issuer for any transaction or chain of transactions that, although in technical compliance with these rules, is part of a plan or scheme to evade the registration provisions of the Act. In such cases, registration under the Act is required.

[As adopted in Release No. 33-6389, March 8, 1982, 47 F.R. 11251.]

¶ 10,851 Definitions and Terms Used in Regulation D

Reg. §230.501. As used in Regulation D, the following terms shall have the meaning indicated:

(a) <u>Accredited investor</u>. "Accredited investor" shall mean any person who comes within any of the following categories, or who the issuer reasonably believes comes within any of the following categories, at the time of the sale of the securities to that person:

(1) Any bank as defined in section 3(a)(2) of the Act whether acting in its individual or fiduciary capacity; insurance company as defined in section 2(13) of the Act; investment company registered under the Investment Company Act of 1940 or a business development company as defined in section 2(a)(48) of that Act; Small Business Investment Company licensed by the U.S. Small Business Administration under section 301(c) or (d) of the Small Business Investment Act of 1958; employee benefit plan within the meaning of Title I of the Employee Retirement Income Security Act of 1974, if the investment decision is made by a plan fiduciary, as defined in section 3(21) of such Act, which is either a bank, insurance company, or registered investment adviser, or if the employee benefit plan has total assets in excess of $5,000,000;

(2) Any private business development company as defined in section 202(a)(22) of the Investment Advisers Act of 1940;

(3) Any organization described in Section 501(c)(3) of the Internal Revenue Code with total assets in excess of $5,000,000;

(4) Any director, executive officer, or general partner of the issuer of the securities being offered or sold, or any director, executive officer, or general partner of a general partner of that issuer;

(5) Any person who purchases at least $150,000 of the securities being offered, where the purchaser's total purchase price does not exceed 20 percent of the purchaser's net worth at the time of sale, or joint net worth with that person's spouse, for one or any combnation of the following: (i) cash, (ii) securities for which market quotations are readily available, (iii) an unconditional obligation to pay cash or securities for which market quotations are readily available which obligation is to be discharged within five years of the sale

Appendix B: Regulation D and Form D

of the securities to the purchaser, or (iv) the cancellation of any indebtedness owed by the issuer to the purchaser;

(6) Any natural person whose individual net worth, or joint net worth with that person's spouse, at the time of his purchase exceeds $1,000,000;

(7) Any natural person who had an individual income in excess of $200,000 in each of the two most recent years and who reasonably expects an income in excess of $200,000 in the current year; and

(8) Any equity in which all of the equity owners are accredited investors under paragraph (a)(1), (2), (3), (4), (6), or (7) of this §230.501.

(b) Affiliate. An "affiliate" of, or person "affiliated" with a specified person shall mean a person that directly, or indirectly through one or more intermediaries, controls or is controlled by, or is under common control with, the person specified.

(c) Aggregate offering price. "Aggregate offering price" shall mean the sum of all cash, services, property, notes, cancellation of debt, or other consideration received by an issuer for issuance of its securities. Where securities are being offered for both cash and non-cash consideration, the aggregate offering price shall be based on the price at which the securities are offered for cash. If securities are not offered for cash, the aggregate offering price shall be based on the value of the consideration as established by bona fide sales of that consideration made within a reasonable time, or, in the absence of sales, on the fair value as determined by an accepted standard.

(d) Business combination. "Business combination" shall mean any transaction of the type specified in paragraph (a) of Rule 145 under the Act (17 CFR 230.145) and any transaction involving the acquisition by one issuer, in exchange for all or a part of its own or its parent's stock, of stock of another issuer if, immediately after the acquisition, the acquiring issuer has control of the other issuer (whether or not it had control before the acquisition).

(c) Calculation of number of purchasers. For purposes of calculating the number of purchasers under §§230.505(b) and 230.506(b) only, the following shall apply:

(1) The following purchasers shall be excluded:

(i) Any relative, spouse or relative of the spouse of a purchaser who has the same principal residence as the purchaser;

(ii) Any trust or estate in which a purchaser and any of the persons related to him as specified in paragraph (e)(1)(i) or (e)(1)(iii) of this §230.501 collectively have more than 50 percent of the beneficial interest (excluding contingent interests);

(iii) Any corporation or other organization of which a purchaser and any of the persons related to him as specified in paragraph (e)(1)(i) or (e)(1)(ii) of this §230.501 collectively are beneficial owners of more than 50 percent of the equity securities (excluding directors' qualifying shares) or equity interests; and

(iv) Any accredited investor.

(2) A corporation, partnership or other entity shall be counted as one purchaser. If, however, that entity is organized for the specific purpose of acquiring the securities offered and is not an accredited investor under paragraph (a)(8) of this §230.501, then each beneficial owner of equity securities or equity interests in the entity shall count as a separate purchaser for all provisions of Regulation D.

Note: The issuer must satisfy all the other provisions of Regulation D for all purchasers whether or not they are included in calculating the number of purchasers. Clients of an investment adviser or customers of a broker or dealer shall be considered the "purchasers" under Regulation D regardless of the amount of discretion given to the investment adviser or broker or dealer to act on behalf of the client or customer.

(f) <u>Executive officer</u>. "Executive officer" shall mean the president, any vice president in charge of a principal business unit, division or function (such as sales, administration or finance), any other officer who performs a policy making function, or any other person who performs similar policy making functions for the issuer. Executive officers of subsidiaries may be deemed executive officers of the issuer if they perform such policy making functions for the issuer.

(g) <u>Issuer</u>. The definition of the term "issuer" in section 2(4) of the Act shall apply, except that in the case of a proceeding under the Federal Bankruptcy Code [11 U.S.C. 101 et seq.], the trustee or debtor in possession shall be considered the issuer in an offering under a plan or reorganization, if the securities are to be issued under the plan.

(h) <u>Purchaser representative</u>. "Purchaser representative" shall mean any person who satisfies all of the following conditions or who the issuer reasonably believes satisfies all of the following conditions:

(1) Is not an affiliate, director, officer or other employee of the issuer, or beneficial owner of 10 percent or more of any class of the equity securities or 10 percent or more of the equity interest in the issuer, except where the purchaser is:

(i) A relative of the purchaser representative by blood, marriage or adoption and not more remote than a first cousin;

(ii) A trust or estate in which the purchaser representative and any persons related to him as specified in paragraph (h)(1)(i) or (h)(1)(iii) of this §230.501 collectively have more than 50 percent of the beneficial interest (excluding contingent interest) or of which the purchaser representative serves as trustee, executor, or in any similar capacity; or

(iii) A corporation or other organization of which the purchaser representative and any persons related to him as specified in paragraph (h)(1)(i) or (h)(1)(ii) of this §230.501 collectively are the beneficial owners of more than 50 percent of the equity securities (excluding directors' qualifying shares) or equity interests;

(2) Has such knowledge and experience in financial and business matters that he is capable of evaluating, alone, or together with other purchaser representatives of the purchaser, or together with the purchaser, the merits and risks of the prospective investment;

(3) Is acknowledged by the purchaser in writing, during the course of the transaction, to be his purchaser representative in connection with evaluating the merits and risks of the prospective investment; and

(4) Discloses to the purchaser in writing prior to the acknowledgment specified in paragraph (h)(3) of this §230.501 any material relationship between himself or his affiliates and the issuer or its affiliates that then exists, that is mutually understood to be contemplated, or that has existed at any time during the previous two years, and any compensation received or to be received as a result of such relationship.

Note 1: A person acting as a purchaser representative should consider the applicability of the registration and antifraud provisions relating to brokers and dealers under the Securities Exchange Act of 1934 ("Exchange Act") [15 U.S.C. 78a et seq., as amended] and relating to investment advisers under the Investment Advisers Act of 1940.

Note 2: The acknowledgment required by paragraph (h)(3) and the disclosure required by paragraph (h)(4) of this §230.501 must be made with specific reference to each prospective investment. Advance blanket acknowledgment, such as for "all securities transactions" or "all private placements," is not sufficient.

Note 3: Disclosure of any material relationships between the purchaser representative or his affiliates and the issuer or its affiliates does not relieve the purchaser representative of his obligation to act in the interest of the purchaser.

[As adopted in Release No. 33-6389, March 8, 1982, 47 F.R. 11251.]

¶ 10,855 General Conditions to be Met

Reg. §230.502. The following conditions shall be applicable to offers and sales made under Regulation D:

(a) <u>Integration</u>. All sales that are part of the same Regulation D offering must meet all of the terms and conditions of Regulation D. Offers and sales that are made more than six months before the start of a Regulation D offering or are made more than six months after completion of a Regulation D offering will not be considered part of that Regulation D offering, so long as during those six month periods there are no offers or sales of securities by or for the issuer that are of the same or a similar class as those offered or sold under Regulation D, other than those offers or sales of securities under an employee benefit plan as defined in Rule 405 under the Act [17 CFR 230.405].

Note: The term "offering" is not defined in the Act or in Regulation D. If the issuer offers or sells securities for which the safe harbor rule in paragraph (a) of this §230.502 is unavailable, the determination as to whether separate sales of securities are part of the same offering (i.e. are considered "integrated") depends on the particular facts and circumstances.

The following factors should be considered in determining whether offers and sales should be integrated for purposes of the exemptions under Regulation D:

(a) whether the sales are part of a single plan of financing;

(b) whether the sales involve issuance of the same class of securities

(c) whether the sales have been made at or about the same time;

(d) whether the same type of consideration is received; and

(e) whether the sales are made for the same general purpose.

<u>See</u> Release No. 33-4552 (November 6, 1962) (27 FR 11316).

(b) **Information requirements.**

(1) **When information must be furnished.**

(i) If the issuer sells securities either under §230.504 or only to accredited investors, paragraph (b) of this §230.502 does not require that specific information be furnished to purchasers.

(ii) If the issuer sells securities under §230.505 or 230.506 to any purchaser that is not an accredited investor, the issuer shall furnish the information specified in paragraph (b)(2) of this §230.502 to all purchasers during the course of the offering and prior to sale.

(2) **Type of information to be furnished.**

(i) If the issuer is not subject to the reporting requirements of section 13 or 15(d) of the Exchange Act, the issuer shall furnish the following information, to the extent material to an understanding of the issuer, its business, and the securities being offered:

(A) **Offerings up to $5,000,000.** The same kind of information as would be required in Part I of Form S-18 [17 CFR 239.28], except that only the financial statements for the issuer's most recent fiscal year must be certified by an independent public or certified accountant. If Form S-18 is not available to an issuer, then the issuer shall furnish the same kind of information as would be required in Part I of a registration statement filed under the Act on the form that the issuer would be entitled to use, except that only the financial statements for the most recent two fiscal years prepared in accordance with generally accepted accounting principles shall be furnished and only the financial statements for the issuer's most recent fiscal year shall be certified by an independent public or certified accountant. If an issuer, other than a limited partnership, cannot obtain audited financial statements without unreasonable effort or expense, then only the issuer's balance sheet, which shall be dated within 120 days of the start of the offering, must be audited. If the issuer is a limited partnership and cannot obtain the required financial statements without unreasonable effort or expense, it may furnish financial statements that have been prepared on the basis of federal income tax requirements and examined and reported on in accordance with generally accepted auditing standards by an independent public or certified accountant.

(B) <u>Offerings over $5,000,000</u>. The same kind of information as would be required in Part I of a registration statement filed under the Act on the form that the issuer would be entitled to use. If an issuer, other than a limited partnership, cannot obtain audited financial statements without unreasonable effort or expense, then only the issuer's balance sheet, which shall be dated within 120 days of the start of the offering, must be audited. If the issuer is a limited partnership and cannot obtain the required financial statements without unreasonable effort or expense, it may furnish financial statements that have been prepared on the basis of federal income tax requirements and examined and reported on in accordance with generally accepted auditing standards by an independent public or certified accountant.

(ii) If the issuer is subject to the reporting requirements of section 13 or 15(d) of the Exchange Act, the issuer shall furnish the information specified in paragraph (b)(2)(ii)(A) or (b)(2)(ii)(B), and in either event the information specified in paragraph (b)(2)(ii)(C) of this §230.502:

(A) The issuer's annual report to shareholders for the most recent fiscal year, if such annual report meets the requirements of §240.14a-3 or 240.14c-3 under the Exchange Act, the definitive proxy statement filed in connection with that annual report, and, if requested by the purchaser in writing, a copy of the issuer's most recent Form 10-K [17 CFR 249.310] under the Exchange Act.

(B) The information contained in an annual report on Form 10-K under the Exchange Act or in a registration statement on Form S-1 [17 CFR 239.11] under the Act or on Form 10 [17 CFR 249.210] under the Exchange Act, whichever filing is the most recent required to be filed.

(C) The information contained in any reports or documents required to be filed by the issuer under sections 13(a), 14(a), 14(c), and 15(d) of the Exchange Act since the distribution or filing of the report or registration statement specified in paragraph (A) or (B), and a brief description of the securities being offered, the use of the proceeds from the offering, and any material changes in the issuer's affairs that are not disclosed in the documents furnished.

(iii) Exhibits required to be filed with the Commission as part of a registration statement or report, other than an annual report to shareholders or parts of that report incorporated by reference in a Form 10-K report, need not be furnished to each purchaser if the contents of the exhibits are identified and the exhibits are made available to the purchaser, upon his written request, prior to his purchase.

(iv) At a reasonable time prior to the purchase of securities by any purchaser that is not an accredited investor in a transaction under §230.505 or 230.506, the issuer shall furnish the purchaser a brief description in writing of any written information concerning the offering that has been provided by the issuer to any accredited investor. The issuer shall furnish any portion or all of this information to the purchaser, upon his written request, prior to his purchase.

(v) The issuer shall also make available to each purchaser at a reasonable time prior to his purchase of securities in a transaction under §230.505 or 230.506 the opportunity to ask questions and receive answers concerning the terms and conditions of the offering and to obtain any additional information which the issuer possesses or can acquire without unreasonable effort or expense that is necessary to verify the accuracy of information furnished under paragraph (b)(2)(i) or (ii) of this §230.502.

(vi) For business combinations, in addition to information required by paragraph (b)(2) of this §230.502, the issuer shall provide to each purchaser at the time the plan is submitted to security holders, or, with an exchange, during the course of the transaction and prior to sale, written information about any terms or arrangements of the proposed transaction that are materially different from those for all other security holders.

(c) <u>Limitation on manner of offering</u>. Except as provided in §230.504(b)(1), neither the issuer nor any person acting on its behalf shall offer or sell the securities by any form of general solicitation or general advertising, including, but not limited to, the following:

(1) Any advertisement, article, notice or other communication published in any newspaper, magazine, or similar media or broadcast over television or radio; and

(2) Any seminar or meeting whose attendees have been invited by any general solicitation or general advertising.

(d) <u>Limitations on resale</u>. Except as provided in §230.504(b)(1), securities acquired in a transaction under Regulation D shall have the status of securities acquired in a transaction under section 4(2) of the Act and cannot be resold without registration under the Act or an exemption therefrom.

The issuer shall exercise reasonable care to assure that the purchasers of the securities are not underwriters within the meaning of section 2(11) of the Act, which reasonable care shall include, but not be limited to, the following:

(1) Reasonable inquiry to determine if the purchaser is acquiring the securities for himself or for other persons;

(2) Written disclosure to each purchaser prior to sale that the securities have not been registered under the Act and, therefore, cannot be resold unless they are registered under the Act or unless an exemption from registration is available; and

(3) Placement of a legend on the certificate or other document that evidences the securities stating that the securities have not been registered under the Act and setting forth or referring to the restrictions on transferability and sale of the securities.

[As adopted in Release No. 33-6389, March 8, 1982, 47 F.R. 11251.]

¶ 10,861 Filing of Notice of Sales

Reg. §230.503.

(a) The issuer shall file with the Commission five copies of a notice on Form D [17 CFR 239.500] at the following times:

(1) No later than 15 days after the first sale of securities in an offering under Regulation D;

(2) Every six months after the first sale of securities in an offering under Regulation D, unless the final notice required by paragraph (a)(3) of this §230.503 has been filed; and

(3) No later than 30 days after the last sale of securities in an offering under Regulation D.

(b) If the offering is completed within the 15 day period described in paragraph (a)(1) of this §230.503 and if the notice is filed no later than the end of that period but after the completion of the offering, then only one notice need be filed to comply with paragraphs (a)(1) and (3) of this §230.503.

(c) One copy of every notice on Form D shall be manually signed by a person duly authorized by the issuer.

(d) If sales are made under §230.505, the notice shall contain an undertaking by the issuer to furnish to the Commission, upon the written request of its staff, the information furnished by the issuer under §230.502(b)(2) to any purchaser that is not an accredited investor.

(e) If more than one notice for an offering is required to be filed under paragraph (a) of this §230.403, notices after the first notice need only report the issuer's name and the information required by Part C and any material change in the facts from those set forth in Parts A and B of the first notice.

(f) A notice on Form D shall be considered filed with the Commission under paragraph (a) of this §230.503:

(1) As of the date on which it is received at the Commission's principal office in Washington, D.C.; or

(2) As of the date on which the notice is mailed by means of United States registered or certified mail to the Commission's Office of Small Business Policy, Division of Corporation Finance, at the Commission's principal office in Washington, D.C., if the notice is delivered to such office after the date on which it is required to be filed.

[As adopted in Release No. 33-6389, March 8, 1982, 47 F.R. 11251.]

¶ 10,865 Exemption for Limited Offers and Sales
of Securities Not Exceeding $500,000

Reg. §230.504.

(a) <u>Exemption</u>. Offers and sales of securities that satisfy the conditions in paragraph (b) of this §230.504 by an issuer that is not subject to the reporting requirements of section 13 or 15(d) of the Exchange Act and that is not an investment company shall be exempt from the provisions of section 5 of the Act under section 3(b) of the Act.

(b) <u>Conditions to be met</u>.

(1) <u>General conditions</u>. To qualify for exemption under this §230.504, offers and sales must satisfy the terms and conditions of §§230.501 through 230.503, except that the provisions of §§230.502(c) and (d) shall not apply to offers and sales of securities under this §230.504 that are made exclusively in one or more states each of which provides for the registration of the securities and requires the delivery of a disclosure document before sale and that are made in accordance with those state provisions.

(2) <u>Specific condition</u>.

(i) <u>Limitation on aggregate offering price</u>. The aggregate offering price for an offering of securities under this §230.504, as defined in §230.501(c), shall not exceed $500,000, less the aggregate offering price for all securities sold within the twelve months before the start of and during the offering of securities under this §230.504 in reliance on any exemption under section 3(b) of the Act or in violation of section 5(a) of the Act.

Note 1: The calculation of the aggregate offering price is illustrated as follows:

<u>Example 1</u>. If an issuer sold $200,000 of its securities on June 1, 1982 under this §230.504 and an additional $100,000 on September 1, 1982, the issuer would be permitted to sell only $200,000 more under this §230.504 until June 1, 1983. Until that date the issuer must count both prior sales towards the $500,000 limit. However, if the issuer made its third sale on June 1, 1983, the issuer could then sell $400,000 of its securities because the June 1, 1982 sale would not be within the preceding twelve months.

Example 2. If an issuer sold $100,000 of its securities on June 1, 1982 under this §230.504 and an additional $4,500,000 on December 1, 1982 under §230.505, the issuer could not sell any of its securities under this §230.504 until December 1, 1983. Until then the issuer must count the December 1, 1982 sale towards the limit of $500,000 within the preceding twelve months.

Note 2: If a transaction under this §230.504 fails to meet the limitation on the aggregate offering price, it does not affect the availability of this §230.504 for the other transactions considered in applying such limitation. For example, if the issuer in Example 1 made its third sale on May 31, 1983, in the amount of $250,000, this §230.504 would not be available for that sale, but the exemption for the prior two sales would be unaffected.

[As adopted in Release No. 33-6389, March 8, 1982, 47 F.R. 11251.]

¶ 10,871 Exemption for Limited Offers and Sales
of Securities Not Exceeding $5,000,000

Reg. §230.505.

(a) Exemption. Offers and sales of securities that satisfy the conditions in paragraph (b) of this §230.505 by an issuer that is not an investment company shall be exempt from the provisions of section 5 of the Act under section 3(b) of the Act.

(b) Conditions to be met.

(1) General conditions. To qualify for exemption under this §230.505, offers and sales must satisfy the terms and conditions of §§230.501 through 230.503.

(2) Specific conditions.

(i) Limitation on aggregate offering price. The aggregate offering price for an offering of securities under this §230.505, as defined in §230-501(c), shall not exceed $5,000,000, less the aggregate offering price for all securities sold within the twelve months before the start of and during the offering of securities under this §230.505 in reliance on any exemption under section 3(b) of the Act or in violation of section 5(a) of the Act.

Note: The calculation of the aggregate offering price is illustrated as follows:

Example 1. If an issuer sold $2,000,000 of its securities on June 1, 1982 under this §230.505 and an additional $1,000,000 on September 1, 1982, the issuer would be permitted to sell only $2,000,000 more under this §230.505 until June 1, 1983. Until that date the issuer must count both prior sales towards the $5,000,000 limit. However, if the issuer made its third sale on June 1, 1983, the issuer could then sell $4,000,000 of its securities because the June 1, 1982 sale would not be within the preceding twelve months.

Example 2. If an issuer sold $500,000 of its securities on June 1, 1982 under §230.504 and an additional $4,500,000 on December 1, 1982 under this §230.505, then the issuer could not sell any of its securities under this §230.505 until June 1, 1983. At that time it could sell an additional $500,000 of its securities.

(ii) <u>Limitation on number of purchasers</u>. The issuer shall reasonably believe that there are no more than 35 purchasers of securities from the issuer in any offering under this §230.505.

Note: See §230.501(e) for the calculation of the number of purchasers and §230.502(a) for what may or may not constitute an offering under this section.

(iii) <u>Disqualifications</u>. No exemption under this §230.505 shall be available for the securities of any issuer described in §230.252(c), (d), (e), or (f) of Regulation A, except that for purposes of this §230.505 only:

(A) The term "filing of the notification required by §230.255" as used in §230.252(c), (d), (e) and (f) shall mean the first sale of securities under this §230.505;

(B) The term "underwriter" as used in §230.252(d) and (e) shall mean a person that has been or will be paid directly or indirectly remuneration for solicitation of purchasers in connection with sales of securities under this §230.505; and

(C) Paragraph (b)(2)(iii) of this §230.505 shall not apply to any issuer if the Commission determines upon a showing of good cause, that it is not necessary under the circumstances that the exemption be denied. Any such determination shall be without prejudice to any other action by the Commission in any other proceeding or matter with respect to the issuer or any other person.

[As adopted in Release No. 33-6389, March 8, 1982, 47 F.R. 11251.]

¶ 10,875 Exemption for Limited Offers and Sales Without Regard to Dollar Amount of Offering

Reg. §230.506.

(a) <u>Exemption</u>. Offers and sales of securities by an issuer that satisfy the conditions in paragraph (b) of this §230.506 shall be deemed to be transactions not involving any public offering within the meaning of section 4(2) of the Act.

(b) <u>Conditions to be met</u>.

(1) <u>General conditions</u>. To qualify for exemption under this §230.506, offers and sales must satisfy all the terms and conditions of §§230 501 through 230.503.

(2) <u>Specific conditions</u>.

(i) <u>Limitation on number of purchasers</u>. The issuer shall reasonably believe that there are no more than 35 purchasers of securities from the issuer in any offering under this §230.506.

Note: See §230.501(e) for the calculation of the number of purchasers and §230.502(a) for what may or may not constitute an offering under this section 230.506.

(ii) <u>Nature of purchasers</u>. The issuer shall reasonably believe immediately prior to making any sale that each purchaser who is not an accredited investor either alone or with his purchaser representative(s) has such knowledge and experience in financial and business matters that he is capable of evaluating the merits and risks of the prospective investment.

[As adopted in Release No. 33-6389, March 8, 1982, 47 F.R. 11251.]

U. S. SECURITIES AND EXCHANGE COMMISSION
Washington, D. C. 20549

OMB APPROVAL
OMB # 3235-0076
Expires January 31, 1988

SEC USE ONLY

SEC USE ONLY SERIAL
21-

NOTICE OF SALES OF SECURITIES
PURSUANT TO REGULATION D OR SECTION 4(6)

Nature of this filing with respect to this offering.

INSTRUCTION: Please check the box(es) corresponding to the exemptive provision applicable to this offering.

Rule 504 ☐   Rule 505 ☐   Rule 506 ☐   Section 4(6) ☐

INSTRUCTION: Circle "N" for a new filing or "A" for an amended filing.

ORIGINAL 1 N/A   COMBINED ORIGINAL AND FINAL 2 N/A   SIX-MONTH UPDATE 3 N/A   FINAL 4 N/A

INSTRUCTIONS: The issuer shall file with the Commission five copies of this notice at the following times: (a) no later than 15 days after the first sale of securities in an offering under Regulation D or Section 4(6); (b) every six months after the first sale of securities in an offering under Regulation D or Section 4(6), unless a final notice has been filed; and (c) no later than 30 days after the last sale of securities in an offering under Regulation D or Section 4(6), *except that if the offering is completed within the 15-day period described in "(a)" above, and if the notice is filed no later than the end of that period but after the completion of the offering, then only one notice need be filed*. If more than one notice for an offering is required to be filed, notices after the first notice need only report the issuer's name, information in response to Part C and any material changes from the facts previously reported in Parts A and B. This notice shall be deemed to be filed with the Commission for purposes of the rule as of the date on which the notice is received by the Commission, or if delivered to the Commission after the date on which it is due, as of the date on which it is mailed by means of United States registered or certified mail to the Office of Small Business Policy, Division of Corporation Finance, U.S. Securities and Exchange Commission, Washington, D.C. 20549.

A. Basic Identification of Issuer.

INSTRUCTION: State the address of the issuer's executive offices and, if different, the address at which the issuer's principal business operations are conducted or proposed to be conducted.

NAME			
ADDRESS OF EXECUTIVE OFFICES			
CITY		STATE	ZIP
AREA CODE	TELEPHONE NUMBER		
ADDRESS OF PRINCIPAL BUSINESS OPERATIONS			
CITY		STATE	ZIP
AREA CODE	TELEPHONE NUMBER		

INSTRUCTION: Please list the full name and address of the following persons: each promoter of the issuer involved in the offering of securities as to which sales pursuant to Regulation D or Section 4(6) are reported on this notice, the issuer's chief executive officer, and each of the issuer's affiliates. Indicate the status of each person named by placing an "X" in the applicable box(es) opposite such person's name. The term "promoter" includes: . . .

(a) Any person who, acting alone or in conjunction with one or more other persons, directly or indirectly takes the initiative in founding and organizing the business or enterprise of an issuer; or

(b) Any person who, in connection with the founding or organizing of the business or enterprise of an issuer, directly or indirectly receives in consideration of services or property, or both services and property, 10 percent or more of any class of securities of the issuer or 10 percent or more of the proceeds from the sale of any class of securities. However, a person who receives such securities or proceeds either solely as brokerage commissions or solely in consideration of property shall not be deemed a promoter within the meaning of this paragraph if such person does not otherwise take part in founding and organizing the enterprise.

SEC 1972 (2-85)

FORM D

NOTICE OF SALES OF SECURITIES PURSUANT TO REGULATION D OR SECTION 4(6)

Page 2

NAME			
ADDRESS	CITY	STATE	ZIP
NAME			
ADDRESS	CITY	STATE	ZIP

CEO	Aff	Pro

CEO	Aff	Pro

1. Has the issuer filed any periodic reports pursuant to Section 13 or 15(d) of the Securities Exchange Act of 1934?   YES ☐   NO ☐

   If yes, please indicate the file number of the docket in which the periodic reports are filed. _____

2. **Please indicate the issuer's IRS employer identification number.** If an application for such number is pending, please enter "00-0000000."

3. Please briefly describe the issuer's business.

   _____

   _____

   _____

4. Please indicate the issuer's type of business organization.
   a. corporation   b. partnership   c. business trust   d. other, *please specify* _____

5. Please indicate the issuer's Standard Industrial Classification (SIC) at the 3 or 4 digit level. If the issuer has more than one SIC, please enter the issuer's primary SIC. If a 3 digit SIC is given, enter "X" in the left-most box.

6. In what year was the issuer incorporated or organized?

7. In what state is the issuer incorporated or organized? Please enter the standard two letter U.S. Postal Service abbreviation. Enter "CN" if the issuer is incorporated or organized in Canada; "FN" if the issuer is incorporated or organized in another foreign jurisdiction.

8. Has the issuer been assigned a CUSIP number for its securities?   YES ☐   NO ☐

   If yes, please specify the first six (6) digits. If no, please enter "000000."

9. Please check the appropriate box for each exchange or market, if any, where the issuer's securities are traded.
   - American Stock Exchange . . . . a. ☐
   - New York Stock Exchange . . . . b. ☐
   - Other National Securities Exchanges . . . . c. ☐
   - Over-the-Counter (including
     National Association of Securities Dealers Automated Quotations System) . . d. ☐
   - Other   *Please Specify* . . . . e. ☐

   SEC USE ONLY

   - None . . . . f. ☐

| FORM D | **NOTICE OF SALES OF SECURITIES PURSUANT TO REGULATION D OR SECTION 4(6)** | Page 3 |

B. Statistical Information About the Issuer

INSTRUCTION: Please enter the letter for the appropriate response to each item in Part B in the box indicated. If the issuer's first fiscal year has not yet ended, furnish the requested information as of a date, or as to a period ending on a date, no more than 90 days prior to the first sale of securities in this offering.

1. What were the issuer's gross revenues for its most recently ended fiscal year? ☐

    a. $500,000 or less   b. $500,001 – $1,000,000   c. $1,000,001 – $3,000,000
    d. $3,000,001 – $5,000,000   e. $5,000,001 – $25,000,000   f. $25,000,001 – $100,000,000
    g. Over $100,000,000

2. What were the issuer's total consolidated assets as of the end of its latest fiscal year? ☐

    a. $500,000 or less   b. $500,001 – $1,000,000   c. $1,000,001 – $3,000,000
    d. $3,000,001 – $5,000,000   e. $5,000,001 – $25,000,000   f. $25,000,001 – $100,000,000
    g. Over $100,000,000

3. What was the issuer's net income, or income before partners' compensation, for its most recently ended fiscal year? ☐

    a. None or net loss   b. $1 – $50,000   c. $50,001 – $250,000   d. $250,001 – $1,000,000
    e. $1,000,001 – $5,000,000   f. Over $5,000,000

4. What was the issuer's shareholders' or partners' equity at the end of its latest fiscal year? ☐

    a. Negative   b. $1 – $50,000   c. $50,001 – $250,000   d. $250,001 – $1,000,000
    e. $1,000,001 – $3,000,000   f. $3,000,001 – $10,000,000   g. Over $10,000,000

5. How many shareholders or partners did the issuer have at the end of its latest fiscal year? ☐

    a. 0 – 4   b. 5 – 9   c. 10 – 24   d. 25 – 99   e. 100 – 299
    f. 300 – 499   g. 500 or more

6. What percentage of shares outstanding were held by non-affiliated shareholders at the end of the issuer's latest fiscal year? [1] ☐

    a. None   b. Less than 5.0%   c. 5.0% – 9.9%   d. 10.0% – 24.9%
    e. 25.0% – 49.9%   f. 50.0% – 74.9%   g. 75.0% or more   h. Not applicable

7. How many shares were outstanding at the end of the issuer's latest fiscal year? ☐

    a. 500,000 or less   b. 500,001 – 1,500,000   c. 1,500,001 – 2,500,000
    d. 2,500,001 – 3,500,000   e. 3,500,001 – 5,000,000   f. Over 5,000,000   g. Not applicable

8. How many full-time equivalent employees did the issuer have at the end of its latest fiscal year? [2] ☐

    a. None   b. 1 – 5   c. 6 – 10   d. 11 – 20   e. 21 – 50   f. 51 – 100
    g. 101 – 500   h. 500 or more

---

[1] A non-affiliated person is defined to be anyone other than a person that directly or indirectly, through one or more intermediaries, controls or is controlled by the issuer or is under common control with such person.

[2] Full-time equivalent employees is defined to equal the sum of the number of full-time employees plus the number of part-time employees working 25 or more hours per typical work week.

FORM D

NOTICE OF SALES OF SECURITIES PURSUANT TO REGULATION D OR SECTION 4(6)

Page 4

C. Section 3(b) or 4(6) Sales Limit and Other Information About the Offering

INSTRUCTION: If a response to any item is "none" or "zero," please enter zero ("0") in the corresponding space.

1. Type and aggregate offering price of securities intended to be sold pursuant to Regulation D or Section 4(6) in this offering.

   a. Debt . . . . $ _____

   b. Equity . . . . $ _____

   c. Convertible . . . . $ _____

2. Number of accredited and non-accredited investors who have purchased securities in this offering in reliance on Rules 505 or 506 and aggregate dollar amounts of their purchases to date. For sales in reliance on Rule 504 or Section 4(6), please enter the number of persons who have purchased securities and aggregate dollar amounts of their purchases to date on the accredited investor lines.

	Number of Investors (A)	Aggregate Dollar Amount (B)
Accredited investors	_____	$ _____
Non-accredited investors	_____	_____
Total	_____	$ _____

3. If this offering is being made pursuant to Rule 504 or 505, report by exemption and type of security *(i.e., debt, equity, convertible)* the dollar amount of all Section 3(b) sales of securities *(other than sales reported in Item C.2 above)* occurring from twelve (12) months prior to the first sale of securities in this offering to date.

	Type (A)	Dollar Amount (B)
Rule 505	_____	$ _____
Regulation A	_____	_____
Rule 504	_____	_____
Total		$ _____

4. Please list the full name and address of each person who has been or will be paid or given directly or indirectly any commission or similar remuneration for solicitation of purchasers in connection with sales of securities in this offering pursuant to Regulation D or Section 4(6). If a person to be listed is an associated person of a broker or dealer registered with the Commission and/or with a state or states, then please also list the name of that broker or dealer. If more than five (5) persons to be listed are associated persons of a broker or dealer registered with the Commission and/or a state or states, then the issuer may list the name and address of only such broker or dealer. Please also list, using the standard two-letter Postal Service abbreviation the state or states in which each person, or if an associated broker or dealer is listed, each such broker or dealer, intends to or is offering securities in this offering; if all states, enter "all."

NAME				SEC USE ONLY
ADDRESS	CITY	STATE	ZIP	8-□□□□□
NAME OF ASSOCIATED BROKER OR DEALER				
STATES				
NAME				SEC USE ONLY
ADDRESS	CITY	STATE	ZIP	8-□□□□□
NAME OF ASSOCIATED BROKER OR DEALER				
STATES				

FORM D

NOTICE OF SALES OF SECURITIES PURSUANT TO REGULATION D OR SECTION 4(6)

Page 5

5. a. Aggregate offering price of securities, from C.1 above $ ☐ _____.

   b. Furnish a reasonably itemized statement of all expenses in connection with the issuance and distribution of the securities being offered in this offering. Please exclude any amounts relating solely to the organizational expenses of the issuer. Insofar as practicable, give amounts for the categories listed below. The information may be given as subject to future contingencies. If the expenditure in any category is not known, furnish an estimate and place an "X" in the box to the left of the amount given.

      a. Blue Sky Fees and Expenses . . . . $ ☐ _____.
      b. Transfer Agents' Fees . . . .   ☐ _____.
      c. Printing and Engraving Costs . . . .   ☐ _____.
      d. Legal Fees . . . .   ☐ _____.
      e. Accounting Fees . . . .   ☐ _____.
      f. Engineering Fees . . . .   ☐ _____.
      g. Sales Commissions *(including Finders' Fees)* . . . .   ☐ _____.
      h. Other Expenses *(Identify)*

         _____   ☐ _____.
         _____   ☐ _____.

                                    Total $ ☐ _____.

   c. Enter the difference between the aggregate offering price in 5.a. and total costs in 5.b. This difference is the "adjusted gross proceeds to the issuer." $ ☐ _____.

6. Indicate below the amount of the adjusted gross proceeds to the issuer *(other than amounts specified in Item 5.b. above)* proposed to be used or used for each of the purposes listed below. If the amount to be used for any purpose is not known, furnish an estimate and place an "X" in the box to the left of the amount given.

		Payments to officers, directors and affiliates (A)	Payments to others (B)
a.	Salaries and fees	$ ☐ _____.	$ ☐ _____.
b.	Purchase of real estate	☐ _____.	☐ _____.
c.	Purchase, rental or leasing and installation of machinery and equipment	☐ _____.	☐ _____.
d.	Construction or leasing of plant building and facilities	☐ _____.	☐ _____.
e.	Development expense *(product development, research, patent costs, etc.)*	☐ _____.	☐ _____.
f.	Purchase of raw materials, inventories, supplies, etc.	☐ _____.	☐ _____.
g.	Selling, advertising, and other sales promotion	☐ _____.	☐ _____.
h.	Acquisition of other businesses *(including the value of securities involved in this offering which may be used in exchange for the assets or securities of another issuer pursuant to a merger)*	☐ _____.	☐ _____.
i.	Repayment of loans	☐ _____.	☐ _____.
	Other — *please specify*		
j.	_____	☐ _____.	☐ _____.
k.	_____	☐ _____.	☐ _____.
l.	_____	☐ _____.	☐ _____.
m.	_____	☐ _____.	☐ _____.
	Total	$ ☐ _____.	$ ☐ _____.

| FORM D | **NOTICE OF SALES OF SECURITIES**
PURSUANT TO REGULATION D OR SECTION 4(6) | Page 6 |

D. Undertaking by issuers filing pursuant to Rule 505.

The undersigned issuer hereby undertakes to furnish to the Securities and Exchange Commission, upon the written request of its staff, the information furnished by the issuer to any non-accredited person pursuant to paragraph (b)(2) of Rule 502.

ISSUER _____

SIGNATURE _____

NAME _____

TITLE _____

E. The issuer has duly caused this notice to be signed on its behalf by the undersigned duly authorized person.

DATE OF NOTICE: _____

ISSUER _____

SIGNATURE _____

NAME _____

TITLE _____

INSTRUCTION: Print the name and title of the signing representative under his signature. One copy of every notice on Form D shall be manually signed. Any copies not manually signed shall bear typed or printed signatures.

---**ATTENTION**---
Intentional misstatements or omissions of fact constitute Federal Criminal Violations (See 18 U.S.C. 1001).

FORM D Continuation Sheet	NOTICE OF SALES OF SECURITIES PURSUANT TO REGULATION D OR SECTION 4(6)	Page 7
Item of Form *(identify)*	Answer	

FORM D Continuation Sheet	NOTICE OF SALES OF SECURITIES PURSUANT TO REGULATION D OR SECTION 4(6)	Page 8
Item of Form (identify)	Answer	

APPENDIX C

Rule 147

§230.147 "Part of an Issue," "Person Resident," and "Doing Business Within" for purposes of section 3(a)(11).

Preliminary Notes

1. This rule shall not raise any presumption that the exemption provided by Section 3(a)(11) of the Act is not available for transactions by an issuer which do not satisfy all of the provisions of the rule.

2. Nothing in this rule obviates the need for compliance with any state law relating to the offer and sale of the securities.

3. Section 5 of the Act requires that all securities offered by the use of the mails or by any means or instruments of transportation or communication in interstate commerce be registered with the Commission. Congress, however, provided certain exemptions in the Act from such registration provisions where there was no practical need for registration or where the benefits of registration were too remote. Among those exemptions is that provided by Section 3(a)(11) of the Act for transactions in "any security which is a part of an issue offered and sold only to persons resident within a single State or Territory, where the issuer of such security is a person resident and doing business with *** such State or Territory." The legislative history of that Section suggests that the exemption was intended to apply only to issues genuinely local in character, which in reality represent local financing by local industries, carried out through local investment. Rule 147 is intended to provide more objective standards upon which responsible local businessmen intending to raise capital from local sources may rely in claiming the section 3(a)(11) exemption.

All of the terms and conditions of the rule must be satisfied in order for the rule to be available. These are: (i) That the issuer be a resident of and doing business within the state or territory in which all offers and sales are made; and (ii) that no part of the issue be offered or sold to nonresidents within the period of time specified in the rule. For purposes of the rule the definition of "issuer" in section 2(4) of the Act shall apply.

All offers, offers to sell, offers for sale, and sales which are part of the same issue must meet all of the conditions of Rule 147 for the rule to be available. The determination whether offers, offers to sell, offers for sale and sales of securities are part of the same issue (i.e., are deemed to be "integrated") will continue to be a question of fact and will depend on the particular circumstances. See Securities Act of 1933 Release No. 4434 (December 6, 1961) (26 FR 9158). Securities Act Release No. 4434 indicsted that in determining whether offers and sales should be regarded as part of the same issue and thus should be integrated any one or more of the following factors may be determinative:

(i) Are the offerings part of a single plan of financing;

(ii) Do the offerings involve issuance of the same class of securities;

(iii) Are the offerings made at or about the same time;

(iv) Is the same type of consideration to be received; and

(v) Are the offerings made for the same general purpose.

Subparagraph (b)(2) of the rule, however, is designed to provide certainty to the extent feasible by identifying certain types of offers and sales of securities which will be deemed not part of an issue, for purposes of the rule only.

Persons claiming the availability of the rule have the burden of proving that they have satisfied all of its provisions. However, the rule does not establish exclusive standards for complying with the Section 3(a)(11) exemption. The exemption would also be available if the issuer satisfied the standards set forth in relevant administrative and judicial interpretations at the time of the offering but the issuer would have the burden of proving the availability of the exemption. Rule 147 relates to transactions exempted from the registration requirements of Section 5 of the Act by section 3(a)(11). Neither the rule nor section 3(a)(11) provides an exemption from the registration requirements of section 12(g) of the Securities Exchange Act of 1934, the anti-fraud provisions of the federal securities laws, the civil liability provisions of section 12(2) of the Act or other provisions of the federal securities laws.

Finally, in view of the objectives of the rule and the purposes and policies underlying the Act, the rule shall not be available to any person with respect to any offering which,

Appendix C: Rule 147

although in technical compliance with the rule, is part of a plan or scheme by such person to make interstate offers or sales of securities. In such cases registration pursuant to the Act is required.

4. The rule provides an exemption for offers and sales by the issuer only. It is not available for offers or sales of securities by other persons. Section 3(a)(11) of the Act has been interpreted to permit offers and sales by persons controlling the issuer, if the exemption provided by that section would have been available to the issuer at the time of the offering. See Securities Act Release No. 4434. Controlling persons who want to offer or sell securities pursuant to section 3(a)(11) may continue to do so in accordance with applicable judicial and administrative interpretations.

(a) <u>Transactions Covered</u>. Offers, offers to sell, offers for sale and sales by an issuer of its securities made in accordance with all of the terms and conditions of this rule shall be deemed to be part of an issue offered and sold only to persons resident within a single state or territory where the issuer is a person resident and doing business within such state or territory, within the meaning of section 3(a)(11) of the Act.

(b) <u>Part of an issue</u>. (1) For purposes of this rule, all securities of the issuer which are part of an issue shall be offered, offered for sale or sold in accordance with all of the terms and conditions of this rule.

(2) For purposes of this rule only, an issue shall be deemed not to include offers, offers to sell, offers for sale or sales of securities of the issuer pursuant to the exemption provided by section 3 or section 4(2) of the Act or pursuant to a registration statement filed under the Act, that take place prior to the six month period immediately preceding or after the six month period immediately following any offers, offers for sale or sales pursuant to this rule, <u>Provided</u>, That, there are during either of said six month periods no offers, offers for sale or sales of securities by or for the issuer of the same or similar class as those offered, offered for sale or sold pursuant to the rule.

Note: In the event that securities of the same or similar class as those offered pursuant to the rule are offered, offered for sale or sold less than six months prior to or subsequent to any offer, offer for sale or sale pursuant to this rule, see Preliminary Note 3 hereof as to which offers, offers to sell, offers for sale, or sales are part of an issue.

(c) <u>Nature of the Issuer</u>. The issuer of the securities shall at the time of any offers and the sales be a person resident and doing business within the state or territory in which all of the offers, offers to sell, offers for sale and sales are made.

(1) The issuer shall be deemed to be a resident of the state or territory in which:

(i) It is incorporated or organized, if a corporated, limited partnership, trusat or other form of business organization that is organized under state or territorial law;

(ii) Its principal office is located, if a general partnership or other form of business organization that is not organized under any state or territorial law;

(iii) His principal residence is located if an individual.

(2) The issuer shall be deemed to be doing business within a state or territory if:

(i) The issuer derived at least 80 percent of its gross revenues and those of its subsidiaries on a consolidated basis.

(A) For its most recent fiscal year, if the first offer of any part of the issue is made during the first six months of the issuer's current fiscal year; or

(B) For the first six months of its current fiscal year or during the twelve month fiscal period ending with such six month period, if the first offer of any part of the issue is made during the last six months of the issuer's current fiscal year from the operation of a business or of real property located in or from the rendering of services within such state or territory; provided, however, that this provision does not apply to any issuer which has not had gross revenues in excess of $5,000 from the sale of products or services or other conduct of its business for its most recent twelve month fiscal period;

(ii) The issuer had at the end of its most recent semiannual fiscal period prior to the first offer of any part of the issue, at least 80 percent of its assets and those of its subsidiaries on a consolidated basis located within such state or territory;

(iii) The issuer intends to use and uses at least 80 percent of the net proceeds to the issuer from sales made pursuant to this rule in connection with the operation of a business or of real property, the purchase of real property located in, or the rendering of services within such state or territory; and

(iv) The principal office of the issuer is located within such state or territory.

(d) <u>Offerees and Purchasers: Person Resident</u>. Offers, offers to sell, offers for sale and sales of securities that are part of an issue shall be mde only to persons resident within the state or territory of which the issuer is a resident. For purposes of determining the residence of offerees and purchasers:

(1) A corporation, partnership, trust or other form of business organization shall be deemed to be a resident of a state or territory if, at the time of the offer and sale to it, it has its principal office within such state or territory.

(2) An individual shall be deemed to be a resident of a state or territory if such individual has, at the time of the offer and sale to him, his principal residence in the state or territory.

(3) A corporation, partnership, trust or other form of business organization which is organized for the specific purpose of acquiring part of an issue offered pursuant to this rule shall be deemed not to be a resident of a state or territory unless all of the beneficial owners of such organization are residents of such state or territory.

(e) <u>Limitation of Resales</u>. During the period in which securities that are part of an issue are being offered and sold by the issuer, and for a period of nine months from the date of the last sale by the issuer of such securities, all resales of any part of the issue, by any person, shall be made only to persons resident within such state or territory.

Notes: 1. In the case of convertible securities resales of either the convertible security, or if it is converted, the underlying security, could be made during the period described in paragraph (e) only to persons resident within such state or territory. For purposes of this rule a conversion in reliance on section 3(a)(9) of the Act does not begin a new period.

2. Dealers must satisfy the requirements of Rule 15c2-11 under the Securities Exchange Act of 1934 prior to publishing any quotation for a security, or submitting any quotation for publication, in any quotation medium.

(f) <u>Precautions Against Interstate Offers and Sales.</u> (1) The issuer shall, in connection with any securities sold by it pursuant to this rule:

(i) Place a legend on the certificate or other document evidencing the security stating that the securities have not been registered under the Act and setting forth the limitations on resale contained in paragraph (e) of this section;

(ii) Issue stop transfer instructions to the issuer's transfer agent, if any, with respect to the securities, or, if the issuer transfers its own securities make a notation in the appropriate records of the issuer; and

(iii) Obtain a written representation from each purchaser as to his residence.

(2) The issuer shall, in connection with the issuance of new certificates for any of the securities that are part of the same issue that are presented for transfer during the time period specified in paragraph (e), take the steps required by paragraphs (f)(1)(i) and (ii) of this section.

(3) The issuer shall, in connection with any offers, offers to sell, offers for sale or sales by it pursuant to this rule, disclose, in writing, the limitations on resale contained in paragraph (e) and the provisions of paragraphs (f)(1)(i) and (ii) and paragraph (f)(2) of this section.

[39 FR 2356, Jan. 21, 1974.]

APPENDIX D
Regulation A

REGULATION A — GENERAL EXEMPTIONS

Definition of Terms in this Regulation

Reg. §230.251. As used in §§230.251 to 230.262, the following terms shall have the meaning indicated:

Affiliate. An "affiliate" of an issuer is a person controlling, controlled by or under common control with such issuer. An individual who controls an issuer is also an affiliate of such issuer.

Parent. A "parent" of a specified person is an affiliate controlling such person directly, or indirectly through one or more intermediaries.

Predecessor. A "predecessor" of an issuer is (a) a person the major portion of whose assets have been acquired directly or indirectly by the issuer, or (b) a person from which the issuer acquired directly or indirectly the major portion of its assets.

Promoter. The term "promoter" includes—

(a) Any person who, acting alone or in conjunction with one or more other persons, directly or indirectly takes the initiative in founding and organizing the business or enterprise of an issuer;

(b) Any person who, in connection with the founding or organizing of the business or enterprise of an issuer, directly or indirectly receives in consideration of services or property, or both services and property, 10 percent or more of any class of securities of the issuer or 10 percent or more of the proceeds from the sale of any class of securities. However, a person who receives such securities or proceeds either solely as underwriting commissions or solely in consideration of property shall not be deemed a promoter within the meaning of this paragraph if such person does not otherwise take part in founding and organizing the enterprise.

Province. A "Province" is any Province or Territory of Canada.

Resident. A "resident" of a specified country is an individual resident of such country or a corporation or other organization which is incorporated or organized under the laws of such country or any of its political subdivisions.

State. A "State" is any State, Territory or insular possession of the United States, or the District of Columbia.

Underwriter. The term "underwriter" shall have the meaning given in Section 2(11) of the Act.

[As last amended in Release No. 33-6340, August 7, 1981, effective September 17, 1981, 46 F.R. 41766.]

Securities Exempted

Reg. §230.252.

(a) Except as hereinafter provided in §§230.251 to 230.262, securities issued by any of the following persons shall be exempt from registration under the Act if offered in accordance with the terms and conditions of §§230.251 to 230.262:

   (1) Any corporation, unincorporated association or trust (i) which is incorporated or organized under the laws of the United States or Canada or any State or Province thereof and (ii) which has or proposes to have its principal business operations in the United States or Canada; or

   (2) Any individual who is a resident of, and has or proposes to have his principal business operations in, any State or Province; or

   (3) In the case of an offering to existing security holders on a pro rata basis pursuant to warrants or rights, any direct or indirect majority-owned subsidiary of any issuer specified in (1) above which has securities registered on a national securities exchange pursuant to the provisions of the Securities Exchange Act of 1934.

(b) No exemption under this regulation shall be available for any of the following securities:

   (1) Fractional undivided interests in oil or gas rights as defined in §230.300, or similar interests in other mineral rights;

   (2) Securities of any investment company registered or required to be registered under the Investment Company Act of 1940, or any company which has elected to be regulated as a business development company under the Investment Company Act of 1940 or has notified the Commission that it intends to elect to be regulated as a business development company pursuant to section 54 of the Investment Company Act of 1940.

(c) No exemption under §§230.251 to 230.262 shall be available for the securities of any issuer if such issuer, any of its predecessors or any affiliated issuer—

(1) Has filed a registration statement which is the subject of any pending proceeding or examination under section 8 of the act, or is the subject of any refusal order or stop order thereunder within five years prior to the filing of the notification required by §§230.255;

(2) Is subject to any pending proceeding under §230.261 or any similar rule adopted under section 3(b) of the act, or to an order entered thereunder within five years prior to the filing of such notification;

(3) Has been convicted within five years prior to the filing of such notification of any felony or misdemeanor in connection with the purchase or sale of any security or involving the making of any false filing with the Commission;

(4) Is subject to any order, judgment, or decree of any court of competent jurisdiction temporarily or preliminarily restraining or enjoining, or is subject to any order, judgment or decree of any court of competent jurisdiction, entered within five years prior to the filing of such notification, permanently restraining or enjoining, such person from engaging in or continuing any conduct or practice in connection with the purchase or sale of any security or involving the making of any false filing with the Commission; or

(5) Is subject to a United States Postal Service false representation order entered under section 3005 of title 39, United States Code, within five years prior to the filing of the notification required by §230.255; or is subject to a temporary restraining order or preliminary injunction entered under section 3007 of title 39, United States Code, with respect to conduct alleged to have violated section 3005 of title 39, United States Code.

This paragraph (c) of §230.252 shall not apply to any order, judgment, or decree contemplated by paragraphs (1) through (5) hereunder because of its entry against any affiliated entity before the affiliation with the issuer arose, if the affiliated entity is not in control of the issuer and if the affiliated entity and the issuer are not under the common control of a third party who was in control of the affiliated entity at the time the order, judgment, or decree was entered against it.

(d) No exemption under §§230.251 to 230.264 shall be available for the securities of any issuer, if any of its directors, officers, general partners, or beneficial owners of ten percent or more of any class of its equity securities (beneficial ownership meaning the power to vote or direct the vote and/or the power to dispose or direct the disposition of such securities), any of its promoters presently connected with it in any capacity, any underwriter of the securities to be offered, or any partner, director, or officer of any such underwriter—

(1) Has been convicted within ten years prior to the filing of the notification required by §230.255 of any felony or misdemeanor in connection with the purchase or sale of any security, involving the making of a false filing with the Commission, or arising out of the conduct of the business of an underwriter, broker, dealer, municipal securities dealer, or investment adviser;

(2) Is subject to any order, judgment, or decree of any court of competent jurisdiction temporarily or preliminarily enjoining or restraining, or is subject to any order, judgment, or decree of any court of competent jurisdiction, entered within five years prior to the filing of such notification, permanently enjoining or restraining such person from engaging in or continuing any conduct or practice in connection with the purchase or sale of any security, involving the making of a false filing with the Commission, or arising out of the conduct of the business of an underwriter, broker, dealer, municipal securities dealer, or investment adviser;

(3) Is subject to an order of the Commission entered pursuant to section 15(b), 15B(a), or 15B(c) of the Securities Exchange Act of 1934; or is subject to an order of the Commission entered pursuant to section 203(e) or (f) of the Investment Advisers Act of 1940;

(4) Is suspended or expelled from membership in, or suspended or barred from association with a member of an exchange registered as a national securities exchange pursuant to section 6 of the Securities Exchange Act of 1934, an association registered as a national securities association under section 15A of the Securities Exchange Act of 1934, or a Canadian securities exchange or association for any act or omission to act constituting conduct inconsistent with just and equitable principles of trade; or

(5) Is subject to a United States Postal Service false representation order entered under section 3005 of title 39, United States Code, within five years prior to the filing of the notification required by §230.255; or is subject to a restraining order or preliminary injunction entered under section 3007 of title 39, United States Code, with respect to conduct alleged to have violated section 3005 of title 39, United States Code.

(e) No exemption under §§230.251 to 230.264 shall be available for the securities of any issuer if any underwriter of such securities was, or was named as, an underwriter of any securities:

(1) Covered by any registration statement which is the subject of any pending proceeding or examination under section 8 of the act, or is the subject of any refusal order or stop order entered thereunder within five years prior to the filing of the notification required by §230.255; or

Appendix D: Regulation A

(2) Covered by any filing which is subject to any pending proceeding under §230.261 or any similar rule adopted under section 3(b) of the act, or to an order entered thereunder within five years prior to the filing of such notification.

(f) No exemption under §§230.251 to 230.264 shall be available for the securities of an isuer which is subject to the requirements of section 13, 14, 15(d) of the Securities Exchange Act of 1934, unless such issuer has filed all reports required by those sections to be filed during the 12 calendar months preceding the filing of the notification required by §230.255 (or for such shorter period that the issuer was required to file such reports).

(g) Paragraph (c), (d), (e), or (f) of this section shall not apply to the securities of any issuer if the Commission determines, upon a showing of good cause, that it is not necessary under the circumstances that the exemption be denied. Any such determination by the Commission shall be without prejudice to any other action by the Commission in any other proceeding or matter with respect to the issuer or any other person.

[As last amended in Release No. 33-6546, August 30, 1984, 49 F.R. 35342.]

Special Requirements for Certain Offerings

Reg. §230.253.

(a) The following provisions of this rule shall apply to any offering under §§230.251 to 230.262 of securities of any issuer which—

    (1) was incorporated or organized within one year prior to the date of filing the notification required by §230.255 and has not had a net income from operations; or

    (2) was incorporated or organized more than one year prior to such date and has not had a net income from operations, of the character in which the issuer intends to engage, for at least one of the last two fiscal years.

(b) If the issuer conducts or proposes to conduct its principal business operations in Canada, the securities to be offered hereunder shall be qualified or made eligible for offering in the Province in which such operations are or will be conducted. The securities of any other issuer incorporated or organized under the laws of Canada or any Province thereof shall be qualified or made eligible for offering in the Province in which the issuer has its principal office or principal place of business in Canada. All securities subject to this paragraph shall be offered in the Province in which they are qualified or made eligible for offering, concurrently with the offering in the United States. Issuers engaged in extractive or manufacturing enterprises shall be deemed to have their principal business operations in the Province in which their principal plants or other properties are located.

(c) In computing the amount of securities which may be offered hereunder, there shall be included, in addition to the securities specified in §230.254—

    (1) all securities issued prior to the filing of the offering statement, a proposal to be issued, for a consideration; consisting in whole or in part of assets or services and held by the person to whom issued; and

    (2) all securities issued to and held by or proposed to be issued, pursuant to options or otherwise, to any director, officer or promoter of the issuer, or to any underwriter, dealer or security salesman:

Provided, that such securities need not be included to the extent that effective provision is made, by escrow arrangements or otherwise, to assure that none of such securities or any interest therein will be reoffered to the public within one year after the commencement of the offering hereunder and that any reoffering of such securities will be made in accordance with the applicable provisions of the Act.

(d) None of the securities to be offered hereunder shall be offered for the account of any person other than the issuer of such securities.

(e) §230.257 shall not apply to any offering of securities under §§230.251 to 230.262 by any issuer which is subject to this rule.

[As last amended in Release No. 33-6340, August 7, 1981, effective Septemper 17, 1981, 46 F.R. 41766.]

Amount of Securities Exempted

Reg. §230.254.

(a) For determining the requisite amount:

    (1) The aggregate offering price of all securities of the issuer offered or sold pursuant to this regulation and any other securities offered or sold within one year prior to the commencement of the proposed offering pursuant to any

other exemption under Section 3(b) of the Act or in violation of Section 5(a) of the Act, shall not exceed the following amounts:
   (i) $1,500,000 if the securities are offered or sold by or on behalf of the issuer, or by the estate of a decedent who owned the securities at death if offered within two years after the death of the decedent, or by affiliates of issuer; provided that the aggregate offering price of securities offered or sold by or on behalf of any one affiliate, other than an estate shall not exceed $100,000; and
   (ii) $100,000 if the securities are offered or sold by or on behalf of any person other than the issuer or its affiliates; provided that the aggregate offering price of all such securities offered or sold by or on behalf of all such other persons shall not exceed $300,000 and provided that the aggregate offering price of securities offered or sold by or on behalf of an estate pursuant to this paragraph and paragraph (i) above shall not exceed $500,000.

(2) When two or more persons agree to act in concert for the purpose of selling securities of the issuer, all securities of the same class sold for the account of all such persons during any 12-month period shall be aggregated for the purpose of determining the limitation on the amount of securities sold.

(3) The following definitions shall apply for the purposes of this rule:
   (i) The term "securities of the issuer" shall include securities issued by any predecessor of the issuer or by any affiliate of the issuer which was organized or became such an affiliate within the past two years.
   (ii) The term "person" when used with reference to a person who offers securities in reliance upon the exemption provided by this rule includes, in addition to such person, all of the following persons:
      (a) Any relative or spouse of such person, or any relative of such spouse, any one of whom has the same home as such person;
      (b) Any trust or estate in which such person or any of the persons specified in (a) collectively own ten percent or more of the total beneficial interest or of which any of such persons serve as trustee, executor or in any similar capacity; and
      (c) Any corporation or other organization (other than the issuer) in which such person or any of the persons specified in (i) are the beneficial owners collectively of ten percent or more of any class of equity securities or ten percent or more of the equity interest.

(b) The aggregate offering price of securities which have a determinable market value shall be computed upon the basis of such market value as determined from transactions or quotations on a specified date within 15 days prior to the date of filing the offering statement or the offering price to the public, whichever is higher; *Provided*, That the aggregate gross proceeds actually received from the public for the securities offered hereunder shall not exceed the maximum aggregate offering price permitted in the particular case by paragraph (a) of this section.

(c) Where securities which have no determinable market value offered in exchange for outstanding securities, claims, property, or services, the aggregate offering price thereof shall be computed at the public offering price of securities of the same class for cash, or if no cash offering is to be made, then upon the basis of the value of the securities, claims, property or services to be received in exchange, as established by bona fide sales made within a reasonable time, or in the absence of such sales, upon the basis of the fair value of the securities, claims, property or services to be received in exchange, as determined by some accepted standard.

(d) The following securities need not be included in computing the amount of securities which may be offered under this regulation:
   (1) Unsold securities the offering of which has been withdrawn with the consent of the Commission by amending the pertinent offering statement to reduce the amount stated therein as proposed to be offered;
   (2) Securities acquired or to be acquired, otherwise than for distribution, by a single holder of the majority of the outstanding voting stock of the issuer in connection with a pro rata offering to stockholders;
   (3) In the case of an offering by an issuer to its existing security holders on a pro rata basis pursuant to warrants or rights, that portion of the offering made outside of the United States and Canada;
   (4) In the case of an offering of interests in an unincorporated theatrical production, interests in any affiliated unincorporated theatrical production; or
   (5) In the case of an offering of interests in an unincorporated issuer organized to hold title to, lease, operate or improve specific real property, interests in any affiliated issuer organized to hold title to, lease, operate or improve other specific real property.

[As last amended in Release No. 33-6340, August 7, 1981, effective September 17, 1981, 46 F.R. 41766.]

Appendix D: Regulation A

Filing of Offering Statement

Reg. §230.255.

(a) At least 10 days (Saturdays, Sundays and holidays excluded) prior to the date on which the initial offering or sale of any securities is to be made under this regulation, there shall be filed with the Regional Office of the Commission specified below five copies of the offering statement required by this Regulation which shall consist of Part I—Notification, Part II—Offering Circular, and Part III—Exhibits. The Commission may, however, in its discretion, authorize the commencement of the offering prior to the expiration of such 10-day period upon a written request for such authorization.

(b) The offering statement shall be signed by the issuer and each person, other than the issuer, for whose account any of the securities are to be offered. If the offering statement is signed by any person on behalf of any other person, evidence of authority to sign on behalf of such other person shall be filed with the offering statement, except where an officer of the issuer signs on behalf of the issuer. At the time of filing an offering statement, the application shall pay to the Commission at the Regional Office where the offering statement is filed a fee of $100.00, no part of which shall be refunded.

(c) The offering statement shall be filed with the Regional Office for the region in which the issuer's principal business operations are conducted or are proposed to be conducted in the United States; *Provided however,* that if the registrant's principal business operations are conducted or proposed to be conducted in the region covered by the Philadelphia Regional Office, the offering statement may be filed either at the Commission's principal office in Washington, D.C. or with the Atlanta or the New York Regional Office. The offering statement of any issuer having or proposing to have its principal business operations in Canada shall be filed with the Regional Office nearest the place where the issuer's principal business operations are conducted or proposed to be conducted, unless the offering is to be made through a principal underwriter located in the United States, in which case the offering statement shall be filed with the Regional Office for the region in which such underwriter has its principal office. If the application of the previous sentence would require a filing with the Philadelphia Regional Office, such filing may be made either at the Commission's principal office in Washington, D.C. or with the Atlanta or the New York Regional Office.

(d) An amendment to any part of the offering statement will necessitate the filing of an amended offering statement which shall be signed in the same manner as the original offering statement. Five copies of such amendment shall be filed with the same Regional Office as the original offering statement at least 10 days prior to any offering or sale of the securities subsequent to the filing of such amendment, or such shorter period as the Commission, in its discretion, may authorize upon a written request for such authorization.

(e) An offering statement or any other document filed as a part thereof may be withdrawn upon application unless the offering statement is subject to an order under §230.261 at the time the application is filed or becomes subject to such an order within 15 days (Saturdays, Sundays and holidays excluded) thereafter, *Provided* That an offering statement may not be withdrawn after any of the securities proposed to be offered thereunder have been sold. Any such application shall be signed in the same manner and filed with the same Regional Office as the offering statement.

(f) The manually signed original (or in the case of duplicate originals, one duplicate original) of all offering statements, reports, or other documents filed shall be numbered sequentially (in addition to any internal numbering which otherwise may be present) by handwritten, typed, printed, or other legible form of notation from the cover page of the document through the last page of that document and any exhibits or attachments thereto. Further, the total number of pages contained in a numbered original shall be set forth on the first page of the document.

(g) Each offering statement shall contain an exhibit index, which should immediately precede the exhibits filed with such offering statement. The index shall list each exhibit filed and identify by handwritten, typed, printed, or other legible form of notation in the manually signed original, the page number in the sequential numbering system described in paragraph (f) of this section where such exhibit can be found or where it is stated that the exhibit is incorporated by reference. Further, the first page of the manually signed offering statement shall list the page in the filing where the exhibit index is located.

[As last amended in Release No. 33-6639, April 14, 1986, effective May 16, 1986, 51 F.R. 12842.]

Filing and Use of the Offering Circular

Reg. §230.256.

(a) Except as provided in paragraph (c) of this section and in §230.257 of this part:

  (1) No written offer of securities of any issuer shall be made under this regulation unless an offering circular containing the information specified in Part II of the offering statement is concurrently given or has previously been

given to the person to whom the offer is made, or has been sent to such person under such circumstances that it would normally have been received by him at or prior to the time of such written offer; and

(2) No securities of such issuer shall be sold under this regulation unless such an offering circular is furnished to the person to whom the securities are expected to be sold at least 48 hours prior to the mailing of the confirmation of sale to such person, or is sent to such person under such circumstances that it would normally be received by him 48 hours prior to his receipt of confirmation of the sale; provided however, if the issuer is required to file reports pursuant to Section 13(a) or 15(d) of the Securities Exchange Act of 1934, as amended, the offering circular may be furnished with or prior to the confirmation of sale.

(b) In the case of transactions effected on a securities exchange, delivery of the offering circular (offering statement—Part II) shall be deemed to have been made if prior to such transactions a reasonable number of copies of the offering circular have been furnished to the exchange for delivery to any person or persons requesting copies thereof.

(c) Any written advertisement or other written communication, or any radio or television broadcast, which states from whom an offering circular containing the information specified in Part II of the offering statement may be obtained and in addition contains no more than the following information may be published, distributed or broadcast at or after the commencement of the public offering to any person prior to sending or giving such person a copy of such circular:

(1) the name of the issuer of such security;

(2) the title of the security, the amount being offered, and the per-unit offering price to the public;

(3) the identity of the general type of business of the issuer; and

(4) a brief statement as to the general character and location of its property.

(d) If the offering is not complete within nine months from the date of the offering circular (offering statement—Part II) a revised offering circular shall be prepared, filed and used in accordance with these rules as for an original offering circular, except that in the case of offerings under stock purchase, savings, stock option or other similar plans for the benefit of employees, if the offering is not completed within 12 months from the date of the offering circular, a revised offering circular shall be prepared, filed and used in accordance with these rules as for an original offering circular. In no event shall an offering circular be used which is false or misleading in light of the circumstances then existing.

(e) If the original offering circular (offering statement—Part II) is revised or amended, such revised or amended circular shall be filed as an amendment to the offering statement, as provided by §230.255(d), with the appropriate Regional Office of the Commission at least 10 days prior to its use, or such shorter period as the Commission may, in its discretion, authorize upon a written request for such authorization.

(f) Sales by a dealer (including an underwriter no longer acting as an underwriter in respect of the security involved in such transaction) of securities of an issuer not subject, immediately prior to the time of filing an offering statement, to the provisions of section 13(a) or 15(d) of the Securities Exchange Act of 1934, as amended, offered pursuant to this regulation and taking place prior to the expiration of ninety days after the first date upon which the securities were bona fide offered to the public, shall not be exempt pursuant to this regulation unless: (1) the dealer furnishes a copy of the then current offering circular (offering statement—Part II) to the purchaser prior to or with the purchaser's receipt of the confirmation of the sale; or (2) the offering circular has previously been mailed or delivered to such purchaser. Failure by a dealer to comply with the provision of this subparagraph shall not otherwise affect the availability of the exemption for any other person, including the aggregate amount of securities exempted pursuant to Rule 254.

(g) The issuer or, if there is an underwriter, the underwriter shall provide reasonable quantities of copies of the offering circular (offering statement—Part II) to any dealer on request prior to the expiration of ninety days after the first date upon which securities of such issuer were bona fide offered to the public pursuant to this regulation.

(h) An offering circular filed pursuant to paragraph (e) of this section may be distributed prior to the expiration of the 10-day waiting period for offerings provided for in §230.255(a) and (d) and paragraph (e) of this section and such distribution may be accompanied or followed by oral offers related thereto, provided the conditions in paragraphs (1) through (4) are met. For the purposes of this section, any offering circular distributed prior to the expiration of the ten day waiting period is called a Preliminary Offering Circular. Such Preliminary Offering Circular may be used to meet the requirements of paragraph (a)(2) of §230.256: *Provided,* That if a Preliminary Offering Circular is inaccurate or inadequate in any material respect, a revised Preliminary Offering Circular or an offering circular of the type referred to in paragraph (4) of this section, shall be furnished to all persons to whom the securities are to be

Appendix D: Regulation A 395

sold at least 48 hours prior to the mailing of any confirmation of sale to such persons, or shall be sent to such persons under such circumstances that it would normally be received by them 48 hours prior to their receipt of confirmation of the sale.

(1) Such Preliminary Offering Circular contains substantially the information required by this section to be included in an offering circular, or contains substantially that information except for the omission of information with respect to the offering price, underwriting discounts or commissions, discounts or commissions to dealers, amounts of proceeds, conversion rates, call prices, or other matters dependent upon the offering price. For issuers not subject to the reporting provisions under section 13(a) or 15(d) of the Securities Exchange Act of 1934, the disclosure on the outside front cover page of the Preliminary Offering Circular should include a bona fide estimate of the range of the maximum offering price and maximum number of shares or other units of securities to be offered or should include a bona fide estimate of the principal amount of debt securities to be offered.

(2) The outside front cover page of the Preliminary Offering Circular shall bear the caption "Preliminary Offering Circular," the date of its issuance, and the following statement which shall run along the left hand margin of the page and be printed perpendicular to the text, in boldface type at least as large as that used generally in the body of such offering circular:

An offering statement pursuant to Regulation A relating to these securities has been filed with the Securities and Exchange Commission. Information contained in this Preliminary Offering Circular is subject to completion or amendment. These securities may not be sold nor may offers to buy be accepted prior to the time an offering circular which is not designated as a Preliminary Offering Circular is delivered. This Preliminary Offering Circular shall not constitute an offer to sell or the solicitation of an offer to buy nor shall there by any sales of these securities in any state in which such offer, solicitation or sale would be unlawful prior to registration or qualification under the securities laws of any such state.

(3) The Preliminary Offering Circular relates to a proposed public offering of securities which is to be sold by or through one or more underwriters who are broker-dealers registered under section 15 of the Securities Exchange Act of 1934, each of whom has furnished a signed Consent and Certification in the form prescribed as a condition to the use of such offering circular.

(4) An offering circular which contains all of the information specified in Part II of the offering statement and which is not designated as a Preliminary Offering Circular is furnishing with or prior to delivery of the confirmation of sale to any person who has been furnished with a Preliminary Offering Circular pursuant to this paragraph.

[As last amended in Releast No. 33-6340, August 7, 1981, effective September 17, 1981, 46 F.R. 41766.]

Offerings Not in Excess of $100,000

Reg. §230.257. Except as to issues specified in paragraph (a) of §230.253 and issues of assessable stock, the offering circular (offering statement—Part II) need not be filed or used in connection with an offering of securities under this regulation if the aggregate offering price of all securities of the issuer, its predecessors and affiliates offered or sold without the use of such an offering circular does not exceed $100,000, computed in accordance with §230.254, provided the following conditions are met:

(a) In addition to filing Part I—Notification and Part III—Exhibits, there shall be filed as an exhibit five copies of a statement setting forth the information (other than financial statements) required by Part II—Offering Circular of the offering statement.

(b) No advertisement, article or other communication published in any newspaper, magazine or other periodical and no radio or television broadcast in regard to the offering shall contain more than the following information:

(1) the name of the issuer of such security;

(2) the title of the security, amount offered, and the per-unit offering price to the public;

(3) the identity of the general type of business of the issuer;

(4) a brief statement as to the general character and location of its property; and

(5) by whom orders will be filled or from whom further information may be obtained.

[As last amended in Release No. 33-6340, August 7, 1981, effective September 17, 1981, 46 F.R. 41766.]

Sales Material to Be Filed

Reg. §230.258. Four copies of each of the following communications prepared or authorized by the issuer or anyone associated with the issuer, and of its affiliates or any principal underwriter for use in connection with the offering of any securities under §§230.251 to 230.265 shall be filed, with the office of the Commission with which the offering statement is filed, at least five days (exclusive of Saturdays, Sundays and holidays) prior to any use thereof, or such shorter period as the Commission, in its discretion, may authorize:

(a) every advertisement, article or other communication proposed to be published in any newspaper, magazine or other periodical;

(b) the script of every radio or television broadcast; and

(c) every letter, circular or other written communication proposed to be sent, given or otherwise communicated to more than ten persons, except an offering circular (offering statement—Part II) filed pursuant to §230.256(e).

[As last amended in Release No. 33-6340, August 7, 1981, effective September 17, 1981, 46 F.R. 41766.]

Statement Required in all Offering Circulars

Reg. §230.259. There shall be set forth on the cover page of every offering circular the following statement in capital letters printed in boldface roman type at least as large as ten-point modern type and at least two points leaded;

"THE UNITED STATES SECURITIES AND EXCHANGE COMMISSION DOES NOT PASS UPON THE MERITS OF OR GIVE ITS APPROVAL TO ANY SECURITIES OFFERED OR THE TERMS OF THE OFFERING, NOR DOES IT PASS UPON THE ACCURACY OR COMPLETENESS OF ANY OFFERING CIRCULAR OR OTHER SELLING LITERATURE. THESE SECURITIES ARE OFFERED PURSUANT TO AN EXEMPTION FROM REGISTRATION WITH THE COMMISSION; HOWEVER, THE COMMISSION HAS NOT MADE AN INDEPENDENT DETERMINATION THAT THE SECURITIES OFFERED HEREUNDER ARE EXEMPT FROM REGISTRATION."

[As last amended in Release No. 33-6340, August 7, 1981, effective September 17, 1981, 46 F.R. 41766.]

Reports of Sales Hereunder

Reg. §230.260. Within 30 days after the end of each six-month period following the date of the original offering circular (offering statement—Part II) required by §230.256, or of the statement required by §230.257, the issuer or other person for whose account the securities are offered shall file with the Regional Office of the Commission with which the offering statement was filed four copies of a report on Form 2-A containing the information called for by that form. A final report shall be made upon completion or termination of the offering and may be made prior to the end of the six-month period in which the last sale is made.

[As last amended in Release No. 33-6340, August 7, 1981, effective September 17, 1981, 46 F.R. 41766.]

Suspension of Exemption

Reg. §230.261.

(a) The Commission may, at any time after the filing of an offering statement, enter an order temporarily suspending the exemption, it has reason to believe that—

(1) no exemption is available under §§230.251 to 230.262 for the securities purported to be offered hereunder or any of the terms or conditions of §§230.251 to 230.262 have not been complied with, including failure to file any report as required by §230.260.

(2) the offering statement or any other sales literature contains any untrue statement of a material fact or omits to state a material fact necessary in order to make the statements made, in the light of the circumstances under which they are made, not misleading;

(3) the offering is being made or would be made in violation of Section 17 of the Act;

(4) any event has occurred after the filing of the offering statement which would have rendered the exemption hereunder unavailable if it had occurred prior to such filing;

(5) any person specified in paragraph (c) of §230.252 has been indicted for any crime or offense of the character specified in subparagraph (3) thereof, or any proceeding has been initiated for the purpose of enjoining any such person from engaging in or continuing any conduct or practice of the character specified in subparagraph (4) of such paragraph;

Appendix D: Regulation A

(6) any person specified in paragraph (d) of §230.252 has been indicted for any crime or offense of the character specified in subparagraph (1) thereof, or any proceeding has been initiated for the purpose of enjoining any such person from engaging in or continuing any conduct or practice of the character specified in subparagraph (2) of such paragraph; or

(7) the issuer or any promoter, officer, director or underwriter has failed to cooperate, or has obstructed or refused to permit the making of an investigation by the Commission in connection with any offering made or proposed to be made hereunder.

(b) Upon the entry of an order under paragraph (a) of this section the Commission will promptly give notice to the persons on whose behalf the offering statement was filed (1) that such order has been entered, together with a brief statement of the reasons for the entry of the order, and (2) that the Commission, upon receipt of a written request within 30 days after the entry of such order, will, within 20 days after the receipt of such request, set the matter down for hearing at a place to be designated by the Commission. If no hearing is requested and none is ordered by the Commission, the order shall become permanent on the thirtieth day after its entry and shall remain in effect unless or until it is modified or vacated by the Commission. Where a hearing is requested or is ordered by the Commission, the Commission will, after notice of an opportunity for such hearing, either vacate the order or enter an order permanently suspending the exemption.

(c) The Commission may, at any time after notice of and opportunity for hearing, enter an order permanently suspending the exemption for any reason upon which it could have entered a temporary suspension order under paragraph (a) of this rule. Any such order shall remain in effect until vacated by the Commission.

(d) All notices required by this rule shall be given to the person or persons on whose behalf the offering statement was filed by personal service, registered or certified mail or confirmed telegraphic notice at the addresses of such persons given in the offering statement.

[As last amended in Release No. 33-6340, August 7, 1981, effective September 17, 1981, 46 F.R. 41766.]

Consent to Service of Process

Reg. §230.262.

(a) If the issuer, any of its directors or officers, any person for whose account any of the securities are to be offered, or any underwriter of the securities to be offered, is not a resident of the United States, each such non-resident person shall, at the time of filing the offering statement required by §230.255, furnish to the Commission in a form prescribed by or acceptable to it, a written irrevocable consent and power of attorney which—

(1) designates the Securities and Exchange Commission as an agent upon whom may be served any process, pleadings, or other papers in any civil suit or action brought against the person executing the consent and power of attorney or to which he has been joined as defendant or respondent, in any appropriate court in any place subject to the jurisdiction of the United States, where the cause of action (i) accrues on or after the effective date of this rule, and (ii) arises out of any offering made or purported to be made under §§230.251 to 230.262 or any purchase or sale of any security in connection therewith; and

(2) stipulates and agrees that any such civil suit or action may be commenced by the service of process upon the Commission and the forwarding of a copy thereof as provided in paragraph (b) of this rule, and that the service as aforesaid of any such process, pleadings, or other papers upon the Commission shall be taken and held in all courts to be as valid and binding as if due personal service thereof had been made.

(b) Service of any process, pleadings or other papers on the Commission under this rule shall be made by delivering the requisite number of copies thereof to the Secretary of the Commission or to such other person as the Commission may authorize to act in its behalf. Whenever any process, pleadings or other papers as aforesaid are served upon the Commission, it shall promptly forward a copy thereof by registered or certified mail to the appropriate defendants at their last address of record filed with the Commission. The Commission shall be furnished a sufficient number of copies for such purpose, and one copy for its files.

[As last amended in Release No. 33-6340, August 7, 1981, effective September 17, 1981, 46 F.R. 41766.]

Notice of Delayed or Suspended Offering and Sale

Reg. §230.263. If within three business days after the issuer has received notice that the Commission has no further comments with respect to the offering statement a bona fide effort is not made to proceed with the offering and sale of the securities proposed to be offered under this regulation, or if the offering or sale of such securities is suspended by the issuer or any underwriter within 15 days after the issuer has received such notice, a notice of the delay or suspension, stating the reasons therefor, shall be filed by the issuer or underwriter with the Regional Office of the Commission with which the offering statement was filed, unless such information is set forth in the offering statement. Such notice shall be sent promptly by telegraph or air mail and if sent by telegraph shall be confirmed in writing within a reasonable time by the filing of a signed copy of the notice.

[As last amended in Release No. 33-6340, August 7, 1981, effective September 17, 1981, 46 F.R. 41766.]

Procedure with Respect to Abandoned Offering Statement

Reg. §230.264. When an offering statement under §§230.251 to 230.265, of the latest substantive amendment thereto, if any, has been on file with the Commission for a period of nine months from its filing date and the offering has not commenced, the Commission may, in its discretion, proceed in the following manner to determine whether such filing has been abandoned by the issuer;

(a) Notice will be sent to the issuer, and to any counsel for the issuer named in the offering statement, by registered or certified mail, return receipt requested, addressed to the most recent addresses for issuer and issuer's counsel as reflected in the offering statement. Such notice will inform the issuer and issuer's counsel that the offering statement or amendments thereto is out of date and must be either amended to comply with applicable requirements of §§230.251 to 230.265 or be withdrawn within thirty days after the date of such notice.

(b) If the issuer or issuer's counsel fails to respond to such notice by filing a substantive amendment or withdrawing the offering statement or does not furnish a satisfactory explanation as to why the issuer has not done so within thirty days, the Commission may, where consistent with the public interest and the protection of investors, enter an order declaring the offering statement abandoned.

(c) When such an order is entered by the Commission, the papers comprising the offering statement and any amendment thereto will not be removed from the files of the Commission but will be plainly marked in the following manner: "Declared abandoned by order dated ....".]

[As last amended in Release No. 33-6340, August 7, 1981, effective September 17, 1981, 46 F.R. 41766.]

Appendix D: Regulation A

FORM 1-A

OMB APPROVAL
OMB Number: 3235-0286
Expires: January 31, 1989

[As last amended in Release No. 33-6340, August 7, 1981, effective September 17, 1981, 46 F.R. 41766.]

Date Filed _____

File No. _____

SECURITIES AND EXCHANGE COMMISSION
Washington, D.C. 20549

REGULATION A OFFERING STATEMENT
Under the Securities Act of 1933

_____
(Exact name of issuer as specified in charter)

_____
(Address of principal executive offices)

_____
(Address of principal place of business or intended principal place of business)

_____
(Name and address of agent for service)

_____
(State other jurisdiction of incorporation)   (Date of incorporation or organization)

_____
(Standard industrial classification code number)*   (IRS employer I.D. number)*

GENERAL INSTRUCTIONS

A. Rule as to Use of the Offering Statement

(a) This form is to be used for securities offerings made pursuant to Regulation A [17 CFR §§230.251 et seq.] under the Securities Act of 1933. Attention is directed to the rules applicable to offerings made pursuant to Regulation A which describe, among other things, the kinds of securities that may be sold, those issuers which may utilize Regulation A, and the amount of securities that may be exempted thereunder.

(b) Issuers utilizing Regulation A shall prepare an offering statement. All issuers shall provide the information which is called for by Part I—Notification and Part III—Exhibits, of the offering statement. Depending on the type of issuer, the kind of securities being issued, and the nature of the transaction in which the securities are being issued, issuers will be required to provide information required by the appropriate items of Part II—Offering Circular of the offering statement.

B. Preparation of Offering Statement

(a) Part I—Notification

Part I of the offering statement shall contain the numbers and captions of the items in Part I of the offering statement, but the text of the items may be omitted provided the answers are so prepared to indicate to the reader the coverage of the items without the necessity of referring to the text of the items or the instructions thereto.

_____
*If, at any time of filing, the issuer is unable to supply its standard industrial classification code number or its IRS employer I.D. number, such information may be omitted and supplied by amendment prior to the commencement of the offering.

(b) Part II—Offering Circular

Part II of the offering statement shall contain the information called for by items 1 through and including 13 which are applicable to the issuer pursuant to General Instruction B(b), except that no reference need be made to inapplicable items and negative answers to any item may be omitted. Information provided in the offering circular should be presented in textual form rather than presenting item-by-item answers. The text of the items should be omitted from the offering circular.

The information required in the offering circular need not follow the order of the items or other requirements in Part II. Such information shall not, however, be set forth in such fashion as to obscure any of the required information or any information necessary to keep the required information from being incomplete or misleading. Where an item requires information to be given in tabular form it shall be given in substantially the tabular form specified in the item. All information contained in the offering circular shall be set forth under appropriate captions or headings reasonably indicative of the principal subject matter set forth thereunder. Except as to financial statements and other tabular data, all information set forth in the offering circular shall be divided into reasonably short paragraphs or sections.

Unless indicated otherwise, information set forth in any part of the offering circular need not be repeated elsewhere in the offering circular. Where necessary or desirable to call attention to information contained elsewhere in the offering circular, this may be done by an appropriate cross-reference.

(c) Part III—Exhibits

Part III of the offering statement shall include the index to exhibits and all exhibits required by that part. The text of the items in Part III need not be repeated in Part III provided the index clearly identifies each exhibit and the exhibits are in readable form.

(d) Printing

The offering statement may be printed, mimeographed, lithographed, or typewritten or prepared by any similar process which will result in clearly legible copies.

C. Documents Comprising the Offering Statement

The offering statement shall consist of the cover page, Part I—Notification, Part II—Offering Circular, Part III—Exhibits, the required signatures, and any other information or documents which are required or which the issuer may file as a part of the offering statement.

Each part of the offering statement may be amended independent of the other parts of the offering statement. Each amendment should indicate which part(s) is being amended. An amendment to any part will, however, necessitate the filing of a new signature page.

D. Supplemental Information

Supplemental information submitted pursuant to any item in Part I—Notification, Part II—Offering Circular, or Part III—Exhibits of the offering statement will be returned to the person who submitted it provided a request for its return is made at the time such information is submitted to the Commission and provided further that return of such information is consistent with the protection of investors and the provisions of the Freedom of Information Act [5 U.S.C. 552]. In addition, issuers may request confidential treatment of supplemental information submitted to the Commission [17 CFR 200.83].

The following is presented as a brief checklist for complying with the supplemental informational requirements of Regulation A. The issuer shall refer to the text of the item for a full description of the requirements.

The issuer shall supplementally furnish the Commission:

(1) A statement as to whether or not the amount of compensation to be allowed or paid to the underwriter has been cleared with the NASD (Part II, Item 2, instruction 3).

(2) Any engineering, management or similar report, or a statement as to the absence thereof (Part II, Item 6(a)(3)(b)).

(3) Under special circumstances, a letter describing the nature and amount of any adjustments other than normal recurring adjustments (Part II, Item 13(b)).

(4) Written advice, when shares are placed in escrow, that none of the deposited shares or interests therein have been transferred (Form 7-A, paragraph 4).

The staff may under appropriate circumstances request additional supplemental information where necessary to a more complete understanding of the offering statement.

PART I—NOTIFICATION

Item 1. Significant Parties

(a) List the full name and business and residential addresses for (1)-(3) below. List the full name and business address for (4)-(13) below:
  (1) the issuer's directors;
  (2) the issuer's officers;
  (3) the issuer's general partners;
  (4) record owners of 10 percent or more of any class of the issuer's equity securities or any other person who has or shares the right to vote or direct the voting of such securities;
  (5) promoters currently connected with the issuer;
  (6) predecessors of the issuer;
  (7) affiliates of the issuer;
  (8) counsel to the issuer in connection with the proposed offering;
  (9) each managing underwriter in connection with the proposed offering;
  (10) the underewriter's directors;
  (11) the underwriter's officers;
  (12) the underwriter's general partners;
  (13) counsel to the underwriter.

Item 2. Application of Rule 252(c)-(e)

(a) State whether any of the individuals or entities identified pursuant to Item 1 are subject to any disability described in Rule 252(c)-(e).

(b) If any such individual or entity is subject to the provisions of Rule 252:
  (1) provide a full description including pertinent names, dates and other details; and
  (2) state whether or not an application has been made pursuant to Rule 252(f) for a waiver of the applicable provisions of Rule 252 and whether such application has been granted or denied.

Item 3. Application of Rule 253(a) and (b)

State whether or not the issuer is subject to the provisions of Rule 253(a) or (b).

Item 4. Jurisdictions in Which Securities Are to Be Offered

(a) List the jurisdictions in which the securities are to-be offered by underwriters, dealers or salespersons.

(b) List the jurisdictions in which the securities are to be offered other than by underwriters, dealers or salesmen and state the method by which such securities are to be offered.

(c) If the offering or any part thereof is to be made by use of the facilities of any securities exchange, identify the exchange.

(d) If the issuer is subject to Rule 253(b), state the Province(s) in which the securities have been or will be qualified or made eligible for offering.

Instruction: In the event an offering is to be made in jurisdictions or on exchanges not previously identified pursuant to this item, an amendment to the offering statement should be filed which identifies the new jurisdictions and exchanges.

Item 5. Unregistered Securities Issued or Sold Within One Year

(a) As to any unregistered securities issued by the issuers within one year prior to the filing of this notification, state:
  (1) the name of such issuer;
  (2) the title and amount of securities issued;
  (3) the aggregate offering price or other consideration for which they were issued and the basis for computing the amount thereof;

(4) the names of the persons or the identity of the class of persons to whom the securities were issued.

Instruction: In responding to this subsection, issuers should consider the effect of the grant or exercise of options, warrants, or rights with regard to the issuer's securities.

(b) As to any unregistered securities of the issuer or any of its predecessors or affiliated issuers which were sold within one year prior to the filing of this notification by or for the account of any person who at the time was a director, officer, promoter or principal security holder of the issuer of such securities, or was an underwriter of any securities of such issuer, furnish the information specified in 1 through 4 of paragraph (a).

(c) Indicate the section of the Act or rule or regulation of the Commission under which exemption from registration was claimed with respect to such securities and state briefly the facts relied upon for the exemption.

Item 6. Other Present or Proposed Offerings

State whether or not the issuer or any of its affiliated issuers is currently offering or currently contemplates the offering of any securities in the United States or Canada in addition to those covered by this notification. If so, describe fully the present or proposed offering.

Item 7. Marketing Arrangements

(a) Briefly describe any arrangement known to the issuer or to any person named in answer to Item 4(d) or 10(a) of Part II made for any of the following purposes:

(1) To limit or restrict the sale of other securities of the same class as those to be offered for the period of distribution.

(2) To stabilize the market for any of the securities to be offered.

(3) For withholding commissions, or otherwise to hold each underwriter or dealer responsible for the distribution of his participation.

(b) Identify any principal underwriter that intends to confirm sales to any accounts over which it exercises discretionary authority and include an estimate of the amount of securities so intended to be confirmed.

Instructions: 1. If the information required by subsection (b) is not available at the time the offering statement is filed, an amendment to Part I—Notification, including such information, should be made prior to the commencement of the offering.

2. If the answer to this item is contained in an exhibit, the item may be answered by a cross-reference to the relevant paragraphs of the exhibit.

Item 8. Relationship with Issuer of Experts Named in Offering Statement

If any expert named in the offering statement as having prepared or certified any part thereof was employed for such purpose on a contingent basis or, at the time of such preparation or certification or at any time thereafter, had a material interest in the registrant or any of its parents or subsidiaries or was connected with the registrant or any of its subsidiaries as a promoter, underwriter, voting trustee, director, officer or employee furnish a brief statement of the nature of such contingent basis, interest or connection.

PART II—OFFERING CIRCULAR

Item 1. Cover Page

The cover page of the offering circular shall include the following information:

(a) Name of the issuer;

(b) The mailing address of the issuer's principal executive offices including the zip code and the issuer's telephone number;

(c) Date of the offering circular;

(d) Description and amount of securities offered (*Note:* this description should include, for example, appropriate disclosure of redemption and conversion features of debt securities);

(e) The statement required by Rule 259;

(f) The table(s) required by Item 2;

(g) The name of the underwriter or underwriters;

Appendix D: Regulation A

(h) Any materials required by the law of any state in which the securities are to be offered;

(i) If applicable, identification of material risks in connection with the purchase of the securities; and

(j) Approximate date of commencement of proposed sale to the public.

Instruction: Where the name of the registrant is the same as the name of another well-known company or indicates a line of business in which the registrant is not engaged or is engaged to only a limited extent, a statement should be furnished to that effect. In some circumstances, however, disclosure may not be sufficient, and a change of name may be the only way to cure its misleading character.

Item 2. Distribution Spread

(a) The information called for by the following table shall be given, in substantially the tabular form indicated, on the outside front cover page of the offering circular as to all securities being offered (estimate, if necessary).

	Price to public	Underwriting discounts and commissions	Proceeds to issuer or other persons
Per unit			
Total			

If the securities are to be offered on a best efforts basis the cover page should set forth the termination date, if any, of the offering, any minimum required sale and any arrangements to place the funds received in an escrow, trust, or similar arrangement. The following tabular presentation of the total maximum and minimum securities to be offered should be combined with the table required above:

	Price to public	Underwriting discounts and commissions	Proceeds to issuer or other persons
Total Minimum			
Total Maximum			

Instructions: 1. The term "commissions" shall include all cash, securities, contracts, or anything else of value, paid, to be set aside, disposed of, or understandings with or for the benefit of any other persons in which any underwriter is interested, made in connection with the sale of such security.

2. Only commissions paid by the issuer in cash are to be indicated in the table. Commissions paid by other persons or any form of non-cash compensation shall be briefly identified in a note to the table with a cross-reference to a more complete description elsewhere in the offering circular.

3. Prior to the commencement of sales pursuant to Regulation A, the issuer shall inform the Commission whether or not the amount of compensation to be allowed or paid to the underwriters, as described in the offering statement, has been cleared with the National Association of Securities Dealers, Inc.

4. If the securities are not to be offered for cash, state the basis upon which the offering is to be made.

5. If it is impracticable to state the price to the public, the method by which it is to be determined shall be explained.

(b) Any finder's fees or similar payments shall be disclosed on the cover page with a reference to a more complete discussion in the offering circular. Such disclosure should identify the finder, the nature of the services rendered and the nature of any relationship between the finder and the issuer, its officers, directors, promoters, principal stockholders and underwriters (including any affiliates thereof).

(c) The amount of the expenses of the offering borne by the issuer, including underwriting expenses to be borne by the issuer, should be disclosed in a footnote to the table.

Item 3. Summary Information, Risk Factors and Dilution

(a) Where appropriate to a clear understanding by investors, there should be set forth in the forepart of the offering circular, under an appropriate caption, a carefully organized series of short, concise paragraphs, summarizing the principal factors which make the offering one of high risk or speculative. *Note:* These factors may be due to such matters as an absence of an operating history of the issuer, an absence of profitable operations in recent periods, an erratic financial history, the financial position of the issuer, the nature of the business in which the issuer is engaged or proposes to engage, conflicts of interest with management, reliance on the efforts of a single individual, or the method of determining the market price where no market currently exists. Issuers should *avoid* generalized statements and include only those factors which are unique to the issuer.

(b) Where there is a material disparity between the public offering price and the effective cash cost to officers, directors, promoters and affiliated persons for shares acquired by them in a transaction during the past three years, or which they have a right to acquire, there should be included a comparison of the public contribution under the proposed public offering and the effective cash contribution of such persons. In such cases, and in other instances where the extent of the dilution makes it appropriate, the following shall be given: (1) the net tangible book value per share before and after the distribution; (2) the amount of the increase in such net tangible book value per share attributable to the cash payment made by purchasers of the shares being offered; and (3) the amount of the immediate dilution from the public offering price which will be absorbed by such purchasers.

Item 4. Plan of Distribution

(a) If the securities are to be offered through underwriters, give the names of the principal underwriters, and state the respective amounts underwritten. Identify each such underwriter having a material relationship to the issuer and state the nature of the relationship. State briefly the nature of the underwriters' obligation to take the securities.

(b) State briefly the discounts and commissions to be allowed or paid to dealers, including all cash, securities, contracts or other consideration to be received by any dealer in connection with the sale of the securities.

(c) Outline briefly the plan of distribution of any securities being issued which are to be offered through the selling efforts of brokers or dealers or otherwise than through underwriters.

(d) If any of the securities are to be offered for the account of security holders, indicate on the cover page the total amount to be offered for their account and include a cross-reference to a fuller discussion elsewhere in the offering circular. Such discussion should identify each selling security holder, state the amount owned by him, the amount offered for his account and the amount to be owned after the offering.

(e) (1) Describe any arrangements for the return of funds to subscribers if all of the securities to be offered are not sold; if there are no such arrangements, so state.

(2) If there will be a material delay in the payment of the proceeds of the offering by the underwriter to the issuer, the salient provisions in this regard and the effects on the issuer should be stated.

Instruction: Attention is directed to the provisions of Rules 10b-9 [17 CFR §240.10b-9] and 15c2-4 (17 CFR §240.15c2-4] under the Securities Exchange Act of 1934. These rules outline, among other things, antifraud provisions concerning the return of funds to subscribers and the transmission of proceeds of an offering to a seller.

Item 5. Use of Proceeds to Issuer

State the principal purposes for which the net proceeds to the issuer from the securities to be offered are intended to be used, and the approximate amount intended to be used for each such purpose.

Instructions: 1. If any substantial portion of the proceeds has not been allocated for particular purposes, a statement to that effect shall be made together with a statement of the amount of proceeds not so allocated and how the registrant expects to employ such funds not so allocated.

2. Include a statement as to the use of the actual proceeds if they are not sufficient to accomplish the purpose set forth and the order of priority in which they will be applied. However, such statement need not be made if the underwriting arrangements are such that, if any securities are sold to the public, it can be reasonably expected that the actual proceeds of the issue will not be substantially less than the estimated aggregate proceeds to the issuer as shown under Item 2.

3. If any material amounts of other funds are to be used in conjunction with the proceeds, state the amounts and sources of such other funds.

4. If any material part of the proceeds is to be used to discharge indebtedness, describe the terms of such indebtedness. If the indebtedness to be discharged was incurred within one year, describe the use of the proceeds of such indebtedness.

5. If any material amount of the proceeds is to be used to acquire assets, otherwise than in the ordinary course of business, briefly describe and state the cost of the assets. If the assets are to be acquired from affiliates of the issuer or their associates, give the names of the persons from whom they are to be acquired and set forth the principle followed in determining the cost to the issuer.

6. The issuer may reserve the right to change the use of proceeds provided that such reservation is due to certain contingencies which are adequately disclosed.

Appendix D: Regulation A   405

Item 6. Description of Business
- (a) Narrative description of business.
    - (1) Describe the business done and intended to be done by the issuer and its subsidiaries and the general development of the business during the past five years or such shorter period as the issuer may have been in business. Such description should include, but not be limited to, a discussion of the following factors if such factors are material to an understanding of the issuer's business:
        - (a) The principal products produced and services rendered and the principal markets for and method of distribution of such products and services.
        - (b) The status of a product or service if the issuer has made public information about a new product or service which would require the investment of a material amount of the assets of the issuer or is otherwise material.
        - (c) The estimated amount spent during each of the last two fiscal years on company-sponsored research and development activities determined in accordance with generally accepted accounting principles. In addition, state the estimated dollar amount spent during each of such years on material customer-sponsored research activities relating to the development of new products, services or techniques or the improvement of existing products, services or techniques.
        - (d) The number of persons employed by the issuer, indicating the number employed full time.
        - (e) The material effects that compliance with Federal, State and local provisions which have been enacted or adopted regulating the discharge of materials into the environment, or otherwise relating to the protection of the environment, may have upon the capital expenditures, earnings and competitive position of the issuer and its subsidiaries. The issuer shall disclose any material estimated capital expenditures for environment control facilities for the remainder of its current fiscal year and for such further periods as the issuer may deem material.
    - (2) The issuer should also describe those distinctive or special characteristics of the issuer's operation or industry which may have a material impact upon the issuer's future financial performance. Examples of factors which might be discussed include dependence on one or a few major customers or suppliers (including suppliers of raw materials or financing), existing or probable governmental regulation, material terms of and/or expiration of material labor contracts or patents, trademarks, licenses, franchises, concessions or royalty agreements, unusual competitive conditions in the industry, cyclicality of the industry and anticipated raw material or energy shortages to the extent management may not be able to secure a continuing source of supply.
    - (3) The following requirement in subparagraph (a) applies only to issuers (including predecessors) which have not received revenue from operations during each of the three fiscal years immediately prior to the filing of the offering statement.
        - (a) Describe, if formulated, the issuer's plan of operation for the twelve months following the commencement of the proposed offering. If such information is not available, the reasons for its unavailability shall be stated. Disclosure relating to any plan should include, among other things, a statement indicating whether, in the issuer's opinion, the proceeds from the offering will satisfy its cash requirements and whether, in the next six months, it will be necessary to raise additional funds.
        - (b) Any engineering, management or similar reports which have been prepared or provided for external use by the issuer or by a principal underwriter in connection with the proposed offering should be furnished to the Commission at the time of filing the offering statement or as soon as practicable thereafter. There should also be furnished at the same time a statement as to the actual or proposed use and distribution of such report or memorandum. Such statement should identify each class of persons who have received or will receive the report or memorandum, and state the number of copies distributed to each such class. If no such report or memorandum has been prepared, the Division should be so informed in writing at the time the report or memorandum would otherwise have been submitted.
- (b) Segment Data. If the issuer is required to include segment information in its financial statements, an appropriate cross-reference shall be included in the description of business.

Item 7. Description of Property

State briefly the location and general character of the principal plants, and other materially important physical properties of the issuer and its subsidiaries. If any such property is not held in fee or is held subject to any major encumbrance, so state and briefly describe how held.

Instruction: What is required is information essential to an investor's appraisal of the securities being offered. Such information should be furnished as will reasonably inform investors as to the suitability, adequacy, productive capacity and extent of utilization of the facilities used in the enterprise. Detailed descriptions of the physical characteristics of individual properties or legal descriptions by metes and bounds are not required and should not be given.

Item 8. Directors, Executive Officers and Significant Employees

(a) List the names and ages of each of the following persons stating his term of office and any periods during which he has served as such and briefly describe any arrangement or understanding between him and any other person(s) (naming such person(s)) pursuant to which he was or is to be selected to his office or position:

   (1) directors;

   (2) persons nominated or chosen to become directors;

   (3) executive officers;

   (4) persons chosen to become executive officers;

   (5) significant employees.

Instructions: 1. No nominee or person chosen to become a director or person chosen to be an executive officer who has not consented to act as such should be named in response to this item.

2. The term "executive officer" means the president, secretary, treasurer, any vice-president in charge of a principal business function (such as sales, administration, or finance) and any other person who performs similar policy making functions for the issuer.

3. The term "significant employee" means persons such as production managers, sales managers, or research scientists, who are not executive officers, but who make or are expected to make significant contributions to the business of the issuer.

(b) Family relationships. State the nature of any family relationship between any director, executive officer, person nominated or chosen by the issuer to become a director or executive officer or any significant employee.

Instruction: The term "family relationship" means any relationship by blood, marriage, or adoption, not more remote than first cousin.

(c) Business experience. Give a brief account of the business experience during the past five years of each director, person nominated or chosen to become a director or executive officer, and each significant employee, including his principal occupations and employment during that period and the name and principal business of any corporation or other organization in which such occupations and employment were carried on. When an executive officer or significant employee has been employed by the issuer for less than five years, a brief explanation should be included as to the nature of the responsibilities undertaken by the individual in prior positions to provide adequate disclosure of his prior business experience. What is required is information relating to the level of his professional competence which may include, depending upon the circumstances, such specific information as the size of the operation supervised.

(d) Involvement in certain legal proceedings. Describe any of the following events which occurred during the past five years and which are material to an evaluation of the ability or integrity of any director, person nominated to become a director or executive officer of the issuer.

   (1) A petition under the Bankruptcy Act or any State insolvency law was filed by or against, or a receiver, fiscal agent or similar officer was appointed by a court for the business or property of such person, or any partnership in which he was general partner at or within 2 years before the time of such filing, or any corporation or business association of which he was an executive officer at or within two years before the time of such filing;

   (2) Such person was convicted in a criminal proceeding (excluding traffic violations and other minor offenses).

Item 9. Remuneration of Directors and Officers

(a) Furnish, in substantially the tabular form indicated, the aggregate annual remuneration of each of the three highest paid persons who are officers or directors as a group during the issuer's last fiscal year. State the number of persons in the group referred to above without naming them.

Name of individual or identity of group	Capacities in which remuneration was received	Aggregate remuneration

Appendix D: Regulation A

Instruction: 1. In case of remuneration paid or to be paid otherwise than in cash, if it is impracticable to determine the cash value thereof, state in a note to the table the nature and amount thereof. 2. This item is to be answered on an accrual basis if practicable; if not so answered, state the basis used.

(b) Briefly describe all remuneration payments proposed to be made in the future pursuant to any ongoing plan or arrangement to the individuals and group specified in Item 9(a). The description should include a summary of how each plan operates, any performance formula or measure in effect (or the criteria used to determine payment amounts), the time periods over which the measurements of benefits will be determined, payment schedules, and any recent material amendments to the plan. Information need not be furnished with respect to any group life, health, hospitalization, or medical reimbursement plans which do not discriminate in scope, terms or operation in favor of officers or directors of the registrant and which are available generally to all salaried employees.

Item 10. Security Ownership of Management and Certain Security-Holders

(a) Voting securities and principal holders thereof.

Furnish the following information, in substantially the tabular form indicated, with respect to voting securities held of record by:

(1) each of the three highest paid persons who are officers and directors of the issuer; *Note* — In the event none of the issuer's officers or directors have received a salary in the past twelve months, this item should be responded to for every officer and director;

(2) all officers and directors as a group;

(3) each shareholder who owns more than 10% of any class of the issuer's securities, including those shares subject to outstanding options.

(1) Title of class	(2) Name and address of owner	(3) Amount owned before the offering	(4) Amount owned after the offering	(5) Percent of class

Instruction: Column (4) need not be responded to if the information would be the same as that appearing under column (3).

(b) If, to the knowledge of the issuer, any other person holds or shares the power to vote or direct the voting of securities described pursuant to subsection (a) above, appropriate disclosure should be made. In addition, if any person other than those named pursuant to subsection (a) holds or shares the power to vote 10% or more of the issuer's voting securities, the information required by the table should be provided with respect to such person.

(c) Non-voting securities and principal holders thereof. Furnish the same information as required in subsection (a) above with respect to securities that are not entitled to vote.

(d) Options, warrants and rights. Furnish the information required by the table as to options, warrants or rights to purchase securities from the issuer or any of its subsidiaries held by each of the individuals and referred to in subsection (a) above:

Name of holder	Title and amount of securities called for by options, warrants or rights	Exercise price	Date of exercise

Instruction: Where the total market value of securities called for by all outstanding options, warrants or rights does not exceed $10,000 for any officer, director, or principal shareholder named in answer to this item, or $50,000 for all officers and directors as a group, this item need not be answered with respect to options, warrants or rights held by such person or group. If the issuer cannot ascertain the market value of its securities, the offering price may be used for purposes of this subsection. If, as is the case with offerings of debt securities, the offering price cannot be determined at the time of filing the offering statement, the issuer may utilize any reasonable method of valuation.

(e) List all parents of the issuer, showing the basis of control and as to each parent the percentage of voting securities owned or other basis of control by its immediate parent, if any.

Item 11. Interest of Management and Others in Certain Transactions

Describe briefly any transactions during the previous two years or any presently proposed transactions, to which the issuer or any of its subsidiaries was or is to be a party, in which any of the following persons had or is to have a direct or indirect material interest, naming such person and stating his relationship to the issuer, the nature of his interest in the transaction and, where practicable, the amount of such interest;

    (1) any director or officer of the issuer;

    (2) Any nominee for election as a director;

    (3) Any principal security holder named in answer to Item 10(a);

    (4) If the issuer was incorporated or organized within the past three years, any promoter of the issuer;

    (5) Any relative or spouse of any of the foregoing persons, or any relative of such spouse, who has the same house as such person or who is a director or officer of any parent or subsidiary of the issuer.

Instruction: 1. No information need be given in answer to this item as to any transaction where:

    (a) The rates of charges involved in the transaction are determined by competitive bids, or the transaction involves the rendering of services as a common or contract carrier fixed in conformity with law or governmental authority;

    (b) The transaction involves services as a bank depositary of funds, transfer agent, registrar, trustee under a trust indenture, or similar services;

    (c) The amount involved in the transaction or a series of similar transactions, including all periodic installments in the case if any lease or other agreement providing for periodic payments or installments does not exceed $50,000; or

    (d) The interest of the specified person arises solely from the ownership of securities of the issuer and the specified person receives no extra or special benefit not shared on a pro-rata basis by all of the holders of securities of the class.

2. It should be noted that this Item calls for disclosure of indirect as well as direct material interests in transactions. A person who has a position or relationship with a firm, corporation, or other entity which engages in a transaction with the issuer or its subsidiaries may have an indirect interest in such transaction by reason of such position or relationship. However, a person shall be deemed not to have a material indirect interest in a transaction within the meaning of this Item where:

    (a) the interest arises only (i) from such person's position as a director of another corporation or organization (other than a partnership) which is a party to the transaction, or (ii) from the direct or indirect ownership by such person and all other persons specified in subparagraphs (1) through (5) above, in the aggregate, of less than a 10 percent equity interest in another person (other than a partnership) which is a party to the transaction, or (iii) from both such position and ownership;

    (b) the interest arises only from such person's position as a limited partner in a partnership in which he and all other persons specified in (1) through (5) above had an interest of less than 10 percent; or

    (c) the interest of such person arises solely from the holding of an equity interest (including a limited partnership interest but excluding a general partnership interest) or a creditor interest in another person which is a party to the transaction with the issuer or any of its subsidiaries and the transaction is not material to such other person.

3. Include the name of each person whose interest in any transaction is described and the nature of the relationships by reason of which such interest is required to be described. The amount of the interest of any specified person shall be computed without regard to the amount of the profit or loss involved in the transaction. Where it is not practicable to state the approximate amount of the interest, the approximate amount involved in the transaction shall be disclosed.

4. Information should be included as to any material underwriting discounts and commissions upon the sale of securities by the issuer where any of the specified persons was or is to be a principal underwriter or is a controlling person, or member, of a firm which was or is to be a principal underwriter. Information need not be given concerning ordinary management fees paid by underwriters to a managing underwriter pursuant to an agreement among underwriters the parties to which do not include the issuer or its subsidiaries.

5. As to any transaction involving the purchase or sale of assets by or to any issuer or any subsidiary, otherwise than in the ordinary course of business, state the cost of the assets to the purchaser and, if acquired by the seller within two years prior to the transaction, the cost thereof to the seller.

6. Information shall be furnished in answer to this item with respect to transactions not excluded above which involve remuneration from the issuer or its subsidiaries, directly or indirectly, to any of the specified persons for services in any capacity unless the interest of such persons arises solely from the ownership individually and in the aggregate of less than 10 percent of any class of equity securities of another corporation furnishing the services to the issuer or its subsidiaries.

Item 12. Securities Being Offered

    (a) If capital stock is being offered, state the title of the class and furnish the following information:

        (1) Outline briefly: (i) dividend rights; (ii) voting rights; (iii) liquidation rights; (iv) preemptive rights; (v) conversion rights; (vi) redemption provisions; (vii) sinking fund provisions; and (viii) liability to further calls or to assessment by the issuer.

(2) Briefly describe potential liabilities imposed on shareholders under state statutes or foreign law, e.g., to laborers, servants or employees of the registrant, unless such disclosure would be immaterial because the financial resources of the registrant are such as to make it unlikely that the liability will ever be imposed.

(b) If debt securities are being offered, outline briefly the following:

(1) Provisions with respect to interest, conversion, maturity, redemption, amortization, sinking fund or retirement.

(2) Provisions with respect to the kind and priority of any lien securing the issue, together with a brief identification of the principal properties subject to such lien.

(3) Provisions restricting the declaration of dividends or requiring the maintenance of any ratio of assets, the creation or maintenance of reserves or the maintenance of properties.

(4) Provisions permitting or restricting the issuance of additional securities, the withdrawal of cash deposited against such issuance, the incurring of additional debt, the release or substitution of assets securing the issue, the modification of the terms of the security, and similar provisions.

Instruction: In the case of secured debt there should be stated (i) the approximate amount of unbonded property available for use against the issuance of bonds, as of the most recent practicable date, and (ii) whether the securities being issued are to be issued against such property, against the deposit of cash, or otherwise.

(c) If securities described are to be offered pursuant to warrants, rights, or convertible securities, state briefly:

(1) the amount of securities called for by such warrants, convertible securities or rights;

(2) the period during which and the price at which the warrants, convertible securities or rights are exercisable;

(3) the amounts of warrants, convertible securities or rights outstanding; and

(4) any other material terms of such securities.

(d) In the case of any other kind of securities, appropriate information of a comparable character.

Item 13. Financial Statements

Furnish the following financial statements of the issuer, or of the issuer and its predecessors, prepared in accordance with generally accepted accounting principles and practices in the United States or, in the case of a Canadian company, a reconciliation to such shall U.S. GAAP shall be filed as part of the financial statements. The statements required for the issuer's latest fiscal year shall be certified by an independent public accountant or certified public accountant in accordance with Regulation S-X if the issuer has filed or is required to file with the Commission certified financial statements for such fiscal year; the statements filed for the period or periods preceding such latest year need not be certified. If audited financial statements are filed by an issuer which is not subject to the reporting requirements of Sections 13 or 15(d) of the Securities Exchange Act of 1934 such audited financial statements need not comply with the requirements of Regulation S-X, except the qualifications and reports of an independent accountant shall comply with the requirements of Article 2 of Regulation S-X

(a) A balance sheet shall be furnished as of a date within 90 days prior to the filing of an offering statement or such longer period of time, not exceeding six months, as the Commission may permit at the written request of the issuer upon a showing of good cause therefor. For filings made after 90 days subsequent to the end of the issuer's most recent fiscal year the filings shall include a balance sheet as of the end of such recent fiscal year.

(b) Statements of income, statements of changes in financial conditions, and statements of other stockholders' equity for each of the two fiscal years preceding the date of the most recent balance sheet being filed and for the interim period, if any, between the end of the most recent of such fiscal years and the date of the most recent balance sheet being filed, or for the period of the issuer's existence if less than the period specified above.

If an unaudited income statement for an interim period is filed, a statement shall be made that in the opinion of management all adjustments necessary for a fair statement of the results for the interim period have been included. If all such adjustments are of a normal recurring nature, a statement to that effect shall be made; otherwise there shall be furnished as supplementary information, but not as a part of the offering statement, a letter describing in detail the nature and amount of any adjustments other than normal recurring adjustments entering into the determination of the results shown.

(c) Past succession to other businesses.

(1) If, during the period for which its income statements are required, the issuer has by purchase or by pooling of interests succeeded to one or more businesses which in the aggregate would meet the test for significant subsidiary ((C)(2) below), the additions, eliminations and other changes effected in the succession shall be appropriately set forth in a note or supporting schedule to the balance sheet being filed, and, if a purchase has been effected during the most recent fiscal year or in a subsequent period, pro forma statements of

income reflecting the combined operations of the entities shall be furnished in columnar form for the latest fiscal year and any interim periods. In addition, furnish income statements, separate or combined as appropriate, for such business or businesses for such period prior to the purchase as may be necessary when added to the time, if any, for which income statements after the purchase are filed to cover the same period for which income statements of the issuer are required in Item (b) above.

Note: This subsection (c)(1) shall not apply with respect to the issuer's succession to the business of any totally held subsidiary or to the succession of one or more businesses which, considered in the aggregate, would not meet the test of a significant subsidiary.

(2) The term "significant subsidiary" means (a) a subsidiary or (b) a subsidiary and its subsidiaries which meet any of the conditions described below based on (i) the most recent annual financial statements, including consolidated financial statements, of such subsidiary which would be required to be filed if such subsidiary were an issuer and (ii) the most recent annual consolidated financial statements of the issuer being filed:

1. the parent's and its other subsidiaries' investments in and advances to, or their proportionate share (based on their equity interests) of the total assets (after intercompany elimination) of, the subsidiary exceed 10 percent of the total assets of the parent and its consolidated subsidiaries.

2. the parent's and its other subsidiaries' proportionate share (based on their equity interests) of the total sales and revenues (after intercompany eliminations) of the subsidiary exceeds 10 percent of the total sales and revenues of the parent and its consolidated subsidiaries.

3. the parents' and its other subsidiaries' equity in the income before income taxes and extraordinary items of the subsidiary exceeds 10 percent of such income of the parent and its consolidated subsidiaries, provided, that if such income of the parent and its consolidated subsidiaries is at least 10 percent lower than the average of such income for the last five fiscal years such average income may be substituted in the determination.

(d) Future successions to other businesses.

(1) If, after the date of the most recent balance sheet filed pursuant to paragraph (a) above, the issuer by purchase or by pooling of interests succeeded or is about to succeed to one or more businesses or acquired or is about to acquire an investment in a business the investment in which is required to be accounted for by the equity method, there shall be filed for such business financial statements, combined if appropriate, which would be required if they were the issuer. In addition, to reflect the succession to any businesses, there shall be filed in columnar form (i) a balance sheet of the issuer, (ii) the balance sheets of the constituent businesses, (iii) the changes to be effected in the succession, and (iv) the pro forma balance sheet of the issuer giving effect to the plan of succession. There shall also be filed pro forma statements of income in columnar form for the periods for which the results of operations of the acquired business would have been included in the issuer's income statement for a pooling of interests or would have been presented on a pro forma basis for a purchase had succession occurred on the date of the latest balance sheet filed. By a note to the financial statements, or otherwise, a brief explanation of the changes shall be given.

(2) The acquisition of securities shall be deemed to be the acquisition of a business if such securities give control of the business or combined with securities already held give such control.

(3) No financial statements need be filed, however, for any business acquired or to be acquired, or for any business in which an investment acquired or to be acquired is required to be accounted for by the equity method, from a totally held subsidiary. In addition, the statements of any one or more such businesses may be omitted if the businesses, considered in the aggregate, would not meet the test of a significant subsidiary as defined above.

PART III—EXHIBITS

Item 1. Index to Exhibits

(a) An index to the exhibits filed should be presented immediately following the cover page of Part III.

(b) Each exhibit should be listed in the exhibit index according to the number assigned to it under Item 2.

(c) The index to exhibits should identify the location of the exhibit under the sequential numbering system.

(d) Where exhibits are incorporated by reference, the reference shall be made in the index to exhibits.

Instructions: (1) Any document or part thereof filed with the Commission pursuant to any Act administered by the Commission may, subject to the limitations of Rule 24 of the Commission's **Rules of Practice,** be incorporated by reference as an exhibit to any offering statement. (2) If any modification has occurred in the text of

Appendix D: Regulation A

any document incorporated by reference since the filing thereof, the issuer shall file with the reference a statement containing the text of such modification and the date thereof.

Item 2. Description of Exhibits

Set forth below is a description of each document for which copies should be filed, where appropriate:

(1) *Underwriting agreement*—Each underwriting contract or agreement with a principal underwriter or letter pursuant to which the securities are to be distributed; if the terms of such documents have not been determined, the proposed forms thereof.

(2) *Charter and by-laws*—The charter and by-laws of the issuer or instruments corresponding thereto as presently in effect and any amendments thereto.

(3) *Instruments defining the rights of security holders*—

  (a) All instruments defining the rights of (a) holders of the equity or debt securities being issued; (2) holders of long-term debt of the issuer, and of all subsidiaries for which consolidated or unconsolidated financial statements are required to be filed; and (3) holders of a new class of securities or indebtedness, the creation of which was required to be disclosed in a periodic report.

  (b) Where the instrument defines the rights of holders of long-term debt of the issuer and all of its subsidiaries for which consolidated financial statements are required to be filed, there need not be filed (1) any instrument with respect to long-term debt not being issued if the total amount of securities authorized thereunder does not exceed 5% of the total assets of the issuer and its subsidiaries on a consolidated basis and if there is filed an agreement to furnish a copy of such agreement to the Commission upon request; (2) any instrument with respect to any class of securities if appropriate steps to assure the redemption or retirement of such class will be taken prior to or upon delivery by the issuer of the securities being issued; or (3) copies of instruments evidencing scrip certificates for fractions of shares.

(4) *Voting trust agreement*—Any voting trust agreements and amendments thereto.

(5) *Material contracts*—

  (a) Every contract not made in the ordinary course of business which is material to the issuer and is to be performed in whole or in part at or after the filing of the offering statement or was entered into not more than two years before such filing. Only contracts need be filed as to which the issuer or subsidiary of the issuer is a party or has succeeded to a party by assumption or assignment or in which the issuer or such subsidiary has a beneficial interest.

  (b) If the contract is such as ordinarily accompanies the kind of business conducted by the issuer and its subsidiaries, it is made in the ordinary course of business and need not be filed unless it falls within one or more of the following categories, in which case it should be filed except where immaterial in amount or significance:

   (1) Any contract to which directors, officers, promoters, voting trustees, security holders named in the offering statement or report, or underwriters are parties except where the contract merely involves the purchase or sale of current assets having a determinable market price, at such market price;

   (2) Any contract upon which the issuer's business is substantially dependent, as in the case of continuing contracts to sell the major part of issuer's products or services or to purchase the major part of issuer's requirement of goods, services or raw materials or any franchise or license or other agreement to use a patent, formula, trade secret, process or trade name upon which issuer's business depends to a material extent;

   (3) Any contract calling for the acquisition or sale of any property, plant or equipment for a consideration exceeding 10% of all such assets of the issuer and its subsidiaries; or

   (4) Any lease under which a significant part of the property described in the offering statement as held by the issuer.

  (c) Any management contract or any remunerative plan, contract or arrangement including but not limited to plans relating to options, warrants or rights, pension, retirement or deferred compensation or bonus, incentive or profit sharing (or if not set forth in any formal document, a written description thereof) shall be deemed material and shall be filed except the following:

   (1) Ordinary purchase and sales agency agreements.

   (2) Agreements with managers of stores in a chain organization or similar organization.

   (3) Contracts providing for labor or salesmen's bonuses or payments to a class of security holders, as such.

(4) Any remunerative plan, contract or arrangement which pursuant to its terms is available to employees generally and which in operation provides for the same method of allocation of benefits between management and non-management participants.

(6) *Material foreign patents*—Each material foreign patent for an invention not covered by a United States patent. If the filing is an offering statement and if a substantial part of the securities to be offered or if the proceeds therefrom have been or are to be used for the particular purposes of acquiring, developing or exploiting one or more material patents or patent rights, furnish a list showing the number and a brief identification of each such patent or patent right.

(7) *Plan of acquisition, reorganization, arrangement, liquidation, or succession*—Any material plan of acquisition, disposition, reorganization, readjustment, succession, liquidation or arrangement and any amendments thereto described in the offering statement.

(8) *Statement concerning issuer's financing*—If any of the securities proposed to be offered hereunder are to be offered for the account of any person other than the issuer, a written statement signed by the issuer representing that the proposed offering will not interfere with any needed financing by the issuer under this regulation.

(9) *Escrow agreements*—
   (a) Any escrow agreement or similar arrangement which has been executed in order to effect compliance with Rule 253(c) shall be filed and may be prepared in conformity with Form 7-A.
   (b) In the event the offering is contingent upon a minimum purchase requirement, any escrow agreement applicable to the proceeds received up to the minimum amount required.

(10) *Consents*—
   (a) Experts—(i) If any accountant, engineer, geologist, or appraiser, or any person whose profession gives authority to a statement made by him, is named as having prepared or certified any part of the offering statement or is named as having prepared or certified a report or evaluation, whether or not for use in connection with the offering statement; (ii) if any portion of the report of an expert is quoted or summarized as such in the offering statement, the written consent of the expert shall expressly state that the expert consents to such quotation or summarization; (iii) if it is stated that any information contained in the offering statement has been reviewed or passed upon by any persons and that such information is set forth in the offering statement upon the authority of or in reliance upon such persons as experts, the written consents of such persons shall be filed with the offering statement.
   (b) Consent and certification by underwriter—A written consent and certification, in the form set forth below, signed by each underwriter of the securities proposed to be offered hereunder. All underwriters may, with appropriate modifications, sign the same consent and certification or separate consents and certifications may be signed by any underwriter or group of underwriters.

Consent and Certification by Underwriter

1. The undersigned hereby consents to being named as underwriter in an offering statement filed with the Securities and Exchange Commission by (name of issuer) pursuant to Regulation A in connection with a proposed offering of (title of securities) to the public.

2. The undersigned hereby certifies that it furnished the statements and information set forth in such offering statement with respect to the undersigned, its directors and officers or partners, that such statements and information are accurate, complete and fully responsive to the requirements of Parts I, II and III of the Offering Statement thereto, and do not omit any information required to be stated therein with respect of any such persons, or necessary to make the statements and information therein with respect to any of them not misleading.

_____
(Underwriter)

Date _____ By _____

3. If a Preliminary Offering Circular will be distributed as permitted by Rule 256(i), the Consent and Certification by Underwriter shall include the following additional paragraph:

   The undersigned hereby undertakes, in connection with any distribution of the Preliminary Offering Circular as permitted by Rule 256(i),

Appendix D: Regulation A

(a) to keep an accurate and complete record of the name and address of each person furnished such Preliminary Offering Circular and

(b) if such Preliminary Offering Circular is inaccurate or inadequate in any material respect, to furnish a revised Preliminary Offering or an offering circular of the type referred to in Rule 256(i)(4) to all persons to whom the securities are to be sold at least 48 hours prior to the mailing of any confirmation of sale to such persons, or to send such a circular to such persons under circumstances that it would normally be received by them 48 hours prior to their receipt of confirmation of the sale.

(c) Consent of non-resident—Each consent to service of process required by Rule 262 shall be filed. Each such consent shall be prepared and executed in conformity with the appropriate form prescribed therefor.

(d) Formal requirements—All written consents filed shall be dated and manually signed.

(e) Application to dispense with the consent—An application to the Commission to dispense with any written consent of an expert shall be made by the issuer and shall be supported by an affidavit or affidavits establishing that the obtaining of such consent is impracticable or involves undue hardship on the issuer.

SIGNATURE

This offering statement has been signed in the City of _____ State (or Province) of _____ on _____, 19_____.

_____
(Issuer)

By _____
(Name and title)

_____
(Selling security holder)

OMB APPROVAL
OMB Number: 3235-0286
Expires: January 31, 1989

SECURITIES AND EXCHANGE COMMISSION
Washington, D.C. 20549

FORM 2-A

[As last amended in Release No. 33-3663, July 23, 1956.]

REPORT PURSUANT TO RULE 260 OF REGULATION A

1. Name of issuer _____
2. Name of underwriter _____
3. Date of this report _____
4. (a) Date offering commenced _____
   (b) Date offering completed, if completed _____
   (c) If offering has not commenced, state reasons briefly _____
   _____
5. (a) Total number of shares or other units offered hereunder _____
   (b) Number of such shares or other units sold from commencement of offering to date _____
   _____
   (c) Number of such shares or other units still being offered _____
6. (a) Total amount received from public from commencement of offering to date .... $ _____
   (b) Underwriting discount allowed .... $ _____
   (c) Expenses paid to or for the account of the underwriters ..... $ _____
   (d) Other expenses paid to date by or for the account of the issuer:
       (1) Legal (including organization) .... $ _____
       (2) Accounting .... $ _____
       (3) Engineers' fees incurred prior to offering .... $ _____
       (4) Printing and advertising .... $ _____
       (5) Other .... $ _____
   (e) Total costs and expenses [(b), (c) and (d)] .... $ _____
   (f) Proceeds to issuer after above deductions [(a) minus (e)] ... $ _____
7. Use of net proceeds from commencement of offering to date:

	Payments to officers, directors and affiliates	Payments to others
(a) Salaries and fees...	$ _____	$ _____
(b) Purchase of real estate	$ _____	$ _____
(c) Purchase and installation of machinery and equipment	$ _____	$ _____
(d) Construction of plant buildings and facilities................	$ _____	$ _____
(e) Development expense (product development, research, patent costs, etc.)	$ _____	$ _____
(f) Purchase of raw materials, inventories, supplies, etc.........	$ _____	$ _____
(g) Selling, advertising, and other sales promotion	$ _____	$ _____
(h) Other disbursements	$ _____	$ _____

SEC 816 (3-86)

    (i) Totals .... $ _____ $ _____

    (j) Balance of cash proceeds on hand .... $ _____

    Instructions. 1. If the issuer is a mining company, substitute for captions (e), (f) and (g) the following captions: "Road building," "Exploration expense (other than drilling)," "Exploratory drilling" and "Mine development."

    2. If the issuer is an oil or gas company, substitute for captions (e), (f) and (g) the following caption: "Exploratory and other drilling."

8. State briefly the nature and extent of each type of the issuer's principal activity to date.

_____
_____
_____
_____
_____

    Instruction. Mining companies shall include exploratory activity, showing the aggregate footage of exploratory drilling and number of holes drilled. Oil and gas companies shall include the number of wells drilled and their depth. Other companies shall include information as to plant construction, development, production and sales.

9. State whether the offering has been discontinued, and if so, state the date and describe briefly the reasons for such discontinuance:

_____
_____
_____
_____
_____

10. List the names and addresses of all brokers and dealers who have, to the knowledge of the issuer or underwriters, participated in the distribution of the securities offered during the period covered by this report.

    Instruction. In reports made subsequent to the initial report, the information need be given only with respect to persons not previously reported.

11. State the number of shares held by each promoter, director, officer or controlling person of the issuer, if different from the amount stated in the offering circular.

                                                                                                                  (Issuer)*

Date _____   By _____
                                                                                                                 (Name and Title)*

Date _____   _____
                                                                                                           (Selling security holder)*

---

*At least one copy of the report shall be signed manually by each person whose signature is required. Any copies not manually signed shall bear typed or printed signatures.

OMB APPROVAL
OMB Number: 3235-0286
Expires: January 31, 1989

SECURITIES AND EXCHANGE COMMISSION
Washington, D.C. 20549

FORM 3-A

[As adopted in Release No. 33-3663, July 23, 1956.]

IRREVOCABLE APPOINTMENT BY INDIVIDUAL OF AGENT FOR SERVICE OF PROCESS, PLEADINGS AND OTHER PAPERS

(Pursuant to Regulation A under Securities Act of 1933)

1. I _____ of _____,
   (Name)   (Address)
   hereby designate and appoint, without power of revocation, the United States Securities and Exchange Commission as my agent upon whom may be served all process, pleadings and other papers in any civil suit or action brought against me arising out of any offering made or purported to be made under Regulation A, adopted by the United States Securities and Exchange Commission under the Securities Act of 1933, or any purchase or sale of any securities in connection therewith, in any court of competent jurisdiction, Federal, State or Territorial, located in the United States or in its territories.

2. I hereby consent, stipulate and agree, without power of revocation—

   (a) that any civil suit or action brought against me arising out of any offering made or purported to be made under Regulation A, adopted by the United States Securities and Exchange Commission under the Securities Act of 1933, or any purchase or sale of any securities in connection therewith, may be commenced against me in any court of competent jurisdiction, Federal, State, or Territorial, located in the United States or in its territories as defined by the Securities Act of 1933, by service of process upon the United States Securities and Exchange Commission;

   (b) that service of process, pleadings or other papers upon the United States Securities and Exchange Commission, as aforesaid, shall be taken and held in all courts to be as valid and as binding upon me as if due personal service had been made upon me; and

   (c) that service upon the United States Securities and Exchange Commission may be effected by delivering copies of said process, pleadings, or other papers to the Secretary of the said Commission or any other person designated by it for such purpose, and that the certificate of the Secretary of the United States Securities and Exchange Commission or of such other person reciting that said process, pleadings or other papers were received by the United States Securities and Exchange Commission and that a copy of each such process, pleading, or other paper was forwarded to me at the last address supplied by me shall constitute evidence of such service upon me.

   IN WITNESS WHEREOF, I have executed this irrevocable power of attorney, consent, stipulation and agreement at _____ this _____ day of _____, A.D. 19_____.

   _____(Seal)

---

*Notary Public or other official authorized by law to administer oaths.

Note: The person executing this irrevocable power of attorney, consent, stipulation and agreement should appear before a person authorized to administer acknowledgments in the jurisdiction in which it is executed and acknowledge that he executed it as his free and voluntary act. The acknowledgment should be in the form prescribed by the law of the jurisdiction in which it is executed. The form of acknowledgment suggested should be used only if it is consistent with the requirements of the law of such jurisdiction.

The failure of any acknowledgment to meet applicable requirements shall not affect the validity or effect of the foregoing irrevocable power of attorney, consent, stipulation and agreement.

SEC 1900 (3-86)

PROVINCE (or State) of _____

County of _____ } ss.

I, _____, _____* in (Name) (Official position)*
and for said County in the State (or Province) aforesaid, do hereby certify that _____
(Name of Individual Appointing
_____ personally appeared before me this day and signed and sealed the above
Agent for Service)
instrument as his free and voluntary act for the uses and purposes therein set forth.

Given under my hand and seal this _____ day of _____ A.D., 19_____.

_____
(Official Position)

My commission (or office) expires:

_____
(Date)

OMB APPROVAL
OMB Number: 3235-0286
Expires: January 31, 1989

SECURITIES AND EXCHANGE COMMISSION
Washington, D.C. 20549

FORM 4-A

[As adopted in Release No. 33-3663, July 23, 1956.]

IRREVOCABLE APPOINTMENT BY CORPORATION*
OF AGENT FOR SERVICE OF PROCESS, PLEADINGS, AND OTHER PAPERS

(Pursuant to Regulation A under Securities Act of 1933)

1. The _____, a corporation duly organized
(Name of Corporation)
and existing by virtue of the laws of _____, hereby designates and appoints,
(Name of State or Province)
without power of revocation, the United States Securities and Exchange Commission, as the agent of said corporation upon whom may be served all process, pleadings and other papers in any civil suit or action brought against said corporation arising out of any offering made or purported to be made under Regulation A, adopted by the United States Securities and Exchange Commission under the Securities Act of 1933, or any purchase or sale of any securities in connection therewith, in any court of competent jurisdiction, Federal, State, or Territorial, located in the United States or in its territories.

2. Said corporation, _____ hereby consents, stipulates and agrees,
(Name of Corporation)
without power of revocation—

   (a) that any civil suit or action brought against it arising out of any offering made or purported to be made under Regulation A, adopted by the United States Securities and Exchange Commission under the Securities Act of 1933, or any purchase or sale of any securities in connection therewith, may be commenced against it in any court of competent jurisdiction, Federal, State, or Territorial, located in the United States or in its territories as defined by the Securities Act of 1933, by service of process upon the United States Securities and Exchange Commission;

   (b) that service of process, pleadings or other papers upon the United States Securities and Exchange Commission, as aforesaid, shall be taken and held in all courts to be as valid and as binding upon it as if due personal service thereof had been duly made upon it; and

   (c) that service upon the United States Securities and Exchange Commission may be effected by delivering copies of said process, pleadings, or other papers to the Secretary of the said Commission or any other person designated by it for such purpose, and that the certificate of the Secretary of the United States Securities and Exchange Commission or of such other person reciting that said process, pleadings or other papers were received by the United States Securities and Exchange Commission and that a copy of each such process, pleading, or other paper was forwarded to this corporation at the last address supplied by it shall constitute evidence of such service upon this corporation.

   IN WITNESS WHEREOF, the President and Secretary of _____.
   (Name of Corporation)

---

*In the case of an association or other form of organization, appropriate revisions should be made.
**Notary Public or other official authorized by law to administer oaths.

Note: The person (or persons) executing this irrevocable power of attorney, consent, stipulation and agreement should appear before a person authorized to administer acknowledgments in the jurisdiction in which it is executed and acknowledge that he (or they) executed it as his (or their) free and voluntary act. The acknowledgment should be in the form prescribed by the law of the jurisdiction in which it is executed. The form of acknowledgment suggested should be used only if it is consistent with the requirements of the law of such jurisdiction.
   The failure of any acknowledgment to meet applicable requirements shall not affect the validity or effect of the foregoing irrevocable power of attorney, consent, stipulation and agreement.

SEC 1901 (3-86)

by the authority and direction of the Board of Directors of said corporation, have executed this irrevocable power of attorney, and consent, stipulation and agreement, for and on behalf of the said corporation, at _____ _____ this _____ day of _____, A.D. 19_____.

Attest _____
(Secretary)

_____
(Corporate name)

By _____
(President)

(Corporate Seal)

STATE (or PROVINCE) OF _____

County of _____ } ss.

I, _____, a _____ in
(Name)   (Official Position)**
and for said County in the State (or Province) aforesaid, do hereby certify that _____
(Name of President)
and _____ personally appeared before me this day, stated that they are respectively the
(Name of Secretary)
President and Secretary of the _____, and that they are the same persons
(Name of Corporation)
named in the foregoing instrument as the President and Secretary of said corporation and that they have been duly authorized to execute said instrument for the corporation, and signed and sealed said instrument for and on behalf of said corporation as its free and voluntary act for the uses and purposes therein set forth.

Given under my hand and seal this _____ day of _____ A.D., 19_____.

_____

_____
(Official Position)

My commission (or office) expires:

_____
(Date)

OMB APPROVAL
OMB Number: 3235-0286
Expires: January 31, 1989

SECURITIES AND EXCHANGE COMMISSION
Washington, D.C. 20549

FORM 5-A

[As adopted in Release No. 33-3663, July 23, 1956.]

CERTIFICATE OF RESOLUTION AUTHORIZING IRREVOCABLE APPOINTMENT BY CORPORATION* OF AGENT FOR SERVICE OF PROCESS, PLEADINGS AND OTHER PAPERS

(Pursuant to Regulation A under Securities Act of 1933)

At a duly constituted meeting of the Board of Directors of _____,
(Name of Corporation)
a corporation organized and existing by virtue of the laws of _____,
(Name of State or Province)
held at the office of said corporation at _____

on the _____ day of _____, A.D. 19_____, the following resolution was adopted:

BE IT RESOLVED that the President and Secretary of this corporation, _____.
(Name of Corporation)
be and hereby are authorized and directed to execute in legal form, and to deliver to the United States Securities and Exchange Commission, on behalf of this corporation, in such wording as may be prescribed by or acceptable to the United States Securities and Exchange commission,

(1) a power of attorney designating and appointing, without power of revocation, the United States Securities and Exchange Commission as the agent of this corporation upon whom may be served all process, pleadings and other papers in any civil suit or action brought against this corporation arising out of any offering made or purported to be made under Regulation A, adopted by the United States Securities and Exchange Commission under the Securities Act of 1933, or any purchase or sale of any securities in connection therewith, in any court of competent jurisdiction, Federal, State, or Territorial, located in the United States or in its territories as defined by the Securities Act of 1933;

(2) a stipulation, consent and agreement, likewise without power of revocation, that any civil suit or action brought against this corporation arising out of any offering made or purported to be made under Regulation A, adopted by the United States Securities and Exchange Commission under the Securities Act of 1933, or any purchase or sale of any securities in connection therewith, may be commenced against this corporation in any court of competent jurisdiction, Federal, State, or Territorial, located in the United States or in its territories as defined by the Securities Act of 1933, by service of process upon the United States Securities and Exchange Commission; and

(3) a stipulation, consent and agreement that service upon the United States Securities and Exchange Commission may be effected by delivering copies of said process, pleadings or other papers to the Secretary of the United States Securities and Exchange Commission or any other person designated by it for such purpose, that the certificate of the Secretary of the United States Securities and Exchange Commission or of such other person reciting that said process, pleadings or other papers were received by the United States Securities and Exchange Commission and that a copy of each such

---

*In the case of an association or other form of organization, appropriate revisions should be made.
**Notary Public or other official authorized by law to administer oaths.
Note: This certificate of resolution should be executed and verified before a person authorized to administer oaths in the jurisdiction in which it is executed. The verification should be in the form prescribed by the law of the jurisdiction in which it is executed. The form of acknowledgment suggested should be used only if it is consistent with the requirements of the law of such jurisdiction.
    The failure of any verification to meet applicable requirements shall not affect the validity or effects of the foregoing certificate of resolution

SEC 1902 (3-86)

process, pleading or other paper was forwarded to this corporation at the last address supplied by it shall constitute evidence of such service upon this corporation, and that service of process, pleadings and other papers upon the United States Securities and Exchange Commission, as aforesaid, shall be taken and held in all courts to be as valid and binding upon this corporation as if due personal service thereof had been duly made.

STATE (or PROVINCE) OF _____ } ss.
County of _____

I, _____, being duly sworn, depose and say that I am Secretary of
                                 (Name)
_____ , and that the foregoing is a true and correct copy
                     (Name of Corporation)
of a resolution adopted by the Board of Directors of said corporation on the _____ day of _____
A.D., 19_____, as the same appears on the records of said corporation now in my custody and control.

IN WITNESS WHEREOF, I have hereunto set my hand and affixed the seal of said corporation.

_____
(Secretary)

(Corporate Seal)

Subscribed and sworn to before me this _____ day of _____ A.D., 19_____.

(Seal)
_____

_____
(Official Position)**

My commission (or office) expires:

_____
(Date)

OMB APPROVAL
OMB Number: 3235-0286
Expires: January 31, 1989

SECURITIES AND EXCHANGE COMMISSION
Washington, D.C. 20549

FORM 6-A

[As adopted in Release No. 33-3663, July 23, 1956.]

IRREVOCABLE APPOINTMENT BY PARTNERSHIP OF AGENT FOR SERVICE OF PROCESS, PLEADINGS AND OTHER PAPERS

(Pursuant to Regulation A under Securities Act of 1933)

1. The undersigned, jointly and severally, as follows,

_____, _____, _____
(Name)   (Name)   (Name)

_____, _____, _____
(Name)   (Name)   (Name)

members of a partnership doing business as _____,
(Firm Name)

having its principal place of business at _____

hereby designate and appoint without power of revocation, the United States Securities and Exchange Commission as the agent of the partnership, and as the agent of each of them individually, upon whom may be served all process, pleadings and other papers in any civil suit or action brought against said partnership firm, or against said persons, jointly or severally, arising out of any offering made or purported to be made under Regulation A, adopted by the United States Securities and Exchange Commission under the Securities Act of 1933, or any purchase or sale of any securities in connection therewith, in any court of competent jurisdiction, Federal, State or Territorial, located in the United States or in its territories as defined by the Securities Act of 1933.

2. The undersigned, jointly and severally, and as members of a partnership doing business as _____

_____ hereby consent, stipulate and agree, without power of revocation—
(Firm Name)

 (a) that any civil suit or action arising out of any offering made or purported to be made under Regulation A, adopted by the United States Securities and Exchange Commission under the Securities Act of 1933, or any purchase or sale of any securities in connection therewith, may be commenced against said partnership firm, or against said persons, jointly or severally, in any court of competent jurisdiction located in the United States or in its territories as defined by the Securities Act of 1933, by service of process upon the United States Securities and Exchange Commission;

 (b) that service of process, pleadings or other papers upon the United States Securities and Exchange Commission, as aforesaid, shall be taken and held in all courts to be as valid and as binding on said partnership firm, and on said persons, jointly and severally, as if due personal service had been duly made; and

 (c) that service upon the United States Securities and Exchange Commission may be effected by delivering copies of said process, pleadings, or other papers to the Secretary of the said Commission or any other person designated by it for such purpose, and that the certificate of the Secretary of the United States Securities and Exchange Commission or

---

*Notary Public or other official authorized by law to administer oaths.

Note: The person (or persons) executing this irrevocable power of attorney, consent, stipulation and agreement should appear before a person authorized to administer acknowledgments in the jurisdiction in which it is executed and acknowledge that he (or they) executed it as his (or their) free and voluntary act. The acknowledgment should be in the form prescribed by the law of the jurisdiction in which it is executed. The form of acknowledgment suggested should be used only if it is consistent with the requirements of the law of such jurisdiction.

The failure of any acknowledgment to meet applicable requirements shall not affect the validity or effect of the foregoing irrevocable power of attorney, consent, stipulation and agreement.

SEC 1903 (3-86)

such other person reciting that said process, pleadings or other papers were received by the United States Securities and Exchange Commission and that a copy of each such process, pleading, or other paper was forwarded to said partnership firm and to each said person at the last address supplied by said partnership firm and by each such person shall constitute evidence of such service upon said partnership firm and each said person.

IN WITNESS WHEREOF, the undersigned, individually and as members of said partnership doing business as _____ have executed this irrevocable power of attorney and
(Firm Name)
consent, stipulation and agreement for the purposes herein set forth at _____
_____ this _____ day of _____, A.D. 19_____.

_____(Seal)   _____(Seal)

_____(Seal)   _____(Seal)

_____(Seal)   _____(Seal)

STATE (or PROVINCE) OF _____

County of _____ } ss.

I, _____, _____ in
          (Name)   (Official Position)*
and for said County in the State (or Province) aforesaid, do hereby certify that _____
                                                                                  (Name)

_____, _____, _____
(Name)   (Name)   (Name)

_____, _____, personally appeared before me this day
(Name)   (Name)
and signed and sealed the above instrument as their free and voluntary act, and as the free and voluntary act of each of them, for the uses and purposes therein set forth.

Given under my hand and seal this _____ day of _____ A.D., 19_____.

_____
_____
(Official Position)

My commission (or office) expires:

_____
(Date)

| OMB APPROVAL |
| OMB Number: 3235-0286 |
| Expires: January 31, 1989 |

SECURITIES AND EXCHANGE COMMISSION
Washington, D.C. 20549

FORM 7-A

[As adopted in Release No. 33-6340, August 7, 1981, effective September 17, 1981, 46 F.R. 41766.]

OPTIONAL FORM OF ESCROW FOR SECURITIES THAT ARE SUBJECT TO THE PROVISIONS OF RULE 253(c) OF REGULATION A

(Pursuant to Regulation A under Securities Act of 1933)

This escrow agreement entered into this _____ day of _____, 19____, between _____, a corporation organized under the laws of the State of
(the issuer)
_____, hereinafter referred to as the "Corporation," and _____
(the purchaser)
of _____, hereinafter referred to as "Purchaser,"
(address)
and _____ of _____,
(independent agent)   (address)
hereinafter referred to as the "escrow agent," witnesseth:

Whereas in order to comply with the provisions of Rule 253(c) of the General Rules and Regulations under the Securities Act of 1933, as amended, hereinafter referred to as the "General Rules and Regulations," the Corporation simultaneously with the execution of this agreement is depositing with the escrow agent _____ shares
(number)
of the _____ stock of the Corporation issued in the name of Purchaser and bearing certificate,
(class)
No. _____, the deposit of which is hereby acknowledged by the escrow agent:

Now, therefore, the parties hereto agree as follows:

1. The escrow agent hereby accepts said shares in escrow and agrees to hold and keep said shares in accordance with the terms and conditions hereof and for the uses and purposes herein set forth, and to deliver said shares upon the performance of the conditions hereinafter set forth.

2. The escrow agent shall not be held to take notice of any terms of any agreement or any rights stated with respect to the deposited shares unless expressly stated in writing herein.

3. During the period of holding the deposited shares in escrow, no transfer or any other disposition of any said shares or of any interest therein is to be made whether subject to this escrow agreement or otherwise but all of said shares are to be held intact as issued and placed in escrow hereunder.

4. The escrow agent is hereby authorized and instructed to hold the deposited shares in escrow, pursuant to Rule 253(c) of the General Rules and Regulations, until such date as shall be one year from the date, shown on a definitive offering circular, of an offering of shares of stock of the Corporation in accordance with the provisions of the General Rules and Regulations. Thereafter upon receipt of written advice by the Corporation and Purchaser to the escrow agent (and to the Securities and Exchange Commission) that none of the deposited shares or any interests therein have been transferred or otherwise disposed of and that the deposited shares are registered under the Securities Act of 1933, as amended, or covered by a filing pursuant to the provisions of Regulation A under the General Rules and Regulations, or are otherwise exempt from registration or are not then required to be registered and that a copy of such advice has been delivered to the Securities and Exchange Commission, said shares will be delivered to Purchaser by escrow agent. If a registration statement is not then in effect and if an appropriate filing under Regulation A has

not been completed under said Act with respect to the deposited shares, prior to delivery of the deposited shares to Purchaser by escrow agent, (i) Corporation and Purchaser will advise escrow agent that Corporation and Purchaser have instructed the transfer agent for the deposited shares to the effect that no transfer of the deposited shares shall be made unless a registration statement under the Securities Act of 1933, as amended, with respect to such shares is in effect or an exemption from the registration requirements of such Act is in fact applicable to such shares and (ii) Corporation shall impress upon the face of the certificate or certificates representing the deposited shares and upon all certificates issued in exchange therefor the following legend:

"No sale, offer to sell or transfer of the shares represented by this certificate shall be made unless a registration statement under the Federal Securities Act of 1933, as amended, with respect to such shares is then in effect or an exemption from the registration requirements of such Act is then in fact applicable to such shares."

5. The fee of the escrow agent for its services hereunder shall be $_____, payable at the time of the execution of this agreement, to be borne by _____.

6. In performing any of its duties hereunder, the escrow agent shall not incur any liability to anyone for any damages, losses, or expenses except for willful default or negligence, and it shall accordingly not incur any such liability with respect (i) to any action taken or omitted in good faith upon advice of its counsel or counsel for the Corporation given with respect to any questions relating to the duties and responsibilities of the escrow agent under this agreement, or (ii) to any action taken or omitted in reliance upon any instrument, including the written advices provided for herein, not only as to its due execution and the validity and effectiveness of its provisions but also as to the truth and accuracy of any information contained therein, which the escrow agent shall in good faith believe to be genuine, to have been signed or presented by a proper person or persons and to conform with the provisions of this agreement.

7. The Corporation and Purchaser, jointly and severally, hereby agree to indemnify and hold harmless escrow agent against any and all losses, claims, damages, liabilities and expenses, including reasonable costs of investigation and counsel fees and disbursements, which may be imposed upon escrow agent or incurred by escrow agent in connection with its acceptance of appointment of escrow agent hereunder, or the performance of its duties hereunder, including any litigation arising from this agreement or involving the subject matter hereof or the shares deposited hereunder.

IN WITNESS WHEREOF, _____ and _____ have
                                      (Corporation)   (escrow agent)

caused this agreement to be executed by their respective officers, thereunto duly authorized, _____
                                                                                                            (Purchaser)

has signed this agreement as of the day and year first above written.

                                                          (Corporation)
                                                          By: _____
                                                                              (Title)

                                                          (Escrow Agent)
                                                         By: _____
                                                                              (Title)

                                                        _____(I.S.)

APPENDIX E

Form S-11

OMB APPROVAL
OMB Number: 3235-0067
Expires: September 30, 1988

SECURITIES AND EXCHANGE COMMISSION
Washington, D.C. 20549

FORM S-11

FOR REGISTRATION UNDER THE SECURITIES ACT OF 1933 OF SECURITIES OF CERTAIN REAL ESTATE COMPANIES

GENERAL INSTRUCTIONS

A. Rule as to Use of Form S-11.

This form shall be used for registration under the Securities Act of 1933 of (i) securities issued by real estate investment trust, as defined in Section 856 of the Internal Revenue Code, or (ii) securities issued by other issuers whose business is primarily that of acquiring and holding for investment real estate or interests in real estate or interests in other issuers whose business is primarily that of acquiring and holding real estate or interest in real estate for investment. This form shall not be used, however, by any issuer which is an investment company registered or required to register under the Investment Company Act of 1940.

B. Application of General Rules and Regulations

(a) Attention is directed to the General Rules and Regulations under the Securities Act, particularly those comprising Regulation C thereunder (17 CFR 230.400 to 230.494). That Regulation contains general requirements regarding the preparation and filing of registration statements.

(b) Attention is directed to Regulation S-K (17 CFR Part 229) for the requirements applicable to the content of the non-financial statement portions of registration statements under the Securities Act. Where this Form directs the registrant to furnish information required by Regulation S-K and the item of Regulation S-K so provides, information need only be furnished to the extent appropriate.

C. Exchange Offers

If any of the securities being registered are to be offered in exchange for securities of any other issuer, the prospectus also shall include the information which would be required by Items 9 to 16, and Item 18 if securities of such other issuer were being registered on this form. Item 26 also shall be answered as to any promoter, director, officer or security holder of such other issuer who is an affiliated person of the registrant.

D. Definitions.

Unless the context clearly indicates the contrary, the following definitions apply:

Affiliated person. The term "affiliated person" means any of the following persons: (i) any director or officer of the registrant; (ii) any person directly or indirectly controlling or under direct or indirect common control with the registrant; (iii) any person owning of record or known by the registrant to own beneficially 10 percent or more of any class of equity securities or the registrant; (iv) any promoter of the registrant directly or indirectly connected with the registrant in any capacity; (v) any principal underwriter of the securities being registered; (vi) any person performing general management or advisory services for the registrant; and (vii) any associate of any of the foregoing persons.

Director. The term "director" means any director of a corporation, trustee of a trust, general partner of a partnership, or any person who performs for an organization functions similar to those performed by the foregoing persons.

Governing instruments. The term "governing instruments" means the Charter, trust agreement, partnership agreement, bylaws or other instruments under which the registrant was organized or created or under which it will operate.

Mortgage. The term "mortgage" means any mortgage, deed of trust or other evidence of indebtedness secured by a lien upon real estate or upon any interest in real estate.

Share. The term "share" means a share of stock in a corporation, a share or other unit of beneficial interest in a trust or unincorporated association, a limited partnership interest, or any similar equity interest in any other type of organization.

E. Foreign Issuers

A non-Canadian foreign private issuer eligible to use Form 20-F may comply with Items 19, 20, 21, 22 and 26 of this Form by furnishing the information specified in Items 3, 4, 10, 11 and 18, respectively, of Form 20-F (§249.220f of this chapter).

SEC 907 (2-87)

SECURITIES AND EXCHANGE COMMISSION
Washington, D.C. 20549

FORM S-11

REGISTRATION STATEMENT
Under the Securities Act of 1933

_____

(Exact name of registrant as specified in governing instruments)
_____

(Address of principal executive offices)
_____

(Name and address of agent for service)

Approximate date of commencement of proposed sale to the public _____

CALCULATION OF REGISTRATION FEE

Title of securities being registered	Amount being registered	Proposed maximum offering price per unit	Proposed maximum aggregate offering price	Amount of registration fee

The registrant hereby amends this registration statement on such date or dates as may be necessary to delay its effective date until the registrant shall file a further amendment which specifically states that this registration statement shall thereafter become effective in accordance with Section 8(a) of the Securities Act of 1933 or until the registration statement shall become effective on such date as the Commission, acting pursuant to said Section 8(a), may determine.*

PART I. INFORMATION REQUIRED IN PROSPECTUS

Item 1. Forepart of Registration Statement and Outside Front Cover Page of Prospectus.

    (a) Set forth on the outside front cover page of the prospectus the information required by Item 501 of Regulation S-K (§229.501 of this chapter).

    (b) If there are any limitations on the transferability of the securities being registered, so state on the outside front cover page of the prospectus and refer to a statement elsewhere in the prospectus as to the nature of such limitations. If there is no market for securities of the same class as those being registered, so state on the outside front cover page of the prospectus; otherwise, state elsewhere in the prospectus the nature of the market for such securities and the market price thereof as of the latest practicable date prior to the filing of the registration statement or amendment thereto.

Item 2. Inside Front and Outside Back Cover Pages of Prospectus.

Set forth on the inside front cover page of the prospectus or, where permitted, on the outside back cover page, the information required by Item 502 of Regulation S-K (§229.502 of this chapter).

Item 3. Summary Information, Risk Factors and Ratio of Earnings to Fixed Charges.

    (a) Furnish the information required by Item 503 of Regulation S-K (§229.503 of this chapter).

    (b) Where appropriate to a clear understanding by investors, an introductory statement shall be made in the forepart of the prospectus, in a series of short, concise paragraphs, summarizing the principal factors which make the offering speculative. Where appropriate, statements with respect to the following shall also be set forth:

_____
*Inclusion of this paragraph is optional. See Rule 473.

(1) A comparison in percentages of the securities being offered to the public and those issued or to be issued to affiliated persons;

(2) The extent to which security holders may be liable for the acts or obligations of the registrant;

(3) Allocation of cash distributions between the public security holders and security holders who are affiliated persons;

(4) The compensation and other forms of compensation and benefits to be received, directly or indirectly, by affiliated persons, including in the case of underwriters a comparison of the aggregate compensation to be received by them with the aggregate net proceeds from the sale of the securities being registered.

Item 4. Determination of Offering Price.

Furnish the information required by Item 505 of Regulation S-K (§229.505 of this chapter).

Item 5. Dilution.

Furnish the information required by Item 506 of Regulation S-K (§229.506 of this chapter).

Item 6. Selling Security Holders.

Furnish the information required by Item 507 of Regulation S-K (§229.507 of this chapter).

Item 7. Plan of Distribution.

Furnish the information required by Item 508 of Regulation S-K (§229.508 of this chapter).

Item 8. Use of Proceeds.

Furnish the information required by Item 504 of Regulation S-K (§229.504 of this chapter).

Item 9. Selected Financial Data.

Furnish the information required by Item 301 of Regulation S-K (§229.301 of this chapter).

Instruction. If, pursuant to this Item, a statement showing the pro forma taxable operating results of the registrant is included in the rgistration statement, the Commission or its staff may request as supplemental information, which the registrant should be prepared to furnish promptly upon request, a schedule reconciling such pro forma results with the historical operating results (*see* Rule 3-14 of Regulation S-X).

Item 10. Management's Discussion and Analysis of Financial Condition and Results of Operations.

Furnish the information required by Item 303 of Regulation S-K (§229.303 of this chapter).

Item 11. General Information as to Registrant

(a) State the name and form of organization of the registrant and the name of the State or other jurisdiction the laws of which govern with respect to the organization of the registrant.

(b) State the date on which the governing instruments became operative and the date on which they will expire. If the duration of the registrant may be sooner terminated or may be extended, outline briefly the pertinent provisions.

(c) If the registrant is not a corporation state briefly the provisions of the governing instruments with respect to the holding of annual or other meetings of security holders. If the governing instruments do not provide for such meetings state the policy or porposed policy of the registrant with respect to holding annual or other meetings of security holders.

(d) If the registrant was organized within the last five years, give the full names of all promoters and indicate all positions and offices with the registrant now held or intended to be held by each such promoter.

Instruction. If any person named as a promoter is no longer connected with the registrant in any capacity, so state.

Item 12. Policy with Respect to Certain Activities

Describe the policy of the registrant with respect to each of the following types of activities, indicating whether such policy may be changed by the officers and directors without a vote of security holders. Indicate the extent to which the registrant proposes to engage in such activities and the extent to which it has engaged in such activities during the past three years.

Appendix E: Form S-11   429

    (a) To issue senior securities.

    (b) To borrow money.

    (c) To make loans to other persons.

    (d) To invest in the securities of other issuers for the purpose of exercising control.

    (e) To underwrite securities of other issuers.

    (f) To engage in the purchase and sale (or turnover) of investments.

    (g) To offer securities in exchange for property.

    (h) To repurchase or otherwise reacquire its shares or other securities.

    (i) To make annual or other reports to security holders, indicating the nature and scope of such reports and whether they will contain financial statements certified by independent public accountants.

    Instructions.

        1. The policy or proposed policy of the registrant with respect to each activity shall be described separately. If the registrant does not propose to engage in a particular activity, a specific statement to that effect shall be made. The information shall be given in such manner and detail as will be meaningful to investors.

        2. For the purpose of (c), the purchasing of a portion of publicly distributed bonds, debentures or other securities, whether or not the purchase was made upon the original issuance of the securities, is not to be considered the making of a loan by the registrant.

Item 13. Investment Policies of Registrant.

Describe the policy of the registrant with respect to investing in each of the following types of investments, indicating whether such policy may be changed by the directors without a vote of security holders, the percentage of assets which the registrant may invest in any one type of investment and, in the case of securities, the percentage of securities of any one issuer which the registrant may acquire and the principles and procedures the registrant will employ in connection with the acquisition of assets.

    (a) *Investments in real estate or interests in real estate.*

    Instructions.

        1. Indicate the geographic area or areas in which the registrant proposes to acquire real estate or interests in real estate.

        2. The types of real estate and interests in real estate in which the registrant may invest shall be indicated; for example, office buildings, apartment buildings, shopping centers, industrial and commercial properties, special purpose buildings and undeveloped acreage.

        3. The method or proposed method of operating and financing the registrant's real estate shall be briefly described. Indicate any limitations on the number or amount of mortgages which may be placed on any one piece of property.

        4. The answer to this item shall be such as will be appropriate in view of the nature of the registrant's business, its history and its experience and the proposed nature of its business and activities.

        5. Include a specific statement as to whether or not it is the registrant's policy to acquire assets primarily for possible capital gain or primarily for income.

        6. State the registrant's policy as to the amount or percentage of assets which will be invested in any specific property.

        7. Include a statement with respect to any other material policy with respect to real estate activities.

    (b) *Investments in real estate mortgages.*

    Instructions.

        1. Indicate the types of mortgages; for example, first or second mortgages and whether such mortgages are to be insured by the Federal Housing Administration or guaranteed by the Veterans Administration or otherwise guaranteed or insured, and the proportion of assets which may be invested in each type of mortgage or in any single mortgage.

        2. Include a description of each type of mortgage activity in which the registrant intends to engage such as originating, servicing and warehousing of mortgages and its portfolio turnover policy.

3. Indicate the types of properties subject to mortgages in which the registrant invests or proposes to invest; for example, single family dwellings, apartment buildings, office buildings, bowling alleys, commercial properties and unimproved land.

(c) *Securities of or interests in persons primarily engaged in real estate activities.*

Instructions.

1. Indicate separately the types of securities of or interest in persons engaged in real estate activities (for example, common stock, interests in real estate investment trusts, partnership interests, joint venture interests) in which the registrant may invest and the proportion of its assets which may be invested in each such type of security or interest.

2. Indicate the primary activities of persons in which the registrant will invest such as mortgage sales, investment in office buildings or investments in undeveloped acreage and the investment policies of such persons.

3. State the criteria followed in the purchase of such securities and interests (for example, securities listed on a national securities exchange, minimum net income requirements, period of operation of issuer).

(d) *Investments in other securities.*

Instructions.

1. Indicate the type of securities (for example, bonds, preferred stocks, common stocks) and the industry groups in which the registrant may invest and the percentage of its assets which it may invest in each such type or industry group.

2. Instruction 3 to paragraph (c) shall also apply to this paragraph.

Item 14. Description of Real Estate.

(a) State the location and describe the general character of all materially important real properties now held or intended to be acquired by or leased to the registrant or its subsidiaries. Include information as to the present or proposed use of such properties and their suitability and adequacy for such use. Properties not yet acquired shall be identified as such.

(b) State the nature of the registrant's or subsidiary's title to, or other interest in, such properties and the nature and amount of all material mortgages, or other liens or encumbrances against such properties. Set forth briefly the current principal amount of each such material encumbrance, its interest and amortization provisions, its pre-payment provisions and its maturity date and balance to be due at maturity assuming no payment has been made on principal in advance of its due date.

(c) Outline briefly the principal terms of any lease of any of such properties or any option or contract to purchase or sell any of such properties.

(d) Outline briefly any proposed program for the renovation, improvement or development of such properties, including the estimated cost thereof and the method of financing to be used. If there are no present plans for the improvement or development of any unimproved or undeveloped property, so state and indicate the purpose for which the property is to be held or acquired.

(e) Describe the general competitive conditions to which the properties described above are or may be subject.

Instructions.

1. What is required is information essential to an investor's understanding of the securities being registered. Detailed descriptions of the physical characteristics of individual properties or legal descriptions by metes and bounds are not required and should not be given. If the registrant has a number of properties, the information may be given in tabular form to the extent that it is practicable to do so.

2. The information shall be furnished separately as to each property the book value of which amounts to ten percent or more of the total assets of the registrant and its consolidated subsidiaries or the gross revenue from which for the last fiscal year amounted to ten percent or more of the aggregate gross revenues of the registrant and its consolidated subsidiaries for the registrant's last fiscal year. With respect to other properties the information shall be given by such classes or groups and in such detail as will reasonably convey the information required.

3. Include a statement as to whether, in the opinion of the management of the registrant the properties are adequately covered by insurance.

Item 15. Operating Data.

Furnish the following information with respect to each improved property which is separately described in answer to Item 14.

Appendix E: Form S-11

(a) Occupancy rate expressed as a percentage for each of the last five years.

(b) Number of tenants occupying ten percent or more of the rentable square footage and principal nature of business of such tenant.

(c) Principal business, occupations and professions carried on in, or from the building.

(d) The principal provisions of the leases between the tenants referred to in (b) above including, but not limited to: rental per annum, expiration date, and renewal options.

(e) The average effective annual rental per square foot or unit for each of the last five years prior to the date of filing.

(f) Schedule of the lease expirations for each of the ten years starting with the year in which the registration statement is filed, stating (i) the number of tenants whose leases will expire, (ii) the total area in square feet covered by such leases, (iii) the annual rental represented by such leases, and (iv) the percentage of gross annual rental represented by such leases.

(g) Each of the properties and components thereof upon which depreciation is taken, setting forth the (i) Federal tax basis, (ii) rate, (iii) method, and (iv) life claimed with respect to such property or component thereof for purposes of depreciation.

(h) The realty tax rate, annual realty taxes and estimated taxes on any proposed improvements.

Instruction. Instruction 3 to Item 14 shall apply to this Item.

Item 16. Tax Treatment of Registrant and Its Security Holders.

(a) Briefly describe the material aspects of the tax treatment of registrant under Federal income tax laws and the Federal tax treatment of registrant's security holders with respect to distributions by registrant, including the tax treatment of gains from the sale of securities or property and distributions in excess of annual net income.

(b) If any of the securities being registered are to be offered in exchange for other securities or property indicate the tax effect upon such exchanges of the Federal income tax laws.

Item 17. Market Price of and Dividends on the Registrant's Common Equity and Related Stockholder Matters.

Furnish the information required by Item 201 of Regulation S-K §229.201 of this chapter).

Item 18. Description of Registrant's Securities.

Furnish the information required by Item 202 of Regulation S-K (§229.202 of this chapter).

Item 19. Legal Proceedings.

Furnish the information required by Item 103 of Regulation S-K (§229.103 of this chapter).

Item 20. Security Ownership of Certain Beneficial Owners and Management.

Furnish the information required by Item 403 of Regulation S-K (§229.403 of this chapter).

Item 21. Directors and Executive Officers.

Furnish the information required by Item 401 of Regulation S-K (§229.401 of this chapter).

Item 22. Executive Compensation.

Furnish the information required by Item 402 of Regulation S-K (§229.402 of this chapter).

Item 23. Certain Relationships and Related Transactions.

Furnish the information required by Item 404 of Regulation S-K (§229.404 of this chapter). If the information prescribed by Instruction 5 to Item 404(a) is included and the assets have been acquired by the seller within five years prior to the transaction, disclose the aggregate depreciation claimed by the seller for federal income tax purposes.

Item 24. Selection, Management and Custody of Registrant's Investments.

(a) Describe the arrangements made or proposed to be made by the registrant with respect to the following:

(1) Management of the registrant's real estate, including arranging for purchases, sales, leases, maintenance and insurance.

(2) The purchase, sale and servicing of mortgages for the registrant.

(3) Investment advisory services.

(b) If any of the services specified in paragraph (a) are performed or to be performed by any affiliated person, furnish the following information as to such person:

(1) Name and address.

(2) Nature of principal business.

(3) Principal occupations during the last five years.

(4) Nature of all existing direct or indirect material interests in or business connections with the registrant or any of its other affiliated persons.

(5) Nature of all services rendered to the registrant and its subsidiaries.

(6) Aggregate compensation received from the registrant and its subsidiaries, directly or indirectly, during the registrant's last fiscal year and the capacities in which such remuneration was received.

Instructions.

1. If any person whose principal occupations during the last five years are described in answer to paragraph (b)(3) is a corporation or other organization, include the name and principal occupations during the last five years of each principal executive officer of such corporation or other organization.

2. The information required by paragraph (b) need not be furnished with respect to any director or officer of the registrant who performs the services specified solely in his capacity as such director or officer and who receives no additional compensation directly or indirectly for such services.

Item 25. Policies with Respect to Certain Transactions.

Outline briefly any provisions of the governing instruments limiting any director, officer, security holder or affiliate of the registrant, or any other person in the following respects. If the governing instruments contain no such provisions, describe the policy of the registrant with respect to such matters.

(a) Having any direct or indirect pecuniary interest in any investment to be acquired or disposed of by the registrant or any of its subsidiaries or in any transaction to which the registrant or any of its subsidiaries is a party or has an interest.

(b) Engaging for their own account in business activities of the types conducted or to be conducted by the registrant and its subsidiaries.

Item 26. Limitations of Liability.

Outline briefly the principal provisions of the governing instruments or of any contract or arrangement to which the registrant or a subsidiary is a party with respect to limitations on the liability of affiliated persons or any of their directors, officers or employees.

Instructions. If any of such provisions are broad enough to cover liability arising under the Securities Act of 1933, the effect of Section 14 of that Act upon such provisions should be indicated.

Item 27. Financial Statements and Information.

Include in the prospectus the financial statements required by Regulation S-X, the supplementary financial information required by Item 302 of Regulation S-K (§229.302 of this chapter) and the information concerning changes in and disagreements with accountants on accounting and financial disclosure required by Item 304 of Regulation S-K (§229.304 of this chapter).

Item 28. Interests of Named Experts and Counsel.

Furnish the information required by Item 509 of Regulation S-K (§229.509 of this chapter).

Appendix E: Form S-11

Item 29. Disclosure of Commission Position on Indemnification for Securities Act Liabilities.

Furnish the information required by Item 510 of Regulation S-K (§229.510 of this chapter).

PART II. INFORMATION NOT REQUIRED IN PROSPECTUS

Item 30. Other Expenses of Issuance and Distribution.

Furnish the information required by Item 511 of Regulation S-K (§229.511 of this chapter).

Item 31. Sales to Special Parties.

Name each person or specify each class of persons (other than underwriters or dealers, as such) to whom any securities have been sold within the past six months, or are to be sold, by the registrant or any security holder for whose account any of the securities being registered are to be offered, at a price varying from that at which securities of the same class are to be offered to the general public pursuant to this registration. State the consideration given or to be given by each such person or class.

Item 32. Recent Sales of Unregistered Securities.

Furnish the information required by Item 701 of Regulation S-K (§229.701 of this chapter).

Item 33. Indemnification of Directors and Officers.

Furnish the information required by Item 702 of Regulation S-K (§229.702 of this chapter).

Item 34. Treatment of Proceeds from Stock Being Registered.

If the capital shares are being registered hereunder and any portion of the consideration to be received by the registrant for such shares is to be credited to an account other than the appropriate capital share account, state to what other account such portion is to be credited and the estimated amount per share. If the consideration from the sale of par value shares is less than par value, state the amount per share involved and its treatment in the accounts.

Item 35. Financial Statements and Exhibits.

(a) List all financial statements filed as part of the registration statement, indicating those included in the prospectus.

(b) Furnish the exhibits required by Item 601 of Regulation S-K (§229.601 of this chapter).

Item 36. Undertakings.

Furnish the information required by Item 512 of Regulation S-K (§229.512 of this chapter).

SIGNATURES

Pursuant to the requirements of the Securities Act of 1933, the registrant certifies that it has reasonable grounds to believe that it meets all of the requirements for filing on Form S-11 and has duly caused this registration statement to be signed on its behalf by the undersigned, thereunto duly authorized, in the City of _____, State of _____, on _____, 19_____.

_____
(Issuer)

By

_____
(Signature and Title)

Pursuant to the requirements of the Securities Act of 1933, this registration statement has been signed by the following persons in the capacities and on the dates indicated.

_____
(Signature)

_____
(Title)

_____
(Date)

Instructions.

1. The registration statement shall be signed by the registrant, its principal executive officer or officers, its principal financial officer, its controller or principal accounting officer, and by at least a majority of the board of directors or persons performing similar functions. If the registrant is a foreign person, the registration statement shall also be signed by its authorized representative in the United States. Where the registrant is a limited partnership, the registration statement shall be signed by a majority of the board of directors of any corporate general partner signing the registration statement.

2. The name of each person who signs the registration statement shall be typed or printed beneath his signature. Any person who occupies more than one of the specified positions shall indicate each capacity in which he signs the registration statement. Attention is directed to Rule 402 concerning manual signatures and Item 601 of Regulation S-K concerning signatures pursuant to powers of attorney.

APPENDIX F
Guide 5

[¶ 12,041] **Preparation of Registration Statements Relating to Interests in Real Estate Limited Partnerships**

Guide 5. References to the General Partner and its affiliates, also referred to as sponsors, are intended to include references to the General Partner(s), promoters of the partnership, and all persons that, directly or indirectly, through one or more intermediaries, control or are controlled by, or are under common control with, such General Partner(s) or promoters.

It is suggested that where appropriate, the information in the prospectus be presented in the same order as the following comments. Where the registrant believes that specific comments are not relevant or are otherwise inappropriate, the registrant should bring this to the staff's attention in a letter indicating the reasons therefor.

1. COVER PAGE

A. The disclosure on the cover page should be as succinct and brief as possible.

B. The cover page should set forth, in addition to basic information about the offering, the termination date of the offering, any minimum required purchase and any arrangements to place the funds received in an escrow trust or similar arrangement.

C. The cover page should contain a tabular presentation of the total maximum and minimum interests to be offered:

	Price to Public	Selling Commissions	Proceeds to the Partnership
Per Limited Partnership Interest			
Total Minimum			
Total Maximum			

D. The cover page also should contain brief identification of the material risks involved in the purchase of the securities with cross-reference to further discussion in the prospectus. The most significant risk factors should be identified where applicable, for example:

   i) Tax Aspects
     For example:
        There are material income tax risks associated with the offering.
   ii) Use of Proceeds
     For example:
        The proceeds of the offering are insufficient to meet the requirements for funds as set forth in the partnership's investment objectives.

iii) Conflicts of Interests
For example:
> The operation of the partnership involves transactions between the partnership and the General Partner or its affiliates which may involve conflicts of interest.

2. SUITABILITY STANDARDS

Standards, if any, to be utilized by the registrant ("suitability standards") in determining the acceptance of subscription agreements should be described immediately following the cover page. Suitability standards should include those established by the registrant, if any, or by any self-regulatory organization or state agency having jurisdiction over the offering of the securities. Registrant should disclose the method(s) it intends to employ to assure adherence to the suitability standards by persons selling the interests and should briefly discuss the factors pertaining to the need for such standards such as lack of liquidity (resale or assignment of securities), importance of the investor's Federal income tax bracket in terms of the tax-benefits to be derived, the long term nature of the investment and possible adverse tax consequences of premature sale of the interests. If suitability standards apply to resale of the interests, this should be discussed.

3. SUMMARY OF THE PARTNERSHIP AND USE OF PROCEEDS

A two-part, concise outline summary relating to the partnership and a tabular summary of use of proceeds should follow the Suitability section of the prospectus. These summaries may replace the Introductory Statement and Use of Proceeds Sections required by the relevant Form if such sections would merely repeat the information in the summaries.

A. *Summary of the Partnership.* The following information should be disclosed in outline form with appropriate cross-references, where applicable:

i) Name, address and telephone number of the General Partner and names of persons making investment decisions for the partnership;

ii) The intended termination date of the partnership;

iii) State, if true, that the General Partner and its affiliates will receive substantial fees and profits in connection with the offering;

iv) If current distributions are an investment objective, state the estimated maximum time from the closing date that the investor might have to wait to receive such distributions;

v) Describe briefly the properties to be purchased. If a material portion of the minimum net proceeds of the offering (allowing for reserves) is not committed to specific properties, so indicate;

vi) Describe the depreciation method to be used;

vii) State the maximum leverage expected to be used by the partnership as a whole and on individual properties, where it may differ;

viii) Include a cross-reference to the Glossary.

B. *Use of Proceeds.* The use of proceeds tabular summary will vary according to the partnership but should include, where appropriate, estimates of the public offering expenses (both organizational and sales), the amount available for investment, nonrecurring initial investment fees, prepaid items and financing fees, cash down payments, reserves, and acquisition fees including those paid by the seller. Estimated amounts to be paid to the General Partner and its affiliates should be identified. The summary should include both dollar amounts and percentages of the maximum and minimum proceeds of the offering. Inclusion of percentages of the estimated maximum and minimum total assets is optional. An example of a summary of Use of Proceeds is attached as Appendix I, but the summary will vary according to the circumstances.

4. COMPENSATION AND FEES TO THE GENERAL PARTNERS AND AFFILIATES

A. This section should include a summary tabular presentation, itemizing by category and specifying dollar amounts where possible, of all compensation, fees, profits, and other benefits (including reimbursement of out-of-pocket expenses) which the General Partner and its affiliates may earn or receive in connection with the offering or operation of the partnership. If more detailed information is required it should be located in the Summary of Partnership Agreement section with cross-reference to that Summary. The presentation should identify the person, including affiliations with the General Partner, who will receive such compensation, fees, profits or benefits and the services to be performed by such person.

The summary should be organized so as to indicate clearly whether the compensation relates to the offering and organizational stage, the developmental or acquisition stage, the operational stage or the termination and liquidation stage of the partnership. Separate subcaptions are recommended.

The type of compensation, fees, profits or other benefits that should be disclosed includes, but is not limited to, the following: disbursements incident to the purchase and sale of the limited partnership interests, including sales commissions, reimbursements for expenses, and real estate commissions; finder's fees; fees for property acquisitions, marketing or leasing up of properties, financing or refinancing, management for properties, insurance and miscellaneous services; commissions and other fees to be paid upon sale of the partnership's properties; participation by the General Partner in cash flow or profits and losses or capital gains and losses arising out of the operation, refinancing or sale of properties; fees or builder's profits; overhead absorption and/or land write-ups; and all profits on the purchase of investments for the partnership from the General Partner or its affiliates. If the partnership agreement limits the losses the General Partner and its affiliates can sustain, this should be discussed.

B. Maximum aggregate dollar front-end fees to be paid during the first fiscal year of operations should be disclosed upon the assumption that the partnership's maximum leverage is utilized.

C. Where compensation arrangements are based upon a formula or percentage, the terms of such arrangements should be disclosed and illustrated. The assumptions underlying the dollar figures should be disclosed and the calculations underlying the figures should be submitted to the staff supplementally with the initial filing. Compensation based upon a given return (percentage of contributed investor capital) to investors should disclose whether such return is cumulative or non-cumulative.

D. Where the General Partner or an affiliate receives a disproportionate interest in the partnership in relation to its own contribution, registrant's attention is directed to Item 506 of Regulation S-K. A bar chart comparison of the various interests and contributors should be provided.

5. CONFLICTS OF INTEREST

A. This section should include a summary of each type of transaction which may result in a conflict between the interests of the public investors and those of the General Partner and its affiliates, and of the proposed method of dealing with such conflict. The types of conflicts of interest which should be disclosed and discussed, if appropriate, include, but are not limited to:

i) The General Partner is a general partner or an affiliate of the general partner in other investment entities (public and/or private) engaged in making similar investments or otherwise makes or arranges for similar investments.

ii) The General Partner has the authority to invest the partnership's funds in other partnerships in which the General Partner or an affiliate is the general partner or has an interest.

iii) Properties in which the General Partner or its affiliates have an interest are brought from or partnership properties are sold to the General Partner or its affiliates or entities in which they have an interest. Where appraisals are used in connection with any such transaction, it should be made clear that appraisals are only estimates of value and should not be relied on as measures of realizable value. If the appraiser is named as an expert, a consent to the use of his name should be furnished. If specific appraised values are included in the registrant statement, the appraiser should be named as an expert, his consent furnished and the appraisals filed as exhibits to the registration statement. If a statement that the purchase price of the property does not exceed its appraised value is included and the appraiser is not named and specified values are not cited, there need not be furnished a consent to use the appraiser's name. In that event, a copy of the appraisal should be submitted supplementally with the registration statement. If any relationship exists between the appraiser and the General Partner or its affiliates this should be stated. If the General Partner intends to buy any properties in which the General Partner or any of its affiliates have a material interest, such properties should be appropriately described in the prospectus along with the investment objectives of the partnership (see paragraph 10, Investment Objectives and Policies). If it is disclosed in the prospectus that the partnership may purchase properties in which the General Partner or its affiliates have a material interest, but no properties are described, and such properties are thereafter purchased for the partnership, the General Partner will have the heavy burden of demonstrating that it did not intend to purchase such property at the time the registration statement became effective.

Appendix F: Guide 5

iv) The General Partner or its affiliates own or have an interest in properties adjacent to those to be purchased and developed by the partnership.

v) Affiliates of the General Partner who act as underwriters, real estate brokers or managers for the partnership, act in such capacities for other partnerships or entities.

vi) An affiliate of the General Partner places mortgages for the partnership or otherwise acts as a finance broker or as insurance agent or broker receiving commissions for such services.

vii) An affiliate of the General Partner acts (a) as an underwriter for the offering, or (b) as a principal underwriter for the offering thereby creating conflicts in performance of the underwriter's due diligence inquiries under the Securities Act.

viii) The compensation plan for the General Partner may create a conflict between the interests of the General Partner and those of the partnership.

B. An organization chart should be included in this section showing the relationship between the various organizations managed or controlled by the General Partner or its affiliates that will do business with the partnership where the relationships are so complex that a graphic display would assist investors in understanding such relationships.

6. *FIDUCIARY RESPONSIBILITY OF THE GENERAL PARTNER*

A. A discussion of the fiduciary obligation owed by the General Partner to the Limited Partners should be set forth. The following disclosure is suggested with appropriate modification for the laws of the state of organization:

A General Partner is accountable to a limited partnership as a fiduciary and consequently must exercise good faith and integrity in handling partnership affairs. This is a rapidly developing and changing area of the law and Limited Partners who have questions concerning the duties of the General Partner should consult with their counsel.

B. Where the limited partnership agreement contains an exculpatory provision and/or the right to indemnification, the following disclosure is suggested, as modified to reflect the substance of such provisions:

Exculpation

i) The General Partner may not be liable to the Partnership or Limited Partners for errors in judgment or other acts or omissions not amounting to willful misconduct or gross negligence, since provision has been made in the Agreement of Limited Partnership for exculpation of the General Partner. Therefore, purchasers of the interests have a more limited right of action than they would have absent the limitation in the Partnership Agreement.

Indemnification

ii) The Partnership Agreement provides for indemnification of the General Partner by the Partnership for liabilities he incurs in dealings with third parties on behalf of the partnership. To the extent that the indemnification provisions purport to include indemnification for liabilities arising under the Securities Act of 1933, in the opinion of the Securities and Exchange Commission, such indemnification is contrary to public policy and therefore unenforceable.

Registrant's attention is also directed to Items 510 and 512(i) of Regulation S-K relating to disclosure of indemnification agreements.

7. *RISK FACTORS*

A. This section should include a carefully organized series of short, concise sub-captioned paragraphs, with cross-references to fuller discussion where appropriate, summarizing the principal risk factors applicable to the offering and to the partnership's particular plan of operations. The risk factors section should be brief.

B. This subsection should summarize each material risk of adverse tax consequences with appropriate cross-references to fuller discussions in the Federal tax section. For example:

i) Where no Internal Revenue Service (IRS) ruling as to partnership tax status has been applied for or obtained, the risk that the IRS may on audit determine that for tax purposes the partnership is an association taxable as a corporation, in which case, investors would be deprived of the tax benefits associated with the offering. As part of this disclosure, it should be stated that a material risk of IRS classification as a corporate association may exist even though registrant relies on an opinion of counsel as to partnership tax status as such opinion is not binding on the IRS. It may also be stated that IRS classification of the partnership as a corporate association would deprive investors of the tax benefits of the offering only if the IRS determination is upheld in court or otherwise becomes final. Any such additional disclosure should explain that contesting an IRS determination may impose representation expenses on investors. (See Federal tax section, p. 12.)

ii) Where the IRS has advised registrant that it proposes not to rule, or to rule adversely, on any tax issue as to which a ruling was applied for, the risk that investors may lose some or all tax benefits associated with the offering. (See Federal tax section, p. 12.)

iii) The risk that after some years of partnership operations an investor's tax liabilities may exceed his cash distributions in corresponding years and that to the extent of such excess the payment of such taxes will be out-of-pocket expenses.

iv) Upon a sale or other disposition (*e.g.*, by gift) of a partnership interest or, upon a sale (including a foreclosure sale) or other disposition of partnership property, the risk that an investor's tax liabilities may exceed the cash he receives and that to the extent of such excess the payment of such taxes will be out-of-pocket expenses. The disclosure should indicate to what extent the gain may be taxed as ordinary income, to what extent as capital gain. (See Federal tax section, p. 19.)

v) The risk that an audit of the partnership's information return may result in an audit of an investor's own tax return. (See Federal tax section, p. 20.)

C. Risk factors relating to the specific partnership might include, where applicable:

i) Management's lack of relevant experience, or management's lack of success with similar partnerships or other real estate investments;

ii) Where the proceeds of the offering will be insufficient to meet the requirements of the partnership's investment objectives, a discussion of the additional sources of capital for the partnership and of the risk of not being able to satisfy the partnership's objectives as a result of not obtaining additional necessary funds;

iii) Where the partnership has high risk investment objectives, including high leveraging, these should be explained;

iv) The risk that no public market for interests is likely to develop and that holders of interests may not be able to liquidate their investment quickly;

v) Risks associated with contemplated rent stabilization programs, fuel or energy requirements or regulations, and construction in areas that are subject to environmental or other federal, state or local regulations, actual or pending;

vi) Where a material portion of the minimum net proceeds of the offering is not committed to specific properties, disclosure of the particular risk associated with an investment in such an offering. Such disclosure should include the increased uncertainty and risk to investors since they are unable to evaluate the manner in which the proceeds are to be invested and the economic merit of the particular real estate projects prior to investment. Also it should be disclosed that there may be a substantial period of time before the proceeds of the offering are invested and therefore a delay to investors in receiving a return on their investment.

D. Risk factors relating to real estate limited partnership offerings in general should be briefly discussed after those relating to the specific partnership. Such risks might include, where applicable: the risks associated with the ownership of real estate, including uncertainty of cash flow to meet fixed and maturing obligations, adverse local market conditions, risks of "leveraging," and uninsured losses.

8. *PRIOR PERFORMANCE OF THE GENERAL PARTNER AND AFFILIATES*

A narrative summary of the "track record" or prior performance of programs sponsored by the General Partner and its affiliates ("sponsors") containing the information set forth below should be included in the text of the prospectus. Tables following the format of those in Appendix II, relating to historical use of proceeds of prior programs, compensation to the sponsors, operations of prior programs, and acquisitions and sales of properties by prior programs, should be included at the back of the prospectus or in Part II of the registration statement as specified in paragraph B "Prior Performance Tables" hereunder.

Sponsors are urged not to include in the prospectus information about prior performance beyond that required by this Guide except for such further material information as may be necessary to make the required statements, in light of the circumstances under which they are made, not misleading.

Terms used in the Guide. "Public" programs include all offerings registered under the Securities Act of 1933, all programs required to report under Section 15(d) of the Securities Exchange Act of 1934 ("Exchange Act"), all programs with a class of equity securities registered pursuant to Section 12(g) of the Exchange Act, and all other programs with at least 300 security holders of record that initially raised at least $1 million.

Programs with "similar investment objectives" are those with similar objectives as set forth in the prospectus. Generally, the sponsor has the responsibility to determine which previous programs had "similar investment objectives," taking into consideration the materiality of information about the prior programs in analyzing the registrant's proposed activities.

A sponsor would be considered to have a "public track record" if it has sponsored at least three programs with investment objectives similar to those of the registrant that file reports under Section 13(a) or Section 15(d) of the Exchange Act and at least two public programs with investment objectives similar to those of the registrant that had three years of operations after investment of 90% of the amount available for investment. In addition, at least two of the public offerings for programs with investment objectives similar to those of the registrant must have closed in the previous three years.

A. *Narrative Summary.*

1. The narrative summary in the text of the prospectus should include a description of the sponsor's experience in the last ten years with all other programs, both public and nonpublic, that have invested primarily in real estate, regardless of the investment objectives of the programs. This summary should include at least (a) the number of programs sponsored, (b) the total amount of money raised from investors, (c) the total number of investors, (d) the number of properties purchased and location by region, (e) the aggregate dollar amount of property purchased, (f) the percentage (based on purchase prices rather than on number) of properties that are commercial (broken out by shopping centers, office buildings and others) and residential, (g) the percentage (based on purchase prices) of new, used or construction properties, and (h) the number of properties sold. Aggregate figures should be presented separately for public and nonpublic programs. In addition, the narrative should indicate the approximate percentage of the overall data that represents activities of programs with investment objectives similar to those of the registrant. The summary also should cross-reference the prior performance tables.

2. The narrative summary should include a discussion of those major adverse business developments or conditions experienced by any prior program, either public or nonpublic, that would be material to investors in this program. The narrative summary also should include a cross-reference to further information that may be found in Appendix II as part of Table III.

3. The narrative summary should include a list of all prior public programs sponsored by the General Partner and its affiliates and an undertaking to provide upon request, for no fee, the most recent Form 10-K Annual Report filed with the Commission by any prior public program that has reported to the Commission within the last twenty-four months and to provide, for a reasonable fee, the exhibits to each such Form 10-K.

4. The narrative summary should include a summary of acquisitions of properties by programs in the most recent three years as set forth in Table VI of Appendix II. The summary should include the number of properties purchased, the type, location and method of financing. Reference should be made to the more detailed description

of these acquisitions in Part II of the registration statement, and the registrant should undertake to provide the more detailed description from Part II without fee upon request.

B. *Prior Performance Tables.* The information required by the tables set forth in Appendix II should be included in the format shown. Tables should appear at the back of the prospectus except for Table VI, which should appear only in Part II of the registration statement. The instructions to the tables specify the programs and time periods about which information is required.

9. MANAGEMENT

A. If a material portion of the maximum net proceeds (allowing for reserves) is not committed to specific properties, disclosure should be made of the identity of the individuals who will make the investment decisions with appropriate background information including that required by Item 401(f) of Regulation S-K.

B. Any substantial reliance on a nonaffiliate in running the operations of the partnership should be disclosed and any relevant prior experience should be discussed. If material amounts of compensation or fees are to be paid to nonaffiliates, a separate heading should be provided entitled, "Fees and Compensation Arrangements with Nonaffiliates" and a tabular presentation describing such fees should be provided.

C. If there is provision in the partnership agreement or otherwise for a change in the management of the partnership, a description of how such change could be accomplished should be included.

D. The amount of, and reason for, any contingent liabilities of the General Partner and its affiliates with regard to prior programs now in existence should be disclosed. If this information appears in the financial statements it may be incorporated hereunder by reference.

10. INVESTMENT OBJECTIVES AND POLICIES

A. Disclosure should be made of the nature of the property intended to be purchased (*e.g.*, commercial, residential) and the criteria (*e.g.*, method of depreciation, location) to be utilized in evaluating proposed investments.

B. If there is provision in the partnership agreement or otherwise for change in the investment objectives of the partnership, a description of how such change could be made should be included.

C. Generally, where the net proceeds of the offering will be invested in nonspecified properties or in properties that do not have any significant operating histories, it is not appropriate to make any statement setting forth a rate of return on the investment.

11. DESCRIPTION OF REAL ESTATE INVESTMENTS

A. Risks associated with specified properties, such as competitive factors, environmental regulation, rent control regulation, fuel or energy requirements and regulation should be noted.

B. If a material portion of the minimum net proceeds (allowing for reasonable reserves) is not committed to specific properties, the issuer should clearly so indicate in the prospectus.

Where a reasonable probability exists that a property will be acquired and the funds to be expended represent a material portion of the net proceeds of the minimum offering, the issuer should describe such property in the registration statement at the time of filing. Where after the registration statement has been filed but prior to its effectiveness a reasonable probability arises that a property will be acquired, a description of such property should be included in a pre-effective amendment to the registration statement. Where a reasonable probability that a property will be acquired arises after the effectiveness of the registration statement and during the distribution period, a 424(c) supplement or post-effective amendment, as appropriate, should be promptly filed. (See Undertaking D.)* Whether adequate disclosure of properties to be acquired has been timely made can only be determined by an examination of the facts in each case. This may vary due to different business practices particular to each issuer. Thus, as in all other situations, the burden of making adequate and timely disclosure rests solely with the issuer.

12. *FEDERAL TAXES*

A. *General Instructions.* This section should summarize under a series of appropriate headings all material Federal income tax aspects of the offering. State tax aspects need usually be summarized only to the extent required by Subsection L, below. Proper citations should be used whenever reference is made to sections of the Internal Revenue Code (the "Code"), the Treasury regulations, decided cases or other sources. An opinion of counsel as to all material tax aspects of the offering should be filed as an exhibit. Such opinion should cite relevant authority for any conclusions expressed. The tax sections of the prospectus should summarize or restate the tax information contained in the opinion.

The function of the tax opinion is to inform investors of the tax consequences they can reasonably expect from an investment in the partnership. If, with respect to an intended tax benefit, counsel are unable to express an opinion that such benefit will be available because of uncertainty in the law or for other reasons, the opinion should so state and also disclose that there is or may be a material tax risk the particular benefit will be disallowed on audit. The tax effect of such disallowance should be explained. Each material risk of disallowance of an intended tax benefit should be disclosed in the tax opinion and under the appropriate heading in the prospectus.

Tax counsel should be aware that their opinion speaks as of the effective date of the registration statement. Such opinion should be updated for any material changes or events occurring subsequent to filing and prior to the effective date. Ruling requests

---

* It has come to the staff's attention that on a number of occasions issuers have identified properties to be purchased and have delayed proceeding with the purchase in order to avoid the necessary disclosure. In the staff's opinion, such practice is not consistent with the obligation of the issuer to disclose material facts relating to the offering.

(including amendments) and rulings should also be filed as exhibits with the original filing, or by amendment as soon thereafter as available.

B. *Partnership Status.* This subsection should state whether an IRS ruling has been requested as to the entity's classification as a partnership for Federal income tax purposes. The contents of any ruling, including any conditions therein, should be summarized. Where a ruling or opinion of counsel as to partnership status is conditioned on the maintenance of certain net worth or other standards, there should be disclosure as to how these standards will be maintained in the future. If no IRS ruling as to partnership tax status has been requested or obtained, counsel's opinion as to partnership tax status should be summarized and the risk of IRS classification of the entity as a corporate association, referred to in the Risk Factors section, should be discussed.

C. *Taxation of Limited Partners.* Insofar as necessary to an understanding of the intended tax benefits and any material risks of their disallowance, this subsection should summarize basic rules of partnership taxation, e.g., that a partnership is not a taxable entity, that a partner will be required to report on his Federal tax return his distributive share of partnership income, gain, loss, deductions or credits, whether or not any actual distribution is made to such partner during his taxable year. The tax treatment of cash distributions to partners should also be explained.

If the partnership agreement provides special allocations among partners of distributive shares of income, gain, loss, deductions or credits, this subsection should set forth an opinion of counsel to the effect that the principal purpose of the allocations is not tax avoidance or evasion under Code Sec. 704(b)(2), and/or a risk disclosure to the effect that the IRS may on audit disallow any special allocation which it determines to have tax avoidance or evasion as its principal purpose. The tax consequences to partners of disallowance of a special allocation should be explained. Where applicable, the tax consequences of retroactive allocations to new partners should be discussed.

D. *Basis.* This subsection should explain that a partner may deduct his share of partnership losses only to the extent of the adjusted basis of his interest in the partnership. Inclusion of a partner's share of the partnership's nonrecourse debt in the adjusted basis of his partnership interest should be explained. If there is a question as to whether the partnership's nonrecourse debt will enter into bases of the limited partners' interests, that should be disclosed.

Where appropriate, there should be an explanation of the consequences to a limited partner of a reduction in his share of the partnership's nonrecourse debt as may result, for example, from a change in his profit sharing ratio.

E. *Depreciation and Recapture.* This subsection should explain the method or methods of depreciation to be used by the partnership on its depreciable property as well as the basis for determining useful lives of such property. Any material risks that the IRS may challenge useful lives chosen by the partnership should be disclosed together with an explanation of the possible tax consequences of applying longer useful lives to partnership property. If methods of depreciation available only to a "first-user" are to be utilized, the basis of such "first-user" status should be explained. Depreciation recapture may be explained here with appropriate cross-reference to subsections on Sale or Other Disposition of Partnership Property and Sale or Other Disposition of a Partnership Interest.

F. *Deductibility of Prepaid and Other Expenses.* As to prepaid interest, possible nondeductibility in the year of payment should be discussed. It should be explained that if a partnership takes a large deduction for prepaid interest in its first year of operation, having little or no income in such year, the IRS may determine that the prepayment created a material distortion of income at the partnership level and require that it be allocated over the term of the loan.

As to other material partnership expenses (e.g., interim commitment fees, management fees, permanent mortgage fees, etc.) it should be stated which are deductible, which are nondeductible and as to which deductibility is uncertain. Where applicable, the possible nondeductibility of guaranteed payments under Code Sec. 707(c) should be discussed.

G. *Tax Liabilities in Later Years.* This subsection should discuss the Risk Factors disclosure that after some years of partnership operations an investor's tax liabilities may exceed cash distributions in corresponding years. The tax problems that will arise after partnership property reaches the point when the partnership's nondeductible mortgage amortization payments exceed its depreciation deductions (the crossover point) should be explained.

It should also be explained that where partnership losses offset an investor's earned income taxable at a 50 percent rate, partnership income in later years may be taxed to the investor at a higher rate.

H. *Sale or Other Disposition of a Partnership Interest.* This subsection should begin with a restatement of the Risk Factors disclosure that an investor may be unable to sell his partnership interest as there may be no market for it. The subsection should then discuss the Risk Factors disclosure that taxes payable on a sale of a partnership interest may exceed cash received. The discussion should explain the tax effect on a partner of being relieved from his share of the partnership's nonrecourse liabilities. The discussion should also state to what extent the gain recognized will be taxed as ordinary income, to what extent as capital gain.

Whether or not the partnership plans to make the Sec. 754 election should be disclosed together with an explanation of the possible tax consequences on a transferee Limited Partner should the election not be made.

This subsection should also explain that a gift of an interest in a partnership holding leveraged property may result in Federal income tax (as well as Federal gift tax) liability to the donor. It should be explained that the IRS is likely to consider that a partner who gives away his partnership interest is relieved of his share of the partnership's nonrecourse liabilities and that he may realize a taxable gain on the gift to the extent that his share of such liabilities exceeds his adjusted basis in his partnership interest. It should be stated to what extent the gain will be taxed as ordinary income, to what extent as capital gain.

I. *Sale or Other Disposition of Partnership Property.* This subsection may use cross-reference to, or be combined with, subsection H in order to avoid repetition.

The subsection should discuss the Risk Factors disclosure that upon a sale (including a foreclosure sale) or other disposition of partnership property an investor's tax liability may exceed cash he would receive. The discussion should explain that the amount received by the partnership on sale (including a foreclosure sale) or other disposition of property will include any nonrecourse indebtedness to which the property was subject. It should be stated to what extent the gain will be taxed as ordinary income, to what extent as capital gain.

If appropriate, the tax treatment of dealer property should be explained. Should the sale of condominium units by the partnership be contemplated, it should be pointed out such units may be treated as dealer property.

J. *Section 183*. The possible impact of this Code section on investors lacking a profit objective in investing in any tax shelter program which is expected to generate annual net losses for tax purposes for a period of years should be discussed. The discussion should note that the section may apply to the Limited Partners of a partnership notwithstanding any profit objective the partnership itself may be deemed to have.

K. *Liquidation or Termination of the Partnership*. The tax consequences to a Limited Partner of partnership liquidation or termination should be explained.

L. *State, Local and Foreign Taxes*. It should be disclosed whether partners will be required to file tax returns and/or be subject to tax in any state or states other than their state of residence, or in any foreign countries. Where applicable, state and foreign tax rates should be noted.

M. *Tax Returns and Tax Information*. It should be disclosed what kind of tax information will be supplied to Limited Partners and when, and whether the same kind of information will also be supplied to assignees who are not substitute limited partners.

It should be explained that the information return filed by the partnership may be audited and that such audit may result in adjustments or proposed adjustments. Any adjustment of the partnership information return would normally result in adjustments or proposed adjustments of a partner's own return. Any audit of a partner's return could result in adjustments of nonpartnership as well as partnership income and losses.

N. *Other Headings*. Where applicable the tax section should also discuss the limitation on deductions of investment interest, the minimum tax on tax preference income, the impact of tax preference items on the maximum tax on earned income, and any other tax information deemed material in the particular offering.

13. GLOSSARY

If terms are used in the prospectus that are technical in nature or are susceptible to varying methods of computation, e.g., acquisition fees, book value, capital contribution, cash flow, cash available for distribution, construction fees, cost of property, development fee, net worth, organization and offering expenses, profit, partnership management fee and property management fee, definitions should be provided. For purposes of uniformity, it is suggested that these definitions conform to those that appear in the Statement of Policy Regarding Real Estate Programs of the North American Securities Administrators Association, or that any variations, and the economic effect thereof, be disclosed.

14. SUMMARY OF PARTNERSHIP AGREEMENT

A brief summary of the material provisions of the Limited Partnership Agreement should be included.

15. REPORTS TO LIMITED PARTNERS

The registrant should identify all reports and other documents that will be furnished to Limited Partners as required by the partnership's Limited Partnership Agreement and the undertakings to the registration statement. In particular, registrant should disclose: (1) whether the financial information contained in such reports will be prepared on an accrual basis in accordance with generally accepted accounting principles, with a reconciliation with respect to information furnished to limited partners for income tax purposes; (2) whether independent certified public accountants will audit the financial statements to be included in the annual report; (3) whether the annual report will be provided to limited partners within 90 days following the close of the partnership's fiscal year; (4) that a detailed statement of any transactions with the General Partner or its affiliates, and of fees, commissions, compensation and other benefits paid, or accrued to the General Partner or its affiliates for the fiscal year completed, showing the amount paid or accrued to each recipient and the services performed, will be furnished to each limited partner at least on an annual basis pursuant to the registrant's undertaking; (5) that the information specified by Form 10-Q (if such report is required to be filed with the Commission) will be furnished to limited partners within 45 days after the close of each quarterly fiscal period pursuant to the registrant's undertaking; and (6) if the registrant has applied for, but not received an IRS ruling as to the tax status at the time of effectiveness of the registration statement, that the registrant will promptly notify each limited partner, in writing, pursuant to its undertaking of the receipt of the ruling or of an adverse ruling or refusal to rule by the IRS.

16. THE OFFERING—DESCRIPTION OF THE UNITS

In addition to the disclosure required by the relevant items of Form S-1 or S-11, disclosure should be made of all restrictions on transfer of the interests, including those in the Partnership Agreement, those imposed by state suitability standards or blue sky laws, and those resulting from the tax laws.

17. REDEMPTION, REPURCHASE AND RIGHT OF PRESENTMENT AGREEMENTS

There should be a discussion of any provisions in the partnership agreement that allow the General Partner or its affiliates to redeem or repurchase the offered security or that allow the investor to seek redemption or repurchase. The conditions of formulae used, *e.g.*, purchase price less capital returns, should also be disclosed. Registrant should be careful to appropriately describe the investor's right—whether it be redemption, repurchase, or merely a right of presentment. The discussion should include the following factors:

(1) That appraisals are simply estimates of value and may not necessarily correspond to realizable value;

(2) The order in which redemption requests will be honored (post mark or other objective standard);

(3) Whether the General Partner and its affiliates will defer their redemption requests until requests for redemption by the Limited Partner public investors have been met;

(4) The source and amount of funds (together with any legal or practical limitations) available for this purpose;

(5) The circumstances under which a later request will be honored, while an earlier request is still pending;

(6) Tax consequences related to redemption;

(7) The period of time during which a redemption request may be pending prior to its being granted or rejected;

(8) Whether there is to be allocation of funds among partners requesting redemption in circumstances where redemption requests exceed funds available for this purpose. If so, state and briefly describe the allocation process;

(9) Whether Limited Partners must hold an interest in the partnership for a specified period prior to making a redemption request; and

(10) A detailed statement of the procedure that must be followed in order to redeem or seek repurchase of the interest, including the forms that must be presented, and whether signature guarantees will be required.

18. *PLAN OF DISTRIBUTION*

A. If there is an understanding or arrangement, whether written or oral, between the registrant and any broker or dealer, relating to the distribution of the interests, which is intended to be finalized after effectiveness of the registration statement, such understanding or arrangement should be disclosed.

B. If, after the registration statement becomes effective, the registrant enters into any selling arrangement which calls for the payment of more than the usual and customary compensation, a sticker supplement (Rule 424(c)) describing such arrangement should be filed.

C. If the registrant intends to pay referral or similar fees to any professional or other persons in connection with the distribution of the interests, this fact should be disclosed.

D. If the General Partner or its affiliates intend to purchase interests, and such interests will be included in satisfying the minimum offering requirements, it should be disclosed whether such interests are intended to be resold, and if so, the period of time these interests will be held prior to being resold. Depending on the circumstances, such interests may be considered to be unsold allotments under Section 4(3) of the Act. (See Securities Act Release 4150.)

19. *SUMMARY OF PROMOTIONAL AND SALES MATERIAL*

A. The sales material should present a balanced discussion of both risk and reward. The contents of the sales material or sales meetings or seminars should be consistent with the representations in the prospectus.

B. A section which identifies all written sales material proposed to be transmitted to prospective investors orally or in writing should be included. The sales material should be appropriately identified by title and character and should be separately categorized either as the registrant's material or that of another person. If material provided by the latter is to be used, state the name of the author and publication and the date of prior publication, if any, identify any persons who are quoted without being identified, and, except in the case of a public official document or statement, state whether or not the consent of the author and publication have been obtained for the use of the material as sales material. Sales materials include memoranda, summary descriptions, graphics, supplemental exhibits, media advertising, charts and pictures relating to the offering of the security and proposed to be transmitted to prospective investors.

C. If any other material is to be used subsequent to the effective date, a "sticker" supplement (424(c) prospectus) should be filed to describe any such sales material.

D. Any sales material that is intended to be furnished to investors orally or in writing, other than that which is used for internal purposes of the registrant, and including all material described in paragraph B above, should be submitted to the staff supplementally, prior to its use. For purposes of this paragraph only, sales material includes all marketing memoranda that are sent by the General Partner or its affiliates to broker/dealers or other sales personnel and may include material labeled "for broker/dealer use only." Staff comments, if any, will be promptly communicated to the registrant. Registrant should check with the staff before using sale material that has been submitted to the staff.

E. Wherever public sales meetings or seminars are to be employed to discuss the offering, individually or in conjunction with other tax sheltered offerings, the staff should be provided, as supplemental information, copies of any written scripts or outlines which are prepared for use in such meetings a reasonable time prior to their use.

F. Reference in sales material or at such sales meetings or seminars to Federal income tax treatment of the partnership and its investors should refer to either a ruling of the IRS or an opinion of counsel. Counsel should be named, his acknowledgement furnished supplementally with respect to such use, and any qualification contained in counsel's opinion should be referred to in such material by cross-referencing to the prospectus. Where the program has not sought a ruling as to the tax status (partnership) from the IRS and is relying on an opinion of counsel, it should be indicated that an opinion of counsel is not binding on the IRS.

20. UNDERTAKINGS

A. The following undertaking should be included in the registration statement if the securities to be registered are to be offered in a continuous offering over an extended period of time:

The registrant undertakes (a) to file any prospectuses required by Section 10(a)(3) as post-effective amendments to the registration statement, (b) that for the purpose of determining any liability under the Act each such post-effective amendment may be deemed to be a new registration statement relating to the securities offering therein and the offering of such securities at that time may be deemed to be the initial bona fide offering thereof, (c) that all post-effective amendments will comply with the applicable forms, rules and regulations of the Commission in effect at the time such post-effective amendments are filed, and (d) to remove from registration by means of a post- effective amendment any of the securities being registered which remain at the termination of the offering.

B. The following undertaking should be included in every registration statement:

The registrant undertakes to send to each limited partner at least on an annual basis a detailed statement of any transactions with the General Partner or its affiliates, and of fees, commissions, compensation and other benefits, paid, or accrued to the General Partner or its affiliates for the fiscal year completed, showing the amount paid or accrued to each recipient and the services performed.

C. The following undertaking should be included in every registration statement:

The registrant undertakes to provide to the limited partners the financial statements required by Form 10-K for the first full fiscal year of operations of the partnership.

D. The following undertakings relating to investment of the proceeds of an offering in which a material portion of the maximum net proceeds (allowing for reasonable reserves) is not committed (i.e., subject to a binding purchase agreement) to specific properties should be included in the registration statement:

The registrant undertakes to file a sticker supplement pursuant to Rule 424(c) under the Act during the distribution period describing each property not identified in the prospectus at such time as there arises a reasonable probability that such property will be acquired and to consolidate all such stickers into a post-effective amendment filed at least once every three months, with the information contained in such amendment provided simultaneously to the existing Limited Partners. Each sticker supplement should disclose all compensation and fees received by the General Partner(s) and its affiliates in connection with any such acquisition. The post-effective amendments shall include audited financial statements meeting the requirements of Rule 3-14 of Regulation S-X only for properties acquired during the distribution period.

The registrant also undertakes to file, after the end of the distribution period, a current report on Form 8-K containing the financial statements and any additional information required by Rule 3-14 of Regulation S-X, to reflect each commitment (i.e., the signing of a binding purchase agreement) made after the end of the distribution period involving the use of 10% or more (on a cumulative basis) of the net proceeds of the offering and to provide the information contained in such report to the Limited Partners at least once each quarter after the distribution period of the offering has ended.

Note Offers and sales of the interests may continue after the filing of a post-effective amendment containing information previously disclosed in sticker supplements to the prospectus, as long as the information disclosed in a current sticker supplement accompanying the prospectus is as complete as the information contained in the most recently filed post-effective amendment.

E. If the registrant has applied for a ruling from the IRS as to tax status, and has not received it at the time of effectiveness:

The registrant undertakes to promptly notify each limited partner, in writing, of the receipt of the ruling or of an adverse ruling or refusal to rule by the IRS, and undertakes to file with the Commission a Form 8-K describing such event.

APPENDIX I
EXAMPLE OF SUMMARY OF THE USE OF PROCEEDS SECTION
Estimated Application of Proceeds of This Offering

	Minimum Dollar Amount	Per Cent	Maximum Dollar Amount	Per Cent
Gross Offering Proceeds	$	100.00%	$	100.00%
Public Offering Expenses: Underwriting Discount and Commissions Paid to Affiliate Organizational Expenses (1)				
Amount Available for investment	$	%	$	%
Prepaid Terms and Fees Related to Purchase of Property (2)				
Cash Down Payment (Equity)				
Acquisition Fees (Real Estate Commissions) (3)				
Working Capital Reserve				
Proceeds Invested				
Public Offering Expenses				
Total Application of Proceeds	$	%	$	100.00%

The Corporate General Partner and its affiliates may receive a maximum of $ (%) if the minimum dollar amount is sold and $ (%) if the maximum dollar amount is sold from the sellers of the properties as Real Estate Commissions on purchases of properties. Real estate commissions are normally paid by the seller of a property rather than the buyer. However, the price of a property will generally be adjusted upward to take into account this obligation of the seller so that in effect the Partnership, as purchaser, will bear all or a portion of the commission in the purchase price of the property. The partnership also expects to pay commissions in connection with the sale of properties which will reduce the net proceeds to the Partnership of any such sales.

(1) Includes a $ non-recurring organization fee to be received by the Corporate General Partner and legal, accounting, printing and other expenses of this offering. To the extent, if any, that expenses of the offering exceed $ per interest, the excess will be paid by

(2) Includes prepaid interest, points, loan commitment fees and legal and other costs of acquisition. The percentage of such items to be capitalized is . . . .%.

(3) "Real Estate Commission" is defined as the total of all fees and commissions paid by any person to any person, including the Corporate General Partner or affiliates in connection with the selection, purchase, construction or development of any property by the Partnership, whether designated as real estate commission, acquisition fees, finders fees, selection fees, development fees, construction fees, non-recurring management fees, consulting fees or any other similar fees or commissions howsoever designated and howsoever treated for tax or accounting purposes. (See "Compensation to Management.")

APPENDIX II
PRIOR PERFORMANCE TABLES
Instructions to Appendix II

1. The prior performance tables should be preceded by a narrative introduction that cross-references the narrative summary in the text, explains the significance of the track record and the tables, explains where additional information (Part II of the registration statement or Form 10-K Annual Reports for prior programs) can be obtained on request and includes a glossary of terms used in the tables.

This introduction also should include a discussion of the factors the sponsor considered in determining which previous programs had "similar investment objectives" to those of the registrant.

2. Each of the tables should be introduced by a brief narrative explaining the objective of the table and what it covers so that the investor will be able to understand the significance of the information presented. There also should be set forth with or in each table any further material information that may be necessary to make the required tabular data, in light of the circumstances under which it is presented, not misleading.

Table I. Experience in Raising and Investing Funds (on a percentage basis)
Instructions:

1. Include information only for programs the offering of which closed in the most recent three years.

2. Sponsors with a "public track record" should include information relating only to public programs with investment objectives similar to those of the registrant.

3. If the sponsor does not have a "public track record," information must be given for each prior program, public or nonpublic, with investment objectives similar to those of the registrant. If the sponsor has not sponsored at least five such programs, then information must be given for each prior program, public or nonpublic, even if the investment objectives for those programs are not similar to those of the registrant. In that case, nonpublic programs with investment objectives that are not similar to those of the registrant should be grouped together according to investment objective and information about those programs presented on an aggregate basis by year. If so presented, the number of programs that have been aggregated should be disclosed. The sponsor

also should indicate by note if the investment objectives of any program are not similar to those of the registrant and should briefly describe those investment objectives.

	Program X	Program Y
Dollar amount offered		
Dollar amount raised (100%)		
Less offering expenses:		
Selling commissions and discounts		
Retained by affiliates		
Organizational expenses		
Other (explain)		
Reserves		
Percent available for investment		
Acquisition costs:		
Prepaid items and fees related to purchase of property		
Cash down payment		
Acquisition fees		
Other (explain)		
Total acquisition cost		
Percent leverage (mortgage financing divided by total acquisition cost)		
Date offering began		
Length of offering (in months)		
Months to invest 90% of amount available for investment (measured from beginning of offering)		

Table II. Compensation to Sponsor

Instructions: 1. Include in a separate column for each program aggregated payments made to the sponsor only by real estate programs the offering of which closed in the most recent three years. Include in another separate column aggregate payments to the sponsor in the most recent three years from all other programs and indicate the number of programs involved.

    2. Sponsors with a "public track record" should include information relating only to public programs with investment objectives similar to those of the registrant.

    3. If the sponsor does not have a "public track record," information must be given for each prior program, public or nonpublic, with investment objectives similar to those of the registrant. If the sponsor has not sponsored at least five such programs, then information must be given for each prior program, public or nonpublic, even if the investment objectives for those programs are not similar to those of the registrant. In that case, nonpublic programs with investment objectives that are not similar to those

Appendix F: Guide 5

of the registrant should be grouped together according to investment objectives and information about those programs presented on an aggregate basis by year. If so presented, the number of programs that have been aggregated should be disclosed. The sponsor also should indicate by note if the investment objectives of any program are not similar to those of the registrant and should briefly describe those investment objectives.

4. The table should include any real estate commissions and other fees paid to the sponsor in connection with the acquisition or disposition of any properties by the program by entities other than the program itself.

Type of Compensation	Program X	Program Y	Other Programs
Date offering commenced			
Dollar amount raised			
Amount paid to sponsor from proceeds of offering:			
Underwriting fees			
Acquisition fees			
—real estate commissions			
—advisory fees			
—other (identify and quantify)			
Other			
Dollar amount of cash generated from operations before deducting payments to sponsor			
Amount paid to sponsor from operations:			
Property management fees			
Partnership management fees			
Reimbursements			
Leasing commissions			
Other (identify and quantify)			
Dollar amount of property sales and refinancing before deducting payments to sponsor			
—cash			
—notes			
Amount paid to sponsor from property sales and refinancing:			
Real estate commissions			
Incentive fees[1]			
Other (identify and quantify)			

[1] Explain subordinated commissions in a note.

Table III. Operating Results of Prior Programs

Instructions:

    1. Include information only for programs the offerings of which closed in the most recent five years. Financial data for each program should be presented separately for each year.

    2. Sponsors with a "public track record" should include information relating only to public programs with investment objectives similar to those of the registrant.

    3. If the sponsor does not have a "public track record," information must be given for each program, public or nonpublic, with investment objectives similar to those of the registrant. If the sponsor has not sponsored at least five such programs, then information must be given for each prior program, public or nonpublic, even if the investment objectives for those programs are not similar to those of the registrant. In that case, nonpublic programs with investment objectives that are not similar to those of the registrant should be grouped together according to investment objective and information about those programs presented on an aggregate basis by year. If so presented, the number of programs that have been aggregated should be disclosed. The sponsor also should indicate by note if the investment objectives of any program are not similar to those of the registrant and should briefly describe those investment objectives.

    4. Information should be presented on the basis of generally accepted accounting principles ("GAAP") where indicated. However, where information about nonpublic programs is required to be included, such information may be presented on a tax basis if the program's books have not been kept on a GAAP basis. If there are any significant differences in operating results between accounting on a tax and GAAP basis they should be explained. This explanation should provide the reader with any additional information about the particular programs presented that may be necessary to make the information contained in the Table not materially misleading in light of the circumstances under which the information is given.

	Program X		
	year 1	year 2	year 3
Gross Revenues			
Profit on sale of properties			
Less: Operating expenses			
Interest expense			
Depreciation			
Net Income—GAAP Basis			
Taxable Income			
—from operations			
—from gain on sale			
Cash generated from operations[1]			
Cash generated from sales			

Cash generated from refinancing
Cash generated from operations,
   sales and refinancing
Less: Cash distributions to investors
       —from operating cash flow
       —from sales and refinancing
       —from other
Cash generated (deficiency) after cash
   distributions
Less: Special items (not including
   sales and refinancing)
   (identify and quantify)
Cash generated (deficiency) after cash
   distributions and special items

Tax and Distribution Data Per $1000 Invested

Federal Income Tax Results:
      Ordinary income (loss)
        —from operations
        —from recapture
      Capital gain (loss)
Cash Distributions to Investors
      Source (on GAAP basis)
        —Investment income
        —Return on capital
      Source (on cash basis)
        —Sales
        —Refinancing
        —Operations
        —Other
Amount (in percentage terms) remaining invested in program properties at the end of the last year reported in the Table (original total acquisition cost of properties retained divided by original total acquisition cost of all properties in program).

---

[1] Indicate in a note what amount is from sources other than operations, such as guaranteed rents or interest.

Table IV. Results of Completed Programs

Instructions:
     1. Include programs that have completed operations (no longer hold properties) in the most recent five years, even if they still hold notes.

2. Sponsors with a "public track record" should include information relating only to public programs with investment objectives similar to those of the registrant.

3. If the sponsor does not have a "public track record," information must be given for each prior program, public or nonpublic, with investment objectives similar to those of the registrant. If the sponsor has not sponsored at least five such programs, then information must be given for each prior program, public or nonpublic, even if the investment objectives for those programs are not similar to those of the registrant. In that case, nonpublic programs with investment objectives that are not similar to those of the registrant should be grouped together according to investment objective and information about those programs presented on an aggregate basis by year. If so presented, the number of programs that have been aggregated should be disclosed. The sponsor also should indicate by note if the investment objectives of any program are not similar to those of the registrant and should briefly describe those investment objectives.

Program Name
    Dollar Amount Raised
    Number of Properties Purchased
    Date of Closing of Offering
    Date of First Sale of Property
    Date of Final Sale of Property
Tax and Distribution Data Per $1000 Investment Through...
    Federal Income Tax Results:
        Ordinary income (loss)
            —from operations
            —from recapture
        Capital Gain (loss)[1]
        Deferred Gain[2]
            Capital
            Ordinary
Cash Distributions to Investors
    Source (on GAAP basis)
        —Investment income
        —Return of capital
    Source (on cash basis)
        —Sales
        —Refinancing
        —Operations
        —Other
Receivable on Net Purchase Money Financing[3]

---

[1] Note 60% capital gain exclusion.
[2] Explain in a note deferred capital gain.
[3] Explain in a note the terms of notes taken back and annual payments, and the fact that the amounts presented are face amounts and do not represent discounted current value.

Table V. *Sales or Disposals of Properties*

Instructions:
1. Include all sales or disposals of property by programs with similar investment objectives within the recent three years.
2. Sponsors with a "public track record" should only include information relating to public programs. If the sponsor does not have a "public track record," then information should be given about sales or disposals of properties by public and nonpublic programs. Where properties held by nonpublic programs are included, information should be on a GAAP basis where feasible without undue effort or expense.

Property	Date Acquired	Date of Sale[1]	Selling Price, Net of Closing Costs and GAAP Adjustments					Cost of Properties Including Closing and Soft Costs			Excess (Deficiency) of Property Operating Cash Receipts Over Cash Expenditures[6]
			Cash received net of closing costs	Mortgage balance at time of sale	Purchase money mortgage taken back by program[2]	Adjustments resulting from application of GAAP[3]	Total[4]	Original mortgage financing	Total acquisition cost, capital improvement, closing and soft costs[5]	Total	

[1]Note if sales of properties are to related parties.
[2]Indicate in a note that the amounts shown are face amounts and do not represent discounted current value. In addition, describe the terms of purchase money mortgages taken by the partnership, including the interest rate, any balloon payment requirements and other special provisions. Also, describe those sales made with a leaseback or any other guarantees which require continued seller involvement.
[3]Include an explanation of any GAAP adjustments.
[4]Note the allocation of the taxable gain between ordinary and capital, and identify those sales that are being reported for tax purposes on the installment basis.
[5]Identify real estate commissions carried but not taken. Indicate that the amounts shown do not include pro rata share of original offering costs.
[6]Do not include amounts otherwise included under "Selling Price, Net of Closing Costs and GAAP Adjustments" or "Cost of Properties Including Closing and Soft Costs." Costs incurred in the administration of the partnership not related to the operation of properties need not be included if so indicated in a note to the Table.

Table VI. Acquisitions of Properties by Programs

Instructions:
      1. Include the following table only in Part II of the registration statement.
      2. Include all properties acquired by any prior programs with similar investment objectives in the most recent three years.
      3. Sponsors with a "public track record" should only include information relating to public programs.
If the sponsor does not have a "public track record," then information should be given about properties acquired by public and nonpublic programs.

Program X
    Name, location, type of property
    Gross leasable space (sq. ft.) or number of units and total square feet of units
    Date of purchase
    Mortgage financing at date of purchase
    Cash down payment
    Contract purchase price plus acquisition fee
    Other cash expenditures expensed
    Other cash expenditures capitalized
    Total acquisition cost
    [As last amended in Release No. 33-6465, April 22, 1983, 48 F. R. 19873.]

APPENDIX G

Form U-4

Uniform Application for Securities Industry Registration or Transfer

HOW TO USE FORM U-4

How the Form Works

An individual applies for registration for the first time by filing a complete Form U-4 with the Central Registration Depository (CRD). After an individual has filed a complete Form U-4 with the CRD, a change of employment or association from one broker-dealer to another is effected by filing only pages 1, 3 and 4 of this form. Since the data contained on page 2 is primarily of an historical nature, it need not be resubmitted with each successive filing.

To keep the CRD current, page 1 (item 12) requires the applicants to provide their current address and update their broker-dealer employment history to report the termination from their previous firm(s). This information will update the individual's record and lessen the probability of application deficiencies. Both initially and with each subsequent change of employment or association to another broker-dealer, the filing must be accompanied by a fingerprint card unless exempt from the fingerprint requirement pursuant to SEC Rule 17f-2.

Additionally, if the applicant has other changes to employment history (Item 19) or other affiliations (Item 20) which are not covered in item 12, the new information should be submitted on page 2 along with the balance of the filing.

Information contained on Form U-4 must be kept current. As changes occur, the CRD should be updated by an amendment filing. Amendments are accomplished by filing the appropriate page(s) containing only the information in need of revision.

Complete Filings

File a complete Form U-4 if any of the following circumstances apply:
1. the applicant has never been registered;
2. the applicant has previously been registered but not within the last 120 calendar days;
3. the applicant has been continuously registered but has never filed a complete Form U-4 with the CRD; or
4. the applicant has been continuously registered, but has amendments to page 2 data not covered by Items 4 and 12 on page 1.

Partial Filings

In all other cases, file only pages 1, 3 and 4 of Form U-4.

The 120 calendar day time frame mentioned above has no bearing upon filing deadlines which are specified as part of the Temporary Agent Transfer Program (TAT). It only serves to specify the period during which a partial filing (pages 1, 3 and 4) is acceptable. Notwithstanding the applicability of the Temporary Agent Transfer Program, all individuals meeting the partial filing criteria should file only pages 1, 3 and 4.

For information regarding the TAT Program call NASD Information Services at (202) 728-8800.

Amendment Filings

Amendment filings are required to:
1. correct deficiencies in a previous filing;
2. update and keep current the information required by the form;
3. request additional registrations with jurisdictions or self-regulatory organizations; and
4. request an examination (See General Instructions Number 5).

Amendments are made by filing the appropriate page(s) of the form answering only the item(s) which are in need of revision. Each amendment page must be manually signed in accordance with the instructions found on the respective page(s).

Supplements to Form BD:

Page 2 of this form is required to be filed on behalf of any natural person listed on Schedule A, B or C of Form BD who does not require registration.

When filing Page 2 of this form for such an individual, the broker-dealer name must appear in the Business and Personal History section (Item 19) or in Item 20 as may apply. Signatures on those Page 2 filings are not required; however, the filing must be accompanied by an Execution Page of Form BD.

GENERAL INSTRUCTIONS

1. All information must be typed or neatly printed in BLACK INK.
2. All information required by Form U-4 must be submitted on the officially prescribed form, or mechanical reproduction thereof. All pages containing this information may be mechanically reproduced by any method producing clear, legible copies of identical type size.
3. All questions must be answered. Enter "none" or "N/A" ("not applicable") where this is the appropriate response. Failure to complete all required items may cause the form to be returned unprocessed or considered deficient.
4. An applicant must use all space provided on the form before using the Form U-4 Attachment Sheet. Except for copies of supporting documents, additional and/or explanatory information must be submitted on the Form U-4 Attachment Sheet. Copied documents must be clearly identified with the applicant's name and CRD# or Social Security #, as well as the item # being answered.
5. All required signatures must be original. Mechanical reproductions of signatures will not be accepted. Page 1, when it is being used **only** to request an exam, requires no signature.
6. **An applicant is under a continuing obligation to update information required by Form U-4 as changes occur. To amend information, file the appropriate page(s) of Form U-4 bearing the updated data.**
7. For purposes of this form, the term "jurisdiction" means a state, territory, the District of Columbia, the Commonwealth of Puerto Rico, a province of the Dominion of Canada or any subdivision or regulatory body thereof.
8. For purposes of this form, the terms "self-regulatory organization" or "organization" mean any national securities and commodities exchange, any national securities association (e.g., the NASD), or any registered clearing agency.
9. For purposes of this form, the term "Control" means the power to direct or cause the direction of the management or policies of a company, whether through ownership of securities, by contract, or otherwise. Any individual or firm that is a director, partner or officer exercising executive responsibility (or having similar status or functions) or that directly or indirectly has the right to vote 25 percent or more of the voting securities or is entitled to 25 percent or more of the profits is presumed to control that company.
10. For purposes of this form, "appropriate signatory" means the individual designated by the broker-dealer or futures sponsor who is authorized to execute Form U-4 on behalf of the broker-dealer or futures sponsor. Such individual must meet the criteria, if any, for acting as the "appropriate signatory" as established by the jurisdictions or self-regulatory organizations requiring this form to be filed.

SPECIFIC INSTRUCTIONS

Items 1-12 must be completed by employer.

Item

5. Specify applicant's initial date (month, day and year) of employment or association with the firm.

8. If the answer to Item 8 is "Yes", consult the rules and statutes of the appropriate self-regulatory organizations and jurisdictions for prohibitions and liability provisions. Employment with other broker-dealers must be listed in the Business and Personal History item on page 2.

9. When an applicant seeks **simultaneous** registration with more than one broker-dealer under common ownership or control, list the primary broker-dealer under Item 4 and affiliated firms under Item 9. If the registrations requested under Item 10 are common to all firms, the CRD will process them from this single form filing. However, if the applicant seeks registration with a different set of self-regulatory organizations and jurisdictions for the affiliates, a separate page 1 for each affiliate **must** accompany the application.

10. Indicate the self-regulatory organizations and jurisdictions where registration is being sought. The checking of a box in Item #10 constitutes an application for registration via the CRD and will cause the applicable fee to be charged to the broker-dealer's CRD account.

    In the case of a Temporary Agent Transfer (TAT), failure to check those jurisdictions and self-regulatory organizations for which a TAT is in effect will result in expiration without registration. However, additional registrations may be requested in the same filing.

11. An applicant may apply for one or more categories of registration in a filing with the CRD. If an applicant does not qualify for the category of registration requested, the required examination will be scheduled and the examination fee(s) charged to the broker-dealer's CRD account.

    The "Reschedule Exam Series" box should be used to:
    1. request re-examination, or
    2. schedule an examination for an individual whose current exam qualifications are not accepted by a specific jurisdiction or self-regulatory organization.

12. **Item 12 must be completed in all partial filings.**

Items 13 through 22 must be completed by applicant.

15. Include any names by which you are or have been known other than your current legal name. This includes any nicknames, maiden names or married names by which you are now or have been known since adulthood.

20. The following information should be furnished:
    1. the full name and address of the business;
    2. the nature of the business;
    3. your title or position;
    4. a brief description of your duties;
    5. the amount of time you devote to the business; and
    6. whether it is during securities trading hours.

22. For each question answered "Yes", supply the following information in complete detail:
    1. who was involved (e.g., the parties to any proceedings);
    2. when it happened;
    3. what the circumstances were, in your own words;
    4. what the final disposition was, if any, and the date on which that disposition was made; and
    5. a copy of any applicable documents such as any complaint, plea, order, agreement of settlement, verdict or other findings made, and sanctions or sentences imposed.

FORM U-4
UNIFORM APPLICATION FOR SECURITIES INDUSTRY REGISTRATION OR TRANSFER

If there is an amendment to this page, complete only Items 1, 2, 3, 4 and Items being amended.

① LAST NAME | JR./SR., etc. | FIRST NAME | MIDDLE NAME (SPECIFY IF NONE) | ② APPLICANT'S CRD #
SOC. SEC. #
③ FIRM CRD # | ④ FIRM NAME (Do not include this employment under item 19, page 2) | APPLICANT'S NFA #
FIRM NFA # | | ⑤ EMPLOYMENT DATE
⑥ FIRM MAIN ADDRESS | STREET | CITY | STATE | ZIP
⑦ BRANCH I.D. # | OFFICE OF EMPLOYMENT ADDRESS | STREET | CITY | STATE | ZIP

⑧ Will applicant maintain registration with another Broker-Dealer not under common ownership or control with the firm named in Item 4 above? ☐ Yes ☐ No
(If "Yes", list in item 19)
If "Yes", has/have the firm(s) been contacted? ☐ Yes ☐ No

⑨ Will applicant maintain multiple registrations with Broker-Dealers under common ownership or control with the firm named in Item 4 above? ☐ Yes ☐ No
If "Yes", fill in information below:
Firm CRD # _____ Name of Firm _____
Firm CRD # _____ Name of Firm _____
Firm CRD # _____ Name of Firm _____

⑩ TO BE REGISTERED WITH THE FOLLOWING:

SRO: ☐ ASE ☐ BSE ☐ CBOE ☐ CSE ☐ MSE ☐ NASD ☐ NFA ☐ NYSE ☐ PHLX ☐ PSE ☐ OTHER (Specify)

STATE:
☐ AL ☐ AK ☐ AZ ☐ AR ☐ CA ☐ CO ☐ CT ☐ DE ☐ DC ☐ FL ☐ GA ☐ HI ☐ ID
☐ IL ☐ IN ☐ IA ☐ KS ☐ KY ☐ LA ☐ ME ☐ MD ☐ MA ☐ MI ☐ MN ☐ MS ☐ MO
☐ MT ☐ NE ☐ NV ☐ NH ☐ NJ ☐ NM ☐ NY ☐ NC ☐ ND ☐ OH ☐ OK ☐ OR ☐ PA
☐ RI ☐ SC ☐ SD ☐ TN ☐ TX ☐ UT ☐ VT ☐ VA ☐ WA ☐ WV ☐ WI ☐ WY ☐ PR

⑪ TYPE OF EXAMINATION/REGISTRATION REQUESTED (check all applicable categories)

☐ S-3 (CR) Commodity Futures
☐ S-4 (OP) Registered Options Principal
☐ S-5 (IO) Interest Rate Options
☐ S-6 (IR) Investment Company and Variable Contracts Products Representative
☐ S-7 (GS) Full Registration/General Securities Representative
☐ S-8 (SU) General Securities Sales Supervisor
☐ S-8 (BM) Branch Office Manager (NYSE)
☐ S-15 (FC) Foreign Currency Options

☐ S-16 (SA) Supervisory Analyst
☐ S-22 (DR) Direct Participation Programs Representative
☐ S-24 (GP) General Securities Principal
☐ S-26 (IP) Investment Company and Variable Contracts Products Principal
☐ S-27 (FN) Financial and Operations Principal
☐ S-39 (DP) Direct Participation Programs Principal
☐ S-41 (AM) Allied Member
☐ S-42 (OR) Options Representative

☐ S-52 (MR) Municipal Securities Representative
☐ S-53 (MP) Municipal Securities Principal
☐ S-54 (FM) Municipal Securities Financial and Operations Principal
☐ S-62 (CS) Corporate Securities Representative
☐ S-63 (AG) Agent
☐ Member Exchange
☐ Reschedule Exam Series _____
☐ Other _____

THIS PORTION MUST BE COMPLETED FOR ALL PARTIAL FILINGS

⑫ APPLICANT'S CURRENT ADDRESS: _____ STREET _____ CITY _____ STATE _____ ZIP _____ FROM MONTH YEAR

FIRM(S) APPLICANT IS TRANSFERRING FROM: _____ TERMINATION DATE: (Mo./Day/Yr.)

☐ CHECK IF THIS U-4 IS BEING FILED TO MAKE PERMANENT A TEMPORARY REGISTRATION 'TAT').

The appropriate signatory area *DOES NOT* have to be completed *UNLESS* this page is being submitted as an amendment.

MONTH DAY YEAR | SIGNATURE OF APPROPRIATE SIGNATORY

TYPE OR PRINT NAME OF APPROPRIATE SIGNATORY | CRD USE ONLY

Rev Form U-4 4/85

FORM U-4
UNIFORM APPLICATION FOR SECURITIES INDUSTRY REGISTRATION OR TRANSFER

If there is an amendment to this page, complete only Items 13, 14 and the Items being amended.

⑬ FIRM CRD #	SOCIAL SECURITY #	APPLICANT'S CRD #
FIRM NFA #		APPLICANT'S NFA #

PERSONAL DATA

⑭ LAST NAME	JR./SR. ETC.	FIRST NAME	MIDDLE NAME	⑮ OTHER NAMES KNOWN BY	
⑯ DATE OF BIRTH (Month, Day, Year)		⑰ SEX	HEIGHT	WEIGHT	HAIR COLOR	EYE COLOR

RESIDENTIAL HISTORY

⑱ GIVE **ALL** ADDRESSES FOR THE PAST FIVE YEARS, STARTING WITH CURRENT ADDRESS.

STREET	CITY	STATE	ZIP	FROM MONTH YEAR	TO MONTH YEAR
					PRESENT

EMPLOYMENT AND PERSONAL HISTORY

⑲ **ACCOUNT FOR ALL TIME FOR THE PAST TEN YEARS.** Give all employment experience starting with your previous employer and working back ten years. Include full and part-time work, self-employment, military service, unemployment and full-time education. (If this page is being filed as part of a Form BD, start with your present employer instead.)

		FROM MONTH YEAR	TO MONTH YEAR	POSITION HELD
NAME				
CITY	STATE			
NAME				
CITY	STATE			
NAME				
CITY	STATE			
NAME				
CITY	STATE			
NAME				
CITY	STATE			
NAME				
CITY	STATE			
NAME				
CITY	STATE			
NAME				
CITY	STATE			
NAME				
CITY	STATE			
NAME				
CITY	STATE			
NAME				
CITY	STATE			

⑳ Are you currently engaged in any other business (not shown above) either as a proprietor, partner, officer, director, trustee, employee, agent or otherwise?
☐ YES ☐ NO. If "YES", please explain below:

The appropriate signatory area *DOES NOT* have to be completed *UNLESS* this page is being submitted as an amendment.

MONTH DAY YEAR | SIGNATURE OF APPROPRIATE SIGNATORY

TYPE OR PRINT NAME OF APPROPRIATE SIGNATORY | CRD USE ONLY

FORM U-4
UNIFORM APPLICATION FOR SECURITIES INDUSTRY REGISTRATION OR TRANSFER
If there is an amendment to this page, complete only Item 21 and Items being amended.

(21) FIRM CRD #

SOCIAL SECURITY #

APPLICANT'S CRD #

FIRM NFA #

APPLICANT'S NFA #

IF THE ANSWER TO ANY OF THE FOLLOWING QUESTIONS IS "YES", ATTACH COMPLETE DETAILS.

(22) **DEFINITIONS**
- **Charged** — Accused of a crime in a formal complaint, information, or indictment.
- **Investment or Investment-Related** — Pertaining to securities, commodities, banking, insurance, or real estate (including, but not limited to acting as or being associated with a broker-dealer, investment company, investment adviser, futures sponsor, bank, or savings and loan association).
- **Involved** — Doing an act or aiding, abetting, counseling, commanding, inducing, conspiring with or failing reasonably to supervise another in doing an act.

		YES	NO	
22A.	Have you been convicted of or plead guilty or nolo contendere ("no contest") to:			
	(1) a felony or misdemeanor involving: investments or an investment-related business, fraud, false statements or omissions, wrongful taking of property, or bribery, forgery, counterfeiting or extortion?	☐	☐	1
	(2) gambling?	☐	☐	2
	(3) any other felony?	☐	☐	3
B.	Have you, or an organization over which you exercised management or policy control, ever been charged with any felony or charged with a misdemeanor specified in question A(1) or (2)?	☐	☐	4
C.	Has any court ever:			
	(1) enjoined you in connection with any investment-related activity?	☐	☐	5
	(2) found that you were involved in a violation of investment-related statutes or regulations?	☐	☐	6
D.	Has the U.S. Securities and Exchange Commission or the Commodity Futures Trading Commission ever:			
	(1) found you to have made a false statement or omission?	☐	☐	7
	(2) found you to have been involved in a violation of investment-related regulations or statutes?	☐	☐	8
	(3) found you to have been a cause of an investment-related business having its authorization to do business denied, suspended, revoked, or restricted?	☐	☐	9
	(4) entered an order denying, suspending or revoking your registration or disciplined you by restricting your activities?	☐	☐	10
E.	Has any other Federal regulatory agency or any state regulatory agency ever:			
	(1) found you to have made a false statement or omission or been dishonest, unfair or unethical?	☐	☐	11
	(2) found you to have been involved in a violation of investment regulations or statutes?	☐	☐	12
	(3) found you to have been a cause of an investment-related business having its authorization to do business denied, suspended, revoked, or restricted?	☐	☐	13
	(4) entered an order against you in connection with investment-related activity?	☐	☐	14
	(5) denied, suspended, or revoked your registration or license or otherwise prevented you from associating with an investment-related business, or disciplined you by restricting your activities?	☐	☐	15
	(6) revoked or suspended your license as an attorney, accountant or federal contractor?	☐	☐	16
F.	Has any self-regulatory organization or commodities exchange:			
	(1) found you to have made a false statement or omission?	☐	☐	17
	(2) found you to have been involved in a violation of its rules?	☐	☐	18
	(3) found you to have been the cause of an investment-related business having its authorization to do business denied, suspended, revoked or restricted?	☐	☐	19
	(4) disciplined you by expelling or suspending you from membership, barring or suspending your association with its members, or restricting your activities?	☐	☐	20
G.	Has any foreign government, court, regulatory agency, or exchange ever entered an order against you related to investments or fraud?	☐	☐	21
H.	Have you ever been the subject of an investment-related, consumer-initiated complaint or proceeding that:			
	(1) alleged compensatory damages of $10,000 or more, fraud, or wrongful taking of property?	☐	☐	22
	(2) was settled or decided against you for $5,000 or more, or found fraud or the wrongful taking of property?	☐	☐	23
I.	Are you now the subject of any complaint, investigation, or proceeding that could result in a "yes" answer to parts A-H of this item?	☐	☐	24
J.	Has a bonding company denied, paid out on, or revoked a bond for you?	☐	☐	25
K.	Do you have any unsatisfied judgments or liens against you?	☐	☐	26
L.	Have you or a firm that you exercised management or policy control over, or owned 10% or more of the securities of, failed in business, made a compromise with creditors, filed a bankruptcy petition or been declared bankrupt?	☐	☐	27
M.	Has a broker or dealer firm that you exercised management or policy control over, or owned 10% or more of the securities of, been declared bankrupt, had a trustee appointed under the Securities Investor Protection Act, or had a direct payment procedure initiated?	☐	☐	28
N.	Have you been discharged or permitted to resign because you were accused of:			
	(1) violating investment-related statutes, regulations, rules, or industry standards of conduct?	☐	☐	29
	(2) fraud or the wrongful taking of property?	☐	☐	30
	(3) failure to supervise in connection with investment-related statutes, regulations, rules or industry standards of conduct?	☐	☐	31

The applicant and appropriate signatory area *DOES NOT* have to be completed *UNLESS* this page is being submitted as an amendment.

MONTH   DAY   YEAR   SIGNATURE OF APPLICANT

TYPE OR PRINT NAME OF APPLICANT

MONTH   DAY   YEAR   SIGNATURE OF APPROPRIATE SIGNATORY

TYPE OR PRINT NAME OF APPROPRIATE SIGNATORY | CRD USE ONLY

Rev. Form U-4 4/85

FORM U-4
UNIFORM APPLICATION FOR SECURITIES INDUSTRY REGISTRATION OR TRANSFER
If there is an amendment to this page, complete only Item 23 and Items being amended.

㉓ FIRM CRD #	SOCIAL SECURITY #	APPLICANT'S CRD #
FIRM NFA #		APPLICANT'S NFA #

THE APPLICANT MUST READ THE FOLLOWING VERY CAREFULLY

1. I swear or affirm that I have read and understand the items and instructions on this form and that my answers (including attachments) are true and complete to the best of my knowledge. I understand that I am subject to administrative, civil or criminal penalties if I give false or misleading answers.

2. I hereby apply for registration with the organizations and states indicated in Item 10 as may be amended from time to time and, in consideration of such organizations and states receiving and considering my application, I submit myself to the jurisdiction of such states and organizations and hereby certify that I agree to abide by, comply with, and adhere to all the provisions, conditions and covenants of the statutes, constitutions, certificates of incorporation, by-laws and rules and regulations of the states and organizations as they are and may be adopted, changed or amended from time to time, and I agree to comply with, be subject to and abide by all such requirements and all rulings, orders, directives and decisions of, and penalties, prohibitions and limitations imposed by such states and organizations, subject to right of appeal as provided by law; and I agree that any decision of such states and organizations as to the results of any examination(s) that I may be required to pass will be accepted by me as final.

3. I further agree that neither the states or organizations nor their officers, employees, and others acting on their behalf shall be liable to me for action taken or omitted to be taken in official capacity or in the scope of employment, except as otherwise provided in the statutes, constitutions, certificates of incorporation, by-laws or the rules and regulations of such states and organizations.

4. I authorize the states and organizations to make available to any employer or prospective employer, or to any federal, state or municipal agency, or any securities or commodities industry self-regulatory organization any information they may have concerning me; and I release the states and organizations, their employees and agents, from any and all liability of whatever nature by reason of furnishing such information.

5. I agree to arbitrate any dispute, claim or controversy that may arise between me and my firm, or a customer, or any other person, that is required to be arbitrated under the rules, constitutions, or by-laws of the organizations with which I register, as indicated in item 10 as may be amended from time to time.

6. I, the undersigned, for the purpose of complying with the laws of the State(s) designated in Item 10 as may be amended from time to time, relating to sale of securities or commodities, hereby irrevocably appoint the administrator, of each of those State(s), or such other person designated by law, and the successors in such office, my attorney in said State(s) upon whom may be served any notice, process or pleading in any action or proceeding against me arising out of or in connection with the offer or sale of securities or commodities, or out of the violation or alleged violation of the aforesaid laws of said State(s) and I do hereby consent that any such action or proceeding against me may be commenced in any court of competent jurisdiction and proper venue within said State(s) by service of process upon said appointee with the same effect as if I were a resident in said States and had lawfully been served with process in said State(s). It is requested that a copy of any notice, process or pleading served hereunder be mailed to me at my residence.

7. I authorize and request any and all of my former employers and any other person to furnish to the agency, jurisdiction or organization with which this application is being filed, or any agent acting on its behalf, any information they may have concerning my credit worthiness, character, ability, business activities, education background, general reputation, together with, in the case of former employers, a history of my employment by them and the reasons for the termination thereof. Moreover, I hereby release each such employer and each such other person from any and all liability of whatever nature by reason of furnishing such information to the agency, jurisdiction or organization or any agent acting on its behalf. Further, I recognize that I may be the subject of an investigative consumer report ordered by the agency, jurisdiction, or organization with which this application is being filed, and as to which I hereby waive any requirement of prior notification. I understand that I have the right to request complete and accurate disclosure by such agency, jurisdiction or organization of the nature and scope of the investigation requested.

8. I understand and certify that the representations herein apply to all employers with whom I seek registration as shown in Items 4 and 9 of this form. I agree to update Form U-4 by causing an amendment to be filed on a timely basis whenever changes occur to answers previously reported on the form. Further, I represent that to the extent any information previously submitted is not amended, such information is currently accurate and complete.

9. If I have become temporarily registered as an agent, I acknowledge that this application for registration with the state(s) and/or organization(s) indicated in Item 10 is separate and distinct from any temporary registration already obtained with the state(s) and/or organization(s). I further understand that under the law(s) of the state(s) and/or the regulation(s) of the organization(s), my registration may be denied, suspended or revoked.

Month	Day	Year	SIGNATURE OF APPLICANT
			TYPE OR PRINT NAME OF APPLICANT

THE FIRM MUST COMPLETE THE FOLLOWING

To the best of my knowledge and belief, the applicant is currently bonded where required, and, at the time of approval, will be familiar with the statute(s), constitution(s), rules and by-laws of the agency, jurisdiction or self-regulatory organization with which this application is being filed, and the rules governing registered persons, and will be fully qualified for the position for which application is being made herein. I agree that, notwithstanding the approval of such agency, jurisdiction or organization which hereby is requested, I will not employ the applicant in the capacity stated herein without first receiving the approval of any authority which may be required by law. This firm has communicated with all of the applicant's previous employers for the past three years (five years for commodities).

EMPLOYER	NAME OF PERSON CONTACTED	POSITION OF PERSON CONTACTED	EMPLOYED FROM	TO	HOW CONTACTED PHONE	LETTER	INTERVIEW

IN ADDITION, I HAVE TAKEN APPROPRIATE STEPS TO VERIFY THE ITEMS AND ATTACHMENTS CONTAINED IN THIS APPLICATION.
THE APPROPRIATE SIGNATORY AREA *MUST BE* COMPLETED ON ALL INITIAL, TRANSFER OR AMENDMENT FILINGS.

CRD USE ONLY

MONTH	DAY	YEAR	SIGNATURE OF APPROPRIATE SIGNATORY
			TYPE OR PRINT NAME OF APPROPRIATE SIGNATORY

Rev. Form U-4 4/85

FORM U-4
UNIFORM APPLICATION FOR SECURITIES INDUSTRY REGISTRATION OR TRANSFER
ATTACHMENT SHEET

LAST NAME	JR./SR., etc.	FIRST NAME	MIDDLE NAME (Specify if none)
CRD #	NFA #	SOCIAL SECURITY #	FIRM CRD #

Use this Attachment Sheet to report details of affirmative responses or to continue an item from Form U-4. Be sure to identify the item number you are referencing. Whenever this sheet is used, make sure the individual's identifying data is completed.

ITEM OF FORM (IDENTIFY)	ANSWER

MONTH   DAY   YEAR   SIGNATURE OF APPLICANT

Rev. Form U-4 4/85   ATTACHMENT SHEET

APPENDIX H

State Security Administrators

ALABAMA - 100 Commerce Street, 1st Southern
  Federal Tower, Suite 1000, Montgomery,
  Alabama 36130.................................... 205-261-2984
  R. Frank Ussery, Director

ALASKA - Division of Banking & Securities
  333 Willoughby Street, Pouch "D", Juneau
  Alaska 99811....................................
  Richard A. Lyon, Commissioner of Commerce and
  Economic Development........................... 907-465-2500
  Willis F. Kirkpatrick, Administrator of
  Securities..................................... 907-465-2521

ARIZONA - 1200 West Washington Street, Phoenix
  Arizona 85007.................................... 602-255-4242
  Matthew J. Zale, Director of Securities
  Victoriano Rodarte, Assistant Director

ARKANSAS - Heritage Plaza, West 201 East Markham,
  Little Rock, Arkansas 72201.................... 501-371-1011
  Lee Thalheimer, Securities Commissioner
  Nancy J. Jones, Assistant Commissioner
  Tom Bull, Broker-Dealer Registration

CALIFORNIA - Department of Corporations - 1025 P Street,
  Suite 205, Sacramento
  California 95814................... Information 916-445-8200
  Franklin Tom, Commissioner of Corporations
    Los Angeles.....................................213-736-3481
  Christine Bender, Chief Deputy Commissioner
    Los Angeles.....................................213-736-3481
  Jack A. Carlson, Assistant Commissioner
    Financial Services Division.......Los Angeles 213-736-2776
  Robert E. LaNoue, Assistant Commissioner,
    Office of Policy....................Sacramento 916-322-3633
  Jerry L. Baker, Assistant Commissioner,
    Securities Regulations Division...Los Angeles 213-736-2713
  G.W. McDonald, Assistant Commissioner,
    Enforcement Division..............Los Angeles 213-736-2511
  David C. Woods, Assistant Commissioner
    Health Care Service Plans.........Los Angeles 213-736-3133
  Robert L. Hansen, Chief Administrative Officer
    Sacramento..................................... 916-445-5541
  OTHER OFFICES
  600 S. Commonwealth Ave., Los Angeles, CA 90005
    Information.................................... 213-737-2741
  1390 Market St., San Francisco, CA 94102
    Information.................................... 415-557-3787
  1350 Front St., San Diego, CA 92101
    Information.................................... 619-236-7341

Appendix H: State Security Administrators

COLORADO - Division of Securities, 1560 Brohouay,
   Suite 1450, Denver
   Colorado 80202....................................303-866-2607
   Royce O. Griffin, Securities Commissioner

CONNECTICUT - Banking Department, Division of Securities and
   Business Investments, State Office Building,
   165 Capitol Avenue, Hartford, Connecticut 06106
   Brian J. Woolf, Banking Commissioner
   Howard B. Brown, Deputy Commissioner
   Caleb L. Nichols, Division Director
   Cynthia A. Antanaitis, Assistant Counsel.......203-566-4560

DELAWARE - Division of Securities, State Office Building,
   820 North French Street, 8th Floor,
   Wilmington, Delaware 19801....................302-571-2515
   Donald L. Bruton, Securities Commissioner

DISTRICT OF COLUMBIA - 451 Indiana Avenue, N.W.,
   Suite 323, Washington, DC 20001...............202-727-3066
   James F. Whitescarver, Jr., Esquire,
    Director of Securities
   Roy E. Bussey, Administrator

FLORIDA - Division of Securities, Department of
    Banking and Finance,
   1402 The Capitol, Tallahassee, Florida.........904-488-9805
   E. C. (Chris) Anderson, Director
   Don Saxon, Assistant Director
   Geraldine Harrison, Chief, Bureau of Securities
    Registration
   William F. Reilly, Jr., Chief, Bureau of Dealer/
    Agent Registration and Examination

GEORGIA - Securities Division, West Tower, 2 Martin
    Luther King, Jr. Drive, Suite 802,
   Atlanta, Georgia 30334........................404-656-2894
   Max Cleland, Secretary of State
   H. Wayne Howell, Director
   James F. Gullion, Assistant Director (Regulation)
   Edwin J. Wilson, Assistan Director (Enforcement)

HAWAII - Department of Commerce and Consumer Affairs,
   1010 Richards Street, Honolulu,
   Hawaii 96813....................................808-548-6521
   Russel H. Yamashita, Deputy Securities
    Commissioner

IDAHO - Statehouse, Boise, Idaho 83720.............208-334-3684
   Tom D. McEldowney, Director of Finance.........208-334-3313
   Gavin M. Gee, Bureau Chief, Securities
    Bureau......................................208-334-3684

ILLINOIS - Illinois Securities Department, 840 S. Spring
   Street, Suite 130, Springfield,
   Illinois 62704....................................217-782-2258
   Philip Howe, Acting Director

INDIANA - One North Capitol, Suite 560,
   Indianapolis, Indiana 46204....................317-232-6681
   O. Wayne Davis, Securities Commissioner........317-232-6690
   Susan K. Sheets, Administrative Assistant
      to Commissioner..............................317-232-6690
   Phil McCool, Chief Deputy Commissioner.........317-232-6685
   Connie Goodwin, Deputy Commissioner............317-232-6587
   Sue E. Stemen, Staff Attorney..................317-232-6696
   Patrick Sanders, Staff Attorney................317-232-6687
   Larry Dunlap, Staff Attorney...................317-232-6683
   Keith Feller, Chief Investigator...............317-232-6686
   Susan Rosemeyer, Director of Licensing.........317-232-6688
   Russell Pope, Director, Collection Agencies....317-232-6682

IOWA - Lucas State Office Building, Des Moines,
   Iowa 50319.......................................515-281-4441
   Craig Goettsch, Superintendent of Securities
   Anton Veldman, Attorney
   Gary Marquett, Attorney
   Greg Theobald, Attorney
   Dennis Britson, Attorney
   Brad Osmundson, Attorney
   Cheryl Friedman, Attorney
   Tom Alberts, Attorney
   Robert Halferty, Accountant

KANSAS - 109 West 9th Street, Suite 501, Topeka,
   Kansas 66612.....................................913-296-3307
   John R. Wurth, Securities Commissioner
   Larry V. Christ, Chief Counsel..................913-296-3307

KENTUCKY - 911 Leawood Drive, Frankfort,
   Kentucky 40601...................................502-564-2180
   Ronda Paul, Director
   Bill Doyle, Legal Counsel
   Lewis Kelly, Registration
   Ruth Kittinger, Broker-Dealer and Agent Licensing

LOUISIANA - 315 Louisiana State Office Building,
   New Orleans, Louisiana 70112....................504-568-5515
   Hunter O. Wagner, Commissioner of Financial
      Institutions and Ex-Officio Commissioner of
      Securities
   Harry C. Stansbury, Securities Deputy Commissioner

MAINE - State House Station 36, Augusta,
   Maine 04333......................................207-289-2261
   Alden H. Mann, Director of Securities Division

Appendix H: State Security Administrators 471

MARYLAND - Munsey Building, 2nd Floor, 7 North
    Calvert Street
    Baltimore, Maryland 21202......................301-576-6360
    Susan Merrick Rittenhouse, Securities Commissioner
    Jeffrey S. Chernow, Assistant Attorney General
    Clinton R. Black, Assistant Attorney General
    Lucy Weisz, Special Assistant, Attorney General
    Della A. Burke, Staff Attorney
    Marjory Silverman, Examiner

MASSACHUSETTS - The Commonwealth of Massachusetts,
    Secretary of the Commonwealth, Securities
    Division, John W. McCormack Building
    Room 1719, One Ashburton Place, Boston,
    Massachusetts 02108............................617-727-3548
    Michael Unger, Director

MICHIGAN - Corporation & Securities Bureau,
    Department of Commerce, P.O. Box 30222, 6546
    Mercantile Way, Lansing, Michigan 48909.......517-373-0880
    E.C. Mackey, Director

MINNESOTA - 500 Metro Square Building, St. Paul,
    Minnesota 55101................................612-296-2594
    Michael A. Hatch, Chairman, Department of Commerce
    Gary A. LaVasseur, Deputy Commissioner
      (Enforcement)
    Samuel G. Crecelius, Deputy Commissioner
      (Registration)

MISSISSIPPI - 401 Mississippi Street, P.O. Box 136,
    Jackson, Mississippi 39205.....................601-359-1374
    Dick Molpus, Secretary of State
    Peyton D. Prospere, Assistant Secretary of State
    Herb Irvin, Staff Attorney

MISSOURI - Harry S. Truman Office Building,
    Jefferson City, Missouri 65102.................314-751-4136
    James C. Kirkpatrick, Secretary of State
    John R. Perkins, Commissioner of Securities

MONTANA - Room 270, Mitchell Building, 126 North Sanders,
    Helena, Montana 59601..........................406-444-2040
    E. V. "Sonny" Omholt, State Auditor & Ex-Officio
      Securities Commissioner
    R. G. "Rick" Tucker, Chief Deputy Securities
      Commissioner
    Renee Jacques, Administrative Assistant
    Patricia J. Lewis, Securities Investigator/Examiner
    S. Jimmy Weg, Securities Investigator/Examiner
    Julie R. Toney, Broker/Dealer & Salesman Registration
    Teresa A. Turner, Secretary

NEBRASKA - 301 Centennial Mall South, P.O. Box 95006
   Lincoln, Nebraska 68509........................402-471-3445
      Patricia A. Humlicek Herstein, Acting Assistant
        Director of Banking & Finance, Legal Counsel,
        Enforcement Division
      Jack E. Herstein, Securities Examiner
      Reed M. Kohl, Asst. Director, Broker-Dealer &
        Agent Examiner
      Thomas A. Sindelar, Securities Examiner & Business
        Opportunity Examiner
      Karen D. Mayo, Registration Assistant, Exemptions
      Julie A. Halloran, Registration Assistant,
        Broker-Dealers
      Elaine M. Cerbus, Registration Assistant,
        CRD Operator
      Beverly McGhghy, Registration Assistant, Securities

NEVADA - State Capitol, Carson City,
   Nevada 89710...................................702-885-5203
      William S. Swackhamer, Secretary of State
      Abner W. Sewell, Deputy Secretary of State
      Helen M. Stecker, Securities Investigator
      Jackie Reese, Securities Investigator
        Las Vegas Office - 2501 East Sahara, Las Vegas,
        Nevada 89104................................702-386-5301

NEW HAMPSHIRE - 169 Manchester Street, Concord,
   New Hampshire 03301............................603-271-2261
      Louis E. Bergeron, Insurance and Securities
        Commissioner
      Robert R. Robitaille, Supervisor, Securities Division

NEW JERSEY - 80 Mulberry Street, Room 308, Newark,
   New Jersey 07102...............................201-648-2040
      James McLelland Smith, Chief, Bureau of
        Securities

NEW MEXICO - Securities Bureau, Lew Wallace Building,
   Santa Fe, New Mexico 87503.....................505-827-7750
      Tommy D. Hughes, Chief of Securities Bureau
      Margaret Armijo, Agent Licensing
      Matias Gonzales, Senior Securities Analyst
      John J. Martinez, Securities Analyst
      Terri Orton, Securities Analyst
      Nick Rael, Securities Analyst
      Maria A. Rael, Secretary
      Fernando F. Rivera, Securities Investigator

Appendix H: State Security Administrators 473

NEW YORK - Two World Trade Center, New York,
   New York 10047.................................212-488-2921
   Robert Abrams, Attorney General
   Orestes J. Mihaly, Assistant Attorney General in
     Charge Bureau of Investor Protection & Securities
   Harvey J. Golubock, Deputy, Bureau of Investor Protection
     & Securities
   David L. Crawford, Chief, Enforcement..........212-488-4487
   Martin S. Weber, Chief, Registration...........212-488-7412
   Elizabeth Block, Theatrical Financing..........212-488-3450
   Judith Schultz, Takeover Bids..................212-488-7493
   Sheldon Horowitz, Franchises...................212-488-7415
   Eric Zanier, Investment Advisers...............212-488-5207
   James M. Morrissey, Assistant Attorney General
     in Charge
     Real Estate Financing Bureau.................212-488-3310

NORTH CAROLINA - Office of the Secretary of State, Securities
   Division, 300 North Salisbury Street, Room 302, Raleigh,
   North Carolina 27611...........................919-733-3924
   Thad Eure, Secretary of State & Securities
     Administrator................................919-733-3924
   F. Daniel Bell, III, Deputy Securities
     Administrator................................919-733-3924
   Amy D. Foreman, Securities Examiner............919-733-3924
   Stephen M. Wallis, Securities Examiner.........919-733-3924
   Roland Jones, Securities Investigator..........919-733-3956
   Linda Douglas, Licensing Clerk.................919-733-3955

NORTH DAKOTA - State Capitol, Bismarck,
   North Dakota 58505.............................701-224-2910
   Peter A. Quist, Securities Commissioner

OHIO - Two Nationwide Plaza, Columbus,
   Ohio 43215.....................................614-466-3440
   Rodger A. Marting, Commissioner of
     Securities...................................614-466-3440
   Philip D. Lehmkuhl, Assistant Commissioner
     Registration & Enforcement...................614-466-6140
   Paul Tague, Attorney Inspector, Enforcement
     Section......................................614-466-6140
   Robert Bibler, Supervisor of Registration......614-466-3440
   Dale Jewell, Supervisor of Broker-Dealer &
     Examinations.................................614-466-3466

OKLAHOMA - Securities Commission, 2915 North Lincoln,
   Oklahoma City, Oklahoma 73105..................405-521-2451
   P. David Newsome, Jr., Administrator

OREGON - Department Commerce, Corporation Division,
  158 - 12th Street, N.E., Salem,
  Oregon 97310
  Jane Edwards, Corporation Commissioner.........503-378-4900
  Thomas Y. Higashi, Deputy Commissioner.........503-378-4900

PENNSYLVANIA - 333 Market Street, 14th Floor,
  Harrisburg, Pennsylvania 17100.................717-787-8061
  Robert M. Lam, Chairman
  Cole B. Price, Jr., Commissioner
  Frederick H. Plank, Commissioner
  Nancy L. Diana, Secretary
  Elliott Klein, Chief Counsel
  G. Philip Rutledge, Director, Division of Corporation
    Finance
  J. Ernest Cole, Director, Division of Licensing
  Mark N. Cohen, Director - Enforcement
    Philadelphia................................. 215-351-2088

  OTHER OFFICES:
  1109 State Office Building, Philadelphia Pennsylvania 19130
  806 State Office Building, Pittsburgh, Pennsylvania 15222

PUERTO RICO - Dept. of Treasury, P.O. Box S-4145, San Juan,
  Puerto Rico 00905..............................809-721-2020
  Fidencio Quiles, Director, Bureau of
    Securities...................................809-721-4075
                                                   (Ext. 2380)

RHODE ISLAND - 100 North Main Street, Providence,
  Rhode Island 02903.............................401-277-3048
  William F. Carroll, Director
  Thomas J. Corrigan, Chief Securities Examiner

SOUTH CAROLINA - 816 Keenan Building, Columbia,
  South Carolina 29201...........................803-758-2833
  John T. Campbell, Secretary of State and
    Securities Commissioner
  Stanley V. Lewis, Deputy Securities Commissioner
  Cooper Smith, Securities Analyst

SOUTH DAKOTA - Capitol Building, Pierre,
  South Dakota 57501.............................605-773-3177
  David Haberling, Director......................605-773-4823
  Debra M. Bollinger, Deputy Director............605-773-4823
  Chuck Van Gerpen, Securities Registration
    Specialist...................................605-773-4823
  Judi Pollard, Franchise Administrator..........605-773-4823
  Melita Bisbee, Registration Assistant..........605-773-4823
  Dorthy Adams, Licensing Assistant..............605-773-4013

Appendix H: State Security Administrators 475

TENNESSEE - Department of Commerce & Insurance,
114 State Office Building, Nashville,
Tennessee 37219................................615-741-2947
James C. Meyer, Assistant Commissioner
  Securities
Catherine L. Rogers, Chief Broker-Dealer/Agent
  Registration
William O. Mitchell, Chief of Enforcement

TEXAS - Box 13167, Capitol Station, Austin,
Texas 78711-3167...............................512-474-2233
Richard D. Latham, Securities Commissioner
Lee Poison, Deputy Commissioner
William H. Kuntz, Director, Securities Registration Division
Sue B. Roberts, Director, Enforcement Division
Peggy Peters, Director, Dealer Registration Division
Denise Voigt Crawford, General Counsel

UTAH - Herber M. Wells Building, 160 E. 300 South,
Salt Lake City, Utah 84111.....................801-530-6600
John B. Hiatt, Director
Sherwood Cook, Head Examiner
Sharon Abbot, Examiner
Patty Lovie, Examiner
Wendy Brown, Receptionist

VERMONT - State Office Building, Montpelier,
Vermont 05602..................................802-828-3301
Harry E. Lantz, Securities Administrator

VIRGINIA - 11 South 12th Street, Richmond, Virginia 23219
  Lewis W. Brother, Jr., Director, Securities
    Division....................................804-786-7751
  Robert G. Lewis, Deputy, Director,
    Securities Division.........................804-786-7752
  Ronald W. Thomas, Examination Coordinator.....804-786-7751
  Max Zoeckler, Investigation Coordinator.......804-786-7751
  Irene Hague, Licensing Supervisor.............804-786-7751
  Joel Perk.....................................804-786-0152

WASHINGTON - Securities Division, Business and Professions
    Administration
    P.O. Box 648, Olympia, Washington 98504.....206-753-6928
    Jack L. Beyers, Securities Administrator

WEST VIRGINIA - Room 205-W, State Capitol Building,
    Charleston, West Virginia 25305.............304-348-2257
    Glen B. Gainer, Jr., Commissioner of Securities
    Robert W. Geake, Esq. Deputy Commissioner of Securities
      and Administrator
    Jack Hall, Assistant Deputy Commissioner
    Gary Burdett, Investigator
    David Vidoni, Investigator
    Fred Sallnier, Chief Analyst

WISCONSIN - P.O. Box 1768, Madison,
   Wisconsin 53701................................608-266-3431
   Richard R. Malmgren, Commissioner of
      Securities..................................608-266-3433
   Stephen L. Morgan, Deputy Commissioner.........608-266-3432
   Randall E. Schumann, General Counsel...........608-266-2139
   Richard P. Carney, Administrator, Licensing
      & Regulation Division.......................608-266-7824
   James R. Fischer, Administrator Securities
      Registration Division.......................608-266-3289
   William C. Lloyd, Staff Attorney, Enforcement
      Division....................................608-266-7968
   Alan E. Korpady, Chief Attorney, Franchise
      Investment Division.........................608-266-3414
   Janet K. Murphy, Administrator, Administration
      Division....................................608-266-3583

WYOMING - State Capitol Building, Cheyenne,
   Wyoming 82002..................................307-777-7370
   Thyra Thomson, Secretary of State & Securities
      Administrator
   Harry Wales, Assistant Securities Commissioner
   F. Parker West, Examiner
   Thomas Cowan, Enforcement Officer
   Dona Clary, Broker/Dealer and Agent Registrar

APPENDIX I

Work of the SEC

INTRODUCTION

The Securities and Exchange Commission (SEC) was created on July 2, 1934 by an act of Congress entitled the Securities Exchange Act of 1934. It is an independent, bipartisan, quasi-judicial agency of the United States Government.

The Commission is composed of five members not more than three of whom may be members of the same political party. They are appointed by the President, with the advice and consent of the Senate, for five-year terms, the terms being staggered so that one expires on June 5th of each year. The Chairman is designated by the President.

The Commission's staff is composed of lawyers, accountants, security analysts and examiners, engineers and other professionals, together with administrative and clerical employees. The staff is divided into Divisions and Offices (including nine Regional Offices), each under charge of officials appointed by the Chairman.

The laws administered by the Commission relate in general to the field of securities and finance, and seek to provide protection for investors and the public in their securities transactions. They include (in addition to the Securities Exchange Act of 1934) the Securities Act of 1933 (administered by the Federal Trade Commission until September 1934), the Public Utility Holding Company Act of 1935, the Trust Indenture Act of 1939, the Investment Company Act of 1940, and the Investment Advisers Act of 1940. The Commission also serves as advisor to Federal courts in corporate reorganization proceedings under Chapter 11 of the Bankruptcy Reform Act of 1978 and, in cases commenced prior to October 1, 1979, Chapter X of the National Bankruptcy Act.

The Commission reports annually to the Congress. These reports contain a review of the Commission's administration of the several laws.

It should be understood that the securities laws were designed to facilitate informed investment analyses and prudent and discriminating investment decisions <u>by the investing public</u>. It is the investor, <u>not</u> the Commission who must make the ultimate judgment of the worth of securities offered for sale. The Commission is powerless to pass upon the merits of securities; and assuming proper disclosure of the financial and other information essential to informed investment analysis, the Commission cannot bar the sale of securities which such analysis may show to be of questionable value.

It is hoped that the following description of the nature and scope of the Commission's work and authority will contribute both to a better understanding of the laws and to their objective of investor protection.

SECURITIES ACT OF 1933

This "truth in securities" law has two basic objectives: (a) to provide investors with material financial and other information concerning securities offered for public sale; and (b) to prohibit misrepresentation, deceit and other fraudulent acts and practices in the sale of securities generally (whether or not required to be registered).

Registration of Securities

The first objective applies to securities offered for public sale by an issuing company or any person in a control relationship to such company. Before the public offering of such securities, a registration statement must be filed with the Commission by the issuer, setting forth the required information. When the statement has become effective, the securities may be sold. The purpose of registration is to provide disclosure of financial and other information on the basis of which investors may appraise the merits of the securities. To that end, investors must be furnished with a prospectus (selling circular) containing the salient data set forth in the registration statement to enable them to evaluate the securities and make informed and discriminating investment decisions.

Exemptions From Registration

The registration requirement applies to securities of both domestic and foreign private issuers, as well as to securities of foreign governments or their instrumentalities. There are, however, certain exemptions from the registration requirement. Among these are: (1) private offerings to a limited number of persons or institutions who have access to the kind of information registration would disclose and who do not propose to redistribute the securities, (2) offerings restricted to the residents of the State in which the issuing company is organized and doing business, (3) securities of municipal, State, Federal and other governmental instrumentalities, of charitable institutions, of banks, and of carriers subject to the Interstate Commerce Act, (4) offerings not in excess of certain specified amounts made in compliance with regulations of the

Commission discussed below, and (5) offerings of "small business investment companies" made in accordance with rules and regulations of the Commission. The anti-fraud provisions referred to above, however, apply to all sales of securities involving interstate commerce or the mails, whether or not the securities are exempt from registration.

Purpose of Registration

Registration of securities does not insure investors against loss in their purchase, nor does the Commission have the power to disapprove securities for lack of merit -- and it is unlawful to represent otherwise in the sale of securities. The only standard which must be met in registration of securities is an adequate and accurate disclosure of the material facts concerning the company and the securities it proposes to sell. The fairness of the terms of securities (whether price, promoters' or underwriters' profits, or otherwise), the issuing company's prospects for successful operation, and other factors affecting the merits of securities, have no bearing on the question whether securities may be registered.

The purpose of registration is to provide disclosure of these and other important facts so investors may make a realistic appraisal of the merits of the securities and thus exercise an informed judgment in determining whether to purchase them. Assuming proper disclosure, the Commission cannot deny registration or otherwise bar the securities from public sale whether or not the price or other terms of the securities are fair or the issuing company offers reasonable prospects of success. These are factors which the investor must assess for himself in the light of the disclosures provided; and if the facts have been fully and correctly stated, the investor assumes whatever risks may be involved in the purchase of the securities.

Nor does registration guarantee the accuracy of the facts represented in the registration statement and prospectus. The law does, however, prohibit false and misleading statements under penalty of fine or imprisonment, or both. In addition, if an investor suffers loss in the purchase of a registered security, the law provides him with important recovery rights if he can prove that there was incomplete or inaccurate disclosure of material facts in the registration statement or prospectus. These rights must be asserted in an appropriate Federal or State court (not before the Commission, which has no power to award damages); and if such misstatements are proved, the issuing company, its responsible directors and officers, the underwriters, controlling interests, the sellers of the securities, and others (or one or more of such persons) would be liable to the purchaser of the securities for losses sustained in their purchase.

The Registration Process

To facilitate the registration of securities by different types of issuing companies, the Commission has prepared special registration forms which vary in their disclosure requirements to provide disclosure of the essential facts pertinent in a given type of offering while at the same time minimizing the burden and expense of compliance with the law. In general, the registration forms call for disclosure of information as (1) a description of the registrant's properties and business, (2) a description of the significant provisions of the security to be offered for sale and its relationship to the registrant's other capital securities, (3) information about the management of the registrant, and (4) financial statements certified by independent public accountants.

The registration statement and prospectus become public immediately on filing with the Commission; but it is unlawful to sell the securities until the effective date. After the filing of the registration statement, the securities may be offered orally or by certain summaries of the information in the registration staterment as permitted by rules of the Commission. The Act provides that registration statements shall become effective on the 20th day after filing (or on the 20th day after the filing of the last amendment thereto); but the Commission, in its discretion, may advance the effective date if, considering the adequacy of information theretofore publicly available, the ease with which the facts about the new offering ccan be disseminated and understood, and the interests of investors and the public, such action is deemed appropriate.

Registration statements are examined by the Division of Corporation Finance for compliance with the disclosure requirements. If a statement appears to be materially incomplete or inaccurate, the registrant usually is informed by letter and given an opportunity to file correcting or clarifying amendments. The Commission however, has authority to refuse or suspend the effectiveness of any registration statement if it finds, after hearing, that material representations are misleading, inaccurate or incomplete. Accordingly, if material deficiencies in a registration statement appear to stem from a deliberate attempt to conceal and mislead, or if the deficiencies otherwise are of such nature as not to lend themselves readily to correction through the informal letter process, the Commission may conclude that it is in the public interest to resort to a hearing to develop the facts by evidence and to determine on the evidence whether a stop order should issue refusing or suspending effectiveness of the statement.

A stop order is not a permanent bar to the effectiveness of the registration statement or sale of the securities, for the order must be lifted and the statement declared effective if amendments are filed correcting the statement in accordance with the stop order decision. The Commission may issue stop orders after the sale of securities has been commenced or completed. Although losses which may have been suffered in the purchase of securities are not restore to investors by the stop order, the Commission's decision and the evidence on which it is based may serve to put investors on notice of their rights and aid in their own recovery suits.

This examination process naturally contributes to the general reliability of the registration disclosures -- but it does not give positive assurance of the accuracy of the facts reported. Even if such a verification of facts were possible, the task, if not actually prohibitive, would involve such a tremendous undertaking (both in time and money) as to seriously impede the financing of business ventures through the public sale of securities.

Small Issue Exemption

Among the special exemptions from the registration requirement is one adopted by Congress as an aid primarily to small business. The law provides that offerings of securities not exceeding $2 million in amount may be exempted from registration, subject to such conditions as the Commission prescribes for the protection of investors. The Commission's Regulation A permits certain domestic and Canadian companies to make exempt offerings not exceeding $1,500,000 in amount. Offerings on behalf of controlling persons are limited in amount to $100,000 for each such person, not to exceed $1,500,000 in all. Offerings on behalf of persons other than an Issuer or its affiliates are limited to $100,000 for each such person, not to exceed a total of $300,000, which is not included in the $1,500,000 ceiling limitation. Under certain circumstances an estate may offer up to $1,500,000 of securities. The exemption is available provided certain specified conditions are met, including the prior filing of a "Notification" with the appropriate Regional Office of the Commission and the use of an offering circular containing certain basic information in the sale of the securities. A similar regulation is available for offerings not exceeding $500,000 by small business investment companies licensed by the Small Business Administration. In addition, the Commission has, through its rulemaking authority, adopted several other provisions designed to facilitate capital formation by small businesses.

Interpretations and Rulemaking

As a part of its activities under this Act, the Division of Corporation Finance also renders administrative interpretations of the law and regulations thereunder to members of the public, prospective registrants and others, to help them decide legal questions about the application of he law and the regulations to particular situations and to aid them in complying with the law. This advice, for example, might include an informal expression of opinion about whether the offering of a particular security is subject to the registration requirements of the law and, if so, advice as to compliance with the disclosure requirements of the applicable registration form. Other Divisions render similar advice and assistance.

The Commission's objective of effective disclosure with a minimum of burden and expense calls for constant review of the practical operations of the rules and registration forms adopted by it. If experience shows that a particular requirement fails to achieve its objective, or if a rule appears unduly burdensome in relation to the benefits resulting from the disclosure provided, the Division of Corporation Finance presents the problem to the Commission for consideration of possible modification of the rule or other requirement. Many suggestions for rule modification follow extensive consultation with industry representatives and others affected. In addition, the Commission normally gives advance public notice of proposals for the adoption of new or amended rules or registration forms and affords opportunity for interested members of the public to comment thereon. The same procedure is followed under the other Acts administered by the Commission.

The scope and importance of the Commission's work in the accounting field under the several statutes are discussed below under "Office of the Chief Accountant."

Fraud Prohibitions

Generally speaking, the fraud prohibitions of the Securities Act are similar to those contained in the Securities Exchange Act of 1934, under which topic the Commission's investigation and enforcement activities are discussed.

SECURITIES EXCHANGE ACT OF 1934

By this Act, Congress extended the "disclosure" doctrine of investor protection to securities listed and registered for public trading on our national securities exchanges; and the enactment in August 1964 of the Securities Acts Amendments of 1964 applied the disclosure and reporting provisions to equity securities of hundreds of companies traded over-the-counter (if their assets exceed $1 million and their shareholders number 500 or more).

Corporate Reporting

Companies which seek to have their securities listed and registered for public trading on such an exchange must file a registration application with the exchange and the Commission. A similar registration form must be filed by companies whose equity securities are traded over-the-counter if they meet the size test referred to. The Commission's rules prescribe the nature and content of these registration statements, including certified financial statements. These data are generally comparable to, but less extensive than, the disclosures required in Securities Act registration statements. Following the registration of their securities, such companies must file annual and other periodic reports to keep current the information contained in the original filing. Copies of any of the reported data may be obtained from the Commission at nominal cost as indicated below.

The law prescribes penalties for filing false statements and reports with the Commission, as well as provision for recovery by investors who suffer losses in the purchase or sale of registered securities in reliance thereon.

Proxy Solicitations

Another provision of this law governs the solicitation of proxies (votes) from holders of registered securities (both listed and over-the-counter), whether for the election of directors or for approval of other corporate action. In any such solicitation, whether by the management or minority groups, disclosure must be made of all material facts concerning the matters on which such holders are asked to vote; and they must be afforded an opportunity to vote "Yes" or "No" on each matter. Where a contest for control of the management of a corporation is involved, the rules require disclosure of the names and interests of all "participants" in the proxy contest. Holders of such securities thus are enabled to vote intelligently on corporate actions requiring their approval. The Commission's rules require that proposed proxy material be filed in advance for examination by the Commission for compliance with the disclosure requirements.

Tender Offer Solicitations

In 1968, Congress amended the Exchange Act to extend its reporting and disclosure provisions to situations where control of a company is sought through a tender offer or other planned stock acquisition of over 10 percent of a company's equity securities. The amount was reduced to 5 percent by an amendment in 1970. These amendments and Commission rules thereunder require disclosure of pertinent information, by the person seeking to acquire over 5 percent of the company's securities by direct purchase or by tender offer, as well as by any persons soliciting shareholders to accept or reject a tender offer. Thus, as with the proxy rules, public investors who hold stock in the subject corporation may now make informed decisions on take-over bids.

Insider Trading

The protection provided the investing public through disclosure of financial and related information concerning the securities of registered companies is supplemented by provisions of the law designed to curb misuse of corporate information not available to the general public. To that end, each officer and director of such a company, and each beneficial owner of more than 10 percent of its registered equity securities, must file an initial report with the Commission (and with the exchange on which the stock may be listed) showing his holdings of each of the company's equity securities. Thereafter, they must file reports for any month during which there was any change in such holdings. In addition, the law provides that profits obtained by them from purchases and sales (or sales and purchases) of such equity securities within any six months period may be recovered by the company or by any security holder on its behalf. This recovery right must be asserted in the appropriate United States District Court. Such "insiders" are also prohibited from making short sales of their company's equity securities.

Margin Trading

The statute also contains provisions governing margin trading in securities. It authorizes the Board of Governors of the Federal Reserve System to set limitations on the amount of credit which may be extended for the purpose of purchasing or carrying securities. The objective is to restrict the excessive use of the nation's credit in the securities markets. While the credit restrictions are set by the Board, investigation and enforcement is the responsibility of the Commission.

Market Surveillance

The Securities Exchange Act also provides a system for regulating securities trading practices in both the exchange and the over-the-counter markets. In general, transactions in securities which are effected otherwise than on national securities exchanges are said to take place "over the counter." Designed to protect the interests of investors and the public,

Appendix I: Work of the SEC

these provisions seek to curb misrepresentations and deceit, market manipulation and other fraudulent acts and practices and to establish and maintain just and equitable principles of trade conducive to the maintenance of open, fair and orderly markets.

While these provisions of the law establish the general regulatory pattern, the Commission is responsible for promulgating rules and regulations for their implementation. Thus, the Commission has adopted regulations which, among other things, (1) define acts or practices which constitute a "manipulative or deceptive device or contrivance" prohibited by the statute, (2) regulate short selling, stabilizing transactions and similar matters, (3) regulate the hypothecation of customers' securities and (4) provide safeguards with respect to the financial responsibility of brokers and dealers.

Registration of Exchanges and Others

In addition, the law as amended requires registration with the Commission of (1) "national securities exchanges" (those having a substantial securities trading volume); (2) brokers and dealers who conduct securities business in interstate commerce; (3) transfer agents; (4) clearing agencies; (5) municipal brokers and dealers; and (6) securities information processors.

To obtain registration, exchanges must show that they are so organized as to be able to comply with the provisions of the statute and the rules and regulations of the Commission and that their rules contain provisions which are just and adequate to insure fair dealing and to protect investors.

Each exchange is a self-regulatory organization, and its rules, among other things, must provide for the expulsion, suspension or other disciplining of member broker-dealers for conduct inconsistent with just and equitable principles of trade. While the law contemplates that exchanges shall have full opportunity to establish self-regulatory measures insuring fair dealing and the protection of investors, it empowers the Commission by order, rule or regulation to amend the rules of exchanges with respect to various phases of their activities and trading practices if necessary to effectuate the statutory objective. For the most part, exchange rules and revisions thereof suggested by exchanges or by the Commission reach their final form after discussions between representatives of the exchange and the Commission without resort to formal proceedings.

By an amendment to the law enacted in 1938, Congress also provided for creation of a self-regulatory organization to prevent fraudulent and manipulative acts and practices, to promote just and equitable principles of trade among over-the-counter brokers and dealers. One such association, the National Association of Securities Dealers, Inc., is registered with the Commission under this provision of the law. The establishment, maintenance and enforcement of a voluntary code of business ethics is one of the principal features of this provision of the law.

Not all broker-dealer firms are members of the NASD; thus, some are not subject to supervision and control by that agency. To equalize the regulatory pattern, Congress provied in the 1964 Amendments that the Commission should undertake to establish investor safeguards applicable to non-NASD firms comparable to those applicable to NASD members. Among the controls adopted by the Commission is a requirement that persons associated with non-NASD firms meet certain qualification standards similar to those applied by the NASH to its members.

Broker-Dealer Registration

Applications for registration as broker-dealers and amendments thereto are examined by the Office of Reports and Information Services with the assistance of the Division of Market Regulation. The registration of brokers and dealers engaged in an interstate over-the-counter securities business also is an important phase of the regulatory plan of the Act. They must conform their business practices to the standards prescribed in the law and the Commission's regulations for the protection of investors (as well as to the fair trade practice rules of their association); in addition, as will be seen later, they may violate these regulations only at the risk of possible loss of registration with the Commission and the right to continue to conduct an interstate securities business, or of suspension or expulsion from the association and loss of the benefits of such membership.

Investigation and Enforcement

It is the duty of the Commission under the laws it administers to investigate complaints or other indications of possible law violations in securities transactions, most of which arise under the Securities Act of 1933 and the Securities Exchange Act of 1934. Investigation and enforcement work is conducted both by the Commission's Regional Offices and the Division of Enforcement.

Most of the Commission's investigations are conducted privately, the facts being developed to the fullest extent possible through informal inquiry, interviewing of witnesses, examination of brokerage records and other documents, reviewing and trading data and similar means. The Commission however, is empowered to issue subpoenas requiring sworn testimony and the production of books, records and other documents pertinent to the subject matter under investigation; in the event of refusal to respond to a subpoena, the Commission may apply to a Federal court for an order compelling obedience thereto.

Inquiries and complaints of investors and the general public provide one of the primary sources of leads for detection of law violations in securities transactions. Another is the surprise inspections by Regional Offices of the books and records of brokers and dealers to determine whether their business practices conform to the prescribed rules. Still another is the conduct of inquiries into market fluctuations in particular stocks which appear not to be the result of known developments affecting the issuing company or of general market trends.

The more general types of investigations concern the sale without registration of securities subject to the registration requirement of the Securities Act, and misrepresentations or omission of material facts concerning securities offered for sale (whether or not registration is required). The anti-fraud provisions of the law also apply equally to the _purchase_ of securities, whether involving outright misrepresentations or the withholding or omission of pertinent facts to which the seller was entitled. For example, it is unlawful in certain situations to purchase securities from another person while withholding material information which would indicate that the securities have a value substantially greater than that at which they are being acquired. Such provisions of the law apply not only to transactions between brokers and dealers and their customers but also to the reacquisition of securities by an issuing company or its "insiders."

Other types of inquiries relate to the manipulation of the market prices of securities; the misappropriation or unlawful hypothecation of customers' funds or securities; the conduct of a securities business while insolvent; the purchase or sale of securities by a broker-dealer, from or to his customers, at prices not reasonably related to the current market prices therefor; and violation by the broker-dealer of his responsibility to treat his customers fairly.

The most common of the latter type of violation involves the broker-dealer who, on gaining the trust and confidence of a customer and thereby establishing an agency relationship demanding the highest degree of fiduciary duty and care, takes secret profits in his securities transactions with or for the customer over and above the agreed brokerage (agency) commission. For example the broker-dealer may have purchased securities from customers are prices far below, or sold securities to customers at prices far above, their current market prices. In most such cases, the broker-dealer subjects himself to no risk of loss, since his purchases from customers are made only if he can make simultaneous sales of the securities at prices substantially in excess of those paid to the customers, and his sales to customers are made only if he can make simultaneous purchases of the securities at prices substantially lower than those charged the customer. Or the firm may engage in large-scale in-and-out transactions for the customer's account ("churning") to generate increased commissions, usually without regard to any resulting benefit to the customer.

There is a fundamental distinction between a broker and a dealer; and it is important that investors should understand the different. The <u>broker</u> serves as the customer's <u>agent</u> in buying or selling <u>for</u> his customer. As such, he owes the customer the highest fiduciary responsibility and care and may charge only such agency commission as has been agreed to by the customer. On the other hand, a <u>dealer</u> acts as a principal and buys securities <u>from</u> or sells securities <u>to</u> his customers. In such transactions, the dealer's profit is measured by the difference between the prices at which he buys and sells securities. Since the dealer is operating for his own account, he normally may not charge the customer a fee or commission for services rendered. Even in the case of such dealer transactions, however, the Commission and the courts have held that the conduct of a securities business carries with it the implied representation that customers will be dealt with fairly and that dealers may not enter into transactions with customers at prices not reasonably related to the prevailing market. The law requires that there be delivered to the customer a written "confirmation" of each transaction disclosing whether the securities firm is acting as a principal for its own account or as an agent for the customer (and, if the latter, the broker's compensation from all sources).

Statutory Sanctions

It should be understood that Commission investigations (which for the most part are conducted in private) are essentially fact-finding inquiries. The facts so developed by the staff are considered by the Commission only in determining whether there is <u>prima facie</u> evidence of a law violation and whether an action should be commenced to determine whether, in fact, a violation actually occurred and, if so, whether some sanction should be imposed.

Assuming that the facts show possible fraud or other law violation, the laws provide several courses of action or remedies which the Commission may pursue:

a. <u>Civil injunction</u>. The Commission may apply to an appropriate United States District Court for an order enjoining those acts or practices alleged to violate the law or Commission rules.

b. <u>Criminal prosecution</u>. If fraud or other willful law violation is indicated, the Commission may refer the facts to the Department of Justice with a recommendation for criminal prosecution of the offending persons. That Department, through its local United States Attorneys (who frequently are assisted by Commission attorneys), may present the evidence to a Federal grand jury and seek an indictment.

c. <u>Administrative remedy</u>. The Commission may, after hearing, issue orders suspending or expelling members from exchanges or the over-the-counter dealers association; denying, suspending or revoking the registrations of broker-dealers; or censuring individuals for misconduct or barring them (temporarily or permanently) from employment with a registered firm.

Broker-Dealer Revocations

All of these sanctions may be applied to any person who engages in securities transactions violative of the law, whether or not he is engaged in the securities business. However, the administrative remedy is generally only invoked in the case of exchange or association members, registered brokers or dealers, or individuals who may associate with any such firm. In any such administrative proceeding, the Commission issues an order specifying the acts or practices alleged to have been committed in violation of law and directing that a hearing be held for the purpose of taking evidence thereon. At the hearing, counsel for the Division of Enforcement (often a Regional Office attorney) undertakes to establish for the record those facts which support the charge of law violation, and the respondents have full opportunity to cross-examine witnesses and to present evidence in defense. The procedure followed in the conduct of such proceedings is discussed below under "Administrative Proceedings." If the Commission in its ultimate decision of the case finds that the respondents violated the law, it may take remedial action as indicated above. Such action may effectively bar a firm from the conduct of a securities business in interstate commerce or on exchanges, or an individual from association with a registered firm -- subject to the respondent's right to seek judicial review of the decision by the appropriate United States Court of Appeals.

In its investigation and enforcement actions, the Commission cooperates closely with other Federal, State and local law enforcement officials, as well as with such private agencies as the Better Business Bureaus.

The many instances in which these sanctions of the law have been invoked present a formidable record. However, of perhaps greater significance to the investing public is the deterrent or prophylactic effect of the very existence of the fraud prohibitions of the law and the Commission's powers of investigation and enforcement. These provisions of the law, coupled with the disclosure requirements applicable to new security offerings and to other registered securities, tend to inhibit fraudulent stock promotions and operations. They also increase public confidence in securities as an investment medium, thus facilitating financing through the public sale of securities, which contributes to the industrial growth of the nation.

Commission Not a Collection Agency

Communications from the investing public are very helpful to the C in connection with its statutory duties and the Commission appreciates receiving them. However, because the Commission receives many inquiries and complaints from investors urging it to intercede in their behalf in an attempt to recover losses in the purchase of securities, it is appropriate to point out that the Commission in no sense is to be considered a collection agency. While the laws provide investors with important recovery rights if they have been defrauded, and although the Commission's administration of the laws operates in many instances to uncover facts indicating the possible existence of such rights, recovery may be sought only through the assertion of claims by investors before a court of competent jurisdiction. Further, the Commission cannot give advice as to the merits of securities, whether or not they are registered. Through enactment of the securities laws Congress sought to provide disclosure of much of the basic information on which the merits of particular securities, and the risks inherent in their purchase, might be realistically appraised. But the responsibility for examining the information and determining the investment merit of securities and the risks involved in their purchase rests with the investor.

Administrative Interpretations and Rulemaking

As previously indicated, the Commission not only consults and advises with industry representatives and others concerning legal interpretive problems arising under the securities laws and with respect to the adoption of new or amended rules and regulations, but also gives public notice of suggested rules and invites comments and criticisms which are considered in determining the nature and scope of rules to be adopted. The

Commission constantly reviews its rules in light of the experience gained in their administration, to the end that they will provide maximum investor protection with a minimum of interference with the proper functioning of the securities markets.

The examination of the periodic report and proxy statements of companies whose shares are listed or traded over-the-counter (except those of investment companies), as well as the reports of insiders, is conducted by the Division of Corporation Finance, while the investigative, enforcement and regulatory work under this law is carried on by the Division of Enforcement, the Division of Market Regulation and the Regional Offices.

PUBLIC UTILITY HOLDING COMPANY ACT OF 1935

Purpose of Act

This statute was enacted by Congress to correct the many abuses which Congressional inquiries had disclosed in the financing and operation of electric and gas public-utiliity holding-company systems.

When the Act became law in 1935, some 15 holding company systems controlled 80 percent of all electric energy generation, 98.5 prcent of all transmission of electric energy across State lines, and 80 percent of all natural-gas pipeline mileage in the United States. Many of the huge utility empires then in existence controlled subsidiaries operating in many widely-separated States and which no economic or functional relationship to each other. Holding companies were pyramided layer upon layer, many of them serving no useful or economic purpose; and many systems had very complicated corporate and capital structures, with control often lodged in junior securities having little or no equity. These conditions ranked high among the abuses which the Act was designed to correct.

Registration

Interstate holding companies which are engaged through their subsidiaries in the electric utility business or in the retail distribution of natural or manufactured gas are subject to regulation under the statute. The Act requires that they register with the Commission and file initial and periodic reports containing detailed data about the organization, financial structure and operations of each such holding company and of its subsidiaries. Once the holding companies are registered, they and their subsidiaries become subject to regulation by the Commission in accordance with statutory standards designed for the protection of investors, consumers, and the public interest. If, however, a holding company or a subsidiary thereof meets certain specifications, it may be exempted from part or all the duties and obligations otherwise imposed on it by statute.

Integration and Simplification

From the standpoint of their impact on the electric and gas utility industries, the most important provisions of the Act are its requirements for the physical integration and corporate simplification of holding company systems. The integration standards of the statute restrict a holding company's operations to an "integrated utility system," which is defined in the Act as one capable of economical operation as a single coordinated system confined to a single area or region in one or more states and not so large as to impair (considering the state of the art) the advantages of localized management, efficient operation and effectiveness of local regulation. Additional systems or incidental businesses are retainable only under certain limited conditions. The corporate simplification provisions of the Act require action to insure that the capital structure and the continued existence of any company in a holding-company system do not unduly or unnecessarily complicate the corporate structure of the system or unfairly or inequitably distribute voting power among security holders of the system.

The integration and simplification provisions of the Act direct the Commission to determine what action, if any, must be taken by registered holding companies and their subsidiaries to comply with these requirements; and the Commission may apply to Federal courts for orders compelling compliance with Commission directives made on the basis of such determinations. However, many divestments of nonretainable subsidiaries and properties, recapitalizations, dissolutions of companies and other adjustments required to comply with the Act have been accomplished by the holding company systems through voluntary reorganization plans for which the Act also provides. If a voluntary plan is found by the Commission to be fair and equitable to all affected persons and to be necessary to further the objectives of the Act, the Commission may approve the plan. Thereafter, if the company requests, the Commission applies to a Federal district court for an order approving the plan and directing its enforcement. All interested persons, including State commissions and other governmental agencies, are accorded full opportunity to be heard in proceedings before the Commission and before the Federal courts.

The overall effect of the Commission's administration of the integration and simplification provisions of the law has been far-reaching and unparalleled.

Since 1938, more than 2,500 companies have been subject to the Act as registered holding companies or subsidiaries thereof at one time or another. Included in this total were over 227 holding companies, 1,046 electric and gas utility companies and 1,210 other companies engaged in a wide variety of pursuits. Among the latter were brick works, laundries, experimental orchards, motion picture theaters and even a baseball club. Today the picture is strikingly different. Only 14 holding company systems are now registered. They are comprised of 13 registered holding companies which function solely as holding companies, 5 holding companies which also are engaged in utility operations, 60 electric and/or gas subsidiary companies, 70 nonutility subsidiaries and 20 inactive companies, making a total of 168 companies with aggregate assets of $48 billion. Further, these 14 systems now account for only about one-fifth of the aggregate assets of the privately-owned electric and gas utility and gas pipeline industries of the nation. Most electric and gas utility companies, which formerly were associated with registered holding companies, now operate as independent concerns.

Property & Financial Transactions

The acquisition of securities and utility assets by holding companies and their subsidiaries may not be authorized by the Commission unless the following standards are met:

1. The acquisition must not tend toward interlocking relations or concentration of control to an extent detrimental to the public interest or the interest of investors or consumers;

2. Any consideration paid for the acquisition, including fees, commissions and other remuneration, must not be unreasonable.

3. The acquisition must not complicate the capital structure of the holding company system;

4. The acquisition must tend toward the economic and efficient development of an integrated public utility system.

The issue and sale of securities by holding companies and their subsidiaries are subject to regulation by the Commission under prescribed standards of the law. The tests which a proposed security issue must meet are: (1) the security must be reasonably adapted to the security structure of the issuer and of other companies in the same holding company system; (2) the security must be reasonably adapted to the earning power of the company; (3) the proposed issue must be necessary and appropriate to the economical and efficient operation of the company's business; (4) the fees, commissions and other remuneration paid in connection with the issue must not be unreasonable; and (5) the terms and conditions of the issue or sale of the security must not be detrimental to the public interest or the interest of investors or consumers. In certain cases where there has been an approval by a State regulatory commission, the law directs the Commission to exempt security issues of subsidiary companies, subject to imposition of such terms and conditions as the Commission may deem necessary for the protection of investors or consumers.

To implement these objectives and to eliminate investment banker control and assure maintenance of competitive conditions as required, the Commission has promulgated a rule requiring (with certain exceptions) that in the sale of new securities by registered holding companies and their subsidiaries, as well as in the sale by such holding companies of securities held in their investment portfolio, the issuer or seller shall invite sealed competitive bids for the securities.

Other Regulatory Provisions

Other phases of the Act provide for the regulation of dividend payments (in circumstances where such payment might result in corporate abuses), inter-company loans, solicitation of proxies, consents and other authorizations, and insiders' trading. "Upstream" loans from subsidiaries to their parents and "upstream" or "cross-stream" loans from public-utility companies to any holding company in the same holding-company system are expresslyt forbidden. The Act also requires that all services performed for any company in a holding company system by a service company in that system be rendered at cost fairly and equitable allocated. Thus, the Act deals effectively with the problem of excessive service charges levied on operating electric and gas companies by their parent holding companies, a problem with which State commissions had experienced considerable difficulty.

The Commission is assisted in the administration of the Holding Company Act by its Division of Corporate Regulation, which analyzes legal, financial, accounting, engineering and other problems arising under the Act. The Division participates in hearings to develop the factual records; where necessary, files briefs and participates in oral arguments before the Commission; and makes recommendations with respect to the Commission's findings and decisions in cases which arise in he administration of the law. All hearings are conducted in accordance with the Commission's Rules of Practice discussed below under "Administrative Proceedings."

TRUST INDENTURE ACT OF 1939

This Act applies in general to bonds, debentures, notes, and similar debt securities offered for pubic sale which are issued pursuant to trust indentures under which more than $1 million of securities may be outstanding at any one time. Even though such securities may be registered under the Securities Act, they may not be offered for sale to the public unless the trust indenture conforms to specified statutory standards of this Act designed to safeguard the rights and interests of the purchasers.

The Act was passed after studies by the Commission had revealed the frequency with which trust indentures failed to provide minimum protections for security holders and absolved so-called trustees from minimum obligations in the discharge of their trusts. It requires that the indenture trustee be free of conflicting interests which might interfere with the faithful exercise of its duties in behalf of the purchasers of the securities. It requires also that the trustee be a corporation with minimum combined capital and surplus; imposes high standards of conduct and responsibility on the trustee; precludes preferential collection of certain claims owing to the trustee by the issuer in the event of default; provides for the issuer's supplying evidence to the trustee of compliance with indenture terms and conditions such as those relating to the release or substitution or mortgaged property, issuance of new securities or satisfaction of the indenture; and provides for reports and notices by the trustee to security holders. Other provisions of the Act prohibit impairment of the security holders' right to sue individually for principal and interest except under certain circumstances, and require the maintenance of a list of security holders which may be used by them to communicate with each other regarding their rights as security holders.

Applications for qualification of trust indentures are examined by the Division of Corporation Finance for compliance with the applicable requirements of the law and the Commission's rules thereunder.

INVESTMENT COMPANY ACT OF 1940

This legislation, together with the Investment Advisers Act of 1940, discussed below, resulted from a study of the activities of investment companies and investment advisers conducted by the Commission pursuant to direction of Congres contained in the Holding Company Act. The results of this study were reported to Congress in a series of reports filed in 1938, 1939 and 1940, the legislation being supported both by the Commission and the investment company industry.

Under this Act, the activities of companies engaged primarily in the business of investing, reinvesting and trading in securities and whose own securities are offered and sold to and held by the investing public, are subject to certain statutory prohibitions and to Commission regulation in accordance with prescribed standards deemed necessary to protect the interests of investors and the public.

It is important for investors to understand, however, that the Commission does not supervise the investment activities of these companies and that regulation by the Commission does not imply safety of investment in such companies.

In addition to a requirement that such companies register with the Commission,* the law requires disclosure of their financial condition and investment policies to afford investors full and complete information about their activities; prohibits such companies from changing the nature of their business or their investment policies without the approval of the stockholders; bars persons guilty of security frauds from serving as officers and directors; prevents underwriters, investment bankers or brokers from constituting more than a minority of the directors of such companies; requires management contracts (and material changes therein) to be submitted to security holders for their approval; prohibits transactions between such companies and their directors, officers, or affiliated companies or persons, except on approval by the Commission as being fair and involving no overreaching; forbids the issuance of senior securities by such companies except under specified conditions and upon specified terms; and prohibits pyramiding of such companies and cross-ownership of their securities.

Other provisions relate to sales and repurchases of securities issued by investment companies, exchange offers, and other activities of investment companies, including special provisions for periodic payment plans and face-amount certificate companies.

With respect to plans of reorganization of investment companies, the Commission is authorized to prepare advisory

---

*A list of registered investment companies, showing their classification, assets size and location, may be purchased from the Commission in photocopy form (cost furnished upon request).

reports as to the fairness of their terms and provisions if requested by the company or 25 percent of its stockholders; and it may institute court proceedings to enjoin a plan of reorganization if it appears grossly unfair to security holders. The Commission may also institute court action to remove management officials who may be guilty of gross misconduct or gross abuse of trust.

The securities of investment companies are also required to be registered under the Securities Act; and the companies must file periodic reports and are subject to the Commission's proxy and "insider" trading rules.

The Division of Investment Management is the staff unit concerned with administration of this law and with the processing of investment company registration statements under the Securities Act as well as their proxy statements and periodic reports.

INVESTMENT ADVISERS ACT OF 1940

This law establishes a pattern of regulation of investment advisers which is similar in many respects to Securities Exchange Act provisions governing the conduct of brokers and dealers. It requires, with certain exceptions, that persons or firms who engage for compensation in the business of advising others about their securities transactions shall register with the Commission and conform their activities to statutory standards designed to protect the interests of investors.

The registration of investment advisers may be denied, suspended or revoked by the Commission if, after notice and hearing, it finds that a statutory disqualification exists and that such action is in the public interest. Disqualifications include a conviction for certain financial crimes or securities violations, the existence of injunctions based on such activities, a conviction for violation of the Mail Fraud Statute, the willful filing of false reports with the Commission, and willful violations of this Act, the Securities Act or the Securities Exchange Act. In addition to the administrative sanction of denial, suspension or revocation, the Commission may obtain injunctions restraining violations of this law and may recommend prosecution by the Department of Justice for fraudulent misconduct or willful violation of the law or rules as may be prescribed by the Commission, and it authorizes the Commission to conduct inspections of such books and records.

The Commission is aided in the administration of this law by the Office of Reports and Information Services and the Division of Investment Management.

CORPORATE REORGANIZATIONS

Under Chapter X of the Bankruptcy Act and Chapter 11 of the Bankruptcy Reform Act of 1978, the Commission serves as adviser to United States district courts in connection with proceedings for the reorganization of debtor corporations in which there is a substantial public interest. It participates as a party to these proceedings, either at the request or with the approval of the courts. It renders independent, expert advice and assistance to the courts, which do not maintain their own staffs of expert consultants.

Representatives of the Commission follow closely the progress of reorganization proceedings in which it is a participant, nd confer with the court-appointed trustees and their counsel and with other interested parties in the solution of the various problems which arise in the administration of the affairs of the debtor corporation and in the formulation of plans of reorganization. In addition to the advice and assistance which the Commission renders, both to the court and to the parties, in connection with the preparation of plans of reorganization, the Commission also presents its views and recommendations on such matters as the qualifications and independence, the need for appointment of trustees or examiners and their fee allowances to the various parties, including the trustees and their counsel, sales of properties and other assets, interim distributions to security holders, and other financial or legal matters. The Commission has no independent right of appeal from court rulings.

In cases pending under Chapter X, where the scheduled liabilities of the debtor exceed $3 million, the plan of reorganization must be, and in other cases may be, referred by the court to the Commission for preparation of an advisory report on the fairness and feasibility of the plan. This advisory report is filed with the court for its assistance and is distributed to creditors and security holders to enable them to exercise an informed judgment in considering whether to vote for or against acceptance of the plan. In cases under Chapter 11, where the debtor, official committees, and institutional creditors can negotiate the terms of a plan without complying with the "fair and equitable" standard, the principal safeguard for public investors will be the adequacy of the statutory disclosure statement which must now be transmitted by the proponent in connection with soliciting votes on the plan. The Commission presents its views and recommendations on whether disclosure statements contain sufficient information to enable public investors to make an informed judgment about the plan. Underlying the Commission's recommendations in each case is a thorough study and analysis of the debtor's operations, financial condition, the terms of the plan, and its prospective effect on public investors.

Because of the predominantly local character of reorganization cases, court appearances, consultations with the parties, investigations and examinations are handled primarily by the Commission's Regional Offices, subject to supervision by the Division of Corporate Regulation and approval by the Commission.

ADMINISTRATIVE PROCEEDINGS

All formal administrative proceedings of the Commission are conducted in accordance with its Rules of Practice, which conform to the Administrative Procedure Act and are designed to establish procedural, "due process" safeguards which will protect the rights and interests of parties to each such proceeding. Among these are requirements for timely notice of the proceeding and for a sufficient specification of the issues or charges involved to enable each of the parties adequately to prepare his case. All parties, including counsel for the interested Department or Office of the Commission, may appear at the hearing and present evidence and cross-examine witnesses in much the same manner as in the ordinary trial of court actions. In addition, other interested persons may be permitted to intervene or be given limited rights of participation. In some cases, the relevant facts may be stipulated in lieu of the conduct of an evidentiary hearing.

Hearings are conducted before a Hearing Officer who is normally an Administrative Law Judge appointed by the Commission; he serves independently of the interested Division or Office and rules on the admissibility of evidence and on other issues arising during the course of the hearing. At the conclusion of the hearing, the parties and participants may urge, in writing, specific findings of fact and conclusions of law for adoption by the Hearing Officer. Thereupon, the Hearing Officer prepares and files an initial decision (unless waived), setting forth his conclusions as to the facts established by the evidence and including an order disposing of the issues involved in the proceeding. Copies of the initial decision are served on the parties and participants, who may seek Commission review thereof. If review is not sought and the Commission does not order review on its own motion, the initial decision becomes final and the Hearing Officer's order becomes effective.

In the event of Commission review of the initial decision, the parties and participants may file briefs and be heard in oral argument before the Commission. On the basis of an independent review of the record, the Commission prepares and issues its own decision; the Office of Opinions and Review aids the Commission in this decisional process. The laws provide that any person or firm aggrieved by a decision order of the Commission may seek review thereof by the appropriate United States court of appeals. The initial decisions of Hearing Officers as well as the Commission's decisions are made public. Ultimately, the Commission's decisions (as well as initial decisions which have become final and are of precedential significance) are printed by the Government Printing Office and published in the Commission's "Decisions and Reports."

OFFICE OF THE GENERAL COUNSEL

The General Counsel is the chief legal officer of the Commission. The duties of his office include representing the Commission in judicial proceedings; handling legal matters which cut across the lines of work of the several operating Divisions; and providing advice and assistance to the Commission, its operating Divisions, and Regional Offices with respect to statutory interpretation, rule-making, legislative matters and other legal problems, public or private investigations and Congressional hearings and investigations. The Office also reviews cases where criminal prosecution is recommended. The General Counsel directs and supervises all contested civil litigation (except United States district court proceedings under Chapter 11 of the Bankruptcy Reform Act and, in cases commenced prior to October 1, 1979, Chapter X of the Bankruptcy Act) and represents the Commission in all cases in the appellate courts, filing briefs and presenting oral arguments in behalf of the Commission. In addition, in cases between private parties involving the statutes the Commission administers, the Office represents the Commission where it participates as a friend of the court in cases involving legal issues of general importance.

The Commission from time to time recommends revisions in the statutes which it administers. In addition, it prepares comments on any proposed legislation which might affect its work or where it is asked for its views by Congressional Committees. The Office of the General Counsel, together with the Division assisting the Commission in the function which may be affected by such legislation, prepares this legislative material.

OFFICE OF THE CHIEF ACCOUNTANT

The Chief Accountant is the Commission's chief consulting officer on accounting matters, advising the Commission with respect to accounting problems which arise in the administration of the Acts, particularly in matters involving new accounting policy determination. The Chief Accountant has general supervision over the execution of Commission policy with respect to the accounting principles and procedures applicable to the financial statements filed with the Commission and to the auditing standards and practices observed by the independent public accountants who examine and render an opinion on these statements.

A major objective of the Commission has been to improve accounting and auditing standards and to maintain high standards of professional conduct by the independent accountants through cooperation with the accounting profession and by the rule-making process. In furtherance of this policy the Chief Accountant consults with representatives of the accounting profession regarding the promulgation of new or revised accounting and auditing standards and drafts rules and regulations which prescribe requirements for financial statements. Many of the rules are embodied in a basic accounting regulation entitled Regulation S-X adopted by the Commission which, together with a number of opinions issued as "Accounting Series Releases," governs the form and content of most of the financial statements filed with it.

The Chief Accountant administers the Commission's rules which require that accountants who examine financial statements filed with it be independent of their clients, and makes recommendations on cases arising under the Commission's Rules of Practice which specify that an accountant may be denied the privilege of practicing before the Commission because of lack of character or integrity or qualifications to represent others, or because of unethical or unprofessional conduct. He also supervises the procedures followed in accounting investigations conducted by the Commission's staff.

DIRECTORATE OF ECONOMIC & POLICY ANALYSIS

The primary function of this office is to assist the Commission in dealing with the economic and empirical issues which are inextricably associated with the Commission's regulatory activities. For the most part, the Directorate carries out this function by supporting and working closely with the Divisions responsible for rule proposals. Whether working with one of the operating Divisions or serving the Commission independently, the Directorate accomplishes its function by performing empirical studies, economic analysis of regulatory impact analysis. In addition, in conformance with the Commission's concerns for responsive and informed regulation, the Directorate provides a general capability to analyze impacts and benefits of proposed regulations and conducts studies on specific rules.

More specifically, the Directorate analyzes rule changes and engages in long-term research and policy planning, builds and maintains diverse computer data bases, designs programs to access data, and develops and tests alternative methodologies. In the area of economic monitoring, the Directorate assesses the impact of securities market regulations on issuers (in particular, small or high technology issuers), broker-dealers, investors, and the economy in general. One area monitored by the Directorate is the impact of competitively-determined commission rates and changes in regulations which affect the ability of small businesses to raise capital. The Directorate also collects, processes and publishes in its SEC Monthly Statistical Review data on the financial condition of the securities industry, registered securities issues, private placement of corporate securities, quarterly assets of non-insured pension funds and property and liability insurance companies, volume and value of trading of exchange-listed equity securities, quarterly stock transactions of selected non-financial institutions, and annual estimated market value of stock outstanding.

PUBLIC INFORMATION

Corporate Reports Available

Quarterly (10Q) and annual (10K) reports, registration statements, proxy material and other reports filed by corporations, mutual funds or broker-dealers with the SEC are available for inspection in the Public Reference Room of the Commission's Headquarters Office in Washington, D.C. Copies of portions or all of such public documents may be obtained for a handling charge of 10 cents per page ($5.00 minimum). Estimates of the cost of copying specific documents will be provided on request to the Public Reference Section, Securities and Exchange Commission, Washington, D.C. 20549.

Current annual and other periodic reports (including financial statements) filed by companies whose securities are listed on exchanges also are available for inspection in the Commission's New York, Chicago and Los Angeles Regional Offices as are the registration statements (and subsequent reports) filed by those companies whose securities are traded over-the-counter which register under the 1964 Amendments to the Exchange Act. Moreover, if the issuer's principal office is located in the area served by the Atlanta, Boston, Denver, Fort Worth or Seattle Regional Office, its filings also may be examined at the appropriate Regional Office. In addition, prospectuses covering recent public offerings of securities registered under the Securities Act may be examined in all Regional Offices; and copies of broker-dealer and investment adviser registrations, as well as Regulation A notifications and offering circulars, may be examined in the Regional Office in which they were filed.

SEC Regional Offices

REGION 1 NEW YORK REGIONAL OFFICE
26 Federal Plaza
New York, N.Y. 10278
212-264-1636
Region: New York and New Jersey

REGION 2 BOSTON REGIONAL OFFICE
150 Causeway Street
Boston, Massachusetts 02114
617-223-2721
Region: Maine, New Hampshire, Vermont, Massachusetts, Rhode Island and Connecticut

REGION 3 ATLANTA REGIONAL OFFICE
1375 Peachtree Street, N.E.
Suite 788
Atlanta, Georgia 30367
404-881-4768
Region: Tennessee, Virgin Islands, Puerto Rico, North Carolina, South Carolina, Georgia, Alabama, Mississippi, Florida and Louisiana east of the Atchafalaya River

MIAMI BRANCH OFFICE
Dupont Plaza Center
300 Biscayne Blvd., Way, Suite 1114
Miami, Florida 33131
305-350-65765

REGION 4 CHICAGO REGIONAL OFFICE
Everett McKinley Dirksen Bldg.
219 South Dearborn Street, Room 1204
Chicago, Illinois 60604
312-353-7390
Region: Michigan, Ohio, Kentucky, Wisconsin, Indiana, Iowa, Minnesota, Missouri, and Kansas City (Kansas) and Illinois

DETROIT BRANCH OFFICE
1044 Federal Bldg.
Detroit, Michigan 48226
313-226-6070

REGION 5 FORT WORTH REGIONAL OFFICE
411 W. Seventh St.
Fort Worth, Texas 76102
817-334-3821
Region: Oklahoma, Arkansas, Texas west of the Atchafalaya River and Kansas (except Kansas City)

Appendix I: Work of the SEC

HOUSTON BRANCH OFFICE
Federal Office and Courts Bldg.
515 Rusk Avenue, Room 5615
Houston, Texas 77002
713-226-4986

REGION 6   DENVER REGIONAL OFFICE
410 17th Street
Suite 700
Denver, Colorado 80202
303-837-2071
Region: North Dakota, South Dakota, Wyoming, Nebraska, Colorado, New Mexico, and Utah

SALT LAKE BRANCH OFFICE
Boston Bldg. Suite 810
Nine Exchange Place
Salt Lake City, Utah 84111
701-524-5796

REGION 7   LOS ANGELES REGIONAL OFFICE
10960 Wilshire Blvd.
Suite 1710
Los Angeles, California 90024
213-473-4511
Region: Nevada, Arizona, California, Hawaii and Guam

SAN FRANCISCO BRANCH OFFICE
450 Golden Gate Avenue, Box 36042
San Francisco, California 94102
415-556-5264

REGION 8   SEATTLE REGIONAL OFFICE
3040 Federal Building
915 Second Avenue
Seattle, Washington 98174
206-442-7990
Region: Montana, Idaho, Washington, Oregon, and Alaska

REGION 9   WASHINGTON REGIONAL OFFICE
Ballston Center Tower 3
4015 Wilson Blvd.
Arlington, Virginia 22203
703-557-8201
Region: Pennsylvania, Delaware, Maryland, Virginia, West Virginia, and District of Columbia

PHILADELPHIA BRANCH OFFICE
William J. Green, Jr. Federal Bldg.
600 Arch Street, Room 2204
Philadelphia, Pennsylvania 19106
215-597-2278

U.S. SECURITIES & EXCHANGE COMMISSION

500 North Capitol Street
Washington, D.C. 20549

INVESTOR COMPLAINTS	Office of Consumer Affairs (202-523-5516)
FILINGS BY REGISTERED COMPANIES	Public Reference Room 1100 L Street, N.W. (202)523-5360
FORMS AND PUBLICATIONS	Public Reference Room (202)523-3761

PERSONNEL LOCATOR
655-4000

CONSUMER TELECOMMUNICATIONS
FOR THE DEAF-TTY-VOICE
523-5516

A Publication of the
U.S. Securities and Exchange Commission
Office of Public Affairs
(202)272-2650

APPENDIX J
NASAA Guidelines

North American Securities Administrators Association, Inc.
on October 2, 1985, Effective January 1, 1986

I. INTRODUCTION
   A. Application
      1. The rules contained in these guidelines apply to qualifications and registrations of real estate programs in the form of limited partnerships (herein sometimes called "PROGRAM" or "partnerships") and will be applied by analogy to real estate programs in other forms. While applications not conforming to the standards contained herein shall be looked upon with disfavor, where good cause is shown certain guidelines may be modified or waived by the ADMINISTRATOR.

         COMMENT: The purpose of the guidelines is to establish uniform and consistent standards to be applied by the various state securities ADMINISTRATORS throughout the country. These standards are primarily designed for public real estate syndications and PROGRAMS which make or invest in mortgage loans. With respect to PROGRAMS which make or invest in mortgage loans, all provisions of these guidelines are applicable thereto, unless specifically excluded or modified.

      2. Where the individual characteristics of specific PROGRAMS warrant modification from these standards they will be accommodated, insofar as possible while still being consistent with the spirit of these guidelines. The Cross Reference Sheet in the form set forth in Section IX.H. Real Estate Guidelines Cross Reference Sheet shall be furnished with the application.
      3. Where these guidelines conflict with requirements of the Securities and Exchange Commission, the guidelines will not apply.
   B. Definitions
      1. ACQUISITION EXPENSES—expenses including but not limited to legal fees and expenses, travel and communications expenses, costs of appraisals, non-refundable option payments on property not acquired, accounting fees and expenses, title insurance, and miscellaneous expenses related to selection and acquisition of properties, whether or not acquired.

ORIGINALLY ISSUED 10/22/84   LATEST REVISION 10/24/85   REVISION NUMBER 4

COMMENT: Definition utilized in section IV.C. making clear that all expenses incurred in acquiring properties for the PROGRAM be included in FRONT-END FEES.

2. ACQUISITION FEE—the total of all fees and commissions paid by any party in connection with the making or investing in mortgage loans or the purchase or development of property by a PROGRAM, except a development fee paid to a PERSON not affiliated with a SPONSOR in connection with the actual development of a project after acquisition of the land by the PROGRAM. Included in the computation of such fees or commissions shall be any real estate commission, selection fee, development fee, nonrecurring management fee, or any fee of a similar nature, however designated.

3. ADMINISTRATOR—the official or agency administering the securities law of a state.

4. AFFILIATE—means (i) any PERSON directly or indirectly controlling, controlled by or under common control with another PERSON (ii) any PERSON owning or controlling 10% or more of the outstanding voting securities of such other PERSON (iii) any officer, director, partner of such PERSON and (iv) if such other PERSON is an officer, director or partner, any company for which such PERSON acts in any such capacity.

5. ASSESSMENTS—additional amounts of capital which may be mandatorily required of or paid at the option of a PARTICIPANT beyond his subscription commitment.

6. AUDITED FINANCIAL STATEMENTS—financial statements (balance sheet, statement of income, statement of partners' equity and statement of changes in financial position) prepared in accordance with generally accepted accounting principles and accompanied by an auditor's report containing an unqualified opinion or an opinion containing no material qualification of an independent certified public accountant or independent public accountant.

7. CAPITAL CONTRIBUTION—the gross amount of investment in a PROGRAM by a PARTICIPANT, or all PARTICIPANTS as the case may be.

8. CARRIED INTEREST—is "an equity interest taken in a program by a PERSON other than the promotional interest provided for in Sections IV.C.3(a), IV.E.1 and IV.E.2, for which full consideration is not paid or to be paid."

9. CASH FLOW—PROGRAM cash funds provided from operations, including lease payments on net leases from builders and sellers, without deduction from depreciation, but after deducting cash funds used to pay all other expenses, debt payments, capital improvements and replacments.

COMMENT: With respect to Programs which make or invest in mortgage loans, only funds which constitute interest payments shall be included in CASH FLOW. Funds which may be deemed to constitute interest payments are (i) contractual current interest payments; (ii) interest accrued or deferred, when received, and (iii) contingent interest based upon the PROGRAM'S share of the gross or net income from properties on which the PROGRAM has made a loan. All other funds shall be considered to be net proceeds from a sale or refinancing.

10. CASH AVAILABLE FOR DISTRIBUTION—CASH FLOW less amount set aside for restoration or creation of reserves.

11. COMPETITIVE REAL ESTATE COMMISSION—that real estate or brokerage commission paid for the purchase or sale of property which is reasonable, customary and competitive in light of the size, type and location of the property.

12. CONSTRUCTION FEE—a fee for acting as general contractor to construct improvements on a PROGRAM's property either initially or at a later date.

13. CROSS REFERENCE SHEET—A compilation of the guideline sections, referenced to the page of the PROSPECTUS, partnership agreement, or other exhibits, and justification of any deviation from the guidelines.

14. DEVELOPMENT FEE—a fee for the packaging of a PROGRAM's property, including negotiating and approving plans, and undertaking to assist in obtaining zoning and necessary variances and necessary financing for the specific property, either initially or at a later date.

15. FINANCING—shall be defined as: "The indebtedness encumbering program properties, the principal amount of which is scheduled to be paid over a period of not less than 48 months, and not more than 50 percent of the principal amount of which is scheduled to be paid during the first 24 months. Nothing in this definition shall be construed as prohibiting a bona-fide pre-payment provision in the financing agreement."

16. FRONT-END FEES—Fees and expenses paid by any party for any services rendered during the PROGRAM's organizational or acquisition phase including ORGANIZATION AND OFFERING EXPENSES, ACQUISITION FEES, ACQUISITION EXPENSES, and any other similar fees, however designated by the SPONSOR.

17. INVESTMENT IN PROPERTIES—The amount of CAPITAL CONTRIBUTIONS used to make or invest in mortgage loans or the amount actually paid or allocated to the purchase, development, construction or improvement of properties acquired by the PROGRAM (including the purchase of properties, working capital reserves allocable thereto (except that working capital reserves in excess of 5% shall not be included), and other cash payments such as interest and taxes but excluding FRONT-END FEES).

18. NET WORTH—the excess of total assets over total liabilities as determined by generally accepted accounting principles, except that if any of such assets have been depreciated, then the amount of depreciation

relative to any particular asset may be added to the depreciated cost of such asset to compute total assets, provided that the amount of depreciation may be added only to the extent that the amount resulting after adding such depreciation does not exceed the fair market value of such asset.

19. NON-SPECIFIED PROPERTY PROGRAM—a PROGRAM where, at the time a securities registration is ordered effective, less than 75% of the net proceeds from the sale of PROGRAM INTERESTS is allocable to the purchase, construction, or improvement of specific properties, or a PROGRAM in which the proceeds from any sale or refinancing of properties may be reinvested. Reserves shall be included in the non- specified 25%.

20. ORGANIZATION AND OFFERING EXPENSES - those expenses incurred in connection with and in preparing a PROGRAM for registration and subsequently offering and distributing it to the public, including sales commissions paid to broker-dealers in connection with the distribution of the PROGRAM and all advertising expenses.

    COMMENT: ALL advertising expenses, except related to PROGRAM property management, charged to a PROGRAM is included within the definition.

21. PARTICIPANT—the holder of a PROGRAM INTEREST

22. PERSON—any natural PERSON, partnership, corporation, association or other legal entity.

23. PROGRAM—a limited or general partnership, joint venture, unincorporated association or similar organization other than a corporation formed and operated for the primary purpose of investment in and the operation of or gain from an interest in real property including such entities formed to make or invest in mortgage loans.

24. PROGRAM INTEREST—the limited partnership unit or other indicia of ownership in a PROGRAM.

25. PROGRAM MANAGEMENT FEE—a fee paid to the SPONSOR or other PERSONS for management and administration of the PROGRAM.

26. PROPERTY MANAGEMENT FEE—the fee paid for day-to-day professional property management services in connection with a PROGRAM's real property projects.

27. PROSPECTUS—shall have the meaning given to that term by Section 2(10) of the Securities Act of 1933, including a preliminary PROSPECTUS; provided, however, that such term as used herein shall also include an offering circular as described in Rule 256 of the General Rules and Regulations under the Securities Act of 1933 or, in the case of an intrastate offering, any document by whatever name known, utilized for the purpose of offering and selling securities to the public.

Appendix J: NASAA Guidelines

28. PURCHASE PRICE OF PROPERTY—the price paid upon the purchase or sale of a particular property, including the amount of ACQUISITION FEES and all liens and mortgages on the property, but excluding points and prepaid interest.

29. SPONSOR—a "SPONSOR" is any PERSON directly or indirectly instrumental in organizing, wholly or in part, a PROGRAM or any PERSON who will manage or participate in the management of a PROGRAM, and any AFFILIATE of any such person, but does not include a PERSON whose only relation with the PROGRAM is as that of an independent property manager, whose only compensation is as such. "SPONSOR" does not include wholly independent third parties such as attorneys, accountants, and underwriters whose only compensation is for professional services rendered in connection with the offering of syndicate interests.

II. REQUIREMENTS OF SPONSORS

A. Experience. The SPONSOR, the general partner or their chief operating officers shall have at least two years relevant real estate or other experience demonstrating the knowledge and experience to acquire and manage the type of assets being acquired, and any of the foregoing or any AFFILIATE providing services to the PROGRAM shall have had not less than four years relevant experience in the kind of service being rendered or otherwise must demonstrate sufficient knowledge and experience to perform the services proposed.

COMMENT: "Relevant real estate or other experience" should be interpreted to include actual direct experience by the chief executive officer, or other PERSONS at the management level, either as a principal or agent in performing the services to be provided to the PROGRAM. This would include acquiring and managing real estate for one's own account or acting as an agent in acquiring and managing real estate comparable to that which the PROGRAM will acquire. If the PROGRAM will be in the business of acquiring shopping centers and office buildings, "relevant real estate experience" would not include experience in buying or selling houses. It is apparent that a different level of sophistication and knowledge is required.

B. NET WORTH Requirement of SPONSOR. The financial condition of the SPONSOR liable for the debts of the PROGRAM must be commensurate with any financial obligations assumed in the offering and in the operation of the PROGRAM. As a minimum, such SPONSOR shall have an aggregate financial NET WORTH, exclusive of home, automobile and home furnishings, of the greater of either $50,000 or an amount at least equal to 5% of the gross amount of all offerings sold within the prior 12 months plus 5% of the gross amount of the current offering, to an aggregate maximum NET WORTH of such SPONSOR of one million dollars. In determining NET WORTH for this purpose, evaluation will be made of contingent liabilities and the use of promissory notes, to determine the appropriateness of their inclusion in computation of NET WORTH.

> COMMENT: The inclusion of promissory notes may be insufficient to satisfy the NET WORTH requirements where the maker of the notes is inadequately capitalized.

C. Reports to ADMINISTRATOR. Each application for registration shall contain a commitment, executed by the SPONSOR, to submit to the ADMINISTRATOR upon request any report or statement required to be distributed to limited partners pursuant to VII.C.

> COMMENT: The SPONSOR need not file with the ADMINISTRATOR all reports that will be filed with the limited partners, but should retain copies of such reports or information and make them available to the ADMINISTRATOR as required. The length this information must be retained will vary from state to state depending upon its requirements.

D. Liability and Indemnification

(a) The partnership agreement shall not provide for indemnification of the SPONSOR for any liability or loss suffered by the SPONSOR, nor shall it provide that the SPONSOR be held harmless for any loss or liability suffered by the partnership, unless all of the following conditions are met:

(1) The SPONSOR has determined, in good faith, that the course of conduct which caused the loss or liability was in the best interests of the partnership, and

(2) such liability or loss was not the result of negligence or misconduct by the SPONSOR, and

(3) such indemnification or agreement to hold harmless is recoverable only out of the assets of the partnership and not from the limited partners.

(b) Indemnification of the SPONSORS or their affiliates will not be allowed for any liability imposed by judgment, and costs associated therewith, including attorneys' fees, arising from or out of a violation of state or federal securities laws associated with the offer and sale of partnership units. Indemnification will be allowed for settlements and related expenses of lawsuits alleging securities law violations, and for expenses incurred in successfully defending such lawsuits, provided that a court either:

(1) approves the settlement and finds that indemnification of the settlement and related costs should be made, or

(2) approves indemnification of litigation costs if a successful defense is made.

Every application for registration must contain an undertaking that such parties seeking indemnification will apprise the court of the positions of the ADMINISTRATOR and the SEC with respect to indemnification for securities laws violations, before seeking court approval for indemnification.

The PROGRAM may not incur the cost of that portion of liability insurance which insures the SPONSOR for any liability as to which the SPONSOR is prohibited from being indemnified under this section.

E. Fiduciary Duty

The program agreement shall provide that the SPONSOR shall have fiduciary responsibility for the safekeeping and use of all funds and assets of the program, whether or not in the SPONSOR'S possession or control, and that the SPONSOR shall not employ, or permit another to employ such funds or assets in any manner except for the exclusive benefit of the PROGRAM.

In addition, the PROGRAM shall not permit the PARTICIPANT to contract away the fiduciary duty owed to the PARTICIPANT by the SPONSOR under the common law.

F. Terminated SPONSOR

Upon the occurrence of a terminating event, the partnership may be required to pay to the terminated SPONSOR all amounts then accrued and owing to the terminated SPONSOR. Additionally, the partnership may terminate the SPONSOR'S interest in partnership income, losses, distributions, and capital by payment of an amount equal to the then present fair market value of the terminated SPONSOR'S interest determined by agreement of the terminated SPONSOR and the partnership, or, if they cannot agree, by arbitration in accordance with the then current rules of the American Arbitration Association. The expense of arbitration shall be borne equally by the terminated SPONSOR and the partnership.

The method of payment to the terminated SPONSOR must be fair; and must protect the solvency and liquidity of the partnership. Where the termination is voluntary, the method of payment will be deemed presumptively fair where it provides for a non-interest bearing unsecured promissory note with principal payable, if at all, from distributions which the terminated SPONSOR otherwise would have received under the partnership agreement had the SPONSOR not terminated. Where the termination is involuntary, the method of payment will be deemed presumptively fair where it provides for an interest bearing promissory note coming due in no less than 5 years with equal installments each year.

III. SUITABILITY OF THE PARTICIPANT

A. Standards to be Imposed. Given the limited transferability, the relative lack of liquidity, and the specific tax orientation of many real estate PROGRAMS, the SPONSOR and its selling representatives should be cautious concerning the PERSONS to whom such securities are marketed. Suitability standards for investors will, therefore, be imposed which are reasonable in view of the foregoing and of the type of PROGRAM to be offered. SPONSORS will be required to set forth in the PROSPECTUS the investment objectives as a PROGRAM, a description of the type of PERSON who could benefit from the PROGRAM and the suitability standards to be applied in marketing it. The suitability standards proposed by the SPONSOR will be reviewed for fairness by the ADMINISTRATOR in processing the application. In determining how restrictive the standards must be, special attention will be given to the existence of such factors as high leverage, tax implications, balloon payment financing, excessive investments in unimproved land, and uncertain or no CASH FLOW from PROGRAM property. As a general rule, PROGRAMS structured to give deductible tax losses of 50% or more of the CAPITAL CONTRIBUTION of the PARTICIPANT in the year of investment should be sold only to PERSONS in higher income tax brackets considering both state and federal income taxes.

PROGRAMS which involve more than ordinary investor risk should emphasize suitability standards involving substantial NET WORTH of the investor.

B. Sales to Appropriate PERSONS. The SPONSOR and each PERSON selling PROGRAM interests on behalf of the SPONSOR or PROGRAM shall make every reasonable effort to assure that those PERSONS being offered or sold the PROGRAM INTERESTS are suitable, in light of the standards set forth as required above, and the PROGRAM INTERESTS are appropriate for the customers' investment objectives and financial situations.

The SPONSOR or his representatives shall ascertain that the investor can reasonably benefit from the PROGRAM, and the following shall be evidence thereof:

1. The investor has the capacity of understanding the fundamental aspects of the PROGRAM, which capacity may be evidenced by the following:
   (a) The nature of employment experience;
   (b) Educational level achieved;
   (c) Access to advice from qualified sources, such as, attorney, accountant and tax advisor;
   (d) Prior experience with investments of a similar nature.
2. The SPONSOR or his representatives shall ascertain that the investor has apparent understanding:
   (a) of the fundamental risks and possible financial hazards of the investment;
   (b) of the lack of liquidity of this investment;

Appendix J: NASAA Guidelines

(c) that the investment will be directed and managed by the SPONSOR; and
(d) of the tax consequences of the investment.

3. The PARTICIPANT can reasonably benefit from the PROGRAM in view of his overall investment objectives and portfolio structure.

4. The PARTICIPANT is able to bear the economic risk of the investment. For purposes of determining the ability to bear the economic risk, unless the ADMINISTRATOR approves a lower suitability standard, PARTICIPANTS shall have a minimum annual gross income of $30,000 and a NET WORTH of $30,000, or in the alternative, a NET WORTH of $75,000. In high risk or principally tax oriented offerings, higher suitability standards may be required. In the case of sales to fiduciary accounts, the suitability standards shall be met by the fiduciary or by the fiduciary account or by a donor who directly or indirectly supplies the funds to purchase the PROGRAM INTERESTS. NET WORTH shall be determined exclusive of home, home furnishings and automobiles.

COMMENT: A modified suitability standard may be used where it is demonstrated to the administrator that the potential risk to the investor justifies a decrease or increase in one or more of the suitability standards contained in Section III.B.4.

C. Maintenance of Records. The SPONSOR shall maintain a record of the information obtained to indicate that a PARTICIPANT meets the suitability standards employed in connection with the offer and sale of its interests and a representation of the PARTICIPANT that he is purchasing for his own account or, in lieu of such representation, information indicating that the PARTICIPANTS for whose account the purchase is made meet such suitability standards. Such information may be obtained from the PARTICIPANT through the use of a form which sets forth the prescribed suitability standards in full and which includes a statement to be signed by the PARTICIPANT in which he represents that he meets such suitability standards and is purchasing for his own account. However, where the offering is underwritten or sold by a broker-dealer, the SPONSOR shall obtain a commitment from the banker-dealer to maintain the same record of information required of the SPONSOR.

IV. FEES - COMPENSATION - EXPENSES

A. Fees, Compensation and Expenses to be Reasonable.

1. The total amount of consideration of all kinds which may be paid directly or indirectly to all parties shall be reasonable.

2. The PROSPECTUS must fully disclose and itemize all consideration which may be received from the PROGRAM directly or indirectly by the

SPONSOR, its AFFILIATES and underwriters, what the consideration is for and how and when it will be paid. This shall be set forth in one location in tabular form.

B. ORGANIZATION AND OFFERING EXPENSES. ALL ORGANIZATION AND OFFERING EXPENSES incurred in order to sell PROGRAM interests shall be reasonable and shall comply with all statutes, rules and regulations imposed in connection with the offering of other securities in the state.

C. INVESTMENT IN PROPERTIES
   1. The SPONSOR shall be required to commit a substantial portion of the PROGRAM'S CAPITAL CONTRIBUTIONS toward INVESTMENT IN PROPERTIES. The remaining CAPITAL CONTRIBUTIONS may be used to pay FRONT-END FEES. When ACQUISITION FEES are paid by the seller of properties, such fees shall not be included in satisfying the required minimum INVESTMENT IN PROPERTIES. Additionally, in determining the amount committed to INVESTMENT IN PROPERTIES, such calculation shall not take into account any FRONT-END FEES.

   If CAPITAL CONTRIBUTIONS are paid on an installment basis, the FRONT-END FEE shall be paid to the SPONSOR pro rata as installments are paid.

   2. At a minimum, the SPONSOR shall commit a percentage of the CAPITAL CONTRIBUTIONS to INVESTMENT IN PROPERTIES which is equal to 82% for PROGRAMS which make or invest in mortgage loans and for all other PROGRAMS is equal to the greater of:
      (a) 80% of the CAPITAL CONTRIBUTIONS reduced by .1625% for each 1% of financing of PROGRAM properties; or
      (b) 67% of the CAPITAL CONTRIBUTIONS.

      COMMENT: The expenses incurred and level of effort required in locating and funding mortgages is not as high as that which is required in locating and closing upon real properties. In addition, the fees traditionally payable in the mortgage funding and acquisition area are much lower than those payable in real property acquisitions. For example, real estate commissions which can represent a large portion of the front-end fees in a traditional PROGRAM are not present in a mortgage PROGRAM. Consequently, the FRONT END FEES permissible in a mortgage PROGRAM are less than those permissible in the more traditional real estate equity PROGRAMS.

   3. If the SPONSOR enters into an INVESTMENT IN PROPERTIES commitment in excess of that specified in Section 2. above, the following mutually exclusive forms of compensation are viewed as not unreasonable alternatives to FRONT END FEES:

(a) the SPONSOR may take an additional promotional interest in the net proceeds remaining from the sale or refinancing of the properties after payment of such proceeds to PARTICIPANTS in an amount equal to 100% of CAPITAL CONTRIBUTIONS, equal to 1% for each 1% of additional INVESTMENT IN PROPERTIES; or

(b) the SPONSOR may take a CARRIED INTEREST which participates in the net proceeds remaining from the sale or refinancing of properties only after payment of such proceeds to PARTICIPANTS in an amount equal to 100% of CAPITAL CONTRIBUTIONS, equal to 1% for the first 2% of additional INVESTMENT IN PROPERTIES, plus 1% for the next 1.5% of additional INVESTMENT IN PROPERTIES, plus 1% for each 1% of additional INVESTMENT IN PROPERTIES thereafter; or

(c) the SPONSOR may take a fully participating CARRIED INTEREST equal to 1% for the first 2.5% of additional INVESTMENT IN PROPERTIES, 1% for the next 2% of additional INVESTMENT IN PROPERTIES, and 1% for each 1% of additional INVESTMENT IN PROPERTIES thereafter.

COMMENT: A CARRIED INTEREST may not be taken other than on the basis of the foregoing.

4. For PROGRAMS whose total CAPITAL CONTRIBUTIONS do not exceed 2 million, the ADMINISTRATOR may reduce the required amount of INVESTMENT IN PROPERTIES to that permitted by 2 (b) above notwithstanding the level of indebtedness encumbering the PROGRAM'S properties.

COMMENT: The purpose of the section is to require the SPONSOR to invest a specified percentage of CAPITAL CONTRIBUTIONS in the acquisition of properties and use the balance for FRONT-END FEES in any manner he wishes, or defer a portion of the FRONT-END FEES to a promotional interest.

This will avoid the necessity of having no attempt to establish the reasonableness of the various FRONT- END FEES on an individual basis. However, the formula continues the tradition of the Guidelines by allowing the SPONSOR's fee to increase as leverage is employed to acquire properties. The PROSPECTUS should include an example demonstrating the mechanics of the formula.

To calculate the percent of financing of PROGRAM properties in Section 2., divide the amount of financing of by the PURCHASE PRICE OF PROPERTY, excluding FRONT-END FEES. The Quotient is multiplied by .1625% to determine the percentage to be deducted from 80%.

The following are examples of application of the formula using CAPITAL CONTRIBUTIONS of $1 Million in each case:

(1) No financing—80% to be committed to INVESTMENT IN PROPERTIES.
(2) 50% financing—50 × .1625% = 8.125%
80% − 8.125% = 71.875% to be committed to INVESTMENT IN PROPERTIES.
(3) 80% financing—80 × .1625% = 13%
80% − 13% = 67% to be committed to INVESTMENT IN PROPERTIES.

Notwithstanding the language in sub. 4 above, the 2 million dollar limitation is intended to be a benchmark figure and may be adjusted upward or downward by an Administrator based on the marketplace in his jurisdiction.

D. PROGRAM MANAGEMENT FEE
1. A general partner of a PROGRAM OWNING unimproved land shall be entitled to annual compensation not exceeding 1/4 of 1% of the cost of such unimproved land for operating the PROGRAM until such time as the land is sold or improvement of the land commences by the limited partnership. In no event shall this fee exceed a cumulative total of 2% of the original cost of the land regardless of the number of years held.
2. A general partner of a PROGRAM holding property in government subsidized projects shall be entitled to annual compensation not exceeding 1/2 of 1% of the cost of such property for operating the PROGRAM until such time as the property is sold.
3. PROGRAM MANAGEMENT FEES other than as set forth above shall be prohibited.

E. Promotional Interest. An interest in the PROGRAM will be allowed as a promotional interest and PROGRAM MANAGEMENT FEE, provided the amount or percentage of such interest is reasonable. Such an interest will be considered presumptively reasonable if it is within the limitations expressed below:
1. An interest equal to 25% of cash to be distributed from the net proceeds remaining from the sale or refinancing of properties after payment to investors from such proceeds, an amount equal to 100% of CAPITAL CONTRIBUTIONS, plus an amount equal to 6% of CAPITAL CONTRIBUTIONS per annum cumulative (the 6% cumulative return may be reduced, but not below zero, by the aggregate amount of prior distributions to investors from CASH AVAILABLE FOR DISTRIBUTION); or

COMMENT: The SPONSOR should not participate in sale or refinancing proceeds until the PARTICIPANTS have received a minimum return on their CAPITAL CONTRIBUTIONS.

However, the 6% subordination requirement may be waived in the situation where the PROGRAM invests more than 60% of its CAPITAL

Appendix J: NASAA Guidelines

CONTRIBUTIONS in newly constructed or totally rehabilitated properties, including housing subsidized under the National Housing Act or similar such programs.

2. An interest equal to:
   (i) 10% of distributions from CASH AVAILABLE FOR DISTRIBUTION; and
   (ii) 15% of cash to be distributed from the net proceeds remaining from the sale or refinancing of properties after payment to investors from such proceeds, an amount equal to 100% of CAPITAL CONTRIBUTIONS, plus an amount equal to 6% of CAPITAL CONTRIBUTIONS per annum cumulative. The 6% cumulative return may be reduced, but not below zero, by the aggregate amount of prior distributions to investors from CASH AVAILABLE FOR DISTRIBUTION.

   COMMENT: In addition to a 6% per annum cumulative return, investors in traditional equity real estate limited partnerships receive:
   (i) Capital gains through product appreciation:
   (ii) Federal income taxation deductions during the early years of property operations leading to all or a portion of cash distributions being treated as a return of capital for taxation purposes:
   (iii) Equity buildup through a reduction of mortgage loans.

   Since Programs which make or invest in mortgage loans are income oriented and investors in such Programs forego a major portion of the benefits set forth in (i) through (iii) above, the per annum cumulative return for such Programs shall be 10%.

3. For purposes of this Section, the CAPITAL CONTRIBUTION of the investors shall only be reduced by a cash distribution to investors of the proceeds from the sale or refinancing of properties. In addition, the cumulative return to each investor shall commence no later than the end of the calendar quarter in which his CAPITAL CONTRIBUTION is made.

4. Dissolution and liquidation of the partnership. The distribution of assets upon dissolution and liquidation of the partnership shall conform to the applicable subordination provisions of subsections 1 and 2(ii) herein, and appropriate language shall be included in the partnership agreement.

   COMMENT: For PROGRAMS which make or invest in mortgage loans, all funds which constitute repayment of loan principal or which represent an equity interest in sale or refinancing proceeds of a real property underlying a loan shall be subordinated and apportioned in the same manner as provided in Section IV.E.1. or 2.(ii) above.

F. Real Estate Brokerage Commissions on Resale or Property. The total compensation paid to all PERSONS for the sale of a PROGRAM property shall be limited to a COMPETITIVE REAL ESTATE COMMISSION, not to exceed 6% of the contract price for the sale of the property. If the SPONSOR provides a substantial amount of the services in the sales effort, he may receive up to one-half of the COMPETITIVE REAL ESTATE COMMISSION, not to exceed 3%, and subordinated as in E. above. If the SPONSOR participates with an independent broker on resale, the subordination requirement shall apply only to the commission earned by the SPONSOR.

> COMMENT: If the SPONSOR provides a substantial amount of services in connection with the sale, he may then receive up to 1/2 of the brokerage commission, to a maximum of 3%, with the fee subordinated, to a return of 100% of CAPITAL CONTRIBUTIONS plus a 6% annual cumulative return, regardless of the type of property acquired by the PROGRAM.

G. PROPERTY MANAGEMENT FEE. Should the SPONSOR or its AFFILIATES perform property management services permitted under section IV.A.1.g. of these guidelines, the fees paid to the SPONSOR or its AFFILIATES shall be the lesser of the maximum fees set forth in subsection 1. through 3. below or the fees which are competitive for similar services in the same geographic area. Included in such fees shall be bookkeeping services and fees paid to non-related persons for property management services.

1. In the case of a residential property, the maximum PROPERTY MANAGEMENT FEE (including all rent-up, leasing, and re-leasing fees and bonuses, and leasing related services, paid to any person) shall be 5% of the gross revenues from such property.

2. In the case of industrial and commercial property, except as set forth in 3. below, the maximum PROPERTY MANAGEMENT FEE from such leases shall be 6% of the gross revenues where the SPONSOR or its AFFILIATES includes leasing, re-leasing and leasing related services. Conversely the maximum PROPERTY MANAGEMENT FEE from such leases shall be 3% of the gross revenues where the SPONSOR or its AFFILIATES do not perform the leasing, re-leasing and leasing related services with respect to the property.

3. In the case of industrial and commercial properties which are leased on a long term (ten or more years) net (or similar) bases, the maximum PROPERTY MANAGEMENT FEE from such leases shall be 1% of the gross revenues, except for a one time initial leasing fee of 3% of the gross revenues on each lease payable over the first five full years of the original term of the lease.

> COMMENT: This section provides a method to calculate the allowable fees for property management by the SPONSOR. The amount of the fee will be based upon, if competitive, the kinds of property management services performed by the SPONSOR for various types of rental

properties and lease arrangements. This section prohibits the SPONSOR from receiving fees for the same service, for which the project has incurred costs to any other PERSON. The salary and fringe benefits of the on-site property personnel may be separately charged, as an operating expense, so long as such manager is not an officer, director, or controlling person of the SPONSOR.

This section is not intended to preclude the charging of a separate competitive fee for the one-time initial rent-up or leasing-up of a newly constructed property if such service is not included in the PURCHASE PRICE OF PROPERTY paid by the PROGRAM. New construction could include a total rehabilitation.

Under Section 3., the initial leasing fee may be taken during each of the first five years on any lease which may include exercised renewals during that period; however, no initial leasing fee may be collected beyond five years for renewals or extensions with the same tenant or tenants's assignee.

The fee limitation would be considered presumptively reasonable unless the SPONSOR can demonstrate, to the satisfaction of the ADMINISTRATOR, thru empirical data that a higher competitive fee in the geographic area for the service rendered, the type of property to be acquired and the terms of the management contract is justified.

H. Insurance Services.

The SPONSOR or his AFFILIATE may provide insurance brokerage services in connection with obtaining insurance on the PROGRAM'S property so long as the cost of providing such service, including cost of the insurance, is no greater than the lowest quote obtained from two unaffiliated insurance agencies and the coverage and terms are likewise comparable. In no event may such services be provided by the SPONSOR or his AFFILIATE unless they are independently engaged in the business of providing such services to other than AFFILIATES and at least 75% of their insurance brokerage service gross revenue is derived from other than AFFILIATES.

I. Mortgage Servicing Fee - The SPONSOR or his AFFILIATE may provide mortgage services in programs which make or invest in mortgage loans for which he may be paid a fee which when added to all other fees paid in connection with the servicing of a particular mortgage does not exceed the lesser of the customary, competitive fee for the provision of such mortgage services on that type of mortgage or 1/4 of 1% of the principal outstanding in such loan.

V. CONFLICTS OF INTEREST AND INVESTMENT RESTRICTIONS

A. Sales, Leases and Loans.

1. Sales and Leases to PROGRAM

A PROGRAM shall not purchase or lease property in which a SPONSOR has an interest unless:

a. The transaction occurs at the formation of the PROGRAM and is fully disclosed in its PROSPECTUS or offering circular, and

b. The property is sold upon terms fair to the PROGRAM and at a price not in excess of its appraised value, and

c. The cost of the property and any improvements thereon to the SPONSOR is clearly established. If the SPONSOR's cost was less than the price to be paid by the program, the price to be paid by the PROGRAM will not be deemed fair, regardless of the appraised value, unless some material change has occurred to the property which would increase the value since the SPONSOR acquired the property. Material factors may include the passage of a significant amount of time (but in no event less than 2 years), the assumption by the promoter of the risk of obtaining a re-zoning of the property and its subsequent re-zoning, or some other extraordinary event which in fact increases the value of the property.

d. The provisions of this subsection notwithstanding, the SPONSOR may purchase property in its own name (and assume loans in connection therewith) and temporarily hold title thereto for the purpose of facilitating the acquisition of such property or the borrowing of money or obtaining of financing for the PROGRAM, or completion of construction of the property, or any other purpose related to the business of the PROGRAM, provided that such property is purchased by the PROGRAM for a price no greater than the cost of such property to the SPONSOR, except compensation in accordance with Section IV above of these Rules, and provided there is no difference in interest rates of the loans secured by the property at the time acquired by the SPONSOR and the time acquired by the PROGRAM, nor any other benefit arising out of such transaction to the SPONSOR apart from compensation otherwise permitted by these Rules.

2. Sales and Leases to SPONSOR. The PROGRAM will not ordinarily be permitted to sell or lease property to the SPONSOR except that the PROGRAM may lease property to the SPONSOR under a lease-back arrangement made at the outset and on terms no more favorable to the SPONSOR than those offered other persons and fully described in the PROSPECTUS.

3. Loans. No loans may be made by the PROGRAM to the SPONSOR or an AFFILIATE. PROGRAMS which make or invest in mortgage loans may provide such loans to PROGRAMS formed by or affiliated with such persons in those circumstances in which such activities have been fully justified to the ADMINISTRATOR. These affiliated transactions must at the minimum meet the following conditions:

   (a) the circumstances under which the loans will be made and the actual terms of the loans must be fully disclosed in the prospectus or;

(b) an independent and qualified adviser must issue a letter of opinion to the effect that any proposed loan to an AFFILIATE of the PROGRAM is fair and at least as favorable to the PROGRAM as a loan to an unaffiliated borrower in similar circumstances. In addition, the SPONSORS will be required to obtain a letter of opinion from the independent adviser in connection with any disposition, renegotiation or other subsequent transaction involving loans made to a SPONSOR or an AFFILIATE of the SPONSOR. The adviser's compensation must be paid by the SPONSOR and not reimburseable by the PROGRAM.

> COMMENT A: Full disclosure of the terms of the loans and the circumstances under which they will be made includes, but is not limited to, identification and description of the borrower(s) and the property(s) securing the loan(s).
>
> COMMENT B: Model loan documents, or, at a minimum, a discussion of the parameters within which loans will be made to SPONSORS or AFFILIATES should be included in the prospectus for purposes of V.A.3.(b).
>
> In order for the adviser to be considered qualified and independent the following conditions must be met:
> (i) The adviser must be a long established, nationally recognized investment banking firm, accounting firm, mortgage banking firm, bank, real estate financial consulting firm or advisory firm:
> (ii) The adviser must have a staff of real estate professionals;
> (iii) The compensation of the adviser must be determined and embodied in a written contract before an opinion is rendered.
> (iv) If an adviser has been engaged to render a fairness opinion who is not the adviser previously engaged to render this or the preceding fairness opinion, the SPONSOR shall inform the investors (by no later than the next annual report) of the date when such new adviser was engaged, and whether there were any disagreements with the former adviser on any matters of valuation, assumptions, methodology, accounting principles and practice, or disclosure, which disagreements, if not resolved to the satisfaction of the former adviser would have caused him to make reference, in connection with the fairness opinion, to the subject matter of the disagreement or decline to give an opinion.
> (v) The compensation of the adviser must be paid by the SPONSOR and the SPONSOR may not claim reimbursement from the PROGRAM for such expenses.

(vi) The adviser, directly or indirectly, has no interest in, nor any material business or professional relationship with, the PROGRAM, the SPONSOR, the borrower, or any AFFILIATES thereof. Independence will be considered to be impaired if, for example, during the period of the adviser's engagement, or at the time of expressing his opinion, he or his firm: (i) had, or was committed to acquire any direct or indirect ownership interest in the PROGRAM, SPONSOR, borrower, or AFFILIATES thereof, or (ii) had any joint closely held business investment with the PROGRAM, SPONSOR, borrower, or any AFFILIATE thereof, which was material in relation the adviser's net worth; or, (iii) had any loan to or from the PROGRAM, SPONSOR, borrower, or AFFILIATES thereof.

The foregoing examples are not intended to be all-inclusive. However, for purposes of determining whether or not the business or professional relationship or joint investment is material, the gross revenue derived by the adviser from the PROGRAM, the SPONSOR, the borrower, and their AFFILIATES shall be deemed material per se if it exceeds 5% of the annual gross revenue derived by the adviser from all sources or exceed 5% of the individual's or the adviser's net worth (on an estimated fair market value basis).

(c) Loans made to third parties, the proceeds of which are used to purchase or refinance property in which the SPONSOR or an AFFILIATE has an equity or security interest, must meet the requirements of V.A.3.(a) or (b).

COMMENT: In this circustance, compliance with V.A.3.(a) would require additional disclosure of the SPONSORS' or the AFFILIATES' interest in such property along with a description of the terms and the circumstances surrounding such interest.

4. Dealing with Related PROGRAMS. A PROGRAM shall not acquire property from a PROGRAM in which the SPONSOR has an interest.

COMMENT: This provision prohibits transactions among PROGRAMS where the SPONSOR has an interest whereas section V.A.1. above relates to properties where the SPONSOR has an interest.

B. Exchange of Limited Partnership Interests. The PROGRAM may not acquire property in exchange for limited partnership interests, except for property which is described in the PROSPECTUS which will be changed immediately upon effectiveness. In addition, such exchange shall meet the following conditions:

1. A provision for such exchange must be set forth in the partnership agreement, and appropriate disclosure as to tax effects of such exchange are set forth in the PROSPECTUS;

Appendix J: NASAA Guidelines 525

2. The property to be acquired must come within the objectives of the PROGRAM;

3. The purchase price assigned to the property shall be no higher than the value supported by an appraisal prepared by an independent qualified appraiser;

4. Each limited partnership interest must be valued at no less than market value if there is a market or if there is no market, fair market value of the PROGRAM's assets as determined by an independent appraiser within the last 90 days, less its liabilities, divided by the number of interests outstanding;

5. No more than one-half of the interests issued by the PROGRAM shall have been issued in exchange for property;

6. No securities sales or underwriting commissions shall be paid in connection with such exchange.

C. Exclusive Agreement. A PROGRAM shall not give a SPONSOR an exclusive right to sell or exclusive employment to sell property for the PROGRAM.

D. Commissions on Reinvestment or Distribution. A PROGRAM shall not pay, directly or indirectly, a commission or fee (except as permitted under section IV) to a SPONSOR in connection with the reinvestment or distribution of the proceeds of the resale, exchange, or refinancing of PROGRAM PROPERTY.

COMMENT: This section clarifies that financing, refinancing, or servicing fees are subject to the limitations of section IV.C.

E. Services Rendered to the Program by the SPONSOR.

1. Expenses of the PROGRAM.

   (a) All expenses of the PROGRAM shall be billed directly to and paid by the PROGRAM. The SPONSOR may be reimbursed for the actual cost of goods and materials used for or by the PROGRAM and obtained from entities unaffiliated with the SPONSOR. The SPONSOR may be reimbursed for the administrative services necessary to the prudent operation of the PROGRAM provided that the reimbursement shall be at the lower of the SPONSOR'S actual cost or the amount the PROGRAM would be required to pay to independent parties for comparable administrative services in the same geographic location. No reimbursement shall be permitted for services for which the SPONSOR is entitled to compensation by way of a separate fee. Excluded from the allowable reimbursement (except as permitted under IV.C.1.) shall be:

   (i) rent or depreciation, utilities, capital equipment, other administrative items; and

   (ii) salaries, fringe benefits, travel expenses, and other administrative items incurred or allocated to any controlling persons of the SPONSOR or AFFILIATES.

Controlling person, for purpose of this section, includes but is not limited to, any person, whatever their title, who performs functions for the SPONSOR similar to those of:

(1) Chairman or member of the Board of Directors;

(2) Executive Management, such as the
    (1) President,
    (ii) Vice-President or Senior Vice-President,
    (iii) Corporate Secretary,
    (iv) Treasurer;

(3) Senior Management such as the Vice-President of an operating division who reports directly to Executive Management; or

(4) Those holding 5% or more equity interest in the SPONSOR or a person having the power to direct or cause the direction of the SPONSOR, whether through the ownership of voting securities, by contract, or otherwise.

(b) The annual PROGRAM report must contain a breakdown of the costs reimbursed to the SPONSOR. Within the scope of the annual audit of the SPONSOR'S financial statement, the independent certified public accountants must verify the allocation of such costs to the PROGRAM. The method of verification shall at minimum provide:

(1) A review of the time records of individual employees, the costs of whose services were reimbursed;

(2) A review of the specific nature of the work performed by each such employee.

The methods of verification shall be in accordance with generally accepted auditing standards and shall accordingly include such tests of the accounting records and such other auditing procedures which the SPONSOR'S independent certified public accountants consider appropriate in the circumstance. The additional costs of such verification will be itemized by said accountants on a PROGRAM by PROGRAM basis and may be reimbursed to the SPONSOR by the PROGRAM in accordance with this subsection only to the extent that such reimbursement when added to the cost for admistrative services rendered does not exceed the competitive rate for such services as determined above.

The PROSPECTUS must disclose in tabular form an estimate of such proposed expenses for the next fiscal year together with a breakdown by year of such expenses reimbursed in each of the last five public programs formed by the SPONSOR.

    COMMENT: This section permits the SPONSOR to be reimbursed for a portion of the costs incurred in performing certain administrative functions for the PROGRAM provided the SPONSOR is both qualified to perform such functions and does so at a cost no greater to the PROGRAM than that which an unaffiliated PERSON would charge the PROGRAM. Regardless of the capacity in which controlling persons of the SPONSOR serve the PROGRAM, their salaries may not be allocated to the PROGRAM.

2. Other Services. No other services may be performed by the SPONSOR for the program except in extraordinary circumstances fully justified to the ADMINISTRATOR. As a minimum, self-dealing arrangements must meet the following criteria:

   a. the compensation, price or fee therefore must be comparable and competitive with the compensation, price or fee of any other PERSON who is rendering comparable services or selling or leasing comparable goods which could reasonably be made available to the PROGRAMS and shall be on competitive terms, and
   b. the fees and other terms of the contract shall be fully disclosed, and
   c. the SPONSOR must be previously engaged in the business of rendering such services or selling or leasing such goods, independently of the PROGRAM and as an ordinary and ongoing business, and
   d. all services or goods for which the SPONSOR is to receive compensation shall be embodied in a written contract which precisely describes the services to be rendered and all compensation to be paid, which contract may only be modified by a vote of the majority of the limited partners. Said contract shall contain a clause allowing termination without penalty on 60 days notice.

   COMMENT: Where the services are available elsewhere from unaffiliated parties, there would be a presumption that there are no extraordinary circumstances. Extraordinary circumstances would only be presumed where there is an emergency situation requiring immediate action by the SPONSOR, and the service is not immediately available from unaffiliated parties. Extraordinary circumstances shall, in no event, include general and administrative expenses, except as otherwise provided herein.

F. Rebates, Kickbacks and Reciprocal Arrangements.

   1. No rebates or give-ups may be received by the SPONSOR nor may the SPONSOR participate in any reciprocal business arrangements which would circumvent these Rules. Furthermore the PROSPECTUS and PROGRAM charter documents shall contain language prohibiting the above as well as language prohibiting reciprocal business arrangements which would circumvent the restrictions against dealing with AFFILIATES or promoters.
   2. No SPONSOR shall directly or indirectly pay or award any commissions or other compensation to any PERSON engaged by a potential investor for investment advice as an inducement to such advisor to advise the purchaser of interests in a particular PROGRAM; provided, however, that this clause shall not prohibit the normal sales commissions payable to

a registered broker-dealer or other properly licensed PERSON for selling PROGRAM INTERESTS.

G. Commingling of Funds. The funds of a PROGRAM shall not be commingled with the funds of any other PERSON. Nothing contained in this Section however, shall prohibit a SPONSOR from establishing a master fiduciary account pursuant to which separate subtrust accounts are established for the benefit of affiliated limited partnerships, provided, that PROGRAM funds are protected from claims of such other partnerships and/or creditors. The prohibition of this Section shall not apply to investments meeting the requirements of Section V.H.

H. Investments of Other PROGRAMS.

1. Investments in limited partnership interests of another PROGRAM shall be prohibited; however, nothing herein shall preclude the investment in general partnerships or ventures which own and operate a particular property provided the PROGRAM acquires a controlling interest in such other ventures or general partnerships (except as permitted by subsection 3.). In such event, duplicate property management or other fees shall not be permitted.

2. Such prohibitions shall not apply to PROGRAMS participating in the subsidized housing provisions of the National Housing Act or any similar programs that may be enacted, but unless prohibited by the applicable federal statute, such partnership (herein referred to as lower tier partnership) shall provide for its limited partners all of the rights and obligations required to be provided by the original PROGRAM in Section VII of these guidelines.

    COMMENT: The investment by a limited partnership in another limited partnership is restricted to investment in those PROGRAMS which have been organized and are regulated pursuant to the subsidized housing provisions of the National Housing Act, or similar state law. This position is based on the recognition that these PROGRAMS have strict compensation parameters outlined by the applicable legislation, and historically have been organized as multiple level limited partnerships. These PROGRAMS will continue to be monitored to determine that duplicative management or other fees are not being paid.

3. The PROGRAM shall be permitted to invest in joint venture arrangements with another PROGRAM formed by the SPONSOR if all the following conditions are met:

    a. The two PROGRAMS have substantially identical investment objectives.
    b. There are no duplicate property management or other fees.
    c. The SPONSOR compensation should be substantially identical in each PROGRAM.

d. The PROGRAM must have a right of first refusal to buy if the other PROGRAM wishes to sell property held in the joint venture.
e. The investment of each PROGRAM is on substantially the same terms and conditions.
f. The PROSPECTUS must disclose the potential risk of impasse on joint venture decisions since neither PROGRAM controls and the potential risk that while one PROGRAM may buy the property from the other joint venturer, in the event of a sale, it may not have the resources to do so.

> COMMENT: In certain situations, it would be to the advantage of the PROGRAM to be able to invest in a joint venture with another PROGRAM where neither PROGRAM has sufficient money to make the entire investment even if the PROGRAM does not acquire a controlling interest. However, in order to provide the necessary protections, there is a need to not only require full disclosure of the joint venture arrangements but also to set out substantive standards that must be adhered to in order to assure these protections.
>
> For PROGRAMS which make or invest in mortgage loans, joint venture arrangements are permitted so long as joint venture arrangements with affiliates satisfy the requirements of Section V.A.3. herein.

I. Lending Practices.
  1. On loans, made available to the PROGRAM by the SPONSOR, the SPONSOR may not receive interest or similar charges or fees in excess of the amount which would be charged by unrelated lending institutions on comparable loans for the same purpose, in the same locality of the property if the loan is made in connection with a particular property. No prepayment charge or penalty shall be required by the SPONSOR on a loan to the PROGRAM secured by either a first or a junior or all-inclusive trust deed, mortgage or encumbrance on the property, except to the extent that such prepayment charge or penalty is attributable to the underlying encumbrance. The sponsor shall be prohibited from providing FINANCING for the PROGRAM, except:
     a. As permitted by subsection 2 of this section V.I.1.; or
     b. Where FINANCING is being provided by or acquired from an affiliated PROGRAM which makes or invests in mortgage loans. In such instances, the provisions of section V.A.3. of the Guidelines shall be applicable; and, to recognize potential conflicts of interest, there will be independent advisers for each publicly registered party to the transaction.

     > COMMENT: Where financing is being provided by a mortgage pool program affiliated with the SPONSOR, the provisions of

V.A.3. of the Guidelines shall be applicable. In addition, in such instances, to provide for arms length negotiation, there will be independent advisers for both the lender and borrower.

2. An "all-inclusive" or "wrap-around" note and deed of trust (the "all-inclusive note" herein) may be used to finance the purchase of property by the PROGRAM only if the following conditions are complied with:

   a. The SPONSOR under the all-inclusive note shall not receive interest on the amount of the underlying encumbrance included in the all-inclusive note in excess of that payable to the lender on that underlying encumbrance;

   b. The PROGRAM shall receive credit on its obligation under the all-inclusive note for payments made directly on the underlying encumbrance, and

   c. A paying agent, ordinarily a bank, escrow company, or savings and loan, shall collect payments (other than any initial payment of prepaid interest or loan points not to be applied to the underlying encumbrance) on the all-inclusive note and make disbursements therefrom to the holder of the underlying encumbrance prior to making any disbursement to the holder of the all-inclusive note, subject to the requirements of subparagraph a. above, or, in the alternative, all payments on the all-inclusive and underlying note shall be made directly by the PROGRAM.

J. Development or Construction contract. The SPONSOR will not be permitted to construct or develop properties, or render any services in connection with such development or construction unless all of the following conditions are satisfied:

1. The transactions occur at the formation of the PROGRAM.

2. The specific terms of the development and construction of identifiable properties are ascertainable and fully disclosed in the PROSPECTUS.

3. The purchase price to be paid by the PROGRAM is based upon a firm contract price which in no event can exceed the cost of the land and the SPONSOR's cost of construction. For the purposes of this subdivision, cost of construction includes the contractor or CONSTRUCTION FEE customarily paid for services as a general contractor, provided, however, that any overhead of the general contractor is not charged to the PROGRAM or included in the cost of construction.

4. In the case of construction, the only fees paid to the SPONSOR in connection with such project shall consist of a CONSTRUCTION FEE for action as a general contractor, which fees must be comparable and competitive with the fee of disinterested PERSONS rendering comparable services (excluding, however, any overhead of the contractor) and a real estate commission in connection with the acquisition of the land, if ap-

Appendix J: NASAA Guidelines 531

propriate under the circumstances. Any such real estate commission shall be subject to the provisions of Section IV.C..

5. The SPONSOR demonstrates the presence of extraordinary circumstances as required by subsection 2. of Section V.E. and otherwise complies with subdivisions b., c., and d. thereunder.

K. Completion Bond Requirements.

(a) The completion of property acquired which is under construction shall be guaranteed at the price contracted by an adequate completion bond or other satisfactory arrangements.

(b) For purposes of this Section, satisfactory arrangements include, but are not limited to, the following:

(1) A written guarantee of completion by a person, supported by financial statements demonstrating sufficient net worth or adequately collateralized by other real or personal properties or other persons guarantees.

(2) A retention of a reasonable portion of the purchase consideration as a potential offset to such purchase consideration in the event the seller does not perform in accordance with the purchase and sale agreement.

(c) Other satisfactory arrangements to guarantee completion may be made, provided they are disclosed in the prospectus and the prior written approval of the ADMINISTRATOR has been obtained.

L. Requirement for Real Property Appraisal.

All real property acquisitions must be supported by an appraisal prepared by a competent, independent appraiser. The appraisal shall be maintained in the SPONSOR's records for at least five years, and shall be available for inspection and duplication by any PARTICIPANT. The PROSPECTUS shall contain notice of this right.

M. Mortgage Loan PROGRAMS. A PROGRAM will not be permitted to invest in or make mortgage loans unless a real property appraisal is obtained as provided for in Paragraph L of this Section for each mortgage loan and a mortgagee's or owner's title insurance policy or commitment as to the priority of a mortgage or the condition of title is obtained. Further, the sponsor of mortgage loan programs shall observe the following policies in connection with investing in or making mortgage loans:

1. The PROGRAM may not invest in or make mortgage loans on any one property which would exceed, in the aggregate, an amount equal to 20% of the CAPITAL CONTRIBUTIONS to be raised by the program;

2. The PROGRAM may not invest in or make mortgage loans to or from any one borrower which would exceed, in the aggregate, an amount greater than 20% of the CAPITAL CONTRIBUTIONS to be raised by the program;

3. The PROGRAM shall not invest in real estate contracts of sale otherwise known as land sale contracts unless such contracts of sale are in recordable form and are appropriately recorded in the chain of title;

4. The PROGRAM may not invest in or make mortgage loans on unimproved real property in an amount in excess of 25% of the CAPITAL CONTRIBUTIONS to be raised by the program;

5. The PROGRAM shall not make or invest in mortgage loans on any one property if the aggregate amount of all mortgage loans outstanding on the property, including the loans of the PROGRAM, would exceed an amount equal to 85% of the appraised value of the property as determined by an independent appraisal unless substantial justification exists because of the presence of other underwriting criteria;

   COMMENT: This restriction applies to all loans including construction loans.

6. The PROGRAM is permitted to borrow money to the extent necessary to prevent defaults under existing loans; when the program has taken over the operation of property and there is a need for additional capital; to pay organizational and/or offering expenses.

   COMMENT: This Section provides certain minimum standards in connection with the investment in or making of mortgage loans by a program. The standards may be exceeded for a particular registration if the mortgage loans are supported by sound underwriting criteria, such as the net worth of the borrower; the credit rating of the borrower based on historical financial performance; or collateral adequate to justify waiver from application of this section. The standards may also be exceeded where program mortgage loans are or will be insured or guaranteed by a government or a government agency; where the loan is secured by the pledge or assignment of other real estate or another real estate mortgage; where rents are assigned under a lease where a tenant or tenants have demonstrated through historical net worth and cash flow the ability to satisfy the terms of the lease; or where similar criteria is presented satisfactory to the Administrator.

VI. NON-SPECIFIED PROPERTY PROGRAMS. The following special provisions shall apply to NON-SPECIFIED PROPERTY PROGRAMS:

   A. Minimum Capitalization. A NON-SPECIFIED PROPERTY PROGRAM shall provide for a minimum gross proceeds from the offering of not less than $1,000,000.00 to be available for INVESTMENT IN PROPERTIES.

   B. Experience of SPONSOR. For NON-SPECIFIED PROPERTY PROGRAMS, the SPONSOR or at least one of its principals must establish that he has had the equivalent of not less than five years experience in the real estate business in an executive capacity and two years experience in the management and acquisition of the type of properties to be acquired or otherwise must demonstrate to the satisfaction of the ADMINISTRATOR that he has sufficient knowledge and experience to acquire and manage the type of properties proposed to be acquired by the NON-SPECIFIED PROPERTY PROGRAM.

C. Statement of Investment Objectives. A NON-SPECIFIED PROPERTY PROGRAM shall state types of properties in which it proposes to invest, such as first-user apartment projects, subsequent-user apartment projects, shopping centers, office buildings, unimproved land, etc., and the size and scope of such projects shall be consistent with the objectives of the PROGRAM and the experience of the SPONSORS. As a minimum the following restrictions on investment objectives shall be observed.

1. Unimproved or non-income producing property shall not be acquired except in amounts and upon terms which can be financed by the PROGRAM's proceeds or from cash available for distribution from operations. Investments in such property shall not exceed 10% of the gross proceeds of the offering. Properties which are expected to produce income within a reasonable period of time shall not be considered non-income producing. For purposes of this subsection two years shall be deemed to be presumptively reasonable.

2. Investments in junior trust deeds and other similar obligations shall be prohibited, except for junior trust deeds which arise from the sale of PROGRAM properties.

> COMMENT: This provision shall not be applicable to: (1) those PROGRAMS formed solely to make or invest in mortgage loans, and (2) in the case of programs whose objectives are to invest in mortgage loans and acquire real properties to that portion of net offering proceeds which are utilized to make or invest in mortgage loans. The restrictions on these PROGRAMS are governed, in part, by Section V.M. of these GUIDELINES.

3. The manner in which acquisitions will be financed including the use of an all-inclusive note or wrap-around, and the leveraging to be employed shall all be fully set forth in the statement of investment objectives.

4. The Statement shall indicate whether the PROGRAM will enter into joint venture arrangements and the projected extent thereof.

D. Period of Offering and Expenditure of Proceeds. No offering of securities in a NON-SPECIFIED PROPERTY PROGRAM may extend for more than one year from the date of effectiveness. While the proceeds of an offering are awaiting investment in real property, the proceeds may be temporarily invested in short-term highly liquid investments where there is appropriate safety of principal, such as U.S. Treasury Bonds or Bills. Any proceeds of the offering of securities not invested within two years from the date of effectiveness (except for necessary operating capital) shall be distributed pro rata to the partners as a return of capital so long as the adjusted INVESTMENT IN PROPERITES is in compliance with section IV.C..

E. Multiple Programs. The method for the allocation of the acquisition of properties by two or more programs of the same SPONSOR seeking to acquire similar types of properties shall be reasonable. The method also shall be described in the prospectus.

VII. RIGHTS AND OBLIGATIONS OF PARTICIPANTS.
  A. Meetings. Meetings of the PROGRAM may be called by the SPONSOR or the PARTICIPANTS holding more than 10% of the then outstanding limited partnership interests, for any matters for which the PARTICIPANTS may vote as set forth in the limited partnership agreement. A list of the names and addresses of all PARTICIPANTS shall be maintained as part of the books and records of the limited partnership and shall be made available on request to any PARTICIPANT or his representative at his cost. Upon receipt of a written request either in PERSON or by certified mail stating the purpose(s) of the meeting, the SPONSOR shall provide all PARTICIPANTS within ten days after receipt of said request, written notice (either in PERSON or by certified mail) of a meeting and the purpose of such meeting to be held on a date not less than fifteen nor more than sixty days after receipt of said request, at a time and place convenient to PARTICIPANTS.
  B. Voting Rights of Limited partners. To the extent the law of the state in question is not inconsistent, the limited partnership agreement must provide that a majority of the then outstanding limited partnership interests may, without the necessity for concurrence by the SPONSOR, vote to: (1) amend the limited partnership agreement, (2) dissolve the PROGRAM, (3) remove the SPONSOR and elect a new SPONSOR, and (4) approve or disapprove the sale of all or substantially all of the assets of the PROGRAM. The agreement should provide for a method of valuation of the SPONSOR interest, upon removal of the SPONSOR, that would not be unfair to the PARTICIPANTS. The agreement should also provide for a successor SPONSOR where the only SPONSOR of the PROGRAM is an individual.
  C. Reports to Holders of Limited Partnership Interests. The partnership agreement shall provide that the SPONSOR shall cause to be prepared and distributed to the holders of PROGRAM INTERESTS during each year the following reports:
    1. In the case of a PROGRAM registered under SECTION 12(g) of the Securities Exchange Act of 1934, within sixty days after the end of each quarter of the PROGRAM, a report containing:
      (i) a balance sheet, which may be unaudited,
      (ii) a statement of income for the quarter then ended, which may be unaudited, and
      (iii) a CASH FLOW statement for the quarter then ended, which may be unaudited, and
      (iv) other pertinent information regarding the PROGRAM and its activities during the quarter covered by the report;

2. In the case of all PROGRAMS, within 75 days after the end of each PROGRAM's fiscal year, all information necessary for the preparation of the limited partners' federal income tax returns;

3. In the case of all PROGRAMS, within 120 days after the end of each PROGRAM's fiscal year, an annual report containing: (i) a balance sheet as of the end of its fiscal year and statements of income, partners' equity, and changes in financial position and a CASH FLOW statement, for the year then ended, all of which, except the CASH FLOW statement, shall be prepared in accordance with generally accepted accounting principles and accompanied by an auditor's report containing an opinion of an independent certified public accountant, (ii) a report of the activities of the PROGRAM during the period covered by the report, and (iii) where forecasts have been provided to the holders of limited partnership interests, a table comparing the forecasts previously provided with the actual results during the period covered by the report. Such report shall set forth distributions to limited partners for the period covered thereby and shall separately identify distributions from: (a) CASH FLOW from operations during the period, (b) CASH FLOW from operations during a prior period which had been held as reserves, (c) proceeds from disposition of property and investments, (d) lease payments on net leases with builders and sellers, and (e) reserves from the gross proceeds of the offering originally obtained from the limited partners.

    COMMENT: See the additional reporting requirements of Section V.E.1.(b).

4. Where ASSESSMENTS have been made during any period covered by any report required by paragraphs 1., 2., and 3. hereof, then such report shall contain a detailed statement of such ASSESSMENTS and the application of the proceeds derived from such ASSESSMENTS.

D. Access to Records. Every limited partner shall at all times have access to the records of the partnership and may inspect and copy any of them. A list of the names and address, of all of the limited partners shall be maintained as part of the books and records and shall be mailed to any limited partner upon request. A reasonable charge for copy work may be charged by the PROGRAM.

E. Admission of PARTICIPANTS. Admission of PARTICIPANTS to the PROGRAM shall be subject to the following:

1. Admission of original PARTICIPANTS. Upon the original sale of partnership units by the PROGRAM, the purchasers should be admitted as limited partners not later than 15 days after the release from impound of the purchaser's funds to the PROGRAM, and thereafter purchasers should be admitted into the PROGRAM not later than the last day of the calendar month following the date their subscription was accepted by the PROGRAM. Subscriptions shall be accepted or rejected by the PROGRAM within 30 days of their receipt; if rejected, all funds should be returned to the subscriber within ten (10) business days.

2. Admission of substituted limited partners and recognition of assignees. The PROGRAM shall amend the certificates of limited partnership at least once each calendar quarter to effect the substitution of substituted PARTICIPANTS, although the SPONSOR may elect to do so more frequently.

In the case of assignments, where the assignee does not become a substituted limited partner, the PROGRAM shall recognize the assignment not later than the last day of the calendar month following receipt of notice of assignment and required documentation.

F. Redemption of PROGRAM INTERESTS. Ordinarily, the PROGRAM and the SPONSOR may not be mandatorily obligated to redeem or repurchase any of its PROGRAM INTERESTS, although the PROGRAM and the SPONSOR may not be precluded from purchasing such outstanding interests if such purchase does not impair the capital or the operation of the PROGRAM. Notwithstanding the foregoing, a real estate PROGRAM may provide for mandatory redemption rights under the following necessitous circumstances:

1. death or legal incapacity of the owner, or
2. a substantial reduction in the owner's NET WORTH or income provided that: (i) the PROGRAM has sufficient cash to make the purchase, (ii) the purchase will not be in violation of applicable legal requirements, and (iii) not more than 15% of the outstanding units are purchased in any year. Where the purchase price is not mutually agreed upon, the matter shall be submitted to arbitration.

G. Transferability of PROGRAM INTERESTS. Restrictions on assignment of limited partnership interests will not be allowed. Restrictions on the substitution of a limited partner are generally disfavored and will be allowed only to the extent necessary to preserve the tax status of the partnership and any restriction must be supported by opinion of counsel.

H. ASSESSMENTS and Defaults.

1. ASSESSMENTS. ASSESSMENTS will not be allowed for NON-SPECIFIED PROGRAMS. In the case of SPECIFIED PROGRAMS, ASSESSMENTS shall be permitted only when specific circumstances demonstrate a need. If the anticipated CASH FLOW from property (after payment of debt service and all operating expenses) is not sufficient to pay taxes and/or special ASSESSMENTS imposed by governmental or quasi-government units, the PROGRAM agreement may include a provision for assessability to meet such deficiencies, including those obligations of a defaulting PARTICIPANT. Assessability must be limited to the foregoing obligations, and all amounts derived from such ASSESSMENTS must be applied only to satisfaction of said obligations.
2. Defaults. In the event of a default in the payment of ASSESSMENTS by a PARTICIPANT his interests shall not be subject to forfeiture, but may be subject to a reasonable penalty for failure to meet his commit-

ment. Provided that the arrangements are fair, this may take the form of reducing his proportionate interest in the PROGRAM, subordinating his interest to that of nondefaulting partners, a forced sale complying with applicable procedures for notice and sale, the lending of the amount necessary to meet his commitment by the other PARTICIPANTS or a fixing of the value of his interest by independent appraisal or other suitable formula with provision for a delayed payment to him for his interest not beyond a reasonable period, but a debt security issued for such interest should not have a claim prior to that of the other investors in the event of liquidation.

> COMMENT: A limited partner will be reinstated to his full status as a limited partner upon payment of the delinquent ASSESSMENT with interest at the maximum rate allowed by law, within 30 days of the date of default. Default would be the failure to pay the ASSESSMENT within 30 days of the date of notice requesting the ASSESSMENT.

I. Dividend Reinvestment Plans. A PROGRAM may offer participants the opportunity to elect to have cash distributions reinvested in the PROGRAM or subsequent programs if the following conditions are met:
  1. The PROGRAM and subsequent programs in which the participants reinvest are registered or exempted under the state's blue sky laws.
  2. Counsel for the PROGRAM submits an opinion that the pooling of the funds for reinvestment is not in itself a security.
  3. The subsequent program has substantially identical investment objectives as the original PROGRAM.
  4. The participants are free to elect or revoke reinvestment within a reasonable time and such right is fully disclosed in the offering documents.
  5. Prior to each reinvestment the participants receive a current updated disclosure document which contains at a minimum the following information:
     a. The minimum investment amount.
     b. The type or source of proceeds (e.g. cash distributions from operations or the sale or disposition of properties) which may be reinvested.
     c. The tax consequences of the reinvestment to the participants.
  6. Counsel for the PROGRAM submits an opinion that different consideration paid on reinvestment is not in violation of the state law (the difference arises when one participant agrees to payment of commission to the broker-dealer and another participant does not agree to payment of commisson).
  7. The broker-dealer or the issuer assumes responsibility for blue sky compliance and performance of due diligence responsibilities and has contacted the participants to ascertain whether the participants continue

to meet the state's suitability standard for participation in each reinvestment.

8. If a broker-dealer is involved it shall obtain in writing an agreement from the client by which the client agrees to the payment of compensation to the broker-dealer in connection with individual reinvestment.

J. Within 60 days after the end of each quarter during which there have been real property acquisitions, a "Special Report" (which may be part of the quarterly report) shall be sent to all PARTICIPANTS until the proceeds of the offering are committed or returned to the investors. The report shall contain the following information:

(a) the location and a description of the general character of all materially important real properties acquired or presently intended to be acquired by or leased to the program, during the quarter.

(b) the present or proposed use of such properties and their suitability and adequacy for such use.

(c) the terms of any material lease affecting the property.

(d) the proposed method of financing, including estimated down payment, leverage ratio, prepaid interest, balloon payment(s), prepayment penalties, due-on-sale or encumbrance clauses and possible adverse effects thereof and similar details of the proposed financing plan, and

(e) a statement that title insurance and any required construction, permanent or other financing and performance bonds or other assurances with respect to builders have been or will be obtained on all properties acquired.

> COMMENT: When a PROGRAM is making or investing in mortgage loans then information should be included in these reports not only about the terms and present status of the loan but also such information reasonably available about the underlying property which could influence the value of the loan.

VIII. DISCLOSURE AND MARKETING REQUIREMENTS.

A. Sales Promotional Efforts.

1. Sales Literature. Sales literature, sales presentations (including prepared presentations to prospective investors at group meetings) and advertising used in the offer or sale of partnership interests shall conform in all applicable respects to requirements of filing, disclosure and adequacy currently imposed on sales literature, sales presentations and advertising used in the sale of corporate securities.

2. Group Meetings. All advertisements of and oral or written invitations to "seminars" or other group meetings at which PROGRAM INTERESTS are to be described, offered or sold shall clearly indicate that the purpose of such meeting is to offer such PROGRAM INTERESTS for sale, the minimum purchase price thereof, and the name of the

SPONSOR, underwriter or selling agent. No cash, merchandise or other item of value shall be offered as an inducement to any prospective PARTICIPANTS to attend any such meeting. In connection with the offer or sale of PROGRAM INTERESTS, no general offer shall be made of "free" or "bargain price" trips to visit property in which the PROGRAM or proposed PROGRAM has invested or intends to invest.

All written or prepared audio-visual presentations (including scripts prepared in advance for oral presentations) to be made at such meetings must be submitted in advance to the ADMINISTRATOR not less than three business days prior to the first use thereof. The foregoing paragraphs 1. and 2. shall not apply to meetings consisting only of representatives of securities broker-dealers.

B. Contents of PROSPECTUS. The PROSPECTUS shall meet the requirements of Guide 5 as of the Securities and Exchange Commission. The description of the method for the allocation of the acquisition of properties by two or more programs of the same sponsor shall meet the requirements of Section VI.E. The ADMINISTRATOR may require additional disclosure if, in the ADMINISTRATORS' opinion, specific facts concerning the offering require it.

C. Forecasts.

1. Use of Forecasts. The presentation of predicted future results of operations of real estate PROGRAMS shall be permitted but not required for specified property PROGRAMS investing primarily in improved property and shall be prohibited for NON-SPECIFIED PROPERTY PROGRAMS or specified property PROGRAMS investing primarily in unimproved land. The covers of the PROSPECTUS must contain in bold face language one of the following statements:

    (i) for SPECIFIED PROPERTY PROGRAMS:

    FORECASTS ARE CONTAINED IN THIS PROSPECTUS (OFFERING CIRCULAR). ANY PREDICTIONS AND REPRESENTATIONS, WRITTEN OR ORAL, WHICH DO NOT CONFORM TO THOSE CONTAINED IN THE PROSPECTUS (OFFERING CIRCULAR) SHALL NOT BE PERMITTED.

    (ii) for NON-SPECIFIED PROPERTY and unimproved land programs:

    THE USE OF FORECASTS IN THIS OFFERING IS PROHIBITED. ANY REPRESENTATIONS TO THE CONTRARY AND ANY PREDICTIONS, WRITTEN OR ORAL, AS TO THE AMOUNT OR CERTAINTY OF ANY PRESENT OR FUTURE CASH BENEFIT OR TAX CONSEQUENCE WHICH MAY FLOW FROM IN INVESTMENT IN THIS PROGRAM IS NOT PERMITTED.

Forecasts for specified property PROGRAMS shall be included in the PROSPECTUS, offering circular or sales material of the PROGRAM only if they comply with the following requirements:

a. General

Forecasts shall be realistic in their predictions and shall clearly identify the assumptions made with respect to all material features of the presentation. Forecasts should be reviewed by an independent certified public accountant in accordance with the Guide For A Review Of A Financial Forecast as promulgated by the American Institute of Certified Public Accountants, and that person or firm should be identified in the PROSPECTUS or offering circular as being responsible for the review of the forecasts. No forecasts shall be permitted in any sales literature which does not appear in the PROSPECTUS or offering circular. If any forecasts are included in the sales literature, all forecasts must be presented.

COMMENT: If predicted future results of operations are used, they shall be prepared in the form of a forecast by expert using standard criteria and format.

b. Material Information

(1) Annual predicted revenue by source; including the occupancy rate used in predicting rental revenue;

(2) Annual predicted expenses;

(3) Mortgage obligation—annual payments for principal and interest, points and financing fees, shown as dollars, not percentages;

(4) The required occupancy rate in order to meet debt service and all expenses;

(5) Predicted annual CASH FLOW; stating assumed occupancy rate;

(6) Predicted annual depreciation and amortization with full description of methods to be used;

(7) Predicted annual taxable income or loss and a simplified explanation of the tax treatment of such results; assumed tax brackets may not be used;

(8) Predicted construction costs—including disclosure regarding contracts;

(9) Accounting policies—e.g., with respect to points, financing costs and depreciation.

c. Presentation

(1) Caveat. Forecasts shall prominently display a statement to the effect that they represent a mere prediction of future events based on assumptions which may or may not occur and may not be relied upon to indicate the actual results which will be obtained.

(2) Additional Guidelines. Explanatory notes describing assumptions made and referring to risk factors should be integrated with tabular and numerical information.
(3) Sale-leasebacks. When a sale-leaseback is employed, the statement that the seller is assuming the operating risk and consequently may have charged a higher price for the property must be included.

d. Additional Disclosures and Limitations
(1) Forecasts shall be for a period at least equivalent to the anticipated holding period for the property, or 10 years, whichever is shorter, and project a resale occurrence, including depreciation recapture, if applicable. The forecasted resale price must be reasonable.
(2) Adequate disclosure shall be made of the changing economic effects upon the limited partners resulting principally from federal income tax consequences over the life of the partnership property, e.g., substantial tax losses in early years followed by increasing amount of taxable income in later years.
(3) Forecasts shall disclose all possible undesirable tax consequences of an early sale of the PROGRAM property (such as, depreciation recapture or the failure to sell the property at a price which would return sufficient cash to meet resulting tax liabilities of the PARTICIPANTS).
(4) In computing the return to investors, no appreciation, so called "equity buildup", or any other benefits from unrealized gains or value shall be shown or included.

2. Unimproved Land — Forecasts shall not be allowed for unimproved land. Instead, a table of deferred payments specifying the various holding costs, i.e., interest, taxes, and insurance shall be inserted. However, where the PROGRAM intends to develop and sell the land as its primary business, a detailed CASH FLOW statement showing the timing of expenditures and anticipated revenues shall be required. Additionally, the consequences of a delayed selling PROGRAM shall be shown.

IX. MISCELLANEOUS PROVISIONS

A. Deferred Payments. Deferred payments or similar arrangements on account of the purchase price of PROGRAM INTERESTS shall not be allowed in the case of NON-SPECIFIED PROGRAMS, and, in the case of SPECIFIED PROGRAMS may be allowed only when warranted by the investment objectives of the partnership, but in any event such arrangements shall be subject to the following conditions:

1. The period of deferred payments shall coincide with the anticipated cash needs of the PROGRAM.

2. Selling commissions paid upon deferred payments are collectible when payment is made on the note.
3. Deferred payments shall be evidenced by a promissory note of the investor. Such notes shall be with recourse and shall not be negotiable and shall be assignable only subject to defenses of the maker. Such notes shall not contain a provision authorizing a confession of judgment.
4. The PROGRAM shall not sell or assign the deferred obligation notes at a discount to meet financing needs of the PROGRAM.
5. In the event of a default in the payment of deferred payments by a PARTICIPANT, his interests may be subjected to a reasonable penalty, as set forth in Section VII.H. of these Guidelines.

B. Reserves. Provision should be made for adequate reserves in the future by retention of a reasonable percentage of proceeds from the offering and regular receipts for normal repairs, replacements and contingencies. Normally, not less than 3% of the offering proceeds will be considered adequate. However, in PROGRAMS that invest in or make mortgage loans, reserves in an amount greater than 1% of the offering proceeds will be considered adequate.

C. Reinvestment of CASH FLOW (excluding proceeds resulting from a disposition or refinancing of property) shall not be allowed. The partnership agreement and the PROSPECTUS shall set forth that reinvestment of proceeds resulting from a disposition or refinancing will not take place unless sufficient cash will be distributed to pay any state or federal income tax (assuming investors are in a specified tax bracket) created by the disposition or refinancing of property. Such a prohibition must be contained in the PROSPECTUS.

> COMMENT: In the case of PROGRAMS which invest in or make mortgage loans any reinvestment must be structured to terminate when the PROGRAM terminates.

D. Financial Information Required on Application. In any offering of interests by a PROGRAM, the PROGRAM shall provide as an exhibit to the application the following financial information:
1. Cash Flow Statement. If the PROGRAM has been formed and owns assets, an unaudited CASH FLOW statement for each of the last three fiscal years shall be part of the PROSPECTUS. If the PROGRAM has operated less than three fiscal years, the statement(s) shall cover the period from organization to a current date.
2. Financial Statements of Program. The PROSPECTUS shall include an audited balance sheet of the PROGRAM as of the end of its most recent fiscal year.
3. Balance Sheet of Corporate Sponsor. A balance sheet of any corporate SPONSORS as of the end of their most recent fiscal year, examined and reported upon by an independent certified public accountant and

prepared in accordance with generally accepted accounting principles. An unaudited balance sheet as of a date not more than one hundred thirty-five days prior to the date of filing should also be prepared. Such statements shall be included in the PROSPECTUS.

4. Other SPONSORS. A balance sheet for each non-corporate SPONSOR (including individual partners or individual joint ventures of a SPONSOR) as of a time not more than one hundred thirty-five days prior to the date of filing an application; such balance sheet shall be examined and reported upon by an independent certified public accountant under the limited review standards set forth by the American Institute of Certified Public Accountants, and shall be signed and sworn to by such SPONSORS. A representation of the amount of such NET WORTH must be included in the PROSPECTUS, or in the alternative, a representation that such SPONSOR meet the NET WORTH requirements of Section II.B.

> COMMENT: It is not intended that financial statements of affiliates of the SPONSOR be required to be disclosed unless appropriate in order to comply with the NET WORTH requirements of Section II.B.
>
> COMMENT: Section IX.E.4. requires a balance sheet for each non-corporate SPONSOR prepared by an independent certified public accountant under the limited review standards set forth by the AICPA. This will add consistency to the form and structure of non-corporate SPONSOR balance sheets. Currently, unaudited financial statements for non-corporate SPONSORS vary in style and content making consistent evaluation difficult. Applying limited review standards will give uniformity to such financial statements, making evaluation of a SPONSORS financial condition more constant. More importantly, limited review standards offer a higher analysis of a non-corporate SPONSOR's financial condition. Concern has been expressed by ADMINISTRATORS over the validity and reliability of unaudited balance sheets currently being submitted by non-corporate SPONSORS. Limited review standards will allow for greater reliability on this financial information which is needed in determining whether a SPONSOR meets the NET WORTH requirements of Section II.B.

5. Interim Financial Information. Where the audited balance sheet is as of a date more than 90 days prior to the date of filing, an unaudited balance sheet as of a date not more than 90 days prior to the date of filing shall also be provided. Interim unaudited statements of income, partners' equity, and changes in financial position shall also be provided with the unaudited balance sheet in instances where such statements for the last fiscal year. When a program has operated less than one fiscal year, audited financial information is not required unless requested by the ADMINISTRATOR.

6. Filing of Other Statements. The ADMINISTRATOR may permit the omission of one or more of the statements required under this Section and the filing (in substitution thereof) of appropriate statements verifying financial information having comparable relevance to an investor in determining whether to invest in the PROGRAM. Such substitution will only be allowed where the ADMINISTRATOR finds this would be consistent with the protection of investors.

E. Opinions of Counsel. The application for qualification and registration shall contain a favorable ruling from the Internal Revenue Service or an opinion of independent counsel to the effect that the issuer will be taxed as a "partnership" and not as an "association" for federal income tax purposes. An opinion of counsel shall be in form and substance satisfactory to the ADMINISTRATOR and shall be unqualified except to the extent permitted by the ADMINISTRATOR. However, an opinion of counsel may be based on reasonable assumptions, such as:

(1) facts or proposed operations as set forth in the offering circular or PROSPECTUS and organizational documents; (2) the absence of future changes if applicable laws; (3) the securities offered are paid for; (4) compliance with certain procedures such as the execution and delivery of certain documents and the filing of a certificate of limited partnership or an amended certificate; and (5) the continued maintenance of or compliance with certain financial, ownership, or other requirements by the issuer of SPONSOR. The ADMINISTRATOR may request from counsel as supplemental information such supporting legal memoranda and an analysis as he shall deem appropriate under the circumstances. To the extent the opinion of counsel or Internal Revenue Service ruling is based on the maintenance of or compliance with certain requirements or conditions by the issuer of SPONSOR the offering circular or PROSPECTUS shall contain representations that such requirements or conditions will be met and the partnership agreement shall, to the extent practicable, contain provisions requiring such compliance.

There shall be included also an opinion of independent counsel to the effect that the securities being offered are duly authorized or created and validly issued interests in the user, and that the liability of the public investors will be limited to their respective total agreed upon investment in the issuer.

The ADMINISTRATOR may request an opinion of counsel concerning tax aspects when this appears necessary for the protection of investors.

F. Provisions of Partnership Agreement. The requirements and/or provisions of appropriate portions of the following sections shall be included in a partnership agreement: II.C.; II.D.; II.E.; II.F.; IV.C.; IV.D.; IV.E.; IV.F.; IV.G.; IV.H.; IV.I.; V.A.; V.B.; V.C.; V.D.; V.E.; V.F.; V.G.; V.H.; V.I.; V.L.; VI.C.; VI.D.; VII.A.; VII.B.; VII.C.; VII.D.; VII.E.; VII.F.; VII.H.; VII.J.; IX.A.; IX.B.; and IX.C.

GENERAL INSTRUCTIONS

NASAA REAL ESTATE GUIDELINES

H.
1. The Cross Reference Sheet should be completed with the Application for Registration.
2. Sections which are not applicable should be noted as such.
3. Provisions of the program which vary from the Guidelines must be explained by footnote; for example, if the program uses a defined term which is different from the Guidelines definition, the variance must be explained. Footnotes should be numbered sequentially in the column designated Footnotes and should be presented on a rider identified as Footnotes with each Footnote on the rider numerically corresponding to the Footnote identified on the Cross Reference Sheet.
4. A section is provided at the bottom of each page of the Cross Reference Sheet for additional or supplemental Cross References. Lines are provided in the event additional Cross References are needed with respect to subsections of the Guidelines not specifically identified on the top of the page, or in the event there were insufficient lines to present all relevant cross references with respect to an item appearing on that page.
5. The last page of the Cross Reference Sheet should be executed by preparer.
6. These General Instructions should be <u>removed</u> before filing with the State Administrator.

REAL ESTATE GUIDELINES CROSS REFERENCE SHEET

NAME OF APPLICANT: _____

Footnote See Instruction 3.	Page Number Prospectus	Section Number Partnership Agreement	Guideline Section
			I.B. DEFINITIONS
_____	_____	_____	1. Acquisition expenses
_____	_____	_____	2. Acquisition fee
_____	_____	_____	5. Assessments
_____	_____	_____	6. Capital contribution
_____	_____	_____	7. Cash flow
_____	_____	_____	8. Cash available for distribution
_____	_____	_____	10. Construction fee
_____	_____	_____	12. Development fee
_____	_____	_____	13. Front-end fees
_____	_____	_____	14. Investment in properties
_____	_____	_____	17. Organization and offering expenses
_____	_____	_____	21. Program interest
_____	_____	_____	22. Program management fee
_____	_____	_____	23. Property management fee
_____	_____	_____	25. Purchase price of property
			II. REQUIREMENTS OF SPONSORS
_____	_____		A. Experience
_____	_____		B. Net worth
_____	_____	_____	C. Reports to administrators
_____	_____	_____	D. Liability
_____	_____	_____	E. Fiduciary duty
_____	_____	_____	F. Termination
			III. SUITABILITY OF THE PARTICIPANT
_____	_____		A. Standards
_____	_____		C. Maintenance of records
_____	_____		D. Minimum investment

ADDITIONAL OR SUPPLEMENTAL CROSS REFERENCES

_____ _____ _____   _____
_____ _____ _____   _____
_____ _____ _____   _____

Appendix J: NASAA Guidelines   547

REAL ESTATE GUIDELINES CROSS REFERENCE SHEET (Cont'd)

Footnote See Instruction 3.	Page Number Prospectus	Section Number Partnership Agreement	Guideline Section
			IV. FEES - COMPENSATION - EXPENSES
_____	_____		B. Organization & offering expenses
_____	_____	_____	C. Investment in properties
_____	_____	_____	D. Program management fee
_____	_____	_____	E. Promotional interest
			2. (i) Interest in cash available for distribution
_____	_____	_____	(ii) Interest in sale or refinancing proceeds
			3. Definition of capital contributions and date for commencement of calculating the preferred return
_____	_____	_____	4. Dissolution and liquidation
_____	_____	_____	F. Real estate brokerage commissions on resale of property
_____	_____	_____	G. Property management fee
_____	_____	_____	H. Insurance services
_____	_____	_____	I. Mortgage servicing fee
			V. CONFLICTS OF INTEREST AND INVESTMENT RESTRICTIONS.
_____	_____	_____	A. 1. Sales and leases to program
_____	_____	_____	2. Sales and leases to sponsor
_____	_____	_____	3. Loans
_____	_____	_____	4. Dealing with related programs
_____	_____	_____	B. Exchange of limited partnership interests
_____	_____	_____	C. Exclusive agreements
_____	_____	_____	D. Commissions on reinvestment or distribution

ADDITIONAL OR SUPPLEMENTAL CROSS REFERENCES

_____ _____ _____ _____

_____ _____ _____ _____

_____ _____ _____ _____

REAL ESTATE GUIDELINES CROSS REFERENCE SHEET *(Cont'd)*

Footnote See Instruction 3.	Page Number Prospectus	Section Number Partnership Agreement	Guideline Section
			E. Services rendered to the program by the sponsor
_____	_____	_____	1. (a) Expenses billed to program
_____	_____	_____	(b) Annual program report
_____	_____	_____	2. Other services
_____	_____	_____	F. Rebates, kickbacks and reciprocal arrangements
_____	_____	_____	G. Commingling of funds
_____	_____	_____	H. Investments in other programs
_____	_____	_____	I. Lending practices
_____	_____	_____	J. Development or construction contracts
_____	_____	_____	K. Completion bond requirements
_____	_____	_____	L. Appraisals
_____	_____	_____	M. Mortgage loan programs
			VI. NON-SPECIFIED PROPERTY PROGRAMS
_____	_____	_____	A. Minimum capitalization
_____	_____		B. Sponsor experience
_____	_____	_____	C. Investment Objectives
_____	_____	_____	1. Unimproved or non-income producing property program
_____	_____	_____	2. Junior trust deeds
_____	_____	_____	3. Financing
_____	_____	_____	4. Joint ventures
_____	_____		D. Offering period
_____	_____	_____	E. Multiple programs

ADDITIONAL OR SUPPLEMENTAL CROSS REFERENCES

_____	_____	_____	_____
_____	_____	_____	_____
_____	_____	_____	_____

Appendix J: NASAA Guidelines 549

REAL ESTATE GUIDELINES CROSS REFERENCE SHEET (Cont'd)

Footnote See Instruction 3.	Page Number Prospectus	Section Number Partnership Agreement	Guideline Section
			VII. RIGHTS AND OBLIGATIONS OF PARTICIPANTS
____	____	____	A. Meetings
____	____	____	B. Voting rights
____	____		C. Reports
____		____	1. 12(g) programs, quarterly reports
____		____	2. Other programs, semi-annual reports
____		____	3. Limited partners tax information
____		____	4. Annual report
____		____	5. Assessment reports
____		____	6. Report to sponsor services
____	____	____	D. Access to records
____	____	____	E. Admission of participants
____	____	____	1. Original participants
____	____	____	2. Substitute limited partners
____	____	____	F. Redemption of program interests
____	____	____	G. Transferability of program interest
____	____	____	H. 1. Assessments
____	____	____	2. Defaults
____	____		I. Dividend Reinvestment Plan
____		____	J. Special Reports
			IX. MISCELLANEOUS PROVISIONS
____	____	____	A. Deferred payments
____	____	____	B. Reserves
____	____	____	C. Reinvestment of cash flow

ADDITIONAL OR SUPPLEMENTAL CROSS REFERENCES

____   ____   ____   ____

____   ____   ____   ____

____   ____   ____   ____

RESPONSE TO THIS CROSS REFERENCE SHEET HAS BEEN PREPARED BY:

NAME: _____

TITLE: _____

REAL ESTATE INVESTMENT SUBCOMMITTEE
OF THE NASAA MERIT REGULATION COMMITTEE

ADVISORY—I

adopted by
North American Securities Administrators Association, Inc.
on April 23, 1983

The NASAA Real Estate Investment Subcommittee ("Subcommittee") at its meeting of May 12, 1982, has adopted a procedure whereby the Subcommittee will from time to time issue interpretations of the NASAA Real Estate Guidelines ("Guidelines"). As with the Guidelines themselves, and even to a greater degree with respect to these interpretations, each state administrator will retain the discretion with respect to the interpretations and implementation of the Guidelines. However, for those administrators who are seeking to increase the degree of uniformity of interpretations of the Guidelines and/or seeking additional guidance with respect to the interpretation of the Guidelines, the Subcommittee has prepared the following interpretations:

INTERPRETATION 1

When a sponsor's promotional interest in liquidation proceeds is subordinated to a higher return to the limited partners than is specified under Sections IV.E.1 and IV.E.2(ii) of the Guidelines, the compensation permitted the sponsors by this section or other sections of the Guidelines should not be increased as a result of this type of arrangement unless specifically justified under Section I.A.2.

INTERPRETATION 2

When a sponsor takes an increased promotional interest pursuant to Section IV.C.3 of the Guidelines, but subordinates the payment of such fees to a higher return to the investors than is specified under such section, the compensation permitted sponsors by this section or other sections of the Guidelines should not be increased as a result of this type of arrangement unless specifically justified under Section I.A.2.

INTERPRETATION 3

When a sponsor takes a share of cash distributions from operations under Section IV.E.2(i) of the Guidelines, but subordinates this interest to a specified return to the investors (which is not required by the Guidelines), the compensation permitted sponsors by this section or other sections of the Guidelines should not be increased as a result of this type of arrangement unless specifically justified under Section I.A.2.

COMMENT ON INTERPRETATIONS 1 THROUGH 3 ABOVE

The Subcommittee believes that the Guidelines create a substantial opportunity for the sponsor to exchange one form of compensation for another form of compensation. For example, there is substantial latitude as to the "mix" in the front-end fees permitted, and the front-end fees can be deferred entitling the sponsor to a larger liquidation fee. In addition, the maximum compensation permitted to sponsors under the Guidelines is liberal and sponsors are permitted and in fact do, in many instances, package programs with sponsors' compensation well below the maximum permitted by the Guidelines. Therefore, in general, the Subcommittee does not believe that it is necessary or appropriate to create an additional standard for modification of the compensation based upon the sponsor increasing subordination beyond that specified in Sections IV.E.1, IV.E.2, and IV.C.3 of the Guidelines. The fact that a sponsor may increase the subordination of his share of cash distributions could be meaningful only when an accurate forecast of annual cash distributions from operations and net proceeds from liquidation could be forecasted, and thus show the "real trade-off" involved in a particular arrangement. Nevertheless, even if a very reliable forecast of the future timing and amount of proceeds from operations and the sale of the property could be made, the Subcommittee believes that the sponsor's willingness to subject its return to a higher subordination than is required under the Guidelines should be considered a response to the pressures of the competitive marketplace and not a trade-off in compensation entitling the sponsor to a larger share somewhere else.

INTERPRETATION 4

When applying the suitability standards under Section III.B.4. of the Guidelines to a participant which is an IRA or Keogh plan, the participant for the purposes of suitability is the beneficiary of the IRA or Keogh Plan.

COMMENT ON INTERPRETATION 4

Suitability standards for investors are imposed because of factors such as the limited transferability, relative lack of liquidity, degree of risk, and specific tax orientation of a real estate program. When an investment in a real estate program is made through an IRA or Keogh plan the investor or participant is considered to be the beneficiary. The beneficiary is the real investor in interest. The beneficiary is the person who supplies the funds to purchase the partnership interest and is the person at risk on the selection and performance of the investment. In the case of self-directed plans or accounts, the beneficiary makes the investment decision. In a fiduciary account the ability to bear the loss as reflected by the beneficiary's financial status is more relevant to the application of a suitability standard than the trustee's financial status or ability to understand the investment risks to the beneficiary.

APPENDIX K

NASD Offices

National Headquarters: National Association of Securities Dealers, Inc.
1735 K Street, N.W.
Washington, DC 20006
(202) 728-8000

NASD District Offices

District No. 1
One Union Square, Suite 1911
Seattle, Washington 98101
(206) 624-0790
Bradford M. Patterson, Director

District No. 2N
425 California Street, Room 1400
San Francisco, California 94101
(415) 781-3434
Theodore F. Schmidt, Director

District No. 2S
727 W. Seventh Street
Los Angeles, California 90017
(213) 627-2122
Kye Hellmers, Director

District No. 3
1401 17th Street, Suite 700
Denver, Colorado 80202
(303) 298-7234
Frank J. Birgfeld, Director

District No. 4
120 W. 12th Street, Suite 900
12 Wyandotte Plaza
Kansas City, Missouri 64105
(816) 421-5700
Jack Rosenfield, Director

District No. 5
1004 Richards Building
New Orleans, Louisiana 70112
(504) 522-6527
Edward J. Newton, Director

District No. 6
1999 Bryan Street
Olympia & York Tower, Suite 1450
Dallas, Texas 75201
(214) 969-7050
Peter M. Walker, Director

District No. 7
250 Piedmont Avenue, N.E.
Atlanta, Georgia 30308
(404) 658-9191
Bennett Whipple, Director

District No. 8
Three First National Plaza,
Suite 1680
Chicago, Illinois 60602
(312) 236-7222
E. Craig Dearborn, Director

District No. 9
1940 East 6th Street, Fifth Floor
Cleveland, Ohio 44114
(216) 694-4545
George W. Mann, Jr., Director

District No. 10
1125 15th Street, N.W.
Washington, DC 20006
(202) 728-3145
Thomas P. Forde, Director

District No. 11
1818 Market Street, 12th Floor
Philadelphia, Pennsylvania 19103
(215) 665-1180
John P. Nocella, Director

District No. 12
Two World Trade Center
South Tower, 98th Floor
New York, New York 10048
(212) 839-6200
George J. Bergen, Vice President,
Director

District No. 13
260 Franklin Street, 20th Floor
Boston, Massachusetts 02110
(617) 482-0466
William S. Clendenin, Director

NASDAQ Data Center
80 Merritt Boulevard
Trumbull, Connecticut 06611
(203) 385-4500
Frank T. Coyle, Vice President

APPENDIX L
Glossary

Acquisition Fee: Money paid to the syndicator or affiliates for services in arranging for the acquisition or property.

Appreciation: Any increase in value due to inflation and supply and demand factors.

Blind Pool: See non-specified offering.

Blue Sky Law: A state law regulating solicitation and sale of securities.

Broker: In real estate, one who is licensed by the state real estate commission to purchase and sell real estate on behalf of others and earn commission income for such services.

Broker-Dealer: Any person who is licensed by state and/or federal securities regulators to effect transactions in securities for his own account or for the account of others.

Capital Gains: An incentive to long term investment which limits taxation to only forty percent of profits earned.

Cash Flow: Income remaining after payment of all investment carrying costs.

Certificate of Limited Partnership: A summary of a limited partnership agreement, required to be filed with the county recorder and/or the state officials.

Corporation: A business entity which has been formed and authorized by law to act as a single person although constituted by one or more persons and legally endowed with various rights and duties.

Depreciation: A bookkeeping method which enables an investor to claim a loss in income equivalent to the projected decline in value of a given investment due to aging.

Disclosure Document: That material which informs the buyer of all pertinent facts regarding a securities issue.

Due Diligence: Investigation by a Broker-Dealer of the background, pertinent facts and truthfulness regarding a securities issue. Such investigation is required by law before an issue can be sold to the public.

Equity: That amount remaining when total debt owed from an investment is subtracted from total value.

Finder's Fee: Fee paid to an individual for finding or referring a buyer to a seller.

General Partner: The individual(s) or entity who has full liability and responsibility for managing the affairs of a partnership.

General Partnership: An entity organized pursuant to law in which all partners are jointly and severally liable for the obligations of the partnership.

Guide 5: Issued by the SEC as a model format for preparing a limited partnership disclosure document.

Intrastate Offering: A securities offering made pursuant to the rules for the intrastate offering exemption from registration with the SEC, i.e. all partnership business is done within a single state. The rules for the intrastate offering exemption are detailed in SEC's Rule 147.

IRS: Internal Revenue Service, the tax-collecting arm of the U.S. government.

Issue: A securities offering, e.g., a limited partnership.

Issuer: The entity in which interests are being offered.

Issuer's Exemption: An exemption from the requirement to register as a securities broker-dealer which may be given to one who sells only his own securities offering (issue).

Leverage: The use of borrowed moneys to help finance the purchase of properties.

Limited Liability: Financial responsibility limited by statute.

Limited Partner: An investor in a limited partnership whose personal liability may be limited to the amount of his investment.

Limited Partnership: A partnership which comprises one or more general partners who are responsible for management and control of the enterprise and one or more limited partners who have neither management nor control. While the general partners in such an enterprise have unlimited liability, the limited partners' liability may not exceed their investment.

Registration: Filing necessary documents to obtain securities administrator approval as a public offering.

RESSI: Real Estate Securities and Syndication Institute, an affiliate of the National Association of Realtors.

Appendix L: Glossary

Security: As defined in the Federal Securities Act of 1933: "Any note, stock, treasury stock, bond debenture, evidence of indebtedness, certificate of interest or participation in any profit-sharing agreement, collateral-trust certificate, pre-organization certificate or subscription, transferable share, investment contract, voting-trust certificate, certificate of deposit for a security." Limited partnership and corporation interests are considered securities because of the dependence upon centralized management which is implied in such organizations.

SEC: Securities and Exchange Commission, a U.S. government regulatory and enforcement agency which supervises investment trading activities and administers securities statutes.

Specified Offering: A syndicate organized to make a specified investment.

Sponsor: The entity which is responsible for establishment and management of a venture.

Subordinated Interest: A claim on benefits from an investment which may only be made after other interests have received some priority claim.

Subscription Agreement: A contract binding the subscriber to purchase an interest in a syndication.

Suitability: Investor standards such as net worth, business sophistication, and financial condition, which must be met before a syndicate issue is offered or sold.

Syndicate: Any general or limited partnership, joint venture, unincorporated association, or similar organization, formed for the purpose of investment or gain.

Tax Loss: Bookkeeping loss which the individual may show in his tax return to offset other income.

Tax Shelter: A factor (such as special depreciation allowances) that reduces taxes on current earnings.

Tombstone Ad: An advertisement which gives only the base data of the subject being promoted -- no hype. Advertisements for securities offerings are restricted by law to such form.

NASAA: The North American Securities Administrators Association, a regulatory body composed of the securities administrators from all of the U.S. states.

NASAA Guidelines: Guidelines established by the state securities administrators to promote full disclosure and fairness in limited partnership offerings.

NASD: The National Association of Securities Dealers, a quasi-official regulatory body for the securities industry.

Negative Cash Flow: Funds required to service financial obligations in excess of those which may be paid from investment income.

Net Worth: Total assets less total liabilities.

Non-Specified Offering: A syndicate organized without commitment to purchase any specified investment; where the money is raised before the investment is made. Also referred to as unspecified offering or blind pool.

Offering: Syndication (securities) issue for sale to investors.

Offering Document: The document which describes the syndication interests offered for sale. Depending upon how the offering is made the offering document carries a different name:

>   Private   Offering Memorandum
>   Intrastate Public   Offering Circular
>   Interstate Public   Prospectus

Partnership Agreement: Agreement between partners setting forth their rights and duties.

Passive Investor: An investor who has no involvement with management and control of the venture.

Private Offering: A securities offering made pursuant to the rules for the private offering exemption from registration with the SEC, i.e. a limited number of investors and no public solicitation. The rules for the private offering exemption are detailed in the SEC's Regulation D.

Public Offering: A securities offering which has been registered with appropriate federal and state securities administrators. Public offerings may be interstate or intrastate.

APPENDIX M

Survey of NASAA Real Estate Guidelines

SURVEY

ON STATE IMPLEMENTATION AND APPLICATION
OF THE CURRENT

NASAA REAL ESTATE GUIDELINES

April 1, 1987

**SUBCOMMITTEE ON REAL ESTATE PROGRAMS
ABA STATE REGULATION OF SECURITIES COMMITTEE**

PREPARED BY JOSEPH P. HILDEBRANDT, CHAIRMAN

The data contained herein is for general informational purposes only and should not be relied upon in lieu of independent verification. To report any changes in the data, please contact Joseph P. Hildebrandt at (608) 258-4232.

Printed by: R. R. Donnelley & Sons Company (Chicago, Illinois)

* *Source:* "Survey on State Implementation and Application of the Current NASAA Real Estate Guidelines," Subcommittee on Real Estate Programs-ABA State Regulation of Securities Committee; prepared by Joseph P. Hildebrandt, Chairman, with the assistance of Ronald J. Burtch, April 1. The data contained herein is for general informational purposes only and should not be relied upon in lieu of independent verification.

STATE	Are you a "merit review" state?	Has your state adopted the Guidelines: Formally?	Has your state adopted the Guidelines: Informally?	If your state has not adopted the Guidelines, do you expect it will, and if so, when do you expect adoption?	Law/Rule citation if Guidelines formally adopted?	Does your application of the Guidelines vary from NASAA's published version?	If you apply the Guidelines differently, what are the differences?	Do you apply the Guidelines to: National Public Offerings?	Do you apply the Guidelines to: Intrastate Offerings?	Do you apply the Guidelines to: Private Offerings filed with you?	How Does Your State Apply Each of the Particular Requirements of the Guidelines? Always and Absolutely (Without Waiver)	How Does Your State Apply Each of the Particular Requirements of the Guidelines? Usually and Strictly (Waivers Rarely)	How Does Your State Apply Each of the Particular Requirements of the Guidelines? Occasionally and Moderately (Waivers Frequently)	How Does Your State Apply Each of the Particular Requirements of the Guidelines? Seldom and Loosely (Occasionally Applied)	Comments
Alabama	Yes	No	Yes	Adoption is now being considered.		No		Yes	Yes	No		X			Private Placement Offerings exempt from "Merit Standards;"—only Full Disclosure Required.
Alaska	Yes	No	Yes	No		No		Yes	Yes	Yes			X		The Guidelines provide a frame of reference for examination of offerings. The administrator will entertain arguments and justification on exceptions to Guidelines. State requires that a Cross-Reference Sheet be submitted and all exceptions to Guidelines noted thereon.
Arizona	Yes	No	Yes			No		Yes	Yes	No		X			Private Placement Offerings not subject to Registration Requirements of Merit Review.
Arkansas	Yes	Yes				No		Yes	Yes	No		X			
California	Yes	No	No	*		No	Apply California Rules and NASAA Guidelines.	No	No	No					*NASAA Guidelines and California Real Estate Program Rules will be coordinated in many areas by amendments to the NASAA Guidelines effective January 1, 1986 and by a California rule revision project commencing in April, 1986. Substantial differences will still exist in regulations governing acquisition fees and compensation.
Colorado	No	No	No	No		No		No	No	No					Interstate offerings are exempt from registration. Intrastate offerings that file for registration are reviewed for "disclosure" only.
Connecticut	No	No	Yes	No		Yes	The Guidelines are not used as strict parameters but are used to determine disclosure offering terms.	Yes	Yes	Yes			X		
Delaware	No	No	No	No				No	No	No					Rule 9 B 9 II (April 15, 1982) exempts all Reg. D offerings.
District of Columbia	No	No	No	No											Registration of securities not required.
Florida	Yes	No	Yes			Yes	We use them only as a guide.	No	Yes*	Yes*			X		*The Guidelines only are applied to those offerings required to register. Such offerings only are required to register if they do not comply with the Florida exemption.
Georgia	No	No	No	No		Yes	Disclosure use only.	No	Yes	No				X	The Guidelines are used only as a reference point for examiners to determine that full and adequate disclosure has been provided.
Hawaii	No	No	No	No									X		
Idaho	Yes	No	Yes	No		No		Yes	Yes	No					

Appendix M: Survey of NASAA Real Estate Guidelines

STATE	Are you a "merit review" state?	Has your state adopted the Guidelines: Formally?	Has your state adopted the Guidelines: Informally?	If your state has not adopted the Guidelines, do you expect it will, and if so, when do you expect adoption?	Law/Rule citation if Guidelines formally adopted?	Does your application of the Guidelines vary from NASAA's published version?	If you apply the Guidelines differently, what are the differences?	National Public Offerings?	Intrastate Offerings?	Private Offerings filed with you?	Always and Absolutely (Without Waiver)	Usually and Strictly (Waivers Rarely)	Occasionally and Moderately (Waivers Frequently)	Seldom and Loosely (Occasionally Applied)	Comments
Illinois	No	No	No	No		No		No	No	No					
Indiana	Yes	*	Yes		*	No		Yes	Yes	Yes		X			*Public hearing on formal adoption scheduled for March 24, 1987. Proposed rule 710 IAC 1-12-8.
Iowa	No*	No	Yes	Yes (date uncertain)		No		Yes	Yes	No (unless registered by qualification)		X			*Disclosure plus substantive review per Uniform Act standards. Guidelines applied to compensation arrangements, conflicts of interest and accountability to investor more so than other aspects of offering (per "promoter's participation" and "tend to work a fraud"). Cross Reference Sheets should be provided with registration applications.
Kansas	Yes		Yes			No		Yes	Yes	Yes		X			
Kentucky	Yes		Yes			No		Yes	No	No		For suitability standards & voting rights.	For all other aspects.		
Louisiana	No	No	No	No		No		Yes	Yes	No					
Maine	Yes*	No	Yes	Possibly		No		Yes				X			*Merit review provided for by 32 M.R.S.A. §10406(1). Suitability standards will be proposed for private offerings.
Maryland	No	No	No	No											See CCH for various releases issued from time to time re: real estate.
Massachusetts	Maybe		Yes	Yes		No		Yes	Yes	No		X			Division's review of private offerings will be from a tend-to-work-a-fraud perspective and concerns relative to abusive tax shelters.
Michigan	Yes	No	Yes	No		No		Yes	Yes	No		X			We are more strict in following the Guidelines in the areas of conflicts of interest and accountability to the investors than we are in the area of compensation.
Minnesota	Yes		Yes	No	M.S. 80 A.31 Rule 2875.8450	Yes	Reviewed on a case by case basis. Guidelines applied in some instances (see Rule 2875.8450)	Yes	Yes	No		X			Rule 2875.8450 allows the flexibility to accept programs which are in compliance with the NASAA Guidelines.

STATE	Are you a "merit review" state?	Has your state adopted the Guidelines: Formally?	Informally?	If your state has not adopted the Guidelines, do you expect it will, and if so, when do you expect adoption?	Law/Rule citation if Guidelines formally adopted?	Does your application of the Guidelines vary from NASAA's published version?	If you apply the Guidelines differently, what are the differences?	National Public Offerings?	Intrastate Offerings?	Private Offerings filed with you?	Always and Absolutely (Without Waiver)	Usually and Strictly (Waivers Rarely)	Occasionally and Moderately (Waivers Frequently)	Seldom and Loosely (Occasionally Applied)	Comments
Mississippi	Yes	Yes			Rule 725	No		Yes	Yes	Yes			X		The staff in this state takes a cooperative approach in the review of these filings and does allow "give and take" to occur in negotiating deviations from the Guidelines.
Missouri	Yes	Yes				No		Yes	Yes	No		X			*Guidelines not applied to private offerings filed pursuant to registration exemption. Only sections dealing with compensation to promoters/underwriters are applied.
Montana	Yes, to a limited degree	No	Yes	Portions, within next 12 months	15 CSR 30-52.180(i)(m)	No		Yes	Yes	No*			X		
Nebraska	Yes	No	Yes	No		No		Yes	Yes	No		X			
Nevada	No	No	No	No											
New Hampshire	No	No	No	Yes				Yes		Yes					Just beginning to talk about adopting Guidelines.
New Jersey	No	No	No	No											All persons (including attorneys & accountants receiving finders' fees) selling limited partnership interests must be registered unless an exception is available.
New Mexico	Yes	Yes	No			No		Yes	Yes	No		X			
New York	No	Yes*	No		13 NYCRR Part 16.11*	Yes*	Yes, see 13 NYCRR Part 16.11*	Yes*	Yes*	(Parts only)		X*			*Adopted part of Guidelines for nonspecified programs only.
North Carolina	No*	No	Yes*			No		Yes	Yes	Yes		X			*Offerings are subject to certain merit review (e.g., promoter participation, cheap stock, etc.) but there are no overall "fair, just and equitable" standards.
North Dakota	Yes	No	Yes			No		Yes	Yes	Yes		X			
Ohio	Yes	No	Yes	No		No		Yes	Yes	Yes*		X			*Guidelines apply to private placements not falling within an Ohio private offering exemption.
Oklahoma	No*	Yes	No		R-306 A2f	No		Yes	Yes	No			X		*Offerings are subject to certain merit review pursuant to Section 306(a)(2)(F) of the Oklahoma Securities Act. The guidelines are utilized in the registration review process and variances are noted in comments. Explanations are required for departure from guideline provisions.
Oregon	Yes	No	No	No											Aware of the Guidelines but look at the overall structure of the offering.

Appendix M: Survey of NASAA Real Estate Guidelines

STATE	Are you a "merit review" state?	Has your state adopted the Guidelines: Formally?	Informally?	If your state has not adopted the Guidelines, do you expect it will, and if so, when do you expect adoption?	Law/Rule citation if Guidelines formally adopted?	Does your application of the Guidelines vary from NASAA's published version?	If you apply the Guidelines differently, what are the differences?	Do you apply the Guidelines to: National Public Offerings?	Intrastate Offerings?	Private Offerings filed with you?	Always and Absolutely (Without Waiver)	Usually and Strictly (Waivers Rarely)	Occasionally and Moderately (Waivers Frequently)	Seldom and Loosely (Occasionally Applied)	Comments
Pennsylvania	Yes	No				Yes	For the purpose of Section VI E. Pennsylvania will request information on status of all previous programs.	Yes	Yes	Limited		X			In Section III.B.4. of the Guidelines, each Pennsylvania investor must represent that he has a net worth (exclusive of homes, furnishings and automobiles) of 10 times his investment in non-specified property programs.
Rhode Island	Yes	No	No	No											
South Carolina	Yes	No	Yes					Yes	Yes	Yes			X		Applications should include a sheet tracking the offering and Guidelines.
South Dakota	Yes	No	Yes	Yes (date uncertain)		No		Yes	Yes	No		X	X		Cross-Reference Sheets should be submitted with registration applications.
Tennessee	Yes	Yes			0780-4-3-.06(4)(m)4.	No		Yes	Yes	Yes*		X			*If Tennessee Guidelines found at Rule 0780-4-3-.06(4)(n) do not apply, the Guidelines will be applied to certain private offerings filed pursuant to T.C.A. § 48-2-103(b)(4) and T.C.A. § 48-2-106. Cross-Reference Sheet must be submitted with application for registration.
Texas	Yes	Yes			Rule: Section 117	No		Yes	Yes	No		X			Private Placement Offerings not required to be filed, but filing of certain forms may be required by Rules 109.13(k) and (l).
Utah	Yes	Yes			Rule 11.1	No		Yes	Yes	No		X			
Vermont	No	No	No												
Virginia	Yes	Yes			Rule 602	Yes	Does not apply Guidelines to mortgage related securities.	Yes	Yes	No	*	*	*	*	*Depends on nature of the offering.
Washington	Yes	Yes			WAC-460-31A-410 through 730.	No		Yes	Yes	No		X			
West Virginia	No	Yes			West Virginia Code 32-4-412 and Securities Reg. 14.06	No		Yes	Yes	Yes			X		
Wisconsin	Yes	Yes			Wis. Adm. Code Section SEC 3.11	Yes		Yes	Yes	No		X			The Guidelines are not applied to offerings filed with the SEC which also meet the suitability standards of Section 551.28(7), Wis. Stats. Only the disclosure provisions of the Guidelines are applied to other offerings meeting the suitability standards.
Wyoming	Yes	Yes			Rule-Chapter V, Section 4, (a)-(h)	No		Yes	Yes	Where applicable.		X			

Index

Accelerated Cost Recovery System (ACRS), 25
Accountant(s)
  as finders, 144
  model syndication documents from, 109–10, 113
  selecting an, 123
Accounting file, setting up the, 154
Advertising offerings, 138–39
Allocations, attorney's comments on, 12
Amortization, 10–11
Appreciation, 10
At-risk rules, 25
Attorney(s)
  as finders, 144
  getting the most out of your, 129–31
  model syndication documents from, 109–10, 113
  selecting an, 122–23

Blind pool offerings. *See* Nonspecified offerings
Blue sky laws, 49–51
Broker-dealer
  defined, 44
  exemptions from registration, 45–46
  model syndication documents from, 110
  registration requirements for, 44–45
  selecting a real estate, 125
  selecting a securities, 123–24

Capital gains, 26
Certificate of limited partnership, 287–92
Corporate reorganizations, 498–99
Corporate reports, public access to, 502–3
Corporation
  general partnership and use of a, 81–83
  shell, 82–83

Depreciation schedules, lengthening of, 24–25
Direct Participation Program (DPP), NASD, 47
Disclosure, 34
  document, 41–43
  economic rationale for avoiding registration, 58–59
  Guide 5, 435–60
  importance of full, 59–60
  legal rationale for avoiding registration, 58
  using Guide 5 disclosure in private offerings, 60–61

Fiduciary controls, 23
Financial planners as finders, 144
Finders, 142–45
Form S-11, 426–34
Form U-4, 461–67
Funds, accepting, 97–98

General partnership, 21, 28–30
  importance of written agreement, 80–81
  legal requirements for interest splitting, 79
  reasons for choosing, 74–76
  rules for structuring the, 76–81
  use of a corporation as a, 81–83
General Partnership Understanding document, 161–62
Guide 5 disclosure standards, 41–43
  document of, 435–60
  offering documents and use of, 105–6
  using, in private offerings, 60–61

Income, definition of, 10
Insurance agents as finders, 144
Interests
  free transferability of, 20–21, 26
  selling of, 93–95

Internal Revenue Service
  partnerships and the, 18–19
  tax shelter registration with the, 48–49
Intrastate exemption, 45, 47–48
Intrastate offerings, 39–40
Investment Advisers Act of 1940, 497
Investment basis, determining, 89–92
Investment Company Act of 1940, 495–47
Investment decisions, guidelines for, 149–51
Investment objectives, establishing, 69–70
Investor confidence, winning, 56–57
Investor meetings, conducting, 139–41
Issuer's exemption, 45–46

Liability, limited, 17, 20
Limited partnership(s)
  control by the general partner, 21, 28–30
  disadvantages of, 22–26
  documentation for, 28
  example of certificate of, 287–92
  how to form a, 30
  limited liability and, 17, 20

Index

regulations and attorney's comments on, 15–16, 22–26, 29–31
regulations governing, 27–29
status, tests of, 19–21
tax treatment and, 18–21
title transfer and, 21–22
who can sell partnership interests, 46–47, 72–73
Limited partnerships, structuring
determining how returns will be shared, 87–93
determining how you will make money, 85–87
preparing a preliminary analysis document, 95–98
selling of interests, 93–95
Tax Recovery Act of 1986 and, 99–102
Loss pass-throughs, limits on, 23–24

Market, defining your, 70–72
Marketing of offers, 142–48

NASAA. *See* North American Securities Administrators' Association
NASD. *See* National Association of Securities Dealers
National Association of Realtors (NAR), 110–11, 125
National Association of Securities Dealers (NASD), 44–45
background of the, 52
limited securities license, 47
offices of the, 552
Nonspecified offerings, specified vs., 62–68
North American Securities Administrators' Association (NASAA)
creation of the, 52
guidelines of the, 30, 31, 53–54 111–13, 507–51
importance of a track record and the, 57
record keeping and the, 157
reporting policy and the, 151, 153
survey of real estate guidelines of the, 557–61

Offering documents, 103
attorneys and accountants and, 109–10, 113
NASAA guidelines, 111–13
pre-, 160–74
pros and cons of writing your own, 106–8
sources for model, 108–11
using Guide 5 for, 105–6
Offering package, 41–43
attorney comment on offering memorandum, 246–51
attorney comment on partnership agreement, 282–85
attorney opinion for offering memorandum, 235–45
components of, 175
example of certificate of limited partnership, 287–92
example of offering memorandum, 181–233
example of partnership agreement, 253–81
example of partnership management agreement, 315–16
example of project documents, 314
example of selling agreement, 317–26
example of subscription agreement and materials, 293–313
offering memorandum, 175–76
partnership agreement, 176–77
partnership management agreement, 179
project documents, 178–79
selling agreement, 179
subscription agreement and materials, 177–78
Offers
advertising for, 138–39
conducting investor meetings, 139–41
marketing of, 142–48
private vs. public, 57–62
specified vs. nonspecified, 62–68
tips on public, 137–38
use of public relations for, 141–42
when to make private, 136–37

Partnership agreement, 176–77
attorney comment on, 282–85
certificate of limited partnership, 287–92
example of, 253–81
Partnership management agreement, 179
example of, 315–16
Preliminary analysis document
elements of a, 163–64
example of a, 164–74
preparing a, 95–98
purpose of a, 163
Pre-offering documents, 160–74
Printing, tips on, 132–35
Private offerings, 34–39
using Guide 5 disclosure in, 60–61
vs. public offerings, 57–62
when to make, 136–37
Project documents, 178–79
example of, 314
Public offerings
advertising, 138–39
conducting investor meetings, 139–41
large, 40–41
private vs. public, 57–62
small, 40, 61–62

Public offerings (cont.)
  specified vs. nonspecified, 62–68
  tips on, 137–38
  use of public relations for, 141–42
Public Utility Holding Company Act of 1935, 491–95

Real estate broker, selecting a, 125
Real Estate Investment Trust (REIT), 22
Real estate investment vs. savings certificates, 2–3
Real Estate Securities and Syndication Institute (RESSI), 45, 53
Record keeping, tips on, 154–57
Regulation A, 389–425
Regulation D, 35–37, 42, 57, 356–82
Reorganization, corporate, 498–99
Reporting policy, 151–53
Residency, investor, 47–48
Revised Uniform Limited Partnership Act (RULPA), 28–29
  record keeping and the, 157
Risks, attorney's comments on, 11–12
Rule 147, 39–40, 383–88
Rules 146, 240, 242, 35, 328–55

Sales agents, 145–48
Savings certificates, real estate investment vs., 2–3
Securities Act of 1933, 33
  description of the, 478–82
  Form S-11, 426–34
  intrastate offerings and the, 39–40
  large public offerings and the, 40–41
  private offerings and the, 34–39
  Regulation A, 389–425
  Regulation D, 35–37, 42, 57, 356–82
  Rule 147, 39–40, 383–88
  Rules 146, 240, 242, 35, 328–55
  small public offerings and the, 40
Securities and Exchange Act of 1934, 43
  broker-dealer defined, 44
  description of the, 482–91
  exemptions from registration, 45–46, 47–48
  registration requirements, 44–45
Securities and Exchange Commission (SEC), 44, 45, 51
  administrative proceedings of the, 499–500
  background of the, 477–78
  Directorate of Economic & Policy Analysis of the, 501–2

model syndication documents from, 111
Office of the Chief Accountant of the, 501
Office of the General Counsel of the, 500
public access to corporate reports, 502–3
regional offices of the, 504–6
Securities laws
  origins of, 32–33
  state, 49–51
Selling agreement, 179
  example of, 317–26
Specialists
  controlling, 114–21
  fees of, 127–28
  identifying competent, 121–25
  preparing for meetings with, 125–31
Specialization, attorney's comments on, 11
Specified vs. nonspecified offerings, 62–68
Specimen documents file, 155–56
State securities administrator(s)
  list of, 468–76
  model syndication documents from, 111
State securities laws, 49–51
Structuring. See Limited partnerships, structuring
Subject file, organizing a, 157
Subscription agreement and materials, 177–78
  example of, 293–313
Syndication
  definition of, 14
  reasons for, 7–12
Syndicators
  advantages of, 3–4
  need for, 5–6

Taxation, double, 18
Tax rates, reduction of personal, 24
Tax Recovery Act of 1986 (TRA), 23–26, 92–93
  structuring under the, 99–102
Tax shelter, 10
  registration with the IRS, 48–49
Tax treatment of partnerships, 18–21
Title transfer, 21–22
Track record, maintaining, 57
Trust Indenture Act of 1939, 495
Typing and printing, tips on, 132–35

Uniform Limited Partnership Act (ULPA),
Uniform Partnership Act (UPA), 27–28

Word processors, use of, 134–35